CIVIL PROCEDURE 2019

THIRD CUMULATIVE SUPPLEMENT TO THE 2019 EDITION

Up-to-date generally to 1 October 2019 to the 109th CPR Update

See Publisher's Note for information on the 110th and 111th CPR Updates

SWEET & MAXWELL

Published in 2019 by Thomson Reuters, trading as Sweet & Maxwell.
Thomson Reuters is registered in England & Wales, Company No. 1679046.
Registered Office and address for service: 5 Canada Square, Canary Wharf, London E14 5AQ.
Typesetting by Sweet & Maxwell electronic publishing system.
Printed and bound in the UK by CPI Group (UK) Ltd, Croydon, CR0 4YY.
For further information on our products and services, visit
http://www.sweetandmaxwell.co.uk.

No natural forests were destroyed to make this product; only farmed timber was used and replanted.

British Library Cataloguing in Publication Data
A CIP catalogue record for this book is available from the British Library

ISBN–978-0-414-07459-0

EDITOR-IN-CHIEF
THE RIGHT HONOURABLE SIR GEOFFREY VOS
Chancellor of the High Court

EMERITUS EDITOR
PROFESSOR I. R. SCOTT Q.C. (Hon)
Emeritus Professor, University of Birmingham; Honorary Bencher of Gray's Inn

GENERAL EDITORS
SENIOR MASTER B. FONTAINE
Senior Master of the Senior Courts in the Queen's Bench Division and Queen's Remembrancer; Central Authority for the Hague Conventions on Service and Taking of Evidence; Central Body under the EC Service and Evidence Regulations; Former Member of the Civil Procedure Rule Committee
DR J. SORABJI
Barrister

EDITOR OF CIVIL PROCEDURE NEWS
DR J. SORABJI
Barrister

SENIOR EDITORIAL BOARD
THE RIGHT HONOURABLE LORD JUSTICE COULSON
Lord Justice of Appeal; Deputy Head of Civil Justice
SENIOR COSTS JUDGE A. GORDON-SAKER
Senior Courts Costs Office
THE RIGHT HONOURABLE LORD JUSTICE HAMBLEN
Lord Justice of Appeal
ROBERT N. HILL
Recorder; North Eastern Circuit; Former District Judge and Regional Costs Judge; Former Member of the Civil Procedure Rule Committee
HIS HONOUR NIC MADGE
A Retired Circuit Judge

EDITORS
MASOOD AHMED
Associate Professor, Leicester Law School, University of Leicester; Member of the Civil Procedure Rule Committee
JONATHAN AUBURN
Barrister, 11 King's Bench Walk
HIS HONOUR JUDGE SIMON AUERBACH
Senior Circuit Judge, Employment Appeal Tribunal
DR STUART BARAN
Barrister, Three New Square
JUDGE BARBER
Insolvency and Companies Court Judge
HIS HONOUR JUDGE NIGEL BIRD
Designated Civil Judge for Greater Manchester
MASTER BROWN
Costs Judge of the Senior Courts (Taxing Master); A Deputy Master of the Senior Courts, Queen's Bench Division
SUZANNE BURN
A Deputy District Judge on the South Eastern Circuit; Former Member of the Civil Procedure Rule Committee
GREG CALLUS
Barrister, 5 Raymond Buildings

This is the Third Cumulative Supplement to the 2019 edition of *Civil Procedure*, which published in March 2019. The First Supplement published with the Main Work and the Second Cumulative Supplement published in June 2019. This Third Cumulative Supplement brings both Volumes of the Main Work generally up to date to 1 October 2019, with the exception of the 110th and 111th CPR Updates, which were published as this Supplement went to press (see **Stop Press Note** below).

This Supplement does not cover amendments to civil procedure legislation made by "Brexit", which will follow in a future supplement once the exit process is finalised.

This Supplement incorporates amendments brought into force by two recent statutory instruments and CPR Updates:

- The Civil Procedure (Amendment No. 2) Rules 2019 (SI 2019/1034), which amends Part 57 (Probate, Inheritance & Presumption of Death) in the light of the 108th CPR Update, which includes a new Practice Direction 57C—Proceedings Under the Guardianship (Missing Persons) Act 2017, (effective on 31 July 2019), a new provision that enables families and friends of missing people to look after their property and financial affairs
- The Civil Procedure (Amendment No. 3) Rules 2019 (SI 2019/1118) which brings into force a new Part 53 for Media & Communication Claims from 1 October 2019. This reflects changes made in the Defamation Act 2013 and the formal introduction of the Media and Communications List

A number of Practice Directions and Pre-Action Protocols have been updated following the 109th CPR Update, which makes the following changes:

- Amendment to PD 2B to remove current inconsistency with Parts 65 and 85
- Amendment to PD 3E to provide clearer guidance on the cut-off between budgeted costs and incurred costs
- Amendments to Practice Direction 7A and significant amendments to Practice Direction 40F (for which a new Practice Direction 40F is substituted)
- Introduces two new Practice Directions, PD 53A and PD 53B. The new Part 53 and Practice Directions apply to claims issued from 1 October 2019
- The Electronic Working Pilot Scheme under PD 51O is extended so that, from 1 July 2019, it is mandatory for a party to use electronic working to start or continue any claims within the Central Office of the Queen's Bench Division
- The Pre-Action Protocol for Defamation Claims is substituted by the Pre-Action Protocol for Media and Communications Claims (in force from 1 October 2019)
- The Pre-Action Protocol for Judicial Review is amended (in force on 17 September 2019)

The Supplement also includes the following:

- New commentary on Pt 53 to take account of the Media and Communications List
- A new edition of the Administrative Court Judicial Review Guide 2019, issued July 2019
- A new edition of the Intellectual Property Enterprise Court Guide, issued July 2019
- Further updates to the Chancery Guide 2016

- A new Practice Note (Admiralty: Assessors' Remuneration) of 1 September 2019
- Commentary on the Assured Tenancies and Agricultural Occupancies (Forms) (England) (Amendment) Regulations 2019 (SI 2019/915)
- The Renting Homes (Fees etc.) (Wales) Act 2019 (online only)
- Changes to court fees pursuant to the Court Fees (Miscellaneous Amendments) Order 2019 (SI 2019/1063) from 22 July 2019
- Amendments to the Courts Directory (List of District Registries)

New case law and commentary, including the following decisions:

Part 1

- *Woodward v Phoenix Healthcare Distribution Ltd* [2019] EWCA Civ 985

Part 3

- *Lomax v Lomax* [2019] EWCA Civ 1467
- *Alba Exotic Fruit SH PK v MSC Mediteranean Shipping Co SA* [2019] EWHC 1779 (Comm)
- *Moorjani v Durban Estates Ltd* [2019] EWHC 1229 (TCC)
- *Chief Constable of Avon and Somerset v Gray* [2019] EWHC 1954 (QB)

Part 5

- *Cape Intermediate Holdings Ltd v Dring* [2019] UKSC 38; [2019] 3 W.L.R. 429

Part 6

- *General Dynamics UK Ltd v Libya* [2019] EWCA Civ 1110
- *Gray v Hurley* [2019] EWHC 1636 (QB)
- *Akcil v Koza Ltd* [2019] UKSC 40; [2019] 1 W.L.R. 4830
- *Gulf International Bank BSC v Aldwood* [2019] EWHC 1666 (QB)

Part 12

- *Smith v Berryman Lace Mawer Service Co* [2019] EWHC 1904 (QB)

Part 19

- *Bates v Post Office Ltd (No.5: Common Issues Costs)* [2019] EWHC 1373 (QB); [2019] Costs L.R. 857

Part 20

- *Wolseley UK Ltd v Fiat Chrysler Automobiles NV* [2019] CAT 12

Part 21

- *Barker v Confiance Ltd* [2019] EWHC 1401 (Ch)

Part 25

- *TC Developments (South East) Ltd v Investin Quay House Ltd* [2019] EWHC 1432 (TCC); [2019] Costs L.R. 765

Part 27

- *Kuznetsov v Amazon Services Europe SARL* [2019] EWCA Civ 964

Part 31

- *Bank Mellat v HM Treasury* [2019] EWCA Civ 449
- *Willers v Joyce* [2019] EWHC 937 (Ch); [2019] Costs L.R. 781
- *A v B* [2019] EWHC 2089 (Ch)

Part 35

- *Dodds v Arif* [2019] EWHC 1512 (QB)

Part 36

- *Knight v Knight* [2019] EWHC 1545 (Ch)
- *JLE (A Child) v Warrington & Halton Hospitals NHS Foundation Trust* [2019] EWHC 1582 (QB); [2019] Costs L.R. 829

Part 38

- *Stati v Republic Of Kazakhstan* [2019] EWHC 1715 (Comm)

Part 39

- *Cape Intermediate Holdings Ltd v Dring* [2019] UKSC 38; [2019] 3 W.L.R. 429

Part 44

- *Malmsten v Bohinc* [2019] EWHC 1386 (Ch); [2019] 4 W.L.R. 87
- *West v Stockport NHS Foundation Trust* [2019] EWCA Civ 1220

Part 45

- *Campaign to Protect Rural England v Secretary of State for Communities and Local Government* [2019] EWCA Civ 1230

Part 46

- *Airways Pension Scheme Trustee Ltd v Fielder* [2019] EWHC 29 (Ch); [2019] 4 W.L.R. 9
- *Barker v Confiance Ltd* [2019] EWHC 1401 (Ch)

Part 51

- *Ventra Investments Ltd v Bank Of Scotland Plc* [2019] EWHC 2058 (Comm)
- *Merck Sharp & Dohme Ltd v Wyeth LLC* [2019] EWHC 1692 (Pat)
- *Obaid v Al-Hezaimi* [2019] EWHC 1953 (Ch)
- *Vannin Capital PCC v RBOS Shareholders Action Group Ltd* [2019] EWHC 1617 (Ch)

Part 52

- *Singh v Dass* [2019] EWCA Civ 360
- *Notting Hill Finance Ltd v Sheikh* [2019] EWCA Civ 1337

Part 53

- *Lachaux v Independent Print Ltd* [2019] UKSC 27; [2019] 3 W.L.R. 18

Part 57

- *Sprint Electric Ltd v Buyer's Dream Ltd* [2019] EWHC 1853 (Ch)

Part 81

- *Attorney General v Yaxley-Lennon* [2019] EWHC 1791 (QB)
- *Solicitor General v Holmes* [2019] EWHC 1483 (Admin); [2019] 2 Cr. App. R. 23
- *Isis Housing Co-Operative v Evelyn* [2019] EWCA Civ 1299
- *Discovery Land Co LLC v Jirehouse* [2019] EWHC 1633 (Ch)

Part 83

- *365 Business Finance Ltd v Bellagio Hospitality WB Ltd* [2019] EWHC 1920 (QB)

Future supplements and *Civil Procedure News* will continue to keep you up to date with developments, including "Brexit" amendments if required, for the remainder of the subscription year.

We welcome feedback from subscribers—please email *whitebook@sweetandmaxwell.co.uk* with any comments or suggestions.

The White Book Team
September 2019

As this Supplement went to press, the 110th and 111th CPR Updates were published by the Ministry of Justice.

The 110th Practice Direction Update, in force from 7 October 2019, amongst other things, makes the following changes to PD 47 (Procedure for Detailed Assessment of Costs & Default Provisions) and PD 51O (Electronic Working Pilot Scheme):

- It extends the application of the existing Electronic Working Pilot Scheme (PD 51O) to the Senior Courts Costs Office (SCCO)
- It makes related changes to the Procedure for Detailed Assessment of Costs and Default Provisions (PD 47) by modifying para.5.1A and adding para.5.1B

The key affected paragraphs are reproduced below. These will also be taken into the online *White Book on Westlaw* edition and the consolidated Proview eBook edition of the *White Book*.

PD 47

Replace paragraph 5.1A with:

5.1A Subject to paragraph 5.1B, whenever electronic bills are served or filed at the court—
- (a) they must be served or filed in hard copy, in a manageable paper format as shown in the pdf version of Precedent S; and
- (b) a copy of the full electronic spreadsheet version must at the same time be provided to the paying party, or as appropriate filed at court, by e-mail or other electronic means.

5.1B Whenever an electronic bill is filed at the Costs Office using Electronic Working (see Practice Direction 51O)—
- (a) a copy of the full electronic spreadsheet version and a pdf version must be uploaded; and
- (b) the electronic bill must not be filed at court by any other means.

PD 51O

Replace paragraph 1.1 with (replacing what is already produced in this Supplement):

1.1(1) This Practice Direction is made under rules 5.5, 7.12 and 51.2 of the Civil Procedure Rules ("CPR"). It provides for a pilot scheme ("Electronic Working") to—

(a) operate from 16 November 2015 to 6 April 2020;
(b) operate in—
- (i) the Chancery Division of the High Court, the Commercial Court, the Technology and Construction Court, the Circuit Commercial Court, and the Admiralty Court, at the Royal Courts of Justice, Rolls Building, London (together, "the Rolls Building Jurisdictions");
- (ii) the Central Office of the Queen's Bench Division at the Royal Courts of Justice;
- (iii) the B&PCs District Registries (as defined in paragraph 1.2 of Practice Direction 57AA); and
- (iv) the Senior Courts Costs Office ("the Costs Office"); and
(c) apply—
- (i) to existing proceedings and proceedings started on or after 16 November 2015 in the Rolls Building Jurisdictions;
- (ii) in the Central Office of the Queen's Bench Division, to proceedings started after 1 January 2019, and will not apply to existing proceedings unless ordered by the court;

(iii) in the B&PCs District Registries, to proceedings started on or after 25 February 2019, and will not apply to existing proceedings unless ordered by the court; and

(iv) in the Costs Office, to detailed assessment proceedings in which the request for a hearing is filed on or after 7 October 2019, to applications filed on or after 7 October 2019 and to proceedings started in the Costs Office on or after 7 October 2019.

(2) Electronic Working is a permitted means of electronic delivery of documents to the Court for the purposes of rule 1.46 of the Insolvency (England & Wales) Rules 2016 ("IR 2016").

Replace paragraph 1.2 with:

1.2(1) Electronic Working works within and is subject to all statutory provisions and rules together with all procedural rules and practice directions applicable to the proceedings concerned, subject to any exclusion or revision within this Practice Direction.

(2) In particular, the following provisions of the CPR apply unless specifically excluded or revised by this Practice Direction—

Part 47 (Detailed Assessment of Costs)
Part 49 (Companies Court)
Part 57 (Probate, Inheritance and Presumption of Death)
Part 58 (Commercial Court)
Part 59 (Circuit Commercial Courts)
Part 60 (Technology and Construction Court Claims)
Part 61 (Admiralty Claims)
Part 62 (Arbitration Claims)
Part 63 (Intellectual Property Claims)
Part 63A (Financial List)
Part 64 (Estates, Trusts and Charities)
Part 74 (Enforcement of Judgments in different jurisdictions)
Part 77 (Provisions in support of criminal justice)
Practice Direction – Insolvency Proceedings
Practice Direction: Directors Disqualification Proceedings
EU Competition law Practice Direction

(3) The following provisions of the CPR shall not apply to this Practice Direction—

Part 76 (Proceedings under the Prevention from Terrorism Act 2005)
Part 88 (Proceedings under the Counter-Terrorism and Security Act 2015

(4) Parties will also need to give careful consideration to the Chancery Guide, the Admiralty and Commercial Courts Guide, the Technology and Construction Court Guide, the Financial List Guide, the Circuit Commercial Court Guide, the Patents Court Guide, the Intellectual Property Enterprise Court Guide, the Senior Courts Costs Office Guide and the Queen's Bench Guide (where applicable).

(5) Where the provisions of this Practice Direction conflict with the provisions of Practice Direction 5B, this Practice Direction shall take precedence.

Replace paragraph 2.2 with (replacing what is already produced in this Supplement):

2.2 Electronic Working applies to and may be used to start and/or continue (subject to the provisions in paragraph 1.1(1)(c)) CPR Part 7, Part 8 and Part 20 claims, pre-action applications including applications under rule 31.16, insolvency proceedings, and arbitration claims in the Rolls Building Jurisdictions, the B&PCs District Registries, and in the Central Office of the Queen's Bench Division and detailed assessment proceedings and Part 8 claims in the Costs Office.

Add new paragraphs 2.2D and 2.2E:

2.2D In the Costs Office from 7 October 2019, for a party who is legally represented, as well as for a party who is not legally represented, Electronic Working may be used by that party to start and/or continue any relevant claims, detailed assessment proceedings or applications.

2.2E In the Costs Office from 20 January 2020, for a party who is legally represented, Electronic Working must be used by that party to start and/or continue any relevant claims, detailed assessment proceedings or applications.

Replace paragraph 2.4 with (replacing what is already produced in this Supplement):

2.4 Proceedings issued in the Rolls Building Jurisdictions, the B&PCs District Registries, the Central Office of the Queen's Bench Division and the Costs Office will be stored by the Court as an electronic case file ("the Electronic Working Case File").

The 111th CPR Update amends PD 51R (Online Civil Money Claims Pilot) and PD 51S (County Court Online Pilot), effective from 9 September 2019.

The changes to PD 51R include:

- Extending the pilot to 30 November 2021
- Release of new features, including:
  - A new online Directions Questionnaire
  - A presumption of mediation for certain defended claims as part of an "opt out" online process
  - The expansion of the "Paid in full Defence", so the process will be available in relation to all forms of defence of the whole of the claim

The PD 51S (County Court Online) pilot is extended to 30 November 2021.

All changes can be seen in full at *http://www.justice.gov.uk/courts/procedure-rules/civil*, on *White Book on Westlaw* and on the consolidated Proview eBook version of the *White Book.*

CONTENTS

TABLE OF CASES

TABLE OF STATUTES

TABLE OF EUROPEAN LEGISLATION

VOLUME 1

SECTION A   CIVIL PROCEDURE RULES 1998

PART 1

OVERRIDING OBJECTIVE

Applicability of CPR to all litigants

Replace paragraph with:

1.1.1   The CPR apply to all litigants whether represented or unrepresented. Unrepresented litigants (or litigants-in-person) do not form a "privileged" class of litigants for whom the rules are modified or disapplied: *Nata Lee Ltd v Abid* [2014] EWCA Civ 1652, CA at [53]; *Ogiehor v Belinfantie* [2018] EWCA Civ 2423; [2018] 6 Costs L.R. 1329, CA at [24]. The court, further to the overriding objective, can provide practical assistance to litigants, but must enforce the rules (see *Mole v Hunter* [2014] EWHC 658 (QB) at [107] and following, and para.3.1A.1). Except where rules or Practice Directions "are particularly inaccessible or obscure", an unrepresented litigant is expected to take steps to familiarise themselves with them: *Barton v Wright Hassal LLP* [2018] UKSC 12; [2018] 1 W.L.R. 1119, UKSC.

Duty of the parties (r.1.3)

Replace paragraph with:

1.3.2   Part 1 places a duty on the court to secure the overriding objective's achievement: see r.1.1, r.1.2, 1.4, and also note r.3.1(2)(m)). No such duty is directly imposed on the parties: r.1.3 states that the parties are required "to help the court" further the overriding objective: see *Hallam Estates Ltd v Baker* [2014] EWCA Civ 661; [2014] C.P. Rep. 38 per Jackson LJ at para.12, *Davies v Forrett* [2015] EWHC 1761 (QB); [2017] 3 Costs L.R. 515, and *Emmanuel v Revenue & Customs* [2017] EWHC 1253 (Ch); [2017] 3 Costs L.R. 515, which stress that party-failure to help the court may be visited in costs on the defaulting party or parties. Jackson LJ in *Hallam Estates* further outlined that legal representatives will not be in breach of any duty to their client if they agree reasonable extensions of time, as such agreement furthers r.1.1(2)(e). In commercial litigation, a particularly "high level of realism and co-operation" is expected of parties in their approach to pre-trial case management in order to ensure that wasted court and party costs are not incurred (*McGann v Bisping* [2017] EWHC 2951 (Comm)). A party is not, however, under a duty to inform their opponent of procedural mistakes: see *Barton v Wright Hassall LLP* [2018] UKSC 12; [2018] 1 W.L.R. 1119, *Woodward v Phoenix Healthcare Distribution Ltd* [2019] EWCA Civ 985.

PART 2

APPLICATION AND INTERPRETATION OF THE RULES

Editorial introduction

In the last paragraph, delete the last sentence.

2.0.1

Add new paragraph at end:

Practice Direction 2F—Court Sittings (see para.2FPD.1below) was introduced by CPR Update 104 (February 2019) on 6 April 2019. Prior to that it had beenPD 39B. It was moved to supplement CPR Pt 2, following restructuring of Pt 39. Previous editions of the White Book noted that it had no direct connection with that Part. Other provisions dealing with court sittings are found elsewhere in the CPR; e.g. PD 54D—Administrative Court (Venue) (see para.54DPD.1).

Specialist lists (r.2.3(2))

Replace the first paragraph with:

2.3.14   The Glossary explains that cases are allocated to different "lists" depending on the subject-matter of the proceedings (see Vol.1, Section F below). Such lists are used for administrative purposes and may also have their own procedures and judges. As amended by the Civil Procedure (Amendment No. 5) Rules 2001 (SI 2001/4015), r.2.3(2) states that a reference in the CPR to a "specialist list" is a reference to a list that has been designated as such by "a rule or practice direction". As was explained above (see para.2.1.2), when the CPR came into effect several varieties of proceedings were listed in Pt 49 as "specialist proceedings" and the CPR applied to them "subject to the relevant practice direction". "Specialist lists" are to be distinguished from "specialist proceedings". However, some of the practice directions relevant to "specialist proceedings" provided that those proceedings should be handled through "specialist lists". The coincidence of "proceedings" and "lists" is also apparent in various other procedural contexts; e.g. PD 7A (How to Start Proceedings—The Claim Form), para.3.7 (see para.7APD.2 below). Most of the proceedings originally designated in Pt 49 as "specialist proceedings" now have their own dedicated CPR Parts. Therefore they are no longer subject to Pt 49. More particularly, they are no longer regulated solely by "the relevant practice direction" but are regulated by rules (hence the amendment to r.2.3(2)) referred to above. In some instances, rules in such new Parts state that the proceedings will be assigned to specialist lists. For example, r.53.2 states that the Media and Communications List is a specialist list of the High Court, r.58.2 states that the commercial list is a specialist list for claims proceeding in the Commercial Court, r.59.1 states that Circuit Commercial Court (formerly the Mercantile Court) is a specialist list in the Business and Property Courts (which are defined in PD Business and Property Courts paras 1.3–1.4) and r.60.1 states that Technology and Construction Court claims form a specialist list. The Intellectual Property Enterprise Court is a specialist list established within the High Court's Chancery Division (r.63.2(2)). Rule 63.3 states that claims in the Patents Court form a specialist list "for the purposes of rule 30.5". Planning Court claims also form a specialist list (r.54.22(1)). The Financial List, provided for by Pt 63A and PD 63AA, is a specialist list, and claims in that list may be commenced in the Commercial Court or in the High Court's Chancery Division in London. Numerous references to "specialist lists" are found throughout the CPR and related practice directions (e.g. r.13.4(2) (Transfer of application to set aside judgment to defendant's home court), r.16.3(5) (Statement of value in claim form issued in High Court), r.26.2(2) (Automatic transfer) and r.30.5 (Transfer between Divisions and to and from a specialist list)). Note also, r.14.13(3)(e) (No transfer to defendant's home court of application for re-determination of time and rate of payment in admitted money claim where claim started in specialist list).

PRACTICE DIRECTION 2B—ALLOCATION OF CASES TO LEVELS OF JUDICIARY

Section III—The County Court

Injunctions, Anti-social Behaviour Orders, Committal and Freezing Orders

Replace paragraph 8.1 with:

2BPD.8 **8.1** Applications for orders and interim injunctions which may not be made or granted by a District Judge in the High Court may not be allocated to a District Judge in the County Court save as provided in this Section. In the first instance, the following applications for orders and interim remedies(including injunctions whether interim or final) will be allocated to a District Judge—

(a) proceedings which have been or may be allocated to a District Judge pursuant to paragraph 11.1 below;

(b) injunctions sought in money claims which have not yet been allocated to a track and the amount claimed does not exceed the fast track financial limit;

(c) injunctions that are to be made under any of the following provisions—

(i) sections 36A, 26B or 26C or 91(3) of the Anti-social Behaviour Act 2002;

(ii) section 27(3) of the Police and Justice Act 2009;

(iii) section 3 of the Protection from Harassment Act 1997;

(iv) sections 34, 40 or 41 of the Policing and Crime Act 2009; or

(v) Part 1 of the Anti-social Behaviour, Crime and Policing Act 2014.

Add new Practice Direction 2F:

PRACTICE DIRECTION 2F—COURT SITTINGS

Court Sittings

1.1(1) The sittings of the Court of Appeal and of the High Court shall be **2FPD.1**
four in every year, that is to say
   (a) the Michaelmas sittings which shall begin on 1st October and end
on 21st December;
   (b) the Hilary sittings which shall begin on 11th January and end on
the Wednesday before Easter Sunday;
   (c) the Easter sittings which, subject to sub-paragraph (3), shall begin
on the second Tuesday after Easter Sunday and end on the Friday
before the spring holiday; and
   (d) the Trinity sittings which shall begin on the second Tuesday after
the spring holiday and end on 31st July.

(1A)(a) in subparagraph (1)(a) and (b) the sittings shall begin on the first
Monday after the specified date if the latter falls on a weekend; and
   (b) in subparagraph (1)(a) and (d) the sittings shall end on the Friday
immediately preceding the specified date if the latter falls on a
weekend.

(2) In the above paragraph "spring holiday" means the bank holiday falling on the last Monday in May or any day appointed instead of that
day under section 1(2) of the Banking and Financial Dealings Act
1971.

(3) The Easter sitting in 2011 shall begin on Wednesday, 4th May.

Vacations

The High Court

2.1(1) One or more judges of each Division of the High Court shall sit in **2FPD.2**
vacation on such days as the senior judge of that Division may from
time to time direct, to hear such cases, claims, matters or applications
as require to be immediately or promptly heard and to hear other
cases, claims, matters or applications if the senior judge of that Division determines that sittings are necessary for that purpose.

(2) Any party to a claim or matter may at any time apply to the Court for
an order that such claim or matter be heard in vacation and, if the
Court is satisfied that the claim or matter requires to be immediately
or promptly heard, it may make an order accordingly and fix a date
for the hearing.

(3) Any judge of the High Court may hear such other cases, claims, matters or applications in vacation as the Court may direct.

2.2 The directions in paragraph 3.1 shall not apply in relation to the trial or
hearing of cases, claims, matters or applications outside the Royal Courts of
Justice but the senior Presiding Judge of each Circuit, with the concurrence of
the Senior Presiding Judge, and the Vice-Chancellor of the County Palatine of
Lancaster and the Chancery Supervising Judge for Birmingham, Bristol and
Cardiff, with the concurrence of the Vice-Chancellor, may make such arrangements for vacation sittings in the courts for which they are respectively
responsible as they think desirable.

2.3(1) Subject to the discretion of the Judge, any appeal and any application
normally made to a Judge may be made in the month of September.

(2) In the month of August, save with the permission of a Judge or

under arrangements for vacation sittings in courts outside the Royal Courts of Justice, appeals to a Judge will be limited to the matters set out in paragraph 3.5 below, and only applications of real urgency will be dealt with, for example urgent applications in respect of injunctions or for possession under rule 83.13(3)).

(3)   It is desirable, where this is practical, that applications or appeals are submitted to a Master, District Judge or Judge prior to the hearing of the application or appeal so that they can be marked "fit for August" or "fit for vacation." If they are so marked, then normally the Judge will be prepared to hear the application or appeal in August, if marked "fit for August" or in September if marked "fit for vacation". A request to have the papers so marked should normally be made in writing, shortly setting out the nature of the application or appeal and the reasons why it should be dealt with in August or in September, as the case may be.

Chancery Masters

2FPD.3   **2.4** There is no distinction between term time and vacation so far as business before the Chancery Masters is concerned. The Masters will deal with all types of business throughout the year, and when a Master is on holiday his list will normally be taken by a Deputy Master.

Queen's Bench Masters

2FPD.4   **2.5**(1) An application notice may, without permission, be issued returnable before a Master in the month of August for any of the following purposes—

to set aside a claim form or particulars of claim, or service of a claim form or particulars of claim;
to set aside judgment; for stay of execution;
for any order by consent;
for judgment or permission to enter judgment;
for approval of settlements or for interim payment;
for relief from forfeiture; for charging order; for garnishee order;
for appointment or discharge of a receiver;
for relief by way of interpleader by a sheriff or High Court enforcement officer;
for transfer to the County Court or for trial by Master;
for time where time is running in the month of August;

(2)   In any case of urgency any other type of application notice (that is other than those for the purposes in (1) above), may, with the permission of a Master be issued returnable before a Master during the month of August.

PART 3

The Court's Case and Costs Management Powers

Practice Directions

Add new paragraph at end:

3.0.4   By CPR Update 104 (February 2019), PD 3G was added (with effect from 6 April 2019). It inserted as a Practice Direction the text of a Memorandum of Understanding agreed by the Attorney General and the Lord Chief Justice, dated 19 December 2001, on the appointment of an Advocate to the Court (amicus curiae). The Memorandum was published in previous editions of the *White Book* at paras 39.8.1 to 39.8.4.

I. Case Management

Extending (or shortening) time limits (r.3.1(2)(a))

Add new paragraphs at end:

3.1.2

Extending time limits imposed by unless orders—An unless order is an aggressive form of conditional order (see further, para.3.1.14) which is used where parties are being given one final chance to comply with some obligation previously imposed upon them; it debars parties from pursuing their claim, defence or counterclaim unless, within a specified period of time, they meet the terms of the order. It is more difficult to get relief from sanctions in respect of a breach of an unless order than it is from the breach of a simple conditional order (see *Khandanpour v Chambers* [2019] EWCA Civ 570 noted in para.3.9.4).

In *Everwarm Ltd v BN Rendering Ltd* [2019] EWHC 2078 (TCC) an application was made to extend a deadline imposed by an unless order shortly before that deadline had been reached; it was held that, in these circumstances, the court should follow the approach taken in *Hallam Estates v Baker* (see above) rather than *Denton v TH White* (see above) but should also take into account the powerful public interest there is in ensuring compliance with unless orders.

"An in-time application made shortly after the 'unless' order was first imposed is likely to be treated differently from one made just before the time allowed for compliance was about to expire. However, that factor may carry less significance in a case where the period for compliance was already short" (at [40]).

In *British Gas Trading Ltd v Oak Cash & Carry Ltd* [2016] EWCA Civ 153; [2016] 1 W.L.R. 4530, CA, an application was made to extend a deadline imposed by an unless order shortly after that deadline had passed; the Court of Appeal applied the principles in *Denton v TH White* (see above) and, in doing so, took into account, not just the breach of the order itself, but also the underlying breach which had led to the making of the order; this turned the breach into a major breach and relief from sanctions was withheld (see further, para.3.9.4).

Requiring a party or a party's legal representative to attend the court: r.3.1(2)(c)

In the last paragraph, after the penultimate sentence, add:

An order for personal attendance will usually also be appropriate where the court has made an **3.1.5** order for early neutral evaluation (as to which, see para.3.1.13 and *Lomax v Lomax* [2019] EWCA Civ 1467 at [31]).

Making other orders for the purpose of managing the case and furthering the overriding objective, including hearing an Early Neutral Evaluation (r.3.1(2)(m))

Early neutral evaluation

Replace paragraph with:

Reference to Early Neutral Evaluation ("ENE") was inserted into r.3.1(2)(m) by the Civil **3.1.13** Procedure (Amendment No. 4) Rules 2015 (SI 2015/1569) and came into force on 1 October 2015. ENE is a form of dispute resolution which involves an independent person, with relevant expertise, expressing an opinion about a dispute, or an element of it. Although that opinion does not bind either party, it may assist them to settle the whole or part of the case (see in particular the decision of HH Judge Birss as he then was in *Fayus Inc v Flying Trade Group Plc* [2012] EWPCC 43).

For some years now ENE has been a major component in the Financial Dispute Resolution (FDR) appointment, practised in the Family Division (as to which, see further, Family Procedure Rules 2010 r.9.17 and *Family Dispute Resolution Appointments: Best Practice* published by the Family Justice Council in December 2012 (*https://www.judiciary.uk/wp-content/uploads/2014/10/fjc_financial_dispute_resolution.pdf* [Accessed 6 June 2019])). It is not appropriate for the judge conducting an FDR appointment to determine heavily disputed issues of fact. Also, if settlement is not reached, the judge hearing the FDR appointment has only a very limited role in any further proceedings in the matter.

Before October 2015 ENE was mentioned in the Commercial Court Guide, the Mercantile Court Guide and the TCC Guide as a form of alternative dispute resolution (ADR) which the court would provide if all parties consented and if the court accepted that ENE in that case was appropriate (see Civil Procedure 2014, Vol.2 paras 2A-102, 2B-24 and 2C-84). In *Halsey v Milton Keynes General NHS Trust* [2004] EWCA Civ 576; [2004] 1 W.L.R. 3002, the Court of Appeal decided that the courts have no power to direct parties to participate in mediation and ruled that the hallmark of ADR procedures and perhaps the key to their effectiveness, is that they are processes voluntarily entered into by parties with outcomes, if they so wish, which are non-binding. Each of the Court Guides mentioned above clearly applied the decision in *Halsey* to requests for ENE by providing a draft order for ADR in a form approved in *Halsey* (see Civil Procedure 2014, Vol.2 paras 2A-164, 2B-24 and 2C-157).

In earlier versions of this paragraph, the amendment to r.3.1(2)(m) was described as giving the court power, not merely to conduct ENE, but also to make orders compelling the parties to submit to a judge-led ENE where the court considered it was appropriate to do so. As authority for this point, reference was made to the amended sub-rule itself; the court's inherent jurisdiction (citing an obiter remark by Lord Neuberger in *Frey v Labrouche* [2012] EWCA Civ 881 at [41] that judges are permitted to express preliminary views as to points at issue); views expressed obiter by Norris J in *Seals v Williams* [2015] EWHC 1829 (Ch); [2015] 4 Costs L.O. 423 at [6] and [7]; and r.9.17 of the Family Procedure Rules 2010 (under which an FDR can be ordered without party consent). However, ENE is now mentioned in many Court Guides and, in all of those Guides, it is still said to depend upon the consent of all parties (see the *White Book*, Vol.2 paras 1A-137 (Chancery Guide), 1B-50 (Queen's Bench Guide), 2A-106 (Commercial Court Guide), 2B-24 (Circuit Commercial (Mercantile) Court Guide), 2C-42 (TCC Guide), 2F-135 (Patent Guide) and 2F-150 (IPEC Guide para.2.13); as to the Administrative Court Judicial Review Guide, see the *White Book*, Vol.2, para.1BA-24).

In *Lomax v Lomax* [2019] EWCA Civ 1467, the Court of Appeal ruled that the wording of r.3.1(2)(m) did not contain a requirement for the parties to consent to ENE and it would be contrary to the overriding objective to imply one. ENE was a process which assisted with the fair and sensible resolution of a case. The rules cannot be disapplied by what is said in the court guides. An ENE hearing is not an obstruction to parties' access to the courts; it is part of the court process (*Halsey v Milton Keynes General NHS Trust* [2004] EWCA Civ 576 and *Seals v Williams* [2015] EWHC 1829 (Ch) considered). If an order for ENE is made it will usually be appropriate to include an order for the personal attendance of the parties so that they will hear directly the judge's evaluation of the case ([31]).

Making orders subject to conditions r.3.1(3)

After the third paragraph, add new paragraphs:

3.1.14   In *Gama Aviation (UK) Ltd v Taleveras Petroleum Trading DMCC* [2019] EWCA Civ 119, the Court of Appeal, applying *Goldtrail*, stated that courts had to be cautious about making conditional orders requiring security for all or most of the sum claimed as a condition of being allowed to defend. They should identify the purpose of imposing the condition and be satisfied that it represented a proportionate and effective means of achieving that purpose. They should also give defendants a reasonable opportunity to adduce evidence of their means. Even though the CPR expressly contemplated the possibility of payment conditions being imposed, *Anglo Eastern Trust Ltd v Kermanshahchi (No.2)* [2002] EWCA Civ 198, established that it was not incumbent on defendants to adduce evidence of resources where there had been no prior notice that the claimant was seeking a conditional order. Although *Gama Aviation* concerned the imposition of a condition in the context of a summary judgment application, the same principles apply whenever a court is considering making any order including a condition to pay money into court.

Goldtrail was followed in *Harbour Castle Ltd v David Wilson Homes Ltd* [2019] EWCA Civ 505, noted in para.3.4.3.2.

After the seventh paragraph (beginning "In Deutsche Bank AG v Unitech Global Ltd"), add new paragraph:

As to the distinction between a conditional order and an unless order see *Khandanpour v Chambers* [2019] EWCA Civ 570, noted in para.3.9.4.

In the last paragraph, replace "Ogiehor v Belinfantie [2018] EWCA Civ 2423" with:

Ogiehor v Belinfantie [2018] EWCA Civ 2423; [2018] 6 Costs L.R. 1329

Ordering security (r.3.1(5), (6) and(6A))

Add new paragraph at end:

3.1.16   In *Alba Exotic Fruit SH PK v MSC Mediteranean Shipping Co SA* [2019] EWHC 1779 (Comm) (Judge Rawlings) on the facts, the judge declined to strike out the claim for the claimant's breach of PD 59 in having failed to apply to fix a case management conference four years and seven months after filing its claim form. Instead, it was held that an order under r.3.1(5) that the claimant provide security for the defendant's costs in an amount representing 79% of the defendant's incurred and estimated costs. While 79% was more than the court might award on an application made under r.25.12, it was a proportionate sanction.

Varying or revoking interim orders

In the last paragraph, replace "Catalyst Management Services v Libya Africa Investment Portfolio [2018] EWCA Civ 1676" with:

3.1.17.1   *Catalyst Management Services v Libya Africa Investment Portfolio* [2018] EWCA Civ 1676; [2018] 4 Costs L.R. 807

Varying or revoking final orders

In the fourth paragraph, replace "Salekipour v Paramar [2017] EWCA Civ 2141; [2018] 2 W.L.R. 1090"
with:
    Salekipour v Paramar [2017] EWCA Civ 2141; [2018] Q.B. 833   **3.1.17.2**

After the penultimate paragraph, add new paragraph:
    Findlay was considered and applied in *Salix Homes v Mantato* [2019] EWCA Civ 445; [2019] 1
W.L.R. 3609.

Effect of rule

In the third paragraph, replace "Sub-rule (2)" with:
    Sub-rule (3)   **3.1A.1**

Add new paragraph 3.1A.2:

The appointment of an advocate to the court

A court may properly seek the assistance of an Advocate to the Court when there is a danger of **3.1A.2**
an important and difficult point of law being decided without the court hearing relevant argument
(Practice Direction 3G para.3). This topic most frequently arises where a case involving an
important and difficult point of law has one or more parties acting in person who cannot afford to
pay for representation and either cannot arrange pro bono representation, or does not have sufficient time to do so.

The person appointed as advocate to the court (formerly called amicus curiae or friend to the
court) represents no-one. Their function is to give to the court such assistance as they are able on
the relevant law and its application to the facts of the case. An Advocate to the Court will not
normally be instructed to lead evidence, cross-examine witnesses, or investigate the facts. If the
court considers it appropriate to seek such assistance it may "request" the Attorney General to arrange it, setting out the circumstances which have occurred, identifying the point of law upon
which assistance is sought and the nature of the assistance required (for example, written advice
and/or oral submissions at the hearing).

Practice Direction 3G also covers other cases in which an Advocate to the Court may be appointed, by the Official Solicitor or the Children & Family Court Advisory Service (CAFCASS). It
also deals with two other cases of advocates appointed by the Attorney General who are not
Advocates to the Court: where a point of law which affects a government department is being
argued in a case where the department is not represented; and where the Attorney believes it is
necessary to intervene as a party in the Attorney's capacity as guardian of the public interest. In the
first of these two cases, the court may simply invite the Attorney to make arrangements for some
representation on behalf of the department if so desired. In the second, the court may grant the
Attorney permission to intervene, in person or by an advocate. In each of these two cases the
advocate who attends will be representing the government department or the Attorney General, as
the case may be.

Attempts to re-litigate issues which were raised, or should have been raised, in previous proceedings

Other case examples of the rule in Henderson, decided post 2001 (after Johnson v Gore Wood)

Add new paragraph at end:
    In *Moorjani v Durban Estates Ltd* [2019] EWHC 1229 (TCC), Pepperall J gives a helpful summary **3.4.3.2**
of the proper approach on applications to strike out claims for abuse of process. The judge made
the point that the focus is upon comparing the causes of action relied upon in each case and not
the particulars of breach or loss and damage. New particulars giving further allegations of breach
of the same promise or tort, or further particulars of loss and damage, do not amount to particulars
of a new cause of action.

Previous litigation terminated without any substantive adjudication or settlement

Replace the seventh paragraph with:
    In *Davies v Carillion Energy Services Ltd* [2017] EWHC 3206 (QB); [2018] 1 W.L.R. 1734, the
claimant, acting in person, had brought a claim in 2010 which was struck out for his failure to file
and serve particulars of claim pursuant to an unless order. He did not appeal, nor did he apply for
relief from sanctions. In 2015 he brought a second claim against the same defendant. The second
defendant applied to have the claim struck out as an abuse of process. The district judge dismissed
that application, a ruling upheld on appeal (albeit on different grounds). Morris J gave the following guidance for cases in which a party brings a second action in respect of matters which raised in
a first action where that action had been struck out on procedural grounds and without any
consideration of the merits (see [52] and [55]):
    (1)   Where a first action has been struck out as itself being an abuse of process, a second action

covering the same subject matter will be struck out as an abuse of process, unless there is special reason: *Securum* at [34] and *Aktas* at [48] and [52].

(2)   In this context abuse of process in the first action comprises: intentional and contumelious conduct; or want of prosecution; or wholesale disregard of rules of court: *Aktas* at [72] and [90].

(3)   Where the first action has been struck out in circumstances which cannot be characterised as an abuse of process, the second action may be struck out as an abuse of process, absent special reason. However, in such a case it is necessary to consider the particular circumstances in which the first action was struck out. At the very least, for the second action to constitute an abuse, the conduct in the first action must have been "inexcusable"; *Collins* at [24] and [25] and *Cranway* at [20].

(4)   Having regard to the introduction, since those cases, of amendments to r.1.1 and given the development of the *Denton* principles, the "special reason" exception identified in *Securum* and *Collins* now falls to be more narrowly circumscribed. Where the conduct of the first action has been found to have been an abuse of process or otherwise inexcusable, then the second action will be struck out as an abuse of process, save in "very unusual circumstances". In addition, in a case where the first action was not itself an abuse of process, whether the conduct in that action was "inexcusable" might fall to be assessed more rigorously and in the defendant's favour. However, even post-Jackson, ultimately, the importance of the efficient use of resources does not, in my judgment, trump the overriding need to do justice: see *Aktas* [92].

(5)   A single failure to comply with an unless order is not, of itself, sufficient to conclude that the second action is an abuse of process.

In *Harbour Castle Ltd v David Wilson Homes Ltd* [2019] EWCA Civ 505, the Court of Appeal gave somewhat different guidance as to whether an action is an abuse of process if it includes claims previously raised in an earlier action which was struck out on procedural grounds and without any consideration of the merits. In *Harbour Castle* C brought a claim (the "first action") seeking remedies in respect of an alleged breach of covenant by D. On C's failure to comply with an order to provide security of costs, a new order was made in the unless form, i.e. an order that the first action would be struck out without any further order if, by a new date, C had still not given the security previously ordered. It was common ground that, at all material times, C had not itself possessed the funds to provide security, but that its sole shareholder (X) personally had the resources to do so. The unless order was made prior to the change in practice brought about by the Supreme Court's ruling in *Goldtrail Travel Ltd (In Liquidation) v Aydin* [2017] UKSC 57; [2017] 1 W.L.R. 3014 (as to which see para.3.1.14). For commercial reasons X did not assist C to comply with the unless order, and therefore its claim was automatically struck out in December 2012. In 2016 C commenced new proceedings (the "second action") raising the same claims as before and D applied for an order striking out the second action as an abuse of process. The lower court struck out the second action as an abuse and C's appeal to the Court of Appeal was dismissed.

"[6] The burden of showing that the second action is an abuse lies on the party asserting it, in this case [D], and it must be clearly shown to be an abuse. Whether an action is an abuse is not a question of discretion, but an evaluative assessment to which there can be only one answer. These propositions are established by several decisions of this court, including *Stuart v Goldberg Linde* [2008] EWCA Civ 2, [2008] 1 WLR 823 and *Aktas v Adepta* [2010] EWCA Civ 1170, [2011] QB 894. If it is an abuse, the court has a discretion whether to strike it out, but, as Rix LJ said in *Aktas v Adepta* at [53], once satisfied that the second action is an abuse of process it is likely that the court will strike it out, but it does not necessarily follow."

Bearing in mind the principles set out in *Goldtrail*, the second action would be an abuse of process if C had decided not to comply with the unless order even though it could have raised sufficient funds to do so. The relevant question in this case was whether X would have provided the requisite funds if he had been requested to do so by C. The burden of proof on this sub-issue fell upon C; it was for C to show that it could not have raised the funds from X. The evidence given by X and others in the second action led the lower court to the conclusion that X had been the sole directing mind of C, had financed both C and the litigation up to December 2012, and had continued to finance C after that time. On the basis of this evidence the lower court had concluded that the decision not to comply with the unless order had been made by X in his capacity as the directing mind of C and that if, in that capacity, he had concluded that it was in the interests of C to proceed with the litigation, he would personally have provided the necessary funding. C therefore did have access to funding if it chose to seek it.

For further case authorities on the striking out of second actions as an abuse, see *Hall v Ministry of Defence* [2013] EWHC 4092 (QB), noted in para.3.4.3.6, *Wahab v Khan* [2011] EWHC 908 (Ch) noted in para.3.9.25 and *Re Samuel (Deceased)* [2018] EWHC 3513 (Ch) (Master Teverson).

Delay

Add new paragraph at end:

3.4.3.6   Issuing and maintaining proceedings with no real intention of carrying them through to trial ("warehousing") may amount to an abuse but the court should always examine all the circumstances, including the length of the delay, the degree of the claimant's responsibility for it and the reasons given for it. In *Asturion Foundation v Alibrahim* [2019] EWHC 274 (Ch), C indicated a willingness to delay its present proceedings in order to await the outcome of proceedings which D had commenced in Liechtenstein. D's proceedings sought to undermine entirely the legitimacy of C's claim. D's application to strike out C's claim was refused: in the circumstances C's decision to pause proceedings dependent on the outcome of D's proceedings did not amount to an abuse of process.

Failure to comply with a rule, practice direction or court order (r.3.4(2)(c))

In the fourth paragraph, replace "Mark v Universal Coatings & Services Ltd [2018] EWHC 3206 (QB)," with:
    Mark v Universal Coatings & Services Ltd [2018] EWHC 3206 (QB); [2019] 1 W.L.R. 2376,   **3.4.4**

Consequences of non-payment

In the last paragraph, replace "3.9.6.9" with:
    3.9.21   **3.7.2**

Consequences of non-payment

In the last paragraph, replace "Hyslop v 38/41 CHG Residents Co Ltd, 5 November 2018, unrep., (QB)," with:
    Hyslop v 38/41 CHG Residents Co Ltd [2018] EWHC 3893 (QB),   **3.7A1.3**

Add new paragraph at end:
    In *Alesco Risk Management Services Ltd v Bishopsgate Insurance Brokers Ltd* [2019] QBD, 1 March 2019, unrep., Freedman J, relief from sanctions was granted to claimants who, by inadvertence, had failed to pay the trial fee on time. Applying *Denton*, it was held that, although serious, the breach was at the bottom of the range of seriousness; there was no good reason for the breach; but in all the circumstances it would be just to grant relief from sanctions because it had been an inadvertent mistake, immediate steps had been taken to rectify it, the defendants did not object and no prejudice had been caused. Striking out the claim under CPR r.3.7A1(7) would be a disproportionate response. The judge commended the claimants for immediately rectifying their mistake and for accepting responsibility. The defendants were commended for not taking advantage of the claimants' mistake (and see also *St Peter Parish Council v Holy Cross Sisters Trustees Inc* [2019] EWHC 735 (QB)).

The first stage: assess seriousness and significance of breach

After the penultimate paragraph, add new paragraph:
    In *Khandanpour v Chambers* [2019] EWCA Civ 570, on D's application to set aside a default costs **3.9.4** certificate, the court made an order setting aside the certificate which was conditional upon D paying £10,000 on account to C by 16.00 on a specified date and upon D also serving points of dispute by 16.00 on that date. D served points of dispute and paid £4,000 to C on time but failed to pay the remaining £6,000 until the following morning. The Court of Appeal held that, for the purposes of determining D's application for relief from sanctions, the conditional order made in this case should not be treated as if it was an unless order.
    "[39] ... even if the payment condition was imposed in the light of the appellant's longstanding failure to pay the judgment debt and a history of leaving things until the last minute, he was not in breach of any previous order as to costs. It was not, therefore, a case such as described by Jackson LJ [in *British Gas Trading*] where, having been in breach of previous orders for payment on account of costs, the appellant was now being given a final chance. At stage one, therefore, this was a minor breach, not one which was serious or significant."

Effect of Denton principles on applications to set aside default judgments

In the penultimate paragraph, replace "Cunico Resources NV v Daskalakis [2018] EWHC 3382 (Comm)" with:
    Cunico Resources NV v Daskalakis [2018] EWHC 3382 (Comm); [2019] 1 W.L.R. 2881   **3.9.8**

Add new paragraph at end:
    In *Tenaga Nasional Bhd v Frazer-Nash Research Ltd* [2018] EWHC 2970 (QB); [2019] 1 W.L.R. 946, F applied under r.74.7 to set aside an order of registration of certain foreign judgments. On such an application facts which need to be proved by the evidence of a witness must be proved by a witness statement (rr.32.2(1)(b) and 32.6(1)). Practice Direction 23A—Applications paras 6.11 and 6.13 provide that on interim applications in which evidence or other documents are required to be filed and served, those documents must be filed and served by 16.00 at least two days before the hearing. F filed and served a supplementary witness statement only 26 hours before the hearing.

T's counsel submitted that the supplementary witness statement was inadmissible in evidence unless F obtained relief from sanctions under r.3.9. Pepperall J ruled that no application under r.3.9 was required because PD 23A does not impose a sanction for non-compliance with paras 6.11 and 6.13 (see [34] and [35]; and see further, *Gama Aviation (UK) Ltd v Taleveras Petroleum Trading DMCC* [2019] EWCA Civ 119 at [39] and *Mark v Universal Coatings & Services Ltd* [2018] EWHC 3206 (QB); [2019] 1 W.L.R. 2376, noted in paras 3.9.4 and 3.9.15).

Extension of time: out-of-time application

3.9.15   *In the last paragraph, replace "Mark v Universal Coatings & Services Ltd [2018] EWHC 3206 (QB)" with:*
Mark v Universal Coatings & Services Ltd [2018] EWHC 3206 (QB); [2019] 1 W.L.R. 2376

Effect of Denton principles in all cases of non-compliance

3.9.23   *Add new paragraph at end:*
The *Denton* principles do not fetter or overlay the discretion given to the court by s.33 of the Limitation Act 1980 to disapply a limitation period otherwise applicable to a personal injury or death claim (*Ellis v Heart of England NHS Foundation Trust* [2018] EWHC 3505 (Ch); [2019] P.I.Q.R. P8). Nor do they apply when the court is considering whether to uphold a "limitation amnesty" agreed by the parties to an Inheritance Act claim (*Cowan v Foreman* [2019] EWCA Civ 1336).

Application to be supported by evidence

3.9.24   *Delete the second paragraph.*

Civil restraint orders

3.11.1   *After the sixth paragraph (beginning "Practice Direction 3C"), add new paragraph:*
In *Sartipy v Tigris Industries Inc* [2019] EWCA Civ 225, the Court of Appeal gave guidance on the requirements for making an extended civil restraint order under PD 3C para 3.1 which may be summarised as follows:
(1)   In the course of those proceedings one or more applications may be issued. If the claim itself is totally without merit and if individual applications are also totally without merit, there is no reason why both the claim and individual applications should not be counted for the purpose of considering whether to make an ECRO.
(2)   Although at least three claims or applications are the minimum required for the making of an ECRO, the question remains whether the party concerned is acting "persistently". That will require an evaluation of the party's overall conduct. It may be easier to conclude that a party is persistently issuing claims or applications which are totally without merit if it seeks repeatedly to re-litigate issues which have been decided than if there are three or more unrelated applications many years apart. The latter situation would not necessarily constitute persistence.
(3)   Only claims or applications where the party in question is the claimant (or counterclaimant) or applicant can be counted (although this includes a totally without merit application by the defendant in the proceedings). A defendant or respondent may behave badly, for example by telling lies in his or her evidence, producing fraudulent documents or putting forward defences in bad faith. However, that does not constitute issuing claims or making applications for the purpose of considering whether to make an ECRO. Nevertheless such conduct is not irrelevant as it is likely to cast light on the party's overall conduct and to demonstrate, provided that the necessary persistence can be demonstrated by reference to other claims or applications, that an Extended Civil Restraint Order or even a General Civil Restraint Order, is necessary.
(4)   Approving *CFC 26 Ltd* (above), the term "a party" refers not only to the named party but also to someone who is not a named party but is nevertheless the "real" party who has issued a claim or made an application. The "real party" concept extends to a person who is controlling the conduct of the proceedings and who has a significant interest in their outcome.
(5)   Where the named claimant allows the use of his or her name to issue claims or make applications which are totally without merit, an Extended Civil Restraint Order may be made against the named party notwithstanding that he or she is personally innocent of any misconduct or even ignorant of the claims or applications which the "real" party has been making. By permitting his or her name to be used, the named claimant or applicant takes responsibility for the conduct of the individual who exercises control over the conduct of the proceedings.
(6)   However, in that situation the named claimant is not responsible for claims and applications made by the "real" party in his or her own name in other proceedings.
(7)   When considering whether to make a restraint order, the court is entitled to take into account any previous claims or applications which it concludes were totally without merit,

and is not limited to claims or applications so certified at the time; *R. (Kumar) v Secretary of State for Constitutional Affairs* (below) followed.

Add new paragraphs at end:
In *Middlesbrough Football and Athletic Co (1986) Ltd v Earth Energy Investments LLP (In Liquidation)* [2019] EWHC 226 (Ch); [2019] 1 W.L.R. 3709, Sir Geoffrey Vos C held that the grounds for discharging an Extended Civil Restraint Order were the same grounds as apply on an application under r.3.1(7), namely a material change of circumstances since the order was made and the facts having been misstated to the judge who made the order.

In *Adelaja v Islington LBC* [2019] EWHC 1295 (QB) extended civil restraint orders were made against both a husband and wife. It was clear that the husband was the driving force behind the various claims and applications and it was necessary and proportionate to make an order against him. The claims had been commenced in both names and there was evidence that the wife had been assessed as lacking capacity to conduct litigation and had signed various forms under pressure from her husband. Whilst she may lack litigation capacity, the wife did have sufficient capacity to understand the order.

In *Chief Constable of Avon and Somerset v Gray* [2019] EWHC 1954 (QB) a general civil restraint order (GCRO) was originally made in 2014 and was renewed for a further two years in 2016. On an application for a second renewal for a further two years, Stuart-Smith J declined so to order despite the likelihood that the respondent would bring further civil claims, including unmeritorious claims. It was held that given the evidence of his financial situation, and the requirement to pay a fee to apply for permission to bring a claim, the general civil restraint order acted as an absolute bar on his right to bring proceedings, and that was not its intended purpose. It should be a permission filter and not a bar. It is to be noted that while the individual had brought unmeritorious proceedings, he had brought two cases which were successful. It is submitted that that whilst this decision is justified on its very unusual facts (including that it was on an application to renew a GCRO) the court's approach, if adopted too readily in other cases, would risk undermining the civil restraint order regime. In this very unusual case the judge warned the respondent that if he were to issue proceedings that are clearly unmeritorious, it was highly probable the court would, either of its own motion or on application, impose a further civil restraint order of some description or seek the involvement of the Attorney General under the provisions of s.42 of the Senior Courts Act 1981. Presumably on that further application for a civil restraint order, the respondent's means would no longer be relevant.

II. Costs Management

Prescribed form of costs budget to be used

Delete the third paragraph.   **3.12.4**

In the fourth paragraph, seventh line, after "have not yet", add:
been

Replace the last paragraph with:
As to the adverse consequences of filing a non-compliant budget, see *Page v RGC Restaurants Ltd* [2018] EWHC 2688 (QB); [2019] 1 W.L.R. 22 noted in para.3.14.1.

Distinction between incurred costs and budgeted costs

After the third paragraph, add new paragraph:
With effect from 1 October 2019, PD 3E para.7.4 is amended to state that the court may not ap- **3.12.6** prove costs incurred up to and including the date of the costs management hearing. According to the Ministry of Justice commentary to the 109th Update to the CPR, this amendment is intended to provide clearer guidance on the cut-off between budgeted costs and incurred costs, drawing the line between costs incurred up to and including the date of the first costs management hearing (incurred costs) and costs to be incurred after that date (budgeted costs). This amendment is intended to assist with the approach to the revision of costs budgets.

To the end of the fourth paragraph (beginning "In two cases"), add:
However, in many cases the court merely records its comments upon the incurred costs without adjusting the budgeted costs to take account of those comments (see, for example, *Various Claimants v Sir Robert McAlpine* [2015] EWHC 3543 (QB); [2015] 6 Costs L.R. 1085, especially at [29] and [30]).

Budgets to include all costs up to and including trial unless the court otherwise orders

Replace the second paragraph with:
In some cases parties may find it difficult or impractical to budget accurately all the work which **3.13.2** will later have to be undertaken. The opening words of r.13.3(1) indicate that the court has the

power to direct the parties to exchange and file budgets in some other form or omitting parts of the prescribed form. Moreover, PD 3E para.6(a) provides that:

> "In substantial cases, the court may direct that budgets be limited initially to part only of the proceedings and subsequently extended to cover the whole proceedings."

A party seeking permission to budget for only part of a case must make an application to the court in advance of the deadline for filing budgets. Unless an appropriate direction has been obtained in advance, a party filing a budget which does not include all costs up to and including trial will be in breach of r.13.3(1) and therefore at risk of the court making a costs management order limiting their recoverable costs to court fees only (see r.3.14 and *Page v RGC Restaurants Ltd* [2018] EWHC 2688 (QB); [2019] 1 W.L.R. 22 noted in para.3.14.1).

Effect of rule

3.14.1   *In the fifth paragraph, replace "Page v RGC Restaurants Ltd [2018] EWHC 2688 (QB)," with:*
   Page v RGC Restaurants Ltd [2018] EWHC 2688 (QB); [2019] 1 W.L.R. 22,

"Unless the court otherwise orders"

3.14.2   *Replace paragraph with:*
   A party in default of r.3.14 need not make a separate application for relief from sanctions under r.3.9. Instead, it may seek to invoke the saving provision in r.3.14 itself ("Unless the court otherwise orders") by seeking to persuade the court to adopt that course at the hearing convened for costs management purposes. This saving provision gives the court an express power to disapply the sanction which is additional to the power it has under r.3.9. Whichever application is made, the court should apply the three-stage test set out in *Denton v TH White Ltd* [2014] EWCA Civ 906; [2014] 1 W.L.R. 3296 (as to which, see para.3.9.3). There is an important difference between these two applications: on an application for relief from sanctions under r.3.9, the starting point should be that the sanction has been properly imposed and complies with the overriding objective (*Denton* at [45]); however, on an application under r.3.14, the court is not required to take that starting point unless there has been a prior judicial decision to that effect (*Page v RGC Restaurants Ltd* [2018] EWHC 2688 (QB); [2019] 1 W.L.R. 22 at [138]).

Revising costs budgets

3.15.4   *To the end of the second paragraph, add:*
   This paragraph and *Sharp v Blank* (see below) was applied in *Seekings v Moores* [2019] EWHC 1476 (Comm) (Judge Worster).

In the third paragraph, replace "(Sharp v Blank)." with:
   (*Sharp v Blank*); in a clinical negligence claim, a change of position by the defendant relating to causation justifying the instruction of leading counsel by the claimant (*Zeromska-Smith v United Lincolnshire Hospitals NHS Trust* [2019] EWHC 630 (QB) (Martin Spencer J)).

Replace the fourth and fifth paragraphs with:
   PD 3E para.7.6 describes the documents which must be produced on an application for revision: the draft revised budget and a note of the changes made, the reasons for them and the objections of any other party. In the draft revised budget the "Incurred" columns and "Estimated" columns for phases not being revised will remain as previously approved or amended even though, by the time of the revision application, some costs in those "Estimated" columns will have been incurred. In respect of each phase of the budget sought to be revised, the "Incurred" columns will remain the same as before and, a changed total (whether upwards or downwards) will be shown in the "Estimated" columns (see further, para.3.12.4). With effect from 1 October 2019, amendment to PD 3E para 7.4 provides clearer guidance on the cut-off between budgeted costs and incurred costs, drawing the line between costs incurred up to and including the date of the first costs management hearing (incurred costs) and costs to be incurred after that date (budgeted costs); see para 3.12.6.
   On applications for an upwards budget revision, respondents often challenge the new amount claimed as excessive and submit that some of it must be an overspend on the budgeted costs previously approved or agreed. By itself, the draft revised budget alone will not enable the court to identify with precision which, if any, part of the increase was incurred before the date of the previous budget. Requiring further detail may fall into the vice of micromanagement criticised by Jacobs J in *Yirenkyi v Ministry of Defence* [2018] EWHC 3102 (QB); [2018] 5 Costs L.R. 1177 (see para.3.15.3). It is open to the court to require the applicant to certify that every increase sought is attributable only to the significant developments relied on. Alternatively the applicant may seek to persuade the court that the significant developments which have occurred justify a root and branch revision of the relevant parts of the previous budget. This is the view generally taken on an analogous application, the upward revision of an order for security for costs (see further, *Stokors SA v IG Markets Ltd* [2012] EWHC 1684 (Comm) and other cases noted in para.25.12.13; and see further, *Barts Health NHS Trust v Salmon* [2019] 1 WLUK 529; L.T.L. 29/3/2019, 19 January 2019, unrep. (HH Judge Dight), noted in para.3.18.3).

What amounts to a good reason to depart?

Replace the second paragraph with:

It is arguable that, on adopting the approach suggested in *Harrison*, a costs judge might be **3.18.3** entitled to reach conclusions as to the proportionality of budgeted costs, or as to the reasonableness of the hourly rates upon which they were claimed, which depart from the conclusions reached by the costs managing court. Two decisions by costs judges have been reported on this topic (both available from the bailii website): *RNB v Newham LBC* [2017] EWHC B15 (Costs) and *Nash v Ministry of Defence* [2018] EWHC B4 (Costs). Both decisions support the view that a costs judge may depart from the last approved or agreed budget if satisfied that the total costs incurred are disproportionate. However, they reach opposite conclusions on the significance of a ruling as to hourly rates which are lower than those upon which an approved budget had been drawn. In *RNB* this was held to amount to a good reason to depart from the budget. In *Nash* it was held that hourly rates form only one of a variety of factors taken into account when setting a budget and should not be treated as holding some special status, making it different from the other factors. Neither case is being taken further by way of appeal.

In *Barts Health NHS Trust v Salmon* [2019] 1 WLUK 529; L.T.L. 29/3/2019, 19 January 2019, unrep. (HH Judge Dight) the parties agreed a settlement before all of the budgeted work had been undertaken and the claimant's bill of costs for detailed assessment claimed the budget sub-totals for completed phases and the actual costs incurred for other phases. The learned judge ruled that the non-completion of budgeted work in any phase of the budget can amount to a good reason to depart from the budget sub-total for that phase. The learned judge further ruled that, once the court has decided to depart from a budget sub-total, it may then hear submissions on the sum to be allowed for that phase. That sum (as determined either by way of a line-by-line assessment or in a more broad brush way) may be a sum lower than the costs actually incurred for that phase. There is no requirement to show a second good reason to make this further departure from the budget sub-total.

The fact that a budget contains a substantial overstatement of the hourly rate applied for one or more of the fee earners may amount to a good reason within the meaning of r.3.18 for departing from the budget (*MXX v United Lincolnshire NHS Trust* [2019] EWHC 1624 (QB)).

PRACTICE DIRECTION 3D—MESOTHELIOMA CLAIMS

"show cause procedure"

Replace paragraph with:

This is defined as a requirement by the court, of its own initiative and usually on a "costs in the **3DPD.6.1** case" basis, for the defendant to identify the evidence and legal arguments that give the defendant a real prospect of success. Applying the test for summary judgment, the burden of showing that the defendant has no real prospect of success remains on the claimant. Further, at a show cause hearing it is for the claimant to adduce credible evidence in support of their case, and it is only if they do so that the defendant becomes subject to an evidential burden to show cause: *Silcock v H M Revenue and Customs* [2009] EWHC 3025 (QB). The justification for the court imposing this filter rather that requiring a full blown application under Pt 24 to be initiated by the claimant, is the fact that the RCJ experience has shown that in many claims there is no such defence and a summary judgment application simply duplicates work and increases costs unnecessarily. The requirement to "show cause" may be imposed on successive occasions, i.e. at the first CMC and then at a later substantive "show cause hearing" if the defendant is able to persuade the court to allow more time. The court's order is to show cause not only as to liability but also as to why the usual standard interim payment should not be made.

Any subsequent application for judgment should be made under Pt 24, not under this procedure.

PRACTICE DIRECTION 3E—COSTS MANAGEMENT

D.   Costs management orders

Replace paragraph 7.4 with:

7.4 As part of the costs management process the court may not approve **3EPD.4** costs incurred up to and including the date of the costs management hearing. The court may, however, record its comments on those costs and will take those costs into account when considering the reasonableness and proportionality of all subsequent budgeted costs.

Add new Practice Direction 3G:

PRACTICE DIRECTION 3G—REQUESTS FOR THE APPOINTMENT OF AN ADVOCATE TO THE COURT
This Practice Direction supplements CPR, rule 3.1

Introduction

3GPD.1   **1.** The following provisions are taken from a memorandum agreed between the Attorney General and the Lord Chief Justice dated 19 December 2001. They give guidance about making a request for the appointment of an Advocate to the Court (formerly called an "amicus curiae").

2. In most cases, an Advocate to the Court is appointed by the Attorney General, following a request by the court. In some cases, an Advocate to the Court will be appointed by the Official Solicitor or the Children & Family Court Advisory Service (CAFCASS) (see paragraphs 11 and 12 below).

The role of an Advocate to the Court

3GPD.2   **3.** A court may properly seek the assistance of an Advocate to the Court when there is a danger of an important and difficult point of law being decided without the court hearing relevant argument. In those circumstances the Attorney General may decide to appoint an Advocate to the Court.

4. It is important to bear in mind that an Advocate to the Court represents no-one. Their function is to give to the court such assistance as they are able on the relevant law and its application to the facts of the case. An Advocate to the Court will not normally be instructed to lead evidence, cross-examine witnesses, or investigate the facts. In particular, it is not appropriate for the court to seek assistance from an Advocate to the Court simply because a defendant in criminal proceedings refuses representation.

5. The following circumstances are to be distinguished from those where it will be appropriate for the court to seek the assistance of an Advocate to the Court—

(a)   where a point of law which affects a government department is being argued in a case where the department is not represented and where the court believe that the department may wish to be represented;

(b)   where the Attorney believes it is necessary for them to intervene as a party in the Attorney's capacity as guardian of the public interest;

(c)   where the court believes it is appropriate for a litigant in person to seek free (pro bono) assistance;

(d)   where, in a criminal trial, the defendant is unrepresented and the Advocate to the Court would be duplicating the prosecutor's duty as a minister of justice "to assist the court on all matters of law applicable to the case";

(e)   where in a criminal case in relation to sentencing appeals there are issues of fact which are likely to arise and the prosecution ought to be represented, or it would be reasonable to ask the prosecutor to be present and address the court as to the relevant law.

6. In the first of these five cases, the court may invite the Attorney to make arrangements for the advocate to be instructed on behalf of the department. In the second, the court may grant the Attorney permission to intervene, in which case the advocate instructed represents the Attorney. In neither case is the advocate an Advocate to the Court.

7. In the third case the court may grant a litigant in person an adjournment to enable them to seek free (pro bono) assistance. In doing so, the court should bear in mind that it is likely to take longer to obtain free (pro bono) representation than funded representation. In contrast to an Advocate to the Court, a free (pro bono) legal representative will obtain their instructions from the litigant and will represent the interests of that party. Their role before the court and duty to the court will be identical to that of any other representative of the parties. Accordingly, it will not be appropriate for the court to take such a course where the type of assistance required is that provided by an Advocate to the Court.

8. In the fourth case the prosecutor's special duty is akin to an Advocate to the Court. In the fifth case, in relation to appeals against sentence where the defendant is represented, it may be preferable to request the attendance of the prosecutor who will be able to address the court on issues of fact and law. It would not be proper for an Advocate to the Court to take instructions from the prosecuting authority in relation to factual matters relating to the prosecution. An Advocate to the Court should only be asked to address the court as to the relevant law.

Making a request to the Attorney General

9. A request for an Advocate to the Court should be made by the Court as **3GPD.3** soon as convenient after it is made aware of the point of law which requires the assistance of an Advocate to the Court. The request should set out the circumstances which have occurred, identifying the point of law upon which assistance is sought and the nature of the assistance required. The court should consider whether it would be sufficient for such assistance to be in writing in the form of submissions as to the law, or whether the assistance should include oral submissions at the hearing. The request should ordinarily be made in writing and be accompanied by the papers necessary to enable the Attorney to reach a decision on the basis of a proper understanding of the case.

10. The Attorney will decide whether it is appropriate to provide such assistance and, if so, the form such assistance should take. Before reaching a decision, the Attorney may seek further information or assistance from the court. The Attorney will also ask the court to keep under review the need for such assistance. Where the circumstances which gave rise to the original request have changed, such that the court may now anticipate hearing all relevant argument on the point of law without the presence of an Advocate to the Court, either the Court or the Attorney may ask the Advocate to the Court to withdraw.

Requests to the Official Solicitor or CAFCASS

11. A request for an Advocate to the Court may be made to the Official **3GPD.4** Solicitor or CAFCASS (Legal Services and Special Casework) where the issue is one in which their experience of representing children and adults under disability gives rise to special experience. The division of responsibility between them is outlined in Practice Notes reported at [2001] 2 FLR 151 and [2001] 2 FLR 155.

12. The procedure and circumstances for requesting an Advocate to the Court to be appointed by the Official Solicitor or CAFCASS are the same as those applying to requests to the Attorney General. In cases of extreme urgency, telephone requests may be made. In some cases, the Official Solicitor will be appointed as Advocate to the Court. The Official Solicitor may be given directions by the Court authorising the Official Solicitor to obtain documents, conduct investigations and enquiries and to advise the Court. The Official Solicitor may appear by counsel or an in-house advocate.

Requests for an Advocate to the Court should be addressed as follows—

The Legal Secretary, The Legal Secretariat to the Law Officers, Attorney General's Office, 5-8 The Sanctuary, London SW1P 3JS

Telephone: 020 7271 2492

Office of the Official Solicitor to the Senior Courts, Victory House, 30-34 Kingsway, London WC2B 6EX

Telephone:

Fax: 020 3681 2762

E-mail: enquiries@offsol.gsi.gov.uk

CAFCASS (Legal Services [and Special Casework]) 3rd Floor, 21 Bloomsbury Street, London, WC1B 3HF

Telephone: 0175 323 5272

For information about free (pro bono) services contact:

Bar Pro Bono Unit, 48 Chancery Lane, London WC2A 1JF

Telephone: 020 7092 3960.

PART 5

COURT DOCUMENTS

Brexit

Replace paragraph with:

5.0.1.1   At the time of writing, the Cross-Border Mediation (EU Directive) (EU Exit) Regulations 2019 (SI 2019/469), consequent upon the EU Mediation Directive (2008/52) ceasing to apply upon a no-deal Brexit, will revoke the Cross-Border Mediation (EU Directive) Regulations 2011 (SI 2011/1133). The likely effect will be, subject to any transitional and saving provisions (such as those contained in regs 2 and 5 of the 2019 Regulations), the revocation of r.5.4C(1B), which was introduced consequent to the EU Mediation Directive, see para.5.4C.1 for further detail on that provision.

Details on the amendments to be effected to the CPR and its Practice Directions upon a no-deal Brexit are set out in the Civil Procedure Rules 1998 (Amendment) (EU Exit) Regulations 2019 (SI 2019/521) (*http://www.legislation.gov.uk/uksi/2019/521/contents/made*) and the CPR Update 107 (March 2019) (*http://www.justice.gov.uk/courts/procedure-rules/civil/pdf/update/107-pdmd-no-deal.pdf*). Both the statutory instrument and the Practice Direction Update will only come into force on exit day. If the UK and EU enter into a Withdrawal Agreement, it is assumed that these amending instruments will either be revoked before they enter into force, or will be amended prior to coming into force to take account of any agreement(s) the UK and EU enter into governing their future relationship.

"records of the court"

Replace the second and third paragraphs with:

5.4B.3   In *Concept Ltd v Cape Intermediate Holdings Plc* [2017] EWHC 811 (QB), 6 April 2017 (Master McCloud), on the application of a non-party made without notice, the Master ordered that documents filed at court during the course of litigation be preserved at the court office pending an application by that party. She thereafter held that the court had a jurisdiction at Common Law to allow a party with a legitimate reason to access any documents presented to the court. On appeal to the Supreme Court, reversing the Court of Appeal on the question of jurisdiction, which had disapproved the first instance decision, the court set out the principles and extent of the Common Law jurisdiction and its mode of exercise and also considered the scope of the expression "records of the court". See detailed note at para.5.4C.2.

"court records"

Replace paragraph with:

5.4C.2   See "records of the court", para.5.4B.3 above. See also para.5.4C.10 below. The principles to be applied on a request for access to court documents by a non-party were comprehensively stated by the Supreme Court in the leading case on access to court documents, *Cape Intermediate Holdings Ltd v Dring (for and on behalf of Asbestos Victims Support Groups Forum UK)* [2019] UKSC 38 by which the Supreme Court unanimously departed from a decision of the Court of Appeal in the same case at [2018] EWCA Civ 1795. The Applicant at first instance became aware that a large claim brought by the insurance industry against Cape in relation to the dangers of asbestos as a product had reached the end of trial after six weeks and that judgment had been reserved. Prior to judgment, the parties settled the claim on terms which included provision for the destruction of documents which had been gathered together for the trial and which covered a large part of the twentieth-century history of knowledge as to asbestos product characteristics and what was known by the industry and when. He applied under the above rules for copies of documents held on the records of the court, as a non-party.

Master McCloud restrained the parties to the original claim from removing the documents from court pending a decision on the application: [2017] EWHC 811 (QB). At a subsequent hearing she held, reviewing the history of the authorities on open justice and access to documents in court, that the documents placed before the court in the form of paper copies and which had been lodged at court as "bundles" were either part of the records of the court for the purposes of the rule, or alternatively that the rules did not limit the scope of the Common Law, and applying the principle of openness of justice, the court had a discretion to allow a party with a legitimate interest to have access to any documents which played a role in the claim: [2017] EWHC 3154 (QB).

Having considered whether the applicant had legitimate reasons to seek access to the documents she held that the applicant had a legitimate interest and that the extent of disclosure should extend on the facts of the case to the bundles actually placed before the court (but not to documents which were merely disclosed and not placed before the court), and she weighed the relative interests of the parties and third parties. She directed that a copy of the judge's trial bundle be disclosed (by giving carriage of the bundle to an officer of the court with instructions to omit any marked up pages, if there were any).

On appeal to the Court of Appeal, her decision was reversed, the court holding that the CPR provisions permitted access only to certain categories of material and that there was no discretion to permit wider access as Master McCloud had done, save in relation to some "key" documents ([2018] EWCA Civ 1795) and was critical of the Master's decision. The Supreme Court on further appeal at [2019] UKSC 38 reversed the decision of the Court of Appeal as far as material, holding consistently with the first instance decision, that although:

(i) for the purposes of the rules "the 'records of the court' must [...] refer to those documents and records which the court itself keeps for its own purposes. It cannot refer to every single document generated in connection with a case and filed, lodged or kept for the time being at court." (para.23) nonetheless:

(ii) "There can be no doubt at all that the court rules are not exhaustive of the circumstances in which non-parties may be given access to court documents. They are a minimum and of course it is for a person seeking to persuade the court to allow access outside the rules to show a good case for doing so. However, case after case has recognised that the guiding principle is the need for justice to be done in the open and that courts at all levels have an inherent jurisdiction to allow access in accordance with that principle" (para.34).

(iii) "The constitutional principle of open justice applies to all courts and tribunals exercising the judicial power of the state. It follows that, unless inconsistent with statute or the rules of court, all courts and tribunals have an inherent jurisdiction to determine what that principle requires in terms of access to documents or other information placed before the court or tribunal in question. The extent of any access permitted by the court's rules is not determinative (save to the extent that they may contain a valid prohibition). It is not correct to talk in terms of limits to the court's jurisdiction when what is in fact in question is how that jurisdiction should be exercised in the particular case."

(iv) That whilst "... the court has the power to allow access, the applicant has no right to be granted it (save to the extent that the rules grant such a right). It is for the person seeking access to explain why he seeks it and how granting him access will advance the open justice principle. In this respect it may well be that the media are better placed than others to demonstrate a good reason for seeking access. But there are others who may be able to show a legitimate interest in doing so." (para.45).

(v) "The court has to carry out a fact-specific balancing exercise. On the one hand will be 'the purpose of the open justice principle and the potential value of the information in question in advancing that purpose'. On the other hand will be 'any risk of harm which its disclosure may cause to the maintenance of an effective judicial process or to the legitimate interests of others'. " (paras 45–46).

(vi) "There may be very good reasons for denying access. The most obvious ones are national security, the protection of the interests of children or mentally disabled adults, the protection of privacy interests more generally, and the protection of trade secrets and commercial confidentiality." (para.46).

(vii) "Also relevant must be the practicalities and the proportionality of granting the request. It is highly desirable that the application is made during the trial when the material is still readily available, the parties are before the court and the trial judge is in day to day control of the court process. The non-party who seeks access will be expected to pay the reasonable costs of granting that access." (para.47).

(viii) "In short, non-parties should not seek access unless they can show a good reason why this will advance the open justice principle, that there are no countervailing principles of the sort outlined earlier, which may be stronger after the proceedings have come to an end, and that granting the request will not be impracticable or disproportionate." (para.47).

(ix)   Lastly, "A clean copy of the bundle, if still available, may in fact be the most practicable way of affording a non-party access to the material in question, but that is for the court hearing the application to decide." (para.48).

Accordingly in any request for access to court documents, a party should first consider whether the request falls within the scope of the CPR provisions as part of the "records of the court" (applying the approach taken in the Supreme Court judgment in *Dring*), and then, if not part of the "records of the court" should consider whether the tests for access at Common Law under the court's wider discretion (discussed both at first instance and in the Supreme Court decision). In many instances it may be prudent to apply on both bases until the Rules Committee clarifies the expression "records of the court" which it was encouraged to do at the conclusion of the Supreme Court judgment. The applicant should ensure that it can pay the costs of copying (which may be much reduced when digital bundles become the norm), and should ensure that the application addresses the criteria outlined by the Supreme Court including legitimate reasons for access, and proportionality.

The Supreme Court held that "marked up" documents such as those which are annotated by parties or the judge should not be disclosed without the consent of the person involved. In respect of paper bundles which may be "marked up", the procedure adopted in *Dring* at first instance was that the Master reviewed the bundles to check for any marking up by the judge, and also adopted a procedure whereby a solicitor acting as an officer of the court was permitted to remove them for copying but with instructions not to copy any marked up pages which were located, in the event that any existed. It is suggested that other approaches to the question of the practicality of copying of bundles or other documents may be considered including where possible the use of clean digital copies if such exist, thereby minimising cost of copying, or the use of witness copies of bundles which are typically unmarked.

PART 6

SERVICE OF DOCUMENTS

Brexit

Replace paragraph with:

6.0.1.1   At the time of writing, a number of statutory instruments are likely to affect Pt 6 upon a no-deal Brexit. First, the Service of Documents and Taking of Evidence in Civil and Commercial Matters (Revocation and Saving Provisions) (EU Exit) Regulations 2018 (SI 2018/1257) will revoke the Service Regulation (1393/2007) and Taking of Evidence Regulation (1206/2001) so that they no longer apply to the UK when it leaves the EU. The effect of this will be to require the service of documents to be carried out using some other method, for example under the Hague Convention, where that is applicable. Secondly, the Civil Jurisdiction and Judgments (Amendment) (EU Exit) Regulations 2019 (SI 2019/479) will revoke the Judgments Regulation (1215/2012) and amend domestic legislation so as to cease to apply the Brussels and Lugano Conventions. Thirdly, the Services of Lawyers and Lawyer's Practice (Revocation etc.) (EU Exit) Regulations 2019 (SI 2019/375) will revoke the European Communities (Lawyer's Practice) Regulations 2000 (SI 2000/1119). The anticipated combined effect of these Regulations, subject to any transitional provisions, should they come into force as drafted, will be to require significant revision to Sections II and III of Pt 6 to remove references to European Lawyers and service within the EEA, as well as requiring significant amendments to Section IV of Pt 6, for instance, rr.6.31, 6.33, 6.35, 6.40 and 6.41, to reflect the non-applicability of the Service Regulation, Judgments Regulation, and Brussels and Lugano Conventions.

See para.5.0.1.1 for detail on the amendments to the CPR and its PDs in the event of a no-deal exit.

II. *Service of the Claim Form in the Jurisdiction or in Specified Circumstances Within the EEA*

"jurisdiction"

Replace paragraph with:

6.11.2   In *Royal Petrol Trading Co UK v Total India Pvt Ltd* [2018] EWHC 1272 (Comm), the relevant clause in the contract provided that the solicitors identified by each party had instructions to accept service of proceedings, and that if a party appointed other legal representatives it should give notice within 24 hours. The defendant instructed new solicitors who notified the claimant that they had been instructed to accept service and that the defendant would not make the payment under the agreement. The claimant terminated the contract and the defendant then notified the claimant that its new solicitors were no longer instructed to accept service. The claimant issued proceedings for breach of contract and served the claim form on the defendant's new solicitors. The claimant argued that there had been good service of the proceedings by a contractually agreed method pursuant to CPR r.6.11. The defendant argued that the contract had not provided for an irrevocable appointment of solicitors to accept service and it had not survived termination of the settlement agreement. The judge rejected the defendant's argument, holding that there had been an effective appointment of the new solicitors under the contract. Although the contract did not refer to revocation, there was no magic in the use of that word. The court had to look at the clause in the contract in context. In the instant case, the authority of the new solicitors could not be revoked and the relevant clause survived termination of the contract. It was an ancillary part of the mechanism for dealing with disputes. It was collateral or ancillary to the English law and jurisdiction clause, which it was agreed survived termination, and which was itself collateral or ancillary to the main subject matter of the agreement. There had accordingly been valid service on the defendant's new solicitors.

For the purposes of the CPR generally, and therefore for all Sections of Pt 6, unless the context requires otherwise, "jurisdiction" means England and Wales (see r.2.3).

"relevant step under rule 7.5(1)"

In the second paragraph, second line, replace "jurisdiction) in accordance with" with:
jurisdictions of England & Wales, Scotland and Northern Ireland) in accordance with **6.14.3**

Replace the eighth paragraph (beginning "The effects of") with:
The effects of r.6.14 on the operation of other rules in the CPR, in particular on r.7.5 (Service of a claim form), and vice versa have been considered in several cases at first instance, from which it is apparent that a number of difficulties not admitting of obvious solution arise. Some differences in judicial opinion have emerged. Those cases include: *Ageas (UK) Ltd v Kwik-Fit (GB) Ltd* [2013] EWHC 3261 (QB); *T&L Sugars Ltd v Tate & Lyle Industries* [2014] EWHC 1066 (Comm), 10 April 2014, unrep. (Flaux J); *Heron Bros Ltd v Central Bedfordshire Council* [2015] EWHC 604 (TCC); [2015] B.L.R. 362 (Edwards-Stuart J); *Brightside Group Ltd v RSM UK Audit* [2017] EWHC 6 (Comm); [2017] 1 W.L.R. 1943 (Andrew Baker J). In *Ageas* and *T & L Sugars Ltd* [2014] EWHC 1066 (Comm) it was held that the apparent inconsistency between rr.7.5 and 6.14, when taken together, can be reconciled by holding that the provisions of r.7.5 are concerned with how service of a claim form in compliance with the four-month time limit for service within the jurisdiction is to be accomplished, but that r.6.14 has a different function and is concerned with a different starting date for the calculation of time standards for the progress of proceedings after service in accordance with the relevant procedural rule. Andrew Baker J in *Brightside Group Ltd* took a different approach holding that compliance with the date for service of a claim form or notice of discontinuance under a r.7.7 notice was to be determined by reference to r.6.14 not r.7.5. He noted that there was no prior authority on the relationship between rr.6.14 and 7.7. He held that the decisions in *Godwin v Swindon BC and Anderton v Clwyd CC (No.2)* (above) remain binding and make it clear that the deemed date of service is set out in r.6.14, which is a fixed and irrebuttable date. He distinguished previous authorities, *Ageas* and *T & L Sugars Ltd* on the ground that neither of those decisions was concerned with r.7.7. The decision in *Brightside* was considered by Master McCloud in *Paxton Jones v Chichester Harbour Conservancy* [2017] EWHC 2270 (QB) where she drew attention to "an unfortunate tension" between rr.6.14 and 7.5 and did not follow the decision in *Brightside*. The approach taken in *Ageas, T & L Sugars Ltd* and *Paxton Jones* was also followed by Sir David Eady in *Kennedy v National Trust for Scotland* [2017] EWHC 3368 (QB).

The issue has now been resolved by the decision of the Court of Appeal in *Kennedy v National Trust for Scotland* [2019] EWCA Civ 648 which held that the judge below was correct to follow the reasoning of Flaux J in *T&L Sugars Ltd* and Master McCloud in *Paxton Jones*.

Delete the ninth, tenth and eleventh paragraphs (beginning "The cases referred to above" and ending "commentary following that rule.").

Effect of rule (r.6.15)

Replace the ninth paragraph (beginning "In terms, r.6.15(1)") with:
In terms, r.6.15(1), being free of any reference to "steps" directed to bringing the document to **6.15.1** the notice of the person to be served, the UKSC in *Cameron v Liverpool Victoria Insurance Co Ltd* [2019] UKSC 6, 20 February 2019, affirmed that alternative service as a mode of service must be such as could reasonably be expected to bring the proceedings to the defendant's attention. In so far as the Court of Appeal in *Abbey National Plc v Frost* [1999] 1 W.L.R. 1080, CA, suggested the contrary it was wrongly decided. Also see paras 37 and 38 of Lord Clarke's judgment in *Abela*. And see para.6.15.3.

Retrospective operation—"steps already taken"

Delete the thirteenth, fourteenth and fifteenth paragraphs (beginning "See also Marashen Ltd" and ending **6.15.5** *"take into account.").*

Service out of jurisdiction by an alternative method

After the third paragraph, add new paragraphs:

6.15.7   In *A v B* [2017] EWHC 503 (Comm) (13 January 2017) Knowles J acknowledged that there had to be good reason for service to take place quicker than under the applicable service convention. Further, the relative speed of service by an alternative method as compared with service under the applicable convention was not, of itself, a sufficient reason for an alternative service order. However, it was a factor for the court to take into account.

There are a number of cases that have considered the threshold test for granting an order for service by alternative means where the claim is to be served out of the jurisdiction where the Hague Convention was applicable. These confirmed that the power to serve proceedings by an alternative method in respect of a defendant outside the jurisdiction derives from CPR r.6.37(5)(b)(i) rather than CPR r.6.15. *Marashen Ltd v Kenvett Ltd* [2017] EWHC 1706 (Ch); [2018] 1 W.L.R. 288 held that there was jurisdiction if sufficiently exceptional circumstances existed. But in *Flota Petrolera Ecuatoriana v Petroleos De Venezuala SA* [2017] EWHC 3630 (Comm), Leggatt J rejected the notion that a country being a signatory to the Hague Convention meant that permission to serve by alternative means could only be ordered in exceptional circumstances. Richard Spearman QC, sitting as a Deputy Judge of the High Court, in *Koza v Akcil* [2018] EWHC 384 (Ch) reached a similar conclusion but considered in a Hague Convention case there needed to be a "good reason" for the making of such an order. These cases were considered by Chief Master Marsh in *Punjab National Bank (International) Ltd v Srinivasan* [2019] EWHC 89 (Ch).

III.   Service of Documents other than the Claim Form in the United Kingdom or in Specified Circumstances within the EEA

Effect of rule (r.6.28)

In the fourth paragraph, replace the last sentence with:

6.28.1   Also see *General Dynamics UK Ltd v Libya* [2019] EWCA Civ 1110 where the Court of Appeal held that the court could dispense with service of an order granting permission to enforce an arbitration award, despite the terms of s.12 of the State Immunity Act 1978 (see para.6.44.1 below).

IV.   Service of the Claim Form and other Documents out of the Jurisdiction

Brexit

Replace paragraph with:

6.30.0   The current regime governing service out of the UK to an EU Member State, Switzerland, Norway, Denmark or Iceland is due to be abolished under the Civil Jurisdiction and Judgments (Amendment) (EU Exit) Regulations 2019 (SI 2019/479). At present, the claimant does not require permission to serve the claim form on a defendant in one of those countries, subject to the exclusions contained in r.6.33 (see the summary at para.6.30.10). However, under the 2019 Regulations, the Judgments Regulation (recast), the Brussels Conventions and the Lugano Convention will cease to apply (reg.26 makes separate provision in relation to consumer and employment matters).

Part 6 of the 2019 Regulations provides in effect for the current regime to continue to apply to determine questions of jurisdiction in proceedings of which the court was seised before exit day and which are not concluded before exit day (reg.92(1)(a)). Thus, in the event of the UK departing the EU without a deal, the 2019 Regulations would preserve the current jurisdiction regime in proceedings brought before exit day. Thereafter, in the absence of further legislation, the regime which currently governs service out in non-EU countries would apply (see r.6.33(2B) and (3), r.6.36 and PD 6B).

Article 67 of the draft Agreement on the Withdrawal of the United Kingdom of Great Britain and Northern Ireland from the European Union and the European Atomic Energy Community, as endorsed by leaders at a special meeting of the European Council on 25 November 2018 (the "Draft Withdrawal Agreement") would extend the expiry date of the existing European jurisdictional rules from exit day until the end of the transition period, which is proposed to 31 December 2020 (draft art.126). In the event that the current Draft Withdrawal Agreement were to govern the UK's departure, the current regime would therefore be preserved until 30 December 2020. Again, thereafter, in the absence of further legislation, the non-EU service out, regime would apply.

One aspect of the current regime which will be preserved is the 2005 Hague Convention on Choice of Court Agreements (r.6.33(2B), see para.6.30.5). The UK is not yet a signatory to the 2005 Hague Convention in its own right. It was due to accede to the Convention on 1 April 2019. However the UK gave notice on 29 March 2019 that it was suspending its accession until 13 April or 23 May 2019, and then again gave notice on 12 April 2019 suspending its accession until 1 November 2019. Accession is conditional upon a failure by the UK and the EU to reach agreement over the terms of Britain's departure. The Civil Jurisdiction and Judgments (Hague Convention on Choice of Court Agreements 2005) (EU Exit) Regulations 2018 (SI 2018/1124), made on 30

October 2018 and due to come into force on exit day, provide for the 2005 Hague Convention to apply, even if there is an interruption to the effectiveness of the Convention in respect of the UK as a result of the UK's transition from Member State of the EU as a signatory to independent signatory (regs 4 and 5). If, by contrast, the Draft Withdrawal Agreement were signed and ratified, the Judgments Regulation (recast) would continue to apply until the end of the transition period (draft art.67).

See para.5.0.1.1 for detail on the amendments to the CPR and its PDs in the event of a no-deal exit.

Service of claim form out of the UK—permission not required where court has power to determine claim under EU Conventions and Regulations (r.6.33(1) and (2))

The effect of the "court first seised" rule

Replace the third sentence with:

Provisions in the Judgments Regulation and in the Conventions anticipate this and, in order to **6.30.4.2** deal with the inconvenience and confusion that may arise, provide that, in the event of proceedings being brought in the courts of different States (say, in a French court and in an English court) "any court other than the court first seised shall of its own motion stay its proceedings".

Service of claim form out of the UK—permission not required where court has power to determine claim under the 2005 Hague Convention (r.6.33(2B))

Replace the first paragraph with:

The Convention on Choice of Court Agreements (the "2005 Hague Convention") was concluded **6.30.5** at the Hague on 30 June 2005, was signed on behalf of the EU on 1 April 2009, was ratified on behalf of the EU on 11 June 2015, and entered into force on 1 October 2015 for the Member States of the EU and for Mexico (the only other State which had ratified the Convention at that date—for a current list of countries that have ratified the Convention see *https://www.hcch.net/en/instruments/conventions/status-table/?cid=98* [Accessed 11 May 2019]). For the purpose of providing for the service out of the jurisdiction on defendants where the English court has power to determine claims under the 2005 Hague Convention, with effect from that date para.(2B) was inserted in r.6.33 by the Civil Jurisdiction and Judgments (Hague Convention on Choice of Court Agreements 2005) Regulations 2015 (SI 2015/1644).

Service of claim form in Scotland or Northern Ireland—permission not required where court has power to determine claim under the 1982 Act (r.6.32(1))

Replace the fourth paragraph with:

Schedule 4 contains several rules of jurisdiction (in r.6.32(1)(b), rr.11 and 12 are identified as **6.30.7** "paragraphs"). Rule 1 states that the general rule of jurisdiction is that, subject to the provisions of the Schedule, a person domiciled in a part of the UK shall be sued in the courts of that part. In the circumstances provided for by r.3 of Sch.4 (Special jurisdiction) a person domiciled in a part of the UK may, in another part of the UK, be sued. In the circumstances provided for by r.11 of Sch.4 (Exclusive jurisdiction) courts of a particular part of the UK shall have jurisdiction "regardless of domicile", and r.12 (Prorogation of jurisdiction) provides a means by which parties, regardless of their domicile, may confer jurisdiction on a court or courts by an agreement to the effect that "a court or courts of a part of the United Kingdom" are to have jurisdiction. Schedule 4 contains no rule comparable to that found in art.29 of the Judgments Regulation (recast), and other Conventions, requiring (subject to exceptions) any court "other than the court first seised" of its own motion to stay its proceedings. In *Kleinwort Benson Ltd v City of Glasgow City Council* (C-346/93) [1996] Q.B. 57, ECJ, the European Court of Justice ruled that the interpretation of the rules in Sch.4 is a matter for the UK national courts. (In that case the interpretation and relationship between provisions in what is now r.3 of Sch.4 determined the question whether the Scottish or English courts had jurisdiction.) In contrast to the position where the defendant is domiciled in an EU Member State other than the UK (see para.6.37.27), the court can stay its proceedings on grounds of forum non conveniens where the defendant is domiciled in Scotland (or Northern Ireland) and that is clearly the more appropriate forum for the dispute (*Kennedy v National Trust for Scotland* [2019] EWCA Civ 648).

Grounds of jurisdiction alternative to defendant's domicile

Jurisdiction in matters relating to insurance, over consumer contracts and individual contracts of employment

To the end of the seventh paragraph (beginning "Broadly speaking these provisions enable a consumer"), add:

(In addition these provisions provide rules of jurisdiction where the other party is not domiciled **6.33.7** in any Member State.) The provisions of this Section may be departed from only by an agreement satisfying art.19.

Replace the eighth paragraph with:

In CPR r.6.33(2) express reference is made to a defendant who is not a consumer but is party to a consumer contract within art.17 (r.6.33(2)(b)(ii)). Thereby it is provided that where a consumer party (C) takes advantage of art.17 and sues the other party (D) in an English court, whether or not D is domiciled in a Member State, C may serve the claim form on D out of the UK without permission, provided no proceedings between the parties concerning the same claim are pending in the courts of any other part of the UK or any other Member State (r.6.33(2)(a)).

In the twelfth paragraph (beginning "Broadly speaking these provisions enable an employee"), after "be departed from", add:

only

In the thirteenth paragraph (beginning "In CPR r.6.33(2) express reference is made to a defendant"), replace "D being domiciled in a Member State other than the United Kingdom," with:

whether or not D is domiciled in a Member State,

Exclusive jurisdiction

Replace the second paragraph with:

6.33.8   In CPR r.6.33(2) express reference is made to proceedings within art.24 (r.6.33(2)(b)(iv)). Thereby it is provided that where a claimant (C) takes advantage of art.24 and sues a defendant (D) in an English court, D being domiciled in a Member State other than the UK (see *Integral Petroleum SA v Petrogat FZE* [2018] EWHC 2686 (Comm) and para.6JR.32.1 below), C may serve the claim form on D out of the UK without permission, provided no proceedings between the parties concerning the same claim are pending in the courts of any other part of the UK or any other Member State (r.6.33(2)(a)).

Statement of the grounds on which the claimant is entitled to serve the claim form out of the jurisdiction

Replace the third paragraph with:

6.33.12   In para.1(b) of Appendix 9 to the Admiralty and Commercial Courts Guide it is stressed that, because of the significance of (amongst other things) the concept of "first seisure" in the context of the Judgments Regulation, it is very important that the statement as to the grounds upon which the claimant is entitled to serve the claim form out of the jurisdiction is accurate and made with care (Vol.2 para.2A-175). If entitlement to serve out of the jurisdiction without leave is wrongly asserted, a claimant may be ordered to pay the costs of a defendant's application to strike out the claim or set aside serve of the claim form on an indemnity basis (ibid).

"statement of the grounds" (r.6.34(1)(a))

Replace the first paragraph with:

6.34.2   A close examination of rr.6.32 and 6.33 reveals that there are ten discrete grounds upon which service of a claim form may be effected without the permission of the court on a defendant out the jurisdiction. They are listed in "boxes" in Form **N510**, each with an appropriate statement of facts. The claimant is required to tick the relevant box and to certify that the facts so stated are true. (Form **N510** was introduced with effect from 1 October 2008. Beforehand r.6.19(3) provided that the claim form "must contain" a statement of the grounds on which the claimant is entitled to serve it out of the jurisdiction recommended wording for each of the several grounds was set out in PD 6B. Note that Form **N510** has not been updated to refer to the additional ground for service outside the jurisdiction under the 2005 Hague Convention, at r.6.33(2B).)

Add new paragraph at end:

In *Sullivan v Ruhan* [2019] EWHC 1336 (Comm) the court refused to grant a default judgment for failure to file acknowledgments of service where the claimant was unable to show that he had validly served the claim form on the defendants in the Isle of Man, none of the grounds in r.6.33 which allowed service of the claim form out of the jurisdiction without the court's permission applied and the claim form had not been accompanied by a notice as required under r.6.34.

Effect of rule (r.6.35)

Replace the last paragraph with:

6.35.1   See further para.1(c) and para.6(c) and (d) of Appendix 9 to the Admiralty and Commercial Courts Guide (Vol.2 paras 2A-175 and 2A-180).

The application for permission (r.6.37(1))

Replace the third paragraph with:

6.37.1   In addition to the matters explained immediately below, note also the information contained in the Court Guides as follows: Chancery Guide Ch.7 paras 7-12 to 7-14 (Permission to serve out of the jurisdiction), and Ch.11 paras 11-7 and 11-8 (Service out) (Vol.2 paras 1A-56 and 1A-77); Queen's Bench Guide (Service of the claim form—out of the jurisdiction—with permission) paras 5.4.1–5.4.3 and 5.4.7–5.4.10 (Vol.2 para.1B-27); Admiralty and Commercial Courts Guide Appendix 9 paras 2 to 4 (Application for permission), and paras 7 to 8 (Practice under rule 6.36) (Vol.2 paras 2A-176 and 2A-180.1); Circuit Commercial Court Guide paras 3.10 to 3.12 (Service of the claim form out of the jurisdiction) (Vol.2 para.2B-20).

Application under r.6.36 to serve out—duty of disclosure

In the third paragraph, replace "Appendix 15" with:
  Appendix 9

6.37.4

Claim form marked "not for service out of the jurisdiction"

In the first paragraph, replace "para.4.4.23" with:
  para.5.4.3

6.37.10

Claim falls within the ground relied on ("good arguable case")

In the seventh paragraph (beginning "In Goldman Sachs International"), replace "Kaefer Aislamientos SA de CV v Atlas Drilling Mexico SA de CV [2019] EWCA Civ 10, 17 January 2019, unrep." with:
  Kaefer Aislamientos SA de CV v Atlas Drilling Mexico SA de CV [2019] EWCA Civ 10; [2019] 1 **6.37.16**
  W.L.R. 3514. See also *Coward v Ambrosiadou* [2019] EWHC 2105 (Comm) (Andrew Henshaw QC), 31 July 2019, unrep.

In the ninth paragraph (beginning "In Al Jaber") replace "Al Jaber v Al Ibrahim [2018] EWCA Civ 1690," with:
  Al Jaber v Al Ibrahim [2018] EWCA Civ 1690; [2019] 1 W.L.R. 885,

In the tenth paragraph (beginning "In Flota Petrolera") replace "Flota Petrolera Ecuatoriana v Petroleos de Venezuala S.A. [2017] EWHC 3630 (Comm)" with:
  Flota Petrolera Ecuatoriana v Petroleos de Venezuala SA [2017] EWHC 3630 (Comm); [2017] 2 C.L.C. 759

Replace the last paragraph with:
  Where a question of law arises in connection with a dispute about service out of the jurisdiction and that question of law goes to the existence of the jurisdiction, then the court will normally decide the question of law, as opposed to seeing whether there is a good arguable case on that issue of law, if the facts are clear (*E F Hutton & Co (London) Ltd v Mofarrij* [1989] 1 W.L.R. 488, CA, per Kerr LJ, at p.495; *Altimo Holdings and Investment Ltd v Kyrgyz Mobile Tel Ltd* [2011] UKPC 7; [2012] 1 W.L.R. 1804, PC, at para. 81; *VTB Capital Plc v Nutritek International Corp* [2012] EWCA Civ 808; [2012] 2 Lloyd's Rep. 313, CA, at para.99; *Lungowe v Vedanta Resources Plc* [2017] EWCA Civ 1528; [2017] B.C.C. 787, CA, at para.63; *Airbus SAS v Generali Italia SPA* [2019] EWCA Civ 805, at paras 52 to 53). There are exceptions to this approach where (as on summary judgment applications) the question is a particularly difficult one or is in a controversial or developing area of law (*Flota Petrolera Ecuatoriana v Petroleos de Venezuala SA* [2017] EWHC 3630 (Comm); [2017] 2 C.L.C. 759 (Leggatt J)). The more doubtful the point of law the more cautious the court should be; as to the facts, the court should proceed on the basis of the pleaded case (*Lungowe v Vedanta Resources Plc*, op cit, at para.63). This approach has consistently been applied to cases where jurisdiction has depended on the applicable law of a contract for the purposes of what is now para.3.1(6)(c) of PD 6B. In such cases the court does not consider whether the claimant has a good arguable case that the contract is governed by English law, but rather whether the contract is governed by English law (*Chellaram v Chellaram (No.2)* [2002] EWHC 632 (Ch); [2002] 3 All E.R. 17 (Lawrence Collins J), at para.136).

English court the appropriate forum (forum conveniens)

Treatment of "a legitimate personal or juridical advantage"

Replace the last paragraph with:
  Other significant authorities on the "justice in the foreign jurisdiction" factor, and its possible **6.37.21** relevance not only in "service out cases" but in "service in cases" as well, are: *Connelly v R.T.Z. Corp Plc* [1998] A.C. 854, HL, at p.872G per Lord Goff ("if a clearly more appropriate forum overseas has been identified generally speaking the plaintiff will have to take that forum as he finds it"); *Deripaska v Cherney* [2009] EWCA Civ 849; [2010] 2 All E.R. (Comm) 456, CA, at para.60; *Altimo Holdings and Investment Ltd v Fellowes International Holdings Ltd* [2011] UKPC 7; [2012] 1 W.L.R. 1804, PC, at paras 89 to 102; *Ferrexpo AG v Gilson Investments Ltd* [2012] EWHC 721 (Comm); [2012] 1 Lloyd's Rep. 588 (Andrew Smith J) at para.33; *Lungowe v Vedanta Resources Plc* [2019] UKSC 20; [2019] 2 W.L.R. 1051, at paras 88 to 101.

Jurisdiction agreements

Replace the second paragraph with:

6.37.23 Where the claim is made in respect of a contract which contains a term to the effect that the English court shall have jurisdiction, the claim will almost certainly be subject to the Judgments Regulation (recast) and the prorogation of jurisdiction provisions therein (see para.6JR.34). If the Judgments Regulation (recast) does not apply, the claimant may apply for permission to serve the claim form out of the jurisdiction under para.6.1(6)(d) of PD6B on the ground that the contract contains such a term (see para.6HJ.22).

At the beginning of the third paragraph, replace "Of immediate interest here are" with:

Where (unusually) the Judgments Regulation (recast) does not apply despite the presence of a jurisdiction agreement in favour of the English courts, the jurisdiction clause may be relevant in

In the fourth paragraph, after "jurisdiction agreements generally", add:

(outside the context of the Judgments Regulation (recast))

Modern authorities on doctrine of forum conveniens

At the end of the last paragraph, replace "(see Lungowe v Vedanta Resources Plc [2017] EWCA Civ 1528: [2017] B.C.C. 787, CA, at paras 108 to 117, and authorities referred to there)." with:

6.37.25 but it should not be regarded as a trump card. In *Lungowe v Vedanta Resources Plc* [2019] UKSC 20; [2019] 2 W.L.R. 1051, the Supreme Court was critical of the approach taken in previous cases (in particular *OJSC VTB Bank v Parline Ltd* [2013] EWHC 3538 (Comm), which was followed by the judge at first instance) in circumstances where it was clear that the claimants would in any event continue proceedings against the anchor defendant in England. In those cases, the courts treated the avoidance of irreconcilable judgments as decisive in favour of England as the proper place, even if all other connecting factors favoured a foreign jurisdiction. In *Vedanta*, the Supreme Court found that this approach involved an error of principle. The judge had given insufficient weight to the fact that the anchor defendant had offered to submit to the jurisdiction of the Zambian courts so that the whole case could be tried there. Accordingly, the risk of irreconcilable judgments stemmed from the claimants' decision to pursue the anchor defendant in England. They were entitled to do so, but not necessarily in a way that avoided incurring the risk of irreconcilable judgments (see paras 66 to 87).

Modern authorities on doctrine of forum non conveniens

In the third paragraph, replace "Conversant Wireless Licensing SARL v Huawei Technologies Co Ltd [2018] EWHC 808 (Pat)" with:

6.37.26 *Conversant Wireless Licensing SARL v Huawei Technologies Co Ltd* [2018] EWHC 808 (Pat); [2018] R.P.C. 16

In the fourth paragraph (beginning "There are a number of"), replace "The Owners of the Ship "Al Khattiya" v The Owners And/Or Demise Charterers of the Ship "Jag Laadki" [2018] EWHC 389 (Admlty)" with:

The Owners of the Ship "Al Khattiya" v The Owners And/Or Demise Charterers of the Ship "Jag Laadki" [2018] EWHC 389 (Admlty); [2018] 2 Lloyd's Rep. 243

Forum non conveniens—court's power to stay proceedings on abuse of process grounds

To the end of the last paragraph, add:

6.37.29 For a decision doubting certain statements made in *Ferrexpo AG v Gilson Investments Ltd*, see *Gulf Investment Bank KSC v Sheikh Badr Fahad Ibrahim Aldwood* [2019] EWHC 1666 (QB) (John Kimbell QC), 1 July 2019, unrep.

The court's general discretion

In the last sentence of the first paragraph, after "the principles have", add:

6.37.30 not

Effect of rule (r.6.39)

6.39.1 *In the second paragraph, delete the penultimate sentence.*

Provisions disapplied

Replace paragraph with:

6.39.2 The rules disapplied by para.(1) are provisions that set out the periods for filing an acknowledgment of service, filing or serving an admission, or filing a defence, where permission to serve the claim form out of the jurisdiction either (a) was not required (and the claim form has been served) (r.6.35), or (b) was required and has been granted (r.6.37(5)). Paragraph (2) of r.11, disapplied by para.(2) of this rule, states that a defendant who wishes to dispute the court's jurisdiction, or to argue that the court should not exercise its jurisdiction, must first file an acknowledgment of service.

Service on a defendant out of the United Kingdom (r.6.40(3) and (4))

Replace the second and third paragraphs with:

6.40.5

There is no express provision in Section IV of Pt 6 permitting service of a claim form out of the jurisdiction by an alternative method, but it is now settled that the court has such jurisdiction and that it is derived from the court's power to give directions as to service under r.6.37(5)(b)(i) (*Cecil v Bayat* [2011] EWCA Civ 135; [2011] 1 W.L.R. 3086, CA and *Abela v Baadarani* [2013] UKSC 44; [2013] 1 W.L.R. 2043 (judgment of Lord Clarke, para.20)). This authorises the court to make an order for alternative service (i.e. by a method or at a place not otherwise permitted by Pt 6) pursuant to r.6.15(1), and also to make such an order with retrospective effect pursuant to r.6.15(2). Where the court grants an application made by a claimant under r.6.15 for service of a claim form out of the jurisdiction by an alternative method, the order must specify the matters referred to in r.6.15(4), including the date on which the claim form is deemed served, otherwise the order would be defective (*Bill Kenwright Ltd v Flash Entertainment FZ LLC* [2016] EWHC 1951 (QB), para.61). A method of service "not otherwise permitted by this Part" has been held by the Supreme Court in *Abela v Baadarani* [2013] UKSC 44; [2013] 1 W.L.R. 2043 in the context of service out of the jurisdiction as occurring in cases (and only in cases) where none of the methods provided in r.6.40(3) has been adopted, including of course service by a method permitted by the law of the country in which the claim form or document is to be served. The starting point is that the defendant has not or will not be served by such a method and the question to be asked by the court is whether there is good reason in prospective cases to declare that service by the proposed method or at the proposed place shall be regarded as good service and in retrospective cases that it should be regarded as having amounted to good service. Speed is a relevant consideration but, in general, the desire of a claimant to avoid the delay inherent in service by the methods permitted by r.6.40 cannot of itself justify an order for service by an alternative method (*Cecil v Bayat* op cit). In *Abela v Baadarani* [2013] UKSC 44; [2013] 1 W.L.R. 2043 Lord Clarke made clear that he was saying nothing about the position where a Convention or Treaty applied and Burnton LJ's dicta in *Cecil* that while the fact that proceedings will come to the attention of the defendant more speedily by an alternative method than by service under the Hague Convention is a relevant consideration under r.6.15 it is in general not a sufficient reason for an order for service by an alternative method. In such cases it is of course open to the claimant to use a method permitted by the law of the country in which service is to be effected subject to r.6.40(4). See further para.6.15.7 (Service abroad of domestic process) above.

In *Abela v Baadarani*, op cit, Lord Clarke held that the only bar to the exercise of the discretion under rr.6.15(1) or (2), if otherwise appropriate, is that by r.6.40(4) the court may not authorise anyone to do anything that is contrary to the law of the country where the claim form or document is to be served. An order cannot be made if its effect would be contrary to the law of that country. Thus the proposed method of service may not be one permitted by the law of that country but the bar applies only where it is positively contrary the law of that country to serve by that method; cf *Ferrarini S.p.A. v Magnol Shipping Co Inc (The Sky One)* above. The view expressed in some first instance decisions that the function of r.6.40(3) is only to prevent service by a method forbidden by the law of the place of service so that another method which is not in accordance with that law but is not actually illegal may be adopted (*Shiblaq v Sadikoglu* [2004] EWHC 1890 (Comm); [2004] All E.R. (D) 428 (Comm)), and that it is implicit in r.6.40(4) that the court may permit any alternative method of service abroad so long as it does not contravene the law of the country where service is to be effected (*Habib Bank Ltd v Central Bank of Sudan* [2006] EWHC 1767 (Comm); [2007] 1 W.L.R. 470; [2007] 1 All E.R. (Comm) 53; [2006] 2 Lloyd's Rep. 412), are impliedly confirmed by this interpretation of the effect of r.6.40(4) by the Supreme Court. See also *BNP Paribas SA v Open Joint Stock Company Russian Machines* [2011] EWHC 308 (Comm); [2012] 1 Lloyd's Rep. 61 (Blair J). In *Cruz City 1 Mauritius Holdings v Unitech Ltd* [2013] EWHC 1323 (Comm); [2013] 2 All E.R. (Comm) 1137, the judge relying on the judgment of Tomlinson J in *Kyrgyz Republic Ministry of Transport Department of Civil Aviation v Finrep GmbH* [2006] EWHC 1722 (Comm); [2006] 2 C.L.C. 402 and the Court of Appeal decision in *Joint Stock Asset Management Co v BNP Paribas SA* [2012] EWCA Civ 644; [2012] 1 Lloyd's Rep. 649, confirmed the Commercial Court's practice in the case of an arbitration whose seat is in the jurisdiction, to regard the fact that service on the respondent's lawyers within the jurisdiction is far more speedy than service under a Convention or Treaty or the Service Regulation, as a good reason within r.6.15(1) and (2). See also *Flora Petrolera Ecuatoriana v Petroleos de Venezuala SA* [2017] EWHC 3630 (Comm); [2017] 2 C.L.C 759 (Leggatt J), at para.22.

Change title and replace paragraph with:

Service by postal channels under the Hague Service Convention

6.40.11

The Hague Service Convention permits the sending of "judicial documents by postal channels directly to persons abroad" provided "the state of destination does not object" to such method of service (see arts 10 and 19). Provided therefore that service by post is permitted by and effected in accordance with the law of the country in which service is effected, there is nothing in the Hague Convention which cuts down the scope of this permission (*Noirhomme v Walklate* [1992] 1 Lloyd's Rep. 427). However, it should be noted that many signatories to the Convention have declared their opposition to incoming service under art.10. Any party considering outgoing service to a Hague Service Convention Country by post should consult the HCCH website as to the relevant declarations and reservations.

Service Regulation

In the third paragraph, after "one method may", add:

6.41.2   not

In the seventh paragraph (beginning "In Henderson v Novo Banco SA"), replace "Henderson v Novo Banco SA (C-354/15)" with:
   Henderson v Novo Banco SA (C-354/15) EU:C:2017:157; [2017] 4 W.L.R. 75

Replace the ninth paragraph with:
   Article 9 on "date of service" is sometimes misunderstood. It should be read with para.(15) of the preamble to the Regulation. Article 9.1 provides that the date of service of a document under art.7 is to be calculated according to the law of the Member State that is requested to serve. So, for example, when considering whether or not a claim form issued in this jurisdiction has been validly served in a Member State during its six months' validity or any extension of that period, it is the date of service indicated by the procedural law of the receiving state which is considered. Article 9.2, although it is far from clear from its wording, is only concerned with the few Member States which have a "double date" system of service where the court of that state does not consider itself seized of the proceedings (i.e. the proceedings to have been commenced) until a first date of receipt by the serving entity (huissier or whoever) and therefore the commencement of the service process is provided after which the proceedings can be validly served on a second date provided for by national procedural law. (See para.15 of the preamble.) For the purposes of art.32(2) of the Judgments Regulation the practice of the Foreign Process Section as to the time when a document is received by the FPS as the authority responsible for service is to regard it as received when a faxed copy is received in the FPS: *Arbuthnot Latham & Co Ltd v M3 Marine Ltd* [2013] EWHC 1019 (Comm); [2014] 1 W.L.R. 190 (a case decided under the equivalent provision of the Brussels I Regulation).

Effect of rule (r.6.43)

In the third paragraph, replace "Chare v Fairclough [2003] EWHC 180 (Treacy J.)," with:
6.43.1   Chare v Fairclough [2003] EWHC 180 (QB) (Treacy J),

Actions against foreign states

Replace the last paragraph with:
6.44.1   Section 12 of the 1978 Act provides for service through the Foreign & Commonwealth Office of: "any writ or other document required to be served for instituting proceedings against the State". In *General Dynamics UK Ltd v State of Libya* [2019] EWCA Civ 1110, the facts were that, on the claimant's (C) application under r.62.18 without notice, Teare J made an order under r.6.28 (with liberty to apply) dispensing with service of a court order granting permission to enforce an arbitration award against a foreign state (D) (being a New York Convention award enforceable pursuant to the Arbitration Act 1996 s.101). Teare J found that D was aware of the award and of C's interest in enforcing it and that C would encounter considerable difficulties were they to seek to serve the order in the manner provided for by the 1978 Act. D's application to set aside Teare J's order succeeded before Males J, who held that there was no jurisdiction to dispense with service as this would be contrary to the mandatory terms of s.12. Males J's decision was overturned by the Court of Appeal, which found that there was jurisdiction to dispense with service in an appropriate case, under both CPR 6.16 (claim forms) and 6.28 (other documents), though it would always be appropriate to make arrangements (as Teare J did) to notify the state in question. The Court of Appeal stressed that such notification did not amount to alternative service, which could not be used where the respondent is a state. Where the document was not a claim form and therefore the application fell within CPR 6.28, it could be said that the court had a general discretion, without a requirement for "exceptional circumstances" as under CPR 6.16. However, the court considered that, when the order permitting enforcement was the first time the foreign state received notice of a claimant's attempt to enforce the award, it was "only right and proper" to apply the test of exceptional circumstances.

Effect of rule

Replace the last paragraph with:
6.47.1   In r.6.47(a) the words "a hearing is fixed when the claim form is issued" cannot be read literally

as applying the rule only to fixed date claims where a hearing date is given on issue since few of such actions could be expected to be served abroad (they are largely possession claims). Further, r.6.40(2) does not modify the term "jurisdiction" in this Section but only in Section II, therefore the general definition in Pt 2.3 would seem to apply. Nevertheless it would be odd if the words in r.6.47(b) "out of the jurisdiction" in the context of this rule referred to Scotland and Northern Ireland in circumstances in which service of claim forms in Scotland and Northern Ireland must be under Section II, so that the filing of written evidence as opposed to the certificate of service should not be necessary.

NOTES ON HEADS OF JURISDICTION IN PARAGRAPH 3.1 OF PRACTICE DIRECTION 6B

Introduction

In the last paragraph, replace "out of the jurisdiction, either with or without the court's permission," with:
within the jurisdiction,
6HJ.1

General Grounds (para.3.1(1) to (4A))

Paragraph 3.1(2): Claim for injunction restraining act within the jurisdiction

In the second paragraph, replace "Unlockd Ltd v Google Ireland Ltd [2018] EWHC 1363 (Ch)," with:
Unlockd Ltd v Google Ireland Ltd [2018] EWHC 1363 (Ch); [2019] E.C.C. 1,
6HJ.4

In the third paragraph, replace "(Conversant Wireless Licensing SARL v Huawei Technologies Co Ltd [2018] EWHC 808 (Pat)," with:
(Conversant Wireless Licensing SARL v Huawei Technologies Co Ltd [2018] EWHC 808 (Pat); [2018] R.P.C. 16,

Paragraph 3.1(3): Another person a necessary or proper party to a claim

"necessary or proper party" (para.3.1(3)(b))

Replace the last paragraph with:
In *Dar Al Arkan Real Estate Development Co v Al Refai* [2014] EWCA Civ 715; [2015] 1 W.L.R. **6HJ.7** 135, CA, where an interim injunction obtained by the claimant companies (C) prohibiting disclosure by the defendants (D) of certain information contained undertakings by C, D applied, after the injunction had been discharged, for a declaration that C were in contempt of court for breach of the undertakings and interim orders and for orders that they be fined, and that an individual (X), who was the managing director of one of the claimant companies and a director of the other and was domiciled in Saudi Arabia, be imprisoned. The judge (1) held that the court's power to make a committal order against the officer of a company where an order may be enforced against the company by an order for committal (r.81.4(1) and (3)) extends to officers who are outside the jurisdiction, and (2) granted D permission to serve the committal application on X out of the jurisdiction under para.3.1(3)(b) on grounds that he was a necessary and proper party to the contempt proceedings against C ([2013] EWHC 4112 (QB); [2014] 1 C.L.C. 813). In dismissing X's appeal the Court of Appeal explained that "the real issue" which it was "reasonable for the court to try" was whether D came within the scope of r.81.4 (Enforcement by committal for breach of undertaking). For a similar analysis, see *Integral Petroleum SA v Petrogat FZE* [2018] EWHC 2686 (Comm); [2019] 1 W.L.R. 574 (Moulder J), at paras 89 to 95. See further commentary on r.81.4 in paras 81.4.5 and 81.5.2.

Paragraph 3.1(4A): Claim "arises out of same or closely connected facts"

In the penultimate paragraph, replace "Eurasia Sports Ltd v Aguad [2018] EWCA Civ 1742," with:
Eurasia Sports Ltd v Aguad [2018] EWCA Civ 1742; [2018] 1 W.L.R. 6089,
6HJ.12

Claims in relation to contracts (para.3.1(6) to (8))

Paragraph 3.1(6)(c): Contract "governed by English law"

The Rome I Regulation

Replace the second paragraph with:
The Rome Convention was incorporated into English law by the Contracts (Applicable Law) Act **6HJ.21** 1990 (c.36). (For ease of reference the Convention was set out in Sch.1 to that Act.) The Rome I Regulation came into effect on 17 December 2009 and has direct effect in Member States (with the exception of Denmark) and its rules apply to contractual obligations in civil and commercial mat-

ters "in situations involving a conflict of laws". It replaces the 1990 Act (which was disapplied by the Law Applicable to Contractual Obligations (England and Wales and Northern Ireland) Regulations 2009 (SI 2009/3064) to the extent that the Rome I Regulation applies). The 1990 Act continued to apply to contracts concluded before 17 December 2009.

6HJ.22 *Change title of paragraph:*

Paragraph 3.1(6)(d): Contract with English jurisdiction clause

Replace the third paragraph with:
    Note however that where there is an English jurisdiction clause, the recast Judgments Regulation will almost certainly apply (unless for example it is not a civil or commercial matter and therefore falls outside the scope of the Regulation, but that will be rare in a case where a jurisdiction agreement is concerned) and there will be no need for permission to serve out of the jurisdiction—see para.6.33.9 above.

Delete the fourth paragraph.

In the fifth paragraph, replace "Dell Emerging Markets (EMEA) Ltd v IB Maroc.com SA [2017] EWHC 2397 (Comm)." with:
    Dell Emerging Markets (EMEA) Ltd v IB Maroc.com SA [2017] EWHC 2397 (Comm); [2017] 2 C.L.C. 417.

Delete the sixth paragraph.

Claims in tort (para.3.1(9))

In the seventh paragraph, replace "Lloyd v Google LLC [2018] EWHC 2599 (QB), 8 October 2018, unrep." with:
6HJ.25   *Lloyd v Google LLC* [2018] EWHC 2599 (QB); [2019] 1 W.L.R. 1265

Enforcement (para.3.1(10))

In the third paragraph, replace the last two sentences with:
6HJ.26   The Court was content to say that there may well be considerable force in the view taken by the judge and, in recommending that any uncertainty in this area should be considered by the Rule Committee, expressed the opinion that it must be in the public interest that there should be a specific jurisdictional "gateway" permitting such service on an officer of a company, where the fact that he is out of the jurisdiction is no bar to the making of a committal application; see *Deutsche Bank AG v Vik* [2018] EWCA Civ 2011; [2019] 1 W.L.R. 1737, CA, at paras 84 to 89 per Gross LJ. See also the discussion on this matter in *Integral Petroleum SA v Petrogat FZE* [2018] EWHC 2686 (Comm); [2019] 1 W.L.R. 574 (Moulder J), at paras 85 to 88.

Claims for breach of confidence or misuse of private information (para.3.1(21))

At the end of the second paragraph, replace "SC.)" with:
6HJ.38   SC but the appeal was subsequently withdrawn.)

NOTES ON RULES OF JURISDICTION IN JUDGMENTS REGULATION (RECAST)

A. Introduction

2. Scope and exclusions

In the first paragraph, replace the last sentence with:
6JR.5   In *Hellenic Republic v Kuhn* (C-308/17) [2019] 4 W.L.R. 49, the Claimant acquired bonds issued by the Greek State. Greece passed national legislation as a result of the Greek financial crisis the effect of which was that the terms under which the bonds were held were changed and the Claimant made a considerable loss when the bonds were sold. The Claimant sued the Greek State. The CJEU held that such a claim did not fall within the concept of "civil and commercial matters". See also *Pula Parking d.o.o. v Tederahn* (C-551/15) EU:C:2017:193; [2017] I.L.Pr. 15, ECJ.

(a) Exclusion of proceedings in bankruptcy etc (art.1.2(b))

Replace the third paragraph with:
6JR.6   The ECJ has held that the Insolvency Regulation and the Judgments Regulation (recast) must be interpreted in such a way as to void any overlap between the rules of law that those instruments lay down and any "legal vacuum" (*Nickel & Goeldner Spedition GmbH v "Kintra" UAB* (C-157/13) EU:C:2014:2145; [2015] Q.B. 96, ECJ). Accordingly, actions excluded, under art.1.2(b) of the

Judgments Regulation (recast), from the scope of that Regulation fall within the scope of the Insolvency Regulation; and actions which fall outside the scope of art.3.1 of the Insolvency Regulation fall within the scope of the Judgments Regulation (recast). In *Nickel & Goeldner Spedition GmbH v "Kintra" UAB* (C-157/13) EU:C:2014:2145; [2015] I.L.Pr. 1, the ECJ ruled that art.1.1 of the Judgments Regulation must be interpreted as meaning that an action for the payment of a debt based on the provision of carriage services taken by an insolvent administrator of an insolvent company in the course of insolvency proceedings opened in one Member State and taken against a service recipient established in another Member State comes within the concept of "civil and commercial matters" within the meaning of that provision. In *NK v BNP Paribas Fortis NV* (C-535/17) [2019] I.L.Pr. 10, the CJEU ruled that a claim for damages arising from a wrongful act by a third party brought by the liquidator and the proceeds of which, if successful, accrued to the general body of creditors was a "civil and commercial matter" falling within the scope of the Judgments Regulation. In *Valach v Waldviertler Sparkasse Bank AG* (C-649/16) [2018] I.L.Pr. 9, ECJ, the ruling was that the bankruptcy exclusion encompasses an action for liability in tort brought against the members of a committee of creditors making allegations concerning their conduct in voting on a restructuring plan in insolvency proceedings. The English courts have held that the bankruptcy exclusion excludes nothing more, and nothing less, than what was included within the scope of the Insolvency Regulation (*Re Rodenstock GmbH* [2011] EWHC 1104 (Ch); [2011] Bus. L.R. 1245 (Briggs J); *Fondazione Enasario v Lehman Brothers Finance SA* [2014] EWHC 34 (Ch); [2014] 2 B.C.L.C. 662 (David Richards J)).

(b)   Exclusion of arbitration (art.1.2(d))

In the last paragraph, replace "Nori Holdings Ltd v Bank Okritie Financial Corp [2018] EWHC 1343 (Comm), 6 June 2018, unrep." with:

    Nori Holdings Ltd v Bank Okritie Financial Corp [2018] EWHC 1343 (Comm); [2018] 2 All E.R. **6JR.7** (Comm) 1009

3.   Burden and standard of proof

Replace the second paragraph with:

    In this context the phrase "good arguable case" connotes that one side has a better argument **6JR.8** than the other. (The phrase "much better argument" was used in *Canada Trust v Stolzenberg (No.2)*, op cit, but the adjunct "much" has since been laid to rest: see *Brownlie v Four Seasons Holdings Inc* [2017] UKSC 80; [2018] 1 W.L.R. 192 (at para.7 per Lord Sumption) and *Kaefer Aislamientos SA de CV v AMS Mexico SA de CV* [2019] EWCA Civ 10; [2019] 1 W.L.R. 3514.) Many of the relevant authorities are cases in which the claimant's contention was that the English court had jurisdiction under art.25.1 because the parties (regardless of their domiciles) had agreed in a choice of court agreement that the English court should have jurisdiction (see para.6JR.36 below). Leading and illustrative authorities are: *Bols Distilleries BV v Superior Yacht Services Ltd* [2006] UKPC 45; [2007] 1 W.L.R. 12, PC; *WPP Holdings Italy Srl v Benatti* [2007] EWCA Civ 263; [2007] 1 W.L.R. 2316, CA; *Football Dataco Ltd v Sportradar GmbH* [2010] EWHC 2911 (Ch); [2011] F.S.R 263 (Floyd J); *AK Investment CJSC v Kyrgyz Mobil Tel Ltd* [2011] UKPC 7; [2011] 4 All E.R. 1027, PC; *DSG International Sourcing Ltd v Universal Media Corp (Slovakia) SRO* [2011] EWHC 1116 (Comm); [2011] I.L.Pr. 33 (Steel J); *Global 5000 Ltd v Wadhawan* [2012] EWCA Civ 13; [2012] Lloyd's Rep. 239, CA; *Antonio Gramsci Shipping Corp v Recoletos Ltd* [2012] EWHC 1887 (Comm); [2012] I.L.Pr. 36 (Teare J).

B.   General Jurisdiction: Person to be Sued in Member State Where Domiciled

2.   Connection between person sued and territory of Member State

Replace the fifth paragraph with:

    Where, on the basis of the general rule of jurisdiction, the English court has jurisdiction the **6JR.11** claimant is entitled to sue the defendant despite the absence of any factual or legal connection with this jurisdiction. In *Owusu v Jackson* (C-281/02) [2005] Q.B. 801 (ECJ), where the claimant had founded jurisdiction on art.4 on the basis of one of the defendants' domicile in a Member State, the ECJ ruled that that state could not decline jurisdiction on forum conveniens grounds in favour of the courts of a non-Member State, where the other defendants were not domiciled in a Member State. In *Lungowe v Vedanta Resources Plc* [2019] UKSC 20; [2019] 2 W.L.R. 1051, 10 April 2019, the Supreme Court, upholding the Court of Appeal, emphasised the mandatory nature of the rule in art.4. Although, like the Court below, the Supreme Court did not exclude the possibility of challenging jurisdiction on the basis that the EU rules of jurisdiction were being used abusively, the cases demonstrated the narrowness of this concept which was limited to situations where an EU principle was invoked collusively to subvert other EU law provisions. The fact that art.4 precluded the application of the doctrine of forum non conveniens could not, of itself, be characterised as an abuse of EU law. In *Lucasfilm Ltd v Ainsworth* [2009] EWCA Civ 1328; [2010] 3 W.L.R. 333, CA, the Court of Appeal rejected the claimant's submission that the *Owusu* case decided that, for the EU, the courts of the Member State of the defendant's domicile have, and must exercise, "subject-matter" jurisdiction over any claim in any civil or commercial matter brought against a defendant (in this case, a claim to enforce the claimant's US copyrights) unless it is one of the excluded matters provided for in art.1 of the Judgments Regulation. On appeal, the Supreme Court did not deal with the point but expressed the view that a reference to the ECJ might be required to resolve it (*Lucasfilm Ltd v Ainsworth* [2011] UKSC 39; [2012] 1 A.C. 208, SC). In *Kennedy v National Trust for Scotland* [2019] EWCA Civ 648, the Court of Appeal confirmed that the *Owusu* case did not preclude the court staying its proceedings on grounds of forum non conveniens where proceedings were issued in the English court against a party domiciled in Scotland and Scotland was clearly the more appropriate forum.

3.   Domicile

Add new paragraph at end:

6JR.12   Where the court is unable to identify the defendant's place of domicile and has no firm evidence that the defendant is domiciled outside the EU, art.4 should be read as extending to the defendant's last known domicile: see *Gray v Hurley* [2019] EWHC 1636 (QB), 25 June 2019 (Lavender J).

C.   Special Jurisdiction: Person May be Sued in Another Member State

1.   Special jurisdiction—general (arts 7 and 8)

(a)   Special jurisdiction—particular matters (art.7)

(i) Matters relating to contract (art.7(1))

To the end of the ninth paragraph (beginning "Where a claim was brought in tort"), add:

6JR.15   A claim where a creditor sought a declaration that the transfer by the debtor of an asset to a third party was invalid or ineffective (actio pauliana) was a "matter relating to a contract" (*Feniks sp.Z.o.o. v Azteca Products & Services Ltd* (C-337/17) [2019] I.L.Pr. 1).

In the eleventh paragraph (beginning ""Obligation in question""), replace "XL Insurance Co SE (formerly XL Insurance Co Ltd) v AXA Corporate Solutions Assurance [2015] EWHC 3431 (Comm)" with:
   XL Insurance Co SE (formerly XL Insurance Co Ltd) v AXA Corporate Solutions Assurance [2015] EWHC 3431 (Comm); [2015] 2 C.L.C. 983

(ii) Matters relating to tort, delict or quasi-delict (art.7(2))

Replace the sixth paragraph with:

6JR.16   As to the characterisation of a claim for damages for misrepresentation, both at common law and under the Misrepresentation Act 1967, as claims relating to tort within the meaning of art.7(2), see *Aspen Underwriting Ltd v Credit Europe Bank NV* [2018] EWCA Civ 2590; [2019] 1 Lloyd's Rep. 221 (at para.136 per Gross LJ), and the authorities referred to there, in particular *Alfred Dunhill Ltd v Diffusion Internationale de Maroquinerie de Prestige SARL* [2002] 1 All E.R. (Comm) 950 (Kenneth Rokison QC).

Delete the fourteenth paragraph (beginning "In Aspen Underwriting Ltd").

In the fifteenth paragraph (beginning "The considerations to be borne"), replace "Griffin Underwriting Ltd v Varouxakis [2018] EWHC 3259 (Comm), 28 November 2018, unrep." with:
   Griffin Underwriting Ltd v Varouxakis [2018] EWHC 3259 (Comm); [2019] 1 W.L.R. 2529

Replace the nineteenth paragraph (beginning "In BVC v EWF") with:
   In *BVC v EWF* [2018] EWHC 2674 (QB); [2019] I.L.Pr. 7 (Karen Steyn QC), a British national (C) who currently worked in a South-East Asian country, commenced a claim for damages for misuse of private information and harassment and applied for an interim injunction to restrain the defendant (D) from publishing his private information on a website. The defendant, a British citizen domiciled in Switzerland (a party to the Lugano Convention 2007), acknowledged service but challenged the court's jurisdiction by an application under r.11, raising the question whether, notwithstanding D's domicile, he could be sued in England on the basis that that was the place where the harmful event occurred or may occur. The judge reviewed the relevant authorities on internet publication and dismissed D's application, holding that C had established a good arguable case to that effect England was the Lugano Convention State "in which he had his centre of interests". For a case where the Court held that C had not established a good arguable case that England was the Contracting State "in which he had his centre of interests", see *Said v Groupe L'Express* [2018] EWHC 3593 (QB); [2019] I.L.Pr. 20.

(iv) Activities of a branch or agency (art.7(5))

To the end of the paragraph, add:

6JR.18   In *ZX v Ryanair DAC* (C-464/18) EU:C:2019:311; [2019] W.L.R. 4202, the CJEU held that a claim for compensation made over the internet which was unrelated to the activities of the branch in question (located in Spain) did not fall within the scope of art.7(5).

2. Special Jurisdiction—Insurance, Consumer and Individual Employee Contracts (arts 10 to 23)

(a) Jurisdiction in matters relating to insurance (arts 10 to 16)

Replace the second paragraph with:

6JR.26
Articles 10 to 16 apply to "matters relating to insurance". In *Aspen Underwriting Ltd v Credit Europe Bank NV* [2018] EWCA Civ 2590; [2019] 1 Lloyd's Rep. 221 the Court of Appeal held (dismissing the defendant's appeal) that a claim by an insurer against a bank that a settlement agreement arising out of an insurance claim had been procured by fraudulent misrepresentation was a "matter relating to insurance". However, the defendant bank could not take the benefit of the special protection afforded by art.14. The mere fact that the bank came within a class specifically referred to in art.14 (being a beneficiary under the insurance policy) did not give rise to an irrebuttable presumption that it was a "weaker party" for whom the protection of that provision was designed. The bank, if not strictly an insurance professional, was analogous to an insurance professional and therefore fell outside the protection of the art.14 regime. The Court's judgment contains an extensive explanation of the purpose and the scope this form of special jurisdiction and the related European and domestic jurisprudence (at paras 62 to 80 per Gross LJ).

(c) Jurisdiction over individual contracts of employment (arts 20 to 23)

Delete the fourth paragraph (beginning "In Yukos International BK UV").   **6JR.28**

In the fifth paragraph (beginning "Article 7(1)(a) states"), delete the last sentence.

To the end of the eighth paragraph (beginning "However, in Arcadia Petroleum Ltd"), add:
The defendants appealed to the Supreme Court, which referred various questions to the CJEU for a preliminary ruling including the question of whether it is sufficient to fall within the relevant provisions of the Lugano Convention that a claim could have been pleaded as a breach of the employment contract, even if no such breach was in fact relied on. However, the effect of the CJEU's ruling on a separate question (see below) meant that there was no individual contract of employment in this case and so there was no need to answer the other questions referred.

To the end of the ninth paragraph (beginning "Article 21 preserves"), add:
These provisions may be departed from only by an agreement which is entered into after the dispute has arisen, or which allows the employee to bring proceedings in courts other than those indicated by the provisions (art.23).

After the ninth paragraph, add new paragraph:
In *Merinson v Yukos International UK BV* [2019] EWCA Civ 830 the Court of Appeal held that claims to annul a settlement agreement concluded to settle an employment dispute were "matters relating to individual contracts of employment" within the meaning of art.20, applying the test set out in *Arcadia Petroleum Ltd v Bosworth* [2016] EWCA Civ 818; [2016] C.P. Rep. 48 (above). The court further held that the settlement agreement was not an agreement entered into after the dispute had arisen within the meaning of art.23(1), and so the exclusive jurisdiction clause in the settlement agreement (in favour of the Dutch courts) was not effective to prevent proceedings being brought against the English-domiciled defendant in the English courts under art.21. The applicable test for whether an agreement has been entered into after the dispute has arisen is (i) whether the parties have disagreed on a specific point, which requires that the subject matter of the disagreement has been communicated between them; and (ii) whether legal proceedings in relation to that disagreement are imminent or contemplated. This sets a high threshold for an agreement falling within art.23(1).

Replace the last paragraph with:
In *Bosworth v Arcadia Petroleum Ltd* (C-603/17) [2019] I.L.Pr. 22 on a reference from the UK Supreme Court for a preliminary ruling, the CJEU held that an "individual contract of employment" requires a relationship of subordination between the company and the individual; accordingly, the equivalent provisions under the Lugano Convention (arts 18 to 21) did not apply to a company's directors who were able to determine the terms of their employment contracts and had control and autonomy over the day-to-day operation of the company's business and the performance of their own duties. See also *Holterman Ferho Exploitatie BV v Spies Von Bullesheim* (C-47/14) [2015] I.L.Pr. 44, ECJ on the requirements for an "individual contract of employment" within the equivalent provisions of the Brussels I Regulation (44/2001).

D.   Exclusive Jurisdiction: Jurisdiction Regardless of the Domicile of the Parties (art. 24)

1.   Exclusive jurisdiction regardless of domicile

6JR.29

Replace the first paragraph with:

The provisions as to exclusive jurisdiction contained in art.24 of the Judgments Regulation (recast) provide that in certain proceedings, being proceedings which "have as their object" or which are "concerned with" certain matters, the courts of a particular Member State (or of a State bound by a Convention) shall have exclusive jurisdiction, regardless of the domicile of the parties. Despite the words "regardless of domicile", it seems art.24 only applies where a defendant is domiciled in an EU Member State; see *Choudhary v Bhattar* [2009] EWCA Civ 1176; [2010] 2 All E.R. 1031 in which Sir John Chadwick held that the words "regardless of domicile" in the predecessor to art.24 (art.22 of the Brussels I Regulation) merely overrode a claimant's usual right to sue in the defendant's EU domicile or another EU Member State which had jurisdiction based on a connecting factor; it did not mean that the article applied regardless of where the defendant was domiciled. That decision has been subject to substantial criticism (see *Dar Al Arkan Real Estate Development Co v Al-Refai* [2013] EWHC 4122 (Comm) (Andrew Smith J) and in the Court of Appeal ([2014] EWCA Civ 715; [2015] 1 W.L.R. 135, CA); and *Deutsche Bank AG v Sebastian Holdings Inc (No.2)* [2017] EWHC 459 (Comm); [2017] 1 W.L.R. 3056 (Teare J) at paras 21 to 26 and in the Court of Appeal (*Deutsche Bank AG v Vik* [2018] EWCA Civ 2011; [2019] 1 W.L.R. 1737, CA, at paras 76 to 83 per Gross LJ)). However, in *Integral Petroleum SA v Petrogat FZE* [2018] EWHC 2686 (Comm); [2019] 1 W.L.R. 574 Moulder J held that she was bound to apply the decision in *Choudhary* in a case concerned with art.24 of the recast Judgments Regulation.

In all five different varieties of proceeding are listed in the article (as paras (1) to (5)); for text of this article, see Vol.2 para.5-269.

In the last paragraph, replace "Deutsche Bank AG v Vik [2018] EWCA Civ 2011," with:

Deutsche Bank AG v Vik [2018] EWCA Civ 2011; [2019] 1 W.L.R. 1737,

3.   Decisions of companies and their dissolution etc

6JR.31   *Delete the fourth paragraph.*

Replace the sixth paragraph with:

The authorities on the ambit of art.24(2) were carefully examined in *Worldview Capital Management SA v Petroceltic International Plc* [2015] EWHC 2185 (Comm); [2015] I.L.Pr. 46 (Judge Waksman QC), where it was held that, on a proper analysis, art.24(2) was not engaged and that the question whether the English court had jurisdiction turned on (what is now) art.7(1). In *Akcil v Koza Ltd* [2019] UKSC 40, 29 July 2019, the Supreme Court, reversing the Court of Appeal, held that where the English Court had jurisdiction over one claim ("claim A") under art.24(2), the mere fact that it was linked to another claim ("claim B") was not sufficient to bring that latter claim within art.24(2) unless claim B was inextricably linked to claim A and itself was principally concerned with the validity of the decision of a company with its seat in England.

5.   Enforcement of judgments

In the fifth line, replace "Integral Petroleum SA v Petrogat FZE [2018] EWHC 2686 (Comm), 17 October 2018, unrep." with:

6JR.32.1   *Integral Petroleum SA v Petrogat FZE* [2018] EWHC 2686 (Comm); [2019] 1 W.L.R. 574

6.   "Reflexive" application of art.24

6JR.33

Replace paragraph with:

Article 24 is on the face of it concerned with the jurisdictional position as between Member States. It does not in terms address what should happen where the principal subject matter of proceedings is, say, the validity of decisions of a company with its seat outside the EU, or the validity of entries in a public register kept outside the EU.

In a number of cases in the High Court it has been accepted that art.24 can be applied "reflexively"; in other words, that the Courts of a Member State can decline to exercise jurisdiction in circumstances where the article would apply were the country in which, say, a register is kept, or a company, legal person or association has its seat, a Member State; see *Ferrexpo AG v Gilston Investments Ltd* [2012] EWHC 721 (Comm); [2012] 1 Lloyd's Rep. 588 (Andrew Smith J) (a dispute regarding the ownership of shares in a Ukranian mining company), *Blue Tropic Ltd v Chkhartishvili* [2014] EWHC 2243 (Ch); [2014] I.L.Pr. 33 (Newey J) (a dispute regarding ownership of shares in BVI companies). However, those cases were decided before the recast Judgments Regulation came into force. In *Gulf International Bank BSC v Aldwood* [2019] EWHC 1666 (QB), 1 July 2019, John Kimbell QC (sitting as a deputy High Court judge) held that there is no power to decline jurisdiction in favour of a non-EU court in a case falling outside the express powers in arts 33 and 34 (in that case, despite the presence of an exclusive jurisdiction clause in favour of a non-EU court, so it would have been a reflexive application of art.25 rather than art.24). See also *UCP Plc v Nectrus Ltd* [2018] EWHC 380 (Comm); [2018] 1 W.L.R. 3409 and para.6JR.47 below.

E.   Prorogation of jurisdiction (arts 25 and 26)

2.   Jurisdiction by agreement (choice of court agreement) (art.25.1)

To the end of the eighth paragraph (beginning "For an examination of"), add:

A contract on the terms of a bill of lading said to be implied from the parties' course of conduct   **6JR.35** did not satisfy the formal requirements of art.25(1)(a) since it was not demonstrated that the parties' consent was in writing or evidenced in writing (*Pan Ocean Co Ltd v China-Base Group Co Ltd* [2019] EWHC 982 (Comm), 16 April 2019 (Christopher Hancock QC)).

Replace the ninth paragraph with:

Where the parties have entered into a complex transaction with competing jurisdiction clauses and the dispute is at the commercial centre of the transaction, it is those jurisdiction clauses that are also at its centre which the parties must have intended to apply to the dispute; *UBS AG v HSH Nordbank AG* [2009] EWCA Civ 585; [2009] 2 Lloyd's Rep. 272 CA; see also *ACP Capital Ltd v IFR Capital Plc* [2008] EWHC 1627 (Comm); [2008] 2 Lloyd's Rep. 655 (Beatson J); *Sebastian Holdings Inc v Deutsche Bank AG* [2010] EWCA Civ 998; [2010] I.L.Pr. 52, CA; *Lornamead Acquisitions Ltd v Kaupthing Bank HF* [2011] EWHC 2611 (Comm); [2013] 1 B.C.L.C. 73; *Citibank NA, London Branch v Oceanwood Opportunities Master Fund* [2018] EWHC 305 (Ch) (Mann J). In *Deutsche Bank AG v Comune di Savona* [2018] EWCA Civ 1740; [2018] I.L.Pr. 38, CA, where there were theoretically competing English and foreign jurisdiction agreements which the Court of Appeal found, on the facts, to be mutually exclusive, the Court commented that whilst it is desirable that potentially conflicting jurisdiction clauses be given a mutually exclusive construction, that might not always be possible and a convoluted construction should not be adopted merely to ensure that outcome (at para.31 per Longmore LJ). (See also *BNP Paribas SA v Trattamento Rifiuti Metropolitani SPA* [2019] EWCA Civ 768 to similar effect.)

In the tenth paragraph (beginning "When considering whether"), replace "Apple Sales International v MJA (C-595/17) ECLI EU:C:2018:854, 24 October 2018," with:

Apple Sales International v MJA (C-595/17) EU:C:2018:854; [2019] 1 W.L.R. 2705,

3.   Jurisdiction by agreement—burden and standard of proof

In the last paragraph, replace "Deutsche Bank AG v Asia Pacific Broadband Wireless Communications Inc [2008] EWCA Civ 1091;" with:

Deutsche Bank AG v Asia Pacific Broadband Wireless Communications Inc [2008] EWCA Civ 1091;   **6JR.36** [2009] 2 All E.R. (Comm) 129;

4.   Stay of proceedings where court seised on basis of exclusive jurisdiction agreement

In the second paragraph, replace "under a contract governed by English law, the effect of" with:

in favour of the English court, the effect of   **6JR.37**

F.   Priority of Jurisdiction—Lis Pendens and Related Actions

Change title of paragraph: **6JR.42**

Lis pendens and exclusive jurisdiction—stay of proceedings (art.31)

Same cause of action

To the end of the first paragraph, add:

In *Easy Rent a Car Ltd v Easygroup Ltd* [2019] EWCA Civ 477; [2019] I.L.Pr. 13, the Court of   **6JR.45** Appeal held that a claim in the English Court for passing off and trade mark infringement had the same "cause" as a claim in the Cypriot Court that the effect of a settlement agreement was that the Claimant had consented to the Defendant's use of the trade mark.

Degree to which proceedings must be "related"

Add new paragraph at end:

In *Office Depot International BV v Holdham SA* [2019] EWHC 2115 (Ch), Sir Geoffrey Vos,   **6JR.46** Chancellor, held that an application pursuant to art.30 for a temporary stay of English proceedings pending final determination of related Swedish proceedings was not an application to which the procedure for challenging jurisdiction set out at CPR Pt 11 applied.

Discretionary stay in favour of proceedings before courts of non-EU states (arts 33 and 34)

6JR.47
To the end of the last paragraph, add:
See also *UCP Plc v Nectrus Ltd* [2018] EWHC 380 (Comm); [2018] 1 W.L.R. 3409 in which it was held that arts 33 and 34 did not apply where the court's jurisdiction was based on a non-exclusive English jurisdiction clause, and therefore the court had no power to stay its proceedings despite proceedings having been commenced first in time in a non-member state (the Isle of Man).

PART 7

How to Start Proceedings—The Claim Form

Editorial introduction

7.0.1
To the end of the last paragraph, add:
A party must be named, unless the court permits otherwise, e.g. pursuant to an order made under r.6.16: *Cameron v Liverpool Victoria Insurance Co Ltd* [2019] UKSC 6; [2019] 1 W.L.R. 1471.

Effect of rule

7.5.1
After the second paragraph, add new paragraph:
In *Kennedy v National Trust for Scotland* [2019] EWCA Civ 648 the court concluded that although the deemed date of service of a claim form was outside the limitation period, the actual date of service was on the last day of validity of it, and thus service was effective: to find otherwise would require the construction of a counter-factual history.

PRACTICE DIRECTION 7A—HOW TO START PROCEEDINGS—THE CLAIM FORM

Where to start proceedings

7APD.2 *After 2.9, add new paragraph:*

2.9A(1) Subject to paragraph 2.9, a claim relating to media and communications work (which includes any work which would fall within the jurisdiction of the Media and Communications List if issued in the High Court) may be started in the County Court or High Court; and paragraph 2.1 shall not apply to such a claim.

(2) Such a claim should be started in the High Court if, by reason of the factors set out in paragraph 2.4(1) to (3), the claimant believes that the claim ought to be dealt with by a High Court judge.

(3) If a claimant starts such a claim in the High Court and the court decides that it should have been started in the County Court, the court will normally transfer it to the County Court on its own initiative. This is likely to result in delay.

PRACTICE DIRECTION 7D—CLAIMS FOR THE RECOVERY OF TAXES AND DUTIES

Scope

7DPD.1 *Add new paragraphs at end:*

1.2 This practice direction also applies to claims by the Welsh revenue Authority for the recovery of a devolved tax (as defined by section 116A(4) of the Government of Wales Act 2006) and interest and penalties thereon.

(Section 116A(4) of the Government of Wales Act 2006 defines a devolved tax as a tax which is specified in Part 4A of that Act as a devolved tax. For example, section 116L of the 2006 Act specifies as a devolved tax a tax which is charged on a Welsh land transaction and complies with the requirements of that section.)

At the hearing

After 3.1, add new paragraph:

(Section 168(1) of the Tax Collection and Management (Wales) Act 2016 **7DPD.3** ("the 2016 Act") provides that a certificate of Welsh Revenue Authority that a relevant amount (as defined by section 164 of the 2016 Act) has not been paid to Welsh Revenue Authority is sufficient evidence that the sum mentioned in the certificate is unpaid unless the contrary is proved.)

PART 8

ALTERNATIVE PROCEDURE FOR CLAIMS

Editorial introduction

Replace the fifth and sixth paragraphs with:

Rule 8.1 and para.3.1 of the Pt 8 Practice Direction (see para.8APD.1) provide for two distinct **8.0.1** types of claim in which the Pt 8 procedure may be followed. The first category is where the claim seeks the court's decision on a question which is unlikely to involve a substantial dispute of fact. These claims will normally be heard and disposed of on written evidence. Claims for declarations as to the construction of documents, questions of law and administration of estates are usually appropriate for this procedure.

The second category is where a rule or practice direction requires or permits the use of alternative procedure, e.g. claims under the Inheritance (Provision for Family and Dependants) Act 1975 (CPR r.57.16(1)) or under s.50 of the Administration of Justice Act 1985 (CPR r.64.3). Claims in this category often require substantial disputes of fact to be resolved, so that disclosure and oral evidence may be appropriate.

Unless falling within the second category, contentious claims involving substantial factual dispute will not usually be suitable for the Pt 8 procedure. However, the court may in appropriate circumstances approve a hybrid procedure under which limited factual disputes requiring oral evidence can be accommodated within Pt 8 proceedings—see *Vitpol Building Service v Samen* [2008] EWHC 2283 (TCC); Const. L.J. 2009, 25(4) 319, at [18] and *Forest Heath District Council v ISG Jackson Ltd* [2010] EWHC 322 (TCC) at [10].

After the seventh paragraph (beginning "In essence, the Pt 8 procedure"), add new paragraph:

Whenever a party is contemplating bringing proceedings under Pt 8 which could be brought under Pt 7, the proposed claimant should generally provide the proposed defendant with the following:

(a) notification that the use of Pt 8 is being contemplated;

(b) a brief explanation as to why Pt 8 is considered to more appropriate than Pt 7 in the particular circumstances of the case;

(c) a draft of the precise issue or question which the claimant is proposing to ask the court to decide, for the proposed defendant to comment on;

(d) identification of any agreed facts relevant to the issue or question.

See *Cathay Pacific Airlines Ltd v Lufthansa Technik AG* [2019] EWHC 484 (Ch) at [42].

Brexit

Replace paragraph with:

At the time of writing, the Cross-Border Mediation (EU Directive) (EU Exit) Regulations 2019 **8.0.1.1** (SI 2019/469), consequent upon the EU Mediation Directive (2008/52) ceasing to apply upon a no-deal Brexit, will revoke the Cross-Border Mediation (EU Directive) Regulations 2011 (SI 2011/1133). A further statutory instrument is intended to revoke the other legislation underpinning CPR Pt 78 (European Enforcement Order, European Order for Payment and European Small Claims Procedure (Amendment etc.) (EU Exit) Regulations 2018 (SI 2018/1311)). In the light of this the reference to Pt 78 in r.8.1 ought to become redundant upon Brexit.

See para.5.0.1.1 for detail on the amendments to the CPR and its PDs in the event of a no-deal exit.

PART 10

Acknowledgment of Service

"default judgment"

10.2.1 *In the ninth line, replace "Cunico Resources v Daskalakis [2018] EWHC 3328 (Comm)" with:*
   Cunico Resources v Daskalakis [2018] EWHC 3382 (Comm); [2019] 1 W.L.R. 2881

PART 11

Disputing the Court's Jurisdiction

Effect of Part

11.1.1 *Replace the twelfth paragraph (beginning "Where parties to applications") with:*
   Where parties to applications under r.11 intend to rely on expert opinion evidence on foreign law the court's permission to do so must be obtained. It is important (particularly in heavy applications) that parties seek directions from the court so that the nature of that evidence and the issues to which it is directed can be regularised (*BB Energy (Gulf) DMCC v Al Amoudi* [2018] EWHC 2595 (Comm), 4 October 2018, unrep. (Andrew Baker J) at paras 48 to 52); see also *Deutsche Bank AG v Comune Di Savona* [2018] EWCA Civ 1740; [2018] 4 W.L.R. 151.

   In the fourteenth paragraph (beginning "In Shiblaq v Sadikloglu"), replace "Shiblaq v Sadikloglu (No.1) [2003] EWHC 2128 (Comm)" with:
   Shiblaq v Sadikloglu (No.1) [2003] EWHC 2128 (Comm); [2005] 2 C.L.C. 380

   Add new paragraph at end:
   In *Lady Moon SPV SRL v Petricca & Co Capital Ltd* [2019] EWHC 439 (Ch) (Murray Rosen QC) the court rejected a submission that the question of whether the claimant had an arguable right to seek the relief claimed could be dealt with by way of an application under r.11.

Jurisdiction in strict sense and exercise of jurisdiction (r.11(1))

11.1.3 *After the second paragraph, add new paragraph:*
   In *Office Depot International BV v Holdham SA* [2019] EWHC 2115 (Ch), Sir Geoffrey Vos, Chancellor, held that an application pursuant to art.30 of the recast Judgments Regulation for a temporary stay of English proceedings pending final determination of related Swedish proceedings was not an application to which CPR Pt 11 applied. Accordingly the time limit under CPR r.11(4) did not apply; the application could have been made at any stage of the proceedings (though the later it was made, the less likely it was to succeed).

Periods for acknowledgment of service and application for order

11.1.5 *In the second paragraph, replace "(Cunico Resources NV v Daskalakis [2018] EWHC 3382 (Comm), 7 December 2018, unrep." with:*
   (*Cunico Resources NV v Daskalakis* [2018] EWHC 3382 (Comm); [2019] 1 W.L.R. 2881

   Replace the third and fourth paragraphs with:
   An application under r.11(1) must be made within 14 days after filing an acknowledgment of service (r.11(4)), but within 28 days where the claim is in the commercial list or the financial list (rr.58.7(2) and 63A.4(5)). A defendant may make an application for the extension of that time limit and such an extension can be granted by the court retrospectively despite r.11(4) and (5)) (*Sawyer v Atari Interactive Inc* [2005] EWHC 2351 (Ch); [2006] I.L.Pr. 8 (Lawrence Collins J), paras 42 to 48; *Polymer Vision R & D Ltd v Van Dooren* [2011] EWHC 2951 (Comm); [2012] I.L.Pr. 14 (Beatson J) at para.74; *Taylor v Giovani Developers Ltd*, op cit, at para.13; and *Caine v Advertiser And Times Ltd* [2019] EWHC 39 (QB) (Dingemans J) at para.31). An application for retrospective extension (made out of time) falls to be decided in accordance with the principles of r.3.9 and, hence, the test under *Denton v TH White Ltd* [2014] EWCA Civ 906; [2014] 1 W.L.R. 3926 (*Newland Shipping & Forwarding Ltd v Toba Trading FZC* [2017] EWHC 1416 (Comm) (Ms Sara Cockerill QC), at para.54; *BVC v EWF* [2018] EWHC 2674 (QB); [2019] I.L.Pr. 7 (Karen Steyn QC), at paras 13 to 29; and *Caine v Advertiser And Times Ltd*).
   As to the variation by written agreement between the parties of a time limit relevant to an ap-

plication under r.11(1), see r.2.11 and r.3.8(4). In commercial list proceedings, circuit commercial claims and financial list proceedings, the claimant must notify the court of any such agreement (PD 58 para.7.1, PD 59 para.6.1, PD 63AA para.5.1); these provisions refer only to r.2.11 but the same applies to a variation under r.3.8(4) (*Griffin Underwriting Ltd v Varouxakis* [2018] EWHC 3259 (Comm); [2019] 1 W.L.R. 2529 (Males J), at para.46). In *Griffin Underwriting Ltd v Varouxakis* [2018] EWHC 3259 (Comm); [2019] 1 W.L.R. 2529 op cit, before the expiry of the time limit relevant to the period within which a foreign defendant was required to make an application under r.11(1), the parties' agreed an indefinite stay of the proceedings terminable on 48 hours' notice but failed to notify the court of this agreement. The judge held that in the circumstances the moratorium was not effective to extend the time for the defendant to challenge jurisdiction.

Waiver of right to challenge—submission to jurisdiction

In the last paragraph, replace "Winkler v Shamoon [2016] EWHC 217 (Ch)" with:
    Winkler v Shamoon [2016] EWHC 217 (Ch); 18 I.T.E.L.R. 818

11.1.10

Jurisdiction agreements—procedural contexts

To the end of the fifth paragraph, after the list, add:
    (Note however that where there is an English jurisdiction agreement, or a jurisdiction agreement in favour of another EU Member State, the recast Judgments Regulation will almost certainly apply (unless for example it is not a civil or commercial matter and therefore falls outside the scope of the Regulation, but that will be rare in a case where a jurisdiction agreement is concerned). If the Regulation applies, the English court will be bound to give effect to the clause without regard to the doctrine of forum conveniens. Where the jurisdiction agreement is in favour of the English court there will be no need for permission to serve out of the jurisdiction in any event—see para.6.33.9 above.)

11.1.13

Jurisdiction agreements—service out of jurisdiction with permission—forum conveniens

To the end of the second paragraph, add:
    (Note however that where there is an English jurisdiction agreement, or a jurisdiction agreement in favour of another EU Member State, the recast Judgments Regulation will almost certainly apply (unless for example it is not a civil or commercial matter and therefore falls outside the scope of the Regulation, but that will be rare in a case involving a jurisdiction agreement). If the Regulation applies, the English court will be bound to give effect to the clause without regard to the doctrine of forum conveniens. Where the jurisdiction agreement is in favour of the English court there will be no need for permission to serve out of the jurisdiction in any event—see para.6.33.9 above.)

11.1.14

Foreign jurisdiction agreement—whether English court forum conveniens

In the first paragraph, fourth line, after "for departing from", replace "it." with:
    it (and where the jurisdiction agreement is in favour of the court of an EU Member State, the English court will generally be bound to give effect to it under the recast Judgments Regulation).

11.1.16

In the fifth paragraph (beginning "In Republic of Angola v Perfectbit Ltd"), replace "Republic of Angola v Perfectbit Ltd [2018] EWHC 965 (Comm)" with:
    Republic of Angola v Perfectbit Ltd [2018] EWHC 965 (Comm); [2018] Lloyd's Rep. F.C. 363

PART 12

DEFAULT JUDGMENT

Brexit

Replace paragraph with:
    At the time of writing, the Service of Documents and Taking of Evidence in Civil and Commercial Matters (Revocation and Saving Provisions) (EU Exit) Regulations 2018 (SI 2018/1257), is intended to revoke the Service Regulation (1393/2007) and Taking of Evidence Regulation (1206/2001) so that they no longer apply to the UK when it leaves the EU, assuming a no-deal Brexit. In the light of this the reference to the Service Regulation in r.12.3 ought to become redundant upon Brexit. References to the Judgments Regulation (1215/2012) and Brussels and Lugano Conventions in r.12.11 ought also to become redundant due to the anticipated effect of the Civil Jurisdiction and Judgments (Amendment) (EU Exit) Regulations 2019 (SI 2019/479).
    See para.5.0.1.1 for detail on the amendments to the CPR and its PDs in the event of a no-deal exit.

12.0.1.1

"judgment in default of an acknowledgment of service"

After the third paragraph (beginning "In Cunico Resources NV"), add new paragraph:

12.3.1   In *Smith v Berryman Lace Mawer Service Co* [2019] EWHC 1904 (QB) Master McCloud considered the decision of Andrew Baker J in *Cunico* and adopted the first of the three approaches he outlined as set out above. She also granted permission to appeal. Whether that will be pursued is unknown at present.

Scope of provision

To the end of the last paragraph, add:

12.11.1   In *Therium Capital Management Ltd v E-Tricity Ltd* [2018] EWHC 3216 (Comm) Teare J held that where the claimant had made an application for judgment in default of acknowledgment of service and the court had listed the matter for a short hearing, the fact that the defendants filed an acknowledgment of service six months late on the day before the hearing and applied for an extension of time for filing of the acknowledgment of service did not mean that the court could not refuse the extension of time and enter judgment in default.

PART 13

SETTING ASIDE OR VARYING DEFAULT JUDGMENT

Brexit

Replace paragraph with:

13.0.1.1   At the time of writing, the Service of Documents and Taking of Evidence in Civil and Commercial Matters (Revocation and Saving Provisions) (EU Exit) Regulations 2018 (SI 2018/1257), are intended to revoke the Service Regulation (1393/2007) and Taking of Evidence Regulation (1206/2001) so that they no longer apply to the UK when it leaves the EU, assuming a no-deal Brexit. In the light of this the reference to the Service Regulation in r.13.3 ought to become redundant upon Brexit.

     See para.5.0.1.1 for detail on the amendments to the CPR and its PDs in the event of a no-deal exit.

PART 14

ADMISSIONS

"amend or withdraw an admission"

Add new paragraph at end:

14.1.8   In *Obaid v Al-Hezaimi* [2019] EWHC 1953 (Ch) Falk J considered an application for a declaration that the defendants had not made an admission for the purposes of CPR Pt 14 when it was admitted in a witness statement (but was not pleaded) that Mr Al-Hezaimi had sent two forged emails. It was held that there was no principled distinction between matters dealt with in and outside a statement of case where the allegation is one of fact and in an important element in the case. The judge held that Mr Al-Hezaimi could not be forced to continue to say he was involved in forging documents and must be entitled to provide oral evidence of what he now says is the truth. He should therefore be required to provide a limited further witness statement confined to correcting his story about the forged emails, which could be done under CPR r.32.5.

Rule 14.1A

Add new paragraphs at end:

14.1A.2   In *Royal Automobile Club v Catherine Wright* [2019] EWHC 913 (QB) William Davis J upheld the decision of the Master and refused the appellant employer permission to withdraw an admission made one year after an accident at work of the respondent employee. The appellant had admitted liability over one year after the accident having been informed that the respondent had sustained two breaks in her right leg and chronic pain and would be seeking advice from several medical experts. The employee served a schedule of loss valued at just in excess of £1 million nearly one year later which led the employer to say it was further refining its case and would be alleging contributory negligence. It later invited the employee to consent to the withdrawal of its admission, but she declined to do so. Proceedings were issued based on the admission and the employer applied for permission to withdraw the admission. This was refused by the Master and his decision was upheld on appeal. It was held that the fact that the employer had initially assumed that the claim would be limited to £25,000—an error not contributed to by the employee—and that it now appeared to exceed £1 million was not a good reason to grant permission. It was held that where clear and unequivocal admissions had been made which had led to substantial investigation of quantum and to interim payments being made without question, if permission to withdraw them were made, there would be real damage to the administration of justice.

In *Zagora Management Ltd v Zurich Insurance Plc* [2019] EWHC 205 (TCC) Judge Stephen Davies held that in circumstances where leaseholders had brought claims to recover the costs of remedial works under new home warranties and the judge had held that the warranties amounted to a cap, they should be permitted to pursue a claim for interest on the capped amount as the defendants had never advanced a claim that the claimants were not entitled to statutory interest and the claimants' failure to qualify their acceptance in their closing submissions amounted to inadvertence and not to an admission under CPR Pt 14.

PART 15

DEFENCE AND REPLY

"must file a defence"

At the end of the paragraph, replace "[Accessed 14 January 2019]." with:
   [Accessed 2 August 2019].

15.2.1

PART 16

STATEMENTS OF CASE

Awards of interest

Replace paragraph with:
   See para.16.4.2 ("if the claimant is seeking interest") and, after the text of PD 16, paras 16AI.1 to 16AI.28 ("Notes on Awards of Interest") much of which was formerly set out in the editorial introduction to Pt 7.

16.0.2

Comprehensive response to the particulars of claim

In the third paragraph, replace "(SPI North Ltd v Swiss Post International UK Ltd [2019] EWCA Civ 7," with:
   (*SPI North Ltd v Swiss Post International (UK) Ltd* [2019] EWCA Civ 7; [2019] 1 W.L.R. 2865, CA,

16.5.2

NOTES ON AWARDS OF INTEREST

C.   Interest on judgment debts

1.   Power to award interest on judgment debts

Replace the second paragraph with:
   The County Courts Act 1984 s.74 applies to county court proceedings and states that sums made payable under judgments or orders (including sums payable by instalments) shall carry interest as provided for by Order (see Vol.2 para.9A-563). That power was not exercised until the County Courts (Interest on Judgment Debts) Order 1991 (SI 1991/1184) was enacted, implementing a recommendation made in the *Report of the Civil Justice Review Body* (Cm.394, 1988) that, subject to appropriate exclusions, High Court and county court remedies should be the same in this respect. The 1991 Order has been amended subsequently (see SI 1996/2516, SI 1998/2400, SI 2019/903). (For text of this Order, see Vol.2 para.9B-70.)

16AI.16

3.   Time from which interest on judgment debts begins to run

Replace the third paragraph with:

16AI.18   In *Simcoe v Jacuzzi UK Group Plc* [2012] EWCA Civ 137; [2012] 1 W.L.R. 2393, CA, it was held that, as CPR r.40.8(1) had been enacted without the concurrence of the Treasury as required by the County Courts Act 1984 s.74(1), it was ineffective in the county court and the County Courts (Interest on Judgment Debts) Order 1991 applied, which stipulated that interest was to be paid from the date the order for costs was made and not the date on which the costs were subsequently assessed or agreed. However, the Treasury has now concurred. Since the coming into force of the County Courts (Interest on Judgment Debts) (Amendment) Order 2019 (SI 2019/903) on 27 May 2019, the County Court is enabled to order interest on a judgment debt to run from a different date than the date when the judgment is given or the amount of the judgment is determined. The date can be from a date that is before the date of the judgment. This brings the powers of the County Court into line with those of the High Court. See further para.40.8.2 below.

PART 17

AMENDMENTS TO STATEMENTS OF CASE

The date from which amendments take effect

In the third paragraph, replace "claim: the addition or substitution of a new cause of action or a new party"." with:

17.3.3   claim": the addition or substitution of a new cause of action or a new party.

Amendments to regularise an existing claim by pleading facts which occurred after the claim form was issued

After the third paragraph, add new paragraph:

17.3.3.2   The decision in *Maridive & Oil Services* (see above) was applied by consent in *Currie v Thornley* [2019] EWHC 172 (Ch) (noted in para.17.3.7).

Late amendments

Add new paragraphs at end:

17.3.7   In *The New York Laser Clinic Ltd v Naturastudios Ltd* [2019] EWCA Civ 421, a few weeks before the trial, C sought permission to amend its particulars of claim so as to substitute its original claim (for negligent misstatement) with a new claim (for breach of warranty), thereby increasing its claim for damages from £400,000 to £4.3 million. The lower court allowed the amendment, accepting that C had discharged the heavy burden of justifying an application for permission to allow the late amendment: the changed pleading largely amounted to a re-characterisation of the existing case and the prejudice that D would suffer was outweighed by the potentially serious injustice C would suffer if the amendment was not allowed. The Court of Appeal dismissed D's appeal holding that the lower court had been entitled to grant permission, even though the case for a late amendment here was only borderline.

In *Currie v Thornley* [2019] EWHC 172 (Ch) C sued D in respect of two demands which C had made upon D under a deed of indemnity. One of the demands had been made before the commencement of proceedings and the other had been made shortly thereafter. At the trial D alleged that neither demand satisfied the formalities required by the deed. After the trial, C made two further demands and sought permission to adduce evidence in respect of them and permission to amend his Points of Claim to enable him to rely upon them. D's counsel conceded that claimants are now permitted to raise causes of action which accrue after the commencement of proceedings (*Maridive & Oil Services (SAE) v CNA Insurance Company (Europe) Ltd* [2002] EWCA Civ 369, as to which, see further, para.17.3.3.2) but opposed C's applications giving reasons based upon the laws of evidence and procedural fairness. However, both applications were allowed (see [18] to [18.3]) and C obtained judgment on the basis of the new demands (see [32.2] to [32.5]).

Issue (3): arising out of the same or substantially the same facts?

After the second paragraph, add new paragraphs:

17.4.4.3   A new claim does not arise out of the same or substantially the same facts as the original claim if it puts the defendant in the position of being obliged to investigate facts and obtain evidence well beyond the ambit of the facts that the defendant could reasonably be assumed to have investigated for the purpose of defending the original claim. In *Akers v Samba Financial Group* [2019] EWCA Civ 416; [2019] 4 W.L.R. 54, the liquidators of an insolvent company (C) took proceedings claiming that shares held in the name of their nominee (X) had been transferred to a bank (D) in repayment of debts owed by X to D. The original claim sought an order under the Insolvency Act 1986 s.27 that the transfer by X to D be declared void as a disposition of C's property after the commencement of the winding-up. In that part of the proceedings C did not make any allegations of bad faith against D. In the Supreme Court it was held that the claim as originally formulated had to fail (C's interest in the shares being equitable not legal, the transfer of legal title had not disposed of C's beneficial interest in them even if that interest had been defeated by any beneficial interest D had if D had been a bona fide purchaser for value). The claim was remitted to the High Court to determine whether C could save the action by applying to re-amend the claim. Birss J permitted C to raise a constructive trust claim (i.e. disputing that D was a bona fide purchaser for value) but this amendment was disallowed by the Court of Appeal: the new claim did not arise out the same or substantially the same facts of the original claim; defending it would have required D to investigate facts and obtain evidence well beyond the ambit of the facts that D could reasonably be assumed to have investigated for the purpose of defending the original claim. C's original pleading had not put in issue any factual allegations of an absence of good faith by D. In the vast majority of cases the pleadings are the only or primary source of material for deciding what facts were originally "in issue". In this case several references had been made concerning D's good or bad faith in written submissions and in witness statements. However, these references did not amount to sufficient material on which to find that wide-ranging factual allegations of an absence of good faith were already in issue in the action.

The decision in *Akers v Samba Financial Group* was followed and applied in *Re One Blackfriars Ltd (In Liquidation)* [2019] EWHC 1516 (Ch) (John Kimbell QC sitting as a deputy High Court judge). Floyd LJ in *Akers* and Mr Kimbell QC in *One Blackfriars* both cited a dictum of Hobhouse LJ in *Lloyd's Bank Plc v Rogers* [1997] T.L.R. 154 to the effect that the policy of s.35 of the Limitation Act "was that, if factual issues were in any event going to be litigated between the parties, the parties should be able to rely on any cause of action which substantially arises from those facts".

PART 19

PARTIES AND GROUP LITIGATION

Proceedings may be brought against unnamed defendants

After the third paragraph, add new paragraph:

In *Vastint Leeds BV v Persons Unknown* [2018] EWHC 2456 (Ch); [2019] 4 W.L.R. 2, Marcus **19.1.3** Smith J granted quia timet final injunctions against unknown persons preventing them from entering or remaining on a development site over which the claimant had a right of possession. The order (which was endorsed with a penal notice) made provision for service on the defendants by means of notices affixed to the perimeter of and entrances to the site and personal service was dispensed with. Great care was taken to define the identity of each defendant by reference to that defendant's future act of infringement. A person who came within that definition would, through the very act of infringing the order, become: (i) a party to the proceedings; (ii) bound by the order; and (iii) in breach of it.

Replace the fifth paragraph (beginning "The Court of Appeal held") with:

The majority in the Court of Appeal held that the principle applied in *Bloomsbury Publishing Group Plc* (see above) was not limited to claims for injunctive relief or to claims in which the applicant would, otherwise, have no remedy. In *Cameron v Hussain* [2019] UKSC 6; [2019] 1 W.L.R. 1471, the UKSC, considering this question for the first time, rejected the Court of Appeal's approach: as a general rule proceedings cannot be brought against a person who cannot be identified as a particular person, except where the circumstances would enable a claim to be properly served or dispensed with. Describing an unknown driver of vehicle, as in this case, by something they had done in the past failed to identify anyone. In such circumstances where the defendant is unknown service cannot be effected properly: see paras 16–26.

The Supreme Court's decision in *Cameron* does not affect claims which are brought against unknown persons in order to obtain a quia timet injunction, because, in these cases, the unknown persons are described by reference to their conduct in the future (an act amounting to a breach of the injunction claimed). In *Boyd v Ineos Upstream Ltd* [2019] EWCA Civ 515 the Court of Appeal upheld the grant of quia timet injunctions against persons unknown entering, without the claimants' consent, specified areas of land which the claimants had selected for the purpose of exploration for shale gas by hydraulic fracturing of rock formations ("fracking"). The Court of Appeal also gave general guidance as to the requirements necessary for the grant of a quia timet injunction against unknown persons, whether in the context of the common law or in the context of the ECHR:

1) there must be a sufficiently real and imminent risk of a tort being committed to justify quia timet relief;

2)   it is impossible to name the persons who are likely to commit the tort unless restrained;

3)   it is possible to give effective notice of the injunction and for the method of such notice to be set out in the order;

4)   the terms of the injunction must correspond to the threatened tort and not be so wide that they prohibit lawful conduct;

5)   the terms of the injunction must be sufficiently clear and precise as to enable persons potentially affected to know what they must not do; and

6)   the injunction should have clear geographical and temporal limits.

In *Ineos Upstream*, the defendants' appeal in respect of two injunctions succeeded because of non-compliance with guidelines 4 and 5, above. In respect of the two injunctions intended to prevent trespass to land, the appeal was dismissed but these injunctions were to continue in their present form only until the completion of a further hearing by the lower court to consider two matters: (1) whether the claimants' case reached the higher standard of proof required on applications which might infringe the freedom of speech (see further, the Human Rights Act 1998 s.12(3), the *White Book*, Vol.2, paras 3D-47 and 3D-49); and (2) if so, what time limit should be imposed on the duration of the injunctions.

Delete the last paragraph.

I.   Addition and Substitution of Parties

The Sardinia Sulcis test for mistake (r.19.5(3)(a))

After the list at the end of the fourth paragraph, add new paragraph:

19.5.4   In *Jenkins v JCP Solicitors Ltd* [2019] EWHC 852 (QB) C brought a claim alleging professional negligence in respect of advice he had received on or after October 2011 from a firm of solicitors ("LLP") trading as "JCP Solicitors". In December 2014 LLP's business was transferred to a company ("the Company") and, in April 2015, the Company started trading as "JCP Solicitors". In December 2015 C's new solicitors sent a preliminary notice and letter of claim to the Company. In September 2017 (i.e. less than six years after October 2011) C's claim form was issued naming the Company as defendant. In March 2018 (i.e. more than six years after October 2011) C applied to join LLP as defendant in substitution for the Company. A district judge refused that application but, on appeal, O'Farrell J made an order substituting LLP for the Company; in her judgment, the error made by C in the claim form was clearly an error as to the name of the intended defendant; it was not an error as to the liability of the Company for any wrongdoings of its predecessor. This was indicated by, amongst other things, C's particulars of claim which contained allegations such as "The Defendant failed to advise the Claimant properly as to the options open to him as at 2011 …" (and see further, at [38]). O'Farrell J's judgment also deals with another aspect of this case, a claim in respect of advice given by LLP in April 2011 (i.e., more than six years before any proceedings had been issued).

II.   Representative Parties

Death of a party (r.19.8(1))

Replace the first paragraph with:

19.8.1   The general rule of joinder (r.19.2) applies where a party to proceedings has died and a formal grant of representation (whether probate or letters of administration) is taken out in respect of his estate. In order to make a search for any grant of representation which may have already been made, go to *https://www.gov.uk/search-will-probate* [Accessed 4 June 2019]. In order to make a search for any grant of representation which may have already been made, go to *https://www.gov.uk/search-will-probate* [Accessed 15 January 2019]. Rule 19.8(1) applies where a party to proceedings (whether claimant or defendant) has died and that person has no personal representative. In such a case the court may order (a) the claim is to proceed in the absence of anyone representing the deceased party's estate, or (b) a person to be appointed to represent the estate of the deceased. These orders have the effect of making the deceased's estate bound by any rulings which the court may make in the proceedings (r.19.8(5)). In *Berti v Steele Raymond* [2001] EWCA Civ 2079 Robert Walker LJ stated:

> "it is apparent from the rule [r.19.8] as a whole that it gives the court quite wide powers to dispense with the need for a formal grant of probate or letters of administration after the death of a party. It seems to recognise that, especially with relatively small claims, the need for a formal grant may be disproportionate and cause unnecessary delay and expense."

III.   Group Litigation

Editorial note

Replace paragraph with:

19.11.1   **PF19** should be used with appropriate adaptations. Parties are invited to submit to the Senior

Master or the Chief Chancery Master in advance of the hearing their own draft order, to enable a check to be made on whether the necessary ingredients have been included. In the Chancery Division parties are advised to contact the Chancery Lawyer, Ms Yvonne Jacobs-Jones (Room D01-010 Rolls Building, 100 Fetter Lane, London EC4, tel. 020 7947 6080) at the earliest opportunity if they are contemplating making an application to the Chief Master for a GLO and in the Queen's Bench Division the Senior Master's listing clerk, David Shoulder at david.shoulder@justice.gov.uk.

Cut-off dates

Add new paragraph at end:

19.13.3

In *Hutson v Tata Steel UK Ltd* [2019] EWHC 143 (QB) Turner J granted an extension of the cut-off date to allow a number of additional claimants to join the group litigation. The judge noted that a hard and fast approach to cut-off dates was inappropriate and approved the approach in *Pearce v Secretary of State for Energy and Climate Change* (above). In considering whether to grant an extension where there had been a failure to comply with the formal requirements for entry on the group register in time, it was necessary to consider the prejudice that an extension would cause to a defendant. Where there was such prejudice it would be harder for an applicant to persuade a court to grant an extension. Further, where certain claims had purportedly been entered on the register but the requisite formalities had not, in fact, been complied with before the deadline had passed, and the claims were a nullity on the basis of the decision in *Kimathi v Foreign and Commonwealth Office (No.2)* [2016] EWHC 3005 (QB), it was permissible for a second claim to be brought (subject to argument as to whether it was an abuse of process) and there was a discretion to extend the cut-off date to permit such second claim to be entered on the register. The judge approached that question (expressly without deciding the issue) on the basis of an application for relief from sanction, applying the test in *Denton v TH White Ltd* [2014] EWCA Civ 906; [2014] 1 W.L.R. 3926. Note that in *Kimathi v Foreign and Commonwealth Office* [2017] EWHC 939 (QB) Stewart J applied the test in *Denton* to an application to permit claims to be added to the register after the cut-off date, but Turner J did not refer to this decision in his judgment.

Change title of paragraph:

19.13.6

Group litigation issues

Add new paragraphs at end:

In *Bates v Post Office Ltd (No.2)* [2018] EWHC 2698 (QB), on an unsuccessful application by the defendant to strike out a large part of the lead claimants' evidence, on the grounds that it was not relevant to the common issues Fraser J held that there were good arguments that it should be harder to strike out evidence, not easier, in group litigation. That was because common issues, or the cases of lead claimants, were selected at an early stage in group litigation. Relevance had to be considered against the litigation as a whole; unless that was done, steps in the litigation (such as resolving at trial common issues that would be relevant to hundreds of claimants) might be taken on an artificially narrow basis. For the evidence to be struck out, it had to be quite plain that, no matter how the proceedings might look at trial, the evidence would never appear to be relevant or, if relevant, would never be sufficiently helpful to any of the common issues. That was "quite a heavy burden": *Wilkinson v West Coast Capital (Pre-Trial Review)* [2005] EWHC 1606 (Ch) applied. In the same case the judge reminded the parties that an aggressive and dismissive approach to major group litigation was entirely misplaced. Such litigation had to be conducted in a co-operative fashion and in accordance with the overriding objective in the CPR. In *Bates v Post Office Ltd* the managing judge had ordered that groups of common issues be tried separately.

In *Bates v Post Office Ltd (No.3: Common Issues)* [2019] EWHC 606 (QB) the common issues trial aimed to resolve issues of contractual construction before breach, causation and loss were considered.

In *Bates v Post Office Ltd (No.4: Recusal application)* [2019] EWHC 871 (QB) the defendant applied after the hearing of the first common issues trial for the managing judge to recuse himself from further involvement in the case. Fraser J held that the points made by Longmore LJ in *Otkritie International Investment Management Ltd v Urumov* [2014] EWCA Civ 1315 at [1] and [2] were directly applicable to Group Litigation. Fraser J stated that such litigation is usually massive in scale, will almost certainly never be heard in a single trial and even if test cases are chosen, not all of those may proceed to judgment as individual claims can always be settled, and such litigation is likely to continue for a number of years. Longmore J had held in *Otkritie* that it was important that judges do not recuse themselves too readily in long and complex cases otherwise the convenience of having a single judge in charge of both the procedural and substantial parts of the case will be seriously undermined. Permission to appeal from Fraser J's decision was refused by Coulson LJ on 9 May 2019.

In *Crossley v Volkswagen AG* [2019] EWHC 698 (QB), Waksman J granted the claimant's application for a trial of certain issues of liability, holding that in GLO cases there can be a staged approach for many things, including particular issues, and that a party does not have to show a real prospect of a radically different or a radically shorter trial or no trial before a preliminary issue trial can be ordered. It is enough that the issues are disputes of a central feature of the litigation and in the present case the issues were a huge bone of contention between the parties.

In *Hutson v Tata Steel UK Ltd* [2019] EWHC 1608 (QB) Turner J refused the defendant's application for a preliminary issue trial on limitation. He held that a central consideration is the extent to which the determination of the limitation issue in selected lead cases would be likely to catalyse the early resolution of a high proportion of other claims. The fact that there is a prospect that the defendant may well be successful in some proportion of lead cases in which a preliminary issue of limitation is intended to be raised is not determinative of the merits of the application. In this case about half the claims were not intended to be the subject of the limitation challenge so that the determination of lead cases confined is solely to the issue of limitation would provide new useful guidance to the proper resolution of unaffected cases. Further any adjudication on the limitation position in the lead cases would not be legally determinative of any of the other cases which the defendant claims to be statute barred. There is also a limit to the assistance which the exercise of discretion in lead cases would provide in informing the parties as to the strength of the limitation in right issues arising in other cases. He further held that the costs of hearing preliminary limitation issues were likely to be out of proportion to the perceived benefits.

Costs Sharing Provisions

Add new paragraph at end:

19.13.7   In *Bates v The Post Office (No. 5: Common Issues Costs)* [2019] EWHC 1373 (QB), where the claimants had succeeded on 16 out of 23 common issues, the judge determined that as many of the common issues interlocked or overlapped, and some were more important than others, the only sensible way to reflect this was to make an approximate percentage adjustment downwards from the 100% which a wholly successful claimant would expect to recover. He followed an approach which he described as the modern practice, as approved in *Kastor Navigation Co Ltd v AXA Global Risk (UK) Ltd* [2004] EWCA Civ 277. He applied a reduction to the claimant's costs of 10%, taking into account the fact that the defendant had put facts in issue during the *Common Issues* trial which, it plainly ought not to have done, and which extended the length of the trial significantly.

PART 20

COUNTERCLAIMS AND OTHER ADDITIONAL CLAIMS

Fee

Add new paragraph 20.2.1:

20.2.1   In *Wolseley UK Ltd v Fiat Chrysler Automobiles NV* [2019] CAT 12, the defendants brought Pt 20 claims against a number of parties including Daimler AG seeking indemnity or contribution in the event they were held liable to the claimants. In response, Daimler sought certain declarations against the claimants. The claimants sought an order that Daimler's claims (issued without the court's permission) were improperly issued and so could not proceed. In fact, the CAT struck out Daimler's claims on other grounds, but went on to consider (obiter) whether those claims had been correctly issued (see paras 53–63 of the judgment). The CAT found that the claimants' claim against Daimler was an "additional claim" as defined by CPR 20.2(1)(b), that Daimler's claims against the claimants were additional claims governed by CPR 20.2(1)(c) and that therefore, by CPR 20.7 such claims were to be started by service of a Claim Form and only with the permission of the court. Daimler's argument that it was "a defendant" to the contribution claims making a claim against "the claimant" in the main action and so the claim it made against the claimant was a counterclaim was described as "untenable"; the terms claimant and defendant had to be read in context and could not relate to different "claims". As no permission to issue the additional claim had been given, Daimler's claim was found to have been improperly issued.

"An additional claim shall be treated as if it were a claim for the purposes of these rules" (r.20.3(1))

Replace paragraph with:

20.3.2   See too PD 20, para.3 (see para.20PD.3). Note Pt 9 (Responding to Particulars of Claim), Pt 11 (Disputing The Court's Jurisdiction) and Pt 15 (Defence and Reply). For example, a person served with a Pt 20 claim must file a defence in accordance with r.15.2. A Pt 20 defendant resident out of the jurisdiction can be required to give security for costs *Roto Packing v Latest Technologies* [2004] EWHC 2451 (Ch). However there are exceptions—for example, rr.7.5 and 7.6 (time within which a claim form may be served), r.16.3(5) (statement of value) and Pt 26 (case management—preliminary stage) do not apply. A Pt 20 claim must be accompanied by a statement of truth. The fact that the Pt 20 claim stands on its own means that, for example there is no automatic right to a stay of execution on the claim if there is an outstanding counterclaim; whether or not there will be a stay of execution will depend on the circumstances of a particular case (see *Isovel Contracts Ltd v ABB Build-*

ing Technologies Ltd [2002] 1 B.C.L.C. 390) as an example of a case where a stay was not granted. See also r.36.2. In *Calonne Construction Ltd v Dawnus Southern Ltd* [2019] EWCA Civ 754 at [24] to [32], the Court of Appeal concluded that a defendant's proposed counterclaim must be treated as a claim for the purposes of determining if an offer is a valid Part 36 Offer.

PART 21

CHILDREN AND PROTECTED PARTIES

Effect of rule

Add new paragraph at end:

In *Barker v Confiance Ltd* [2019] EWHC 1401 (Ch) (Morgan J), a claim concerning trusts and **21.2.1** various applications, the judge reviewed the authorities and held that when considering whether to make an order for costs against a litigation friend who had acted for an unsuccessful child party, the general approach was that the litigation friend was expected to be liable for such costs as the relevant party, if they had been an adult, would normally have been required to pay. It was not necessary for the litigation friend to have given an undertaking under r.21.4(3)(c). As the court would have regard to all the circumstances of the case in exercising its discretion as to costs, it was open to the litigation friend to point to any circumstance as to their involvement in the litigation which might justify making a different costs order. Furthermore, the court was not persuaded that a different rule applied where the litigation friend was acting for an unsuccessful child defendant. There was also no general rule that a costs order could not be made against the child personally; in deciding whether to exercise its discretion as to costs, the court had to consider all the circumstances under r.44.2(4).

Replace r.21.12 with:

Expenses incurred by a litigation friend[1]

21.12—(1) Subject to paragraph (1A), in proceedings to which rule 21.11 21.12 applies, a litigation friend who incurs costs or expenses on behalf of a child or protected party in any proceedings is entitled on application to recover the amount paid or payable out of any money recovered or paid into court to the extent that it—

(a) has been reasonably incurred; and

(b) is reasonable in amount.

(1A) Costs recoverable in respect of a child under this rule are limited to—

(a) costs which have been assessed by way of detailed assessment pursuant to rule 46.4(2); or

(b) costs incurred by way of success fee under a conditional fee agreement or sum payable under a damages based agreement in a claim for damages for personal injury where the damages agreed or ordered to be paid do not exceed £25,000, where such costs have been assessed summarily pursuant to rule 46.4(5).

(2) Expenses may include all or part of—

(a) a premium in respect of a costs insurance policy (as defined by section 58C(5) of the Courts and Legal Services Act 1990); or

(b) interest on a loan taken out to pay a premium in respect of a costs insurance policy or other recoverable disbursement.

(3) No application may be made under this rule for costs or expenses that—

---

[1] Introduced by the Civil Procedure (Amendment) Rules 2007 (SI 2007/2204) and amended by the Civil Procedure (Amendment) Rules 2013 (SI 2013/262), the Civil Procedure (Amendment No. 7) Rules 2013 (SI 2013/1974), the Civil Procedure (Amendment No. 8) Rules 2014 (SI 2014/3299), the Civil Procedure (Amendment No. 2) Rules 2015 (SI 2015/670) and the Civil Procedure (Amendment) Rules 2019 (SI 2019/342).

(a)   are of a type that may be recoverable on an assessment of costs payable by or out of money belonging to a child or protected party; but

(b)   are disallowed in whole or in part on such an assessment.

(Costs and expenses which are also "costs" as defined in rule 44.1(1) are subject to rule 46.4(2) and (3).)

(4)   In deciding whether the costs or expenses were reasonably incurred and reasonable in amount, the court will have regard to all the circumstances of the case including the factors set out in rule 44.4(3) and 46.9.

(5)   When the court is considering the factors to be taken into account in assessing the reasonableness of the costs or expenses, it will have regard to the facts and circumstances as they reasonably appeared to the litigation friend or to the child's or protected party's legal representative when the cost or expense was incurred.

(6)   Subject to paragraph (7), where the claim is settled or compromised, or judgment is given, on terms that an amount not exceeding £5,000 is paid to the child or protected party, the total amount the litigation friend may recover under paragraph (1) must not exceed 25% of the sum so agreed or awarded, unless the court directs otherwise. Such total amount must not exceed 50% of the sum so agreed or awarded.

(7)   The amount which the litigation friend may recover under paragraph (1) in respect of costs must not (in proceedings at first instance) exceed 25% of the amount of the sum agreed or awarded in respect of—

(a)   general damages for pain, suffering and loss of amenity; and

(b)   damages for pecuniary loss other than future pecuniary loss, net of any sums recoverable by the Compensation Recovery Unit of the Department for Work and Pensions.

(8)   Except in a case to which Section II, III or IIIA of Part 45 applies, and a claim under rule 45.13 or 45.29J has not been made, no application may be made under this rule for a payment out of the money recovered by the child or protected party until the costs payable to the child or protected party have been assessed or agreed.

Editorial note

Replace paragraph with:

21.12.1   This rule is supplemented by para.11 of PD 21 (see para.21PD.11 below). The rule was amended by the Civil Procedure (Amendment No. 2) Rules 2015 (SI 2015/670) r.11, and the Civil Procedure (Amendment No. 8) Rules 2014 (SI 2014/3299) r.5, which in combination inserted paras (1A), (7) and (8) and made consequential amendments elsewhere in the rule. These amendments came into effect on 6 April 2015, and were made for the purpose of addressing a growth in the number of applications at approval hearings for payment out of the child or protected party's damages to meet the success fee provided for in the conditional fee agreement or entered into between the litigation friend and the solicitor for the child or protected party. Further, clarificatory, amendments were made to rr.21.12(1A) and 21.12(8) by Civil Procedure (Amendment) Rules 2019 (SI 2019/342), with effect from 6 April 2019. The amendment to the former rule makes clear that that rule's restrictions concerning recoverability of costs and expenses only apply where the litigation friend acts on the behalf of a child. The amendment to the latter rule provided that in the event of party failure to agree the amount to be paid by way of disbursement, as per Sections II, III and IIA of Pt 45, did not preclude an application for payment out of damages under r.21.12(1) being determined.

PRACTICE DIRECTION 21—CHILDREN AND PROTECTED PARTIES

Costs or expenses incurred by a litigation friend

Replace paragraph 11.3 with:

21PD.11   **11.3**   Where the application is for payment out of the damages in respect of costs pursuant to rule 21.12(1A) the witness statement must also include (or be accompanied by)—

(1)   a copy of the conditional fee agreement or damages based agreement;

(2) the risk assessment by reference to which the success fee was determined;

(3) the reasons why the particular funding model was selected;

(4) the advice given to the litigation friend in relation to funding arrangements;

(4A) a copy bill or informal breakdown in the form of a schedule of the solicitor and own client base costs incurred;

(5) details of any costs agreed, recovered or fixed costs recoverable by the child; and

(6) confirmation of the amount of the sum agreed or awarded in respect of—

    (a) general damages for pain, suffering and loss of amenity; and

    (b) damages for pecuniary loss other than future pecuniary loss,

net of any sums recoverable by the Compensation Recovery Unit of the Department for Work and Pensions.

PART 24

SUMMARY JUDGMENT

Effect of rule

Delete the second, third and fourth paragraphs. **24.2.1**

"no real prospect of succeeding/successfully defending"

Replace paragraph with:

The following principles applicable to applications for summary judgment were formulated by **24.2.3** Lewison J in *Easyair Ltd v Opal Telecom Ltd* [2009] EWHC 339 (Ch) at [15] and approved by the Court of Appeal in *AC Ward & Sons Ltd v Catlin (Five) Ltd* [2009] EWCA Civ 1098; [2010] Lloyd's Rep. I.R. 301 at 24:

  i) The court must consider whether the claimant has a "realistic" as opposed to a "fanciful" prospect of success: *Swain v Hillman* [2001] 1 All E.R. 91;

  ii) A "realistic" claim is one that carries some degree of conviction. This means a claim that is more than merely arguable: *ED & F Man Liquid Products v Patel* [2003] EWCA Civ 472 at [8];

  iii) In reaching its conclusion the court must not conduct a "mini-trial": *Swain v Hillman*;

  iv) This does not mean that the court must take at face value and without analysis everything that a claimant says in his statements before the court. In some cases it may be clear that there is no real substance in factual assertions made, particularly if contradicted by contemporaneous documents: *ED & F Man Liquid Products v Patel* at [10];

  v) However, in reaching its conclusion the court must take into account not only the evidence actually placed before it on the application for summary judgment, but also the evidence that can reasonably be expected to be available at trial: *Royal Brompton Hospital NHS Trust v Hammond (No.5)* [2001] EWCA Civ 550;

  vi) Although a case may turn out at trial not to be really complicated, it does not follow that it should be decided without the fuller investigation into the facts at trial than is possible or permissible on summary judgment. Thus the court should hesitate about making a final decision without a trial, even where there is no obvious conflict of fact at the time of the application, where reasonable grounds exist for believing that a fuller investigation into the facts of the case would add to or alter the evidence available to a trial judge and so affect the outcome of the case: *Doncaster Pharmaceuticals Group Ltd v Bolton Pharmaceutical Co 100 Ltd* [2007] F.S.R. 3;

  vii) On the other hand it is not uncommon for an application under Pt 24 to give rise to a short point of law or construction and, if the court is satisfied that it has before it all the evidence necessary for the proper determination of the question and that the parties have had an adequate opportunity to address it in argument, it should grasp the nettle and decide it. The reason is quite simple: if the respondent's case is bad in law, he will in truth have no real prospect of succeeding on his claim or successfully defending the claim against him, as the case may be. Similarly, if the applicant's case is bad in law, the sooner that is determined, the better. If it is possible to show by evidence that although material in the form of documents or oral evidence that would put the documents in another light is not currently before the court, such material is likely to exist and can be expected to be available at trial, it would be wrong to give summary judgment because there would be a real, as opposed to a fanciful, prospect of success. However, it is not enough simply to argue that the case should be allowed to go to trial because something may turn up which would have a bearing on the question of construction: *ICI Chemicals & Polymers Ltd v TTE Training Ltd* [2007] EWCA Civ 725.

In *Global Asset Capital Inc v Aabar Block S.A.R.L.* [2017] EWCA Civ 37; [2017] 4 W.L.R. 16 at [27] the Court of Appeal approved a shortened form of the above principles as applicable for the purposes of the issues arising in that case.

No set off in action on dishonoured bill or cheque

24.2.7   *In the first paragraph, first sentence, delete "wholly different".*

"any type of proceedings"

In the first paragraph, replace the first sentence with:

24.3.1   The CPR do not repeat the provisions contained in the RSC which excluded applications for summary judgment in proceedings which included a claim by the claimant for libel, slander, malicious prosecution or false imprisonment (former RSC Ord.14 r.1(2) and CCR Ord.9 r.14(1)(c)).

A conditional order

Replace the third, fourth, fifth, sixth and seventh paragraphs (beginning "The court's jurisdiction" and ending "Anglo Eastern Trust Ltd, above).") with:

24.6.6   The court's jurisdiction to make a conditional order stems from r.3.1(3) (*Deutsche Bank AG v Unitech Global Ltd* [2016] EWCA Civ 119; [2016] 1 W.L.R. 3598). The scope and effect of r.3.1(3) was explained by the Court of Appeal in *Huscroft v P & O Ferries Ltd (Practice Note)* [2010] EWCA Civ 1483; [2011] 1 W.L.R. 939, CA, a judgment subsequently cited with approval in *IPCO (Nigeria) Ltd v Nigerian National Petroleum Corp* [2017] UKSC 16; [2017] 1 W.L.R 970, at [44] (and see further, para.3.1.14, above). In *Huscroft* it was held that, before exercising the power, the court should identify the purpose of imposing a condition and should satisfy itself that the condition it has in mind represents a proportionate and effective means of achieving that purpose, having regard to the order to which it is to be attached. In summary judgment applications against a defendant the purpose of making a conditional order requiring payment in to court is usually to provide security in respect of a particularly weak defence.

In *Gama Aviation (UK) v Taverelas Petroleum Trading DMCC* [2019] EWCA Civ 119 the Court of Appeal held that the following five principles applied when considering whether a conditional order for payment into court or security for costs should be made on an application for summary judgment:

1.   In a case where the defendant has a real prospect of successfully defending the claim, the court must not impose a condition requiring payment into court or the provision of security with which it is likely to be impossible for the defendant to comply.

2.   The burden is on the defendant to establish on the balance of probabilities that it would be unable to comply with a condition requiring payment into court or the provision of equivalent security.

3.   In order to discharge that burden a defendant must show, not only that it does not itself have the necessary funds, but that no such funds would be made available to it, whether (in the case of a corporate defendant) by its owner or (in any case) by some other closely associated person.

4.   Despite the fact that the Rules expressly contemplate the possibility of a payment condition being imposed, it is not incumbent on a defendant to a summary judgment application to adduce evidence about the resources available to it, at any rate in a case where no prior notice has been given that the claimant will be seeking a conditional order.

5.   The court's power to make a conditional order on a summary judgment application is not limited to a case where it is improbable that the defence will succeed. Such an order may be appropriate in other circumstances, for example (and without being exhaustive) if there is a history of failures to comply with orders of the court or there is a real doubt whether the party in question is conducting the litigation in good faith. However, the court needs to exercise caution before making a conditional order requiring a defendant who may have a good defence to provide security for all or most of the sum claimed as a condition of being allowed to defend.

In considering whether the burden imposed under the third principle has been discharged, the Court held that it is important in the case of a corporate defendant to keep well in mind that the question is not whether the company's shareholders can raise the money but whether the defendant company has established that funds to make the payment will not be made available to it by its beneficial owners. As to the kind of evidence which the court would expect to receive when a company seeks to discharge this burden Longmore LJ, cited Lord Wilson in *Goldtrail v Travel Ltd v Aylin* [2010] UKSC 57 at [24]:

"In cases, therefore, in which the respondent to the appeal suggests that the necessary funds would be made available to the company by, say, its owner, the court can expect to receive an emphatic refutation of the suggestion both by the company and, perhaps in particular, by the owner. The court should therefore not take the refutation at face value. It should judge the probable availability of the funds by reference to the underlying realities of the company's financial position; and by reference to all aspects of its relationship with its owner, including, obviously, the extent to which he is directing (and has directed) its affairs and is supporting (and has supported) it in financial terms."

A conditional order requiring a claimant to give security for a defendant's costs can also be made where, had the defendant applied under Pt 25 (Section II) in addition to or instead of his application under Pt 24, his application for security under Pt 25 (Section II) would have been successful (*Allen v Bloomsbury Publishing Plc* [2011] EWHC 770 (Ch); [2011] F.S.R. 222).

In the last paragraph, delete the last sentence.

PART 25

INTERIM REMEDIES AND SECURITY FOR COSTS

Brexit

Replace paragraph with:

25.0.1.1 At the time of writing, the Civil Jurisdiction and Judgments (Amendment) (EU Exit) Regulations 2019 (SI 2019/479) are intended to come into force on exit day assuming a no-deal exit. In the light of this reference to the Judgments Regulation (1215/2012) and Brussels and Lugano Conventions would need to be deleted in terms of the restriction imposed by r.25.13(2) for the grant of security of costs in respect of claimants within countries to which those instruments apply. Transitional provisions will be made to the CPR to secure the continued application of the rule for proceedings commenced before exit day in order to ensure that defendants in such proceedings do not secure a procedural advantage post-Brexit.

See para.5.0.1.1 for detail on the amendments to the CPR and its PDs in the event of a no-deal exit.

I.   Interim Remedies

Interim injunction (r.25.1(1)(a))

Unnamed defendants

After the third paragraph, add new paragraphs:

25.1.12.3 The Supreme Court has clarified that, except in evasion of service cases (including concealment of identity in order to evade service) and those cases where alternative method service may be permissible (CPR r.6.15), or service dispensed with (CPR r.6.16), proceedings and the grant of injunctive relief may only be brought against a person unknown if that person is "anonymous but identifiable": this means that it is possible to communicate with that person and identify them as the person described in the claim form and injunction. Where an interim injunction can be enforced against some property, or by notice to third parties who would necessarily be involved in any contempt, the process of enforcement may be sufficient to bring the proceedings to the Defendant's notice. *Cameron v Liverpool Victoria Insurance Co Ltd* [2019] UKSC 6 at [15] and [25].

Proper consideration must be given to compliance with s.12(3) of the Human Rights Act 1998. In *Boyd v Ineos Upstream Ltd* [2019] EWCA Civ 515 at [34], Longmore LJ (admittedly tentatively) identified the requirements as follows: (1) there must be a sufficiently real and imminent risk of a tort being committed to justify quia timet relief; (2) it is impossible to name the persons who are likely to commit the tort unless restrained; (3) it is possible to give effective notice of the injunction and for the method of such notice to be set out in the order; (4) the terms of the injunction must correspond to the threatened tort and not be so wide that they prohibit lawful conduct; (5) the terms of the injunction must be sufficiently clear and precise as to enable persons potentially affected to know what they must not do; and (6) the injunction should have clear geographical and temporal limits.

Undertaking by defendant in lieu of injunction

Delete the last paragraph.

25.1.14.1

Add new paragraph 25.1.14.2:

Discharge or release from, and appeals in relation to, undertakings

25.1.14.2 In *Birch v Birch* [2017] UKSC 53; [2017] 1 W.L.R. 2959, SC, the Supreme Court clarified that a court has no power to impose any variation of the terms of a voluntary promise. A litigant who wishes to cease to be bound by their undertaking should apply for release from, or discharge, of it, and may accompany the application with an offer of a further undertaking in different terms. The court may decide to accept the further undertaking and, in the light of it, to grant the application for release. Equally, the court may indicate that it will grant the application for release only on condition that the applicant is willing to give an additional undertaking or one in terms different from those of a further undertaking currently on offer.

In the absence of extraordinary circumstances, a claimant who has given an undertaking (however reluctantly) in order to obtain an injunction or other order, is not normally entitled to pursue an appeal against that undertaking. Such a litigant can apply to be released from the undertaking (either unconditionally or on condition of offering a new undertaking), but generally a change in circumstances must be shown: *Schettini v Silvestri* [2019] EWCA Civ 349 at [21].

A litigant who wishes to dispute the contents of an undertaking before an appeal court has two possible routes. (1) To decline to give the undertaking, accepting that the injunction will be refused (or granted only in limited terms pending appeal, as in *Novartis AG v Hospira UK Ltd* [2013] EWCA Civ 583; [2014] 1 W.L.R. 1264); (2) To refuse to give the undertaking, but to invite the judge to make an order in equivalent terms or to make the injunction conditional on fortification. In either case, the refusal or the condition may be challenged on appeal: *Schettini v Silvestri* [2019] EWCA Civ 349 at [20].

Orders in relation to relevant property (r.25.1(1)(c))

Inspection of relevant property (r.25.1(1)(c)(ii))

To the end of the first paragraph, add:

25.1.18   By contrast, in *Goodrich Actuation Systems Ltd v Valente* [2018] EWHC 3241 (Ch), Arnold J held that, after reasonable and proportionate searches by the defendant in course of standard disclosure, the determination of the issue as to what, if any, use had been made by the defendant of confidential information downloaded from the claimant's computer depended on a forensic examination of all the relevant devices. He therefore ordered that the defendant's personal laptop should be examined by a single joint expert, having put in place safeguards to protect the defendant's privileged and private information held on it.

Taking of a sample of relevant property (r.25.1(1)(c)(iii))

After the first paragraph, add new paragraph:

25.1.19   Provision of samples under this rule is covered by the implied undertaking not to use them for a collateral purpose outside the purpose of the proceedings, though the court has jurisdiction to permit wider use if special circumstances so justify: *Shire Pharmaceutical Contracts Ltd v Mount Sinai School of Medicine of New York University* [2011] EWHC 3492 (Pat); [2012] F.S.R. 18 at [29]. See also para.25.5.1 below in relation to applications pre-action or against non-parties.

Carrying out of an experiment on or with relevant property (r.25.1(1)(c)(iv))

To the end of the paragraph, add:

25.1.20   See the preceding note in para.25.1.19 which applies equally to materials supplied under compulsion for the purposes of an experiment.

Freezing injunction (formerly Mareva injunction) (r.25.1(1)(f))

Jurisdiction—generally

Replace the last paragraph with:

25.1.25.1   An order granting an interim remedy in the form of a freezing injunction may be made only by a judge (Practice Direction (Allocation of Cases to Levels of Judiciary), para.2.1, see para.2BPD.1 above). Exceptionally, an application for a freezing order to preserve assets may be made by a director or shareholder of a company which has been struck off the register, but is in the course of an application for restoration (Companies Act 2006 s.1029). The company's assets would have vested in the Crown as bona vacantia, but restoration would be retrospective: *Yuzu Hair & Beauty Ltd v Selvathiraviam* [2019] EWHC 772 (Ch) (Zacaroli J) applying *HMRC v Egleton* [2006] EWHC 2313 (Ch) (Briggs J), a case where the petitioning creditor seeking a winding up order applied for a freezing order against the defendant which was a debtor of the company.

Varying, clarifying or revoking order

To the start of the paragraph, add:

25.1.25.10   If a defendant is unable or unwilling to comply with an order by the time stated, it is not enough to issue an application for a variation of the order and wait for it to be listed. The proper course is to notify the court immediately and to seek an urgent hearing and an extension of time pending determination, to avoid being in breach. At the hearing, the court can then decide whether the non-compliance should be excused and/or whether there should be a variation to the order: *Fundo Soberano De Angola v Dos Santos* [2018] EWHC 1867 (Comm) (Phillips J).

Post judgment freezing orders

Replace the third paragraph with:

25.1.25.13

In *Mobile Telesystems Finance SA v Nomihold Securities Inc* [2011] EWCA Civ 1040; [2012] 1 All E.R. (Comm) 223; [2012] Bus. L.R. 1166, the Court of Appeal held that "it will sometimes and perhaps usually be inappropriate to include an ordinary course of business exception" in an immediately enforceable post judgment asset freezing order. The debtor is of course able to apply to vary the order to include such a exception on proper grounds being shown. On the other hand, a freezing order granted in aid of enforcement of a judgment where enforcement is not presently available (for example, where there is a stay of execution, or where an arbitration award is not yet enforceable because the period under CPR 62.18(9) has not expired) should ordinarily contain the usual exception to permit payments in the ordinary course of business (at [37] per Tomlinson LJ). The impact on the defendant's continuing business is a material consideration (ibid. at [35]). In *Michael Wilson and Partners Ltd v Emmott* [2019] EWCA Civ 219, the Court of Appeal at [57]–[59] confirmed Tomlinson LJ's approach in *Nomihold* at [33] as the correct starting point providing "helpful and appropriately nuanced general guidance" and said that a decision applying it is a discretionary matter reached on a fact specific basis, with which the Appeal Court would be slow to interfere. See also Vol.2, para.15-71.

Search order (formerly Anton Piller order) (r.25.1(1)(h))

After the third paragraph, add new paragraph:

25.1.27

The making of an intrusive order ex parte allowing searches of premises or vehicles is contrary to normal principles of justice and can only be done when there is a paramount need to prevent a denial of justice to the claimant. The absolute extremity of the court's powers is to permit a search of the defendant's dwelling: *Lock International Plc v Beswick* [1989] 1 W.L.R. 1268 per Hoffmann J at p.1281. The court has therefore developed a less intrusive version, known as a doorstep delivery-up order, for when the evidence does not satisfy the high threshold for a search order. In *Hyperama Plc v Poulis* [2018] EWHC 3483 (QB) Pepperall J required the doorstep delivery up of electronic devices to be retained uninspected until after the inter partes hearing.

Effect of rule

Replace "24.4.2" with:

25.4.2

25.4.1

Effect of rule

Replace the first paragraph with:

25.5.1

The court's powers under the statutory provisions referred to in this rule include not merely pre-action inspection, photographing, and preservation of property as to which any question may arise in subsequent proceedings, and the taking of samples and the carrying out of any experiment on or with such property, but also the equivalent relief against persons who are not, and are not likely to be, parties to proceedings.

In *Boehringer Ingelheim Pharma GmbH v Generics (UK) Ltd* [2019] EWHC 584 (Ch), Henry Carr J considered that the provision of samples in that case might have had the effect of avoiding proceedings altogether if the applicant's fears as to infringement turned out to be unjustified, or might enable the parties to focus on the correct issues. Some assistance is to be drawn from the case law under CPR r.31.16 (Pre-action disclosure), for example that on an application under these provisions, it is not necessary for the Court to consider the merits or the "arguability" of the applicant's potential claim: the question is whether the applicant has shown some reason to believe that he may have suffered a compensatable injury, and if so with what degree of likelihood: *Smith v Secretary of State for Energy and Climate Change* [2014] 1 W.L.R. 2283 per Underhill LJ at [28].

In *Boehringer Ingelheim* (above) at [23], it was held that provision of materials under this rule is covered by the implied undertaking not to use them for a collateral purpose outside the purpose of the proceedings, though the court has jurisdiction to permit wider use if special circumstances so justify.

As for the costs of such an application, the starting point is that the applicant should pay the costs of the application and the costs of compliance with the order. That may be displaced if, for example, the respondent unreasonably delays or declines to provide the materials: *Boehringer Ingelheim* (above) at [34].

II.   Security for Costs

Effect of legal expenses insurance on applications for security for costs

In the first paragraph in the first sentence, replace "being taken into account" with:

be taken into account

25.12.9

Subsequent applications concerning security for costs

In the first paragraph, replace the last sentence with:

25.12.13   A further application may be justified if a previous order described the security as being in respect of costs up to a specified stage in the proceedings and that stage had now been reached (*Eli Lilly & Co Ltd v Neopharma Ltd* [2012] EWHC 2297 (Ch)).

Discretionary power to order security for costs

Replace the fourth paragraph with:

25.13.1   In exercising the discretion

"it must be borne in mind that the design of the rules is to protect a defendant (or a claimant placed in a similar position by a counterclaim) who is forced into litigation at the election of someone else against adverse costs consequences of that litigation" (see *Autoweld Systems Ltd v Kito Enterprises LLC* [2010] EWCA Civ 1469 at [59] per Black LJ).

Although the making of such an order is discretionary, it is unlikely to be refused on the basis that the defendants in question are wealthy enough to survive without such protection, or are protected by some other means, such as a right of indemnity against a third person (*LIC Telecommunications Sarl v VTB Capital Plc* [2016] EWHC 1891 (Comm), HH Judge Waksman QC).

Replace the last paragraph with:

On the question whether an order for security for costs may infringe a party's right to a fair trial under ECHR art.6(1), see para.3.1.5 above and para.25.13.4 below. A claimant who alleges that an order for security will stifle the claim must adduce satisfactory evidence that they do not have the means to provide security and that they cannot obtain appropriate assistance to do so from any third party, such as a relative or friend, who might reasonably be expected to provide such assistance if they could (*Al-Koronky v Time Life Entertainment Group Ltd* [2005] EWHC 1688). In *Gama Aviation (UK) v Taverelas Petroleum Trading DMCC* [2019] EWCA Civ 119 the Court of Appeal considered the principles to be applied when considering whether to make a conditional order providing security for costs on an application for summary judgment and the kind of evidence the Court would expect to see (set out in para.24.6.6). On the question whether an order for security of costs may infringe the prohibition of discrimination set out in ECHR art.14, see para.25.13.6 below and *Vedatech Corp v Crystal Decisions (UK) Ltd (formerly Seagate Software IMG Ltd) (Appeal against Security for Costs)* [2002] EWCA Civ 356.

Discretionary factors where both claims and counterclaims are raised

Replace the second paragraph with:

25.13.1.1   In *TC Developments (South East) Ltd v Investin Quay House Ltd* [2019] EWHC 1432 (TCC) Stuart-Smith J held that when determining whether an order for security for costs should be made against a counterclaiming defendant the following propositions were well-established:

i)   An order for costs against a counterclaiming defendant should not ordinarily be made if all the defendant is doing, in substance, is to defend himself: *Hutchison* (see above) at 317d;

ii)   The question may be expressed as "is the defendant simply defending himself, or is he going beyond mere self-defence and launching a cross-claim with an independent vitality of its own": *Hutchison* ibid. An alternative way of expressing the same principle is to ask "whether in the particular case the counterclaim is a cross-action or operates as a defence, that is to say merely operates as a defence": *Hutchison* at 313a per Dillon LJ, with whom Bingham LJ agreed;

iii)   An order for security against a counterclaiming defendant is not precluded because the counterclaim arises out of the same transaction as the claim: *Hutchison* at 311h, 317f;

iv)   The Court should look at the substantial position of the parties and not the form as appearing from the pleadings or otherwise: *Hutchison* at 317e. Thus, for example, the fact that the defendant in the present case has pleaded all material facts in the defence and then adopted a short form of counterclaim is not determinative or even of any real influence if the reality is that it has gone beyond merely defending itself and has launched a cross-claim with an independent vitality of its own;

v)   It is clearly a relevant consideration that if the claimant had not issued proceedings the defendant would have done, because in such a case it may be almost a matter of chance whether a party happens to be the claimant or the defendant; and if the proper inference is that the defendants would have sued anyway, that fortifies the inference that the counterclaim has an independent vitality of its own and is not a mere matter of defence: *Hutchison* at 317g–h. If, however, the proper conclusion is that the claim by the claimant and the cross-claim by the defendant raise essentially the same issues and are going to be litigated anyway so far as one can tell, that would militate against making an order for security: *Crabtree* at 54, per Bingham LJ;

vi)   It is not conclusive that the counterclaim overtops the claim, though this may be a relevant consideration and a marked discrepancy in size between the amount claimed in the action and the very much greater amount claimed by the cross-claim will be a relevant factor: *Hutchison* at 314h, 317f–g.

Stuart-Smith J held that the fact that counterclaim was "very substantially greater" than the claimants' claims supported the inference that the counterclaim would have been worth pursuing whether or not the claimants had made their claims for fees. Further, the independent vitality of the counterclaim became clear on an analysis of what was involved in the claimants' claims and the counterclaim. The claimants' claims were conceptually straightforward and, with one exception, required very limited factual enquiry. By contrast, for the defendant to establish the counterclaim and set-off required much more detailed factual investigation. Such a claim would require both factual and expert-opinion evidence, and such evidence might need to be extensive. The defendant had therefore gone well beyond mere defence in its counterclaim and security for costs was ordered.

In *Dumrul v Standard Chartered Bank* [2010] EWHC 2625 addressing the problem of one-sided litigation identified in *Crabtree*, Hamblen J held that an order for security should only be made if a defendant undertook to consent to the dismissal of the counterclaim in the event of a claimant's claim being dismissed for failure to put up security.

No discrimination against claimants resident in other States

Replace the second paragraph with:

If security is sought on the grounds that there will be obstacles to enforcement, the obstacles **25.13.6**
need to be sufficiently substantial to amount to a real risk of non-enforcement (*Bestfort Developments LLP v Ras Al Khaimah Investment Authority* [2016] EWCA Civ 1099; [2018] 1 W.L.R. 1099; [2017] C.P. Rep. 9).

> "In my judgment, it is sufficient for an applicant for security for costs simply to adduce evidence to show that 'on objectively justified grounds relating to obstacles to or the burden of enforcement', there is a real risk that it will not be in a position to enforce an order for costs against the claimant/appellant and that, in all the circumstances, it is just to make an order for security. Obviously there must be 'a proper basis for considering that such obstacles may exist or that enforcement may be encumbered by some extra burden' but whether the evidence is sufficient in any particular case to satisfy the judge that there is a real risk of serious obstacles to enforcement, will depend on the circumstances of the case. In other words, I consider that the judge was wrong to uphold the Master's approach that the appropriate test was one of 'likelihood', which involved demonstrating that it was 'more likely than not' (i.e. an over 50% likelihood), or 'likely on the balance of probabilities', that there would be substantial obstacles to enforcement, rather than some lower standard based on risk or possibility. A test of real risk of enforceability provides rational and objective justification for discrimination against non-Convention state residents." (per Gloster LJ, para.77).

Obstacles to enforcement give rise to the risk of non-enforcement, and therefore security granted on this ground should be ordered by reference to the costs of the proceedings (*De Beer v Kanaar & Co* [2003] 1 W.L.R. 38 and *Bestfort*, above). The starting point should be that the defendant is entitled to security for the entirety of his costs; it is wrong in principle to reduce the amount as if on a sliding scale depending upon the degree of risk of non-enforcement; however, security might be reduced, or disallowed altogether, because of discretionary factors, such as delay or stifling (*Chernukhin v Danilina* [2018] EWCA Civ 1802).

Replace the last paragraph with:

Formal evidence is not always required in order to prove the obstacles or difficulties of enforcement which may arise. Whilst there must be a proper basis for considering that such problems exist, the court will take note of obvious realities (*Thistle Hotels Ltd v Gamma Four Ltd* [2004] EWHC 322; and see, further, *Kahangi v Nourizadeh* [2009] EWHC 2451 (QB)). In line with the flexible test based on risk and applications for freezing orders, expert evidence did not have to be adduced in compliance with the rules on expert evidence in CPR Pt 35, *Roman Pipia v BGEO Group Ltd* [2019] EWHC 325 (Comm).

Foreign and English co-claimants

In the first paragraph, after "security for costs if, having", replace "grant" with:
regard **25.13.10**

Scope of this rule

25.15.1 *Delete the first paragraph.*

PART 26

CASE MANAGEMENT—PRELIMINARY STAGE

Effect of rule

Add new paragraph at end:

26.8.4 For a case where an application by defendants to transfer an inquiry as to damages for copyright infringement from the IPEC multi-track to the small claims track was refused, see *Twentieth Century Fox Film Corp v Cyclone Events Ltd* [2019] EWHC 1758 (IPEC), 13 June 2019 (HHJ Hacon).

PART 27

THE SMALL CLAIMS TRACK

Related sources

27.0.7 *After the second list item, add:*
  • Part 39 (Miscellaneous Provisions Relating to Hearings)—in particular rr.39.2 and 39.8

Replace r.27.2(1)(h) with:

Extent to which other Parts apply[1]

27.2 **(h) Part 39 (hearings) except rule 39.2 (general rule—hearing to be in public) and rule 39.8 (communications with the court).**

Effect of rule

Add new paragraph at end:

27.2.1 CPR r.27.2(1)(h) ensures that the open justice principles enshrined in CPR Pt 39 apply to claims proceeding in the small claims track. The deletion of PD 27 para.4.1 in the 109th Update of the CPR completes the consistency between the open justice principles in rr.39 and 27. Decisions on whether to hold a small claim hearing in private is governed solely by consideration of the factors in r.39.2(3).

Add new paragraph 27.11.2.1:

"not more than 14 days"

27.11.2.1 The 14-day provision within which a party must make an application to set aside was considered in *Kuznetsov v Amazon Services Europe SARL* [2019] EWCA Civ 964. In a case where the other provisions of r.27.11 were met, because the respondent was only joined as a party at the small claim hearing and was neither represented at it, nor in a position to have made an election under r.27.9(1), as it was not then a party, the court considered r.27.11(2) and confirmed that r.3.1(2)(a) applied. As a result applications to extend the time under r.27.11(2) may be made even after the time for compliance with that provision has expired.

PRACTICE DIRECTION 27—SMALL CLAIMS TRACK

Small Claim Hearing

Replace paragraph 4.1 with:

27PD.4 **4.1** [Omitted.]

---

[1] Amended by the Civil Procedure (Amendment) Rules 2000 (SI 2000/221) and the Civil Procedure (Amendment No.3) Rules 2006 (SI 2006/3435) and the Civil Procedure (Amendment) Rules 2019 (SI 2019/342).

PART 28

THE FAST TRACK

Specimen trial timetable for trial of a case allocated to the fast track

In the last paragraph, replace "48PD.5" with:
44PD.9

28.6.5

Summary assessment of costs at fast-track trial

Replace paragraph with:
The general rule is that the court should make a summary assessment of costs at the conclusion **28.6.6** of a case which has been dealt with on the fast track (see para.44PD.9). It is the duty of the parties and their legal representatives to assist the judge in making the summary assessment by preparing, serving and filing a written statement of costs. The statement of costs must be filed at court and the copies of it must be served as soon as possible and, in any event, not less than two days before a fast track trial (see para.44PD.9).

PART 29

THE MULTI-TRACK

Filing costs estimates

Replace "(N170, as amended in April 2013)" with:
(**N170**, published in May 2014)

29.6.3

Pre-trial review

Replace the first paragraph with:
On receipt of the completed pre-trial check list the court will again consider whether to hold a **29.7.1** pre-trial review or, if one has already been fixed, whether to cancel it. Pre-trial reviews will not be held in every case. However, they are likely to be held in all cases in which the trial is estimated to last more than 10 days, if the case is proceeding in the Queen's Bench Division (Queen's Bench Guide para.10.5.1 (see Vol.2, para.1B-61)), or five days if the case is proceeding in the Chancery Division (Practice Note: Fixed-end trials, see para.B18-001).

Add new paragraph 29.9.2:

Effect of a "debarring" order
In response to major or repeated rule disobedience by a claimant, claims are sometimes struck **29.9.2** out or dismissed with costs. The equivalent sanction for defendants is an order striking out that defendant's defence and debarring that defendant from defending the claim. Subject of course to its precise terms, a debarring order extinguishes any right the debarred defendant would otherwise have to participate in any way in the determination of all the issues which fall for determination at that trial (*Michael v Phillips* [2017] EWHC 1084 (QB)). The order may debar the defendant from making submissions, calling witnesses or cross-examining witnesses called by other parties. The claimants are still required to prove every fact upon which their case depends, except any facts which the debarred defendants had admitted in their struck out pleadings.
A debarring order does not, in fact, override the control which the trial judge always has over procedure at the trial (rr.27.8, 28.7 and 29.9). For example, in *Michael*, at the pre-trial review, which the debarred defendants attended by counsel, Soole J directed that they would be permitted to make submissions at the trial as to what if any order for costs should be made.

PART 30

TRANSFER

Brexit

Add new paragraph at end:

30.0.1.1   See para.5.0.1.1 for detail on the amendments to the CPR and its PDs in the event of a no-deal exit.

PART 31

DISCLOSURE AND INSPECTION OF DOCUMENTS

Add new paragraph 31.0.0 before paragraph 31.0.1:

Relationship with PD51U—Disclosure Pilot Scheme

31.0.0   For cases in the Business and Property Courts, see the disclosure pilot scheme in Practice Direction 51U. This was introduced on 1 January 2019 without transitional provisions, and so applies to all existing proceedings, including even where an initial disclosure order has already been made before that date: *UTB LLC v Sheffield United Ltd* [2019] EWHC 914 (Ch) at [16]–[17] per Vos C. Where the pilot applies, CPR Pt 31 is disapplied in its entirety and issues of disclosure and inspection are governed by Practice Direction 51U. See paras 51.2.10, 51UPD.1, and 57AB.4, and following for details of the pilot scheme and its application. For an example of an application made under this new pilot scheme, see *Merck Sharp & Dohme Ltd v Wyeth LLC* [2019] EWHC 1692 (Pat).

Brexit

Replace paragraph with:

31.0.1.1   At the time of writing, the Cross-Border Mediation (EU Directive) (EU Exit) Regulations 2019 (SI 2019/469), consequent upon the EU Mediation Directive (2008/52/EC) ceasing to apply upon a no-deal Brexit, will revoke the Cross-Border Mediation (EU Directive) Regulations 2011 (SI 2011/1133). A further statutory instrument is intended to revoke the other legislation underpinning CPR Pt 78 (European Enforcement Order, European Order for Payment and European Small Claims Procedure (Amendment etc.) (EU Exit) Regulations 2018 (SI 2018/1311)). In the light of this references to Pt 78 in, for instance, rr.31.3, 31.16 and following will become redundant, subject to any necessary amendments relating to transitional and saving provisions (such as those contained in regs 2 and 5 of the Regulations).

See para.5.0.1.1 for detail on the amendments to the CPR and its PDs in the event of a no-deal exit.

(a)   Communications privileged although no litigation was contemplated or pending—"legal advice privilege"

Solicitor and client

After the third paragraph, add new paragraph:

31.3.6   Communications covered by legal advice privilege include documents which evidence the substance of communications: *Three Rivers DC v Governor and Company of the Bank of England (No.5)* [2003] EWCA Civ 474; [2003] Q.B. 1556 at [19], [21]; *Re Edwardian Group Ltd* [2017] EWHC 2805 (Ch) at [28], [37]. Lawyers' working papers are treated as equivalent to communications to the extent that they convey the tenor of communicated advice: *Re RBS (Rights Issue Litigation)* [2016] EWHC 3161 (Ch) at [99]–[107]; also see *Director of the Serious Fraud Office v Eurasian Natural Resources Corp Ltd* [2017] EWHC 1017 (QB) at [95]–[97] (reversed on other grounds on appeal: [2018] EWCA Civ 2006).

To the end of the fifth paragraph (beginning "This principle from"), add:

Compare earlier cases following *Three Rivers (No.5)*: *National Westminster Bank Plc v Rabobank Nederland* [2006] EWHC 2332 (Comm) at [26]–[29], *Re RBS (Rights Issue Litigation)* [2016] EWHC 3161 (Ch), and *Director of the Serious Fraud Office v Eurasian Natural Resources Corp Ltd* [2017] EWHC 1017 (QB) at [68]–[93] (reversed on other grounds on appeal: [2018] EWCA Civ 2006).

(b) Communications privileged only when litigation was contemplated or pending—"litigation privilege"

Solicitors and non-professional agent or third party

Add new paragraph at end:

31.3.12 Litigation privilege covers communications seeking advice or information for making decisions about whether to settle, but not to purely commercial discussions about settlement: *WH Holding Ltd v E20 Stadium LLP* [2018] EWCA Civ 2652.

Contemplation of criminal prosecution

Add new paragraph at end:

31.3.13.1 It is not necessary that a decision to prosecute has been taken or a defendant knows the full details of what is likely to be unearthed for criminal legal proceedings to be in contemplation: *Director of the Serious Fraud Office v Eurasian Natural Resources Corp Ltd* [2018] EWCA Civ 2006 at [100].

(c) Legal professional privilege generally

Confidential documents

To the start of the paragraph, add:

31.3.15 Communications between a lawyer and client in circumstances where they could not reasonably have expected confidentiality to be maintained are not covered by the privilege, e.g. *Simpkin v Berkeley Group Holdings Plc* [2017] EWHC 1472 (QB); [2017] 4 W.L.R. 116 at [29]–[42].

Challenging a claim to privilege

Add new paragraph at end:

31.3.30.1 For further guidance on how to raise and resolve a challenge to a claim of privilege see *Single Buoy Moorings Inc v Aspen Insurance UK Ltd* [2018] EWHC 1763 (Comm).

Documents tending to incriminate or expose to a penalty

Add new paragraph at end:

31.3.31 In an investigation into suspected tax avoidance and evasion, notices served under the Tax Information Exchange Agreement between Jersey and Norway requesting that Jersey obtain information concerning a number of Jersey-registered companies did not engage the privilege against self-incrimination under ECHR art.6, nor the privilege under Jersey customary law: *Volaw Trust & Corporate Services Ltd v Office of the Comptroller of Taxes* [2019] UKPC 29.

Add new paragraph 31.3.31.1:

Disclosure exposes party to risk of foreign criminal law

31.3.31.1 That disclosure may constitute a breach of foreign law and put the disclosing party at risk of criminal prosecution in another country is a factor to weigh in deciding whether to order disclosure, but is not a necessary bar to disclosure, particularly when the order can be made subject to confidentiality provisions: *Bank Mellat v HM Treasury* [2019] EWCA Civ 449. Foreign law does not override an English court's ability to conduct proceedings in the UK in accordance with English procedures and law. Whether to make such an order is a matter for the discretion of the English court. An order will not lightly be made where compliance may lead to a party breaching foreign criminal law. The court will balance the actual risk of prosecution in the other state against the importance of the documents to the trial being held in England: *Bank Mellat* (ibid).

Documents privileged on the ground that production would be injurious to the public interest

Add new paragraph at end:

31.3.33 Where a lower court has considered material covered by public interest immunity that is not shown to a party, the appellate court will need to consider that material as well: *R. (Haralambous) v St Albans Crown Court* [2018] UKSC 1; [2018] A.C. 236 at [59]; *Competition and Markets Authority v Concordia International RX (UK)* [2018] EWCA Civ 1881.

(d) Other grounds of privilege

Without prejudice communications

Add new paragraph at end:

31.3.40 The protection afforded to communications in aid of settlement can apply across different proceedings. Thus communications marked without prejudice save as to costs, which referred to without prejudice communications in prior proceedings, were covered by the rule; and the communications indicated an intention that the settlement negotiations could be used in a later dispute as to costs: *Willers v Joyce* [2019] EWHC 937 (Ch). The court there also observed that the without prejudice rule is not limited to admissions made against a party's interest, nor limited to statements made in the course of settlement negotiations with the other parties to those negotiations. It extended to statements made in settlement negotiations in earlier proceedings between the parties concerning a matter that remained in issue between them. Further, the court held that once the protection of the without prejudice rule had been waived, the waiver covered the whole of the without prejudice communications and not just those aspects of them that one of the parties had sought to deploy.

Disclosure and inspection of documents subject to search order

To the end of the paragraph, add:

31.6.7   Guidance as to the proper approach to inspection and interrogation of imaged digital data obtained under a search and seizure order was set out in *A v B; Hewlett Packard Enterprise Co v Manchester Technology Data (Holdings) Ltd* [2019] EWHC 2089 (Ch). The court at paras 32–49 also gave guidance as to the factors to consider when deciding which party should first inspect and interrogate the data.

Costs of the application

Replace paragraph with:

31.17.6   The respondent's costs of the application are normally paid by the applicant: r.46.1(2). The court may make a different order, for example if a respondent unreasonably opposed the application or unreasonably refused to comply with a pre-action protocol: r.46.1(3). In an appropriate case the costs of the application could be ordered to be borne by a party whose failure to disclose documents has led to the need for a third-party disclosure application which should have been unnecessary. For costs of *Norwich Pharmacal* applications, see para.31.18.12.

Procedure for bringing a Norwich Pharmacal application

Replace the last paragraph with:

31.18.11   The claimant seeking the name of the wrongdoer will have to pay a blameless defendant's expenses in providing the information. If the defendant has any doubts then they may properly require the matter to be submitted to the court before supplying the information and the claimant will nevertheless be obliged to pay the costs of these proceedings (ibid.).

Add new paragraph 31.18.12:

Costs of Norwich Pharmacal applications

31.18.12   Normally, after a successful *Norwich Pharmacal* application, the applicant should be ordered to pay the costs of the respondent including the costs of complying with the order. (Such applications are not ordinary adversarial proceedings, where the general rule is that the unsuccessful party pays the costs of the successful party; they are akin to proceedings for pre-action disclosure where costs are governed by r.46.1 (formerly r.48.1).) The costs so incurred by an applicant may subsequently be claimed in proceedings against the wrongdoer; see *Totalise Plc v The Motley Fool Ltd* [2001] EWCA Civ 1897; [2002] 1 W.L.R. 1233, CA, at [29]; *Cartier International AG v British Telecommunications Ltd* [2018] UKSC 28; [2018] 1 W.L.R. 3259, UKSC, at [12].
    In the *Norwich Pharmacal* litigation the costs of that litigation were recovered as damages in the subsequent substantive patent infringement action, on the basis that the infringer could or ought to have foreseen that steps by way of investigation and disclosure were likely to result from their wrong (*Morton Norwich Products Inc v Intercen Ltd (No.2)* [1981] F.S.R. 337, HC).

PRACTICE DIRECTION 31C—DISCLOSURE AND INSPECTION IN RELATION TO COMPETITION CLAIMS

Before paragraph 31CPD.1, add new paragraph 31CPD.0:

Introduction

31CPD.0   Note that the 107th Civil Procedure Rules Update provides for related no deal EU exit implications and will only come into force if and when the Civil Procedure Rules 1998 (Amendment) (EU Exit) Regulations 2019 (SI 2019/521) come into force. If this instrument comes into force, it will make changes to Practice Direction 31C—Disclosure and Inspection in relation to Competition Claims.

PART 32

EVIDENCE

Brexit

Replace paragraph with:

32.0.1.1   At the time of writing, the Cross-Border Mediation (EU Directive) (EU Exit) Regulations 2019 (SI 2019/469), consequent upon the EU Mediation Directive (2008/52) ceasing to apply upon a no-deal Brexit, will revoke the Cross-Border Mediation (EU Directive) Regulations 2011 (SI 2011/1133). In the light of this references to CPR rr.78.26 to 78.28 in r.32.7 would be expected to become redundant.

See para.5.0.1.1 for detail on the amendments to the CPR and its PDs in the event of a no-deal exit.

PRACTICE DIRECTION 32—EVIDENCE

Agreed Bundles for Hearings

Add paragraphs 27.3 to 27.15:   **32PD.27**

27.3 Rule 39.5 provides that unless the court orders otherwise, the claimant must file a trial bundle containing documents required by—

(a) a relevant practice direction; and

(b) any court order.

27.4 Rule 39.5 provides that the claimant must file the trial bundle not more than 7 days and not less than 3 days before the start of the trial.

27.5 Unless the court orders otherwise, the trial bundle should include a copy of—

(a) the claim form and all statements of case;

(b) a case summary and/or chronology where appropriate;

(c) requests for further information and responses to the requests;

(d) all witness statements to be relied on as evidence;

(e) any witness summaries;

(f) any notices of intention to rely on hearsay evidence under rule 32.2;

(g) any notices of intention to rely on evidence (such as a plan, photograph etc.) under rule 33.6 which is not—

(i) contained in a witness statement, affidavit or experts' report;

(ii) being given orally at trial; and

(iii) hearsay evidence under rule 33.2;

(h) any medical reports and responses to them;

(i) any experts' reports and responses to them;

(j) any order giving directions as to the conduct of the trial; and

(k) any other necessary documents.

27.6 The originals of the documents contained in the trial bundle, together with copies of any other court orders should be available at the trial.

27.7 The preparation and production of the trial bundle, even where it is delegated to another person, is the responsibility of the legal representative who has conduct of the claim on behalf of the claimant. If the claimant is unrepresented, the court may direct that another party must prepare and produce the trial bundle.

27.8 The trial bundle should be paginated (continuously) throughout, and indexed with a description of each document and the page number. Where the total number of pages is more than 100, numbered dividers should be placed at intervals between groups of documents.

27.9 The bundle should normally be contained in a ring binder or lever arch file. Where more than one bundle is supplied, they should be clearly distinguishable, for example, by different colours or letters. If there are numerous bundles, a core bundle should be prepared containing the core documents essential to the proceedings, with references to the supplementary documents in the other bundles.

27.10 For convenience, experts' reports may be contained in a separate bundle and cross referenced in the main bundle.

27.11 If a document to be included in the trial bundle is illegible, a typed copy should be included in the bundle next to it, suitably cross-referenced.

27.12 The contents of the trial bundle should be agreed where possible. The parties should also agree where possible—

(a) that the documents contained in the bundle are authentic even if not disclosed under Part 3; and

(b) that documents in the bundle may be treated as evidence of the facts stated in them even if a notice under the Civil Evidence Act 1995 has not been served.

Where it is not possible to agree the contents of the bundle, a summary of the points on which the parties are unable to agree should be included.

27.13 The party filing the trial bundle should supply identical bundles to all the parties to the proceedings and for the use of the witnesses.

27.14 Unless the court otherwise directs, contemporaneous documents in the trial bundle relied on by the parties or either of them should be assembled as a single unit in chronological order of creation.

27.15 Unless the court otherwise directs, documents in the trial bundle should be copied double-sided.

PART 33

MISCELLANEOUS RULES ABOUT EVIDENCE

Effect of rule

33.2.1 *Delete the last paragraph.*

PART 34

WITNESSES, DEPOSITIONS AND EVIDENCE FOR FOREIGN COURTS

Brexit

Replace paragraph with:

34.0.2 The Service of Documents and Taking of Evidence in Civil and Commercial Matters (Revocation and Saving Provisions) (EU Exit) Regulations 2018 (SI 2018/1257) come into force on exit day. This means that the EU Service Regulation (1393/2007) and Taking of Evidence Regulation (1206/2001) no longer apply to the UK when it leaves the EU. The Regulations will cease to apply, rather than be saved by the European Union (Withdrawal) Act 2018, given that their operation is dependent upon reciprocity between the UK and the remaining countries of the EU.

The statutory instrument contains transitional provisions which mean that the 2001 and 2007 Regulations will continue to apply to outstanding requests for documents to be served or evidence to be taken in the UK, where those requests were received in the UK before exit day. Accordingly, following the exit of the UK, Section III of Pt 34 will cease to apply. Thereafter the taking of evidence between the UK and the remaining countries of the EU will depend upon whether the countries in question are members of the Hague Convention; see para.34.13.8. All remaining states other than Austria, Belgium and Ireland are contracting states to the Hague (Evidence) Convention. Where the Hague Convention does apply as between the UK and the remaining EU country, it is Section II (Evidence for Foreign Courts) which will apply. Note, however, that the Evidence (Proceedings in Other Jurisdictions) Act 1975 is not confined to countries which are parties to the Hague Convention. Accordingly, Section II would apply to Austria, Belgium and Ireland. Where the person to be examined is out of the jurisdiction in a remaining EU country, r.34.13 will apply following an amendment to r.34.13(1).

As in relation to the other changes foreshadowed by the Brexit statutory instruments, draft Withdrawal Agreement provides for a longer saving period than the 2018 Regulations, and if agreed, would preserve the Service Regulation and the Taking of Evidence Regulation requests for documents to be served or evidence to be taken in the UK which were received before the end of the transition period, rather than exit day as provided in the draft Regulations (draft art.68).

See para.5.0.1.1 for detail on the amendments to the CPR and its PDs in the event of a no-deal exit.

II. Evidence for Foreign Courts

General principles for compliance with foreign request for evidence

To the end of the fifth paragraph (beginning "The English Court has power"), add:
For a case in which the Court deleted certain requests on the grounds of relevance, see *Buzzfeed* **34.21.2** *Inc v Aleksej Gubarev* [2018] EWHC 1201 (QB), (Jay J), 18 May 2018, unrep.

PART 35

EXPERTS AND ASSESSORS

Editorial introduction

To the end of the second paragraph, add:
However, please see the judgment of the Privy Council in *Bergan v Evans* [2019] UKPC 33 **35.0.1** which highlights the distinction between the admissibility of expert evidence and the ability of a party to deploy the same at trial (albeit in the context of the provisions applying in St Kitts and Nevis) [38]–[45].

In the last paragraph, after "Council's Guidance for", add:
the

Expert availability and the trial timetable

Replace paragraph with:
Since April 1999 the Court of Appeal has made it clear that attempts to introduce expert **35.0.2** evidence late in the timetable, or the unavailability of the parties' chosen experts for the trial window or fixed trial date, will only very rarely be sufficient grounds to vary case management directions or trial dates or grant an adjournment. In *Rollinson v Kimberly Clark Ltd* [2000] C.P. Rep. 85 (CA), the Court of Appeal said that it was not acceptable for a solicitor to instruct an expert shortly before trial without checking their availability for the trial date. Where such an expert was unavailable, a different expert should be instructed. In *Matthews v Tarmac Bricks & Tiles Ltd* [1999] C.P.L.R. 463 (CA), Lord Woolf MR indicated that, if the parties were unable to agree on a trial date which was convenient to the parties, their experts and the court, they would need to provide reasons as to why their experts were unable to attend on certain dates:
> "If they hold themselves out as practising in the medico-legal field doctors must be prepared to arrange their affairs to meet the commitments of the courts where this is practical."
Note also the decision in *Robshaw v United Lincolnshire Hospitals NHS Trust* [2015] EWHC 247 (QB); [2015] Med. L.R. 339 (QBD), a clinical negligence case, in which the defendant applied to adjourn the trial on the basis that they would be prejudiced by their inability to cross examine the claimant's paediatric neurologist expert who had a stress related illness and it might not be possible for him to attend trial for the foreseeable future. Foskett J decided that the claimant would have possibly greater forensic and logistical difficulties because of the absence of their expert at trial and as the neurologists had met and prepared a joint statement it would be fair for the trial to proceed rather than adopt the defendant's proposal that the claimant instruct a new expert.

Judicial assessment of expert evidence

In the first paragraph, replace the first two sentences with:
A judge is entitled to prefer the evidence of a witness of fact to that of an expert witness. **35.0.3**

In the second paragraph, after "an appeal court", replace "deals" with:
dealing

In the third paragraph, replace the last sentence with:
When deciding liability for a road traffic accident where the parties and their experts had contended that the accident occurred in one of two ways, the trial judge should not have found that it occurred in a third way which had not been canvassed with the lay or expert witnesses and without inviting submissions on it before delivering his judgment: see *Faunch v O'Donoghue* [2013] EWCA Civ 1698, CA.

In the fourth paragraph, replace the last sentence with:
Additionally, in *Friarwood Ltd v Champagne Cattier SA* [2006] EWCA Civ 1105, CA the trial judge's decision could not stand where he had rejected expert evidence having thought, wrongly, that the expert had applied the incorrect test. Given the issues involved, the case was remitted for retrial.

Replace the last paragraph with:
Where an expert witness completely disregards their duty to the court by failing to follow the court's directions, the court may rule that the party may not rely on that expert's evidence, the effect of which may mean that the party loses the entire action, see *Stevens v Gullis* [2000] 1 All E.R. 527, CA. For a more recent example of the court's approach where an expert has failed to comply with its directions, see *Mayr v CMC Cameron McKenna Nabarro Olswang LLP* [2018] EWHC 3669 (Comm), noted at para.35.12.2.

Experts and the ultimate question

35.0.4 *Replace "Barings Plc (In Liquidation) v Coopers & Lybrand (No.2) [2001] Lloyd's Rep. Bank. 85" with:*
Barings Plc (In Liquidation) v Coopers & Lybrand [2001] Lloyd's Rep. Bank. 85

Related sources

35.0.5 *Replace list with:*
- Part 1 (the Overriding Objective)
- Part 3 (Case Management)
- Part 18 (Further Information)
- Part 23 (General Rules About Applications for Court Orders)
- Part 25 (Interim Remedies)
- Parts 26 to 29 (Case Management on the Tracks)
- Part 32 (Evidence)
- Part 33 (Miscellaneous Rules About Evidence)
- Part 34 (Depositions and Court Attendance by Witnesses)
- Practice Direction (Experts and Assessors) (see para.35PD.1)
- Practice Direction (Fast Track) Appendix (para.28PD.13)
- Practice Direction (The Multi-Track), paras 4 and 5 (paras 29PD.4 and 29PD.5)
- Civil Evidence Act 1972 s.2 (Rules of court with respect to expert reports and oral expert evidence) (see Vol.2, para.9B-1057)
- Civil Evidence Act 1972 s.3 (Admissibility of expert opinion) (see Vol.2, para.9B-1060)
- Senior Courts Act 1981 s.70 (see Vol.2, para.9A-261)
- County Courts Act 1984 s.63, (see Vol.2, para.9A-537)
- Chancery Guide, paras 17.44 to 17.60 (Vol.2, paras 1A-45 to 1A-47)
- Circuit Commercial Courts Guide, paras 12.1 to 12.13 (Vol.2, para.2B-20).
- Queen's Bench Court Guide, paras 10.8.1 to 10.8.15 (Vol.2, para.1B-49).
- Guidance for instruction of experts in civil claims, (Vol.1, paras 35EG.1 to 35EG.23).

Expert evidence held not to be necessary

Small claims

35.1.2 *After "is unnecessary in", add:*
the ordinary case in

Intellectual property

After "cases expert evidence", add:
as to consumer "eye appeal"

Medical evidence

Replace the first, second and third paragraphs with:
Where the issues in question in a stress at work claim were essentially issues of fact, restricting the parties to call one psychiatric expert each was justified, whilst it was noted that should one party adduce further quasi-expert evidence of fact, the other party could seek permission to rely on a further expert (*Heyward v Plymouth Hospital NHS Trust* [2005] EWCA Civ 939; [2006] C.P. Rep. 3, CA, distinguished from *ES v Chesterfield and North Derbyshire Royal Hospital NHS Trust* [2003] EWCA Civ 1284; [2004] C.P. Rep. 9, CA.
In *Casey v Cartwright* [2006] EWCA Civ 1280; [2007] 2 All E.R. 78, CA, at [30]–[36], the Court

of Appeal gave guidance as to how the causation issue should be addressed in low value whiplash claims. There would be no need for expert medical evidence on the causation issue in run-of-the-mill cases. However, where a defendant wished to argue that the nature of the impact was such that it was impossible or very unlikely that injury or any more than trivial injury could have been caused, such that the claimant had fabricated the claim and to adduce expert medical evidence on that issue, it would have to satisfy certain formalities. He or she would have to notify the claimant in writing that it intended to raise the causation issue within three months of receipt of the letter of claim. The defence must expressly raise the issue. Within 21 days of serving the defence, the defendant must file and serve a witness statement identifying the grounds on which the issue is raised. If satisfied that the issue has been properly identified and raised, the court will generally give permission for the claimant to be examined by the defendant's medical expert. On receipt of the resulting report, if the court is satisfied on the totality of the defendant's evidence that he or she has properly identified a case on the causation issue with a real prospect of success, the defendant will generally be granted permission to rely on such evidence at trial, though the court retains the discretion to refuse such permission. The Court of Appeal gave examples of factors which would justify such refusal.

In *Dodds v Arif* [2019] EWHC 1512 (QB) at [23], Master Davison distilled the authorities on the question of when it is appropriate to allow expert statistical evidence on life expectancy in personal injury cases into the following propositions: (1) Where the injury has not itself impacted upon life expectancy, permission will not be given unless the condition in para.5 of the Explanatory Notes to the Ogden Tables is satisfied, namely that there is clear evidence to support the view that the individual is atypical and will enjoy longer or shorter expectation of life. (2) Where the injury has impacted on life expectancy, or the condition in para.5 of the Explanatory Notes is satisfied, the "normal or primary route" for life expectancy evidence is the clinical experts. (3) The methodology which the experts adopt to assess the claimant's life expectancy is a matter for them. (4) Permission for bespoke evidence from an expert in life expectancy will not ordinarily be given unless the clinical experts cannot offer an opinion at all, or for reason state that they require specific input from a life expectancy expert, or where they deploy, or wish to deploy, statistical material, but disagree on the correct approach to it.

Financial and banking

In the eighth line, replace "suitability of financial produces" with:
suitability of financial products

Change title and replace paragraph with:

The nature of expert evidence

In *United Bank of Kuwait Plc v Prudential Property Services Ltd* [1995] E.G. 190 (C.S.) Evans LJ **35.2.1** stated the following:
> "The nature and permissible scope of expert evidence varies widely. In all cases it is admissible to inform the court of relevant practices in an area where the conduct on the particular occasion is said to have been negligent. In other words, such as no reasonably competent practitioner would undertake. Sometimes, however, it may be unnecessary so to inform the court. An obvious example is in the case of a motor accident where private cars and pedestrians are involved. It might be otherwise, however, if a specialist vehicle was involved in the particular case. Another example might be the straightforward need to translate a document from a foreign language. Evidence might be unnecessary in the case of elementary French, whereas it would almost certainly be necessary in the case of even elementary Mandarin Chinese. The object throughout and always is that the Court should reach a fully informed decision... it is a mistake to attempt to include all experts in one category. They range from, for example, the translator of foreign languages to a person who can explain advanced scientific concepts and from describing practices in highly technical areas, including surgery, to those in other areas where the Court has sufficient personal experience of its own."

Effect of rule

Replace paragraph with:
A fundamental problem with the provision of expert evidence prior to the introduction of the **35.3.1** CPR was that expert evidence was not viewed, in many cases, to be sufficiently independent and impartial. Experts were viewed as partisan advocates for the parties instructing them: *Abbey Mortgages Plc v Key Surveyors Nationwide Ltd* [1996] 1 W.L.R. 1534, CA. Rule 35.3 was introduced to reinforce the common law duties imposed on experts that were summarised in *National Justice Compania Naviera SA v Prudential Life Assurance Co Ltd (The "Ikarian Reefer")* [1993] 2 Lloyd's Rep. 68 (Comm Ct) (see para.35.3.3): see *Stevens v Gullis* [2000] 1 All E.R. 527, CA. The overriding duty to the court contained in r.35.3 is thus intended to ensure that where an expert is preparing evidence for court proceedings, or is giving evidence in court, their responsibility is to give such evidence to the court impartially on the matters within their expertise.

No property in an expert witness

Replace paragraph with:

35.3.2   It is contrary to the public interest for a party and an expert to contract that the expert will not act as an expert witness for the other party, see *Lilly ICOS LLC v Pfizer Ltd*, 17 August 2000 (ChD), unrep. In *Lloyd's Syndicate v X* [2011] EWHC 2487 (Comm); [2012] 1 Lloyd's Rep. 123 (Comm Ct) at para.32, it was noted that the authorities established that where an expert had previously acted for one party they could act for another in proceedings if they could do so without having to use privileged material which they obtained during the course of their original instruction. If it could be demonstrated that it was likely that they would be unable to avoid having to resort to such material the court would prevent them from acting for the other party.

Duties and responsibilities of experts

In the first paragraph, replace the third list item with:

35.3.3   3.   An expert witness should state the facts or assumptions on which their opinion is based. They should not omit to consider material facts which could detract from their concluded opinion (*Re J*, above).

Replace the second paragraph with:

Cresswell J's guidance was, with one caveat, expressly endorsed by the Court of Appeal: *National Justice Compania Naviera SA v Prudential Assurance Co Ltd* [1995] 1 Lloyd's Rep. 455. However, they added "one word of caution" in relation to para.4 of his guidance:

"It was evident that in this case the Judge was concerned to confine each expert to his area of expertise; but it is not always possible to do so and where the subject of inquiry is fire, an experienced fire expert, when he is assessing the significance of certain evidence, must be entitled to weigh the probabilities and this may involve making use of the skills of other experts or drawing on his general mechanical or chemical knowledge." (see Stuart-Smith LJ at pp.139–140).

The requirements of this rule emphasise that it is to the court, that the overriding duty is owed irrespective of who instructed or called the expert. The other duties and responsibilities (above) remain to be fulfilled. Practice Direction 35 para.2.1 now includes a paragraph which helpfully summarises Cresswell J's catalogue of duties and which emphasises in particular the need for experts to be independent, objective on matters within their expertise, and to consider all the material facts, including those which might detract from their opinion. See also the requirements as to the contents of an expert's report (r.35.10).

Replace the last paragraph with:

While *The Ikarian Reefer* stressed the fact that experts are not to act as advocates for the party instructing them, it remains apparent that this obligation is breached far too often by experts to the detriment of the party instructing them, see, for instance, *Gee v Depuy International Ltd* [2018] EWHC 1208 (QB); [2018] Med. L.R. 347 (QBD) at [19].

In *Imperial Chemical Industries Ltd v Merit Merrell Technology Ltd (No.2 Quantum)* [2018] EWHC 1577 (TCC); [2018] T.C.L.R. 6 at [237], Fraser J enjoined every expert to read Practice Direction 35. He also provided a list of points to be considered by experts and those instructing them: (1) Experts of like discipline should have access to the same material. (2) It is not for an independent expert to indicate which version of the facts they prefer. (3) Experts should not take a partisan stance in relation to interim applications. (4) The process of experts meeting and producing an agreement (where possible) is governed by the CPR, including the Overriding Objective, and should be constructive and co-operative. The parties and experts must save expense and approach the case proportionately. (5) Should material emerge close to trial such that an expert considers that further analysis, consideration or testing is required, his or her opposite number should be notified as soon as possible. Only in exceptional circumstances rendering it unavoidable should an expert produce a further report during a trial that takes the other side by surprise. (6) The principles in *The Ikarian Reefer* should be adhered to.

Independence issues in relation to experts

35.3.5   *At the end of the third paragraph, delete the last two sentences.*

When an expert fails to comply with their duty—sanctions

At the end of the fourth paragraph, replace "an expert gave their evidence in a thoroughly unsatisfactory manner;" with:

35.3.7   the conduct or evidence of an expert witness raises the question whether they are fit to practise;

Replace the last paragraph with:

Committal for contempt of court: *Liverpool Victoria Insurance Co Ltd v Khan* [2019] EWCA Civ 392, the Court of Appeal gave extremely detailed guidance on sentencing an expert who has been held to be in contempt of court (a great deal of its guidance applies to sentencing non-experts also). The approach of the criminal courts was a useful, though not precise, analogy. Accordingly, the Sentencing Council's definitive guidelines on the imposition of community and custodial sentences and on the discount to be applied for a guilty plea were relevant:

"... the deliberate or reckless making of a false statement in a document verified by a statement of truth will usually be so inherently serious that nothing other than an order for committal to prison will be sufficient." [59], and see para.81.29.1.

Effect of rule

In the third paragraph, replace "r.35.7(3)" with:
   r.35.7(2)

35.4.1

Replace the fifth and sixth paragraphs with:
   Confining expert evidence to one or two specialities may also cause difficulties, even when this seems justifiable on proportionality grounds, especially if the court has decided that a single joint expert will give evidence. It could encourage an expert to step outside their expertise, and to give opinion evidence on matters on which they are not really competent. The uses which parties are permitted to make of expert evidence may vary depending on the nature of the case management track to which proceedings are allocated. The fact that expert evidence is to be relied on in a case, and the extent of that evidence, may affect the question whether a case is allocated to the fast track or to the multi-track. See, further, the provisions as to allocation of a case to an appropriate case management track in Pts 26 to 29 and the Practice Directions supplementing those Parts; note also "Court's permission" below.

Court's permission

Replace paragraph with:
   Permission to call an expert to testify or to put in evidence an expert's report may be given in the court's own case management directions or in response to an application to the court by a party; the court will prompt the parties to consider their intentions regarding the use of expert evidence at an early stage. The requirement to obtain the court's permission to adduce expert evidence cannot be circumvented by seeking to adduce expert evidence within or as an annex to a witness statement, see *New Media Distribution Company Sezc Ltd v Kagalovsky* [2018] EWHC 2742 (Ch) (Marcus Smith J) at para.10, also see para.32.4.5. However, applications for security for costs constitute an exception to the foregoing. In *Pipia v BGEO Group Ltd* [2019] EWHC 325 (Comm) [23]–[25] and [30] it was held that, following the flexible approach to applications for security for costs endorsed by the Court of Appeal in *Bestfort Developments LLP v Ras Al Khaimah Investment Authority* [2016] EWCA Civ 1099; [2017] C.P. Rep. 9, on such applications, expert evidence did not have to be adduced in compliance with Part 35 and could be given by way of witness statements.

35.4.2

After the first paragraph, add new paragraph:

Permission not required where expert not instructed by parties to the proceedings—CPR Pt 35 is not a comprehensive, exclusive code. It only applies where expert evidence is to be adduced from an expert instructed by the parties to the immediate proceedings. Where a party seeks to rely on expert evidence adduced in previous proceedings, they may seek to do so as hearsay evidence. In such a circumstance the court retains a discretion under CPR r.32.1(2) to exclude it, although it should be slow to do so. It could, however, be properly excluded before trial if to permit a party to rely on it would lead to disproportionate cost; see *Rogers v Hoyle* [2014] EWCA Civ 257; [2015] Q.B. 265, CA, at [62]–[63]; *Mondial Assistance (UK) Ltd v Bridgewater Properties Ltd* [2016] EWHC 3494 (Ch) at [22], and, *Illumina Inc v TDL Genetics Ltd* [2019] EWHC 1159 (Pat) at [24]–[25]. Also see para.35.10.6.

Test for permission to adduce expert evidence

In the third paragraph (beginning "In British Airways plc"), after "the claim and proportionality, the", add:
   effect of a judgment either way on the parties, the

Procedure

Replace the first paragraph with:
   Parties are asked to state in the directions questionnaire: (i) whether any party will be seeking to adduce expert evidence, if so (ii) the name, estimated cost and other details of the expert whom the party wishes to use, and (iii) whether the case is suitable for a single joint expert in any field.

Replace the last paragraph with:
   In fast track cases, the matters to be dealt with by directions under r.28.2(1) include expert evidence (r.28.3(1)(c)). In such cases, the principle of proportionality dictates that expert evidence should be particularly limited, generally restricting each party to two experts (r.26.6(5)(b)), with single joint experts being used wherever possible (see r.35.7).

Guidance on experts with a relationship to a party

In the fourth paragraph, replace "para.89." with:

35.4.3   para.83.

Pre-action protocols and disclosure of expert reports

Replace the second, third and fourth paragraphs with:

35.4.4   In *Carlson v Townsend* [2001] EWCA Civ 511; [2001] 1 W.L.R. 2415, CA the Court of Appeal confirmed that the Personal Injury Pre-action Protocol does not require a medical expert, selected in accordance with the protocol, to be jointly instructed, or her report to be disclosed to the defendant. Such reports remain privileged and the court cannot order their production, although the claimant would need the court's permission before relying on another expert's report in the proceedings. But in *Edwards-Tubb v JD Wetherspoon Plc* [2011] EWCA Civ 136; [2011] 1 W.L.R. 1373, CA, a personal injury claim, the claimant, pre-issue, obtained a medical report from one doctor, whose name had been given to the defendant, but after issue disclosed a report from a different doctor. The Court of Appeal ordered the disclosure of the first report as a condition of being permitted to rely on the second because the first one had been obtained when the claimant had embarked on the pre-action protocol procedure. This was very different from a party obtaining advice from an expert pre-protocol, which was outside r.35.2. The court has the same power to impose a condition of disclosure of an earlier report when the change of expert occurred pre-issue as when it occurred post issue (*Beck v Ministry of Defence* [2003] EWCA Civ 1043; [2005] 1 W.L.R. 2206, CA and *Vasiliou v Hajigeorgiou* [2005] EWCA Civ 236; [2005] 1 W.L.R. 2195, CA, considered at para.35.5.2). Expert shopping is to be discouraged. However, in *Bowman v Thomson* [2019] EWHC 269 (QB) at [22] and [27]–[28], a claimant was given permission to adduce expert evidence from a urologist. No conditions were imposed on the grant of permission. The defendant subsequently discovered that the claimant had previously obtained expert evidence from a different expert, which had not been disclosed. The defendant applied for an order requiring the claimant to give specific disclosure of the first expert's evidence. On appeal, the starting point was that no condition had been attached to the grant of permission. Accordingly, there was "no vehicle for the imposition of such a condition under the existing orders" i.e., a retrospective imposition of such a condition. Attempting to rely on the general case management powers under CPR r.3.1(2)(m) or the power to vary the order under r.3.1(7) after the original grant of permission was not permitted.
   The Pre-action Protocols for Low Value Personal Injury Claims in Road Traffic Accidents that came into force on 30 April 2010 for accidents occurring after that date and for Low Value Employment and Public Liability claims for accidents after 30 July 2013 that include a claim for damages for personal injury for less than £25,000 have their own bespoke provisions for medical reports. Again the claimant instructs the expert, but there is no requirement to involve the defendant insurer in the choice of the expert(s).
   The Pre-Action Protocol for Professional Negligence claims encourages parties to co-operate when deciding on appropriate expert specialisations, whether experts might be instructed jointly and whether any reports obtaining pre-action might be shared. The Pre-action Protocol for Construction and Engineering Disputes has similar provisions. The Housing Disrepair Protocol encourages joint selection and instruction of a single joint expert.

Contingency fees

In the third paragraph, replace "Protocol on the Instruction of Experts," with:

35.4.6   Code of Guidance on Expert Evidence,

Direction for expert evidence to be given concurrently

Replace "Re Baby X [2011] EWHC 590 (Fam); [2011] Fam. Law 577 (Fam)" with:

35.4.8   *A Local Authority v A* [2011] EWHC 590 (Fam); [2011] Fam. Law 577 (Fam)

Permission to give oral evidence

Replace the first paragraph with:

35.5.2   In small claims and fast track cases, the general rule is that expert evidence is to be given in a written report prepared by the expert and not, unless the court so directs, by the expert's oral evidence. However, in small claims and fast track cases the court will not give a direction "unless it is necessary to do so in the interests of justice" (r.35.5(2)) and the parties will be expected to make out a strong case for requiring oral expert evidence.

Late Disclosure of expert's report

Replace paragraph with:

35.5.3   It is the general rule that, where a party wishes to use an expert's report at trial, or, having obtained the court's permission, wishes to call the expert to give evidence orally, they must disclose the report to other parties (r.35.13). Prior to the CPR it was not unusual for expert evidence to be served very late, sometimes only days before, or even at, trial. Except in highly unusual circumstances, such conduct is no longer acceptable. Parties can expect that the court will rule that late expert evidence cannot be relied upon (see *Baron v Lovell* [1999] C.P.L.R. 630; [2000] P.I.Q.R. P20, CA; para.35.13.1 and see, e.g. *TQ Delta LLC v ZyXEL Communications UK Ltd* [2019] EWHC 1597 (Pat)). On occasions, to "deal with a case justly", the court will, however, allow an expert to be instructed at a late stage, see, for instance, *Holmes v SGB Services Plc* [2001] EWCA Civ 354, CA.

Exchange or consecutive disclosure

Replace the first and second paragraphs with:

35.5.4

The court has wide powers under its general powers of case management to make orders as to the exchange of experts' reports. This may be simultaneous or sequential. The court may order simultaneous exchange of some reports (e.g on liability) and sequential exchange of others (e.g on quantum). Such order may prescribe the time and date of such exchange and may spell out the consequences of non-compliance. The court will usually impose a sensible but tight timetable for, amongst other things, the exchange of experts' reports and for experts' discussions or meetings. It will do so taking account of the complexity of the case and what may be necessary to enable experts to agree matters that can be agreed, identify matters that cannot be agreed, and to provide a summary of reasons why such matters cannot be agreed (see r.35.12).

In *Beck v Ministry of Defence* [2003] EWCA Civ 1043; [2005] 1 W.L.R. 2206, CA the Court of Appeal allowed the defendant to abandon their first expert's report, although this was favourable to their case, and to instruct a second expert, but on condition that the first expert's report was disclosed. It was emphasised that a party seeking to "replace" an expert has to provide good reasons particularly, as here, where a claimant may be subjected to another medical examination, but that the party does not have to disclose the first report until the court has decided the application for a further expert. However, in *Vasiliou v Hajigeorgiou* [2005] EWCA Civ 236; [2005] 1 W.L.R. 2195, CA, the Court of Appeal held that permission was not needed for the defendant to instruct a different expert than had been canvassed at the case management conference because the judge's directions did not name the expert to be instructed. See also *Edwards-Tubb v JD Wetherspoon Plc* [2011] EWCA Civ 136; [2011] 1 W.L.R. 1373, CA and *Bowman v Thomson* [2019] EWHC 269 (QB) and the notes at para.35.4.4. In *Bowman v Thomson*, it was held that when a clinical negligence claimant had obtained permission to rely on an expert's opinion, the court could not subsequently make that permission conditional upon the claimant disclosing to the defendant the opinion of another expert, whom he had previously instructed and in whom he had lost confidence.

Replace the sixth paragraph with:

Murray v Devenish [2017] EWCA Civ 1016 was a personal injury claim arising out of alleged abuse by a teacher in the 1970s. In 2013, the claimant had sent a letter of claim, at that time relying upon a medical expert whose evidence had recently been criticised in other proceedings. The claimant then issued proceedings, relying upon a report from a second expert. A trial was fixed for late 2015. A few months before trial, having lost confidence in his second expert, the claimant applied to rely on the report of a third expert. The application was refused, in part due to the proximity of trial. The following month, the claimant was given permission to appeal and the month after that, the trial was vacated and the matter stayed. The stay was subsequently lifted. On appeal, the Court of Appeal held that the judge had been correct to dismiss the application as matters had stood at that stage but, two years later, following the lifting of the stay and with no new trial date fixed, the balance of justice had changed and the claimant should not be left with an expert in whom he had lost confidence. He was granted permission to rely on the third expert's evidence on condition of disclosure of the first expert's report (the second expert's report having already been disclosed).

Delete paragraph 35.5.6, "Expert evidence as to foreign law".

Witness summonses

Replace the second paragraph with:

35.5.7

The court has the power to compel the attendance of an expert witness. In exercising that power, the court will have regard to (i) the court is entitled to every witness's evidence, whether of fact or opinion; (ii) the expert's connection with the case; (iii) their willingness to attend; (iv) whether they might have other important work which might be disrupted by attendance and (v) whether another expert of equal calibre is available: *Society of Lloyds v Clemenston (No.2)* [1996] C.L.C. 1205, CA. Save in exceptional circumstances, a witness summons to compel attendance at trial cannot be used to get round a party's obligation to pay the expert: *Brown v Bennett (Witness Summons), Times,* 2 November 2000, Ch D. See further Pt 34 (Witnesses, depositions and evidence for foreign courts).

Delete paragraph 35.5.8, "Inspection of written evidence".

Replace r.35.6(2) with:

Written questions to experts

35.6   **(2)   Written questions under paragraph (1)—**
   (a)   may be put once only;
   (b)   must be put within 28 days of service of the expert's report; and
   (c)   must be for the purpose only of clarification of the report, unless in any case—
      (i)   the court gives permission; or
      (ii)   the other party agrees.

Effect of rule

Replace the first, second and third paragraphs with:

35.6.1   Under r.35.6 a party may put to an expert instructed by another party written questions about his/her report in accordance with the terms of the rule. The answers form part of the report (r.35.6(3)). Where an expert does not answer a question put, r.35.6(4) comes into play.

This is a useful provision, perhaps particularly so in fast track cases (see r.35.5(2)). It enables a party to obtain clarification of a report prepared by an expert instructed by their opponent. In a given case, were it not possible to achieve such clarification of a report, the court, for that reason alone, may feel obliged to direct that the expert witness should testify at trial. The meaning of "clarification" is not explained in the rule or Practice Direction. However, it would seem that questions should not be used to require an expert to carry out new investigations or tests, to expand significantly on his/her report, or to conduct a form of cross-examination by post, including on the expert's credibility unless the court gives express permission. In *Mutch v Allen* [2001] EWCA Civ 76; [2001] C.P. Rep. 77, CA, the Court of Appeal stressed the usefulness of the ability to put written questions to an expert in enabling a party to obtain clarification of a report prepared by an expert instructed by the other side or to arrange for a point not covered in the report, but within the expert's expertise, to be dealt with. Written questions may be put once only (without the court's permission) and must be put within 28 days of receipt of the expert's report. Questions must also be proportionate. Practice Direction 35, para.6.1 (see para.35PD.1) states that, where a party sends a written question or questions direct to an expert, a copy of the questions should, at the same time, be sent to the other party or parties.

Effect of rule

In the second paragraph, replace "Peet v Mid Kent Area Healthcare NHS Trust [2001] EWCA Civ 1703; [2002] 1 W.L.R. 210" with:

35.7.1   *MP v Mid Kent Area Healthcare NHS Trust* [2001] EWCA Civ 1703; [2002] 1 W.L.R. 210

At the end of the third paragraph, replace the last two sentences with:

In *Yearsley v Mid Cheshire Hospitals NHS Trust* [2016] EWHC 1841 (QB), a clinical negligence claim pleaded at around £500,000, Whipple J held that it would not be appropriate to direct that a single joint expert opine as to whether or not the claimant had dementia, as, amongst other things, this was an issue which could potentially go to the heart of the case, being relevant to the question of capacity and of serious importance to quantum. Rather, the parties were given permission to adduce evidence from their own experts [7]–[8].

Replace the fifth paragraph with:

In the light of their report, the parties may agree that the evidence of a single joint expert should not be given at the trial. If the evidence is to be used at trial it may be submitted as a written report without the expert being called. The issue of cross examination of a single joint expert was addressed in *MP v Mid Kent Area Healthcare NHS Trust* [2001] EWCA Civ 1703; [2002] 1 W.L.R. 210, CA. At [28] Lord Woolf LCJ stated that

> "in the normal way the report prepared by the single expert should be the evidence in the case on the issues covered by that expert's report. In the normal way, therefore, there should be no need for that report to be amplified or tested by cross-examination. If it needs amplification, or if it should be subject to cross-examination, the court has a discretion to allow that to happen. The court may permit that to happen either prior to the hearing or at the hearing. But the assumption should be that the single joint expert's report is the evidence. Any amplification or cross-examination should be restricted as far as possible."

Single joint experts and Article 6 of ECHR

Replace paragraph with:

35.7.2   A single joint expert is not a court-appointed expert. Even if it were, the appointment of a court-appointed expert is not contrary to ECHR art.6(1) (*Brandstetter v Austria* (1993) 15 E.H.R.R. 378, ECtHR).

Directions as to single joint expert

Replace the first paragraph with:

35.7.3   For directions as to the appointment of single joint experts which may given by the court in fast track cases, see Practice Direction 28, Appendix (para.28PD.13). In multi-track cases, where appropriate agreed directions on allocation should include provision for the use of a single joint expert, see Practice Direction 29, para.4.8(4) (para.29PD.4). In such cases, where the court gives directions on its own initiative in the circumstances stated in para.4.10 of the Practice Direction, its general approach will be to give directions for a single joint expert on any appropriate issue unless there is good reason not to do so (para.29PD.4).

In the second paragraph, replace "para.H2.4" with:
    para.H2

Obtaining further expert evidence

Replace paragraph with:
    Where the parties give joint instructions to a single expert, whether as a result of a direction **35.7.4** given by the court under r.35.7 or as a result of an agreement to that effect between the parties, it is conceivable that one of the parties may be unhappy with the report produced by the single joint expert. The question may then arise whether that party should be permitted to instruct another expert with a view to their obtaining a report which will enable them to make a decision as to whether or not there were aspects of the report of the single joint expert which they might wish to challenge. In *D (A Child) v Walker* [2000] 1 W.L.R. 1382, CA, Lord Woolf MR indicated that the fact that a party had agreed to a joint expert, did not, of itself, operate as a bar to him or her then seeking further expert evidence. He gave the following guidance (from p.1388):
    "In a substantial case such as this, the correct approach is to regard the instruction of an expert jointly by the parties as the first step in obtaining expert evidence on a particular issue. It is to be hoped that in the majority of cases it will not only be the first step but the last step. If, having obtained a joint expert's report, a party, for reasons which are not fanciful, wishes to obtain further information before making a decision as to whether or not there is a particular part (or indeed the whole) of the expert's report which he or she may wish to challenge, then they should, subject to the discretion of the court, be permitted to obtain that evidence.
    In the majority of cases, the sensible approach will not be to ask the court straight away to allow the dissatisfied party to call a second expert. In many cases it would be wrong to make a decision until one is in a position to consider the situation in the round. You cannot make generalisations, but in a case where there is a modest sum involved a court may take a more rigorous approach. It may be said in a case where there is a modest amount involved that it would be disproportionate to obtain a second report in any circumstances. At most what should be allowed is merely to put a question to the expert who has already prepared a report...
    In a case where there is a substantial sum involved, one starts, as I have indicated, from the position that, wherever possible, a joint report is obtained. If there is disagreement on that report, then there would be an issue as to whether to ask questions or whether to get your own expert's report. If questions do not resolve the matter and a party, or both parties, obtain their own expert's report, then that will result in a decision having to be reached as to what evidence should be called. That decision should not be taken until there has been a meeting between the experts involved. It may be that agreement could then be reached; it may be that agreement is reached as a result of asking appropriate questions."
He noted that calling experts to give oral evidence is a last resort, due to its expense. Factors that may be relevant to the question whether a party should be permitted to adduce further expert evidence were outlined in *Cosgrove v Pattison* [2001] C.P. Rep. 68, Ch D. However, in *Popek v National Westminster Bank Plc* [2002] EWCA Civ 42; [2002] C.P.L.R. 370, CA the Court of Appeal decided that the trial judge was not wrong to refuse the claimant's late application to adduce additional expert evidence to that of the single joint expert, not least because the claimant's case had no prospect of success.

Directions as to inspection, etc.

Replace paragraph with:
    In appointing a single joint expert, the court may give directions about any inspection, examina- **35.8.4** tion or experiments which the expert wishes to carry out (r.35.8(3)(b)). Note also, r.33.6 (inspection of plans, models, photographs, etc).

Conferences and meetings with single joint experts, their attendance at trial and cross-examination

Replace paragraph with:
    Where a single joint expert is instructed, it is impermissible for one party to attend a conference **35.8.5** with the expert in the absence of the other party, unless prior consent to such a meeting is obtained in writing from the party who is to be absent from the meeting, and that consent is fully informed, see *MP v Mid Kent Area Healthcare NHS Trust* [2001] EWCA Civ 1703; [2002] 1 W.L.R. 210, CA at

paras 21–24 and 35, and *Childs v Vernon & Butcher* [2007] EWCA Civ 305, CA at para.18. An unrepresented party would not be in a position to give such consent unless they were fully aware of their rights. Where a single joint expert is instructed there should, usually, be no need to amplify or test the report of a single joint expert at trial by cross-examination, see *MP v Mid Kent Area Healthcare NHS Trust*, op cit., at para.28, albeit obiter, although approved in *Popek v National Westminster Bank Plc* [2002] EWCA Civ 42; [2002] C.P.L.R. 370 at para.28. In *Popek* the Court of Appeal, at para.29, went on to set out that if a single joint expert were, unusually, to be cross-examined then steps should be taken to ensure that they knew in advance of the hearing "what topics are to be covered, and where fresh material is to be adduced for his or her consideration". For an application of this approach, and an example where it would have been inappropriate to appoint a further expert due to the proximity to the trial date as the single joint expert could be cross-examined, see *P French & Co Ltd v Walton Street Trading Co Ltd* [2012] EWHC 4436 (QB), at para.9.

Weight to be given to a single joint expert's report

Replace the first paragraph with:

35.8.6   At [42]–[43] in *Coopers Payen Ltd v Southampton Container Terminal Ltd* [2003] EWCA Civ 1223; [2004] 1 Lloyd's Rep. 331, CA, the Court of Appeal gave the following guidance as to the weight to be attached to the evidence of a single joint expert:

> "All depends upon the circumstances of the particular case. For example, the joint expert may be the only witness on a particular topic, as for instance where the facts on which he expresses an opinion are agreed. In such circumstances it is difficult to envisage a case in which it would be appropriate to decide this case on the basis that the expert's opinion was wrong. More often, however, the expert's opinion will be only part of the evidence in the case. For example, the assumptions upon which the expert gave his opinion may prove to be incorrect by the time the judge has heard all the evidence of fact. In that event the opinion of the expert may no longer be relevant, although it is to be hoped that all relevant assumptions of fact will be put to the expert because the court will or may otherwise be left without expert evidence on what may be a significant question in the case. However, at the end of the trial the duty of the court is to apply the burden of proof and to find the facts having regard to all the evidence in the case which will or may include both evidence of fact and evidence of opinion which may interrelate.
>
> In the instant case the judge did not disregard the evidence of the joint expert. On the contrary, in some respects she accepted it. A judge should very rarely disregard such evidence. He or she must evaluate it and reach appropriate conclusions with regard to it. Appropriate reasons for any such conclusions reached should of course be given."

At the end of the second paragraph, replace "evidence." with:
evidence [36]–[38].

Effect of rule

Replace the first and second paragraphs with:

35.9.1   This rule is a particular application of the overriding objective's aim of securing equality of arms (see r.1.1(2)(a)). It does not provide the means to obtain access to a party's expert report. It simply provides the means to obtain information, which is presumably derived from a source of expertise accessible to the other party. Practice Direction 35, para.4 (see para.35PD.4) states that where the court makes an order under this rule, the document to be prepared recording the information should set out sufficient details of any facts, tests or experiments which underlie any part of the information to enable an assessment and understanding of the significance of the information to be made or obtained.

This rule, which does not appear to be relied upon very often, would seem to apply most readily to situations where one party has researched and developed a technical process over a long period of time and is therefore possessed with particular information and expertise in that area. It might thus be reasonable for the court to require that party to share information as to those matters which might reasonably assist the opposing party's expert without the necessity of time-consuming and expensive research before they can form a view. Any direction under r.35.9 would have to take into account such matters as commercial confidentiality in the use of such information in connection with the proceedings. It is hard to conceive of circumstances whereby such information could be sought by a party before proceedings have commenced. There seems to be no basis upon which a court could order an examination, experiment or tests on the matter in issue before preparing and filing the document recording the information. An application on notice in writing would be made to the court stating what order the applicant is seeking and the reasons relied upon by the applicant. Such an application may be supported by evidence from the applicant's expert setting out their particular difficulties in the absence of such information and the advantage that such information would have as to the just and expeditious resolution of the case. On the face of it, there is nothing to prevent a court of its own motion making such an order under this rule, if it was satisfied upon evidence before it that it was necessary to make such an order to enable the court to deal with the case justly, considering its objectives of ensuring so far as is practical that the parties are on equal footing, expense could be saved and that the matter could be dealt with expeditiously.

Literature to be served with reports

Replace "Breeze v Ahmed [2005] EWCA Civ 223; [2005] C.P. Rep. 29" with:
   Breeze v Ahmad [2005] EWCA Civ 223; [2005] C.P. Rep. 29   **35.10.5**

Composite expert reports

Replace paragraph with:
   In *Rogers v Hoyle* [2013] EWHC 1409 (QB); [2013] Inquest L.R. 75 (QB), Leggatt J permitted **35.10.6** the claimant to rely upon a published investigation report of the Air Accident Investigation Branch of the Department of Transport. This contained statements of fact of witnesses, and opinions of the (not identified) in-house and third-party investigators. The judge permitted reliance as the report contained a "wealth of relevant and potentially important evidence which bears directly or indirectly on whether the claimant's death was caused by the defendant's negligence", and said that it was for the trial judge to make such use of the report as she thought fit. In reaching his decision, Leggatt J at paras 116–118, as approved by Christopher Clarke LJ in *Rogers v Hoyle* [2014] EWCA Civ 257; [2015] Q.B. 265, CA at paras 52–55, stated that, as a matter of principle, where an expert expresses opinions on disputed issues of fact that do not call for expertise to evaluate such opinion, whilst technically inadmissible, should be treated as a matter of weight. Where it is inadmissible it should be given no weight. Any such inadmissible matters should not be required to be excised from expert reports as that would be inconsistent with the overriding objective of saving expense, and hence it was not justified by effective case management. The defendant's arguments that the anonymity of the authors would make the evidence unsafe, and that relying on such reports as evidence in civil proceedings could deter witnesses from co-operating with investigations, were dismissed. And see *Moylett v Geldof* [2018] EWHC 893 (Ch), Ch D for an application of the principle identified by Leggatt J in *Rogers v Hoyle* [2013] EWHC 1409 (QB); [2013] Inquest L.R. 75 (QB). In *A v B* [2019] EWHC 275 (Comm); [2019] 4 W.L.R. 25, Moulder J held that the principle in *Rogers v Hoyle* (that, as a general rule, the whole of an expert's report, including any inadmissible parts, should be placed before the trial judge, rather than the court undertaking an editing exercise at an interim stage) applied to expert reports governed by CPR Pt 35.

Effect of rule

At the end of the paragraph, replace "11-12." with:
   11–14.   **35.11.1**

Replace r.35.12(1)(b) with: **35.12**

Discussions between experts
   (b)   **where possible, reach an agreed opinion on those issues.**

Effect of rule

Replace the second paragraph with:
   In terms, r.35.12 require the experts, not simply to identify those parts of their evidence which **35.12.1** are in issue, but to identify the expert issues in the proceedings and, where possible, to "reach agreement on those issues". Further, the court may specify the issues which the experts must discuss. Narrowing, at an early stage, the issues to be put before the court, including issues of expert opinion, is one of the fundamental purposes of case management (r.1.4(2)(b)). The procedural judge conducting a case management conference should not only direct an experts' meeting but define, with the help of the parties and their legal representatives, the subject matter to be covered.

Replace the last paragraph with:
   An experts' discussion in a clinical negligence claim does not engage the question of a right to a fair trial under ECHR art.6, see *H v Lambeth, Southwark and Lewisham HA* [2001] EWCA Civ 1455; [2001] C.P. Rep. 117, CA, where it was exmplained that this was because the court's power to order a discussion is discretionary, the content of the expert's discussion would not be referred to at trial unless the parties agreed and any agreement reached at the discussion would not be binding on the parties, unless they agreed so to be bound. The Court of Appeal went on to decline to order that the lawyers should attend the discussion on the grounds that their input should be to a well drafted agenda but Hale LJ suggested that when time and costs permitted the appointment of an independent legally qualified person to chair an experts' discussion might be considered.

The joint statement

35.12.2 *In the first paragraph, after "Guidance for the Instruction of Experts", delete "to Give Evidence".*

At the end of the second paragraph, replace "(TCC)." with:
(TCC), [79].

Replace the third paragraph with:
An effective joint statement is best achieved by parties agreeing a single agenda for the experts' discussion, see *Saunders v Central Manchester University Hospitals NHS Foundation Trust* [2018] EWHC 343 (QB); [2018] Med. L.R. 287. It is expected that solicitors will "do their best to agree a single agenda" for a joint meeting of experts. The production of separate agendas by parties should not be routine and may, result in adverse costs consequences being visited on parties; see *Welsh v Walsall Healthcare NHS Trust* [2018] EWHC 1917 (QB) at paras 35–36. Experts are required to ensure they approach the joint meeting in a constructive manner. They are required, as part of the overriding duty to the court (see r.35.3(1)), to ensure that they prepare and agree the joint statement. It is only once the joint statement is completed that the necessity of short supplemental expert's reports can be explored. Failure to comply with these requirements may result in permission to adduce expert evidence being withdrawn, subject to making a successful application for relief from sanctions, see *Mayr v CMS Cameron McKenna Nabarro Olswang LLP* [2018] EWHC 3669 (Comm).

At the end of the fourth paragraph (beginning "The duty owed"), replace "para.9.8 and Denton Hall Legal Services v Fifield [2006] EWCA Civ 169; [2006] Lloyd's Rep. Med. 251, CA." with:
para.9.8.

In the fifth paragraph (beginning "It is not for the parties"), after "a breach of the condition", add:
of the grant of permission

In the penultimate paragraph, delete the last sentence.

Replace the last paragraph with:
In *Transco Plc v Griggs* [2003] EWCA Civ 564; (2003) 147 S.J.L.B. 507, CA both parties' medical experts changed their minds following their discussion. The Court of Appeal said that an expert's willingness to change their opinion in the light of discussion with others, and the evidence as it develops, may be a sign of strength rather than weakness [34]. However in *Stallwood v David* [2006] EWHC 2600 (QB); [2007] 1 All E.R. 206 (QB) a personal injury claim in which the claimant's medical expert changed his opinion after a discussion with the defendant's expert and the statement then read that the experts agreed that the claimant's inability to work full-time was unrelated to the accidents, the claimant was allowed to call a second expert, partly because she had lost confidence in the first one, and partly because the judge had made gratuitous comments at the case management conference that heightened the claimant's sense of grievance. However, at para.17 of the judgment it was stated that
> "the mere fact that an expert has changed or modified his opinion following an experts' meeting cannot by itself be a reason for permitting a party who is disappointed with the change or modification of opinion to adduce evidence from another expert" ,
as cited approvingly in *Guntrip v Cheney Coaches Ltd* [2012] EWCA Civ 392; [2012] C.P. Rep. 26, CA at para.17.

Effect of rule

35.14.1 *Replace paragraph with:*
An expert, in carrying out their function, operates within a framework stipulated by the instructions they have received, by the directions, if any, given by the court, and by the rules in this Part. When, upon a party's application the court grants permission to adduce expert evidence, the court may attach directions (r.35.4). They may also be attached when the court gives a direction for a discussion between experts (r.35.12) and where it gives a direction under r.35.7 for a single joint expert to be used. Within this framework, it is the duty of the expert to help the court; this duty overrides their obligations to others (r.35.3). An expert has to copy any request to the court to their instructing party seven days, and to any other party four days, in advance of filing it. Care should be taken to ensure that this requirement does not result in experts being deprived of direct access to the case management judge.

Consequences of withdrawal of funding

35.14.3 *Replace paragraph with:*
In *MS v Lincolnshire CC* [2011] EWHC 1032 (QB), the claimant's public funding was withdrawn. Neither expert was prepared to continue unless instructed by a solicitor and so no meeting of the experts had taken place. The Court held that it was not right to compare a wilful refusal or dilatory failure by a party or its expert to comply with a court's direction to a situation in which the party was prevented from complying by circumstances beyond his control. The judge should have ap-

proached the application for summary judgment on the basis of the ruling most favourable to the claimant that a trial judge could reasonably make rather than the ruling that the judge himself would be likely to make. The judge should have allowed the claimant to put in his reports on the basis that the weight to be attached to them, if any, would be a matter for the trial judge. Furthermore, it was not accepted that the reports would have no real evidential value; if they contained material that was not effectively challenged, there was no reason why a judge should not rely on that material; see paras 13–16 of the judgment.

Effect of rule

In the first paragraph, replace "assessors on an application of a party" with:
    one or more assessors

35.15.1

In the second paragraph, after "Under r.35.15,", add:
    when read with r.3.3

Replace the third and fourth paragraphs with:
    The court may vary or revoke an order or direction made under this rule (r.3.1(7)). As to assessors in the Admiralty Court, see r.61.13 (see Vol.2). For assessors in Admiralty appeals see para.52.21.9.
    Rule 18A of CPR Sch.2 CCR Ord.49 (Miscellaneous Statutes) states that r.35.15 applies to proceedings under para.5 of Sch.2 to the Telecommunications Act 1984.

Appointment of assessor

At the end of the first paragraph, replace "para.10.2)." with:
    para.10.3).

35.15.2

Replace the second paragraph with:
    In *Balcombe Group Plc v London Development Agency* [2008] EWHC 1392 (TCC); [2008] T.C.L.R. 8 (TCC), Coulson J, at para.6, identified the following principles applicable to the court's wide discretion to appoint an assessor under r.35.15:
    "(a) The court must have regard to the overriding principle (CPR 1.1), and in particular to all questions of proportionality, when considering appointing an assessor. Since the parties will have to pay the costs of an assessor, a court should think twice about imposing an extra layer of cost on the parties, and evaluate the potential benefit of an assessor against that cost, and the amount at stake in the proceedings.
    (b) The appointment of an assessor may be appropriate if the subject matter of the proceedings is technically complex or involves a particular activity which will be unfamiliar to the court. In nautical collision cases, an assessor will often be appointed; see, by way of example, *The Owners of the Ship 'Bow Spring' v The Owners of the Ship Manzanillo II* [2004] EWCA Civ 1007; and *The Owners and Bareboat Charterers of the Vessel 'Global Marina' v The Owners and Bareboat Charterers of the Vessel 'Atlantic Crusader'* [2005] EWHC 380 (Admlty). Assessors can sometimes be appropriate in detailed or complex costs disputes although, depending on the circumstances, their own costs will often be met by the court service, rather than by the parties.
    (c) Where assessors are appointed, it will be important to ensure that both the questions put to the assessor, and the assessor's answers to those questions are shared with the parties and made the subject of counsel's submissions. This can lead to the risk of increased cost and delay which will be 'inherent in the ping-pong of post-hearing exchanges'; see paragraph 16 of the judgment of Gross J in Global Marina (sic).
    (d) In TCC cases in recent years, the appointment of an assessor has been very much the exception rather than the rule..."

Change title to "Guidance for the Instruction of Experts in Civil Claims 2014".

GUIDANCE FOR THE INSTRUCTION OF EXPERTS IN CIVIL CLAIMS 2014

Introduction

Replace paragraph 1 with:
    1. The purpose of this guidance is to assist litigants, those instructing experts **35EG.1** and experts to understand best practice in complying with Part 35 of the Civil Procedure Rules (CPR) and court orders. Experts and those who instruct them should ensure they are familiar with CPR 35 and the Practice Direction (PD35). This guidance replaces the Protocol for the instruction of experts in civil claims (2005, amended 2009).

Selecting and Instructing Experts

Duties and obligations of experts

Replace paragraph 14 with:

35EG.3   **14.**   Experts should inform those instructing them without delay of any change in their opinions on any material matter and the reasons for this (see also paragraphs 64–66).

Replace paragraph 15 with:

15.   Experts should be aware that any failure to comply with the rules or court orders, or any excessive delay for which they are responsible, may result in the parties who instructed them being penalised in costs, or debarred from relying upon the expert evidence (see also paragraphs 89–92).

Acceptance of instructions

Replace paragraph 26 with:

35EG.6   **26.**   Experts should agree the terms on which they are to be paid with those instructing them. Experts should be aware that they will be required to provide estimates for the court and that the court may limit the amount to be paid as part of any order for budgeted costs (CPR 35.4(2) and (4) and 3.15).

Single joint experts

Replace paragraph 34 with:

35EG.10   **34.**   CPR 35.7-8 and PD 35 paragraph 7 deal with the instruction and use of joint experts by the parties and the powers of the court to order their use. The CPR encourage the use of joint experts. Wherever possible a joint report should be obtained. Single joint experts are the norm in cases allocated to the small claims track and the fast track.

Cross-examination of the single joint expert

Replace paragraph 47 with:

35EG.13   **47.**   Single joint experts do not normally give oral evidence at trial but if they do, all parties may ask questions. In general, written questions (CPR 35.6) should be put to single joint experts before requests are made for them to attend court for the purpose of cross-examination.

Experts' reports

Replace paragraph 50 with:

35EG.14   **50.**   PD 35, paragraph 3.1 provides that experts' reports should be addressed to the court and gives detailed directions about their form and content. All experts and those who instruct them should ensure that they are familiar with these requirements.

Written questions to experts

Replace paragraph 67 with:

35EG.19   **67.**   Experts have a duty to provide answers to questions properly put. Where they fail to do so, the court may impose sanctions against the party instructing the expert, and, if there is continued non-compliance, debar a party from relying on the report. Experts should copy their answers to those instructing them.

Discussions between experts

Replace paragraph 73 with:

35EG.20   **73.**   Where there is sequential exchange of expert reports, with the defendant's expert's report prepared in accordance with the guidance at paragraph 63 above, the joint statement should focus upon the areas of disagreement, save for the need for the claimant's expert to consider and respond to material, information and commentary included within the defendant's expert's report.

Replace paragraph 75 with:

75. In multi-track cases the parties, their lawyers and experts should co-operate to produce an agenda for any discussion between experts, although primary responsibility for preparation of the agenda should normally lie with the parties' solicitors.

Experts and conditional and contingency fees

Replace paragraph 88 with:

88. Payment of experts' fees contingent upon the nature of the expert **35EG.22** evidence or upon the outcome of the case is strongly discouraged. In *ex parte Factortame (no8)* [2003] QB 381 at [73], the court said 'we consider that it will be a rare case indeed that the court will be prepared to consent to an expert being instructed under a contingency fee agreement'.

PART 36

OFFERS TO SETTLE

I. Part 36 Offers to Settle

Scope of Part 36

Replace the second paragraph with:

Counterclaims and other additional claims—Rule 36.2(3)(a) now clarifies that Part 36 offers can be **36.2.3** made in respect of counterclaims and other additional claims. This was always the case (see *AF v BG* [2009] EWCA Civ 757; [2009] All E.R. (D) 249; [2010] 2 Costs L.R. 164, CA) but the clarification is welcome in view of the difficulty perceived in the old rules in *F&C Alternative Investments (Holdings) Ltd v Barthelemy (Costs)* [2011] EWHC 2807 (Ch); [2012] Bus. L.R. 891, Ch D (Sales J); overturned on appeal: [2012] EWCA Civ 843; [2013] 1 W.L.R. 548; [2012] 4 All E.R. 1096, CA. The matter is put beyond doubt by the signpost at the end of this rule to rr.20.2 to 20.3 and by the wording of the new Form **N242A**. In *Calonne Construction Ltd v Dawnus Southern Ltd* [2019] EWCA Civ 754; [2019] Costs L.R. 309 the Court of Appeal confirmed that a Part 36 offer could be made in respect of a counterclaim that had not been commenced at the time the offer was made. When making an offer in a case concerning a counterclaim or other additional claim, it is important to make clear whether it is intended to be a claimant's or a defendant's offer. By way of example, a counterclaiming defendant may wish to make a claimant's offer (where the offer is to accept some payment on the counterclaim) or a defendant's offer (where the offer is to pay some money on the claim). Such offer may be limited to the counterclaim or claim; alternatively it may take the other adverse claim into account: see r.36.5(1)(d) to (e). See also the guidance notes on Form **N242A** and *Van Oord UK Ltd v Allseas UK Ltd* [2015] EWHC 3385 (TCC); [2016] 1 Costs L.O. 1 (Coulson J).

Formal requirements for a Part 36 offer

Replace the fourth paragraph with:

Paragraph(1)(d)—While offers can be made pre-issue (see para.36.7.1), an offer in extant proceed- **36.5.1** ings must be made by reference to the pleaded issues. After issue, an offer made in respect of an intimated but unpleaded issue is not therefore made pursuant to Pt 36: *Hertel v Saunders* [2018] EWCA Civ 1831; [2018] 1 W.L.R. 5852; [2018] 4 Costs L.R. 879. Although see *Calonne Construction Ltd v Dawnus Southern Ltd* [2019] EWCA Civ 754; [2019] Costs L.R. 309, noted at para.36.2.3, where the Court of Appeal distinguished *Hertel* and held that it was permissible to make a Part 36 offer in respect of an unpleaded counterclaim. In *White v Wincott Galliford Ltd* [2019] EWHC B6 (Costs), Deputy Master Friston held that an offer in respect of solicitor's hourly rates was a valid offer in respect of a specific issue. Nevertheless, the Deputy Master deprecated the tactical use of Pt 36 to make an offer on the issue of hourly rates in provisional assessment proceedings.

After the seventh paragraph (beginning "Where a claimant's offer"), add new paragraph:
Doubting the decision in *Procter & Gamble* (above), HHJ Paul Matthews held in *Knight v Knight* [2019] EWHC 1545 (Ch), 17 June 2019, unrep., that he was bound by *Mitchell* (above) and *French* (above) to hold that any offer that included terms as to costs was not a valid Part 36 offer.

After the eighth paragraph (beginning "Late offers–"), add new paragraph:
Terms as to interest—Additional terms as to interest payable after the end of the relevant period did not invalidate a Part 36 offer: *Calonne Construction Ltd v Dawnus Southern Ltd* [2019] EWCA Civ 754; [2019] Costs L.R. 309, CA. Equally, a Part 36 offer to accept a sum in costs assessment proceedings exclusive of interest was valid: *Horne v Prescot (No.1) Ltd* [2019] EWHC 1322 (QB); [2019] Costs L.R. 279, Nicol J. While the decision was expressly based on the fact that interest on costs pursuant to the Judgments Act 1838 did not form part of the claim in assessment proceedings, Nicol J observed more generally that additional words that do not conflict with the mandatory requirements of Pt 36 do not invalidate the offer.

Effect of rule

36.13.1
In the last paragraph, replace "Finnegan v Spiers [2018] EWHC 3064 (Ch)" with:
Finnegan v Spiers [2018] EWHC 3064 (Ch); [2018] 6 Costs L.O. 729

Other effects of acceptance

36.14.1
In the last paragraph, replace "Bentley Design Consultants Ltd v Sansom [2018] EWHC 2238 (TCC)," with:
Bentley Design Consultants Ltd v Sansom [2018] EWHC 2238 (TCC); [2018] 6 Costs L.O. 743,

Claimant's offer (rr.36.17(1)(b) and 36.17(4))

36.17.4
Add new paragraphs at end:
On appeal, in *JLE v Warrington & Halton Hospitals NHS Foundation Trust* [2019] EWHC 1582 (QB), 24 June 2019, unrep., Stewart J agreed that it was open to a judge to conclude that it was unjust to order some, but not all, of the orders pursuant to r.36.17(4). The judge added, however, that it would be unusual for the circumstances to yield a different result for some only of the orders.

Making orders pursuant to r.36.17(4) does not interfere with a trustee's claim for indemnity from a trust fund, which is a matter of trust law and not the CPR: *Price v Saundry* [2019] EWHC 1039 (Ch), 25 March 2019, unrep. (HHJ Matthews).

Order for "an additional amount" (r.36.17(4)(d))

36.17.4.4
Add new paragraphs at end:
The high level of the bill of costs (or the claim in the case of a Part 36 offer in the substantive proceedings) by comparison to the award is, save where the inflated claim led the paying party to incur expense before the date of the offer, no reason to refuse to award the additional amount: *Ayton v RSM Bentley Jennison* [2018] EWHC 2851 (QB); [2018] 5 Costs L.R. 915, *Cashman* (above) and *JLE v Warrington & Halton Hospitals NHS Foundation Trust* [2019] EWHC 1582 (QB), 24 June 2019, unrep.

In *White v Wincott Galliford Ltd*, 28 May 2019, unrep., SCCO, Deputy Master Friston held that it was unjust to award the full additional amount in provisional assessment proceedings merely because the receiving parties achieved a decision on the issue of hourly rates that was at least as advantageous as their Part 36 offer. Drawing on *Thinc Group Ltd v Kingdom* [2013] EWCA Civ 1306; [2014] C.P. Rep 8, CA, the Deputy Master held that the words in r.36.17(4) that "unless [the court] considers it unjust" meant "unless and to the extent that". Accordingly, it was open to the court to order a reduced amount under r.36.17(4)(d). Disagreeing, Stewart J held, obiter, in *JLE v Warrington & Halton Hospitals NHS Foundation Trust* [2019] EWHC 1582 (QB), 24 June 2019, unrep. that the additional amount is an "all or nothing" award and that there is no jurisdiction to order a reduced amount under r.36.17(4)(d).

"considers it unjust to do so" (r.36.17(5))

36.17.5
Replace the first paragraph with:
Where an effective Part 36 offer has been made, the court must make the orders referred to in r.36.17(3) (in the case of a claimant failing to obtain a judgment more advantageous than the defendant's Part 36 offer) or r.36.17(4) (in the case of a claimant obtaining a judgment at least as advantageous as their own Part 36 offer), as the case may be, "unless it considers it unjust to do so" (the injustice test). In *Thinc Group Ltd v Kingdom* [2013] EWCA Civ 1306; [2014] C.P. Rep 8, CA at [22], Macur LJ held, in respect of equivalent provisions under the then extant version of Pt 36, that "unless it considers it unjust to do so" means "unless and to the extent of"; see *Horne v Prescot (No.1) Ltd* [2019] EWHC 1322 (QB); [2019] Costs L.R. 279 at [29]–[31]. In considering whether it would be unjust to make the orders, r.36.17(5) requires the court to take into account all the

circumstances of the case including the particular matters listed in that sub-rule. The party at risk is required to establish grounds for rendering it unjust to make the order and such must be found by the court so as to deny the offeror their costs. The question is not whether the offeree had reasonable grounds for not accepting the offer as if there were some unfettered discretion as to costs, but to consider whether the usual order would be unjust (*Matthews v Metal Improvements* [2007] EWCA Civ 215; [2007] C.P. Rep. 27, CA). For a summary of the authorities applicable to the injustice test see *Horne v Prescot (No.1) Ltd* [2019] EWHC 1322 (QB); [2019] Costs L.R. 279 at [20]-[21].

Add new paragraphs at end:
   In *JLE v Warrington & Halton Hospitals NHS Foundation Trust* [2019] EWHC 1582 (QB), 24 June 2019, unrep., Stewart J held, obiter, that the additional amount is an "all or nothing" award and that there is no jurisdiction to order a reduced amount under r.36.17(4)(d).
   Further, in *JLE* (above), Stewart J held that the costs judge had been wrong to take into account the small margin by which the receiving party beat its Part 36 offer in detailed assessment proceedings. To do so ignored the terms of r.36.17(2) that "more advantageous" means "better in money terms by any amount, however small" and risked reintroducing the discredited decision in *Carver v BAA Plc* [2008] EWCA Civ 412; [2009] 1 W.L.R. 113; [2008] 3 All E.R. 911, CA. (See generally the commentary at para.36.17.2.)

Effect of rule

Add new paragraph at end:
   Where a claimant started her claim under the portal even though it was worth in excess of £25,000, she remained limited to fixed costs under Pt 45 upon acceptance of a subsequent Part 36 offer: *Hammond v SIG Plc*, 11 June 2019, unrep., Master Leonard. **36.20.1**

PART 38

DISCONTINUANCE

Editorial introduction

Replace paragraph with:
   CPR 38 gives a claimant a unilateral right to discontinue all or part of a claim upon the filing **38.0.1** and service of a notice of discontinuance (see r.38.2(1)).
   Permission to discontinue is required by the claimant only in the situations prescribed by r.38.2(2). A claimant who discontinues is liable for the defendant's costs unless the court orders otherwise (r.38.6).

Add new paragraph 38.1.2:

claim
   A "claim" is not defined, but it is clear that a claim is to be distinguished from a remedy (*Galazi* **38.1.2** *v Christoforou* [2019] EWHC 670 (Ch), 26 March 2019). If the claimant abandons a remedy, but continues the claim for other remedies, it is not treated as discontinuing all or part of the claim— r.38.1(2).
   For a discussion as to whether the word "claim" in r.38.2 means the entire action outlined in the claim form, or only a cause of action, see *Kazakhstan Kagazy Plc v Zhunus* [2016] EWHC 2363 (Comm). Leggatt J stated that the repeated references to "all or part of a claim" made the latter unlikely. Causes of action are not susceptible to partition in a way that would make discontinuance an appropriate procedure. The appropriate way of discontinuing a cause of action is simply to amend the statement of case. In his judgment, the word "claim" had to refer to the entire action or, at the very least, to all causes of action asserted by a particular claimant against a particular defendant. On the other hand, in *Galazi v Christoforou*, Chief Master Marsh held that the abandonment of an entire cause of action may amount to a partial discontinuance. He stated,
   "With great respect to Leggatt J, it seems to me that the analysis in *Kazakhstan Kagazy Plc v Zhunus* does not consider rule 38 as a whole and does not give sufficient weight to rules 38.2(1) and (3). Part 38 is explicit in saying that a claimant may discontinue part of a claim against one defendant. The later use of the word 'proceedings' in rule 38.5(2) must be treated as a synonym for claim. The rule does not otherwise make sense. A claim is more than particular relief but may be less than the entire claim against a party."

Effect of rule

Add new paragraph at end:
   It is not entirely clear from rr.38.3(1) and 38.5(1) whether a notice of discontinuance is required **38.2.1**

where the court's permission to discontinue must to be obtained. On its face, r.38.3 requires the filing and service of a notice for a discontinuance to take place, whatever the circumstances may be. This is reinforced by r.38.5 which specifies that discontinuance takes effect on service of the notice on the relevant defendant or defendants. The terms of the rule are explicit and it is hard to avoid the conclusion that the filing and service of a notice of discontinuance is required in every case. Obtaining the court's permission, where it is required, is a preliminary step to discontinuance which takes place by filing and service of the notice. Unless and until notice has been filed and served there has not been a discontinuance. However, it may well be, in practice, that the court often implicitly waives the requirement for a notice and deals with costs and any other issues that arise on the permission hearing. Plainly that is a sensible pragmatic approach albeit it is not one that can be found in the rule (*Galazi v Christoforou* per Chief Master Marsh).

Permission to discontinue

Replace the second paragraph with:

38.2.2   In *Kazakhstan Kagazy Plc v Zhunus* [2016] EWHC 2363 (Comm) Leggatt J held that the words "in relation to which ... the court has granted an interim injunction" in r.38.2(2)(a) refer to the part of the claim which the claimant wishes to discontinue. The court's permission is therefore only required when the claim to be discontinued was included within the subject matter of an injunction which is still in force. Permission does not need to be obtained where the claim had historically been included within the subject matter of the injunction, but was no longer included.

Delete the last paragraph.

Effect of rule

To the end of the second paragraph, add:

38.6.1   In the case of partial discontinuance, the default position under r.38.6(2)(b) is that the costs of the discontinuance must not be assessed until the conclusion of the rest of the proceedings.

In the fourth paragraph (beginning "A claimant who wishes to avoid"), after "to pre-action correspondence)).", add:
     This is a "high" hurdle for such a claimant to overcome.

Basis for costs

Replace paragraph with:

38.6.2   In view of CPR r.44.9(1)(c), a costs order following service of a notice of discontinuance is deemed to be on the standard basis, but CPR r.38.6(1) which gives the court power to order otherwise, allows the court to order costs on the indemnity basis if there are exceptional circumstances (*Atlantic Bar and Grill Ltd v Posthouse Hotels Ltd* [2000] C.P. Rep. 32) or there is something in the conduct of the claim or the circumstances of the claim which takes the case out of the norm (*Excelsior Commercial and Industrial Holdings Ltd v Salisbury Hammer Aspden & Johnson* [2002] EWCA Civ 879 at [39] per Waller LJ). It is not necessary for there to have been some sort of lack of moral probity or conduct deserving moral condemnation on the part of the paying party (*Reid Minty v Taylor* [2011] EWCA Civ 1723 at [27] per May LJ). See e.g. *Mireskandari v Law Society* [2009] EWHC 2224 (Ch), where the claim was hopeless from its inception and had been conducted unreasonably, *Two Right Feet Ltd (In Liquidation) v National Westminster Bank Plc* [2017] EWHC 1745 (Ch); [2017] 6 Costs L.O. 735 (where the claim was speculative and weak in fact and law and brought without proper investigation or engaging with the relevant pre-action protocol); *Galazi v Christoforou* [2019] EWHC 670 (Ch), 26 March 2019 and *Stati v Republic Of Kazakhstan* [2019] EWHC 1715 (Comm), QBD, 2 July 2019 (Jacobs J).
     If a claimant is given permission to discontinue after making allegations of fraud, conspiracy and dishonesty, an order for indemnity costs is likely to be the just result, unless some explanation can be given as to why the claimant decided that the allegations were bound to fail (*Clutterbuck v HSBC Plc* [2015] EWHC 3233 (Ch); [2016] 1 Costs L.R. 13 and *PJSC Aeroflot - Russian Airlines v Leeds* [2018] EWHC 1735 (Ch)).

PART 39

Miscellaneous Provisions Relating to Hearings

Editorial introduction

Replace the first paragraph with:

39.0.1   As its title suggests this Part sweeps up various remaining provisions concerning hearings, in particular it reflects the principle of open justice and deals with the circumstances in which hearings may be held in private. It was amended, with effect from 6 April 2019, by Civil Procedure (Amendment) Rules 2019 (SI 2019/342). The amendment substituted a new r.39.1 and inserted new provisions in r.39.2 and new rr.39.8–39.10.

Practice Directions

Replace paragraph with:

39.0.3

Part 39 was originally supplemented by two Practice Directions: PD 39A—Miscellaneous Provisions Relating to Hearings; and PD 39B—Court Sittings. The former supplemented various provisions of Pt 39, the latter had no direct connection with this Part but had been included for reasons of convenience. Practice Direction 39A was deleted by CPR Update 104 (February 2019), with effect from 6 April 2019. Practice Direction 39B—Court Sittings was deleted from this Part and moved to become CPR PD 2F—Court Sittings, with effect from 6 April 2019 by the same CPR PD Update.

Recording of hearings

Replace paragraph with:

39.0.6

Rule 39.9, inserted by Civil Procedure (Amendment) Rules 2019 (SI 2019/342) contains provisions about the recording of hearings and the supply to any party or person of transcripts of recordings. These provisions were previously contained in para.6 of PD 39A, which was deleted as from 6 April 2019 (see para.39.0.3). On 14 February 2014, the Lord Chief Justice issued *Practice Direction (Audio Recordings of Proceedings: Access)* [2014] 1 W.L.R. 632, for the purpose of clarifying the practice and procedure governing access to CD or digital audio recordings of civil and family proceedings in all courts in England and Wales; for text of this Practice Direction, which should be read with r.39.9, see para.39PDAR.1. Paragraph 6 of the 2014 Practice Direction states that an application for permission to listen to or receive a copy of an audio recording will only be granted in exceptional circumstances, for example where there is cogent evidence that the transcript may have been wrongly transcribed. In *Bath v Escott* [2017] EWHC 1101 (Ch) (Matthews J), a party to High Court proceedings, having obtained a written transcript of the judgment of a district judge in those proceedings, and being of the opinion that the transcript did not accurately set out the judgment as delivered by the district judge orally, applied to a High Court judge for an order for the release to him of the recording of the oral judgment. The judge dismissed the application, principally on the ground that the applicant gave no particulars of the differences to which he was referring. In doing so the judge explained that it does not matter if the approved transcript adds to or differs from the actual words used by the judge at the time of giving judgment; what matters is only that it has been considered, revised if necessary, and then approved by the judge; there is no duty on the judge to approve a transcript limited to the exact terms of the words spoken on the day.

Delete paragraph 39.0.7, "Exhibits at trial".

Settlement or discontinuance after the trial date is fixed

Replace paragraph with:

39.0.8

Rule 39.10 requires practitioners, in cases where a date or "window" has been fixed for the trial of a claim, to notify the listing officer immediately where the whole of the claim has been disposed of by settlement or discontinuance. The importance of parties providing the court with such information is obvious. This rule replicates, in clearer language the provisions of what was para.4.1 of PD 39A (see para.39.0.3). In respect of that paragraph, and there is no reason to believe its incorporation into the CPR as r.39.10 has altered this, the Court of Appeal held that the duties of parties are broader than those imposed by what was then para.4.1. In *Yell Ltd v Garton* [2004] EWCA Civ 87; [2004] C.P. 29, CA, it was stressed that parties have an obligation to inform the court if they believe that a case is likely to settle as soon as they become aware of the possibility of settlement. The court held that a considerable amount of time had been wasted in preparing for the appeal, and the parties' legal advisers ought to have contacted the 24-hour switchboard at the Royal Courts of Justice in order to have obtained the telephone number of the clerk to the senior presiding judge so that he could have been notified of the position. Failure to do so may result in the court making an adverse costs order against the parties. The obligations placed upon parties in these respects are reinforced in some of the Court Guides.

Delete paragraph 39.0.9, "Citation of Human Rights authorities".

Replace r.39.1 with:

Interpretation[1]

39.1   **39.1.—(1) In this Part—**

    (a) "hearing" means the making of any interim or final decision by a judge at which a person is, or has a right to be, heard in person, by telephone, by video or by any other means which permits simultaneous communication; and

    (b) "judge" has the same meaning as in rule 2.3(1).

  (2) This Part is subject to rule 62.10 (hearings in arbitration claims).

"hearing" (r.39.1, r.39.2)

Replace paragraph with:

39.1.1   Rule 39.1(1)(a) was amended by Civil Procedure (Amendment) Rules 2019 (SI 2019/342) in order to introduce a new definition of "hearing". The amendment substituted a new r.39.1. Although the previous r.39.1 provided that a reference to a hearing included a reference to a trial, "hearing" was not defined. The previous provision covered interlocutory hearings (*ABC Ltd v Y* [2010] EWHC 3176 (Ch), at para.16). Telephone hearings were not mentioned. While public access to justice has improved in that hearings are no longer routinely held "in chambers", it was felt that that gain should be balanced against the loss of access through increased adjudication on the papers and at video and telephone hearings. The new definition is sufficiently wide enough to capture all forms of communication between the parties and the court and explicitly captures interim as well as final hearings.

    Rule 39.1(2) makes reference to arbitration claims. Rule 62.10(2) expressly excludes the application of the general rule that a hearing is to be heard in public by simply stating that "rule 39.2 does not apply". Rule 62.10(1) provides that the court may order that an arbitration claim may be heard either in public or in private. The reference to arbitration claims was introduced for the sake of clarity. It does not alter the current approach in the High Court to the issue of publicity in arbitration claims: see *Moscow City Council v Bankers Trust Co* [2005] Q.B. 207 (per Mance LJ).

Replace r.39.2 with:

General rule—hearing to be in public[2]

39.2   **39.2—(1) The general rule is that a hearing is to be in public. A hearing may not be held in private, irrespective of the parties' consent, unless and to the extent that the court decides that it must be held in private, applying the provisions of paragraph (3).**

  (2) In deciding whether to hold a hearing in private, the court must consider any duty to protect or have regard to a right to freedom of expression which may be affected.

  (2A) The court shall take reasonable steps to ensure that all hearings are of an open and public character, save when a hearing is held in private.

  (3) A hearing, or any part of it, must be held in private if, and only to the extent that, the court is satisfied of one or more of the matters set out in sub-paragraphs (a) to (g) and that it is necessary to sit in private to secure the proper administration of justice—

    (a) publicity would defeat the object of the hearing;

    (b) it involves matters relating to national security;

    (c) it involves confidential information (including information relating to personal financial matters) and publicity would damage that confidentiality;

    (d) a private hearing is necessary to protect the interests of any child or protected party;

    (e) it is a hearing of an application made without notice and it would be unjust to any respondent for there to be a public hearing;

    (f) it involves uncontentious matters arising in the administration of trusts or in the administration of a deceased person's estate; or

---

[1] Amended by the Civil Procedure (Amendment) Rules 2019 (SI 2019/342).

[2] Amended by the Civil Procedure (Amendment) Rules 2007 (SI 2007/2204) and the Civil Procedure (Amendment) Rules 2019 (SI 2019/342).

(g) the court for any other reason considers this to be necessary to secure the proper administration of justice.

(4) The court must order that the identity of any party or witness shall not be disclosed if, and only if, it considers non-disclosure necessary to secure the proper administration of justice and in order to protect the interests of that party or witness.

(5) Unless and to the extent that the court otherwise directs, where the court acts under paragraph (3) or (4), a copy of the court's order shall be published on the website of the Judiciary of England and Wales (which may be found at www.judiciary.uk). Any person who is not a party to the proceedings may apply to attend the hearing and make submissions, or apply to set aside or vary the order.

Add new paragraph 39.2.0:

Editorial Introduction

39.2.0

Rule 39.2 makes provision for the constitutional principle of open justice; see *Scott v Scott* [1913] A.C. 417; *R. (Mohamed) v Secretary of State for Foreign and Commonwealth Affairs* [2010] EWCA Civ 65; [2011] Q.B. 218, CA, paras 38–40. As originally drafted it was subject to criticism in the *Report of the Super-Injunction Committee* (2011). It recommended that the rule as drafted should be reviewed. That review was ultimately completed in 2018, which resulted in substantial amendments to r.39.2 by the Civil Procedure (Amendment) Rules 2019 (SI 2019/342). The amendments clarified the open justice requirements in relation to hearings in private and reporting restrictions. The amendments also introduced a wider definition of a "hearing" to explicitly take into account technological developments, govern parties communicating with the court, and supplement the provision of transcripts.

"hearing to be in public" (r.39.2)

Replace paragraph with:

39.2.1

Rule 39.2 reflects the principle of open justice which is a fundamental aspect of English and Welsh law. It was amended as from 6 April 2019 (see para.39.2.0) The general rule is that hearings are to be in public (see *Scott v Scott* [1913] A.C. 417 and *R. v Bow County Court, Ex p. Pelling (No.2)* [2001] U.K.H.R.R. 165, QBD Administrative Court and, more recently, *Cape Intermediate Holdings Ltd v Dring (for and on behalf of Asbestos Victims Support Groups Forum UK)* [2018] EWCA Civ 1795). Lord Diplock in *Attorney General v Leveller Magazine Ltd* [1979] A.C. 440 at 449H–450D explained the policy rationale underpinning the principle of open justice when he said:

"The application of this principle has two aspects: as respects proceedings in the court itself it requires that they should be held in open court to which the press and public are admitted and that, in criminal cases at any rate, all evidence communicated to the court is communicated publicly. As respects the publication to a wider public of fair and accurate reports of proceedings that have taken place in court the principle requires that nothing should be done to discourage this."

However, that rule is not absolute. CPR r.39.2(3) is facilitative and permits certain limited exceptions, always assumed to that being subject to the interests of justice. CPR r.39.2(3) is not unlawful or ultra vires. Nor does it breach ECHR arts 6 or 10 (ibid.). See further paras 9–15 of *Practice Guidance: Interim Non-Disclosure Orders* given by Lord Neuberger MR in August 2011 (see para.53PG.1).

The rule, as amended from April 2019, makes clear that the parties cannot agree that a hearing will be held in private or that their mutual consent will in practice be accepted by the judge as sufficient reason to hold the hearing in private, without further consideration of the question; it thus now gives expression to the Court of Appeal's decision in *JIH v News Group Newspapers Ltd (Rev 1)* [2011] EWCA Civ 42; [2011] 1 W.L.R. 1645, para.21(7).

Any derogation from the general rule must be considered by the court in light of the exceptions set out in CPR r.39.2(3). These changes reflect a fundamental culture shift towards a clearer understanding of the importance of the principle of open justice and the need to preserve it.

In *Pink Floyd Music Ltd v EMI Records Ltd* [2010] EWCA Civ 1429; [2011] 1 W.L.R. 770, CA, Lord Neuberger MR stated that a private hearing (or party anonymisation) will be granted in the Court of Appeal only if, and only to the extent that, a member of the Court is satisfied that it is necessary for the proper administration of justice and gave guidance as to the correct procedure to be adopted where a party to an appeal wants a private hearing (or anonymisation) (paras 62–69). Where the court below permitted a private hearing (or anonymisation) the Court would normally pay close regard to the judge's decision, especially if expressed in a reasoned judgment, but was not bound by it.

In libel action where the court is asked to consider the meaning of publications where no evidence except the words themselves is admissible, the court may, in the interest of furthering the overriding objective, dispense with an oral hearing and decide the matter on the papers (*Hewson v Times Newspapers Ltd* [2019] EWHC 650 (QB)). In *Hewson*, Nicklin J noted that this approach would potentially impact on the principle of open justice as explained by Tugendhat J in *Church*. However, Nicklin J held that the difficulties identified in *Church* could be overcome by adopting the following procedure: (a) the court would consider the written submissions of the parties and prepare a judgment to be handed down; (b) the draft judgment would be circulated to the parties in the normal way; (c) the case would be listed, in open court, for judgment to be handed down; (d) at the hand down, the court would make available all written submissions considered, together with copies of the judgment (see paras 16–27 of judgment).

It should be noted that where a court or tribunal has sat in private without justification, the decision made will be unlawful (*Storer v British Has Plc* [2000] 2 All E.R. 440). In *R. (O'Connor) v Aldershot Magistrates Court* [2016] EWHC 2792 (Admin) it was held that the principle of open justice is such that where members of the public are unlawfully excluded from the proceedings, the exclusion means that any decisions taken under those conditions would also be invalid.

The new r.39.2(2) refers to s.12 of the Human Rights Act 1998. It places an obligation on the court to consider the right to freedom of expression which may be affected when deciding whether to hold a hearing in private.

CPR r.39.2(2A), introduced in April 2019, now explains what the obligation to hold hearings in public means for those wishing to attend. See *R. (O'Connor)* op. cit. para.47, where Leggatt J explained that:

"the question of when a hearing ceases to be open to the public is one of fact and degree. In a case where members of the public are unlawfully excluded from the court, we think the essential question is whether the nature and extent of the exclusion are such as to deprive the hearing of its open and public character."

In cases where questions as to whether the court should sit in private for the whole of or part of proceedings arise, questions may also arise as to whether the court should exercise related powers; in particular powers (1) to grant an interim injunction (a) restraining the publication, use or disclosure of categories of confidential information, (b) restraining the publication or disclosure of the existence of the proceedings, and (c) providing for the anonymisation of the parties, and (2) to give directions of the sort commonly used in order to underwrite the security of such injunctions (e.g restricting access to court records). The common law rules and Convention provisions relevant to these related powers of the court were examined by the Court of Appeal in *Donald v Ntuli* [2010] EWCA Civ 1276; [2011] 1 W.L.R. 294; [2011] C.P. Rep. 13. See further Vol.2, paras 15-40 to 15-45.

In *Al-Rawi v Security Service* [2011] UKSC 34; [2011] 3 W.L.R. 388, SC, the claimants brought claims against various emanations of the Crown or government for damages in tort, breach of contract, and breach of statutory duty in respect of their detainment at various locations as suspected terrorists. Amongst other matters, the defence raised issues of public interest immunity.

On public interest grounds, the defendants proposed that a "closed material procedure", similar to that mandated by statutes for control order proceedings and financial restriction proceedings (see CPR Pt 76 and Pt 79), should be adopted, with proceedings being held partly in public and partly in private, and with "open" and "closed" judgments. The Supreme Court, by majority, held that this was not possible because it was only for Parliament, not the courts, to introduce a closed material procedure to replace the existing established process for dealing with public interest immunity in a civil trial for damages, and in doing so upheld, on slightly different grounds, the decision of the Court of Appeal (see [2010] EWCA Civ 492; [2010] 3 W.L.R. 1069, CA). The several judgments handed down by the Supreme Court Justices and the judgment of the Court of Appeal contain extensive accounts of the principle of open justice and derogations from the principle as permitted by statute and other means.

For authority under ECHR art.6(1) on the right to a public hearing, see *Werner v Austria* (1998) 26 E.H.R.R. 310, ECtHR, *Diennet v France* (1996) 21 E.H.R.R. 554, ECtHR, and *Scarth v United Kingdom (33745/96)* (1998) 26 E.H.R.R. CD154, EComHR, confirmed by ECtHR.

The Strasbourg institutions have generally taken the view that interlocutory hearings are not determinative of civil rights and obligations with the meaning of ECHR art.6(1). These hearings are therefore generally not required to be public: *APIS v Slovakia* (2000) 29 E.H.R.R. CD105, ECtHR, 2nd chamber (interim injunction), *Alsterlund v Sweden (12446/86)* (1988) 56 D.R. 229, EComHR (stay of execution), *Noviflora Sweden ab v Sweden (14369/88)* (1993) 15 E.H.R.R. CD6, decision of 12 October 1992, unrep., EComHR (search order), *Ewing v United Kingdom No.11224/84* (1998) 10 E.H.R.R. CD141. The amendments to r.39.1(1)(a) read together with r.39.2 makes clear that that distinction is not replicated in England and Wales.

In *Ewing v The Crown Court sitting at Cardiff and Newport* [2016] EWHC 183 (Admin); [2016] 4 W.L.R. 21; [2016] 1 Cr. App. R. 32 the Divisional Court (dealing with a criminal case) concluded that those who attend public court hearings should be free to take notes and no prior permission to do so is required. The court may prohibit the taking of notes but only where the taking of notes would interfere with the administration of justice (see paras 23 and 24).

For the position under ECHR art.6(1) in relation to public access to judgments see *Pretto v Italy* (1984) 6 E.H.R.R. 182, ECtHR, *Axen v Germany* (1984) 6 E.H.R.R. 195, ECtHR, and *Werner v Austria* (1998) 26 E.H.R.R. 310, ECtHR. The Convention draws a distinction between hearings, which may be held in private in certain circumstances, and judgments, which must be pronounced publicly. This means that they must be available to the public.

Add new paragraph 31.2.1.0:

Access to court documents

The principle of open justice also extends to the obtaining of court documents by non-parties (CPR r.5.4C). When considering an application by a non-party for access to court documents, the court must, when exercising its discretion, have regard to the principle of open justice. In *Cape Intermediate Holdings Ltd v Dring (for and on behalf of Asbestos Victims Support Groups Forum UK)* [2018] EWCA Civ 1795 the Supreme Court considered the extent to which non-parties should have access to documents placed before the court and referred to during a hearing. The Court held that the default position is that the public should be allowed access, not only to the parties' submissions and arguments, but also to the documents which have been placed before the court and referred to during the hearing. It followed that it should not be limited to those which the judge has been asked to read or has said that he has read. The Court also held that, although the court has the power to allow access to documents, the applicant has no right to be granted it (save to the extent that the rules grant such a right) and that it was for the person seeking access to explain why he is seeking it and how granting him access will advance the open justice principle. Following the approaches taken in both *A v BBC* [2014] UKSC 25 and *Kennedy v Information Commissioner* [2014] UKSC 20, the Court in *Cape* held that a fact-specific balancing exercise must be carried out between: (i) the purpose of the open justice principle and the potential value of the information in question in advancing that purpose; and (ii) any risk of harm which disclosure may cause to the maintenance of an effective judicial process or to the legitimate interests of others. In short, a non-party should not seek access unless he can show a good reason why this will advance the open justice principle, that there are no countervailing principles (e.g. national security issues or the need to protect the identity of a child), and that granting the request will not be impracticable or disproportionate.

39.2.1.0

Change title and replace paragraph with:

"A hearing, or any part of it, must be held in private" (r.39.2(3)) Hearings in private under r.39.2(3) are derogations from the principle of open justice and must be ordered only when it is necessary and proportionate to do so, with a view to protecting the rights which claimants (and others) are entitled to have protected by such means. That they must be ordered, as now provided by r.39.2(3) rather than "may" be ordered reflects the decision in *AMM v HXW* [2010] EWHC 2457 (QB) where Tugendhat J confirmed that when a judge is being asked to consider a request to depart from the principle of open justice, the test is one of necessity and not discretion, and that when the subject matter is particularly acute (in this case blackmail) the test to be satisfied is "whether there is sufficient general public interest in publishing a report of the proceedings which identifies [x] to justify any resulting curtailment of his right and his families' right to respect for their private and family life." When such orders are made they must be limited in scope to what is required in the particular circumstances of the case (*G v Wikimedia Foundation Inc* [2009] EWHC 3148 (QB); [2010] E.M.L.R. 14 (Tugendhat J)).

39.2.2

If the test for sitting in private is satisfied, the court must sit in private; if not, it must sit in public. The wording of the new r.39.2(3), "necessary ... to secure the proper administration of justice", is derived from *Practice Direction (Committal for Contempt: Open Court)* [2015] 1 W.L.R. 2195, paras 3 and 4. It was felt by the Civil Procedure Rule Committee that the previous wording may have encouraged the mistaken view that if a case fell into one of the categories covered in (a) to (g), the hearing would be in private. That is not the law. In particular, there is no right to a private hearing where a person's personal finances are under discussion. An issue that requires further consideration is the disclosure of an individual's finances in respect of applications for Judicial Review and other challenges which come under the Aarhus Convention claim provisions. The question is whether the information disclosed warrants a departure from the stated general principle of open justice. In *RSPB v Secretary of State for Justice* [2017] EWHC 2309 (Admin), Dove J concluded that Aarhus Convention claim environmental costs protection regime (ECPR) should be amended, so that the default position is that any hearing of an application to vary costs caps in an Aarhus Convention claim should be held in private. The revised provisions of CPR r.39.2(1) and (4) are sufficient to accommodate cost capping hearings in Aarhus Convention claims which will allow such claims to be listed in private.

Paragraph 1.4 of PD 39A, before it was deleted, stated that the decision as to whether to hold a hearing in public or in private must be made by the judge conducting the hearing having regard to any representations which may have been made to them. Notwithstanding its deletion it is reasonable to assume that this sensible practice will be maintained. Rule 39.2(3) does not give a litigant a right to a hearing in private merely because the case falls within one of the classes identified in the rule. The court has to form a view of the nature of the confidential information, its importance to the party and the damage that would be suffered by its disclosure, before deciding whether it is necessary to hold a hearing in private (In the matter of *Timothy Edward Shuldham* [2012] EWHC 1420 (Ch), Floyd J, noted on Lawtel). See *Smithkline Beecham Plc v Generics (UK) Ltd* [2003] EWCA Civ 1109; [2004] 1 W.L.R. 1479, (patent infringement claim—cross-examination on confidential documents in private).

For consideration of the application of ECHR art.6(1) to a refusal to admit a McKenzie friend to an ex parte hearing in private see *R. v Bow County Court Ex p. Pelling* [1999] 1 W.L.R. 1807, CA. The court should also bear in mind the ECHR principle of proportionality when deciding whether all or part of the hearing should be held in private.

In proceedings to which Pt 76 (Prevention of Terrorism Act 2005), Pt 79 (Financial Restrictions Proceedings Under the Counter-Terrorism Act 2008), or Pt 80 (Terrorism Prevention and Investigation Measures Act 2011) applies, the court is given special powers to hold hearings in private for particular purposes (see, respectively, rr.76.22, 79.17(2) and 80.18)).

An inspector of court administration exercising rights of entry and inspection under the Courts Act 2003 s.61 is not entitled to be present when a county court is hearing proceedings in private.

"confidential information" and "personal financial matters" (r.39.2(3)(c))

Replace the second paragraph with:

39.2.3.1   The Court of Appeal in *XW v XH* [2019] EWCA Civ 549 set out the correct approach to applications for reporting restrictions orders in financial remedy cases heard in the Court of Appeal. From *Norman v Norman* [2017] EWCA Civ 49 the court drew the following propositions: (i) ordinarily, in a financial remedy appeal, a formal application should be made to hear the appeal in private or for there to be a reporting restrictions order; (ii) only exceptionally would an order for anonymity supported by a reporting restrictions order be made in the Court of Appeal: parties were not routinely entitled to anonymity and the preservation of confidentiality in their financial affairs; (iii) parties could not waive the rights of the public by consent: the decision was the court's, having conducted the balancing exercise in *Re S (A Child) (Identification: Restrictions on Publication)* [2004] UKHL 47; (iv) the Court of Appeal would pay close regard to any such order made by the first instance judge, although such orders were not binding, not least because of the different starting points for the respective courts; (v) when considering such an application, only rarely would the Court of Appeal go behind the facts as found by the judge; (vi) having concluded that the parties' ECHR art.8 rights were engaged and having weighed up the competing art.8 and art.10 rights, the interests of a child might render it necessary to restrict public reporting of certain information in financial remedy cases (*K v L (Ancillary Relief: Inherited Wealth)* [2011] EWCA Civ 550).

39.2.4   *Change title of paragraph:*

"matters relating to national security" (r.39.2(3)(c))

39.2.5   *Change title of paragraph:*

"child or protected party" (r.39.2(3)(d))

Replace the first paragraph with:

Where a claim by or on behalf of a child or protected party is compromised etc. by or on behalf of a child or a protected party the approval of the court is required as provided by r.21.10. Rule 39.2(3)(d) states that a hearing, or any part of it, must be in private if that is necessary to protect the interest of any child or patient.

In *Zeromska-Smith v United Lincolnshire Hospitals NHS Trust* [2019] EWHC 552 (QB) the court refused to grant an anonymity order to a mother in a clinical negligence case who was claiming psychiatric injury following the stillbirth of her child. The court held that the open justice principle was not adequately satisfied by publishing only the defendant's name where the party seeking anonymity was not a child or protected person (*Re Guardian News and Media Ltd* [2010] UKSC 1).

After the second paragraph, add new paragraphs:

In *MN v OP* [2019] EWCA Civ 679 the Court of Appeal made clear that anonymity should not be the norm or default position for minor beneficiaries in applications made under the Variation of Trusts Act 1958. However, where it was necessary to provide a measured degree of protection to the rights of the minor beneficiaries until their majority, when they would be introduced to their settlement interests, those privacy rights could be afforded the necessary degree of protection by making an order under Children and Young Persons Act 1933 s.39.

Add new paragraph at end:

The court in *Zeromska-Smith* provided guidance on the proper approach to take to the provision of advance notice of anonymity applications which ought to be followed in future case. In *Zeromska-Smith* the application was made at the start of the trial without notice being given to the Press Association in advance, which did not allow for full consideration of the issues or properly prepared submissions on behalf of the Press Association. The court held that such an application should be made and heard in advance of the trial to give the press a proper opportunity to make representations in advance, whether orally or in writing. In addition, if a claimant in a sensitive case knew that, if the matter went to trial, her name would be published in the press, she might consider that to be an important factor in deciding whether to accept an offer of settlement. In some cases that could tip the balance. An application for anonymity should be made well in advance of the trial and a claimant should not assume that the application would be entertained at the start of the trial, because of the disruption to the trial which might ensue if the application was adjourned to enable the Press Association time to prepare its submissions, nor that it would be approved by the judge where the defendant took a neutral stance and there was only a court reporter in court to represent the interests of the press.

"necessary in the interests of justice" (r.39.2(3)(g))

Replace paragraph with:

39.2.7   See too r.1.1 (the overriding objective). There are a wide range of circumstances in which it may be necessary in the interests of justice for an exception to be made to the general rule that hearings should be in public. Where there is a serious risk of reputational damage if a matter is heard in public, the court will balance the competing interests of those whose reputation is at stake against the public interest in open justice. Whilst the outcome of the exercise depends on the particular circumstances of the case, the principle of open justice will generally prevail, see *Global Torch v Apex Management Limited* [2013] EWCA Civ 819. However, once the court has applied the relevant test, it is, as Tugendhat J stated at first instance in *AMM v HXW* [2010] EWHC 2457 (QB) at [34], under a duty either to grant the derogation or refuse it (also see *Nursing and Midwifery Council v D*, para.39.2.3.1).

Delete paragraph 39.2.8, "Order following a hearing in private".

Delete paragraph 39.2.9 "Transcripts and orders".

Add new paragraphs 39.2.10.1 to 39.2.10.3:

"copy of the order shall be published"

39.2.10.1   CPR r.39.2(5) introduces a new procedural mechanism for determining open justice issues. The procedure allows media organisations or other potential opponents of anonymity orders to be notified of such orders being made. The procedure adopts a similar approach to that set out in *Practice Direction (Committal for Contempt: Open Court)* [2015] 1 W.L.R. 2195.

CPR r.39.2(5) covers those situations where the court has decided to hear cases in private and where the identities of the parties are anonymised. The court is placed under a positive duty to make the orders public by following a simple procedure which will result in an electronic copy of the order being made available on the relevant website. A non-party is thereby able to challenge the order by making an application to the court.

The duty to publish on the website would only arise where the judge acts under CPR r.39.2(3) (sitting in private, including in freezing injunction, and search and seize applications) or grants anonymity to a party or witness. In other cases, the order is on the court file and open to inspection under CPR Pt 5. In many cases the court will properly direct that the order should not be published, or not until served or not without safeguards such as anonymity or redactions.

Placing court orders on the website is established practice. Judges will be required to approve orders in the normal way and send them (with any necessary directions about publication) to be uploaded to the necessary webpage. Media organisations or other members of the public present at a hearing considered likely to be held in private are at present, and should remain, able to make submissions (in public) to the court advocating a public rather than a private hearing. The judge managing the hearing will need to keep the exercise within the bounds of proportionality.

In April 2019, the Master of the Rolls issued Practice Guidance: Publication of Privacy and Anonymity Orders (see para.39.8.0). This Guidance sets out the recommended practice to courts and parties concerning the provision of copies of court orders for publication pursuant to CPR 39.2(5). Any party seeking a private hearing or anonymity pursuant to CPR r.39.2(3) or (4) must ensure that they prepare and submit to the court a draft order which does not contain any information that would undermine the purpose of the order. The courts retains discretion to vary the requirements under CPR 39.2(5) to provide a redacted copy or to set aside the publication requirements.

"provided to the other party or parties or their representatives"

39.2.10.2   There has been an increase in parties communicating with the court (often by email) without copying the other party, and without good reason not to do so. This was a serious denial of open justice of a particular kind; it is self-evidently objectionable, other than in exceptional cases, for a party to engage in a private dialogue with the court without the other party. To exclude the other party from the communication requires compelling justification. As Lord Judge LCJ said in *R. (Mohamed) v Secretary of State for Foreign and Commonwealth Affairs (No. 2)* [2010] EWCA Civ 158, at para.7:

> "It is an elementary rule of the administration of justice that none of the parties to civil litigation may communicate with the court without simultaneously alerting the other parties to that fact ..."

CPR r.39.8 introduces an explicit obligation to copy the other side when communicating with the court and a separate obligation to include in communications sent to the court a statement that the communication has been copied to the other side; other than in cases where there is compelling justification for not doing so (e.g. at an early stage in a without notice freezing order or search and

seize application); in which event the reason should be stated in the communication. The obligation should arise whenever a party makes a representation to the court about a matter of substance
or procedure in the proceedings. The obligation does not apply to communications that are purely
routine, uncontentious and administrative (an email from a party asking in which court or court
building a hearing will take place).

"compilation and sharing of any note or other informal record"

39.2.10.3   CPR r.39.9(5) introduces a new rule which provides assistance to the increasing number of
unrepresented parties appearing before the courts. Transcripts can be difficult and, for many,
costly and time-consuming to obtain. It is rare to have an approved transcript in sufficient time to
consider an appeal on the basis of it. To address these concerns, r.39.9(5) encourages the court and
the parties to assist in providing an adequate interim informal record of the proceedings while
awaiting the approved transcript or, in some cases, as a sufficient substitute, particularly if a note of
the proceedings is agreed and/or approved by the judge.

There are a number of justifications which underpin the rule. Advocates already have a duty to
take an accurate note and therefore the rule does not impose a new duty to make a note, only to
provide it to the other side. Although there is no obligation on the judge to provide a note of a
judgment or hearing or to share his or her notes with the parties, the reference to sharing any note
"made ... by the court" will encourage sharing of informal judicial notes but does not compel the
judge to do so. Where a note is provided by the court, it can easily be prevented from acquiring the
status of a transcript by including a clear warning on the notes that they may not be cited externally
or used for any purpose other than the litigation. The proposal is also an extension of existing
precedents and reflects the duty of the parties to further the overriding objective. See further the
specific provision in family proceedings for preparation of bundles by a represented party instead
of an unrepresented one, even where the latter is an applicant; see CPR PD 27A 3.1:

> "A bundle for the use of the court at the hearing shall be provided by the party in the posi-
> tion of applicant at the hearing (or, if there are cross-applications, by the party whose applica-
> tion was first in time) or, if that person is a litigant in person, by the first listed respondent
> who is not a litigant in person."

Replace paragraph 39.8 and add new paragraphs 39.9 and 39.10:

Communications with the court[1]

39.8   **39.8—(1) Any communication between a party to proceedings and the court
must be disclosed to, and if in writing (whether in paper or electronic format),
copied to, the other party or parties or their representatives.**

**(2) Paragraph (1) applies to any communication in which any representa-
tion is made to the court on a matter of substance or procedure but does not
apply to communications that are purely routine, uncontentious and
administrative.**

**(3) A party is not required under paragraph (1) to disclose or copy a com-
munication if there is a compelling reason for not doing so, and provided that
any reason is clearly stated in the communication.**

**(4) A written communication required under paragraph (1) to be copied to
the other party or parties or their representatives, must state on its face that it
is being copied to that person or those persons, stating their identity and
capacity.**

**(5) Unless the court directs otherwise, a written communication which
does not comply with paragraph (4) will be returned to the sender without being considered by the court, with a brief explanation of why it is being
returned.**

**(6) In addition to returning a communication under paragraph (5), where
a party fails to comply with paragraph (1) the court may, subject to hearing
the parties, impose sanctions or exercise its other case management powers
under Part 3.**

**(7) Paragraph (1) does not apply to communications authorised by a rule
or practice direction to be sent to the court without at the same time being
provided to the other party or parties or their representatives.**

---

[1] Inserted by the Civil Procedure (Amendment) Rules 2019 (SI 2019/342).

Recording and transcription of proceedings[1]

39.9—(1) At any hearing, whether in the High Court or the County Court, the proceedings will be tape recorded or digitally recorded unless the judge directs otherwise. **39.9**

(2) No party or member of the public may use unofficial recording equipment in any court or judge's room without the permission of the court. (To do so without permission constitutes a contempt of court under section 9 of the Contempt of Court Act 1981.)

(3) Any party or person may require a transcript or transcripts of the recording of any hearing to be supplied to them, upon payment of the charges authorised by any scheme in force for the making of the recording or the transcript.

(Paragraph 6(2) of Practice Direction 52C (Appeals to the Court of Appeal) deals with the provision of transcripts for use in the Court of Appeal at public expense.)

(4) Where the person requiring the transcript or transcripts is not a party to the proceedings and the hearing or any part of it was held in private under rule 39(2), paragraph (3) of this rule does not apply unless the court so orders.

(5) At any hearing, whether in public or in private, the judge may give appropriate directions to assist a party, in particular one who is or has been or may become unrepresented, for the compilation and sharing of any note or other informal record of the proceedings made by another party or by the court.

Discontinuance and settlement[2]

39.10—(1) Where a claim is discontinued or settled after a date for the trial or trial window (the period during which it is expected that the trial will take place) has been fixed, the parties must ensure that the listing officer for the trial court is notified immediately. **39.10**

(2) If an order is drawn up giving effect to the discontinuance or settlement, a copy of the order should be filed with the listing officer.

MEMORANDUM FROM THE LORD CHIEF JUSTICE AND THE ATTORNEY GENERAL

Delete "Memorandum from the Lord Chief Justice and the Attorney General" (paragraphs 39.8.1 to 39.8.4).

Add new Practice Guidance: Publication of Privacy and Anonymity Orders:

PRACTICE GUIDANCE: PUBLICATION OF PRIVACY AND ANONYMITY ORDERS

1. This Guidance sets out recommended practice to courts and parties concerning the provision of copies of court orders for publication. It is issued as guidance and not as a Practice Direction by the Master of the Rolls as Head of Civil Justice. **39PG.1**

2. Civil Procedure Rules (CPR) r.39.2(5) provides that, except where the court otherwise directs, a copy of a court order made under CPR r.39.2(3) or r.39.2(4) shall be published on the website of the Judiciary of England and Wales.

3. Any party seeking a private hearing or anonymity pursuant to CPR r.39.2(4) or (5) should ensure that they prepare and submit to the court a draft order which does not contain any information that would

---

[1] Inserted by the Civil Procedure (Amendment) Rules 2019 (SI 2019/342).
[2] Inserted by the Civil Procedure (Amendment) Rules 2019 (SI 2019/342).

undermine the purpose of the order.

4. Copies of orders for publication should be sent by a court officer via email to the Judicial Office at: judicialwebupdates@judiciary.uk. Wherever possible, they should be sent in pdf format. For ease of identification, emails should be headed 'Order for Publication under CPR r.39.2(5)'. Following receipt, they will be uploaded to www.judiciary.uk.

5. Where necessary, to protect the integrity of the order, the court may consider varying, under CPR r.39.2(5), the requirement to provide a copy of the court order for publication to provide for a redacted copy to be published or to set aside the requirement to publish a copy.

Sir Terence Etherton, Master of the Rolls
16 April 2019

PRACTICE DIRECTION 39A—MISCELLANEOUS PROVISIONS RELATING TO HEARINGS

Replace paragraphs 39APD.1 to 39APD.8 with:

39APD.1   Practice Direction 39A has been omitted.

PRACTICE DIRECTION 39B—COURT SITTINGS

Replace paragraphs 39BPD.1 to 39BPD.4 with:

39BPD.1   Practice Direction 39B has been renamed as Practice Direction 2F, and can now be found at para.2FPD.1.

PART 40

JUDGMENTS, ORDERS, SALE OF LAND ETC.

Collection of non-disclosure injunctions information

Replace paragraph with:

40.0.7   Practice Direction 40F (Non-disclosure injunctions information collection scheme) was added to this Part in October 2012. A new PD 40F was substituted by CPR Update 109 (30 June 2019), effective as from 1 October 2019. It provides for a scheme for the recording, and transmission to the Ministry of Justice for analysis, of certain data in relation to injunctions prohibiting publication of private or confidential information. The scheme applies to civil proceedings in the Court of Appeal and the High Court. The purpose of the scheme is to enable the Ministry of Justice to collate and publish, in anonymised form, information about applications for injunctions where the Human Rights Act 1998 s.12 is engaged. The scheme was first introduced as a pilot scheme made under CPR Pt 81, following upon *Practice Guidance: Interim Disclosure Orders* [2012] 1 W.L.R. 1003, issued by the Master of the Rolls in August 2011 (see para.53PG.1 below). Practice Direction 40F is inserted in Pt 40 for convenience. It does not affect the form or content of any order for injunction to which it applies.

I.   Judgments and Orders

Delay in delivering trial judgment

In the first paragraph, replace "Ramnarine v Ramnarine [2013] UKPC 27; see further para.52.10.7 below)." with:

40.2.14   *Ramnarine v Ramnarine* [2013] UKPC 27; [2014] 1 F.L.R. 594, PC; *Nuttal v Kerr* [2019] EWHC 1977 (QB)).

Tomlin orders

Replace the eleventh paragraph (beginning "In a Tomlin order") with:

40.6.2   In a Tomlin order the schedule contains a binding contract between the parties compromising their proceedings. As such it is a simple contract for the purposes of the Limitation Act 1980 i.e., the six-year time limit for enforcement applies. Moreover, an application to enforce obligations contained in the schedule is an application for the court to enforce its own order, to which neither CPR r.17.4 or s.35(3) of the Limitation Act 1980 apply. (*Bostani v Pieper* [2019] EWHC 547 (Comm); [2019] 4 W.L.R. 44 per Jacob J at paras 54–59). The terms of a compromise embodied in a schedule are susceptible to an application for rectification according to the settled principles for the rectification of instruments (e.g *Lloyds TSB Bank Ltd v Crowborough Properties Ltd* [2013] EWCA Civ 107). A settlement contained in a Tomlin order must be construed as a commercial instrument. The aim of the inquiry is not to probe the real intentions of the parties but to ascertain the contextual meaning of the relevant contractual language; the inquiry is objective (*Sirius International Insurance Co (Publ) v FIR General Insurance Ltd* [2004] UKHL 54; [2004] 1 W.L.R. 3251, HL, at [18] per Lord Steyn). In *Community Care North East v Durham County Council* [2010] EWHC 959 (QB); [2012] 1 W.L.R. 338 (Ramsey J), where the submission that the court has a general power to vary the terms of a settlement agreement incorporated in a Tomlin order was rejected (see further para.40.6.3 below), the authorities on the application of contractual remedies to agreements contained in the schedules to such orders (e.g rectification) were explained and applied.

Effect of rule

Replace the third and fourth paragraphs with:

40.8.1 The County Courts Act 1984 s.74 provides for the fixing of the rate of interest payable on judgment debts in County Court proceedings.

In *Simcoe v Jacuzzi UK Group Plc* [2012] EWCA Civ 137; [2012] 1 W.L.R. 2393, CA, the Court of Appeal held that r.40.8(1) was ineffective in the County Court because the CPR were made without the concurrence of the Treasury as required by s.74(1). It held that art.2 of the County Court (Interest on Judgment Debts) Order 1991 (SI 1991/1184) (see Vol.2 para.9B-71), which provided, at that time, that interest on every judgment debt shall carry interest from the date on which the relevant judgment was given, applied and not r.40.8(1). The County Court thus had no power to order otherwise. The 1991 Order was amended, as from 27 May 2019, by the County Courts (Interest on Judgment Debts) (Amendment) Order 2019 (SI 2019/903). The amendments remedy this defect and align the County Court's powers with those of the High Court under r.40.8(1). Under the amended 1991 Order, art.2 and art.2A, provide the County Court with the power to order that interest runs from either a later date than that on which the judgment was given (art.2, as amended) or from a date before the judgment was given (art.2A as inserted). Also see Vol.1 para.16AI.16 and Vol.2 para.9A-565.

Replace Practice Direction 40F with:

PRACTICE DIRECTION 40F—NON-DISCLOSURE ORDERS INFORMATION SCHEME

This Practice Direction supplements CPR Part 40

40FPD.1 **1.** This Practice Direction provides for a scheme for the recording, and transmission to the Ministry of Justice for analysis, of certain data in relation to applications for injunctive relief in civil proceedings to restrain the publication of private or confidential information. The purpose of the scheme is to enable the Ministry of Justice to collate and publish, in anonymised form, information about applications for non-disclosure orders where section 12 of the Human Rights Act 1998 is engaged.

40FPD.2 **2.** The scheme applies in any civil proceedings in the High Court or Court of Appeal in which the court considers an application for a non-disclosure order in civil proceedings to restrain the publication of private or confidential information, the continuation of such an non-disclosure order, or an appeal against the grant or refusal of such an non-disclosure order. The scheme does not apply to proceedings to which the Family Procedure Rules 2010 or the Court of Protection Rules 2017 apply, to immigration or asylum proceedings, to proceedings which raise issues of national security or to proceedings to which Part 21 applies.

40FPD.3 **3.** Except where a direction under paragraph 6 is made, following the hearing of an application for a non-disclosure order or any appeal against the grant or refusal of any such non-disclosure order—

  (a) the legal representatives for the claimant a defendant will agree the information to be included in the Privacy Injunctions Statistics Form in the Annex to this practice direction ("the Form") and the claimant's legal representatives should send the completed Form to the judge or judge's clerk;

(b) the judge will review and record the information specified in paragraph 4 (the information) in a final version of the Form.

40FPD.4   **4.** The information to be included in the Form is—

(a) the application number, parties and claim title (anonymised where appropriate);

(b) whether the hearing was of—

    (i) an application for an interim non-disclosure order;

    (ii) an application for an extension or variation of an interim non-disclosure order or an undertaking to the court;

    (iii) an application for a final non-disclosure order; or

    (iv) an appeal against the grant or refusal of an interim or final non-disclosure order;

(c) whether the hearing was on notice, or without notice to—

    (i) the defendant; or

    (ii) any third party liable to be affected by the order.

(d) whether the parties consented to the order;

(e) whether the defendant was—

    (i) a news media organisation;

    (ii) a social media platform;

    (iii) a search engine;

    (iv) an individual publisher;

    (v) other – please specify;

(f) whether the claimant notified a third party that was—

    (i) a news media organisation;

    (ii) a social media platform;

    (iii) a search engine;

    (iv) an individual publisher;

    (v) other – please specify;

(g) whether any derogations from the principle of open justice were sought, and if so—

    (i) what they were;

    (ii) whether they were granted;

    (iii) if granted whether with the parties' consent.

40FPD.5   **5.** Derogations from the principle of open justice include, but are not limited to—

(a) an order that the hearing be held wholly or partly in private;

(b) an order that the names of one or more of the parties not be disclosed;

(c) an order that access to documents on the court file be restricted (under rule 5.4C or the inherent jurisdiction);

(d) an order that the provision of documents to third parties be restricted (under Practice Direction 25A, paragraph 9.2); and

(e) an order prohibiting disclosure of the existence of the proceedings or the order.

(Rule 39.2 provides for the general rule that a hearing is to be in public, and for the circumstances in which a hearing must be held in private.)

40FPD.6   **6.** Subject to any express direction to the contrary in the order, any order made by the court on an application for a non-disclosure order or appeal from the grant or refusal of such an non-disclosure order shall be deemed to include a provision giving permission to a court officer to transmit the information to the Chief Statistician in the Ministry of Justice in order for it to be analysed and published in such form as does not enable the public identification of the parties to any proceedings.

7. If, in exceptional circumstances, the judge makes any direction under **40FPD.7** paragraph 8, the judge shall report that fact, and the nature of any derogation from open justice contained in the non-disclosure order, to the Master of the Rolls. The Master of the Rolls is, following consultation with the judge, entitled to transmit such information as he sees fit to the Chief Statistician to enable publication by the Ministry of Justice of the bare fact that a non-disclosure order of that type has been made.

8. Once the final version of the Form has been completed, the judge will **40FPD.8** send it or cause it to be sent to the Chief Statistician at the Ministry of Justice.

PART 41

DAMAGES

II. Periodical Payments under the Damages Act 1996

Add new paragraph 41.4.2:

Mesothelioma, payments for ongoing immunotherapy of uncertain cost and duration
 In *Howard v Imperial London Hotels Ltd* [2019] EWHC 202 (QB) Master Thornett sitting in the **41.4.2** specialist Asbestos List in the QBD held that payment for future funding for immunotherapy and chemotherapy for terminal mesothelioma should be by way of interim payments and not by way of the periodical payments procedure.

PART 42

CHANGE OF SOLICITOR

Effect of rule

Replace the second paragraph with:
 Where the solicitor's retainer has been determined but no notice has been given in accordance **42.3.1** with r.42.2, the solicitor can apply for a an order under r.42.3 declaring that they have ceased to act. Having regard to the provisions of r.42.1 and r.42.2(5), the solicitor should do so promptly upon determination of the retainer. The rules do not expressly cater for the situation where someone purports to issue proceedings on behalf of a claimant, giving a solicitor's address for service, without the knowledge and/or authority of the solicitor concerned. On the face of it, CPR r.42.1 treats the unsuspecting solicitor as acting for the claimant until he or she is removed from the record, yet in such circumstances, the solicitor never consciously came on the record. In such circumstances, the lay client is entitled to know if there is a problem which may adversely affect the conduct of the case. Although,

> "it is a moot point whether CPR 42 requires it … the better course in such a situation would be for a formal application to be made by the solicitor to come off the record, under CPR 42.3" (*Jetly v The Secretary of State for the Home Department* [2019] EWHC 204 (Admin)).

PART 44

GENERAL RULES ABOUT COSTS

I. General

The costs which are within the court's discretion—"costs of and incidental to"

Delete the twelfth paragraph (beginning "Normally after a successful").   **44.2.3**

Payment on account of costs (r.44.2(8))

44.2.12   *In the second paragraph, replace "(Allason v Random House UK Ltd [2002] EWHC 1030 (Ch)," with:*
(*Allason v Random House UK Ltd*, 27 February 2002, unrep.,

Proceedings to which the general rule does not apply

44.2.15   *Add new paragraph at end:*
For orders for costs against children and their litigation friends see para.46.4.2.

Judicial review claim—costs at the permission stage

44.2.31   *After the penultimate sentence, add:*
An unsuccessful applicant may be liable for the costs of more than one defendant: *Campaign to Protect Rural England v Secretary of State for Communities and Local Government* [2019] EWCA Civ 1230.

Proportionality

44.3.3   *Replace the first paragraph with:*
When assessing the reasonableness of the costs claimed, the court may, if appropriate and convenient, address the proportionality of any particular item at the same time. That will be a matter for the judge. At the end of the assessment of the reasonableness of the costs, the proportionality of the total figure must be assessed by reference to both rr.44.3(5) and 44.4(1). If the court regards the overall figure as disproportionate, a further assessment is required of those costs which are not properly regarded as unavoidable. Unavoidable costs include court fees and the reasonable element of ATE premiums in clinical negligence cases. That assessment will involve looking at the different categories of costs (such as particular phases or periods) and considering whether the sums allowed as reasonable are nevertheless disproportionate. If they are, they should be reduced as appropriate: *West v Stockport NHS Foundation Trust* [2019] EWCA Civ 1220.

After the second paragraph, add new paragraph:
In considering whether the costs assessed as reasonable are also proportionate, the court may have regard both to its experience of similar cases and to the costs claimed by the opponent. Where both sides have adopted the same approach to costs, it may be that any reduction on the ground of proportionality should be limited: *Malmsten v Bohinc* [2019] EWHC 1386 (Ch).

Proportionality—transitional provisions

44.3.4   *Replace the first paragraph with:*
The test of proportionality provided by r.44.3(2) and (5) does not apply to additional liabilities recoverable under pre-commencement funding arrangements (as defined by r.48.2(1)), in respect of which the test of proportionality set out in r.44.4(2), as it stood before 1 April 2013 (see para.44x.4.2), continues to apply: *BNM v MGN Ltd* [2017] EWCA Civ 1767. The new test does apply to ATE insurance premiums which are recoverable under the Recovery of Costs in Clinical Negligence Proceedings (No. 2) Regulations 2013 (SI 2013/739) in cases commenced on or after 1 April 2013: *Peterborough and Stamford Hospitals NHS Trust v McMenemy* [2017] EWCA Civ 1941. However where the recoverable part of a block-rated premium has been assessed as reasonable, it should be left out of the assessment of the proportionality of the total costs, on the ground that it was an unavoidable cost: *West v Stockport NHS Foundation Trust* [2019] EWCA Civ 1220.

Form for summary assessment (Form N260)

44.6.4   *Add new paragraph at end:*
The court may summarily assess costs in a foreign currency if that properly reflects the party's loss. A party seeking costs in a foreign currency should give proper notice of its intention to do so, explain the basis for seeking them and provide sterling equivalents of the sums claimed: *Cathay Pacific Airlines Ltd v Lufthansa Technik AG* [2019] EWHC 715 (Ch).

Editorial note

44.11.1   *To the end of the fourth paragraph (beginning "So where a solicitor"), add:*
Mistakes or negligence, without more, are insufficient. Where a receiving party's solicitor misstated the risk assessment in the narrative to a bill, but not in a way as to amount to improper or unreasonable conduct, it was appropriate not to make an order under the rule: *Murray v Oxford University Hospitals NHS Trust* [2019] EWHC 539 (QB).

PART 45

FIXED COSTS

IIIA. Claims Which No Longer Continue Under the RTA or EL/PL Pre-Action Protocols and Claims to Which the Pre-Action Protocol for Resolution of Package Travel Claims Applies—Fixed Recoverable Costs

Add new paragraph 45.29I.3:

VAT on medical agency fees

45.29I.3 Where a medical reporting organisation had been instructed to obtain medical records and reports, it was reasonable and proportionate to pay VAT on the whole of the organisation's fee, even if the doctors and hospitals who provided the records and reports were not VAT-registered. The amount at stake was small. The court went on to state that in most cases VAT will be recoverable on the whole of the fees charged by medical reporting agencies: *British Airways Plc v Prosser* [2019] EWCA Civ 547.

Add new paragraph 45.29J.1:

Exceptional circumstances

45.29J.1 The test of "exceptional circumstances" is a high one and the circumstances must be judged against only those cases to which Section IIIA applies and not the totality of cases to which the low value protocols apply: *Ferri v Gill* [2019] EWHC 952 (QB).

VII. Costs Limits in Aarhus Convention Claims

Replace r.45.41(2)(a) with:

Scope and interpretation[1]

45.41 (a) "Aarhus Convention claim" means a claim brought by one or more members of the public by judicial review or review under statute which challenges the legality of any decision, act or omission of a body exercising public functions, and which is within the scope of Article 9(1) or 9(2) or 9(3) of the UNECE Convention on Access to Information, Public Participation in Decision-Making and Access to Justice in Environmental Matters done at Aarhus, Denmark on 25 June 1998 ("the Aarhus Convention");

Effect of Section

In the second paragraph, replace the last sentence with:

45.41.1 The rules in this section were therefore amended further, with effect from 28 February 2017, by extending the scope of the section to include statutory reviews within the scope of art.9(1) or 9(2) and by making provision for the variation of the costs limits and amended again, with effect from 1 October 2019, to include statutory reviews within the scope of art.9(3).

Add new paragraph 45.43.2:

The limits and the assessment of costs

45.43.2 The limits to the amount of costs recoverable do not have a bearing on the approach to the assessment of those costs. On a standard basis assessment the court will allow only those costs which are reasonable and proportionate. Once those costs have been assessed the cap is applied only if the assessed costs would otherwise exceed it: *Campaign to Protect Rural England v Secretary of State for Communities and Local Government* [2019] EWCA Civ 1230.

---

[1] Amended by the Civil Procedure (Amendment) Rules 2017 (SI 2017/95) and the Civil Procedure (Amendment No. 3) Rules 2019 (SI 2019/1118).

PART 46

Costs—Special Cases

I.   Costs Payable by or to Particular Persons

Effect of r.46.1

Add new paragraph at end:

46.1.2   For the costs of *Norwich Pharmacal* applications (applications for disclosure against non-parties in respect of the identity of wrongdoers), see para.31.18.12.

Commercial funders

Add new paragraph at end:

46.2.4   Where the funded party had made unfounded allegations (which had justified an order for costs on the indemnity basis), it was likely that the opponents would incur substantial costs which the funded party would not be able to pay and which would far exceed the amount of the funding and where the funding was structured in such a way that the funder would receive a substantial return on its investment if the funded party succeeded, it was appropriate not to apply the Arkin cap: *Davey v Money* [2019] EWHC 997 (Ch).

Insurers

To the end of the third paragraph (beginning "In a case where insurers of a negligent"), add:

46.2.6   Where professional indemnity insurers continued to fund but relinquished control of the defence of litigation to their insured, and the prospects of success of the insured were assessed as poor, the insurers were ordered to pay the one half of the claimants' costs which were attributable to the way in which the insurers funded the claims: *Various Claimants v Giambrone & Law* [2019] EWHC 34 (QB).

Editorial note

Add new paragraph at end:

46.3.1   Where a trustee was found to be acting in the interests of a pension scheme as a whole by pursuing an appeal to the Supreme Court, it was appropriate for the High Court to make a pre-emptive order in respect of the costs of that appeal. However the estimated costs of the trustee were such that the indemnity should be capped: *Airways Pension Scheme Trustee Ltd v Fielder* [2019] EWHC 29 (Ch).

Add new paragraph 46.4.2:

Costs orders against children and their litigation friends

46.4.2   The litigation friend of an unsuccessful child claimant will usually be ordered to pay the successful defendant's costs: *Slaughter v Talbot* 94 E.R. 839; (1739) Barnes 128. It is doubtful that there was ever a general rule that the litigation friend of an unsuccessful child defendant will not be liable to pay the costs of a successful claimant unless he has been guilty of gross misconduct: *Barker v Confiance Ltd* [2019] EWHC 1401 (Ch). In such a case the court should have regard to all the circumstances when deciding what costs order to make: r.44.2(4). Nor is there a general rule that a child, whether a claimant or a defendant, may not be ordered personally to pay costs unless they have been guilty of fraud or misconduct: *Barker*.

II.   Costs Relating to Legal Representatives

The position of legal representatives acting under conditional fee agreements

To the end of the last paragraph, add:

46.9.4   Affirmed on appeal: [2019] EWCA Civ 527.

PART 47

Procedure for Detailed Assessment of Costs and Default Provisions

VII.   Costs of Detailed Assessment Proceedings

Add new paragraph 47.20.1.1:

Part 36 offers in respect of costs

Although r.36.5(4) provides that Part 36 offers will, with limited exceptions, be treated as **47.20.1.1** inclusive of interest, para.19 of Practice Direction 47 provides that an offer should specify whether or not it is intended to be inclusive of interest and that, unless it states otherwise, an offer will be treated as being inclusive of interest. An offer in relation to costs which expressly excludes interest may still be a valid Part 36 offer, because interest on costs is awarded automatically and is not part of the claim: *Horne v Prescot (No.1) Ltd* [2019] EWHC 1322 (QB); [2019] Costs L.R. 279.

PART 48

Part 2 of the Legal Aid, Sentencing and Punishment of Offenders Act 2012 Relating to Civil Litigation Funding and Costs: Transitional Provision in Relation to Pre-Commencement Funding Arrangements

Effect of CPR Part 48

Replace the second paragraph with:

As indicated above, the significant amendments made by ss.44 and 46 of the 2012 Act relate to **48.0.3** what are defined in r.43.2(1)(k), as it stood before 1 April 2013, as a "funding arrangement", specifically, a CFA providing for the payment of a success fee, an insurance policy taken out against the risk of costs liability, and an agreement with a membership organisation to meet legal costs. The draftsman has met the considerable challenges posed in the drafting of Pt 48 by distinguishing between a funding arrangement as defined by r.43.2(1)(k), made in relation to insolvency-related proceedings, publication or privacy proceedings, or a mesothelioma claim, and a funding arrangement so defined but entered into in relation to other proceedings. Both forms of funding arrangement are defined as a "pre-commencement funding arrangement". In relation to proceedings other than insolvency-related proceedings, publication or privacy proceedings, or a mesothelioma claim, "pre-commencement" means a funding arrangement made before 1 April 2013. In relation to insolvency-related proceedings, publication or privacy proceedings, or a mesothelioma claim, "pre-commencement" means a funding arrangement made at any time before ss.44 and 46 of the 2012 Act come into force; that is to say, at any time before 1 April 2013, or during the subsequent period in which the savings provisions in the 2012 Act and the commencement order explained above may continue to have effect. As noted above (para.48.0.2.4), in relation to insolvency-related proceedings, those saving provisions ceased to have effect on 6 April 2016. In respect of insolvency-related proceedings, ss.44 and 46 came into force on 6 April 2016. In respect of publication and privacy proceedings, s.44 (success fees) came into force on 6 April 2019. However s.46 (after the event insurance premiums) has not as yet been brought into force in respect of those proceedings.

Add new paragraph 48.2.3:

The relevant date for publication and privacy proceedings

In respect of publication and privacy proceedings, s.44 (success fees) but not s.46 (after the event **48.2.3** insurance premiums) came into force on 6 April 2019: Legal Aid, Sentencing and Punishment of Offenders Act 2012 (Commencement No. 13) Order 2018 (SI 2018/1287) art.2.

PART 48

[BEFORE 1 APRIL 2013] COSTS—SPECIAL CASES

Editorial note

Add new paragraph at end:

48x.0.1   The General Principles and Case Law Relating to Costs section has been broken up and parts relocated elsewhere. In particular:
   For the Summary Assessment of Costs, please see para.44SC.1.0.
   For the Guidance Notes on the Application of Section 26(1) of LASPO 2012, please see para.7D-125.
   Pro Bono Costs Guidance is referred to at para.46.7.2.

PART 51

TRANSITIONAL ARRANGEMENTS AND PILOT SCHEMES

Electronic Working Pilot Scheme

Replace the first paragraph with:

51.2.5   Practice Direction 51O made in accordance with r.51.2 was published in CPR Update 82 (October 2015), and supplements r.5.5 (Filing and sending documents), and r.7.12 (Electronic issue of claims), see para.51OPD.1. It originally operated in the Chancery Division of the High Court, the Commercial Court, the Technology and Construction Court, the Circuit Commercial Court, and the Admiralty Court, at the RCJ Rolls Building ("the Rolls Building Jurisdictions"). By CPR Update 100 (September 2018), which substituted the original PD with a new one, it was extended as from 1 January 2019 to proceedings in the Queen's Bench Division. The pilot scheme was further extended by CPR Update 105 (February 2019), with effect from 25 February 2019 to the Business & Property Courts District Registries, as defined in CPR PD 57AA. Guidance on the use of the electronic filing is contained on the website of Her Majesty's Courts and Tribunals Service, see *https://www.gov.uk/guidance/ce-file-system-information-and-support-advice* [Accessed 24 January 2019]. Guidance on the application of the scheme in the Queen's Bench Division is set out in the *Senior Master's Practice Note* of 11 February 2019, see para.51OPN.2. The scheme came into effect on 16 November 2015, and applies to existing claims and claims started on or after that date, save for claims issued in the Queen's Bench Division where it applies to proceedings started after 1 January 2019 unless the court orders its application to existing proceedings. By CPR Update 96 (27 March 2018) the duration of the scheme was extended so that it should run from 16 November 2015 to 6 April 2020. Where there is a conflict between provisions of this Practice Direction and the provisions of Practice Direction 5B (Electronic Communication and Filing of Documents by Email) (para.5BPD.1), the former shall take precedence. Practice Direction 51J (Electronic Working Pilot Scheme), which was made by Update 79 (April 2015) and which operated from 27 April 2015, in the Technology and Construction Court in the High Court at the RCJ Rolls Building was, by Update 81, omitted with effect from 7 December 2015. By CPR Update 109 (30 June 2019) a new para.2.2A was substituted, the effect of which was to make use of the scheme mandatory, as from 1 July 2019, for legally represented parties in the Central Office of the Queen's Bench Division.

Online Civil Money Claims Pilot Scheme

After "pilot scheme's numbering.", add:

51.2.7   Further amendments were made by CPR Update 106 (March 2019), as of 11.00 on 18 March 2019. This update made a number of technical amendments concerning time limits to submit documents. It also introduced a new para.10A, which provides for notification where claims settle.

The County Court Online Pilot

To the end of the paragraph, add:

51.2.8   The pilot scheme was amended by CPR Update 106 (March 2019), as of 11.00 on 18 March 2019. Amendments were made to paras 16, 17.2 and 18 concerning time limits to submit claim forms.

Disclosure Pilot Scheme for the Business and Property Courts

Replace the second paragraph with:

51.2.10   The pilot is operative in the Business and Property Courts only. It applies to proceedings commenced both before and after 1 January 2019. It contains no transitional provisions. The pilot is not, however, of retrospective effect: it does not disturb any disclosure order that had been made before it came into force unless that order is set aside or varied. Where such orders are in place, any further disclosure applications will be subject to the pilot. See the *Chief Master's Practice Note* of 3 December 2018 at [9] (see para.57AB.4); and *UTB LLC v Sheffield United Ltd* [2019] EWHC 914 (Ch), unrep., per Vos C at [16]–[17], where it was stated that

> "[16] The Pilot was deliberately put in place without transitional provisions so that it would apply to all existing proceedings (apart from those specifically excluded) even where an initial disclosure order had been made.
>
> ...
>
> [17] To be clear, I am quite satisfied that the Pilot was intended to apply and does apply, to all relevant proceedings subsisting in the Business and Property Courts, whether started before or after 1st January 2019, even in a case where a disclosure order was made before 1st January 2019 under CPR Part 31."

Also see *UTB LLC v Sheffield United Ltd* [2019] EWHC 914 (Ch), unrep., at [23]–[24] on the approach where proceedings commenced before the pilot scheme came into force. In *Ventra Investments Ltd v Bank Of Scotland Plc* [2019] EWHC 2058 (Comm), unrep., at [35]–[36] Richard Salter QC sitting as a deputy High Court judge noted that the principles underpinning the pilot scheme must not "create a framework for injustice", and that it was necessary to take account of the "significant asymmetry of information between the claimant and defendant" in considering the requirements of para.18.2 of the PD.

The pilot will continue to apply to any proceedings after the pilot concludes to which it applied from 1 January 2019. It does not apply to any proceedings in the County Court. It also does not apply, save where an order to the contrary is made, to the following proceedings: competition claims; public procurement claims; IPEC claims; Admiralty Court claims; claims to which the Shorter and Flexible Trial Scheme applies; claims to which a fixed or capped costs regime applies. Insofar as claims in the Patents Court are concerned, the provisions in CPR PD 63 paras 6.1–6.3 continue to apply, save as modified by the pilot scheme. See para.51UPD.1 and following. For guidance on the application of the pilot scheme to Pt 8 claims, see the *Chief Master's Practice Note* of 27 March 2019 (para.51UPN.1). For guidance on the application of the pilot scheme in the Insolvency and Companies List, see the *Chief Insolvency and Companies Court Judge's Practice Note* of February 2019 (see para.51UPN.2).

Add new paragraph 51.2.13:

New Statement of Costs for Summary Assessment Pilot

51.2.13 Practice Direction 51X made in accordance with r.51.2 was published in CPR Update 104 (February 2019); see para.51XPD.1. Its purpose is to provide, from 1 April 2019 to 31 March 2021, a new Statement of Costs for Summary Assessment. It applies to all claims where "costs are to be summarily assessed, whenever they were commenced"; see PD 51X para.2(b). It provides model Form **N260A** (for costs incurred on an interim application) and Form **N260B** (for costs incurred up to trial), as model statements of costs for use under the pilot scheme.

PRACTICE DIRECTION 51O—THE ELECTRONIC WORKING PILOT SCHEME

General

Replace paragraph 1.1 with:

51OPD.1 **1.1**(1) This Practice Direction is made under rules 5.5, 7.12 and 51.2 of the Civil Procedure Rules ("CPR"). It provides for a pilot scheme ("Electronic Working") to—

(a) operate from 16 November 2015 to 6 April 2020;

(b) operate in—

  (i) the Chancery Division of the High Court, the Commercial Court, the Technology and Construction Court, the Circuit Commercial Court, and the Admiralty Court, at the Royal Courts of Justice, Rolls Building, London (together, "the Rolls Building Jurisdictions");

  (ii) the Central Office of the Queen's Bench Division at the Royal Courts of Justice; and

  (iii) the B&PCs District Registries (as defined in paragraph 1.2 of Practice Direction 57AA); and

(c) apply—

(i)   to existing proceedings and proceedings started on or after 16 November 2015 in the Rolls Building Jurisdictions;

(ii)   in the Central Office of the Queen's Bench Division, to proceedings started after 1 January 2019, and will not apply to existing proceedings unless ordered by the court; and

(iii)   in the B&PCs District Registries, to proceedings started on or after 25 February 2019, and will not apply to existing proceedings unless ordered by the court.

(2)   Electronic Working is a permitted means of electronic delivery of documents to the Court for the purposes of rule 1.46 of the Insolvency (England & Wales) Rules 2016 ("IR 2016").

Usage and operation of Electronic Working

Replace paragraphs 2.2 and 2.2A with:

51OPD.2   **2.2**   Electronic Working applies to and may be used to start and/or continue (subject to the provisions in paragraph 1.1(1)(c)) CPR Part 7, Part 8 and Part 20 claims, pre-action applications including applications under rule 31.16, insolvency proceedings, and arbitration claims in the Rolls Building Jurisdictions, the B&PCs District Registries, and in the Central Office of the Queen's Bench Division.

2.A2   In the Rolls Building Jurisdictions from 1 October 2017—

(a)   for a party who is legally represented, Electronic Working must be used by that party to start and/or continue any relevant claims or applications; and

(b)   for a party who is not legally represented, Electronic Working may be used by that party to start and/or continue any relevant claims or applications.

2.2A   In the Central Office of the Queen's Bench Division—

(a)   from 1 January 2019, for a party who is legally represented, as well as for a party who is not legally represented, Electronic Working may be used by that party to start and/or continue any relevant claims or applications; and

(b)   from 1 July 2019, for a party who is legally represented, Electronic Working must be used by that party to start and/or continue any relevant claims or applications.

Add new paragraphs 2.2B and 2.2C:

2.2B   In the B&PCs District Registries from 25 February 2019, for a party who is legally represented, as well as for a party who is not legally represented, Electronic Working may be used by that party to start and/or continue any relevant claims or applications.

2.2C   In the B&PCs District Registries from 30 April 2019, for a party who is legally represented, Electronic Working must be used by that party to start and/or continue any relevant claims or applications.

Replace paragraph 2.4 with:

2.4   Proceedings issued in the Rolls Building Jurisdictions, the B&PCs District Registries, and the Central Office of the Queen's Bench Division will be stored by the Court as an electronic case file ("the Electronic Working Case File").

Electronic Working and alternate filing methods

Replace paragraph 3.2 with:

51OPD.3   **3.2**   Proceedings which have not been started using Electronic Working may be continued using Electronic Working (subject to the provisions in paragraph

1.1(1)(c)) after documents originally submitted in those proceedings have been converted to PDF format. The proceedings shall then continue as if they had been started using Electronic Working.

General rules regarding issue and filing

Replace paragraph 5.5 with:

5.5 A claim form or other originating application filed by a party using **51OPD.5** Electronic Working will, subject to Acceptance and payment, be issued in the relevant Rolls Building Jurisdiction, B&PC District Registry, or Central Office of the Queen's Bench Division and the claim will proceed in that Court unless it is transferred to another Court.

Service

Replace paragraph 8.2 with:

8.2 Unless the Court orders otherwise, any document filed by any party or **51OPD.8** issued by the Court using Electronic Working in the Rolls Building Jurisdictions, the B&PCs District Registries, and Central Office of the Queen's Bench Division which is required to be served shall be served by the parties and not the Court.

Transfer of proceedings and file transmission

Replace paragraph 9.3 with:

9.3 If proceedings are transferred into one of the Rolls Building Jurisdic- **51OPD.9** tions, or one of the B&PCs District Registries, or the Central Office of the Queen's Bench Division, all filing subsequent to the order transferring those proceedings may be done using Electronic Working after documents originally submitted in those proceedings have been converted to PDF format in accordance with paragraphs 3.2 and 3.3.

PRACTICE DIRECTION 51R—THE ONLINE CIVIL MONEY CLAIMS PILOT

Add entry for Section 10A to the Table of Contents:

Contents of this Practice Direction

Add new paragraph 51RPD.10.1:

Section 10A—Informing the court that the claim has been settled

Informing the court that the claim has been settled

10A.1(1) If the claimant uses the OCMC website to tell the court that the **51RPD.10.1** claim has been settled, the court must notify the defendant. When the court notifies the defendant, it must also tell the defendant that the claim will be stayed, unless the defendant contacts the court, on time, to object.

(2) The defendant contacts the court on time if they contact the court within 19 days after notification by the court.

(3) If the defendant objects on time, the court must transfer the claim out of Online Civil Money Claims to the "CCBC" (as defined).

(4) If the defendant does not object on time, the court must "stay" the proceedings (as defined).

Section 14—Submitting Documents at Court—Timing of Submitting, and Responsibility for Submitting on Time

Submitting documents at court– timing of submitting, and responsibility for submitting on time

Replace paragraph 14.1 with:

51RPD.14   **14.1**(1) If the OCMC website is functioning normally so that it can receive forms and documents, and the court receives a form or document at or after 4p.m., that form or document is treated as submitted before 4p.m. on the next day the court office is open.

(2)   If—

(a) the OCMC website is malfunctioning and cannot receive forms and/or documents;

(b) that malfunction starts before but continues up to or beyond 4 p.m. on a particular day; and

(c) that malfunction alone prevents a person from being able to submit a form or document within a time limit imposed by this practice direction or in "directions" (as defined),

a judge must give directions to alter the time limit for submitting that form or document, so that the time limit does not expire until after the website is again functioning normally. The judge's directions may be expressed to apply to a specific claim, or may apply more generally, for example to any number of claims, or to claims of a particular type.

(3)   If a time limit imposed by this practice direction or in directions expires on a day when the CCBC (as defined) is closed, a form or document is still submitted on time if it is submitted before 4p.m. on the next day the court office is open.

(4)   Where any time limit applies (whether imposed by this practice direction or in any other way) it is the relevant party's responsibility to ensure that a form or document is submitted on time.

(Civil Procedure Rule Practice Direction 2A paragraph 3.2 sets out the days when court offices (including the CCBC) are closed.)

PRACTICE DIRECTION 51S—THE COUNTY COURT ONLINE PILOT

Section 5—Submitting Online Claim Forms at Court—Timing of Submitting and Responsibility for Submitting on Time

Replace paragraphs 16, 17 and 18 with:

51SPD.5   **16.** If the County Court Online website is functioning normally so that it can receive forms, and the court receives an online claim form at or after 4p.m., that form is treated as submitted before 4p.m. on the next day the court office is open.

17. If—

17.1. the County Court Online website is malfunctioning and cannot receive forms;

17.2. that malfunction starts before but continues up to or beyond 4 p.m. on a particular day; and

17.3. that malfunction alone prevents a legal representative from being able to submit an online claim form within a time limit imposed by the Civil Procedure Rules or by the court,

a judge must give directions to alter the time limit for submitting that form, so that the time limit does not expire until after the website is again functioning normally. The judge's directions may be expressed to apply to a specific claim, or may apply more generally, for example to any number of claims, or to claims of a particular type.

18. If a time limit imposed by the Civil Procedure Rules or the court expires on a day when the CCMCC is closed, an online claim form is still submitted on time if it is submitted before 4p.m. on the next day the court office is open.

PRACTICE DIRECTION 51U—DISCLOSURE PILOT FOR THE BUSINESS AND PROPERTY COURTS

Add new paragraph 51UPD.0:

Editorial Introduction

The Disclosure pilot scheme is the result of concerns that reforms to CPR Pt 31 introduced in **51UPD.0** 1999 and then in 2013 had failed to introduce a more proportionate, economical and efficient approach to disclosure. Those concerns resulted in the formation of a Disclosure Working Group in 2016. It identified a number of problems with Pt 31, including a failure on the part of both the courts and parties to use the full range of disclosure options, set out in CPR r.31.5. Standard disclosure too often remained the default. Additionally, Pt 31 was noted to be insufficiently able to deal with e-disclosure.

The pilot scheme is intended to remedy the various problems with disclosure, and not least to ensure that a new, proportionate, culture of disclosure was embedded into the litigation process. As Vos C has made clear the pilot is more than a revision of Pt 31. It is intended to operate "along different lines driven by reasonableness and proportionality" (*UTB LLC v Sheffield United Ltd* [2019] EWHC 914 (Ch), at [75]). Under the pilot, disclosure is to be focused on the key issues for disclosure (see PD 51U paras 2.4 and 7.3). In this way the pilot is intended to strike a better balance between wider disclosure, where and only where that is appropriate, and the aim of reducing the amount of unnecessary documentary disclosure, either because it is irrelevant or peripheral to the issues in dispute. To effect the necessary culture change the court is required to take a more pro-active approach to the case management of the disclosure process (see, for instance, PD 51U paras 6.2, 6.4 and 8.2 in respect of extended disclosure) and parties must ensure that they act consistently with the Disclosure Duties contained in para.3 of PD 51U, and particularly those placed on legal representatives set out in paras 3.2(3) to (5).

Add new paragraph 51UPD.2.1:

Principles and known adverse documents

In *Obaid v Al-Hezaimi* [2019] EWHC 1953 (Ch), Falk J at [43] accepted that "known adverse **51UPD.2.1** documents" (CPR PD51U para.2.8) was a broad concept that could encompass matters not dealt with in statements of case. The judge also noted that important considerations in ensuring that disclosure was reasonable and proportionate such that a fair resolution of civil proceedings could be achieved (see para.2.1) were the need to avoid ambush and to enable parties a proper opportunity to respond to allegations. At [44] Falk J held that the provisions in the pilot scheme concerning adverse documents did not require the court to admit such documents. The pilot scheme and its provisions were subject to the general power set out in CPR r.32.1 to exclude otherwise admissible evidence.

Add new paragraph 51UPD.5.1:

Whether Initial Disclosure should be dispensed with by the parties

Except where one of the justifications set out in PD 51U para.5.3 for dispensing with Initial **51UPD.5.1** Disclosure applies, the provision of Initial Disclosure is required. Parties should consider carefully if one of the reasons for dispensing with Initial Disclosure does apply, see PD 51U paras 5.3 and 5.8.

Add new paragraph 51UPD.6.1:

Consideration of factors to determine whether to order Extended Disclosure

One of the problems identified by the Disclosure Working Party with CPR Pt 31 was that **51UPD.6.1** standard disclosure was too often adopted as a default form of order. Care should be taken by both the court and parties to ensure that a similar approach is not taken to Extended Disclosure i.e., that ordering Extended Disclosure and "Model D" Disclosure, under PD 51U para.8.3, does not become a "default" approach.

When considering whether it is "reasonable and proportionate having regard to the overriding objective", to grant an application for extended disclosure each of the factors set out in para.6.4 of PD 51U are to be given weight. In a complex and important case, the third, fourth and seventh factors are likely to have particular importance (*UTB LLC v Sheffield United Ltd* [2019] EWHC 914 (Ch), at [76]). In *Merck Sharp & Dohme Ltd v Wyeth LLC* [2019] EWHC 1692 (Pat), Arnold J, in considering an application for disclosure, accepted that a wide-ranging search would be both costly and disproportionate. In the circumstances, disclosure on a specific issue was justified. He also noted that a further application for wider disclosure could be made in the future, if justified.

Add new paragraph 51UPD.11.1:

When to seek court guidance

51UPD.11.1 In *Vannin Capital PCC v RBOS Shareholders Action Group Ltd* [2019] EWHC 1617 (Ch), Joanna Smith QC, sitting as a deputy High Court judge, was critical of the parties failure to seek guidance from the court on the question whether an application for further searches under CPR PD51U para.17 fell within the scope of an existing order for extended disclosure. Such guidance could have narrowed issues between the parties. As the parties had explored the issues in correspondence and not resolved the issues between them, such guidance from the court was particularly pertinent and ought to have been sought. If guidance had been sought it could have saved court and party time and costs. As such it would have furthered the aims of the pilot scheme (see para.51UPD.0).

Add new paragraph 51UPD.18.1:

Variation of order for extended disclosure

51UPD.18.1 In *Vannin Capital PCC v RBOS Shareholders Action Group Ltd* [2019] EWHC 1617 (Ch), Joanna Smith QC sitting as a deputy High Court judge, considered applications to vary an order for extended disclosure (CPR PD 51U para.18.1) and for further searches (CPR PD 51U para.17). The judge was critical of the approach to the applications taken by the parties, which was noted to be contrary to the spirit of the pilot scheme. A more co-operative manner was required by the culture change inherent in the pilot scheme's approach (see paras 51UPD.0 and 51UPD.11.1). The judge further held at [8]–[10] that the power to vary orders under CPR r.3.1(7) did not apply to applications to vary orders for extended disclosure: that general power gave way to the specific power to vary set out in CPR PD51U paras 18.1 and 18.2. As such the criteria applicable to applications to vary under CPR r.3.1(7) set out in *Tibbles v SIG Plc* [2012] EWCA Civ 518; [2012] 1 W.L.R. 2591, CA, were not applicable to applications to vary extended disclosure under the pilot scheme. While the power to vary under paras 18.1 and 18.2 was focused more clearly on applications to expand the scope of an order, the judge considered that the power to vary could be applied to reduce the scope of an extant disclosure order. The question to determine, as in this case, where a reduction in the scope of an extant order was sought was whether it was reasonable and proportionate to reduce the scope of the existing order: see [11]–[13].

Add new Practice Note, "Disclosure Pilot Practice Note":

DISCLOSURE PILOT PRACTICE NOTE

51UPN.1 1. This note applies to claims in the following lists in the Business and Property Courts of England and Wales:
- Business List (ChD) (and its sub-lists)
- Insolvency and Companies List
- Intellectual Property List
- Property Trusts and Probate List
- Revenue List

2. Practitioners have expressed uncertainty about whether the disclosure pilot applies to Part 8 claims. This note is intended to provide guidance. It is not, however, authoritative about the meaning of the Practice Direction.

3. The pilot does not directly apply to Part 8 claims because Part 8 contains its own regime for the disclosure of documents that are relied on by the parties.

4. The only statement of case in a Part 8 claim is the claim form. Paragraph 5.1 of the Practice Direction says there is no obligation to give Initial Disclosure with the Part 8 claim form. This is to ensure that the provisions relating to Initial Disclosure do not overlap with, and duplicate, the provisions in Part 8.

5. The court has power to make an order for extended disclosure under the pilot in a case proceeding under Part 8. It will adopt such elements of the Practice Direction as are appropriate to the case and the scope of

disclosure that is sought. The party requesting disclosure will need to identify the issues for disclosure and the Model or Models that apply. It is not expected that the full procedure for extended disclosure, including completion of all elements of the Disclosure Review Document, will normally be required.

Chief Master Marsh
27 March 2019

Add new "Message from the Chief Insolvency and Companies Court Judge":

MESSAGE FROM THE CHIEF INSOLVENCY AND COMPANIES COURT JUDGE

This note relates to Practice Direction 51U - Disclosure Pilot for the Business **51UPN.2** and Property Courts ('the Disclosure Pilot').

The provisions of the Disclosure Pilot apply to the Insolvency and Companies List. The Disclosure Pilot does not apply to Practice Direction 51P that provides the procedure for Insolvency Express Trials.

The Disclosure Pilot applies to Part 7 proceedings with statements of case. Part 7 claims without particulars of claim and Part 8 claims are expressly excluded from certain of its requirements. Forms of originating process familiar to users of the Insolvency and Companies List, such as petitions and applications, are not 'statements of case' for the purpose of the Disclosure Pilot. An exception is made for petitions issued for relief pursuant to sections 994-996 of the Companies Act 2006 and/or for winding up on the just and equitable ground, since these are analogous to Part 7 proceedings with statements of case.

The Court may, as part of its case management powers, consider it appropriate to order disclosure in proceedings commenced by Part 8 claim, petition or application, either of its own motion or on the application of a party. As the Disclosure Pilot replaces Part 31 of the CPR, such disclosure will be in accordance with the Disclosure Pilot's provisions.

February 2019

Add new Practice Direction 51X and Editorial note:

PRACTICE DIRECTION 51X—NEW STATEMENT OF COSTS FOR SUMMARY ASSESSMENT PILOT

General

1. This Practice Direction is made under rule 51.2. It provides for a pilot of **51XPD.1** a new Statement of Costs for Summary Assessment.

2. The pilot scheme will—
a) operate from 1st April 2019 to 31st March 2021;
b) apply to all claims in which costs are to be summarily assessed, whenever they were commenced.

3. Where the provisions of this Practice Direction conflict with other provisions of the rules or other practice directions, this Practice Direction takes precedence.

The Statement of Costs for Summary Assessment Pilot

4. Forms N260A and N260B (annexed to this Practice Direction) are model **51XPD.2** forms of Statement of Costs which may be used for summary assessments while the scheme is in force. The N260A applies when the costs have been incurred on an interim application. The N260B applies when the costs have been incurred up to trial.

5. Forms N260A and N260B contain a documents schedule. The documents schedule may be created from electronic time records by filtering the time that is recorded under the activity described in Schedule 2 to PD47 as '10 - Plan, Prepare, Draft, Review'. This may then be sorted and presented first by grade of fee earner and then chronologically.

6. Where parties or their legal representatives use form N260A or N260B instead of form N260, a reference in the rest of the CPR to form N260 is treated as a reference to form N260A or N260B as appropriate, and a reference to a statement of costs is treated as including a reference to a statement of cost in form N260A or N260B as appropriate.

7. Forms N260A and N260B are available in paper/pdf form and in electronic spreadsheet form. Parties and their legal representatives may use the paper/pdf form only. If they use the electronic spreadsheet form they must file and serve the paper/pdf form and at the same time provide the electronic spreadsheet form to the paying party and to the court, by e-mail or other electronic means.

8. In any case which has been the subject of a costs management order, any party filing form N260B for summary assessment in accordance with Practice Direction 44 paragraph 9.5(4) must also file and serve form Precedent Q at the same time.

Editorial note

51XPD.3   The Annexes attached to this Practice Direction (Annex A Form **N260A** and Annex B Form **N260B**) can be found under Civil Procedure Forms in the online Civil Procedure Forms Volume.

PART 52

Appeals

I. Scope and interpretation

Appeals in contempt proceedings

After the second paragraph, add new paragraph:

52.1.7   In *McKendrick v Financial Conduct Authority* [2019] EWCA Civ 524, Hamblen LJ stated at [37]–[38] that the Court of Appeal would be reluctant to interfere with a judge's decision on sentencing for contempt. He stated that it would generally only do so if the judge had: (i) made an error of principle; (ii) took account of immaterial factors or failed to take account of material ones; or, (iii) reached a sentencing decision that was plainly wrong in that it was outside the range of decisions a judge could reasonably make.

Add new paragraph 52.1.17:

Appeals from undertaking

52.1.17   For appeals from undertakings see para.25.1.14.2, below, and *Schettini v Silvestri* [2019] EWCA Civ 349, CA.

II. Permission to Appeal—General

Effect of rule

To the end of the first paragraph, add:

52.5.1   This rule does not contravene the right to fair trial at common law or under art.6 European Convention on Human Rights, see *R. (Siddiqui) v Lord Chancellor* [2019] EWCA Civ 1040.

Test for permission for first appeals

Replace the fourth paragraph with:

In *Swain v Hillman* [2001] 1 All E.R. 91, CA, Lord Woolf MR discussed the meaning of "real **52.6.2** prospect of succeeding" in r.24.2. The court had to consider whether there was a realistic, as opposed to a fanciful, prospect of success. In *Tanfern Ltd v Cameron-MacDonald (Practice Note)* [2000] 1 W.L.R. 1311, CA, at [21], Brooke LJ cited *Swain v Hillman* and stated that the same approach should be adopted in relation to, what is now, r.52.6(1)(a). In *R. (A Child)* [2019] EWCA Civ 895 at [29]–[31], Peter Jackson LJ in disapproving of the approach taken in *NLW v ARC* [2012] 2 F.L.R. 129 which stated that the test was one that required an appellant to demonstrate that the proposed appeal had a greater than 50/50 prospect of succeeding, re-affirmed that the test for permission to appeal to the Family Court, High Court or Court of Appeal was that set out in *Swain* and in *Tanfern*. As he put it, there is no requirement to demonstrate that success is probable or more likely than not. Where the basis of a permission to appeal application is a challenge to a trial judge's findings of fact, given the requirement that the appeal court will need to be satisfied that those findings were either unsupported by the evidence before the judge or that the decision subject to challenge was one that no reasonable judge court have reached (*The Mayor and Burgesses of the Haringey LBC v Ahmed & Ahmed* [2017] EWCA Civ 1861, CA, at [29]–[31]), meeting the "real prospect of success" test for permission to appeal will be a difficult test to satisfy (also see paras 52.21.3, 52.21.5).

IV. Additional Rules

Effect of rule

Replace the second paragraph with:

In Practice Direction 52C (Appeals to the Court of Appeal), para.30 (Amendment of appeal **52.17.1** notice) and para.8(4) (Respondent's notice) supplement r.52.17 in circumstances where it applies to appeals to the Court of Appeal (paras 52CPD.8 and 52CPD.30 below). Where a proposed amendment raises a power argued in the lower court, if it is sought timeously, it may not prejudice the parties or litigants in other appeals, it may be permitted, subject to the general principles governing amendments. See the commentary to Pt 17. Where a proposed amendment raises a point not argued in the lower court, see para.52.21.1.1.

Delete paragraph 52.17.2, "Point raised below".

Delete paragraph 52.17.3, "Point not raised below".

Add new paragraph 52.21.1.1:

Appeal on point not raised at trial

The stance which the Court of Appeal should take towards a point not raised at trial in the High **52.21.1.1** Court or in the County Court and raised for the first time on appeal in the court, either in the original notice of appeal or on an application to amend the notice, has been explained in a number of authorities. It is a discretion that "ought to be most jealously scrutinised" (per Lord Herschell in *The Tasmania* (1890) 15 App. Cas. 223 at 225). The principles were set out in *Pittalis v Grant* [1989] Q.B. 605, CA, at 611 where the Court of Appeal held that the same principles apply to appeals from the County Court as from the High Court. (For other pre-CPR authorities, see *Supreme Court Practice 1999* Vol.1 paras 59/10/10 and 59/19/5.) They were summarised in *Singh v Dass* [2019] EWCA Civ 360 and *Notting Hill Finance Ltd v Sheikh* [2019] EWCA Civ 1337 at [23]–[26]. As stated by Haddon-Cave LJ in *Singh* at [16]–[18] the principles governing the discretion are:

> "[16] First, an appellate court will be cautious about allowing a new point to be raised on appeal that was not raised before the first instance court.
>
> [17] Second, an appellate court will not, generally, permit a new point to be raised on appeal if that point is such that either (a) it would necessitate new evidence or (b), had it been run below, it would have resulted in the trial being conducted differently with regards to the evidence at the trial (*Mullarkey v Broad* [2009] EWCA Civ 2 at [30] and [49]).
>
> [18] Third, even where the point might be considered a 'pure point of law', the appellate court will only allow it to be raised if three criteria are satisfied: (a) the other party has had adequate time to deal with the point; (b) the other party has not acted to his detriment on the faith of the earlier omission to raise it; and (c) the other party can be adequately protected in costs. (*R (on the application of Humphreys) v Parking and Traffic Appeals Service* [2017] EWCA Civ 24; [2017] R.T.R. 22 at [29])."

Also see *Glatt v Sinclair* [2013] EWCA Civ 241; [2013] 1 W.L.R. 3602. There is no general rule that a case needs to be exceptional for an appellate court to permit a new point to be raised on appeal, see Snowden J in *Notting Hill Finance Ltd* at [26]–[28], explaining the reference to "exceptionality" in May LJ's judgment in *Jones v MBNA International Bank* [2000] EWCA Civ 514 at [52]. Also see *Crane v Sky In-Home Ltd* [2008] EWCA Civ 978 at [18]–[22] where Arden LJ identified a number of factors which would be fatal to an application to raise a new point on appeal. If the appellant wishes to raise a new point on appeal, this may necessitate amendment of the original pleadings. The Court of Appeal has power in an appropriate case to allow such an amendment, even if it was not sought in the court below (*Islington LBC v UCKAC* [2006] EWCA Civ 340; [2006] 1 W.L.R. 1303, at [36]-[41]). Nevertheless, in the absence of permission to amend, the court's jurisdiction is constrained by what is in the grounds of appeal and in the grant of permission (*Gover v Propertycare Ltd* [2006] EWCA Civ 286; [2006] I.C.R. 1073 at [10]). A third party who has been joined in an action, and is therefore bound by findings made between the claimant and the defendant, is entitled to advance on an appeal any defence which might have been available to the defendant had he chosen to appeal (*Den Danske Bank A/S v Surinam Shipping Ltd* [2014] UKPC 10).

Grounds for allowing appeal (r.51.21(3))

In the third paragraph, replace "Manning v Stylianou [2006] EWCA Civ 1655; 26 October 2006, unrep., CA," with:

52.21.5   *Manning v Stylianou* [2006] EWCA Civ 1655

Replace the fifth and sixth paragraphs with:
　　Guidance on the approach an appeal court should take in considering alleged errors of fact by the lower court was given in *Assicurazioni Generali SpA v Arab Insurance Group (Practice Note)* [2002] EWCA Civ 1642; [2003] 1 W.L.R. 577, CA, at [6]-[23] per Clarke LJ and [193]-[197] per Ward LJ. As Lloyd LJ (with whom Sullivan and Laws LJJ agreed) put it in *Cook v Thomas* [2010] EWCA Civ 227 at [48],
　　　　"an appellate court can hardly ever overturn primary findings of fact by a trial judge who has seen the witnesses give evidence in a case in which credibility was in issue".
The degree of deference which is due to the findings of primary fact made by the judge below will, however, depend upon the nature and circumstances of the case. The approach of the court in this kind of case (absent any fresh evidence) should be the same, whether it is conducting a review or a rehearing.
　　Where a judge's evaluation of facts is challenged, it is properly understood to be very difficult for an appellate court to place itself in the position of the trial judge who would have had to take account of both written and oral evidence. As Lord Hoffmann explained it in *Biogen Inc v Medeva Plc* [1997] R.P.C. 1 at 45, an appellate court must be cautious in reversing a trial judge's evaluation of facts, just as it must be in reversing a primary finding of fact. The reasons for this approach, and authorities, are summarised in Lewison LJ's judgment in *Fage UK Ltd v Chobani UK Ltd* [2014] EWCA Civ 5; [2014] E.T.M.R. 26 at [114]-[115]. Authoritative guidance on the approach that appellate courts should take when called upon to assess a trial judge's evaluation of facts was given by the Supreme Court in *Re B (A Child) (Care Proceedings: Threshold Criteria)* [2013] UKSC 33; [2013] 1 W.L.R. 1911, *McGraddie v McGraddie* [2013] UKSC 58; [2013] 1 W.L.R. 2477 and *R. (R) v Chief Constable of Greater Manchester* [2018] UKSC 47; [2018] 1 W.L.R. 4079, and by the Court of Appeal in *IBM United Kingdom Holdings Ltd v Dalgleish* [2017] EWCA Civ 1212; [2018] I.C.R. 1681 at 1764-5. The authorities, and particularly *Re B*, are well-summarised in *Prescott v Potamianos (also known as Re Sprintroom)* [2019] EWCA Civ 932 in a judgment of the court (McCombe, Leggatt and Rose LJJ) at [72]-[78]. The proper approach in the light of the authorities was (at [76]) that
　　　　"... on a challenge to an evaluative decision of a first instance judge, the appeal court does not carry out a balancing task afresh but must ask whether the decision of the judge was wrong by reason of some identifiable flaw in the judge's treatment of the question to be decided, 'such as a gap in logic, a lack of consistency, or a failure to take account of some material factor, which undermines the cogency of the conclusion'".
(Also see para.52.21.2 on assessment of witness evidence.)

At the end of the seventh paragraph (beginning "In Manning v Stylianou"), delete the last sentence.

Delete the eighth paragraph (beginning "As to what constitutes").

In the ninth paragraph, replace "(In re C (A Child) (Adoption: Placement order) (Practice Note) [2013] EWCA Civ 431; [2013] 1 W.L.R. 3720, CA, at para.39 per Sir James Munby P; Piglowska v Piglowski [1999] 1 W.L.R. 1360, HL, at p.1372 per Lord Hoffmann)." with:
　　(*Re C (A Child) (Adoption: Placement order) (Practice Note)* [2013] EWCA Civ 431; [2013] 1 W.L.R. 3720, CA, at [39] per Sir James Munby P; *Piglowska v Piglowski* [1999] 1 W.L.R. 1360, HL, at 1372 per Lord Hoffmann).

Delete the tenth and eleventh paragraphs (beginning "An alternative formulation").

Add new paragraph 52.21.9:

Assessors in Appeals
52.21.9   The Court of Appeal may sit with assessors, such as costs assessors, see para.35.15.1 and following. It may also sit with nautical assessors in appeals from admiralty proceedings: see *Practice Direction (Admiralty Appeals: Assessors)* [1965] 1 W.L.R. 853.

V. Special Provisions Relating to the Court of Appeal

Hear-by dates and listing windows—expedited hearings

Replace the second paragraph with:
    In PD 57AB–Shorter and Flexible Trials Schemes, para.2.60 states that the Court of Appeal will **52.23.3** seek to take into account the fact that a case was in the Shorter Trials Scheme, as provided for by that Practice Direction, and the desire for expedition, in deciding when applications for permission to appeal will be considered and when appeals will be listed (see para.57ABPD.2).

PART 53

After Part 52, add new Part 53 (retaining the existing Part 53):

[Issued from 1 October 2019] Media and Communications Claims

Editorial introduction
    Well over five years since the Defamation Act 2013 came into effect, Pt 53 has finally been **53n.0** brought up to date (by the Civil Procedure (Amendment No. 3) Rules 2019 (SI 2019/1118)) to reflect the changes made in the Act, and to recognise the existence of the Media and Communications List ("the MAC List"). The MAC List is to a degree the successor of the old Jury List, although defamation claims are now tried by judge alone, not by jury, and it encompasses claims for misuse of private information, claims in data protection, and claims in harassment by publication, which were only ever tried by judges.
    There are now two Practice Directions. Practice Direction 53A deals with transfer of proceedings to and from the MAC List, and 53B is a substantially amended update of the old PD 53, giving valuable guidance on a wide range of matters of practice and pleading, extended beyond defamation to cover the new MAC List causes of action.
    However, the new Pt 53, and the new Practice Directions, do not apply to claims issued before 1 October 2019 (see CPR Update 109–Practice Direction Amendments (30 June 2019), para.1(b), (c)). The old Pt 53 and Practice Direction 53 will therefore continue to apply to claims issued before 1 October 2019. For the old Part 53, see para.53.0.1, and for the Practice Direction, and the commentary to it, see para.53PD.1.

Scope of this Part[1]
    53.1—(1) This Part contains rules about media and communications claims. 53n.1
    (2) A "media and communications claim" means a claim which—
        (a) satisfies the requirements of paragraph (3) or (4); and
        (b) has been issued in or transferred into the Media and Communications List.
    (3) A High Court claim must be issued in the Media and Communications List if it is or includes a claim for defamation, or is or includes—
        (a) a claim for misuse of private information;
        (b) a claim in data protection law; or
        (c) a claim for harassment by publication.
    (4) Subject to Part 63 and any other applicable provisions, a claim not falling within paragraph (3) may be issued in the Media and Communications List if the claim arises from—
        (a) the publication or threatened publication of information via the media, online or in speech; or
        (b) other activities of the media,
and the claimant considers it is suitable for resolution in that list.

Scope of Part 53
    Rule 53.1(3) obliges claimants to issue claims in the MAC List if they are or include claims in **53n.1.1** defamation (i.e. libel or slander), misuse of private information, data protection law or harassment by publication. Surprisingly, that excludes malicious falsehood. Less surprisingly, it also excludes claims in breach of confidence, which are often brought in tandem with claims for misuse of

---

[1] Introduced by the Civil Procedure (Amendment No. 3) Rules 2019 (SI 2019/1118).

private information. That is sensible, for if a claim in confidence is coupled with a privacy claim, r.53.1(3) will require it to be issued in the MAC List; but many confidence claims (for example, where trade secrets are concerned) may have little or nothing to do with publication in the media or elsewhere.

The scope of r.53.1(4), which covers claims which claimants may (but are not obliged to) issue in the MAC List, is wide enough to embrace causes of action in malicious falsehood and passing off, as well as suitable claims in confidence. Note, however, that the apparent width of r.53.1(4) is expressly made subject to the provisions of Pt 63, which deals with Intellectual Property Proceedings.

Specialist list[1]

53n.2   **53.2—(1) The Media and Communications List is a specialist list of the High Court.**

(2) One of the Judges of the Queen's Bench Division shall be the Judge in Charge of the Media and Communications List.

(3) A Media and Communications List Judge is a judge authorised by the President of the Queen's Bench Division, in consultation with the Chancellor of the High Court, to hear claims in the Media and Communications List.

(4) All proceedings in the Media and Communications List will be heard by a Media and Communications Judge, or by a Master of the Queen's Bench Division, except that—

> **(a)   another judge of the Queen's Bench Division or Chancery Division may hear urgent applications if no Media and Communications Judge is available; and**

> **(b)   unless the court otherwise orders, any application relating to enforcement of a Media and Communications List order or judgment for the payment of money will be dealt with by a Master of the Queen's Bench Division or District Judge.**

Specialist list

53n.2.1   The requirement of consultation with the Chancellor of the High Court (see r.53.2(3)) envisages that Chancery judges may be appointed as judges of the MAC List. Chancery judges may also hear urgent applications in the list (r.53.2(4)). While High Court MAC List privacy and data protection claims must be issued in the Queen's Bench Division (see r.53.4), there is a wide discretion to order transfer out the MAC List (see 53APD.1 paras 3–5, below).

Application of the Civil Procedure Rules[2]

53n.3   **53.3 These Rules and their practice directions apply to claims in the Media and Communications List unless this Part or a practice direction provides otherwise.**

(Practice Direction 53B makes provision as to statements of case, and for certain kinds of application, in media and communications claims.)

Proceedings in the Media and Communications List[3]

53n.4   **53.4—(1) A media and communications claim that is issued in the High Court must be issued in the Queen's Bench Division, Royal Courts of Justice, and marked in the top left corner "Media and Communications List".**

(2) A media and communications claim that is issued in a District Registry of the High Court must be transferred either to the County Court or to the Royal Courts of Justice (as appropriate).

Proceedings in the Media and Communications List

53n.4.1   This provision will prevent future claimants from issuing privacy claims in the Chancery Division (as Cliff Richard did: *Richard v BBC* [2018] EWHC 1837 (Ch); [2019] Ch. 169). But there will be nothing to stop them applying to transfer the claim out of the MAC List to another court or division: see the wide discretion provided by PD 53A at para.53APD.1 paras 3, 4 and 5. Moreover, there appears to be no reason why a Chancery judge should not be authorised under r.53.2(3) to hear claims in the MAC List. That seems to be envisaged by the requirement of consultation with

---

[1] Introduced by the Civil Procedure (Amendment No. 3) Rules 2019 (SI 2019/1118).
[2] Introduced by the Civil Procedure (Amendment No. 3) Rules 2019 (SI 2019/1118).
[3] Introduced by the Civil Procedure (Amendment No. 3) Rules 2019 (SI 2019/1118).

the Chancellor of the High Court; and see also r.53.2(4)(a), which permits Chancery judges (as well as other judges of the QBD) to hear urgent applications if no MAC judge is available.

Any MAC claims issued in a District Registry must be transferred to the Royal Courts of Justice or to the County Court, as appropriate. No doubt the purpose of this provision is to ensure that case management and interlocutory decisions in complex cases are dealt with by specialist judges, but the width of the provisions for transfer to another court or list (PD 53A, para.5) is such that there is unlikely to be any difficulty in obtaining transfer of the trial of a claim to a court centre more convenient to the parties and witnesses.

Summary disposal under the Defamation Act 1996[1]

53n.5

53.5—(1) This rule provides for summary disposal in accordance with the Defamation Act 1996 ("the Act").

(2) In proceedings for summary disposal under sections 8 and 9 of the Act, rules 24.4 (procedure), 24.5 (evidence) and 24.6 (directions) apply.

(3) An application for summary judgment under Part 24 may not be made if—

> **(a) an application has been made for summary disposal in accordance with the Act, and that application has not been disposed of; or**
>
> **(b) summary relief has been granted on an application for summary disposal under the Act.**

(4) The court may on any application for summary disposal direct the defendant to elect whether or not to make an offer to make amends under section 2 of the Act.

(5) When it makes a direction under paragraph (4), the court must specify the time by which and the manner in which—

> **(a) the election is to be made; and**
>
> **(b) the notification of it is to be given to the court and the other parties.**

Summary disposal

53n.5.1

This rule reproduces the old CPR 53.2, and gives effect to the regime for summary disposal of defamation claims introduced by ss.8 to 10 of the Defamation Act 1996. See also PD 53B para.7 at para.53BPD.7 below.

The summary disposal procedure enables the court to consider the strength of claim and defence at any stage and to dispose of the claim summarily at the instance of either party. It provides an alternative to summary judgment under Pt 24, but it is now very rarely used. For a recent consideration of this "antique procedural weapon", see *Alsaifi v Amunwa* [2017] EWHC 1443 (QB); [2017] 4 W.L.R. 172 at [56], where the procedure was said to have been "largely left to gather dust".

Both procedures share the same basic test, namely whether there is a prospect of success which is not fanciful: *James Gilbert Ltd v MGN Ltd* [2000] E.M.L.R. 680, *Mosley v Focus Magazin Verlag GmbH* [2001] EWCA Civ 1030. Lord Woolf's analysis of Pt 24's "no real prospect of success" in *Swain v Hillman* [2001] 1 All E.R. 91 remains helpful.

In other respects, the two procedures differ markedly. The main differences are these:

1. Under the Act, a claimant may obtain summary relief, which (by s.9) means such of the following as may be appropriate: (a) a declaration that the offending statement was false and defamatory of the claimant; (b) an order that the defendant publish a suitable correction and apology; (c) damages not exceeding £10,000; and (d) an injunction. By contrast, under Pt 24 there is no mechanism for obtaining an order for an apology, but equally there is no statutory limit on damages, which, once liability is established, may be assessed in the normal way.

2. While both procedures allow an action to go to trial if there is some reason (under Pt 24, a "compelling" reason) why it should do so, s.8(4) of the Act obliges the court in considering whether a claim should be tried to have regard to a number of factors (whether all the persons who are or might be defendants are before the court; whether summary disposal of the claim against another defendant would be inappropriate; the extent to which there is a conflict of evidence; the seriousness of the defamation; and whether it is justifiable in the circumstances to proceed to a full trial). There is no equivalent obligation under Pt 24.

3. Pt 24 applications (commonly coupled with an application to strike out under CPR r.3.4(2)) may be used to attack part of a claim (for example, a plea of qualified privilege), whereas applications under the Act are intended to dispose of the claim in its entirety.

The summary disposal regime has in the past been used to dispose of a defence and obtain

---

[1] Introduced by the Civil Procedure (Amendment No. 3) Rules 2019 (SI 2019/1118).

judgment on the claim (e.g. *Downtex v Flatley* [2003] EWCA Civ 1282, where the Court of Appeal was persuaded that a defence of qualified privilege was bound to fail), and to force the claimant to have his claim disposed of summarily rather than by jury trial, in which case the defendant must waive any substantive defence (see e.g. *Milne v Telegraph Group Ltd (No.2)* [2001] E.M.L.R. 30). On a defendant's application, the court must be satisfied that summary relief (in particular, the £10,000 damages ceiling) will adequately compensate the claimant: see s.8(3), *Burstein v Times Newspapers Ltd* [2001] 1 W.L.R. 579 and *Mawdsley v Guardian Newspapers Ltd* [2002] EWHC 1780 (QB) at [16], [56].

Direction to elect whether or not to make offer of amends

53n.5.2   This rule was expressly envisaged by s.10(2)(f) of the Act. It was considered by Gray J in *Green v Times Newspapers Ltd*, 17 January 2001, unrep. For the offer of amends procedure, see paras 5.1 to 5.3 of Practice Direction 53B at para.53BPD.5 below.

Sources of information[1]

53n.6   **53.6 Unless the court orders otherwise, a party will not be required to provide further information about the identity of the defendant's sources of information.**

(Part 18 provides for requests for further information.)

Sources of information

53n.6.1   This rule re-states the old r.53.3. Its practical importance is limited, given the statutory protection of sources provided by s.10 of the Contempt of Court Act 1981.

Add new Practice Direction 53A:

PRACTICE DIRECTION 53A—TRANSFERRING PROCEEDINGS TO AND FROM THE MEDIA AND COMMUNICATIONS LIST

This Practice Direction supplements Part 53

53APD.1   **1.** If a Media and Communications Judge orders proceedings to be transferred to the Media and Communications List—

(1)   the judge will order them to be transferred to the Royal Courts of Justice; and

(2)   the judge may give case management directions.

2. An application by a defendant, including a Part 30 defendant, for an order transferring proceedings to or from the Media and Communications List should be made promptly and normally not later than the first case management conference.

3. A party applying for an order transferring a claim to the Media and Communications List must give notice of the application to the court or list in which the claim is proceeding, and the Media and Communications Judge will not make an order for transfer unless and until satisfied that such notice and any applicable consent has been given.

4. A Media and Communications Judge may decide that the court should consider of its own motion whether a claim should be transferred from the Media and Communications List. If the judge does so, CPR rules 3.3 and 23.8(c) apply.

5. A Media and Communications List Judge deciding whether to transfer a claim to or from the Media and Communications List will consider whether the claim or any part of it—

(1)   falls outside the scope of that list (whether or not it also falls within the scope of Part 63); or

(2)   falls within the scope of the list but would more conveniently be dealt with in another court or list,

and make such order as the court considers appropriate in the light of its conclusions.

6. This practice direction is subject to CPR rule 30.5.

---

[1] Introduced by the Civil Procedure (Amendment No. 3) Rules 2019 (SI 2019/1118).

Note

This Practice Direction does not apply to claims issued before 1 October 2019 (see CPR Update **53APD.2** 109—Practice Direction Amendments (30 June 2019), para.1(b), (c)).

It is subject to CPR r.30.5, which deals with transfer between Divisions of the High Court and transfer to and from a specialist list, as the MAC List is (see r.53.2). Note that while any party seeking to transfer a claim suitable for the MAC List from another court or list must first give notice and obtain any necessary consent from a judge of that court or list, in the case of a claim proceeding in (or to be transferred to) the Chancery Division, the consent of the Chancellor of the High Court must be obtained: see r.30.5(4).

Add new Practice Direction 53B:

PRACTICE DIRECTION 53B—MEDIA AND COMMUNICATIONS CLAIMS
This Practice Direction supplements CPR Part 53

General

1. This practice direction applies to media and communications claims.   **53BPD.1**
(Rule 53.1 defines "media and communications claim".)

Scope of the Practice Direction

The new Practice Directions do not apply to claims issued before 1 October 2019 (see CPR **53BPD.2** Update 109—Practice Direction Amendments (30 June 2019), para.1(b), (c)). The old Practice Direction 53 will therefore continue to apply to claims issued before 1 October 2019.

While the old Practice Direction is confined almost entirely (except for statements in open court) to defamation claims, the new Practice Direction 53B ranges much more widely. It applies to all media and communications (MAC) claims. By r.53.1, MAC claims are claims issued in or transferred into the Media and Communications List (the MAC List) which are claims in defamation, misuse of private information, data protection and harassment by publication, and claims which otherwise arise from the publication or threatened publication of information via the media, online or in speech, or from other activities of the media.

Statements of Case

2.1 Statements of case should be confined to the information necessary to **53BPD.3** inform the other party of the nature of the case they have to meet. Such information should be set out concisely and in a manner proportionate to the subject matter of the claim

(Part 16 and the accompanying practice direction contain requirements for the contents of statements of case.)

2.2 A claimant must in the particulars of claim give full details of the facts and matters on which they rely in support of any claim for damages.

(Rule 16.4(1)(c) requires a claimant seeking aggravated or exemplary damages to include in the particulars of claim a statement to that effect and the grounds for claiming such damages.)

2.3 A claimant who wishes to advance any positive case in response to any facts or matters raised in a defence must file and serve a reply.

(Rule 15.8 contains the requirements for filing and serving a reply.)

(Further requirements as to the statements of case in particular types of claim are set out at paragraphs 4, 8, 9 and 10 below.)

Statements in open court

3.1 This paragraph only applies where a party wishes to accept a Part 36 of- **53BPD.4** fer or other offer of settlement in relation to a claim for—

(1) libel;
(2) slander;
(3) malicious falsehood; or
(4) misuse of private or confidential information.

3.2 A party may apply for permission to make a statement in open court before or after the Part 36 offer or other offer to settle the claim is accepted.

3.3 The statement that the applicant wishes to make must be submitted for the approval of the court and must accompany the notice of application.

3.4 The court may postpone the time for making the statement if other claims relating to the subject matter of the statement are still proceeding.

Statements in court

53BPD.5 Paragraphs 3.1–3.4 are substantially identical to paras 6.1–6.4 of the old Practice Direction 53.

The procedure for reading statements provides valuable means of vindication for a claimant because the statement can be reported freely under the privilege which protects fair and accurate reports of proceedings heard in public, and will normally receive some press and media coverage, even if only in the claimant's home district. It may be unilateral (where the claimant alone makes a statement) or bilateral (where the defendant joins in the making of a statement in agreed terms). The bilateral statement is far more effective, particularly in defamation and malicious falsehood cases, because it almost invariably demands an acceptance by the defendant that the published words were false, and a suitable expression of contrition. In a proper case, which is likely to be rare, a defendant may seek to make a statement in open court in order to obtain vindication in respect of allegations made in the course of litigation: *CTB v News Group Newspapers Ltd* [2011] EWHC 3099 (QB).

For the considerations which apply where a privacy claimant seeks anonymity in a statement in open court, see *Hemsworth (formerly SWS) v DWP* [2018] EWHC 1998 (QB); [2019] E.M.L.R. 2. It is doubtful whether there is a rigid rule that statements will be allowed in privacy cases (see *Hemsworth*).

Statements in open court: procedure

53BPD.6 Statements in open court are made where a party wishes to accept a Part 36 offer, where a claimant has accepted an offer of amends and wishes to make a unilateral statement (see *Winslet v Associated Newspapers Ltd* [2009] EWHC 2735 (QB); [2010] E.M.L.R. 11 and *Murray v Associated Newspapers Ltd* [2015] EWCA Civ 488; [2015] E.M.L.R. 21), and where the action has settled and (generally) one of the terms of settlement provides for a bilateral statement to be made in agreed terms.

A statement has been allowed in Northern Ireland without a claim having been issued: *Campbell College Board of Governors v Independent News & Media (Northern Ireland) Ltd* [2016] NIQB 51. It now appears that this device has been permitted in the English High Court, although the decision is unreported: *Pierdant v Guardian News & Media Ltd* The normal practice is for the applicant to issue an application notice under CPR Pt 23 seeking permission to make a statement in terms approved by the court, but it is doubtful whether the Pt 23 route is proper unless proceedings have been issued. If the claim has settled before proceedings are issued, the best course is to issue a Pt 7 or—perhaps more appropriately—a Pt 8 claim form (see *Hemsworth v DWP*, above, at [10]). That accords with the practice where the court's assistance is invoked under the offer of amends procedure: see para.5.2 and para.53BPD.34 below.

The application should be made to a judge of the Media and Communications List. Permission is required for the making of a statement in open court so that the judge can ensure that the court's process, or the forum it provides, is not abused: *CTB v News Group Newspapers Ltd* (above) at [26]. The notice of application for permission, together with a copy of the proposed statement, whether bilateral or unilateral, should be filed in the judges' Listing Office, Room WG08. A date convenient for both parties is arranged between counsels' clerks or between solicitors, and the signed statement is listed before the judge for mention. It is unusual for a bilateral statement to be refused by the court, but the court will refuse permission if informed that one of the parties proposing to join in the statement believes that it is false:

> "It is one thing for the court to be unable to guarantee that all its judgments or verdicts are the whole truth. It is quite another for the court to permit itself to be used for the making of a statement that the maker is at the same time declaring he believes to be untrue" (per Tugendhat J, *Adelson v Associated Newspapers Ltd (No.3)* [2008] EWHC 278 (QB) [67], [70]).

Where a statement is opposed

53BPD.7 When the claimant applies to make a statement, the defendant has the right to be heard and to object to its wording (but note *Charlton v EMAP*, Times, 11 June 1993, where the defendant was not allowed to insist on a reference to a payment in having been made for "commercial reasons"). Subject to a defendant's objections, the court will generally give permission to make a statement, particularly when the libel has been widely publicised, although if the sum offered is very small compared with the gravity of the libel, permission may be refused (see for instance *Church of Scientology of California v North News Ltd* (1973) 117 S.J. 566, where the claimant accepted a payment of £50 and was refused leave to make a statement). It would be quite exceptional for the court to refuse permission for the making of a reasonable and proportionate statement: see *Phillips v Associated Newspapers Ltd* [2004] EWHC 190 (QB); [2004] 1 W.L.R. 2106. Note that in that case Eady J held that where a claimant has accepted a Part 36 offer, the costs of any application to make a unilateral statement, and of the making of the statement itself, will generally fall to be paid by the defendant as an integral part of the costs of the action.

Where the action has settled, the terms of the statement will usually be agreed, but a second defendant who is not party to the settlement may wish to be heard (as in *Barnet v Crozier* [1987] 1 W.L.R. 272). Where parties reach a bona fide settlement, and ask for permission to make a statement in court, permission ought to be granted unless, taking into account the interests of all parties affected and the risk of prejudice to the fair trial of any outstanding issue, sufficient reason appears from the material before the judge for it to be refused (ibid). A claimant who has reached a bona fide settlement can normally expect to be given permission to make a unilateral statement unless that would give rise to unfairness to the other party: *Murray v Associated Newspapers Ltd* [2015] EWCA Civ 488; [2015] E.M.L.R. 21. A statement in open court, whether unilateral or joint, must be fair and proportionate, should not misrepresent a party's case or the nature of the settlement reached, and must bear in mind the interests of third parties. The court is unlikely to intervene in the absence of any real or substantial unfairness to the objecting party or a third party, and "nitpicks" are to be discouraged: *Murray*, above. A good recent example is *Richard v BBC* [2017] EWHC 1648 (Ch); [2017] E.M.L.R. 25, where the BBC (the first defendant, against which the proceedings remained live) unsuccessfully opposed the reading of a statement by the claimant and second defendant. A third party affected by a statement also has standing to apply to the court not to approve it: see *Virgin Atlantic Airways v British Airways*, 11 January 1993, unrep., in which Drake J allowed a third party to make representations and to make his own statement challenging what was said.

It should be the norm for applications to read unilateral statements, even if opposed, to be dealt with on paper: *Murray v Associated Newspapers Ltd* [2014] EWHC 1170 (QB); [2014] E.M.L.R. 23.

Offer of amends

A statement may also be made where an offer of amends is accepted by the aggrieved party, but there is no agreement on the steps to be taken by way of correction, apology and publication. The aggrieved party may make a unilateral statement if dissatisfied with the terms of the proposed apology: *Winslet v Associated Newspapers Ltd* [2009] EWHC 2735 (QB); [2010] E.M.L.R. 11, *Murray v Associated Newspapers Ltd* [2015] EWCA Civ 488; [2015] E.M.L.R. 21. Alternatively, the offeror may make the correction and apology by a (presumably unilateral) statement in terms approved by the court: Defamation Act 1996 s.3(4). Such a statement would not fall within the terms of para.3 of the Practice Direction. Nonetheless, the application should be issued before a judge of the Media and Communications List. Applications should be made by Pt 23 notice. If there are no existing proceedings, a Pt 8 claim form should be issued: see para 5.2 below. **53BPD.8**

Defamation

Statements of case

4.1(1) In a claim for libel the publication the subject of the claim must be identified in the claim form. **53BPD.9**

(2) In a claim for slander the claim form must so far as practicable identify the person or persons to whom the words were spoken and when.

Claim form: libel and slander

"Publication" is used in the technical sense of the instance of libel (e.g. the particular document, or broadcast programme) which is complained of. For example, in the case of a newspaper article the pleader should claim "Damages for libel published by the defendant on page X of the issue of the Daily Beast dated January 1, 2019". The actual words complained of should be set out in the Particulars of Claim, not the claim form. **53BPD.10**

In the case of slander, the requirement is only to identify the person or persons to whom the words were spoken and when: e.g. "Damages for slander spoken by the defendant to X and Y on [date]". The old Practice Direction (53PD para 2.2(2)) required pleaders in slander cases to set out the actual words complained of in the claim form. The removal of that requirement is welcome.

4.2 The claimant must set out in the particulars of claim— **53BPD.11**

(1) the precise words of the statement complained of, save where the length of the statement makes it impracticable to do so, in which case the words may be set out in a schedule annexed to the particulars of claim, or otherwise identified;

(2) when, how and to whom the statement was published. If the claimant does not know to whom the statement was published or it is impracticable to set out all such persons, then the particulars of claim must include all facts and matters relied upon to show (a) that such publication took

place, and (b) the extent of such publication;

(3)   the facts and matters relied upon in order to satisfy the requirement of section 1 of the Defamation Act 2013 that the publication of the statement complained of has caused or is likely to cause serious harm to the reputation of the claimant, or, in the case of a body that trades for profit, that it has caused or is likely to cause the body serious financial loss;

(4)   the imputation(s) which the claimant alleges that the statement complained of conveyed, both—

(a)   as to its natural and ordinary meaning; and

(b)   by way of any innuendo meaning (that is, a meaning alleged to be conveyed to some person by reason of knowing facts extraneous to the statement complained of). In the case of an innuendo meaning, the claimant must also identify the relevant extraneous facts;

(5)   full details of the facts and matters on which the claimant relies in support of the claim for damages. A claimant who seeks aggravated or exemplary damages must provide the information specified in rule 16.4(1)(c).

Particulars of Claim:precise words to be pleaded

53BPD.12   This requirement reflects the law as it has stood for centuries: see for example *Cook v Cox* 105 E.R. 552; (1814) 3 M. & S. 110 at 113, per Lord Ellenborough CJ (the actual words must be set out "in order that the defendant may know the certainty of the charge, and be able to shape his defence").

"In libel and slander everything may turn on the form of words. ... It is not the fact of the defendant having used defamatory expressions, but the fact of his having used those defamatory expressions alleged, which is the fact on which the case depends" per Lord Coleridge CJ, *Harris v Warre* (1879) 4 C.P.D. 125 at 128.

It is impermissible to plead the effect or gist of the words in the hope of fishing for disclosure, although exactly what is required of the pleader will to some extent depend on the facts of the case. The words relied on must be set out with reasonable certainty, unless the claimant can show by credible evidence that the defendant on a particular occasion and to a particular person made a defamatory statement about him of a specified nature: in that event, the claimant may ascertain the precise words used by seeking an order for further information (*Best v Charter Medical of England Ltd* [2001] EWCA Civ 1588; [2002] E.M.L.R. 18 at [11]). See also *Wissa v Associated Newspapers Ltd* [2014] EWHC 1518 (QB), and for guidance on how to plead a claim on Twitter, see *Monroe v Hopkins* [2017] EWHC 433 (QB); [2017] 4 W.L.R. 68.

Serious harm

53BPD.13   See now *Lachaux v Independent Print Ltd* [2019] UKSC 27; [2019] 3 W.L.R. 18; [2019] E.M.L.R. 22, for the Supreme Court's conclusive view of the meaning and effect of s.1 of the Defamation Act 2013. The claimant's pleaded case should include reference to the claimant's circumstances, the consequences (or probable future consequences) of publication, including the extent of publication, and the impact of the words complained of, or their probable future impact, on those to whom they were published. The inherent tendency of the words remains a relevant factor. There is no reason why inferences of fact as to the seriousness of the harm done to the claimant's reputation should not be drawn from such considerations. A body trading for profit must plead facts showing that the harm done by publication did in fact (or would probably) cause it serious financial loss, which is not the same as special damage (see *Lachaux* at [15]).

Meaning

53BPD.14   The meaning which the claimant contends that the words bear should always be pleaded, however obvious it may be. Pleading the meaning is a difficult art: the meaning should be as high and as specific as possible, but not strained and not too wide. Too narrow or too low a meaning, and the claimant will be constrained in opening the case; too high, and he may face an adverse ruling under para.6(1) of this Practice Direction; too wide, and he may let in a wider defence of truth than would otherwise have been possible (see *Bookbinder v Tebbit (No.1)* [1989] 1 W.L.R. 640).

The traditional rule is that the defendant may not say what he says the words mean. The rule was questioned over 30 years ago by Mustill LJ in *Viscount de L'Isle v Times Newspapers Ltd* [1988] 1 W.L.R. 49, 58C–D:

"... it is submitted that this rule needs re-examination; in many cases one of the crucial issues at trial is the meaning of the words and it would be clearly convenient if the precise issue between the parties was placed on the record in the pleadings before the hearing".

The reasons for defendants' reluctance to state their position had to do with jury trial, and make little sense now that trial by jury is a dead letter. See Nicklin J's characteristically fresh and lively discussion of the issue in *Bokova v Associated Newspapers Ltd* [2018] EWHC 2032 (QB); [2019] E.M.L.R. 6 at [7]–[10].

Natural and ordinary and innuendo meanings

Where words are defamatory on their face, they are said to be defamatory in their natural and ordinary meaning; where they are defamatory only by reason of some special facts known to the person who read or heard them (the "publishee") they are said to be defamatory in an innuendo meaning, often referred to in the authorities as a "legal" innuendo. (Note that confusion has been caused in the past by the use of the word "innuendo", sometimes qualified with the words "popular" or "false", to refer to a natural and ordinary meaning which arises by implication or inference; that usage is best avoided).

53BPD.15

When a legal innuendo is pleaded, para.4.2(4)(b) requires the pleader to set out the special or extraneous facts which are relied on as giving the words their defamatory meaning. The special facts must be matters outside the libel: *Grubb v Bristol United Press* [1963] 1 Q.B. 309. They may be the explanation of a slang word or a technical term, which was understood by the publishee but might not have made sense to most people who heard it; or they may be some additional facts, known to the publishee, which gave the words a defamatory sense. It is usually necessary to identify the publishees who knew the special facts and therefore would have understood the words to bear the innuendo meaning (see *Baturina v Times Newspapers Ltd* [2011] EWCA Civ 308; [2011] E.M.L.R. 19; [2011] 1 W.L.R. 1526); but it may be possible to rely on inference in suitable cases (see *Fullam v Newcastle Chronicle & Journal Ltd* [1977] 1 W.L.R. 651). The claimant cannot rely on special facts which occur or are discovered after the words have been published, because the cause of action is complete on publication: *Grappelli v Derek Block (Holdings) Ltd* [1981] 1 W.L.R. 822 (but see now *Simon v Lyder* [2019] UKPC 38 at [25]–[27]).

An advantage of the legal innuendo is that it has long been proper for counsel to ask publishees at trial what they understood the words to mean, which is not permissible where only a natural and ordinary meaning is pleaded: see *Lewis v Commissioner of Police of the Metropolis* [2011] EWHC 781 (QB) at [56] and following, but compare *Baturina* (above), per Sedley LJ at [56].

Matters relied upon in support of the claim for damages

The advent of Defamation Act 2013 s.1 requires the claimant to plead all matters relied upon to satisfy the requirement of serious harm (see para 4.2(3) and para.53BPD.13 above and *Lachaux v Independent Print Ltd* [2019] UKSC 27; [2019] 3 W.L.R. 18; [2019] E.M.L.R. 22). That will include matters relied upon in support of the claim for damages.

53BPD.16

Even before the 2013 Act, it had become normal to plead fully the claimant's case on general damage. That would typically include any factors which had aggravated damages, including anything relevant to the impact of the libel or slander on the claimant's feelings, such as the way others treated the claimant as a result, and the defendant's own behaviour (e.g. refusal to apologise, repetition of the libel, and malicious conduct, such as spreading a libel with no belief that it is true), and any unusual feature relied on as increasing damage: see, e.g. *Slipper v BBC* [1991] 1 Q.B. 283.

4.3 Where a defendant relies on the defence under section 2 of the Defamation Act 2013 that the imputation conveyed by the statement complained of is substantially true, they must—

53BPD.17

(1) specify the imputation they contend is substantially true; and

(2) give details of the matters on which they rely in support of that contention.

Specifying the meaning to be proved true

From 1 January 2014, the common law defence of justification was abolished for actions where the cause of action arose on or after that date, and replaced by the statutory defence of truth (Defamation Act 2013 s.2). However, the established common law principles continue to apply to the defence of truth (see e.g. *Bokova v Associated Newspapers Ltd* [2018] EWHC 2032 (QB); [2019] 2 W.L.R. 232; [2019] E.M.L.R. 6).

53BPD.18

Defendants must specify the defamatory meaning in which they say that the words are true:

"... the importance of a properly pleaded meaning is difficult to overstate. In virtually every libel action, the meanings are key to the determination and proper conduct of all aspects of the litigation from the initial stages through to ... trial"

(*Ashcroft v Foley* [2012] EWCA Civ 423; [2012] E.M.L.R. 25 at [35], and see *Lucas-Box v News Group Newspapers Ltd* [1986] 1 W.L.R. 147, CA). However, the *Lucas-Box* meanings must not differ from any meaning that has already been determined by the court (*Bokova*, above).

For example, a defence of truth might typically use words such as these, e.g.:

"The words complained of are true in the following meaning, namely that in January 2000 the claimant defrauded the X Bank of a substantial sum of money".

The defendant will then go on (see below) to set out the particulars of truth, namely the material facts replied on in support of his plea. For more detailed guidance on pleading of truth see *Gatley on Libel & Slander*, 12th edn (London: Sweet & Maxwell, 2017), para.27.6 and following.

Although the new Practice Direction no longer says so (cf. the previous wording at PD 53 para 2.6(1)), the meaning to be proved true must be a defamatory meaning: see e.g. *Broadcasting Corp of New Zealand v Crush* [1988] 2 N.Z.L.R. 234 at 237 (proving the truth of a non-defamatory meaning would be a "pointless exercise"), and *Maxwell v Bower*, 10 April 1990, unrep., Michael Davies J.

Pleading the meaning in which the defendant says he will prove the words to be true is different from pleading the meaning which he says the words bear, which is still not the practice, although quaere whether it ought to be: see *Bokova v Associated Newspapers Ltd* (above) at [7]–[10].

Details of the matters relied on in support of a plea of truth

53BPD.19   Once the defendant has decided on the meaning in which he intends to prove that the libel or slander is true, he must set out, plainly and unambiguously, the material facts which he relies on in support of that case. Facts pleaded in particulars of truth must be sufficient (i.e. capable of proving the sting of the defamatory meaning pleaded: see *Simpson v MGN Ltd* [2016] EWCA Civ 772; [2016] E.M.L.R. 26) and properly particularised (a requirement to be judged not by the numbers of particulars but by whether they provide a clear and succinct summary of the essential and relevant facts relied on: see *Ashcroft v Foley* [2012] EWCA Civ 423; [2012] E.M.L.R. 25 at [49]f). On the pleading of fraud, see now *Suresh v Samad* [2016] EWHC 2704 (QB) at [24].

53BPD.20   **4.4** Where a defendant relies on the defence under section 3 of the Defamation Act 2013 that the statement complained of was a statement of honest opinion, they must—

 (1) specify the imputation they seek to defend as honest opinion; and

 (2) set out the facts and matters relied on in support of their case that—

  (a) the statement complained of indicated, in general or specific terms, the basis of the opinion; and

  (b) an honest person could have held that opinion on the basis of any fact which existed at the time it was published or anything asserted to be a fact in a privileged statement published before the statement complained of.

Honest opinion

53BPD.21   The common law of fair comment, briefly known as "honest comment" (*Joseph v Spiller* [2010] UKSC 53; [2011] 1 A.C. 852), was abolished with effect from 1 January 2014 and replaced by a statutory defence of honest opinion, which applies to actions where the cause of action arose on or after that date (Defamation Act 2013 s.3).

Under the new law as under the old, the defendant must specify the defamatory meaning that he intends to defend as honest opinion (a requirement dating from *Control Risks v New English Library* [1990] 1 W.L.R. 183).

The words complained of must indicate (whether in general or specific terms) the basis of the opinion (a principle taken from *Spiller* by s.3(3) of the 2013 Act), and the opinion must be such as could have been held by an honest person on the basis of any fact that existed at the time the words complained of were published (or on anything alleged to be a fact in a privileged statement published before the words complained of): s.3(4). (Curiously, there is no requirement in the Act that the fact should have been known to the person expressing the opinion.) Hence, all facts and matters relied upon in support of that case must be pleaded.

The bounds of acceptable criticism are probably wider, and honest opinion more easily established, where the claimant is a public figure or the words complained of are part of a political debate: see *Mughal v Telegraph Media Group Ltd* [2014] EWHC 1371 (QB). However, there is now no requirement for honest opinion to be expressed on a matter of public interest.

53BPD.22   **4.5** Where a defendant alleges that the statement complained of was, or formed part of, a statement on a matter of public interest under section 4 of the Defamation Act 2013, they must—

 (1) specify the matter of public interest relied upon; and

 (2) give details of all matters relied on in support of any case that they reasonably believed that publishing the statement was in the public interest.

Publication on a matter of public interest

53BPD.23   Defamation Act 2013 s.4 abolished the form of common law privilege known as *Reynolds* privilege (*Reynolds v Times Newspapers Ltd* [2001] 2 A.C. 127; [2000] E.M.L.R. 1) for causes of action which accrued on or after 1 January 2014, and replaced it with a statutory defence of publication on a matter of public interest.

The terms of s.4 oblige the pleader to show that the statement complained of was or formed part of a statement on a matter of public interest, and that the defendant believed on reasonable grounds that publishing the statement was in the public interest. The practice direction requires the matter of public interest to be specified, and the facts and matters relied on for that reasonable belief to be pleaded.

The court must, in determining whether the statement complained of was or formed part of a statement on a matter of public interest, and whether the defendant reasonably believed that publishing the statement was in the public interest, have regard to all the circumstances of the case: s.4(2). Even though s.4 focuses on the publisher's belief that publishing the statement complained of is in the public interest, while the *Reynolds* defence was mainly concerned with the responsibility of the publisher's conduct, it is now clear that the common law principles identified in *Reynolds* and subsequent authority continue to be relevant to the interpretation of s.4: see *Economou v de Freitas* [2018] EWCA Civ 2591; [2019] E.M.L.R. 7. Those would include such matters as the seriousness of the allegation, the extent to which it was a matter of public interest or concern, the source and status of the information, the steps taken to verify it, the urgency of the matter, and the steps taken to obtain and print the claimant's side of the story. Such matters should, if they apply, be pleaded.

4.6 Where a defendant alleges that the statement complained of was published on a privileged occasion, they must specify the circumstances they rely on in support of that contention. **53BPD.24**

Paragraph 4.6

This paragraph repeats the long established obligation to set out all facts and matters relied on for the proposition that the words complained of were published on an occasion of classical duty/interest qualified privilege. This common law qualified privilege is unaffected by the 2013 Defamation Act. **53BPD.25**

Note that if the defendant is a public authority bound by s.6 of the Human Rights Act 1998 to act in accordance with Convention rights, that will have implications for a qualified privilege defence: see *Clift v Slough BC* [2010] EWCA Civ 1484; [2011] 1 W.L.R. 1774; [2011] E.M.L.R. 13.

4.7 Where a defendant relies on a defence under section 2 (truth), section 3 (honest opinion), or section 4 (publication on a matter of public interest) of the Defamation Act 2013, the claimant must serve a reply specifically admitting, not admitting, or denying that defence and setting out the claimant's case in response to each fact alleged by the defendant in respect of it. **53BPD.26**

4.8(1) If the defendant contends that any of the statement complained of, or any part thereof, was honest opinion, or was published on a privileged occasion, and the claimant intends to allege that the defendant did not hold the opinion or acted with malice (as applicable), the claimant must serve a reply giving details of the facts or matters relied on.

(2) If the defendant relies on any other defence, and the claimant intends to allege that the defence is not available because of the defendant's state of mind, the claimant must serve a reply giving details of the facts or matters relied on. This includes—

(a) where a defendant relies on the defence under section 4 of the Defamation Act 2013 and the claimant intends to allege that the defendant did not reasonably believe that the publication was in the public interest;

(b) where a defendant relies on the defence under section 4(2) of the Defamation Act 1996 (offer to make amends) and the claimant intends to allege that the defendant had the state of mind referred to in section 4(3) of the defamation Act 1996.

Reply to defence of publication on a matter of public interest

The claimant faced with the s.4 defence of publication on a matter of public interest should set out in his reply all the circumstances which go to show that the words complained of were not a statement on a matter of public interest, and/or that the defendant did not reasonably believe that publication was in the public interest. Malice is immaterial: the publisher's state of mind will be relevant only to the extent that the defendant must show reasonable belief that publication was in the public interest (ss.4(1)(b) and 4(4) Defamation Act 2013). On reasonable belief, see *Economou v de Freitas* [2018] EWCA Civ 2591; [2019] E.M.L.R. 7. **53BPD.27**

Malice: honest opinion

53BPD.28 Malice in honest opinion has a much narrower scope than in qualified privilege. The statutory defence of honest opinion is defeated if it is proved that the defendant did not hold the opinion: Defamation Act 2013 s.3(5).

Malice: qualified privilege

53BPD.29 Where classical duty/interest qualified privilege is pleaded (but not s.4 public interest privilege: see para.53BPD.27 above), the claimant must give full particulars in his reply of all the facts and matters from which malice is to be inferred. The normal practice is to allege that the defendant published the words complained of with "express malice", and to follow that general plea with particulars of the facts which show, or from which it is to be inferred, that the defendant was driven by some dominant improper motive, or knew that (or was recklessly indifferent as to whether) his words were false, or was otherwise malicious (see *Horrocks v Lowe* [1975] A.C. 135).

No belief that publication was in the public interest

53BPD.30 On reasonable belief that publication was in the public interest, see *Economou v de Freitas* (above).

Malice: offer of amends

53BPD.31 Where a defendant relies on offer of amends, that is a defence (Defamation Act 1996 s.4(2)) unless the claimant can prove that the defendant knew or had reason to believe that the statement complained of referred to the claimant or was likely to be understood as referring to him (that is not usually in issue) and was both false and defamatory of that party: s.4(3). For the relevant state of mind, see *Milne v Express Newspapers Ltd (No.1)* [2002] EWHC 2564 (QB); [2003] 1 W.L.R. 927, Eady J, affirmed [2004] EWCA Civ 664; [2005] 1 W.L.R. 772.

53BPD.32 **4.9** A defendant who relies on an offer to make amends under section 2 of the Defamation Act 1996 as their defence must—

    (1) state in their defence—

        (a) that they are relying on the offer in accordance with section 4(2) of the Defamation Act 1996; and

        (b) that it has not been withdrawn by them or been accepted; and

    (2) attach a copy of the offer made with their defence.

Offer of amends as defence

53BPD.33 The fact that an offer of amends has been made but not accepted is a defence to a defamation claim (Defamation Act 1996 s.4(2)), except where the offeror knew or had reason to believe that the statement complained of (a) referred to the claimant or was likely to be understood as doing so, and (b) was both false and defamatory of the claimant (s.4(3)). This imports a bad faith or malice test, which will rarely be satisfied: see *Milne v Express Newspapers Ltd (No.1)* [2002] EWHC 2564 (QB); [2003] 1 W.L.R. 927, Eady J, affirmed [2004] EWCA Civ 664; [2005] 1 W.L.R. 772. For a case where malice was proved, see *Thornton v Telegraph Media Group Ltd* [2011] EWHC 1884 (QB); [2012] E.M.L.R. 8. Where the defence of offer of amends is relied on, no other defence may be pleaded: s.4(4).

Court's powers in connection with an offer of amends

53BPD.34 **5.1** Sections 2 to 4 of the Defamation Act 1996 make provision for a person who has made a statement which is alleged to be defamatory to make an offer to make amends. Section 3 provides for the court to assist in the process of making amends.

    5.2 A claim under section 3 of the Defamation Act 1996 made other than in existing proceedings may be made under CPR Part 8—

    (1) where the parties agree on the steps to make amends, and the sole purpose of the claim is for the court to make an order under section 3(3) for an order that the offer be fulfilled; or

    (2) where the parties do not agree—

        (a) on the steps to be taken by way of correction, apology and publication (see section 3(4));

        (b) on the amount to be paid by way of compensation (see section 3(5)); or

        (c) on the amount to be paid by way of costs (see section 3(6)).

    (Applications in existing proceedings made under section 3 of the Defamation Act 1996 must be made in accordance with CPR Part 23.)

    5.3(1) A claim or application under section 3 of the Defamation Act 1996 must be supported by written evidence.

(2)　The evidence referred to in paragraph (1) must include—
- (a)　a copy of the offer of amends;
- (b)　details of the steps taken to fulfil the offer of amends;
- (c)　a copy of the text of any correction and apology;
- (d)　details of the publication of the correction and apology;
- (e)　a statement of the amount of any sum paid as compensation;
- (f)　a statement of the amount of any sum paid for costs;
- (g)　why the offer is unsatisfactory.

(3)　Where any step specified in section 2(4) of the Defamation Act 1996 has not been taken, then the evidence referred to in paragraph (2)(c) to (f) must state what steps are proposed by the party to fulfil the offer of amends and the date or dates on which each step will be fulfilled and, if none, that no proposal has been made to take that step.

Offer of amends

This procedure allows a person who has published a statement alleged to be defamatory of another to offer to make amends. An offer of amends must be in writing, must be expressed to be an offer of amends under s.2 and must state whether or not it is qualified (i.e. limited to a specific defamatory meaning which the offeror accepts that the statement conveys); but whatever else the offer may contain, s.2(4) provides that it will be taken to include an offer to make a suitable correction and apology, before service of defence, to publish the correction and apology in a manner that is reasonable and practicable in the circumstances, and to pay the aggrieved party (who need not have issued proceedings) such compensation (if any) and costs as may be agreed or determined. **53BPD.35**

Offer of amends and serious harm

A defendant who wishes to resist a claim on the basis that it fails to meet the threshold of serious harm to reputation created by Defamation Act 2013 s.1 should not serve a defence before taking the serious harm point. If the application to determine the threshold issue fails, then (because no defence has been served) the defendant can still consider making an offer of amends (*Lachaux v Independent Print Ltd* [2015] EWHC 2242 (QB); [2016] Q.B. 402; [2016] 2 W.L.R. 437 at [169]). **53BPD.36**

The section 3 procedure

If the offer is accepted, the s.3 procedure applies. The party accepting the offer may neither bring nor continue defamation proceedings against the offeror in respect of the libel or slander concerned, but can enforce the offer. To do so, any of a number of applications to the court may have to be made. If both parties agree on the steps to be taken to fulfil the offer, the person accepting the offer may apply to the court for an order that the other party should fulfil the offer by taking those steps. If they do not agree, other consequences flow. If they disagree about the steps to be taken by way of correction, apology and their publication, the offeror may make the correction and apology by statement in court in terms approved by the court, and give an undertaking to the court as to the manner in which they are to be published. Equally, the aggrieved party, if dissatisfied by the proposed apology, may make a unilateral statement in court: *Winslet v Associated Newspapers Ltd* [2009] EWHC 2735 (QB); [2010] E.M.L.R. 11, *Murray v Associated Newspapers Ltd* [2015] EWCA Civ 488; [2015] E.M.L.R. 21. An application to make a statement should normally be dealt with on paper: *Murray v Associated Newspapers Ltd*, above. If the parties disagree about the amount of compensation, the court must determine the amount according to the usual principles applying to defamation damages. The same applies, mutatis mutandis, if they disagree about costs. **53BPD.37**

For the principles to be applied on assessment of damages, and the need to avoid a "rough and ready" approach, see *Kareem Abu v MGN Ltd* [2002] EWHC 2345 (QB); [2003] 1 W.L.R. 2201; [2003] 2 All E.R. 864, Eady J and *Nail v News Group Newspapers Ltd* [2004] EWCA Civ 1708; [2005] 1 All E.R. 1040; and for guidance on the practical need for informal discussion between the parties to avoid applications to the court, see *Cleese v Clark* [2003] EWHC 137 (QB); [2004] E.M.L.R. 3, Eady J. It appears that it is not open to a defendant who has made an unqualified offer to argue that the claimant's meanings are untenable: such a challenge should be flagged up by use of a qualified offer (see *Nail v News Group* [2004] EWHC 647 (QB); [2004] E.M.L.R. 20, approved [2004] EWCA Civ 1708; [2005] 1 All E.R. 1040).

Paragraph 5.2 provides that s.3 applications before proceedings have been issued must be made under CPR Pt 8, while applications made after the issue of proceedings should be made under Pt 23; and para.5.3 sets out the requirements for written evidence in support of a s.3 application.

Note that while para.5.3(2)(e) requires that the amount of any sum actually paid as compensation must be included in the supporting evidence, it is preferable for the judge not to be told the competing figures advanced by the parties in without prejudice correspondence: *Cleese v Clark*, above.

There is no provision for "rejection" of the offer, which is either accepted or not accepted. A failure to accept may be construed as non-acceptance. The onus is squarely on the claimant to decide promptly whether or not to accept: see *Loughton Contracts Plc v Dun & Bradstreet Ltd* [2006] EWHC 1224 (QB). However, a reasonable time will be allowed: *Tesco Stores Ltd v Guardian News & Media Ltd* [2009] E.M.L.R. 5, Eady J, 29 July 2008. Once an offer is accepted, the defendant may not resile from it except in rare and special circumstances so different from those contemplated that it would be appropriate to release them from their obligation: *Warren v Random House Group Ltd* [2008] EWCA Civ 834; [2009] Q.B. 600.

A claimant may obtain disclosure of an identified and specific document which is relevant to a pleaded issue and highly material to the decision whether or not to accept the offer of amends, but that is not to sanction routine or wide-ranging applications by claimants faced with that decision: *Rigg v Associated Newspapers Ltd* [2003] EWHC 710 (QB); [2004] E.M.L.R. 4, Gray J.

The section 4 procedure

53BPD.38   If the offer is not accepted, the fact that it was made is a defence (if the offer was qualified, then a partial defence) to defamation proceedings in respect of the publication in question. But there is no defence if the offeror knew or had reason to believe that the allegation complained of referred to the claimant or was likely to be understood as referring to him, and was both false and defamatory of him. The offer of amends regime (which has been much used by the media) is intended to provide an exit route for journalists who have made a mistake and want to put their hands up. It is only intended to shut out those who have acted in bad faith, i.e. maliciously (see *Milne v Express Newspapers Ltd (No.1)* [2002] EWHC 2564 (QB); [2003] 1 W.L.R. 927, Eady J, affirmed [2004] EWCA Civ 664; [2005] 1 W.L.R. 772.

Determination of meaning

53BPD.39   **6.1**   At any time in a defamation claim the court may determine—
(1)   the meaning of the statement complained of;
(2)   whether the statement is defamatory of the claimant at common law;
(3)   whether the statement is a statement of fact or opinion.

6.2   An application for a determination of meaning may be made at any time after the service of particulars of claim. Such an application should be made promptly.

6.3   Where an application is made for a determination of meaning, the application notice must state that it is an application for a determination of meaning made in accordance with this practice direction.

6.4   An application made under this paragraph must be made to a Judge.

(Rule 3.3 applies where the court exercises its powers on its own initiative.)

(Following a determination of meaning the court may exercise its power under rule 3.4.)

Determination of meaning

53BPD.40   The abolition of the right to trial by jury in defamation actions (Defamation Act 2013 s.11) has brought in a salutary new culture, which enables the court to determine the actual meaning of a publication as a preliminary issue. For the many advantages that this brings, see the discussion in *Bokova v Associated Newspapers Ltd* [2018] EWHC 2032 (QB); [2019] 2 W.L.R. 232; [2019] E.M.L.R. 6 at [7]–[10].

The old concept of determining what meaning the words complained of are capable of bearing is redundant: there will rarely if ever (although see *Al Alaoui v Elaph Publishing Ltd* [2017] EWCA Civ 29; [2017] E.M.L.R. 13) be any purpose in seeking a ruling on that question. This proposition was endorsed in *Alsaifi v Amunwa* [2017] EWHC 1443 (QB); [2017] 4 W.L.R. 172 at [40]. Instead, the court will be asked at an early stage to determine the actual meaning of the words.

Malicious falsehood

53BPD.41   Paragraph 6.1 refers only to defamation claims, but a ruling on meaning may also be obtained by way of preliminary issue in a malicious falsehood case: *Ajinomoto Sweeteners Europe SAS v Asda Stores Ltd* [2009] EWHC 781 (QB); [2009] F.S.R. 16 (now reversed on appeal, but to the effect that the single meaning rule in defamation does not apply to malicious falsehood, not on the availability of a ruling as to meaning: [2010] EWCA Civ 609; [2010] E.M.L.R. 23).

Ruling without an oral hearing (CPR 23.8)

53BPD.42   It will not usually be appropriate to deal with a meaning application without an oral hearing, except in a very limited number of cases: *Church v MGN Ltd* [2012] EWHC 693 (QB); [2012] E.M.L.R. 28.

Appeals on meaning

The Court of Appeal has in the past discouraged appeals from rulings as to meaning except in **53BPD.43** cases which are clearly fit for argument in that court, although it will be less reluctant to interfere with a judge's decision where a meaning has been ruled out once and for all (see *Cruise v Express Newspapers Plc* [1999] Q.B. 931 at 936), and where the judge has erred on the side of unnecessary restriction of meaning (*Berezovsky v Forbes Inc* [2001] EWCA Civ 1251; [2001] E.M.L.R. 1030, CA). For a recent appeal from determination of meaning as a preliminary issue, see *Simpson v MGN Ltd* [2016] EWCA Civ 772; [2016] E.M.L.R. 26. In *Bukovsky v CPS* [2017] EWCA Civ 1529; [2018] 4 W.L.R. 13; [2018] E.M.L.R. 5, the court repeated that it should only substitute its own views on meaning for those of the judge when satisfied that the judge was wrong. Meaning was often a matter of impression, defamation judges were well used to applying the relevant tests for determining meaning, and it was undesirable for the Court of Appeal to approach issues of meaning simply on the basis that they might have formed a different view from the judge.

Whether the words complained of are defamatory at common law

It seems unlikely that the question of whether words are defamatory at common law will often **53BPD.44** arise. It is curious that the Practice Direction makes no provision for the far more important question of whether the words are defamatory within s.1 of the Defamation Act 2013, i.e. whether the serious harm threshold has been met. That should not deter practitioners from seeking determination of the serious harm question as a preliminary issue, in cases where that can be done without excessive expenditure of time and cost. Where the issue is likely to involve substantial evidence, it should usually be left to trial. It is not yet clear what the practical impact will be of the Supreme Court's decision in *Lachaux v Independent Print Ltd* [2019] UKSC 27; [2019] 3 W.L.R. 18; [2019] E.M.L.R. 22, but there seems no reason to suppose that the issue of serious harm will not in many cases be suitable for prompt and early determination together with the issue of meaning, as Davis LJ urged in *Lachaux* in the Court of Appeal ([2017] EWCA Civ 1334; [2018] Q.B. 594 at [79]).

Whether the words complained of are a statement of fact or opinion

There tends to be an elaborate cost-benefit calculation involved in deciding whether or not to **53BPD.45** seek determination of issues at an early stage of proceedings, but it is usually relatively inexpensive to resolve issues of fact or opinion, and an early decision may bring real benefits, by ruling in or out, partly or wholly, a defence of truth or honest opinion: see e.g. *British Chiropractic Association v Singh* [2010] EWCA Civ 350; [2011] 1 W.L.R. 133.

Summary disposal

7.1 Where an application is made for summary disposal, the application **53BPD.46** notice must state—

(1) that it is an application for summary disposal made in accordance with section 8 of the Defamation Act 1996; and

(2) the matters set out in paragraph 2(3) of Practice Direction 24.

7.2 An application for summary disposal may be made at any time after the service of particulars of claim.

(This provision disapplies for these applications the usual time restriction on making applications in rule 24.4.)

7.3(1) This paragraph applies where—

(a) the court has ordered the defendant in defamation proceedings to agree and publish a correction and apology as summary relief under section 8(2) of the Defamation Act 1996; and

(b) the parties are unable to agree its content within the time specified in the order.

(2) Where the court grants this type of summary relief under the Act, the order will specify the date by which the parties should reach agreement about the content, time, manner, form and place of publication of the correction and apology.

(3) Where the parties cannot agree the content of the correction and apology by the date specified in the order, then the claimant must prepare a summary of the judgment given by the court and serve it on all the other parties within 3 days following the date specified in the order.

(4) Where the parties cannot agree the summary of the judgment prepared by the claimant they must within 3 days of receiving the

summary –

   (a) file with the court and serve on all the other parties a copy of the summary showing the revisions they wish to make to it; and

   (b) apply to the court for the court to settle the summary.

(5)   The court will then itself settle the summary and the judge who delivered the judgment being summarised will normally do this.

Procedure and evidence

53BPD.47   These paragraphs are almost identical to the previous PD 53 paras 5.1–5.3, except that there is no longer a requirement to state in the application notice should whether or not the defendant has made an offer of amends under s.2 of the Defamation Act 1996 and whether or not it has been withdrawn.

The summary disposal route is becoming an "antique procedural weapon", largely left to gather dust, because of the greater flexibility of the Pt 24 summary judgment procedure: see the discussion in *Alsaifi v Amunwa* [2017] EWHC 1443 (QB); [2017] 4 W.L.R. 172 at [56].

Applications for summary disposal should be made by Pt 23 notice in the usual way. However, the notice must state that it is an application for summary disposal under s.8 of the Defamation Act 1996. That is to ensure that there is no confusion with the Pt 24 summary judgment procedure which is far more frequently employed in defamation cases. It has been said that if the two procedures are invoked in tandem, the applicant may be put to election: see r.53.5(3), and *Clarke v Davey* [2002] EWHC 2342 (QB), Gray J (although a combined application was noted without disapproval by the Court of Appeal in *Downtex v Flatley* [2003] EWCA Civ 1282 and has since been made without comment: *Blackwell v News Group Newspapers Ltd* [2007] EWHC 3098 (QB)). *Clarke v Davey* shows that (at least on a defendant's application) where it makes no practical difference whether the s.8 or Pt 24 procedure is followed, the application should be made solely under Pt 24.

As with a Pt 24 application for summary judgment, the notice (or the accompanying evidence) must, in accordance with Practice Direction 24 para.2(3)(qv), identify any point of law or provision in a document on which the applicant relies, and/or state that the application is made because the applicant believes that the respondent has no real prospect of success on the claim, defence or issue in question, and state that the applicant knows of no other reason why disposal of the claim or issue should await trial. In making that statement, the applicant would be wise to consider carefully the factors to which the court is obliged, by s.8(4) of the 1996 Act, to have regard in considering whether a claim should go to trial, namely whether all the persons who are or might be defendants are before the court; whether summary disposal of the claim against another defendant would be inappropriate; the extent to which there is a conflict of evidence; the seriousness of the alleged wrong (as regards both the content of the statement and the extent of publication); and whether it is justifiable in the circumstances to proceed to a full trial.

An application may be made at any time after service of particulars of claim (para.7.2), and the time restriction for Pt 24 summary judgment applications does not apply. By r.24.4(1), a claimant may generally not make a Pt 24 application until the defendant (the respondent to the application) has filed an acknowledgement of service or a defence: by contrast, the claimant seeking summary disposal under Pt 53 may issue the application without waiting 14 days for the acknowledgement of service or defence. The application may even be made after judgment on liability: see *Loutchansky v Times Newspapers Ltd (No.2)* [2001] EWCA Civ 1805; [2002] Q.B. 783, where the Court of Appeal upheld Gray J's order for summary disposal of assessment of damages following trial of the issues of liability by a jury.

In other respects the procedural requirements of r.24.4 apply to a r.53.5 application, as do the provisions for evidence (r.24.5) and directions (r.24.6): see r.53.5(2). So the respondent must be given at least 14 days' notice of the date fixed for the hearing and the issues to be decided (r.24.4(3)); the respondent must file and serve any written evidence at least seven days before the hearing (r.24.5(1)), and any evidence in reply must be filed and served at least three days before (r.24.5(2)). The application notice must set out the grounds of the application in clear terms: *Armstrong v Times Newspapers Ltd* [2005] EWCA Civ 1007; [2005] E.M.L.R. 33.

The relief which the court may give to a claimant by way of summary disposal of a claim includes a mandatory injunction (Defamation Act 1996 s.9(1)(b): an order that the defendant publish or cause to be published a suitable correction and apology) and an injunction to restrain further publication (s.9(1)(d)). The court may also grant a declaration of falsity under s.9(1)(a), but see *Mahfouz v Brisard (No.3)* [2006] EWHC 1191 (QB) for reasons why it may be reluctant to do so.

Tribunal

53BPD.48   Applications in serious matters (e.g. actions involving the media, police officers or public office holders, or serious or high profile allegations) , or those which seek an order restraining publication, should be filed in the Judges' Listing Office, room WG08, and made to a judge of the Media and Communications List. Applications in other cases may be made to the Master, although if the Master thinks that the application should be heard by a judge, the parties may be asked to argue the point.

Correction and apology

Paragraph 7.3 provides a mechanism for the enforcement of orders for publication of correc- **53BPD.49** tions and apologies as part of the grant of summary relief under s.9 of the 1996 Act. Section 9(2) provides that the content of any correction and apology and the time, manner, form and place of publication are for the parties to agree, but that if they cannot agree the court may direct the defendant to publish a summary of the court's judgment to be agreed by the parties or settled by the court.

Misuse of Private or Confidential Information

8.1 In a claim for misuse of private information, the claimant must specify **53BPD.50** in the particulars of claim (in a confidential schedule if necessary to preserve privacy)—

(1) the information as to which the claimant claims to have (or to have had) a reasonable expectation of privacy;

(2) the facts and matters upon which the claimant relies in support of the contention that they had (or have) such a reasonable expectation;

(3) the use (or threatened use) of the information by the defendant which the claimant claims was (or would be) a misuse; and

(4) any facts and matters upon which the claimant relies in support of their contention that their rights not to have the specified information used by the defendant in the way alleged outweighed (or outweigh) any rights of the defendant to use the information in that manner.

8.2 In a claim for misuse of confidential information or breach of confidence, the claimant must specify in the particulars of claim (in a confidential schedule if necessary to preserve confidentiality)—

(1) the information said to be confidential;

(2) the facts and matters upon which the claimant relies in support of the contention that it was (or is) confidential information that the defendant held (or holds) under a duty or obligation of confidence;

(3) the use (or threatened use) of the information by the defendant which the claimant claims was (or would be) a misuse of the information or breach of that obligation.

Note

Here and at paras 9 and 10 the updated Practice Direction to Pt 53 for the first time provides **53BPD.51** guidance on the pleading of claims other than defamation. It should be noted that in many claims for misuse of private information, a primary concern will be to seek an order anonymising the parties: see CPR r.39.2(4).

Data Protection

9. In any claim for breach of any data protection legislation the claimant **53BPD.52** must specify in the particulars of claim—

(1) the legislation and the provision that the claimant alleges the defendant has breached;

(2) any specific data or acts of processing to which the claim relates;

(3) the specific acts or omissions said to amount to such a breach, and the claimant's grounds for that allegation; and

(4) the remedies which the claimant seeks.

Harassment

10.1 This paragraph applies to claims for harassment arising from publica- **53BPD.53** tion or threatened publication via the media, online, or in speech.

10.2 Rule 65.28(1)(a) shall not apply, and the claim should be commenced under the Part 7 procedure.

10.3 The claimant must specify in the particulars of claim (in a schedule if necessary) the acts of the defendant alleged to constitute a course of conduct which amount to (and which were known or ought to have been known by the defendant to amount to) harassment, including specific details of any actual or threatened communications.

10.4 A defendant must in any defence specifically admit or deny each act alleged in the particulars of claim to constitute part of a course of conduct amounting to harassment.

(Rule 16.5 contains requirements as to the contents of defences.)

Note

53BPD.54 The course of conduct relied upon (para.10.3) must involve conduct on at least two occasions if one person is involved, and if two or more people are claimants, it must involve conduct on at least one occasion with respect to each person: Protection from Harassment Act 1997 s.7(3). "Conduct" includes speech: s.7(4). But claims for harassment by publication are likely to be rare, because to comply with s.3 of the Human Rights Act 1998, the courts will hold that a course of conduct in the form of journalistic speech is reasonable under s.1(3)(c) of the 1997 Act unless the course of conduct is so unreasonable that it is necessary and proportionate to interfere with that speech in pursuit of one of the aims listed in art.10(2): *Trimingham v Associated Newspapers Ltd* [2012] EWHC 1296 (QB). In pleading a claim for harassment by publication, it will be essential to have that test in mind. Two cases where that threshold was crossed are *Hourani v Thomson* [2017] EWHC 432 (QB) and *Ware v McAllister* [2015] EWHC 3068 (QB) (a case involving online publication by a community "activist" and online journalist).

PART 53

Change title:

[ISSUED BEFORE 1 OCTOBER 2019] DEFAMATION CLAIMS

Editorial introduction

Replace paragraph with:

53.0.1 A new CPR Pt 53, and new Practice Directions 53A and 53B (see paras 53APD.1 and 53BPD.1) have been introduced with effect from 1 October 2019. However, they do not apply to claims issued before that date. The existing Pt 53 and Practice Direction 53 will therefore continue to govern claims issued before 1 October 2019.

PRACTICE DIRECTION 53—DEFAMATION CLAIMS

Slander

Add new paragraph at end:

53PD.4 It is interesting to note that the requirement to set out the words complained of in slander cases has been removed from the new PD 53B: see para.53BPD.9.

Pleading the meaning

Replace the second paragraph with:

53PD.6 Note that by s.1(1) of the Defamation Act 2013, a statement is not defamatory unless its publication has caused or is likely to cause serious harm to the reputation of the claimant. The Supreme Court has now determined the meaning and effect of s.1: see *Lachaux v Independent Print Ltd* [2019] UKSC 27; [2019] 3 W.L.R. 18; [2019] E.M.L.R. 22. As well as pleading the meaning of the words, the claimant will have to plead a case sufficient to show that the statement crosses the s.1 threshold. That case should include reference to the claimant's circumstances, the consequences (or probable future consequences) of publication, including the extent of publication, and the impact of the words complained of, or their probable future impact, on those to whom they were published. The inherent tendency of the words remains a relevant factor. There is no reason why inferences of fact as to the seriousness of the harm done to the claimant's reputation should not be drawn from such considerations. A body trading for profit must plead facts showing that the harm done by publication did in fact (or would probably) cause it serious financial loss, which is not the same as special damage (see *Lachaux* at [15]).

Innuendo meanings: extraneous facts

After the penultimate sentence, add:
But see now *Simon v Lyder* [2019] UKPC 38, where the Privy Council stated that the rigid **53PD.8**
exclusionary principle stated by the Court of Appeal in *Grapelli* goes too far.

Specifying the meaning to be proved true

At the end of the first paragraph, replace "(Bokova v Associated Newspapers Ltd [2018] EWHC 2032 (QB); [2019] E.M.L.R. 6)." with:
(*Bokova v Associated Newspapers Ltd* [2018] EWHC 2032 (QB); [2019] 2 W.L.R. 232; [2019] **53PD.12**
E.M.L.R. 6).

Qualified privilege and publication on a matter of public interest

Replace the third paragraph with:
The terms of s.4 oblige the pleader to show that the statement complained of was or formed **53PD.17.1**
part of a statement on a matter of public interest, and that the defendant believed on reasonable
grounds that publishing the statement was in the public interest. Those matters (and the facts
relied upon in support of them) must be pleaded, even though the practice direction in its current
form does not require it.

The court must, in determining whether the statement complained of was or formed part of a
statement on a matter of public interest, and whether the defendant reasonably believed that
publishing the statement was in the public interest, have regard to all the circumstances of the case:
s.4(2). Even though s.4 focuses on the publisher's belief that publishing the statement complained
of is in the public interest, while the *Reynolds* defence was mainly concerned with the responsibility
of the publisher's conduct, it is now clear that the common law principles identified in *Reynolds* and
subsequent authority continue to be relevant to the interpretation of s.4: see *Economou v de Freitas*
[2018] EWCA Civ 2591; [2019] E.M.L.R. 7. Those would include such matters as the seriousness
of the allegation, the extent to which it was a matter of public interest or concern, the source and
status of the information, the steps taken to verify it, the urgency of the matter, and the steps taken
to obtain and print the claimant's side of the story. Such matters should, if they apply, be pleaded.

Damages

Replace paragraph with:
The advent of Defamation Act 2013 s.1 requires the claimant to plead all matters relied upon to **53PD.24**
satisfy the requirement of serious harm (see 53PD.6 above and *Lachaux v Independent Print Ltd*
[2019] UKSC 27; [2019] 3 W.L.R. 18; [2019] E.M.L.R. 22). That will include matters relied upon
in support of the claim for damages.

Even before the 2013 Act, it had become normal to plead fully the claimant's case on general
damage. That would typically include any factors which aggravated damages, including anything
relevant to the impact of the libel or slander on the claimant's feelings, such as the way others
treated the claimant as a result, and the defendant's own behaviour (e.g. refusal to apologise, repetition of the libel, and malicious conduct, such as spreading a libel with no belief that it is true), and
any unusual feature relied on as increasing damage: see, e.g. *Slipper v BBC* [1991] 1 Q.B. 283.

Ruling on meaning

Replace the last paragraph with:
Preliminary issues as to meaning have in recent years commonly been dealt with at the same **53PD.32**
time as the issue of serious harm (see Defamation Act 2013 s.1(1) and *Lachaux v Independent Print
Ltd* [2019] UKSC 27; [2019] 3 W.L.R. 18; [2019] E.M.L.R. 22). It is not yet clear what the practical
impact will be of the Supreme Court's decision in *Lachaux*, but–at the risk of over-optimism–there
seems no reason to suppose that serious harm will not often continue to be suitable for prompt and
early determination together with the issue of meaning, as Davis LJ urged in the Court of Appeal (
[2017] EWCA Civ 1334; [2018] Q.B. 594 at [79]). Where the issue is likely to involve substantial
evidence, it should usually be left to trial.

Statement in court

In the second paragraph, replace "SWS v DWP [2018] EWHC 1998 (QB); [2019] E.M.L.R. 2." with:
Hemsworth (formerly SWS) v DWP [2018] EWHC 1998 (QB); [2019] E.M.L.R. 2. **53PD.41**

Procedure

Replace the first paragraph with:

53PD.42   Statements in open court are made where a party wishes to accept a Pt 36 offer, where a claimant has accepted an offer of amends and wishes to make a unilateral statement (see *Winslet v Associated Newspapers Ltd* [2009] EWHC 2735 (QB); [2010] E.M.L.R. 11 and *Murray v Associated Newspapers Ltd* [2015] EWCA Civ 488; [2015] E.M.L.R. 21), and where the action has settled and (generally) one of the terms of settlement provides for a bilateral statement to be made in agreed terms. A statement has been allowed in Northern Ireland without a claim having been issued: *Campbell College v Independent News & Media (Northern Ireland) Ltd* [2016] N.I.Q.B. 51. It now appears that this device has been permitted in the English High Court, although the decision is unreported: *Pierdant v Guardian News & Media Ltd,* 7 April 2017, unrep. The normal practice is for the applicant to issue an application notice under CPR Pt 23 seeking permission to make a statement in terms approved by the court. However, the Pt 23 route is unsatisfactory when no proceedings have been issued, and in that case the better course is probably to issue a Pt 8 claim form: see *Hemsworth (formerly SWS) v DWP* (above) at [11]. That would accord with the procedure where a statement is to be made following acceptance of an offer of amends: see para.53PD.44 below. The practice is now to make the application to a judge of the Media and Communications list. Permission is required for the making of a statement in open court so that the judge can ensure that the court's process, or the forum it provides, is not abused: *CTB v News Group Newspapers Ltd* (above) at [26]. The notice of application for permission, together with a copy of the proposed statement, whether bilateral or unilateral, should be filed in the judges' Listing Office, Room WG08. A date convenient for both parties is arranged between counsel's clerks or between solicitors, and the signed statement is listed before the judge for mention. It is unusual for a bilateral statement to be refused by the court, but the court will refuse permission if informed that one of the parties proposing to join in the statement believes that it is false:

> "It is one thing for the court to be unable to guarantee that all its judgments or verdicts are the whole truth. It is quite another for the court to permit itself to be used for the making of a statement that the maker is at the same time declaring he believes to be untrue" (per Tugendhat J, *Adelson v Associated Newspapers Ltd (No.3)* [2008] EWHC 278 (QB) [67], [70]).

Where a statement is opposed

In the second paragraph, replace "Richard v BBC [2017] EWHC 1648 (Ch); [2017] E.M.L.R. 1," with:

53PD.43   *Richard v BBC* [2017] EWHC 1648 (Ch); [2017] E.M.L.R. 25,

Offer of amends

Replace paragraph with:

53PD.44   As explained above, a statement may also be made where an offer of amends is accepted by the aggrieved party, but there is no agreement on the steps to be taken by way of correction, apology and publication. The aggrieved party may make a unilateral statement if dissatisfied with the terms of the proposed apology: *Winslet v Associated Newspapers Ltd* [2009] EWHC 2735 (QB); [2010] E.M.L.R. 11; *Murray v Associated Newspapers Ltd* [2015] EWCA Civ 488; [2015] E.M.L.R. 21. Alternatively, the offeror may make the correction and apology by a (presumably unilateral) statement in terms approved by the court: Defamation Act 1996 s.3(4). However, such a statement would not fall within the terms of para.6 of the Practice Direction. *The Queen's Bench Guide 2018*, para.19.6.4, suggests that the application notice should be issued before the Senior Master, who may refer it to the judge. The better course may be to issue it before a judge of the Media and Communications List, whose approval should be obtained since it is in the judge's court that the statement will be read. Note that the application should be made by Pt 23 notice in existing proceedings, but by Pt 8 claim form if no proceedings have been issued.

PART 54

JUDICIAL REVIEW AND STATUTORY REVIEW

I. Judicial Review

Costs at the permission stage

In the third paragraph, replace the last sentence with:

54.12.5   The Court of Appeal has held that more than one defendant, and any person named as an interested party and served with the claim form, may recover the costs of preparing and filing an acknowledgment of service and summary grounds. The court will need to assess whether the costs claimed are reasonable and proportionate. See *R. (Campaign to Protect Rural England - Kent Branch) v Secretary of State for Communities and Local Government* [2019] EWCA Civ 1230.

PART 55

Possession Claims

I. General Rules

Renting homes in Wales

At the end of the last paragraph, replace "April 2019." with:
2020.

II. Accelerated Possession Claims of Property Let on an Assured Shorthold Tenancy

Requirements for use of the accelerated possession procedure

Add new paragraph at end:
In respect of dwellings situated wholly in Wales, s.44(1) of the Housing (Wales) Act 2014 **55.11.4** provides that a Housing Act 1988 s.21(1) or 21(4) notice may be not be given in relation to a domestic dwelling if the landlord is not registered or licensed under Pt 1 of the 2014 Act. To be licensed under the Act, a landlord must be shown to be a fit and proper person and to have undergone training on the law and best practice in relation to the letting of dwellings. It has been decided in the county court that the word "or" in this context should be given its conjunctive meaning, so to give such notice a landlord must be registered and licensed—see *Fleri v Evans* [2019] EW Misc 13 (CC). However, the subsection also makes clear that such a notice may be given on behalf of a registered but unlicensed landlord by a licensed agent appointed to carry out all property management work in respect of the dwelling on the landlord's behalf.

Claim form

Replace the second paragraph with:
Before a judge can make an order for possession under the accelerated procedure, the claimant **55.13.1** must establish that he is entitled to recover possession under s.21 of the 1988 Act (r.55.16(2)(a) and PD 55A para.8.1). For tenancies of properties in England commenced after 1 October 2015, the additional requirements prescribed by the Assured Tenancies and Agricultural Occupancies (Forms) (England) (Amendment) Regulations 2019 (SI 2019/915) apply. They include confirmation that the tenant has "How to rent: the checklist for renting in England", as published by the Department for Communities and Local Government, an energy performance certificate and a gas safety certificate. A revised **N5B England** published in Autumn 2017 allows claimants to incorporate all this information. The **N5B Wales** form requires information as to whether the landlord is registered or licensed under the Housing (Wales) Act 2014 or has appointed a licensed agent to carry out all property management work in respect of the dwelling on the landlord's behalf (see para.55.11.4 above). A claim form which does not show that the landlord is registered and licensed or has appointed such an agent is liable to be struck out.

PART 57

Change title:

Probate, Inheritance, Presumption of Death and Guardianship of Missing Persons

Editorial introduction

Replace paragraph with:
Part 57 is in six Sections. The first Section contains the rules applicable to contentious probate **57.0.1** claims as defined in r.57.1(2)(a). The second and third are concerned with matters other than contentious probate, namely rectification of wills and the removal or substitution of personal representatives. The fourth Section deals with claims under the Inheritance (Provision for Family and Dependants) Act 1975. The fifth deals with applications under the Presumption of Death Act 2013 for a declaration that a missing person is presumed to be dead. The sixth deals with applications for a guardianship order under the Guardianship (Missing Persons) Act 2017 (in force 31 July 2019) in relation to the property and affairs of missing persons. In its expanded form, Pt 57

relates to the property and affairs of the missing as well as the dead. Part 57 is supplemented by three practice directions: Practice Direction 57 (Probate) supplements rules in the first four Sections. Practice Direction 57B (Proceedings under the Presumption of Death Act 2013) and Practice Direction 57C (Proceedings under the Guardianship (Missing Persons) Act 2017) supplement the fifth and sixth Sections respectively. Practice Direction 57 (Probate) in keeping with other CPR Parts having more than one PD is referred to below as Practice Direction 57A (paras 57APD.1 to 57APD.19).

Replace r.57.1(1) with:

Scope of this Part and definitions[1]
57.1 **57.1—(1) This Part contains rules about—**
    (a) probate claims;
    (b) claims for the rectification of wills;
    (c) claims and applications to—
        (i) substitute another person for a personal representative; or
        (ii) remove a personal representative;
    (d) claims under the Inheritance (Provision for Family and Dependants) Act 1975;
    (e) proceedings under the Presumption of Death Act 2013; and
    (f) proceedings under the Guardianship (Missing Persons) Act 2017.

III. Substitution and Removal of Personal Representatives

Editorial note

Add new paragraphs at end:
57.13.1 Unlike CPR r.57.16(1), r.57.13(1) does not state that claims under s.50 must be made by Pt 8 claim. Practice Direction 57A para.13.1(2) requires the claim form to be accompanied by written evidence containing the grounds of the claim together with other specified information concerning the estate. This shows it was intended that the Pt 8 procedure should be used for claims under s.50: *Schumacher v Clarke* [2019] EWHC 1031 (Ch) (Chief Master Marsh).

In practice, most claims under s.50 are disposed of on written evidence alone at a disposal hearing. It is uncommon for s.50 applications to be directed to continue under Pt 7 in order to go to trial. Where a trial is needed it will be confined to issues necessary to determine the s.50 claim and should not be taken as an opportunity to ventilate allegations not relevant to the core issue of by whom the estate should be administered having regard to the interests of the beneficiaries as a whole: *Perry v Neupert* [2018] EWHC 1788 (Ch) (Henry Carr J) at [29]; *Schumacher v Clarke* at [18] and [34].

IV. Claims under the Inheritance (Provision for Family and Dependants) Act 1975

Time-limit for applications

To the end of the paragraph, add:
57.16.0.1 The time limit in s.4 is designed to avoid unnecessary delay in the administration of estates. All factors including whether the claim has a realistic prospect of success must be considered. There is no disciplinary element to s.4. A substantial case must be made out but the application should not be treated as if it were a procedural default requiring relief against sanctions: *Cowan v Foreman* [2019] EWCA Civ 1336.

V. Proceedings under the Presumption of Death Act 2013

Add new paragraphs 57.24, 57.25 and 57.25.1:

Requirement to send copy of declaration to the Public Guardian[2]
57.24 **57.24 Where a declaration of presumed death made under the 2013 Act satisfies section 3(3)(a) or (b) of that Act, the court must send a copy of the declaration to the Public Guardian.**

---

[1] Introduced by the Civil Procedure (Amendment) Rules 2014 (SI 2014/407) and amended by the Civil Procedure (Amendment No. 6) Rules (SI 2014/2044) and the Civil Procedure (Amendment No. 2) Rules 2019 (SI 2019/1034).
[2] Introduced by the Civil Procedure (Amendment No. 2) Rules 2019 (SI 2019/1034).

VI. Proceedings Under The Guardianship (Missing Persons) Act 2017

Scope and interpretation[1]

57.25—(1) This Section contains rules about proceedings under the **57.25** Guardianship (Missing Persons) Act 2017.

(2) In this Section, terms used in the Guardianship (Missing Persons) Act 2017 have the meaning given by that Act, and—

    (a) "the 2017 Act" means the Guardianship (Missing Persons) Act 2017;

    (b) "the missing person" means the person who is or has been asserted to be "missing" within the meaning of the 2017 Act;

    (c) "a claim for a guardianship order" means an application under section 2 (applying for a guardianship order) of the 2017 Act for a guardianship order;

    (d) "an application for a revocation/variation order" means—

        (i) an application under section 12 (variation of a guardianship order) of the 2017 Act for an order varying a guardianship order; or

        (ii) an application under section 13 (revocation of a guardianship order) of the 2017 Act for an order revoking a guardianship order;

    (e) "an application relating to a guardianship order" means any application which relates to the exercise of functions of a guardian but which is not a claim for a guardianship order or an application for a revocation/variation of a guardianship order;

    (f) "an intervener" means either a person who falls within section 21(1) of the 2017 Act and who has given notice of intention to intervene, or a person to whom the court has given permission to intervene.

Editorial note

Section VI was added to Pt 57 by the Civil Procedure (Amendment No. 2) Rules 2019 (SI 2019/ **57.25.1** 1034) and came into effect on 31 July 2019. The rules in this section are supplemented by Practice Direction 57C (Proceedings under the Guardianship (Missing Persons) Act 2017), see para.57CPD.1.

The 2017 Act came into force on 31 July 2019. The Lord Chancellor has published a Code of Practice pursuant to s.22 of the Act containing guidance for persons making applications under the Act. The court must take into account the code if it considers the code is relevant to a question arising in the proceedings. The code contains a useful summary of the Act's provisions.

The Act enables the High Court to appoint a guardian over a missing person's property and financial affairs. This is referred to as a "guardianship order". The period of guardianship must not exceed four years from the day the order is made. A copy of the order must be sent by the court to the Office of the Public Guardian.

The Chancery Division and the Family Division both have jurisdiction to make a guardianship order. The code gives guidance as to the type of cases more suitable to each Division.

Under s.1 of the Act a person is "missing" if the person is missing from his or her usual place of residence and from his or her usual day-to-day activities and either the person's whereabouts are not known or are not known with sufficient precision to enable the person to be contacted or the person is unable to make decisions relating to his or her property and the reason for that is something beyond their control, other than illness, injury or lack of capacity in relation to the matter (within the meaning of the Mental Capacity Act 2005).

The 2017 Act fulfils a different function to the 2013 Act. The 2013 Act enables a declaration to be obtained that a missing person is deemed to have died. It applies where a person is thought to have died or has not been known to be alive for at least seven years. The 2017 Act enables a guardianship order to be made if a person has been "missing" for 90 days but without any presumption the missing person is dead. On the contrary, the missing person may be known or believed to be alive. Where there is real doubt about whether the missing person is alive, r.57.33 permits a claim form to incorporate claims under both the 2013 Act and the 2017 Act provided of course the statutory conditions for each Act are met.

---

[1] Introduced by the Civil Procedure (Amendment No. 2) Rules 2019 (SI 2019/1034).

Add new paragraphs 57.26 to 57.33:

Proceedings to be in the High Court[1]

57.26   57.26—(1) Proceedings under the 2017 Act must be issued in the High Court in either—

    (a)   the Chancery Division; or

    (b)   the Family Division.

(2) The Civil Procedure Rules apply to proceedings under the 2017 Act which are brought in the Family Division, except that in the Family Division the provisions of Part 29 of the Family Procedure Rules 2010 relating to the drawing up and service of orders shall apply instead of the provisions in the Civil Procedure Rules Part 40 and Practice Direction 40B.

Procedure for making claims for a guardianship order[2]

57.27   57.27—(1) A claim for a guardianship order must be made by issuing a claim form in accordance with Part 8.

(2) Following issue, the court shall fix a date for the first hearing of the claim and which shall, unless the court otherwise orders, be not less than 56 days from the date of issue; but any person may apply for the claim or an application to be heard at an earlier date.

(3) In addition to the matters set out in rule 8.2 (contents of the claim form), the claim form must also include the information required by paragraph 1.1 of Practice Direction 57C and be accompanied by a witness statement containing the information required by paragraph 1.2 and, where appropriate, paragraph 1.3 of Practice Direction 57C.

(4) The claim form must name the missing person as the defendant but—

    (a)   the claimant need take no steps to serve the claim form upon the missing person unless the court orders otherwise;

    (b)   the court shall consider at the first hearing what, if any, directions to make regarding service or dispensing with service of the claim form upon the missing person;

    (c)   Rules 6.9, 6.15, 6.16 and 7.5 (rules as to service of the claim form) shall not apply.

(5) Rules 8.3, 8.4 and 8.5 (rules relating to part 8 claims) shall not apply. (Rule 57.29 sets out further steps that a claimant must take.)

Procedure for making applications for revocation/variation of guardianship orders and applications relating to guardianship orders[3]

57.28   57.28—(1) An application for a revocation/variation order and an application relating to a guardianship order must be made in accordance with Part 23 as modified by this rule and by paragraph 2 of Practice Direction 57C.

(2) In addition to the matters set out in rule 23.6 (what an application notice must include), the application notice must also include, or be accompanied by, a witness statement which contains the information required by paragraph 2 of Practice Direction 57C in relation to that type of application.

(3) Following issue, the court shall fix a date for the first hearing of the application which shall, unless the court otherwise orders, be not less than 56 days from the date of issue; but any person may apply for the application to be heard at an earlier date.

(4) The applicant need take no steps to serve the application or any order upon the missing person unless the court orders otherwise.

---

[1] Introduced by the Civil Procedure (Amendment No. 2) Rules 2019 (SI 2019/1034).
[2] Introduced by the Civil Procedure (Amendment No. 2) Rules 2019 (SI 2019/1034).
[3] Introduced by the Civil Procedure (Amendment No. 2) Rules 2019 (SI 2019/1034).

(5) Rules 23.9 and 23.11 apply as modified by paragraphs (6) and (7).

(6) Rule 23.9(2) (service of application where application made without notice) applies as if it did not refer to the missing person as defendant, but did refer also to any interveners.

(7) Rule 23.11 (power of court to proceed in the absence of a party) applies as if the words "or any intervener" were inserted after both references to "any respondent".

(Rules 57.29 and 57.30 set out further steps that applicants must take.)

Giving notice and advertisement of claim for a guardianship order or an application for a revocation/variation order[1]

57.29—(1) The claimant or applicant must, within 14 days of notification of the date of the first hearing of the claim for a guardianship order or of an application for a revocation/variation order— **57.29**

    (a)   send notice of the claim or application to those of the following persons whose identity and current residential or e-mail address or nominated address for service are known to the claimant or applicant—

        (i)   the spouse or civil partner of the missing person;

       (ii)   any parent of the missing person;

     (iii)   any child of the missing person;

     (iv)   any sibling of the missing person;

      (v)   if there are no persons within paragraphs (i) to (iv), the nearest relative of the missing person known to the claimant or applicant;

     (vi)   any guardian or any former guardian of the missing person;

    (vii)   any person who has previously intervened in and/or become a party to these or any proceedings in which a guardianship order was sought in relation to the missing person,

    by sending (subject to any redaction ordered by the court, and subject to paragraph (2)) the material set out in paragraph 3.1 of Practice Direction 57C to the relevant addresses; and

    (b)   advertise notice of the claim or application—

        (i)   in a form which meets the requirements set out in paragraph 4.1 of Practice Direction 57C;

       (ii)   in at least one public news media circulating in or relating to the vicinity of the last known usual place of residence of the missing person;

    being "Advertisement of the claim/application".

(2) If the person has a nominated address for service known to the claimant or applicant, and provided that such address for service has been nominated expressly for the purpose of 2017 Act proceedings, the material need only be sent to that address; and, if the claimant or applicant has no access to any, or no, e-mail address of their own, they need not send the material to any e-mail address.

(3) The claimant or applicant must file at court no later than 7 days before the first hearing of the claim or application, a witness statement—

    (a)   confirming compliance with paragraph (1)(a), and attaching Form N215 (Certificate of Service) completed to describe each method of sending to each person, as if references on that form to "service" were to "sending"; and

[1] Introduced by the Civil Procedure (Amendment No. 2) Rules 2019 (SI 2019/1034).

(b)   confirming compliance with paragraph (1)(b), and containing or attaching evidence of Advertisement of the claim/application, including details of how, where and when it was advertised.

Giving notice and advertisement of applications relating to guardianship orders or the potential exercise of powers under the 2017 Act[1]

57.30   57.30—(1) Unless the court dispenses with the need for notice, notice of an application relating to a guardianship order must be sent to those of the following persons whose identity and current residential or e-mail address or nominated address for service are known to the applicant—

(a)   the spouse or civil partner of the missing person;

(b)   any parent of the missing person;

(c)   any child of the missing person;

(d)   any sibling of the missing person;

(e)   if there are no persons within sub-paragraphs (a) to (d), the nearest relative of the missing person known to the applicant;

(f)   any guardian or any former guardian of the missing person;

(g)   any person who has previously intervened in and/or become a party to these or any proceedings in which a guardianship order was sought in relation to the missing person,

by sending (subject to any redaction ordered by the court, and subject to paragraph (2)) the material set out in paragraph 3.1 of Practice Direction 57C to the relevant addresses within 14 days after the court has notified the date for the hearing of the application.

(2) If the person has a nominated address for service known to the applicant, and provided that such address for service has been nominated expressly for the purpose of 2017 Act proceedings, the material need only be sent to that address; and, if the applicant has no access to any, or no, e-mail address of their own, they need not send the material to any e-mail address.

(3) The applicant must file at court no later than 7 days before the first hearing of the application, a witness statement confirming compliance with paragraph (1) above and attaching Form N215 (Certificate of Service) completed to describe each method of sending to each person as if references on that form to "service" were to "sending".

(4) The court may make—

(a)   a direction for advertisement of the application; and

(b)   any further provision for notification or service of the application.

(5) If the court is considering whether to exercise a power under the 2017 Act without an application having been made, the court may require—

(i)   notice of the matter to be given (in such manner the court may direct) to any of the persons listed in paragraph (1), or to any other person; and

(ii)   the matter to be advertised in such manner as the court may direct.

Interveners[2]

57.31   57.31—(1) A person who is entitled under section 21(1) (right to intervene) of the 2017 Act to intervene in a claim for a guardianship order, an application for a revocation/variation order, or an application relating to a guardianship order should, not less than 14 days before the first hearing date of the claim or application, notify the court and the claimant/applicant of any intention to intervene in accordance with the requirements of paragraph 5.1 of Practice Direction 57C.

---

[1] Introduced by the Civil Procedure (Amendment No. 2) Rules 2019 (SI 2019/1034).
[2] Introduced by the Civil Procedure (Amendment No. 2) Rules 2019 (SI 2019/1034).

(2) On receipt of a notice under paragraph (1) the court may give case management directions.

(3) Failure to comply with paragraph (1) shall not prevent the person from intervening (if they are otherwise entitled to do so) but may be taken into account on any question relating to costs.

(4) Any other person who wishes to intervene in such proceedings must, not less than 14 days before the first hearing date of the claim or application, file with the court and serve on the claimant/applicant an application for permission to intervene in accordance with Part 23 and paragraph 5.2 of Practice Direction 57C.

(5) Within 7 days of receiving an application for permission to intervene—
- (a) from a person who has not been sent or served with the claim form or the application notice, the claimant/applicant must serve a copy of the claim form or application, the evidence in support and notice of the hearing date, upon the person seeking permission to intervene; and in any case
- (b) the claimant or applicant must file with the court and serve upon the person seeking permission to intervene, a statement of whether or not they object and any evidence in support of any objection.

(6) Where the court grants permission to intervene to a person who otherwise has no entitlement to intervene under section 21(1) (right to intervene) of the 2017 Act, it may do so on conditions and may give case management directions.

(7) The court may direct that a person who intervenes in proceedings be added as a claimant (provided that they consent in writing) or defendant to the claim.

Requirement to send copy of all orders made to the Public Guardian[1]

57.32 Where the court makes a guardianship order, a revocation/variation order, an order relating to the functions of a guardian, or an order granting or refusing permission to intervene, it shall send a copy of such order to the Public Guardian. **57.32**

Death of the missing person[2]

57.33—(1) If the missing person has died before or dies after the issue of the claim then, subject to any order of the court, the claim shall not abate or be stayed, and rule 19.8 shall not apply. **57.33**

(2) If the claimant considers that there is real doubt as to whether the missing person is still alive, the claim form may incorporate claims under both the Presumption of Death Act 2013 ("the 2013 Act") and the 2017 Act.

(3) If the court determines at any point in the claim that the missing person has not been known to be alive for a period of seven years whether before or after the issue of the claim, the court may order that the claim should continue as if it had been brought under the 2013 Act.

(4) The court may make an order under or in relation to paragraphs (2) and (3) on such terms and conditions and with such consequential provisions as it considers appropriate.

---

[1] Introduced by the Civil Procedure (Amendment No. 2) Rules 2019 (SI 2019/1034).
[2] Introduced by the Civil Procedure (Amendment No. 2) Rules 2019 (SI 2019/1034).

Add new Practice Direction 57C:

PRACTICE DIRECTION 57C—PROCEEDINGS UNDER THE GUARDIANSHIP (MISSING PERSONS) ACT 2017
This Practice Direction supplements CPR Part 57

Procedure for claims—rules 57.25–57.33

1.1   Claim for guardianship order—rule 57.27

57CPD.1   The claim form for a claim for a guardianship order must include the following—

(1)   information about the claimant—
   (a)   the claimant's name and address, and, if different, their address for service;
   (b)   the relationship of the claimant to the missing person; and
   (c)   if the claimant is not the missing person's spouse, civil partner, parent, child or sibling, or other person within section 19(3) (requirement for applicants to have sufficient interest) of the 2017 Act, details of the claimant's interest in relation to the missing person's property or financial affairs;

(2)   the name and last known address of the missing person (who must be named as a defendant), and when and for how long they have been missing;

(3)   details of the terms of the guardianship order sought including the name of the proposed guardian;

(4)   if applicable, that the claimant seeks a guardianship order on the basis that the urgency condition applies (section 3(3) of the 2017 Act).

1.2   The claimant must also provide the following information, in a witness statement accompanying the claim form, and attaching any relevant evidence—

(1)   as far as the claimant knows—
   (a)   the missing person's name and surname, and any other names by which the missing person is or have formerly been known;
   (b)   the missing person's gender;
   (c)   the missing person's maiden surname (if any);
   (d)   the missing person's date and place of birth;
   (e)   the occupation of the missing person;
   (f)   the existence, name and surname, and the current residential or electronic address and any nominated address for service of—
      (i)   the missing person's spouse or civil partner,
      (ii)   the missing person's parents;
      (iii)   the missing person's siblings;
      (iv)   the missing person's children;
   (g)   the missing person's National Insurance number;
   (h)   the missing person's usual place of residence, and when they became absent from it;
   (i)   the missing person's usual day-to-day activities and when they became absent from them;
   (j)   whether it is asserted that the missing person is in prison or has been detained, and if so where and from what date;
   (k)   the date and circumstances in which the missing person is thought to have become missing; and whether there has been any police investigation, and, if so, whether any such report has been or could be obtained;
   (l)   the missing person's whereabouts, and any evidence or contentions with regard to the matters set out in section 1(2) of the 2017 Act (the missing person's whereabouts—first condition);

(m) any evidence or contentions with regard to the matters set out in section 1(3) of the 2017 Act (the missing person's ability to make relevant decisions—the second condition);

(n) reasons for supposing that the missing person is still alive; and

(o) what, if any, steps are proposed with regard to service of the claim upon or other notification of the claim to be given to the missing person, with reasons for such steps being considered appropriate;

(2) reasons why the claimant considers the court has jurisdiction to hear and determine the claim under section 2(2) (applying for a guardianship order) of the 2017 Act;

(3) reasons why the claimant asserts that they satisfy the requirement to have a sufficient interest in relation to the missing person's property or financial affairs, having regard to section 19 (requirement for applicants to have sufficient interest) of the 2017 Act;

(4) if not the claimant, the name and address of the proposed guardian together with evidence that the person consents to acting as guardian;

(5) details of the missing person's property and financial affairs as are known to the claimant and relevant to the claim for a guardianship order;

(6) reasons why, in all the circumstances, the appointment of a guardian in respect of property or financial affairs of the missing person is in the missing person's best interests (sections 3(2)(c) and 18 of the 2017 Act);

(7) an explanation as to why the proposed guardian meets the requirements to act as guardian set out in section 4 (choice of guardian) of the 2017 Act;

(8) details of any persons referred to in rule 57.29(1)(a) to whom the claimant cannot send notice of the claim and reasons for this;

(9) details of the public news media in which the claimant proposes to advertise the claim (rule 57.29(1)(b)) and reasons why it is appropriate;

(10) details of any registered Lasting Power of Attorney or registered Enduring Power of Attorney, or confirmation that no Lasting Power of Attorney or Enduring Power of Attorney has been registered, by or in relation to the missing person; and

(11) details of any Deputy appointed or confirmation that no Deputy has been appointed on behalf of the missing person under the Mental Capacity Act 2005.

1.3 Where the absence condition is not or may not be met, the witness statement must provide reasons why the claimant considers the urgency condition (section 3(3) of the 2017 Act) is met, and attach any evidence which supports this.

Applications

2.1 Any application must be made in accordance with CPR Part 23 as modi- **57CPD.2**
fied by rule 57.28 and the following paragraphs.

2.2 An application and the evidence in support must set out in detail—

(1) the applicant's name and address;

(2) the applicant's relationship with the missing person;

(3) why the applicant asserts that they satisfy the requirement to have a sufficient interest in relation to the missing person's property or financial affairs, having regard to section 19(3) (requirement for applicants to have sufficient interest) of the 2017 Act;

(4) the reasons for the application and the details of the determination, order or directions sought; and

(5) the persons to or upon whom the applicant proposes to send or serve the application.

2.3   In addition to the matters referred to in paragraph 2.2 above, an application for a revocation/variation order and an application relating to a guardianship order must be supported by a witness statement stating—

    (1)   as far as the applicant knows, the existence, name, surname and current residential and electronic address, and any nominated address for service, of—

        (a)   the missing person's spouse or civil partner;

        (b)   the missing person's parents;

        (c)   the missing person's siblings;

        (d)   the missing person's children;

        (e)   if there are no persons within sub-paragraphs (a) to (d), the nearest relative of the missing person known to the applicant;

        (f)   any guardian or any former guardian of the missing person;

        (g)   any person who has previously intervened in and/or become a party to these or any proceedings in which a guardianship order was sought in relation to the missing person;

    (2)   what, if anything, is known of the location of the missing person; and

    (3)   in the case of an application for a revocation/variation of a guardianship order, details of:

        (a)   any persons referred to in rule 57.29(1)(a) to whom the applicant cannot send notice of the application and reasons for this; and

        (b)   the public news media in which the applicant proposes to advertise the application (see rule 57.29(1)(b)) and reasons why it is appropriate.

Giving of Notice—rule 57.29(1)(a) and rule 57.30

57CPD.3   **3.1**   The material required to be sent as notice by rules 57.29 or 57.30 must include (subject to any redactions ordered by the court) a copy of the claim form or application notice, a copy of the evidence in support, and a letter stating the date of the first hearing of the claim or application and that—

"Any spouse, civil partner, parent, child or sibling of the missing person is entitled to intervene in the matter. Any other person having an interest may apply to the court for permission to intervene in the matter.

If you wish to give notice of intention to intervene or to apply to the court for permission to intervene, you should do so at [COURT ADDRESS] as soon as possible, and no later than 14 days before the date of the first hearing, and serve a copy of that notice or application on the [CLAIMANT/APPLICANT] at the address given below. Delay may harm your prospects of obtaining permission to intervene if you are not entitled to intervene, and in any event, may be taken into account on any question relating to costs."

Advertisement of claim for guardianship order or an application for a revocation/variation order—rule 57.29(1)(b)

57CPD.4   **4.1**   The advertisement of the claim for a guardianship order or an application for a revocation/variation order required by section 20(1) (giving notice of applications) of the 2017 Act and rule 57.29(1)(b) must be in the appropriate form set out below, or contain the equivalent information about the claim or application and the possibility of applying, and where and by when to apply, to the court—

IN THE HIGH COURT OF JUSTICE
IN THE [CHANCERY] [FAMILY] DIVISION

Case Number ...

IN THE MATTER OF AN APPLICATION MADE UNDER THE GUARDIANSHIP (MISSING PERSONS) ACT 2017 [FOR A GUARDIANSHIP ORDER] [TO REVOKE OR VARY A GUARDIANSHIP ORDER] IN RESPECT OF [INSERT MISSING PERSON NAME]

[A claim has been issued in the High Court of Justice, [ ] Division, Claim No. [ ], by [INSERT NAME OF CLAIMANT] for an order that [INSERT NAME OF PROPOSED GUARDIAN] be appointed guardian in respect of [INSERT NAME OF MISSING PERSON ("the missing person")], whose [last usual place of residence] was [INSERT ADDRESS].]

[An application has been issued in the High Court of Justice, [ ] Division, Claim No. [ ], by [INSERT NAME OF APPLICANT] for an order that the Guardianship Order dated [ ] made in respect of [INSERT NAME OF MISSING PERSON ("the missing person")], whose [last usual place of residence] was [INSERT ADDRESS] should be [revoked] [varied].]

The date and venue for the first hearing of the [Claim] [Application] is [ ] at [address].

Any spouse, civil partner, parent, child or sibling of the missing person is entitled to intervene in the matter. Any other person having an interest may apply to the Court for permission to intervene in the matter.

If you wish to give notice of intention to intervene or to apply to the Court for permission to intervene, you should do so at [COURT ADDRESS] as soon as possible, and no later than 14 days before the date of the first hearing, and serve a copy of that notice or application on the [CLAIMANT/ APPLICANT] at the address given below. Delay may harm your prospects of obtaining permission to intervene if you are not entitled to intervene, and, in any event, may be taken into account on any question relating to costs.

Claimant/Applicant's name

[If the claimant/applicant is legally represented]
Name of Claimant/Applicant's Legal Representative and their address for service

[If the claimant/applicant is not legally represented]
Claimant/Applicant's address for service

Interveners—rule 57.31

5.1 A person who is entitled and wishes to intervene in a claim for a **57CPD.5** guardianship order or an application for a revocation/variation order or an application relating to a guardianship order by virtue of section 21(1) (right to intervene) of the 2017 Act (the missing person's spouse, civil partner, parent, child or sibling) should notify their intention to intervene as early as possible, and not later than 14 days before the date of the first hearing, by filing with the court, and serving on the claimant or applicant, notice in writing, specifying—
  (1) the intervener's name and address;
  (2) the intervener's relationship to the missing person;

(3) the reasons for intervening; and

(4) particulars of any determination, order or directions sought.

5.2 An application under rule 57.31(4) for permission to intervene in the proceedings must be filed with the court and served on the claimant or applicant as early as possible and, in any event, no later than 14 days before the date of first hearing of the claim or application, and must specify—

(1) the applicant's name and address;

(2) why the applicant asserts that they satisfy the requirement to have a sufficient interest in relation to the missing person's property or financial affairs, having regard to sections 19 and 21(3) (requirement for applicants to have sufficient interest) of the 2017 Act;

(3) the applicant's relationship to the missing person or other interest in the proceedings;

(4) the reasons for applying for permission to intervene; and

(5) particulars of any determination, order or directions sought.

Case management of a claim for guardianship order and applications

57CPD.6   **6.1** The court may make case management directions in respect of a claim for a guardianship order, an application for the revocation/variation of a guardianship order, or relating to a guardianship order, with or without a hearing as it considers appropriate.

6.2 Applications which are not specifically provided for within Section VI of Part 57 should be made in accordance with Part 23.

Practice Direction 8A (alternative procedure for claims)

57CPD.7   **7.1** Practice Direction 8A (alternative procedure for claims) does not apply to a claim for a guardianship order except for paragraph 5.1 (no defence or reply) and paragraph 8.1 (what court may do on a hearing date).

Practice Direction 23A (applications)

57CPD.8   **8.1** Practice Direction 23A (applications) does not apply to applications for the revocation/variation of a guardianship order or relating to a guardianship order except for paragraphs 1 and 2 (subject to the express provisions of Section VI of Part 57 and this Practice Direction).

Public Guardian to be supplied with court documents relevant to supervision of guardians

57CPD.9   **9.1** Subject to paragraphs 9.2 and 9.5, where the court makes a guardianship order, a revocation/variation order or any order relating to a guardianship order, the Public Guardian is entitled to be supplied by the court with a copy of qualifying documents if the Public Guardian reasonably considers that it is necessary to have regard to them in connection with the discharge of the Public Guardian's functions under section 17 of the 2017 Act in relation to supervision of guardians.

9.2 "Qualifying documents" means the following documents which are filed in court in connection with the proceedings referred to in sub-paragraph 9.1 if not already provided to the Public Guardian—

(a) claim form seeking a guardianship order and any accompanying witness statement;

(b) any application notice seeking a revocation/variation order or an order relating to a guardianship order and any accompanying witness statement;

(c) any notice of intention to intervene or application for permission to intervene.

9.3 The court may direct that the right to be supplied with documents under paragraph 9.1 does not apply in relation to one or more such documents, or descriptions of documents, as the court may specify.

9.4 The court may direct that any document is to be provided to the Public Guardian on a redacted basis.

9.5 A direction under paragraph 9.3 or 9.4 may be given—

(a) either on the court's own initiative or on an application made to it; and

(b) either—

    (i) at the same time as the court makes the order which appoints the guardian, or which varies it; or

    (ii) subsequently.

Security Bonds—guardianship order requiring a guardian to give security for discharge of functions

10.1 Where the court makes a guardianship order which requires the guardian to give security for the discharge of his functions as guardian, the guardian must give the security before discharging any functions under the guardianship order, unless the court permits the security to be given subsequently. **57CPD.10**

10.2 Paragraphs 10.3 to 10.5 apply where the security is required to be given before the guardian discharges any functions under the guardianship order.

10.3 Subject to paragraph 10.4, the security must be given in accordance with the requirements of regulation 33(2)(a) of the Lasting Powers of Attorney, Enduring Powers of Attorney and Public Guardian Regulations 2007 (which makes provision about the giving of security by means of a bond that is endorsed by an authorised insurance company or an authorised deposit-taker).

10.4 The court may impose other requirements in relation to the giving of the security as it considers appropriate (whether in addition to, or instead of, those specified in paragraph 10.3).

10.5 In specifying the date from which the guardianship order referred to in paragraph 10.1 is to take effect, the court will consider the need to postpone that date for such reasonable period as would enable the Public Guardian to be satisfied that—

(1) if paragraph 10.3 applies, the requirements of regulation 34 of the Lasting Powers of Attorney, Enduring Powers of Attorney and Public Guardian Regulations 2007 have been met in relation to the security; and

(2) any other requirements imposed by the court under paragraph 10.4 have been met.

Code of Practice

11.1 Under section 22 of the 2017 Act it is provided that the Lord Chancellor shall issue a Code(s) of Practice and which shall include guidance to persons making applications under the 2017 Act. Attention is drawn to section 22(3) which provides that a court must take into account the relevant provisions of such a Code(s) and any failure to comply with such a Code(s) when deciding any question arising in legal proceedings. Accordingly, claimants, applicants and others should consult the Code(s) at all stages of 2017 Act proceedings, and draw the court's attention to their provisions where and when relevant. **57CPD.11**

PART 57A

BUSINESS AND PROPERTY COURTS

Editorial introduction

Add new paragraph at end:

57A.0.1   For electronic working in the B&PC, and its district registries, see para.51.2.5.

Add new paragraph 57A.0.3:

Pilot Schemes operating in the Business and Property Courts

57A.0.3   For pilot schemes specifically operative in the Business and Property Courts, see: The Electronic Working Pilot Scheme (paras 51.2.5 and 51OPD.1); The Insolvency Express Trials Pilot Scheme (paras 51.2.6 and 51PPD.1); The Disclosure Pilot Scheme (paras 51.2.10 and 51UPD.1); and, The Capped Costs List Pilot Scheme (paras 51.2.12 and 51WPD.1).

PRACTICE DIRECTION 57AB—SHORTER AND FLEXIBLE TRIALS SCHEMES

Transfer into or out from Shorter Trials Scheme

After 2.15, add new paragraph 57ABPD.2.1:

57ABPD.2.1   In considering whether to transfer a claim into or out from the shorter trials scheme, consideration should be given to the overriding objective. Particularly, consideration, in addition to the requirements of para.2.14, should be given to whether allocation to, or a claim remaining on, the shorter trials scheme is likely to further the overriding objective by reducing litigation cost for the parties, promoting proportionality, and enabling the court's resources to be made available to other litigants. See *Family Mosaic Home Ownership Ltd v Peer Real Estate Ltd* [2016] EWHC 257 (Ch); [2016] 4 W.L.R. 37 at [16], a decision made in respect of the scheme when it was a pilot scheme under CPR PD 51N, and see *Sprint Electric Ltd v Buyer's Dream Ltd* [2019] EWHC 1853 (Ch) at [9]–[10]; the latter decision affirming that the court has power under CPR r.3.1(2)(m) to transfer a claim out of the shorter trials scheme. CPR PD 51N was not formally revoked until 6 April 2019 by CPR Update 104. Inadvertently it had not been omitted when PD 57AB was introduced.

After 2.16, add new paragraph 57ABPD.2.2:

Suitability for Shorter Trials Scheme

57ABPD.2.2   In determining whether a claim was suitable for the shorter trial scheme it was appropriate to consider the extent of disclosure; the nature of any expert evidence; the likely trial length, and particularly if the trial could be expected to be no more than four days in length. In doing so it was important to focus on the nature of the shorter trial scheme, such that even where statements of case disclosed a degree of complexity that might suggest the dispute was outside its scope, the overall nature of the dispute i.e., the extent of the evidence, disclosure and likely trial length, could still justify proceeding under the scheme. A decision to transfer a claim to or keep a claim on the shorter trial scheme may be revisited in the light of developments in the course of case management. (*Excel-Eucan Ltd v Source Vagabond System Ltd* [2018] EWHC 3864 (Ch), HHJ Pearce (sitting as a judge of the High Court). Also see *Sprint Electric Ltd v Buyer's Dream Ltd* [2019] EWHC 1853 (Ch), noted at para.57ABPD.2.1.)

PART 64

ESTATES, TRUSTS AND CHARITIES

I.   Claims Relating to the Administration of Estates and Trusts

Variation of Trusts Act 1958—r.64.2(c)

Replace the second paragraph with:

64.2.7   In *MN v OP* [2019] EWCA Civ 679, the Court of Appeal held that anonymity should not be the norm or default position for beneficiaries in applications under the Variation of Trusts Act. It might be appropriate to provide a more measured degree of protection for minor beneficiaries until their majority. This might take the form of an order under s.39(1)(a) and (b) of the Children and Young Persons Act 1933. Save in exceptional circumstances, applications under the 1958 Act will be held in open court. The existing approach and guidance set out in *V v T* [2014] EWHC 3432 (Ch) by Morgan J will continue to apply and be followed.

PART 68

References to the European Court

Brexit

Replace paragraph with:

68.0.1.1 Section 6(1)(b) of the European Union (Withdrawal) Act 2018 provides for the jurisdiction of the Court of Justice of the European Union to cease on exit day. As a consequence, subject to transitional provisions, Pt 68 will become redundant on Brexit. It will therefore be revoked.

See para.5.0.1.1 for detail on the amendments to the CPR and its PDs in the event of a no-deal exit.

PART 70

General Rules about Enforcement of Judgments and Orders

Methods of enforcement

In the first paragraph, after the list, replace the following sentence with:

70.2.1 Save where permission to issue is required (as to which see r.83.2(3)) the first two of these methods (writs and warrants of control) are wholly administrative processe

Simultaneous enforcement

Replace the first paragraph with:

70.2.2 Whilst obviously the judgment creditor can only be paid once, r.70.2(2)(b) confirms that they can use more than one method of enforcement at the same time. A judgment creditor who is unsure which method to use should first consider Pt 71.

Effect of rule

Replace the first paragraph with:

70.2A.1 By the Civil Procedure (Amendment) Rules 2014 (SI 2014/407), rules as to enforcement formerly found in Schs 1 and 2 to the CPR were brought into the main body of the CPR, subject to transitional provisions. The insertion of r.70.2A in Pt 70 was part of that exercise.

PART 71

Orders to Obtain Information from Judgment Debtors

Venue

Replace "in the appropriate issuing court" with:

71.2.3 in the appropriate hearing centre

"produce at court documents in his control" (r.71.2(6))

To the end of the paragraph, add:

71.2.9 The power to order a judgment debtor to produce documents in his control does not extend to ordering production of the judgment debtor's passport for the purpose of testing the truthfulness of the judgment debtor's explanation for failure to attend an earlier hearing of the application: see *Hassan Khan & Co v Al-Rawas* [2018] 12 WLUK 42, Morris J.

Suspended committal order

Replace the first paragraph with:

71.8.1   The most common of the three types of non-compliance listed in r.71.8(1) is the debtor's failure to attend court to be examined. That rule imposes a mandatory requirement that the person under a suspended committal order must be brought before a judge to consider whether to discharge the order, and must be read with PD 71 para.8.5 which states that at that hearing the judge "will discharge the committal order unless he is satisfied beyond reasonable doubt" that the judgment debtor has failed to comply with the order: see *Baz v Singapore Airlines* [2017] 9 WLUK 63. The examination itself would have been before a court officer or District Judge. That person certifies the debtor's failure to attend (PD 71 para.8). The High Court Judge or Circuit Judge, in reliance on that certificate then makes a committal order (r.71.8(2)) but suspends it provided that the debtor attends on a subsequent occasion. If the debtor immediately does so, the examination then takes place, and the suspended committal order is thereupon discharged.

PART 73

CHARGING ORDERS, STOP ORDERS AND STOP NOTICES

I.   Charging Orders

Appropriate court (s.1 of 1979 Act)

To the end of the paragraph, add:

73.3.1   The High Court has jurisdiction to make a final charging order over a sum paid into court by the judgment debtor in separate proceedings where the payment was ordered to be paid in by way of security as a condition of being granted permission to appeal: see *A v B* [2019] EWHC 953 (Comm).

"may make an interim order"

Replace "para.7 of their application. Similarly para.7" with:

73.4.2   para.8 of their application. Similarly para.8

Effect of insolvency

Replace "r.73.8" with:

73.10.4   r.73.8(2)

The Charging Orders (Orders for Sale: Financial Thresholds) Regulations 2013 (SI 2013/491)

Replace paragraph with:

73.10.10   These regulations, made under the Charging Orders Act 1979 s.3A, came into force on 6 April 2013 but are so feeble as to be pointless and of no practical use. They apply where a charging order has been made to secure payment under a "regulated agreement" (within Consumer Credit Act 1974 s.189(1)) and provide that no order for sale can be made to recover an amount less than £1,000. It is hard to imagine that any court would have made such an order. Where the application for a charging order is in relation to a modest judgment debt, it is good practice to set out in the application notice the reasons why the judgment creditor considers that the making of the order would be a proportionate measure, together with details of any other steps that have been taken to secure payment of the debt.

III.   Stop Notices

Effect of rule

Replace the last paragraph with:

73.17.1   A judgment creditor who has obtained a final charging order upon the contingent equitable interest of a judgment debtor in Government and Bank of England Stock standing in the name of a trustee, can issue a stop notice under these rules. In *Adam v Bank of England* (1908) 52 S.J. 682, it was held that the Bank was bound to transfer stock on the direction of the legal owner, notwithstanding a charging order obtained against a person equitably entitled (following *Churchill v Bank of England* (1843) 11 M. & W. 323). Subsequent to this decision Joyce J (9 November 1908) authorised the issue in a Chancery action of a *distringas* notice based upon a final charging order.

PART 74

ENFORCEMENT OF JUDGMENTS IN DIFFERENT JURISDICTIONS

Brexit

Replace the first, second and third paragraphs with:

74.0.3.1   The Judgments Regulation will cease to apply after the UK leaves the EU and will not be saved by the European Union (Withdrawal) Act 2018, as its operation is dependent upon reciprocity between the UK and the remaining countries of the EU. The government has published a statutory instrument, the Civil Jurisdiction and Judgments (Amendment) (EU Exit) Regulations 2019 (SI 2019/479). Its effect ought to see reference to the Judgments Regulation and Brussels and Lugano Conventions within Pt 74 rendered of no effect, subject to transitional provisions. This ought to result in significant amendment to Sections I and IV of Pt 74. Part 6 of the 2019 Regulations provides saving provisions for the application of the various instruments in respect of recognition and enforcement in relation to proceedings under them which commenced prior to exit day. Unless the UK is able to join the Lugano Convention in its own right, applications for registration of foreign judgments would have to be made under the Foreign Judgments (Reciprocal Enforcement) Act 1933 for those EU/EEA Member States to which it applies, (Austria, Belgium, France, Germany, Italy, The Netherlands, Norway), or the Administration of Justice Act 1920 for those EU Member States to which it applies (Cyprus and Malta), unless the Government takes steps to revoke the application of the 1933 Act and 1920 Act to those countries. In respect of other EU Member States not covered by the 1933 Act or 1920 Act, fresh proceedings would have to be brought based on the judgment, in the same way as non-treaty countries.

The EEO Regulation (the European Enforcement Order, European Order for Payment and European Small Claims Procedure (Amendment etc.) (EU Exit) Regulations 2018 (SI 2018/1311)) ought to see reference to the EEO Regulation within Pt 74 rendered of no effect, subject to transitional provisions.

Due to the effect of the Mutual Recognition of Protection Measures in Civil Matters (Amendment) (EU Exit) Regulations 2019 (SI 2019/493), Section VI of Pt 74 would be subject to amendment to take account of the retention of recognition of incoming protection measures, i.e., of those ordered in an EU Member State, within England and Wales. Outgoing protection measures, i.e., those originating in England and Wales, will no longer be capable of recognition under EU legislation absent an exit deal, accordingly the provisions in that section on outgoing protection measures may become redundant.

Add new paragraph at end:

See para.5.0.1.1 for detail on the amendments to the CPR and its PDs in the event of a no-deal exit.

Council Regulation 1896/2006 of December 12, 2006

To the end of the paragraph, add:

74.0.9   European orders for payment are dealt with in CPR Pt 78.

Editorial note

Replace the first paragraph with:

74.1.1   Rule 74.1(5)(d) reflects the adoption of the recast Brussels I Regulation, which deals with cross-border jurisdiction, recognition and enforcement of judgments in civil and commercial matters. The recast Brussels I Regulation (the Judgments Regulation) came into effect on 10 January 2015. The Regulation has direct effect but changes were required to the rules to ensure that domestic legislation is consistent with the provisions of the Regulation as recast.

In the third paragraph, after "Transitional provisions", replace "are" with:

were

Delete the fourth paragraph (beginning "It should be noted that the amendments").

Replace the sixth and seventh paragraphs with:

Subparagraph (g) was added to reflect the coming into force on 1 October 2015 of the Civil Jurisdiction and Judgments (Hague Convention on Choice of Court Agreements 2005) Regulations

2015 (SI 2015/1644). This puts the 2005 Hague Convention into force in England & Wales, Scotland and Northern Ireland by making amendments to the Civil Jurisdiction and Judgments Act 1982 and to the Civil Procedure Rules. For the wording of the 2005 Hague Convention see *https://www.hcch.net/en/instruments/conventions/full-text/?cid=98* [Accessed 11 May 2019]).

That website also contains a list of the countries which have ratified the 2005 Hague Convention.

I.   Enforcement in England and Wales of Judgments of Foreign Courts

Editorial note

Replace the fourth paragraph with:

74.2.1   The provisions of the Lugano Convention are generally parallel in nature to the equivalent provisions in Council Regulation 44/2001 (the previous Judgments Regulation).

Editorial note

Replace "Berhad v Fraser-Nash Research Limited [2018] EWHC 2970 (QB)" with:

74.3.1   Berhad v Fraser-Nash Research Ltd [2018] EWHC 2970 (QB); [2019] 1 W.L.R. 946

The 2005 Hague Convention—evidence

Replace paragraph with:

74.4.1   Practice Direction 74A does not give any further guidance on the evidence in support of an application for registration, and the rule directs the reader to art.13 of the 2005 Hague Convention.

Change title and replace paragraph with:

74.4.2   Registration under the Lugano Convention—evidence Paragraph (6) of r.74.4 is supplemented by Practice Direction 74A para.6A (which came into effect on 10 January 2010), where it is explained that provisions in Title III of the Lugano Convention and Annex V thereof (which are annexed to Practice Direction 74A) set out the evidence needed in support of an application for registration under the Convention. (For text of Convention, see Vol.2 paras 5-392+ et seq.)

In *Percival v Motu Novu LLC* [2019] EWHC 1391 (QB), Murray J held that a master was entitled to conclude that he had sufficient information to dispense with a requirement for an Annex V certificate from the court of origin, under art.55 of the Brussels I Regulation, and was not required to give reasons for that conclusion. He also held that, so long as the applicant was an "interested party" for the purposes of art.38 of the Brussels I Regulation, the court was entitled to register the judgment in full without inquiring into the nature or extent of the applicant's interest. The decision is also likely to be relevant where the application for registration is made under the Lugano Convention, as arts 38 and 55 of that Convention are in very similar terms to the equivalent provisions of the Brussels I Regulation.

Administration of Justice Act 1920

In the second paragraph, replace "Berhad v Fraser-Nash Research Limited [2018] EWHC 2970 (QB)," with:

74.6.2   Berhad v Fraser-Nash Research Ltd [2018] EWHC 2970 (QB); [2019] 1 W.L.R. 946,

At the end of the fourth paragraph, after "to H.M. Dominions", add:
(see para.74.6.6 below)

Countries currently covered for reciprocal enforcement under the Civil Jurisdiction and Judgments Act 1982

74.6.7   *Delete "Denmark" from the list.*

Judgments Regulation

74.6.8   *Delete "as from July 1, 2007:".*

The Lugano Convention

Replace paragraph with:

74.6.8.1   This covers reciprocal enforcement between all EU Member States and Iceland, Norway and Switzerland.

Forms

Replace paragraph with:
74.6.10 The title of the witness statement or affidavit should expressly state whether it is made, "In the Matter of the Administration of Justice Act 1920 Part II", "In the Matter of the Foreign Judgments (Reciprocal Enforcement) Act 1933" or "In the Matter of the Civil Jurisdiction and Judgments Act 1982" or "In the Matter of Council Regulation (EC) No. 44/2001 of 22nd December 2000" or "In the Matter of the Lugano Convention of 30th October 2007": and in each case, the title of the witness statement or affidavit should also identify the judgment by reference to the court in which it was obtained and its date.

No submission to foreign court by appearance

Delete the last paragraph.
74.6.15

Effect of registration

Add new paragraph at end:
74.6.16 In *Islandsbanki HF v Stanford* [2019] 6 WLUK 295, 19 June 2019, unrep. (Fancourt J), however, the court held that a creditor could not petition for bankruptcy on the basis of a foreign judgment, where the period permitted for appeal against registration under art.43(5) of the Lugano Convention had not expired.

Scope of foreign judgments capable of registration

After "shows that it", replace "did." with:
74.6.17 did: see [2012] UKSC 46; [2013] 1 A.C. 236.

Application to set aside registration

In the penultimate paragraph, replace "State Bank of India v Mallya [2018] EWHC 1084 (Comm)" with:
74.7.1 State Bank of India v Mallya [2018] EWHC 1084 (Comm); [2018] 1 W.L.R. 3865

In the last paragraph, replace "Berhad v Fraser-Nash Research Limited [2018] EWHC 2970 (QB)," with:
Berhad v Fraser-Nash Research Ltd [2018] EWHC 2970 (QB); [2019] 1 W.L.R. 946,

Fraud

In the second paragraph, after "evidence that was not available at the trial", add:
74.7.2 (as to which see more recently the Supreme Court decision in *Takhar v Gracefield Developments Ltd* [2019] UKSC 13; [2019] 2 W.L.R. 984)

In the last paragraph, replace "Midtown Acquisitions LP v Essar Global Fund Ltd [2017] EWHC 519 (Comm)" with:
Midtown Acquisitions LP v Essar Global Fund Ltd [2017] EWHC 519 (Comm); [2017] 1 W.L.R. 3083

Public policy

In the penultimate paragraph, replace "Joint Stock Company (Aeroflot-Russian Airlines) v Berezovsky [2014] EWCA Civ 20" with:
74.7.3 Joint Stock Company (Aeroflot-Russian Airlines) v Berezovsky [2014] EWCA Civ 20; [2014] 1 C.L.C. 53

In the last paragraph, replace "Spliethoff's Bevrachtingskantoor BV v Bank of China [2015] EWHC 999 (Comm)" with:
Spliethoff's Bevrachtingskantoor BV v Bank of China [2015] EWHC 999 (Comm); [2016] 1 All E.R. (Comm) 1034

Add new paragraph at end:
In *CDR Creances SAS v Tapie* [2019] EWHC 1266 (Comm), Waksman J held that the French court's failure to refer certain questions of competition law to the ECJ was not a manifest breach of public policy in the sense required, i.e. a manifest breach of the rule of law regarded as essential in the EU legal order.

Immunity from suit

Replace "Sindicato Unico de Pescadores del Municipio v International Oil Pollution Compensation Fund [2015] EWHC 2476 (QB)" with:
74.7.4 Sindicato Unico de Pescadores del Municipio v International Oil Pollution Compensation Fund [2015] EWHC 2476 (QB); [2016] 1 Lloyd's Rep. 332

Appeals

Replace the fourth paragraph with:

74.8.1   In *Citibank NA v Rafidian Bank* [2003] EWHC 1950 (QB); [2003] 2 All E.R. (Comm) 1054 it was held that the two-month time limit under r.74.8 was not unfair and was compliant with art.6 ECHR. In *Verdoliva v JM Van der Hoeven BV* (C-3/05) EU:C:2006:113; [2006] E.C.R. I-1579, the European Court held that the time limit for appealing was "strict and mandatory", and that service of the decision authorising enforcement in accordance with the procedural rules of the contracting state in which enforcement was sought. The Court of Appeal has confirmed that there is no power to extend the two-month time limit for appealing against the registration of a judgment from another EU Member State against a defendant domiciled in the UK or another EU state. The Court followed *Verdoliva* in *Christofi v National Bank of Greece (Cyprus) Ltd* [2018] EWCA Civ 413; [2019] 1 W.L.R. 1435 and held that the provisions of art.43(5) provided a balance between the objective of simplicity and expedition in the recognition and enforcement of judgments and permitting a defendant to exercise an effective right of appeal against a declaration of enforceability. It would undermine the Regulation to permit a general judicial power to extend time beyond that allowed, and the principles behind its exercise would diverge between the Member States, impairing the effectiveness of the scheme for recognising and enforcing judgments.

In the fifth paragraph, replace "La Caisse Regional du Credit Agricole Nord du France v Ashdown [2007] EWHC 528 (QB)" with:
   La Caisse Regional du Credit Agricole Nord du France v Ashdown [2007] EWHC 528 (QB); [2007] I.L.Pr. 23

In the seventh paragraph (beginning "This line of authorities"), after "10 January 2015. Judgments", add:
   in proceedings instituted

In the last paragraph, replace "Lebek v Domino (C-70/15)" with:
   Lebek v Domino (C-70/15) EU:C:2016:524; [2016] W.L.R. 4221

Protective measures

Replace paragraph with:

74.8.2   The case of *Banco Nacional de Comercio Exterior SNC v Empresa de Telecomunicaciones de Cuba SA* [2007] EWHC 19 (Comm); [2007] 2 All E.R. (Comm) 46 concerned the enforcement of an Italian judgment, registered in England pursuant to art.38(2) of the Judgments Regulation. David Steel J considered whether any protective measures must be limited to assets within England. It was held that where a foreign judgment has been registered in England under the Judgments Regulation, art.47 provides "an unrestricted and discrete code for the granting of provisional or protective measures in the context of enforcement", and there was no basis for restricting protective measures to the freezing or disclosure of domestic assets. In *Cyprus Popular Bank v Vgenopoulos* [2018] EWCA Civ 1; [2018] Q.B. 886 the court held that notification of the terms of a judgment or a worldwide freezing order, even if it contained a penal notice, might be a step necessary for subsequent enforcement, but it was not a measure of enforcement within the meaning of "measures of enforcement" in art.47. The provisions of CPR r.74.9(2) and Pt 70 suggested very strongly that "enforcement" of a judgment as a matter of English law entailed the invocation of the process of the English court. There was no ground for distinction between a money judgment and a judgment granting a worldwide freezing order for this purpose. Although this decision relates to the previous Judgments Regulation, the ratio would have the same effect in relation to references to measures of enforcement and protective measures in the 2012 Brussels I (recast) Judgments Regulation.

Enforcement

In the first paragraph, after "for judgments entered", add:
74.9.0   in proceedings instituted

Stay of enforcement

Replace "Banco Nacional de Comercio Exterior S.N.C. v Empresa de Telecomunicaciones de Cuba S.A. [2007] EWHC 2322 (Comm);" with:
74.9.0.1   Banco Nacional de Comercio Exterior S.N.C. v Empresa de Telecomunicaciones de Cuba S.A. [2007] EWHC 2322 (Comm); [2007] 2 C.L.C. 690;

Execution

In the third paragraph, replace "Michael Wilson and Partners v Sinclair [2017] EWCA Civ 55" with:
74.9.2   Michael Wilson and Partners v Sinclair [2017] EWCA Civ 55; [2017] 1 W.L.R. 3069

Recognition of judgments under the 1982 Act, under the Lugano Convention and under the 2005 Hague Convention

In the second paragraph, replace "Prudential Assurance Co Ltd v Prudential Insurance Co of America [2003] EWCA Civ 327," with:
   Prudential Assurance Co Ltd v Prudential Insurance Co of America [2003] EWCA Civ 327; [2003] 1 **74.10.1**
W.L.R. 2295,

Public policy

Delete the third paragraph. **74.10.5**

In the fourth paragraph, replace "Case C-7/98 Dieter Krombach v Andre Bamberski Case C-7/98 Dieter Krombach v André Bamberski [2000] E.C.R. I-1935; [2001] Q.B. 709" with:
   Dieter Krombach v Andre Bamberski (C-7/98) EU:C:2000:164; [2001] Q.B. 709

In the fifth paragraph, after "that decision. In", delete "Case C-38/98".

In the sixth paragraph, replace "Banco Nacional de Comercio Exterior S.N.C. v Empresa de Telecomunicaciones de Cuba S.A. [2007] EWHC 2322 (Comm)" with:
   Banco Nacional de Comercio Exterior S.N.C. v Empresa de Telecomunicaciones de Cuba S.A. [2007] EWHC 2322 (Comm); [2007] 2 C.L.C. 690

In the eighth paragraph, replace "In Orams v Apostolides [2010] EWCA Civ 9," with:
   Orams v Apostolides [2010] EWCA Civ 9; [2011] Q.B. 519,

Replace the last paragraph with:
   In *Meroni v Recoletos Ltd* (C-559/14) EU:C:2016:349; [2017] Q.B. 85, the European Court held that a freezing injunction from another Member State did not infringe art.34(1) of the 2001 Brussels Regulation (public policy) where any third party affected had the right to apply to the original court to vary or discharge the judgment. The appeal against enforcement of the freezing injunction in Latvia was on the basis that the party affected by the order had not been party to the English proceedings, which was alleged to be contrary to its right to a fair trial. The decision confirms the limited scope of public policy as a ground for resisting enforcement of a judgment from another EU Member State.

Default of appearance

In the third paragraph, replace "The position should be simplified by the European Enforcement Order," with:
   Note also the European Enforcement Order, **74.10.7**

Irreconcilable with a judgment in a dispute between the same parties in State in which recognition sought

In the second paragraph, replace "Case C-80/00 Italian Leather SpA (judgment of the court of June 6, 2002)," with:
   Italian Leather SpA (C-80/00) EU:C:2002:342; [2002] I.L.Pr. 41 (judgment of the court of 6 June **74.10.11**
2002),

II. *Enforcement in Foreign Countries of Judgments of the High Court and the County Court*

Editorial note

Replace paragraph with:
   Rule 74.12 sets out the procedure for obtaining certified copy judgments for the purpose of **74.12.1**
enforcement out of the jurisdiction, including where the judgment is one subject to the provisions of the Judgments Regulation.
   In *Weil v Gulacsi* (C-361/18) EU:C:2019:472, the ECJ ruled that a court hearing an application to issue a certificate under art.54 of the Brussels I Regulation must ascertain whether the dispute falls within the scope of the Regulation, if the court which gave the judgment did not determine that point. The same is likely to apply to applications under art.53 of the Judgments Regulation or art.54 of the Lugano Convention.

Judgment entered in the High Court

Replace paragraph with:
   Not every judgment of the High Court can be made the subject of a certificate under the 1933 **74.13.1**
Act. The rule applies to "a judgment under which a sum of money is payable, not being a sum pay-

able in respect of taxes or other charges of a like nature or in respect of a fine or other penalty" (1933 Act s.10).

The enlargement of the county court jurisdiction following the Courts and Legal Services Act 1990 raises the question of whether judgments transferred to the High Court for enforcement and which are to be treated "for all purposes" as a judgment or order of the High Court can be granted certificates for enforcement abroad under this rule and the 1920 and 1933 Acts. As these Acts are based on reciprocity it cannot be assumed that countries with which these reciprocal arrangements exist will enforce judgments other than those of the "High Court" or "Superior Court" as defined in the Acts, however they are described in subsequent domestic legislation which includes the repeal of references to the "Superior Court" in the 1933 Act by s.54 of the Civil Jurisdiction and Judgments Act 1982. A number of countries to which the 1933 Act applies are parties to the Brussels and Lugano Conventions (incorporated into English, Scottish and Northern Irish law by the 1982 Act) under which the certification of county court judgments raises no problems and in such cases applications for certificates should be made to the county court. In respect of countries not party to these conventions it can only be stated with reasonable certainty that the Isle of Man will enforce under the 1933 Act county court judgments transferred to the High Court for enforcement and certified under this rule by the High Court (*Stapleford Flying Club v Kreisky*, 18 April 1991, unrep., High Court of the Isle of Man, Deemster Corrin). In all cases under the 1933 Act concerning county court judgments, application for certificates should be made in the High Court on the transferred county court judgment, though there is a risk, other than in the Isle of Man, that the certificate will be rejected by the receiving country. The Royal Court of Jersey has in fact rejected registration of an English county court judgment transferred to the High Court for enforcement. The basis of rejection was the absence of reciprocity in that a judgment of the Jersey Petty Debts Court would not be amenable to registration in England. Bailiff Bailhache commented that though the English courts might be bound to regard the judgment of the county court as a judgment of the High Court for all purposes, it was not a judgment "given in a superior court" for the purposes of the Jersey legislation (*Re Hardwick* [1995] The Jersey Law Reports 245). The position under the 1920 Act remains unchanged and permits a certificate to be issued only in respect of judgments "obtained in the High Court" which leaves open the question of whether the receiving court will consider a transferred county court judgment to be such a judgment.

IV. Enforcement in England and Wales of European Community Judgments

Community judgments enforceable in the UK

Replace the first paragraph with:

74.26.1   The European Communities (Enforcement of Community Judgments) Order 1972 (SI 1972/1590) (the Order in Council) provides for certain decisions, judgments and orders of Community institutions to be registered and enforced in the UK. The provisions of Section IV of Pt 74 (added to the CPR by the Civil Procedure (Amendment) Rules 2002) replaced the rules previously found in CPR Sch.1, RSC Ord.71, Section II.

From the start of the second paragraph, delete "For the purposes of the Order in Council and of this Order,".

V. European Enforcement Orders

In the first paragraph, replace "Zulfikarpasic v Gajer (C-484/15) (9 March 2017)" with:

74.27.1   *Zulfikarpasic v Gajer* (C-484/15) EU:C:2017:199; [2017] I.L.Pr. 16

Judgment capable of being certified as an EEO

After the third paragraph, add new paragraph:

74.28.2   In *G v de Visser* (C-292/10) EU:C:2012:142; [2013] Q.B. 168, the ECJ held that, although a default judgment was capable of being certified as an EEO, such a judgment could not be certified as an EEO where the defendant's address was unknown. In *RD v SC* (C-518/18) EU:C:2019:546, the ECJ held that the same applied where the proceedings had been served on a guardian *ad litem* appointed to represent the defendant in the proceedings; a guardian *ad litem* was not the debtor's representative within the meaning of art.15 of the EEO Regulation.

Replace the last paragraph with:

But in *Chachani Misti y Pichu Pichu SRL v Hostplanet Ltd* [2016] EWHC 983 (Ch); [2017] I.L.Pr. 34, an application for an EEO certificate was granted, where the claimant did not have a physical address for the defendant but the defendant had requested the claimant to send the documents to him to email. The High Court held that the claimant's non compliance with the procedural requirements of art.14 were cured by the application of art.18(2) which provides that such non-compliance shall be cured if it is proved by the conduct of the debtor in the court proceedings that he has personally received the document to be served in sufficient time to arrange his defence. The defendant had taken no formal steps in the proceedings, such as obtaining documents or challenging jurisdiction. It was held that, if art.18(2) was to have any effect in the case of a default judgment, it had to be construed as extending to conduct in the proceedings going wider than formal steps.

Delete paragraph 74.29.1, "Editorial note".

Enforcement costs following rescission of EEO in court of origin

In the last paragraph, replace "De La Hija v Lee (Executrix of the estate of Lee) [2018] EWHC 1374 (Ch))" with:
De La Hija v Lee (Executrix of the estate of Lee) [2018] EWHC 1374 (Ch); [2019] 1 W.L.R. 175   **74.33.1**

PRACTICE DIRECTION 74A—ENFORCEMENT OF JUDGMENTS IN DIFFERENT JURISDICTIONS

To the end of the second paragraph, add:
A current list of the countries which have ratified the Convention is available at **74APD.16** https://www.hcch.net/en/instruments/conventions/status-table/?cid=98 [Accessed 11 May 2019].

PART 81

APPLICATIONS AND PROCEEDINGS IN RELATION TO CONTEMPT OF COURT

Structure of Pt 81

Delete the sixth paragraph (beginning "Pt 81 and Practice Direction 81").   **81.0.2**

In the last paragraph, replace "(R v Yaxley-Lennon [2018] EWCA Crim 1856; [2018] 2 Cr. App. R. 30," with:
(R. v Yaxley-Lennon [2018] EWCA Crim 1856; [2019] 1 W.L.R. 5400; [2018] 2 Cr. App. R. 30,

II. Committal for breach of a judgment, order or undertaking to do or abstain from doing an act

Scope of Section

After the tenth paragraph (beginning "Procedure in respect"), add new paragraph:
Committal for a breach of a reporting restriction order, such as an order postponing reports **81.4.1** under s.4(2) of the Contempt of Court Act 1981, does not fall within Section 2 of Pt 81, but rather Section 3 of Pt 81: see *Attorney General v Yaxley-Lennon* [2019] EWHC 1791 (QB) at [92]-[101].

"does not do it" or "disobeys"

Replace both instances of "Olu-Williams v Olu-Williams [2018] EWHC 2464 (Fam)" with:
Olu-Williams v Olu-Williams [2018] EWHC 2464 (Fam); [2019] 1 F.C.R. 714   **81.4.2**

Enforcement against body corporate

In the third paragraph, replace "Integral Petroleum SA v Petrogat FZE [2018] EWHC 2686 (Comm)" with:
Integral Petroleum SA v Petrogat FZE [2018] EWHC 2686 (Comm); [2019] 1 W.L.R. 574   **81.4.5**

Effect of rule

In the last paragraph, replace "Deutsche Bank AG v Vik [2018] EWCA Civ 2011" with:
Deutsche Bank AG v Vik [2018] EWCA Civ 2011; [2019] 1 W.L.R. 1737   **81.10.1**

Application notice under Part 23

In the sixth paragraph (beginning "The grounds on which"), replace "R v Yaxley-Lennon [2018] EWCA Crim 1856; [2018] 2 Cr. App. R. 30," with:
R. v Yaxley-Lennon [2018] EWCA Crim 1856; [2019] 1 W.L.R. 5400; [2018] 2 Cr. App. R. 30,   **81.10.2**

In the ninth paragraph (beginning "An order for committal"), replace "R v Yaxley-Lennon [2018] EWCA Crim 1856; [2018] 2 Cr. App. R. 30," with:
> R. v Yaxley-Lennon [2018] EWCA Crim 1856; [2019] 1 W.L.R. 5400; [2018] 2 Cr. App. R. 30,

Service

81.10.4 *In the third paragraph, replace "Deutsche Bank AG v Vik [2018] EWCA Civ 2011" with:*
> Deutsche Bank AG v Vik [2018] EWCA Civ 2011; [2019] 1 W.L.R. 1737

In the fifth paragraph (beginning "In Integral Petroleum SA"), replace "Integral Petroleum SA v Petrogat FZE [2018] EWHC 2686 (Comm)" with:
> Integral Petroleum SA v Petrogat FZE [2018] EWHC 2686 (Comm); [2019] 1 W.L.R. 574

III.   Committal for interference with the due administration of justice

Effect of Section

Replace the sixth, seventh, eighth and ninth paragraphs (beginning "The potential for confusion as to whether, in a particular case" and ending "court will have concurrent jurisdiction.") with:

81.12.1   Three Divisional Courts have had cause to criticise the confusion caused by the drafting of CPR Pt 81: *Simmonds v Pierce (Practice Note)* [2017] EWHC 3126 (Admin); [2018] 1 W.L.R. 1849 at [9]–[32]; *Solicitor General v Holmes* [2019] EWHC 1483 (QB) at [32] and [53]; *Attorney General v Yaxley-Lennon* [2019] EWHC 1791 (QB) at [94]–[97], and the drafting of CPR Pt 81 is now being reconsidered by the Rules Committee.

There is very considerable potential for confusion as between the different Sections of Pt 81. In general, breaches of orders or undertakings will be within Section 2, unless the order is a reporting restriction order or injunction contra mundem, in which case it will more ordinarily be dealt with by an application under Section 3 by the Law Officers to the Divisional Court, or summarily (or, in the criminal courts, under the postponed enquiry procedure under Criminal Procedure Rules 2015 (SI 2015/1490) Pt 48) by the judge who made the order in question: see *Attorney General v Yaxley-Lennon* [2019] EWHC 1791 (QB) at [92]–[97].

Contempt in the face of the court will ordinarily be dealt with under Section 5 of Pt 81 if in the face of a court operating under the CPR, and dealt with by that court, but will be dealt with under Section 3 if the application is made to the High Court (including a Divisional Court) in respect of contempt in the face of an inferior or criminal court: see *Solicitor General v Holmes* [2019] EWHC 1483 (Admin) at [13]–[40].

Where the contempt alleged constitutes both a false statement of truth or a false disclosure statement (such that Section 6 of Pt 81 applies) but also some other interference in the administration of justice (falling within Section 3 of Pt 81), r.81.17(5) provides that Section 3 applies (subject to r.81.17(6)).

Delete the last two paragraphs.

Inferior court proceedings

81.12.2 *Replace "Hughes Jarvis Ltd v Searle [2019] EWCA Civ 1 at [30]-[38]." with:*
> Hughes Jarvis Ltd v Searle [2019] EWCA Civ 1; [2019] 1 W.L.R. 2934.

Criminal proceedings

Replace the fourth sentence (beginning "Thus the jurisdictions") with:

81.12.3   Thus the jurisdictions of the High Court and the Crown Court are to an extent concurrent: see *Solicitor General v Holmes* [2019] EWHC 1483 (Admin) at [13]–[37] confirming that the Divisional Court's jurisdiction in respect of contempt in the face of the Crown Court is not ousted by the infelicitous drafting of r.81.12(1)(e); and for the exercise of the various forms of concurrent jurisdiction of the Divisional Court and the criminal courts in respect of contempt by publication, see *Attorney General v Yaxley-Lennon* [2019] EWHC 1791 (QB).

Divisional Court

In the last paragraph, replace the last sentence with:

81.13.3   The permission of the Divisional Court is required in respect of all applications to that Court under CPR r.81.12(1)(e) made in respect of contempt alleged within criminal proceedings, whether in the face of the court (*Solicitor General v Holmes* [2019] EWHC 1483 (Admin) at [38]–[40]), or by way of publication including breach of reporting restriction orders (*Attorney General v Yaxley-Lennon* [2019] EWHC 1791 (QB) at [92]–[97]). (In the Crown Court, leave to proceed is not required; see Criminal Procedure Rules 2015 (SI 2015/1490) Pt 48.)

Proceedings "which are criminal proceedings"

In the first paragraph, after "Circumstances may arise" replace "where, apparently, the Crown Court" with:
where the Crown Court **81.13.5**

Disposal of application for permission

To the end of the second paragraph, add:
The only difference between permission in respect of false statements under Section 6 of Pt 81, **81.14.5** and permission under Section 3 of Pt 81 is that in the former, the Court of Appeal has affirmed that a "strong prima facie" case is required (see *Zurich Insurance Plc v Romaine* [2019] EWCA Civ 851 at [29]), whereas in respect of the latter, two Divisional Courts have recently held that only a "prima facie" case need be shown: *Solicitor General v Holmes* [2019] EWHC 1483 (Admin) at [41]-[47], and *Attorney General v Yaxley-Lennon* [2019] EWHC 1791 (QB) at [98]-[101].

Replace the fourth paragraph with:
No express provision is made in CPR Pt 81 for the making of renewed applications where permission is refused, or for revocation of permission already granted. However, in *Zurich Insurance Plc v Romaine* [2018] EWHC 3383 (QB), Goose J held that the Court did have the latter power under CPR r.3.1, and revoked permission and declined its regrant. While the substantive decision on permission was overturned on appeal, the Court of Appeal made no adverse comment as to the High Court's jurisdiction to act as it did: see [2019] EWCA Civ 851 at [22]-[23], [35]. A disappointed applicant may apply for permission to appeal against the adverse decision of the single judge or of a Divisional Court (as the case may be) in the normal way.

V. Contempt in the Face of the Court

Effect of Section

In the first paragraph, replace "Hughes Jarvis Ltd v Searle [2019] EWCA Civ 1" with:
Hughes Jarvis Ltd v Searle [2019] EWCA Civ 1; [2019] 1 W.L.R. 2934 **81.16.1**

*In the third paragraph, replace "R v Yaxley-Lennon [2018] EWCA Crim 1856; [2018] Cr. App. R. 30,"
with:*
R. v Yaxley-Lennon [2018] EWCA Crim 1856; [2019] 1 W.L.R. 5400; [2018] Cr. App. R. 30,

"that court has power to commit"

Replace the second paragraph with:
The court in whose "face" the contempt was committed is the court that has jurisdiction to com- **81.16.2** mit for this type of contempt, although the High Court (whether or not sitting as a Divisional Court) enjoys concurrent jurisdiction in respect of contempt in the face of inferior and/or criminal courts: *Solicitor General v Holmes* [2019] EWHC 1483 (Admin) at [13]-[37], albeit at [40] suggesting that only exceptionally should contempt in the face be dealt with other than by the criminal judge, whether summarily or by way of the postponed enquiry procedure in the Criminal Procedure Rules Pt 48. In the High Court and in the County Court the jurisdiction is inherent (see Vol.2, paras 3C-27 and 3C-33).

VI. Committal for Making a False Statement of Truth (Rule 32.14) or Disclosure Statement (Rule 31.23)

Permission of the court

Replace the penultimate paragraph with:
In *Zurich Insurance Plc v Romaine* [2018] EWHC 3383 (QB), (Goose J), it was held that the High **81.18.2** Court had the power under rr.3.1(7) and 3.1(2)(m) to revoke a refusal of permission to bring committal proceedings which had been made on paper, whether the application had been made under Pt 23 or by way of Pt 8 claim form. Although the substantive decision on permission was overturned on appeal, the Court of Appeal implicitly endorsed the High Court's jurisdiction to act as it did: see [2019] EWCA Civ 851 at [22]-[23], [35].

VIII.   General Rules about Committal Applications, Orders for Committal and Writs of Sequestration

Grounds and evidence relied on—burden and standard of proof

Replace the fifth paragraph with:

81.28.4   A person accused of contempt, like the defendant in a criminal trial, has the right to remain silent (*Comet Products UK Ltd v Hawkex Plastics Ltd* [1971] 2 Q.B. 67, CA). It is the duty of the court to ensure that the accused person is made aware of that right and also of the risk that adverse inferences may be drawn from his silence (*Inplayer Ltd v Thorogood* [2014] EWCA Civ 1511, 25 November 2014, CA, unrep., at para.41). In *Discovery Land Co LLC v Jirehouse* [2019] EWHC 1633 (Ch) at [23]-[30], it was held that notwithstanding the terms of CPR r.81.28, an alleged contemnor could not be compelled to submit to cross-examination even if he or she had tendered an affidavit into evidence in the contempt proceedings, nor would he or she be put to an election as to whether to submit or forgo reliance on the affidavit. The drawing of adverse inference in this context is consistent with the jurisprudence of the European Court of Human Rights (*Khawaja v Popat* [2016] EWCA Civ 362, 14 April 2016, CA, unrep., at para.30 per McCombe LJ). If the committal application is heard at the same time as other issues about which the alleged contemnor needs to give evidence, he is placed in the position where he is effectively deprived of the right of silence (ibid). That is a serious procedural error (see also *Hammerton v Hammerton* [2007] EWCA Civ 248; [2007] 2 F.L.R. 1133, CA). In the case of *Re L (A Child)* [2016] EWCA Civ 173; [2017] 1 F.L.R. 1135; [2016] Fam. Law 668, in proceedings for enforcement of a collection order, the paternal uncle (D) of the child concerned was brought before the court on witness summons and gave evidence under compulsion (which was not believed). In proceedings brought by the local authority, in which it was alleged that D had not provided the court with all the information he had about the whereabouts of the child, D was committed for contempt. The Court of Appeal allowed D's appeal, principally on the ground that, at the committal hearing, use was made against him of "the evidence which had been extracted from him under compulsion". See, in the context of a breach of a "gang injunction" under s.34 of the Policing and Crime Act 2009, *Douherty v Chief Constable of Essex Police* [2019] EWCA Civ 55, where the appeal was allowed for failure of the judge to warn the contemnor of his distinct rights to remain silent and of privilege against self-incrimination. However, the Court is entitled to look at evidence already given by a person and civil judgments against them when considering an allegation of contempt by that person, without breaching their right to silence under r.81.28(3), and is not an impermissible collateral use for the purposes of r.31.22: see *Super Max Offshore Holdings Ltd v Malhotra* [2018] EWHC 2979 (Comm).

Effect of rule

In the first paragraph, replace "(R v Yaxley-Lennon [2018] EWCA Crim 1856; [2018] Cr. App. R. 30," with:

81.29.1   (*R. v Yaxley-Lennon* [2018] EWCA Crim 1856; [2019] 1 W.L.R. 5400; [2018] Cr. App. R. 30,

In the second paragraph, after "explained. See e.g.", add:

     Liverpool Victoria Insurance Co Ltd v Zafar [2019] EWCA Civ 392 (the leading modern restatement of sentencing principles in contempt cases); *Sellers v Podstreshnyy* [2019] EWCA Civ 613 (for the relevance of the contemnor's caring responsibilities);

Service of committal order

To the end of the paragraph, add:

81.30.2   A failure to serve the order, or to apply for the court to dispense with such service, will not necessarily invalidate the contemnor's arrest or committal to prison: see *Isis Housing Co-Operative v Evelyn* [2019] EWCA Civ 1299 at [15]-[21].

Application to be discharged from prison

Add new paragraph at end:

81.31.1   In *Podstreshny v Pericles Properties Ltd* [2019] EWHC 1237 (Ch), Marcus Smith J considered and granted an application under CPR r.81.31. However, there was no attestation given by the prison governor or other senior officer at the prison, as is required by r.81.31(2)(a). At [13]-[15], the judge warned that if the same situation occurred in future, it was open to the Court to join the prison authorities as parties, summon them to court to provide an explanation of the failure, with potential costs and other consequences.

Discharge of a person

In the first paragraph, after "at [45] et seq).", add:

81.31.4   In *McKendrick v Financial Conduct Authority* [2019] EWCA Civ 524 the Court of Appeal dismissed an appeal against sentence, but suggested in obiter at [41] that where the sentence comprises both a penal element and a coercive element that the latter is the element which can be remitted where the contemnor purges his contempt.

PART 82

Closed Material Procedure

Editorial introduction

Replace the ninth and tenth paragraphs (beginning "In proceedings in which a declaration") with:

In proceedings in which a declaration under s.6 of the 2013 Act has been made, the questions will arise whether and to what extent art.6 ECHR affects the disclosure that must be given to the excluded party. For discussion of the relevant principles following the making of a s.6 declaration, see *HTF, ZMS v Ministry of Defence* [2018] EWHC 1623 (QB), at [12]-[19]. In proceedings which involve the determination of civil rights and obligations, the 2013 Act and Pt 82 must be read subject to art.6, so that "there will have to be whatever disclosure is necessary for the claimants to have the 'fair hearing' to which article 6 entitles them": *R. (K) v Secretary of State for Defence* [2016] EWCA Civ 1149; [2017] 1 W.L.R. 1671, CA, para.21. The question whether art.6 requires the excluded party to be given "sufficient disclosure to know the nature of the allegations made, to take legal advice and to make an effective challenge to them" (also known as the "irreducible minimum" disclosure requirement or "A-type disclosure," after the decision of the European Court of Human Rights in *A v United Kingdom* (2009) 49 E.H.R.R. 625) is the subject of case law in other statutory contexts. A-type disclosure can, in principle, encompass a requirement for disclosure even where that would damage national security or another important public interest, if such disclosure is required to enable the excluded party not merely to deny, but to refute (insofar as possible) the case against him or her: *Bank Mellat v HM Treasury (No.4)* [2015] EWCA Civ 1052; [2016] 1 W.L.R. 1187, paras 33–37. However, statutory regimes in which such disclosure requirements apply invariably provide for a party ordered to disclose material whose disclosure would damage national security or another important public interest to elect, instead, to make a concession, or to withdraw the part of his or her case to which the disclosure is relevant: above, para.37. A-type disclosure is required in proceedings under Pt 76 to challenge control orders (*Secretary of State for the Home Department v AF (No.3)* [2009] UKHL 28; [2010] 2 A.C. 269, HL); in proceedings under the Terrorist Asset Freezing Act 2010 (*Mastafa v HM Treasury* [2013] 1 W.L.R. 1621 (Collins J)); and in at least some proceedings under Pt 79 challenging financial restrictions orders under the Counter-Terrorism Act 2008 (*Bank Mellat v HM Treasury (No.4)* [2015] EWCA Civ 1052; [2016] 1 W.L.R. 1187, paras 12-28). No right to A-type disclosure arises, however, in employment proceedings (*Tariq v Home Office* [2011] UKSC 35; [2012] 1 A.C. 452, SC); nor in judicial review proceedings to challenge the Home Secretary's refusal to grant a Convention Travel Document to a refugee (*R. (AZ) v Secretary of State for the Home Department* [2017] EWCA Civ 35; [2017] 4 W.L.R. 94, CA). The question whether art.6 requires A-type disclosure in general depends on "context and all the circumstances of the case" (*Kiani v Secretary of State for the Home Department* [2015] EWCA Civ 776; [2016] Q.B. 595, CA, para.23 (Lord Dyson MR)). In proceedings under Pt 82, it is important to place the issues that arise for determination on a "spectrum or scale", from control orders (*AF (No.3)*) and asset-freezing (*Mastafa*) at one end to cases such as *AZ* at the other, with employment cases (*Tariq, Kiani*) in the middle (*R. (K) v Secretary of State for Defence* [2017] EWHC 830 (Admin); [2017] A.C.D. 75, unrep., DC, paras 12–13. In a public law claim brought by persons claiming to have served as interpreters for the UK in Afghanistan to challenge the arrangements made to protect them, A-type disclosure did not apply, but it did not follow that there should be no disclosure which might harm national security. The court may need to strike a balance between the significance of material not otherwise disclosed and the interests of national security (above, para.24).

82.0.1

This Part provides the procedure for closed material procedure (CMP) applications in courts to which the CPR applies. For discussion of recourse to CMP in proceedings in the Supreme Court, see *Bank Mellat v HM Treasury (No.2)* [2013] UKSC 38; [2013] UKSC 39; [2014] 1 A.C. 700, SC; in the Magistrates' Court, Crown Court and High Court dealing with applications for search and seizure warrants, see *R. (Haralambous) v St Albans Crown Court* [2018] UKSC 1; [2018] 2 W.L.R. 357 which was described in *Competition and Markets Authority v Concordia International Rx (UK) Ltd* [2018] EWHC 3448 (Ch) at footnote 2 as having

"succeeded in creating, through the common law, a procedure similar to the statutory procedures [i.e. those provided for in ss.6ff of the Justice and Security Act 2013 and CPR Pt 82] protecting material the disclosure of which would be damaging to the interests of national security";

and in the First-Tier Tribunal, see *Browning v Information Commissioner* [2014] EWCA Civ 1050; [2014] 1 W.L.R. 3848, CA. Those cases contain guidance on the function of closed material procedures generally.

II.   General Provisions

Add new paragraph 82.16.1:

A library of closed judgments has now been established in the Royal Courts of Justice. For practical rules applying to any court or tribunal giving a "closed" judgment following a closed material procedure, whether pursuant to the provisions of Pt 1 of the Justice and Security Act

82.16.1

2013, in the High Court, the Divisional Court or the Court of Appeal; in proceedings in relation to terrorism prevention and investigation measures; in any tribunal established under the Tribunals, Courts and Enforcements Act 2007 (save for the employment tribunal and the Employment Appeals Tribunal) and in any appeals therefrom, see *Practice Direction (Closed Judgments)* [2019] 1 W.L.R. 1351. Secure handling provisions for such judgments are set out in the *Closed Judgments Library–Security Guidance of 2017*, a copy of which can be obtained from the RCJ Senior Information Officer.

PART 83

Writs and Warrants—General Provisions

II.   Writs and Warrants

Add new paragraph 83.4.4:

The priority of a relevant writ

83.4.4   In *365 Business Finance Ltd v Bellagio Hospitality WB Ltd* [2019] EWHC 1920 (QB), the court undertook a detailed consideration of r.83.4(5)(a), the binding of goods under Sch.12 to the Tribunals, Courts and Enforcement Act 2007 and the link between "binding of goods" and "priority" of competing writs. The court concluded that priority is determined by the time and date that the writ is received by the person required to endorse receipt of it and that

> "although the same goods can be bound by multiple writs, it is only once the first writ is satisfied out of proceeds that the surplus (if any) can be applied to the second writ, and so on, in accordance with writ priority".

Effect of rule

Replace the first paragraph with:

83.7.1   This rule distinguishes provisions that relate to writs of control, warrants of control and all types of warrant. It also contains discrete provisions that apply only to the county court (r.83.7(8)–(15)). This rule confers express power on the court to stay execution either absolutely or for such period and subject to such conditions as the court thinks fit, provided that the applicant can satisfy either (a) or (b) in r.83.7(4). It seems that this power is not limited to stays in respect of writs or warrants of control, but may apply to other forms of enforcement (*Michael Wilson & Partners Ltd v Sinclair (No.2)* [2017] EWCA Civ 55; [2018] 1 W.L.R. 3069, CA, at para.15 per McCombe). The exercise of this power is not limited to cases where a writ of control or other warrant has been issued. Instead an application may be made by the debtor (or other party liable to execution of a writ of control or a warrant) "from the moment of the making of the judgment or order for the payment of money" (ibid at para.13 per McCombe LJ).

It is important to note that this rule relates solely to stays of execution and not to a variation of a judgment (albeit that conditions imposed on granting a stay may have that effect e.g. to provide for instalment payments). This may have little practical consequence in the county court as, pursuant to s.71 of the County Courts Act 1984 "Satisfaction of judgments and orders for payment of money", the court may "at any time ... suspend or stay any judgment or order given ...". This provision is incorporated in the CPR at r.40.9A. However, there is no similar statutory provision, and so no equivalent procedural provision, in the High Court. In *Loson v Stack* [2018] EWCA Civ 803 at [17] the court stated, obiter, that

> "any variation of a High Court order for payment of the amount as a single sum must be made under the power contained in CPR 3.1(7) which in most cases will require the applicant for the variation to demonstrate a material change of circumstances" .

(Note that CPR r.40.8A provides for stays of execution in respect of matters that have occurred since the date of judgment).

Rule 40.11 enables a party in both the High Court and the county court to seek a date beyond the prescribed 14 days for payment of money under a judgment or order (including an order for instalment payments) as part of the judgment or order (as opposed to by subsequent variation of a judgment or order). However, this does not operate as an automatic stay of execution e.g. a charging order may be made even if there has been no breach of an order for payment by instalment (see para.73.4.4). Accordingly, an application under r.83.7 should be made when a stay of execution is required.

IV. Warrants

Enforcement of High Court judgments in the County Court

Replace paragraph with:

However, where the sum which it is sought to enforce is less than £600, enforcement by execution must be in the county court (para.8 High Court and County Courts Jurisdiction Order 1991 see Vol.2 para.9B-939) and can be in the county court where that sum is less than £5,000. **83.17.1**

PART 89

ATTACHMENT OF EARNINGS

II. Applications for Attachment of Earnings Orders

Committal

After the second sentence, add:

Section 23(2)(c) provides that a debtor who fails to comply with a notice (**N61**) served pursuant **89.8.2** to s.14(1) commits an offence. The effect of r.89.8(4) is to require the court to serve a notice (**N63**) on a debtor who commits such an offence requiring them to attend a hearing to show cause why they should not be sent to prison. Section 23(1) provides that if a debtor fails to comply with such a notice (**N63**) by failing to attend the "show cause" hearing, the court may adjourn the hearing and order the debtor to attend on the day and at the time specified in the order. If the debtor fails to attend the adjourned hearing (or attends but refuses to be sworn or give evidence) the judge may order that the debtor be imprisoned for up to 14 days. The power to commit pursuant to s.23(1) would appear to be exercisable only where the debtor fails to attend the adjourned hearing. This seems to be consistent with the wording of r.89.9(1) which provides for suspension of a committal order made at an adjourned hearing.

SCHEDULE 1—RSC PROVISIONS

RSC ORDER 109—THE ADMINISTRATION OF JUSTICE ACT 1960

Editorial note

Replace "House of Lords" with:

Supreme Court of the United Kingdom **sc109.4.1**

SECTION C   PRE-ACTION CONDUCT AND PROTOCOLS

The development of the current protocols

C1A-003   *Replace table with:*

Protocol	Came into force
Personal Injury	26 April 1999
Clinical Negligence	26 April 1999
Construction and Engineering	02 October 2000
Defamation (From 1 October 2019 the Defamation Protocol will be replaced by the Pre-Action Protocol for Media and Communications Claims)	02 October 2000
Professional Negligence	16 July 2000
Judicial Review	4 March 2002
Disease and Illness	8 December 2003
Housing Disrepair	8 December 2003
Possession Claims by Social Landlords	2 October 2006
Possession Claims for Mortgage Arrears	19 November 2008
Dilapidation of Commercial Property	1 January 2012
Low Value Personal Injury Road Traffic Accident Claims	30 April 2010 extended from 31 July 2013
Low Value Personal Injury Employers' and Public Liability Claims	31 July 2013
Debt Claims	1 October 2017
Resolution of Package Travel Claims	7 May 2018
Media and Communications Claims	1 October 2019

Considering alternatives to litigation

Replace the third list item with:

C1A-005   • in a commercial dispute where there is a written contract, whether there is an applicable arbitration or mediation clause which could provide a cost and time effective solution;

To the end of the last paragraph, add:

See also *Imperial Chemical Industries Ltd v Merit Merrell Technology Ltd (Costs)* [2018] EWHC 1577 (TCC) where indemnity costs were ordered in part because of an unreasonable refusal to mediate.

Points to note on the application of the protocols

Replace the seventh paragraph with:

C1A-006   Most of the protocols do not require the parties to take specific steps to try to settle the claim pre-issue, either by making an offer to settle (under Pt 36) or by meeting/negotiating. But they all strongly encourage early settlement discussions and use of an ADR approach. The courts are not sympathetic to parties who are unwilling at least to try to narrow the issues or to hold settlement discussions pre-issue. It should be noted also that pre-action Part 36 offers to settle may have the same costs consequences as post-commencement offers, provided the offeror has provided the offeree with sufficient information to enable her to understand and evaluate the offer.

Compliance with the Practice Direction and Protocols: The Court's Role

Add new paragraph at end:

C1A-007   In *Williams v Secretary of State for Business, Energy and Industrial Strategy* [2018] EWCA Civ 852 the Court of Appeal confirmed, in cases where settlement was reached prior to issue of proceedings, that an unreasonable failure to comply with a protocol, would usually result in fixed costs only being awarded, where fixed costs would have applied had the protocol been used.

Pre-action costs

In the third paragraph, first sentence, after "Three", delete "recent".

C1A-011

To the end of the last paragraph, add:
See *Singh v Public Service Commission* [2019] UKPC 18

The Personal Injury Protocol

Scope and content

In the second paragraph, after "fast track cases is £25,000", add new footnote 1:
[1] Previously the limit was £15,000.

C2A-001

The Construction and Engineering Protocol

Replace the first list item with:
* it includes professional negligence disputes against building professionals (the personal injury and clinical negligence protocols do not do so);

C5A-001

The Defamation Protocol

Replace paragraph with:
From 1 October 2019 this protocol is replaced by the Protocol for Media and Communication Claims, to reflect the changes in the Rules and Practice Direction, and the creation of the Media and Communications List.

C6A-001

Replace the Pre-Action Protocol for Defamation with:

PRE-ACTION PROTOCOL FOR MEDIA AND COMMUNICATION CLAIMS

1   Introduction

1.1   This Pre-Action Protocol was updated after a consultation following the formation of the Media and Communications List in 2017. It now applies to cases within the scope of CPR rule 53.1: all cases involving claims in defamation, misuse of private information, data protection law or harassment by publication, and claims in breach of confidence and malicious falsehood which arise from publication or threatened publication by the print or broadcast media, online, on social media, or in speech.

C6-001

1.2   This Protocol is intended to encourage exchange of information between parties at an early stage and to provide a clear framework within which parties to a media and communications claim, acting in good faith, can explore the early and appropriate resolution of that claim.

1.3   The courts will treat the standards set out in this Protocol as the normal reasonable approach for parties to a media and communications claim. Therefore, the courts will expect parties to have complied with this Protocol in good time before proceedings are issued. Should a claim proceed to litigation, the extent to which this Protocol has been followed by the parties will assist the court in dealing with liability for costs and making other orders.

1.4   There are important features which distinguish defamation claims and other media and communications cases from other areas of civil litigation, and these must be borne in mind when both applying, and reviewing the application of, the Pre-Action Protocol. In particular, time is frequently "of the essence" in defamation and other publication claims; the limitation period is (uniquely) only 1 year in defamation and malicious falsehood cases, and often, a Claimant will be seeking an immediate correction and/or apology as part of the process of restoring his/her reputation.

Litigants in Person

C6-002   If a party to the claim does not have a legal representative they should still, in so far as reasonably possible, fully comply with this Protocol.

If a party to a claim becomes aware that another party is a litigant in person, they should send a copy of this Protocol to the litigant in person at the earliest opportunity.

2   Aims of the Protocol

C6-003   The aims of this Protocol are to enable the parties to prospective claims to:
  (a)   understand and properly identify the issues in dispute and to share information and relevant documents;
  (b)   make informed decisions as to whether and how to proceed;
  (c)   try to settle the dispute without proceedings or reduce the issues in dispute;
  (d)   avoid unnecessary expense and control the costs of resolving the dispute; and
  (e)   support the efficient management of proceedings where court proceedings cannot be avoided.

Proportionality

C6-004   **2.2** In formulating both the Letter of Claim and Response and in taking any subsequent steps, the parties should act reasonably to keep costs proportionate to the nature and gravity of the case and the stage the complaint has reached.

3   Pre-action protocols for Media and Communications List causes of action

3.1   Letter of Claim

C6-005   The Claimant should notify the Defendant of his/her claim in writing at the earliest reasonable opportunity.

In respect of all causes of action falling within the Media and Communications List, the Claimant should include the following information:
  •   name of Claimant;
  •   the nature of and basis for the entitlement to the remedies sought by the Claimant;
  •   any facts or matters relevant to England and Wales being the most appropriate forum for the dispute; and
  •   details of any funding arrangement in place.

3.2   Letter of Claim (Defamation, Slander and Malicious Falsehood)

C6-006   The Letter of Claim should additionally include the following information—
  •   sufficient details to identify the specific publication which contained the statement complained of;
  •   the statement complained of and, if known, the date of publication; where possible, a copy or transcript of the statement complained of should be enclosed and, in the case of slander, where and in what circumstances as far as known the statement complained of was spoken;
  •   the imputation the Claimant contends was conveyed by the statement complained of;
  •   factual inaccuracies or unsupportable comment within the statement complained of; the Claimant should give a sufficient explanation to enable the Defendant to appreciate why the statement is inaccurate or unsupportable;
  •   for defamation claims, how or why the Claimant says that the statement complained of has caused or is likely to cause serious harm for the purposes of section 1 Defamation Act 2013 including, when the Claim-

ant is a body that trades for profit, such details as are available of the nature and value of the serious financial loss which the Claimant says has been caused or is likely to be caused by publication of the statement complained of;

- for slander or malicious falsehood claims, how or why the Claimant says that publication of the statement complained of has caused, or is likely to cause, special damage or pecuniary loss, or why publication of the statement is actionable without proof of actual loss; and,
- in malicious falsehood claims an outline of the Claimant's case with regard to malice.
- where relevant, the Letter of Claim should also include—
- any facts or matters which make the Claimant identifiable from the statement complained of; and
- details of any special facts relevant to the interpretation of the statement complained of and/or any particular damage caused by the statement complained of.

3.3 Letter of Claim (Privacy, Breach of Confidence)
The Letter of Claim should additionally include the following information— **C6-007**

- the information or categories of information which is claimed to constitute confidential information or in respect of which the Claimant is said to have a reasonable expectation of privacy;
- sufficient details to identify the publication or proposed publication containing the relevant information;
- details of the circumstances giving rise to confidentiality or a reasonable expectation of privacy (in breach of confidence or misuse of private information claims respectively);
- why the information is claimed to constitute information in respect of which the Claimant has a reasonable expectation of privacy or confidential information of a nature that should not be published or continued to be published, including details of any damage or distress suffered or anticipated, where an interim non-disclosure order or final non-disclosure order to restrain publication is sought; and,
- in claims for misuse of private information, why it is claimed that the Claimant's right to private and family life outweighs the right to freedom of expression; in respect of confidential information, in so far as known, the extent to which the information is already in the public domain; the nature and any available details of any particular damage caused or likely to be caused by the publication, proposed publication or processing complained of.
- When, at the time of sending the letter of claim, the Claimant intends to make an application for dispensation from the requirements of CPR PD16 (Statements of Case) with a view to bringing his/her claim anonymously, this should be indicated in the letter of claim, which should also give an indication of the basis upon which any application would be made. Any response from the Defendant should be provided to the Court upon an application.

3.4 Letter of Claim (Data Protection)
The Letter of Claim should additionally include the following information— **C6-008**

- any further information necessary to identify the data subject;
- the data controller to which the claim is addressed;
- the information or categories of information which is claimed to constitute personal data including, where necessary, the information which is said to constitute sensitive personal data or to fall within a

special category of personal data;
- sufficient details to identify the relevant processing;
- the identification of the duty or duties which are said to have been breached and details of the manner in which they are said to have been breached, including any positive case on behalf of the Claimant;
- why the personal data ought not to be processed/further processed, if applicable;
- the nature and any available details as to any particular damage caused or likely to be caused by the processing/breach of duty complained of; and
- Where a representative data protection claim is intended to be brought on behalf of data subjects, the letter of claim should also: set out the nature of the entity which intends to bring the claim and explain how it fulfils the relevant suitability criteria – see Article 80 of the General Data Protection regulation (GDPR); include details of the data subjects on whose behalf the claim would be brought; and, confirmation that they have mandated the representative body to represent them and receive compensation, where applicable.

3.5   Letter of Claim (Harassment where the course of conduct includes publication)

C6-009   The Letter of Claim should include the following—
- sufficient details about the course of conduct which is claimed to constitute harassment, including sufficient details to identify the publication(s) or proposed publication(s) forming part of the course of conduct;
- how or why the Claimant says that the course of conduct amounts to harassment, including, if relevant how or why it has caused, or is likely to cause, alarm or distress; and
- where relevant, how or why and in what amount the Claimant says that the course of conduct has caused financial loss.

3.6   Defendant's Response to Letter of Claim

C6-010   The Defendant should provide a full response to the Letter of Claim, as soon as reasonably possible. If the Defendant believes that he/she will be unable to respond within 14 days (or such shorter time limit as specified in the Letter of Claim), then he/she should specify the date by which he/she intends to respond.

3.7   The Response should include the following—
- whether or to what extent the Claimant's claim is accepted, whether more information is required or whether it is rejected;
- if the claim is accepted in whole or in part, the Defendant should indicate which remedies it is willing to offer;
- if more information is required, then the Defendant should specify precisely what information is needed to enable the claim to be dealt with and why;
- if the claim is rejected, then the Defendant should explain the reasons why it is rejected, including a sufficient indication of any statutory exemptions or facts on which the Defendant is likely to rely in support of any substantive defence;
- in a defamation or malicious falsehood claim, the defamatory or false imputation(s) the Defendant contends was conveyed by the statement complained of, if any; and
- where the Claimant to a proposed action has indicated his/her intention to make an application to bring the claim anonymously, the Defendant should indicate whether the Defendant accepts such an order would be

appropriate and give an indication of the basis for the Defendant's position.

3.8 Settlement and Alternative Dispute Resolution

Court proceedings should be a last resort. The parties should consider whether some form of alternative dispute resolution (ADR) procedure might enable them to settle their dispute without commencing court proceedings, and if so, endeavour to agree which form to adopt. **C6-011**

Although ADR is not compulsory, the court will expect the parties to have considered ADR. A party's refusal to engage with ADR (including its failure to respond to an invitation to participate in ADR) might be considered unreasonable by the court and could lead to the court ordering that party to pay additional costs.

3.9 Some of the options for resolving disputes without commencing proceedings are—

(a) without prejudice discussions and negotiations between the parties;

(b) mediation – a form of facilitated negotiation assisted by an independent neutral third party;

(c) early neutral evaluation (ENE) - a third party giving an informed opinion on the dispute (for example, a lawyer experienced in the field of defamation or an individual experienced in the subject matter of the claim); and

(d) reference to a press regulator established to deal with complaints from members of the public about the editorial content of newspapers and magazines or an arbitration scheme operated by such a regulator.

3.10 CPR Part 36 (Offers to Settle) permits claimants and defendants to make offers to settle before and after proceedings have been issued. The parties should consider if it is appropriate to make a Part 36 Offer before proceedings are issued. If such an offer is made, the party making the offer must supply sufficient evidence and/or information to enable the offer to be properly considered.

The defendant may make an offer to settle a defamation action through the offers to amend procedure under sections 2 – 4 of the Defamation Act 1996. This procedure requires the defendant to make an offer to publish an apology or a redaction statement. The defendant may also be required to pay damages and costs to the claimant.

Stocktake

3.11 Where the procedure set out in this Protocol has not resolved the dispute between the parties, they should undertake a further review of their respective positions. The parties should consider the state of the papers and the evidence in order to see if proceedings can be avoided and, at the least, narrow the issues between them which can assist efficient case management. **C6-012**

3.12 Further reference

The parties may find reference to the following of particular assistance: **C6-013**

- CPR Part 53 and Practice Direction: Defamation Claims;
- CPR Part 25: Interim Remedies and Security for Costs;
- *Master of the Rolls' Practice Guidance: Interim Non-Disclosure Orders* August 2011 [2012] 1 WLR 1003, SEN CTS (*White Book*, Volume 1, B13-001 onwards);
- CPR PD48 paragraphs 3.1 and 3.2: Part 2 of the Legal Aid, Sentencing and Punishment of Offenders Act 2012 Relating to Civil Litigation Funding and Costs: Transitional Provision and Exceptions – Insolvency-related proceedings and publication and privacy proceedings; and

- 2013 CPR rule 44.15 and PD44.paragraphs 19.1-19.6: Providing information about funding arrangements (*White Book*, Volume 1, 44x.15, 44xPD.3); 2013 Practice Direction – Pre-Action Conduct, paragraph 9.3: Information about funding arrangements (2013 *White Book* Volume 1 C1-008); and, 2013 CPR rule 44.3B(1)(c): Limits on recovery under funding arrangements (*White Book* Volume 1, 44x.3B).

THE JUDICIAL REVIEW PROTOCOL

Replace the second list item with:

C8A-001
- provides advice on when judicial review may not be the appropriate remedy and on when the protocol may not be applicable—including when the proposed defendant does not have the legal power to change the decision being challenged, or in very urgent situations;

PRE-ACTION PROTOCOL FOR JUDICIAL REVIEW

Annex A

Letter before claim

Section 2. Address for sending the letter before claim

Replace the fourth list item with:

C8-006
- Where the claim concerns a decision by a department or body for whom the Treasury Solicitor acts and the Treasury Solicitor has already been involved in the case, a copy should also be sent, quoting the Treasury Solicitor's reference, to—

  The Treasury Solicitor,
  102 Petty France,
  Westminster,
  London SW1H 9GL

- Where the claim concerns a decision by Her Majesty's Revenue and Customs—

  the address on the letter notifying the decision; and
  The General Counsel and Solicitor to HM Revenue and Customs,
  HM Revenue and Customs,
  South West Wing,
  Bush House,
  Strand,
  London WC2B 4RD

THE PROTOCOL FOR LOW VALUE PERSONAL INJURY CLAIMS IN ROAD TRAFFIC ACCIDENTS

Summary of Stage 1 and Stage 2 processes

Add new paragraph at end:

C13A-002   In *Fitton v Ageas*, 8 Nov 2018, unrep. HHJ Parker held that the parties were bound by a figure accepted under the portal procedure even where there had been a mistake on the part of the claimant, and the claimant had not intended to accept the defendant's offer. The transcript is available on Lawtel.

The Protocol for Low Value Personal Injury (Employers' Liability And Public Liability) Claims

Sanctions

Add new paragraph at end:

If the claimant fails to use the Protocol process when he or she should have, the court will likely **C15A-003** award fixed costs only: *Williams v Secretary of State for Business, Energy and Industrial Strategy* [2018] EWCA Civ 852.

VOLUME 2

SECTION A1   PROCEDURAL GUIDES

15.   Insolvency

15.1   Creditors' Winding-up Petitions

Validation of payments

Replace table entry with:

A1.15-001

Insolvency Act 1986 s.127, IPD 2018 para.9.11	Company may apply for order that any disposition of property or payment should not be void in the event of the company being wound up on the hearing of the petition. The application should generally be made to the Insolvency and Companies Court Judge/ district judge.

SECTION 1   COURT GUIDES
SECTION 1A   CHANCERY GUIDE

Chapter 1 Introduction

ABOUT THE CHANCERY DIVISION

Replace paragraph 1.5 with:

1.5 There are currently 16 High Court Judges (including the Chancellor) attached to the **1A-1** Division. There are also six judges who are referred to as Masters (one of whom is the Chief Master), and six Insolvency and Companies Court Judges (ICC Judges) (one of whom is the Chief ICC Judge). Throughout this Guide the term "judge" (initial lower case) includes the High Court Judges, Masters, ICC Judges, judges with s.9 powers sitting as a High Court Judge and deputies. If the context makes it clear, "Judge" (initial capital) may be used to denote a High Court Judge.

Chapter 2 Contact details

IN THE ROLLS BUILDING

THE JUDGES

High Court Judges' Clerks

Replace table with:

Judge	Clerk	Telephone	Email	
Chancellor of the High Court, the Rt Hon Sir Geoffrey Vos	Adam Davis, Diary Secretary Vannina Ettori, Legal Secretary Andrea Dowsett, Private Secretary Natalie Ford, Clerk	6680 7477 7143 7071-5648 6412	*adam.davis@ejudiciary.gsi. gov.uk* *vannina.ettori@judiciary.gsi. gov.uk* *andrea.dowsett@judiciary.uk* *Natalie.ford@justice.gov.uk*	**1A-3**
Mr Justice Mann	Susan Woolley	7964	*susan.woolley@justice.gov.uk*	
Mr Justice Morgan	Natalie Ford	6412	*Natalie.Ford@justice.gov.uk*	
Mr Justice Norris	Pauline Drewett	7073 1789	*pauline.drewett@justice. gov.uk*	
Mr Justice Barling	Katie Dunkley	6675	*katie.dunkley@justice.gov.uk*	

Judge	Clerk	Telephone	Email
Mr Justice Arnold	Pauline Drewett	7073 1789	pauline.drewett@justice.gov.uk
Mr Justice Roth	Irram Khan (Based at	7071 5694 Competition	irram.khan@justice.gov.uk Appeal Tribunal)
Mr Justice Hildyard	Morenike Phillips	6039	morenike.phillips@justice.gov.uk
Mr Justice Birss	Gwilym Morris	7379	Gwilym.Morris2@justice.gov.uk
Mr Justice Nugee	Gary Clark	7200	gary.clark@justice.gov.uk
Mr Justice Snowden	Wendy Simpson	7073 0304	wendy.Simpson@justice.gov.uk
Mr Justice Marcus Smith	Steven Brilliant	7767	steven.brilliant@justice.gov.uk
Mr Justice Zacaroli	Ashley Woodstock	6775	ashley.woodstock@justice.gov.uk
Mr Justice Fancourt	Nazia Malik	6251	nazia.malik@justice.gov.uk
Mr Justice Falk	Supriya Saleem	6419	supriya.saleem@justice.gov.uk

IPEC

Chancery Masters' Clerks

Replace table with:

1A-6

Chief Master Marsh	Hearing room 2	Jack Gunby	jack.gunby@justice.gov.uk
Master Teverson	Hearing room 5	Dani Ince	dani.ince@justice.gov.uk
Master Clark	Hearing room 6	Mohammed Choudhury	mohammed.choudhury5@justice.gov.uk
Master Shuman	Hearing Room 3	Anita Rathod	anita.rathod@justice.gov.uk
Master Kaye	Hearing room 4	Nathalie Drysdale	nathalie.drysdale@justice.gov.uk
Vacant Master	Hearing room 1	Alison Gaby	alison.gaby@justice.gov.uk

1A-7
Replace the first line with:
Contact details for the ICC Judges' Clerks:

Replace email with:
Email – Issue section: rcjcompanies.orders@justice.gov.uk

HIGH COURT INSOLVENCY AND COMPANIES

GROUND FLOOR

1A-14
Replace the first line with:
High Court Insolvency and Companies Delivery Manager (7472)

CHAPTER 3 USERS COMMITTEES AND SUGGESTIONS FOR IMPROVEMENT

INSOLVENCY AND COMPANIES COURT USERS' COMMITTEE

1A-24
Replace paragraph 3.3 with:
3.3 Proposals for changes in insolvency matters fall within the remit of the Insolvency and Companies Court Users' Committee unless they relate to the Insolvency Rules 1986. The members of the Insolvency and Companies Court Users' Committee include members of the Bar, solicitors, the Law Society, the Insolvency Service and the Society of Practitioners of Insolvency. Meetings are held three times a year, and more often if necessary. Suggestions for points to be considered by the committee should be sent to the Chief ICC Judge.

INSOLVENCY RULES COMMITTEE

1A-27
Replace paragraph 3.6 with:
3.6 The Insolvency Rules Committee must be consulted before any changes to the Insolvency Rules 1986 are made. The chairman of the Insolvency Rules Committee is Mr Justice Zacaroli. Proposals for changes in the rules should be sent to The Insolvency Service at insolvency.enquiryline@insolvency.gov.uk, with a copy to the clerk to Mr Justice Zacaroli or the Chief ICC Judge.

Chapter 4 Litigants in person

LEGAL AID AGENCY: CIVIL LEGAL ADVICE

Replace paragraph 4.19 with:

4.19 The LAA is responsible for making sure that legal aid services from solicitors, barristers **1A-40** and the not-for-profit sector are available to those who are eligible. A new online 'eForm' process for applying for legal aid is available. Telephone 0300 200 2020 or email contactcivil@justice.gov. uk.

Chapter 6 The court file

ELECTRONIC FILING

Replace the first paragraph in 6.9 with:

6.9 The Electronic Working Pilot Scheme initially went live on 16th November 2015, enabling **1A-46** parties to commence proceedings and file documents online. It has been extended until 6th April 2020. As from 25th April 2017 (and from 30 April 2019 for the B&PCs outside of London) it is mandatory for all professional court users to use the scheme. Therefore legal representatives must file all documents which are required by the rules or any practice direction to be filed on the court file (apart from original documents), in all courts in the Rolls Building, using Electronic Working. This applies to commencing proceedings and to filing documents in existing cases. Litigants in person are encouraged to use e-filing wherever possible but they still have the option of filing documents in hard copy at present. Electronic working is also now available in the B&PCs outside of London and in the Central Office of the Queens Bench Division.

Replace paragraph 6.13 with:

6.13 It is important to note that where documents are filed and payment of a fee is not required the date and time of filing will be the date and time of issue for all claim forms and the date and time of filing for all other documents for the purposes of any direction under the CPR or of complying with a court order. Where a fee is required the date and time of filing will be deemed to be the date and time at which payment of the court fee is made using Electronic Working. Fees relating to any filing may be paid using the PBA system (details may be obtained from the PBA Support Team, telephone 01633 652125) or by *https://www.gov.uk/government/publications/form-fee-account-application-form-fee-account-customer-application-form* or by credit or debit card.

OTHER COMMUNICATIONS WITH THE COURT

Replace paragraph 6.21 with:

6.21 There have recently been some important changes in the use of emails to the court where **1A-48** electronic working is used. On 3 October 2016 PD 51O was amended, as a step towards the increased use of electronic working by court users, and PD 5B (which enables parties to file certain documents by email and to use email to communicate with the court), was disapplied for all Rolls Building courts. The PD was amended to provide unduly restrictive limits on the use of email. This wording has, however, now been re-amended.

Replace paragraph 6.22 with:

6.22 The new wording of paragraph 3.4(2), is as follows:
(1) The court may refuse to convert documents to PDF format where those documents were originally submitted by other means.
(2) In relation to any document required by the rules, any practice direction or any order of the court to be filed, the court will not accept that document for filing if submitted by e-mail and any such document must be filed through Electronic Working (unless submitted on paper); but if a judge, Master or ICC Judge has requested or permitted the submission of such a document by email then it must be so submitted as well as being filed through Electronic Working (or on paper).

Replace the first paragraph in 6.23 with:

6.23 The effect of this amendment is that "submissions", that is all documents which are required by the rules or any practice direction to be filed on the court file, need to be filed using Electronic Working, but such documents may also to be sent via email if the judge, Master or ICC Judge requests or permits.

Replace paragraph 6.26 with:

6.26 If late submissions need to reach the court urgently (for example last minute filing for a hearing) they may be emailed, if this is acceptable to the judge, Master or ICC Judge, or the clerk. But it is essential that they are also filed using electronic working.

Chapter 8 Issue of the claim form

SHORTER AND FLEXIBLE TRIALS SCHEME

Replace paragraph 8.18 with:

1A-64 **8.18** As from 1 October 2018 a scheme is in operation in all three jurisdictions in the Rolls Building for "business claims" (the term is not defined in the scheme) which will not exceed 4 days, including judicial reading, at trial. Opting into the scheme will lead to the claim being fully docketed to a High Court Judge or, if the parties consent, a Chancery Master, at an early stage. The idea behind the scheme is that for some types of business dispute a simplified procedure will be suitable and the claim will come on for trial in a truncated period. The expense of pursuing a claim is expected to be lower than in ordinary claims and costs management does not apply. For further details of the scheme see Chapter 28 of this guide and PD 57AB. The scheme is only applicable to a Part 7 claim.

Chapter 9 Part 8 claims

DETAILS OF PROCEDURE

CONTINUING UNDER PART 7

1A-68 *Add new paragraph 9.13:*
9.13 Some Part 8 claims are complex and raise a number of issues. Where it would assist the overriding objective, the parties are encouraged to agree the issues to be determined at an early stage. It is unhelpful for parties to be surprised by issues and arguments at the stage skeletons are served. The court will therefore consider making directions to address this. For example, the court may order that the parties file an agreed list of issues which include the position they intend to take on those issues and identifies (in summary form) the basis for the position taken. The list of issues is not intended to cover what would be included in a skeleton argument, but should include (in summary form) any arguments of law that a party intends to raise which would otherwise be likely to take another party by surprise and which ought to be addressed in their skeleton argument.

Chapter 14 Judges/Masters

DEPUTIES

Replace paragraph 14.6 with:

1A-81 **14.6** Deputy High Court Judges are appointed under section 9 of the Senior Courts Act 1981. They may be either senior Circuit Judges who sit as deputies from time to time, or they may be practitioners who are called upon on an ad hoc basis. They carry out the same work as the Judges, although certain cases of particular substance or difficulty will only be tried by a High Court Judge (see Chapter 17 paragraph 29).

ALLOCATION TO A MANAGEMENT TRACK / DOCKETING

Replace paragraph 14.9 with:

1A-83 **14.9** Since January 2015 all cases in the Chancery Division in London are allocated to one of four management tracks:
- Case management and trial by Master (or ICC Judge)
- Case management by Master (or ICC Judge) and trial by High Court Judge
- Full docketing to a particular Judge, so that the Judge deals with all case management and the trial
- (On a pilot basis) a partnership management arrangement under which the prospective trial Judge works with a specified Master (or ICC Judge).

Replace paragraph 14.11 with:
14.11 Most track allocation is undertaken by Masters and ICC Judges, especially at Case Management Conferences. It is, however, open to a Judge to allocate a case at a hearing before him/her, and a supervising Judge may make an allocation decision if the parties request that. The supervising Judges are available to be consulted by Masters and ICC Judges as needed.

Replace paragraph 14.12 with:
14.12 Decisions as to full docketing to Judges are made by full-time Masters, ICC Judges and Judges. Any decision that a case should be given full docketing will be passed to the Chancellor for approval. Assuming that the Chancellor endorses the decision, he will nominate the particular Judge.

Chapter 15 Matters dealt with by Masters

HEARING OF APPLICATIONS BEFORE MASTERS

ORAL APPLICATIONS WITHOUT NOTICE

Replace paragraph 15.15 with:

15.15 The time at which Applications Without Notice ("AWNs") are dealt with will vary depend- **1A-89** ing upon the individual preference of the Master. They are no longer dealt with only at 2.15pm. The times are:

      Chief Master Marsh 10.30am – 10.45am
      Master Teverson 2.00pm – 2.15pm
      Master Clark 10.30am – 10.45am
      Master Shuman 10.30am – 10.45am
      Master Kaye 10.30am – 10.45am
      Vacant Master 2.00pm – 2.15pm

BUNDLES FOR USE AT MASTERS' HEARINGS

Replace paragraph 15.36 with:

15.36 Bundles provided for the use of the Master or ICC Judge should be removed promptly **1A-94** after the conclusion of the hearing unless the Master or ICC Judge directs otherwise.

Chapter 16 Applications to a High Court Judge

APPLICATIONS IN EXISTING PROCEEDINGS

JUDGES' APPLICATION INFORMATION FORM

Replace paragraph 16.13 with:

16.13 An application should not be listed before the Interim Applications Judge if it is suitable **1A-100** for hearing by a Master or ICC Judge. The mere fact that it is urgent is not enough, because both Masters and ICC Judges are available to hear urgent applications. If an application which should be heard by a Master or ICC Judge is listed before the Interim Applications judge, the judge may refuse to hear it.

Chapter 17 Case and costs management

CASE MANAGEMENT DIRECTIONS

DISCLOSURE AND INSPECTION OF DOCUMENTS

Replace paragraph 17.34 with:

17.34 The pilot applies from 1 January 2019 for two years to existing and new proceedings in **1A-121** the B&PCs of England and Wales and the B&PCs in Birmingham, Bristol, Cardiff, Leeds, Liverpool, Manchester and Newcastle; it does not apply in the County Court. The pilot substantially replaces CPR 31 and can be found at CPR PD 51U: *https://www.justice.gov.uk/courts/procedure-rules/ civil/rules/practice-direction-51u-disclosure-pilot-for-the-business-and-property-courts*. Feedback regarding the pilot should be sent by email to **DWG@justice.gov.uk**.

Replace paragraph 17.35 with:

17.35 The pilot does not disturb an order for disclosure made before 1 January 2019 or before the transfer of proceedings into a B&PC, unless that order is varied or set aside. The Chancellor however has made clear in the case of *UTC LLC v Sheffield United & Ors* [2019] EWHC 914 (CH) that the pilot applies to all relevant proceedings in the B&PCs, whether started before or after 1 January 2019, even in a case where a disclosure order was made before 1 January 2019 under CPR Part 31. If proceedings are transferred out of a BP&C into a Court that is not a B&PC, any order for disclosure made under the pilot will stand unless and until any other order is made by the transferee Court.

Replace paragraph 17.37 with:

17.37 As detailed in paragraph 5 of the Practice Direction, unless dispensed with by agreement or order (and subject to several other exceptions), 'Initial Disclosure' of key documents relied upon by the disclosing party (and are necessary for other parties to understand the case against them) will be given with its statement of case. A party wishing to seek disclosure of documents in addition to, or as an alternative to 'Initial Disclosure' must request 'Extended Disclosure' from the Court. The parties and their advisers must then discuss and complete a joint 'Disclosure Review Document' before the first CMC. In an appropriate case where the claimant is acting in person and the defendant is not, the Court may request the legal representatives of the defendant to lead on the preparation of the 'Disclosure Review Document'.

CHAPTER 18 CASE MANAGEMENT FOR SETTLEMENT

EARLY NEUTRAL EVALUATION AND FINANCIAL DISPUTE RESOLUTION

EARLY NEUTRAL EVALUATION

1A-137

Replace paragraph 18.9 with:
   18.9 ENE is offered in the Chancery Division by all judges. The judge providing the ENE may be a full time Chancery judge, a section 9 judge, Chancery Master or ICC Judge. The ENE may be conducted by a judge of the same level as would be allocated to hear the trial, but need not be if the parties agree otherwise.

CHANCERY FDR ("CH FDR")

1A-138

Replace list item 1 in paragraph 18.18 with:
   18.18 IT IS ORDERED THAT:
   1.   The claim shall be listed before the Master/Judge for a without prejudice financial dispute resolution ('FDR') appointment in private on [date] [or a date to be fixed in consultation with counsel's clerks] with a time estimate of [x] hours commencing at 11.00. Judicial pre-reading is estimated to take [x] hours.

CHAPTER 21 TRIALS

LISTING

RESPONSIBILITY FOR LISTING

1A-144

Replace paragraph 21.1 with:
   21.1 Subject to the direction of the Chancellor, the Chancery Judges' Listing Officer (ground floor, Rolls Building), has overall responsibility for listing trials before Judges. All applications relating to listing should, in the first instance, be made to Judges' Listing, who will refer matters, as necessary, to a Judge. Any party dissatisfied with any decision of the Chancery Judges' Listing Officer may, on one clear day's notice to all other parties, apply to the Interim Applications Judge. Any such application should be made within seven days of the decision of the Chancery Judges' Listing Officer and be arranged through the Chancery Judges' Listing Office ("Judges' Listing"). Trials before Masters should be arranged through Masters' Appointments and trials before ICC Judges through Insolvency and Companies Court. It should be borne in mind when fixing a trial that normal court hours are 10.30am to 1pm and 2pm to 4.15pm.

LISTING OF PARTICULAR BUSINESS

—BANKRUPTCY APPLICATIONS

1A-154

Replace paragraph 21.15 with:
   21.15 All applications to the Judge should be lodged in Judges' Listing. Urgent applications without notice for (i) the committal of any person to prison for contempt or (ii) injunctions or the modification or discharge of injunctions will be passed directly to the clerk to the Interim Applications Judge for hearing by that Judge. All applications on notice for (i) and (ii) above, and applications referred to the Judge by the ICC Judge, will be listed by the Chancery Judges' Listing Officer. Applications estimated not to exceed two hours will be heard by the Interim Applications Judge. The Chancery Judges' Listing Officer is to give at least three clear days' notice of the hearing to the applicant and to any respondent who attended before the ICC Judge. Applications over two hours will be placed in the General List and listed accordingly.

—COMPANIES COURT

1A-155

Replace paragraph 21.16 with:
   21.16 Matters for hearing before the Companies Judge, such as applications for an administration order, applications for approval by the court of schemes of arrangement and applications for the appointment of provisional liquidators, may be issued for hearing on any working day in term time (other than the last day of each term). Unopposed applications for the approval of schemes of arrangement will sometimes be heard by a Judge before the start of normal sittings. Other applications may be dealt with by the Interim Applications Judge as Companies Judge. Applications or

petitions which are estimated to exceed two hours are liable to be stood over to a date to be fixed by the Chancery Judges' Listing Officer. Urgent applications will also be dealt with by the Interim Applications Judge. Applications and petitions referred to the Judge by the ICC Judge will be placed in the General List and listed accordingly. Feedback regarding the pilot should be sent by email to **DWG@justice.gov.uk**.

—APPLICATIONS REFERRED TO THE JUDGE

Replace paragraph 21.17 with:
21.17 The proper use of judicial resources dictates that where the Master has jurisdiction in **1A-156** respect of an application he should ordinarily exercise that jurisdiction. The same principles apply to ICC Judge. Applications referred by the Master to the Judge will be added to the Interim Hearings List. The power to refer applications made to the Master and in respect of which the Master has jurisdiction is very sparingly exercised.

Change title of paragraph: **1A-158**

TRIALS BEFORE JUDGES, MASTERS AND ICC JUDGES

ESTIMATES: FIXED-END TRIALS

Replace paragraph 21.20 with:
21.20 All trials in the Chancery Division in London (including trials before Masters and ICC **1A-159** Judges) are now conducted on a fixed-end basis. That means that each trial will, save in exceptional circumstances, be required to be completed within the period allocated to it.

Replace paragraph 21.23 with:
21.23 Where one or more parties to a case propose that the time estimate for a trial should be changed but one or more other parties disagree, the matter must be referred to a Master, ICC Judge or Judge, as appropriate. Judges' Listing cannot change the time estimate given for a trial without either the parties' consent or a direction from a Master, ICC Judge or Judge.

SKELETON ARGUMENTS

Replace the first sentence in 21.77 with:
21.77 *Time for delivery of all skeleton arguments (so that the Judge/Master can read them with the* **1A-175** *papers):*

—FILING BY EMAIL (UNDER 25 PAGES)

Replace list item (a) in 21.79 with:
Filing by email at the Rolls Building of skeleton arguments under 25 pages in length **1A-177**
(a)   Subject to the exception mentioned in (b) below, all skeletons under 25 pages in length for hearings in the Rolls Building should be filed by email to the appropriate address:
  • ChanceryJudgesListing@justice.gov.uk for skeletons for the Applications Court;
  • ChanceryJudgesListing@justice.gov.uk for all other skeletons for Judges' hearings; and
  • *chancery.Mastersappointments@justice.gov.uk* for all skeletons for Masters' hearings.

ROBED AND UNROBED HEARINGS

Replace the first and second paragraphs in 21.97 with:
21.97 Judges wear robes for all hearings. Robes are not worn at hearings before Masters unless **1A-187** the Master is conducting a trial. The daily cause list will specify whether the legal advocate is to be robed before an ICC Judge. The general rule is that robes will be worn before ICC Judges for all trials with oral evidence, appeals from the County Court, public examinations of bankrupts and of directors or other officers of companies; applications for discharge from bankruptcy or for suspension of such discharge; all hearings under the Company Directors Disqualification Act 1986; hearings of petitions to wind up companies in the winding up court; final hearings of petitions for the reduction of capital of companies and in any hearing involving the liberty of the subject. District Judges wear robes for trials and winding up petitions.

CHAPTER 24 APPEALS

GENERAL

Replace paragraph 24.1 with:
24.1 This Chapter is concerned with the following appeals affecting the Chancery Division: **1A-209**

- appeals within the ordinary work of the Division from Masters to High Court Judges;
- appeals within the ordinary work of the Division from High Court Judges to the Court of Appeal;
- specialist appeals in the Insolvency and Companies List from County Court District Judges to ICC Judges;
- specialist appeals in the Insolvency and Companies List from ICC Judges at first instance to High Court Judges; and
- statutory appeals to the Chancery Division.

Proceedings under the Companies Acts (and other legislation relating to companies and limited liability partnerships) are specialist proceedings for the purposes of Part 49 [and therefore as regards the destination of appeals]. [In those cases appeals from final decisions by an ICC Judge go direct to the Court of Appeal: see the table in PD 52A paragraph 3.5. Such appeals are not covered in this Chapter]. Most appeals from tribunals are now dealt with by the Upper Tribunal, which is not covered by this Guide. Appeals from some other bodies (e.g. the Comptroller of Patents and the Pensions Ombudsman) still lie to the court.

Replace the first paragraph in 24.3 with:

24.3 The Access to Justice (Destination of Appeals) Order 2016, which came into effect on 3rd October 2016, has replaced the Destination of Appeals Order 2000. No distinction is now made between interim and final decisions and in general all appeals now lie to the next tier of the judiciary. The introduction of the Insolvency (England and Wales) Rules 2016 (IR 2016) creates a new route of appeal from District Judges in the South-Eastern Circuit to the High Court ICC Judges in respect of corporate insolvency matters; See Rule 12.59 IR 2016. This includes directors' disqualification. In addition the ICC Judges will hear appeals from District Judges on the South-Eastern Circuit in respect of non insolvency corporate law matters: see section III Practice Direction 52A, which provides for appeals from the County Court to the High Court. All appeals from County Court judges therefore now go to the High Court rather than the Court of Appeal, as do all appeals from Chancery Masters, both interim and final. (See Table 1 in PD 52A).

PERMISSION TO APPEAL

Replace paragraph 24.4 with:

1A-210   **24.4** Permission to appeal is required in all cases except: (a) appeals against committal orders and (b) certain statutory appeals. Permission to appeal will be given only where the court considers that the appeal would have a real prospect of success or there is some other compelling reason why the appeal should be heard (CPR rule 52.6(1)). The time in which to lodge an appellant's notice is 21 days after the date the decision of the lower court the appellant wishes to appeal was made, not from the date that the formal order recording the decision was issued (CPR 52.12 (2)(b)).

Attention is drawn to the guidance given by the Court of Appeal in *McDonald v Rose* [2019] EWCA Civ 4 at [21] where a reserved judgment is handed down at a hearing without counsel or parties present. A party wishing to seek permission to appeal should do so before the hand-down hearing. If necessary a party can request an adjournment of the hand-down hearing date to allow the court to consider any application for permission to appeal and any consequential orders. If an adjournment is sought, the party appealing will also need to request an extension of time for filing the appellant's notice, as an adjournment of the hand-down hearing does not automatically extend the 21-day deadline. An application for permission to appeal cannot be made to the lower court if made after the hand-down hearing has concluded without being adjourned. If the lower court refuses permission, or permission is not applied for to the lower court, an application for permission to appeal may be made to the appeal court.

Replace Chapter 25 with:

CHAPTER 25 INSOLVENCY AND COMPANIES LIST

INTRODUCTION TO THE COURTS AND JUDGES

(1) HIGH COURT

1A-219   **25.1** All High Court insolvency and company work is to be heard in the B&PCs, which includes the courts of the Chancery Division. This is a specialist area of work and is assigned to the Insolvency and Companies List (ChD). In London it is heard in the Business and Property Courts of England & Wales, based at the Rolls Building, Royal Courts of Justice. Outside London, it is heard in the B&PCs based in District Registries of the High Court.

25.2 The Insolvency and Companies List comprises two sub-lists: 'Insolvency' and 'Companies'

25.2.1 Insolvency work includes petitions, applications and claims relating to insolvent corporations and individuals. Such work is largely governed by the Insolvency Act 1986 ("IA 1986") and the Limited Liability Partnerships Act 2000 ('LLPA'), but insolvency may involve many other areas of law covered by various pieces of legislation such as: special administration orders, which may be made under specific legislation for companies carrying out statutory functions of a public nature (such as housing, water, finance & education); the Financial Services and Markets Act 2002; the EU Regulations on Insolvency Proceedings 2015; the Cross-Border Insolvency Regulations 2006; the Third Parties (Rights against Insurers) Act 2010; the Debt Relief Orders (Designation of Competent Authority) Regulations 2009; the Charities Act 2011; the Fraud Act 2006 and the Proceeds of Crime Act 2002. It also includes cases concerning the administration of the insolvent estates of deceased persons.

25.2.2 Company work includes claims and applications arising from or concerning: the Companies Act 2006 ("CA 2006"); the Company Directors Disqualification Act 1986 ('CDDA'); the LLPA; the Financial Services and Markets Act 2000, the Financial Services Act 2012 and the Companies (Cross-Border Mergers) Regulations 2007.

25.3 In London, the judges who hear insolvency or companies cases are High Court Judges, the specialist ICC Judges and their respective deputies. As explained in Chapter 24, both High Court Judges and ICC Judges hear appeals, as well as exercising first instance jurisdiction in respect of applications and trials. In Court, a High Court Judge is addressed as "My Lord/Lady" and an ICC Judge as "Judge".

25.4 District Registries do not have ICC Judges. Company and insolvency matters will be assigned between the visiting Chancery High Court Judges, Circuit Judges with section 9 authorisation to sit in the High Court and Chancery District as part of their general Chancery work. In Court, District Judges are addressed as "Sir/Madam".

(2) COUNTY COURT

25.5 Subject to any rule relating to the jurisdiction of the County Court, applications and petitions to commence individual and corporate insolvency proceedings can be presented in a County Court hearing centre having insolvency jurisdiction. The jurisdiction for company work will depend upon the statutory provision or regulation relied upon. Section 1156 of the CA 2006 defines "the court" in England and Wales as "the High Court or the county court".   **1A-220**

25.6 In the County Court at Central London there are specialist Bankruptcy District Judges. Depending upon the nature of the work and the decision of the designated County Court Judge, applications will be first heard either by a District Judge or a Circuit Judge.

(3) DISTRIBUTION OF BUSINESS – PERSONAL AND CORPORATE INSOLVENCY

25.7 The Insolvency Practice Direction (IPD) sets out the court procedures to be followed in England and Wales. It covers applications, petitions and claims concerning personal insolvency, corporate insolvency, office-holder remuneration, unfair prejudice, the Financial Markets and Insolvency (Settlement Finality) Regulations 1999 and appeals. It is available at: **1A-221**
https://www.judiciary.uk/wp-content/uploads/2018/07/pd-insolvency-proceedings-july2018.pdf

25.8 In relation to the distribution of business, there is a four-tier system that provides for the level of judiciary required. The first tier comprises those applications, petitions or claims which may only be listed before a High Court Judge (as defined by paragraphs 1.1(8) and (9) of the IPD):
- applications for committal for contempt
- applications for a search order and freezing order under CPR 25.

25.9 The second tier comprises those applications which may only be listed before a High Court Judge or an ICC Judge but not before a District Judge sitting in a District Registry in the High Court or the County Court. These include:
- applications for an administration order (which include special administration orders)
- applications for the appointment of a provisional liquidator
- ancillary orders under CPR 25

25.10 The third tier comprises those matters which may only be listed before a High Court Judge or ICC Judge or (with the consent of the Supervising Judge for the circuit in which the District Judge is sitting) a District Judge sitting in the High Court District Registry, such as:
- applications for an injunction to restrain presentation or advertisement of a winding up petition
- interim applications and applications for directions or case management after any proceedings have been referred or adjourned to the Judge

25.11 The fourth tier comprises the remainder of insolvency business in which applications or petitions are issued in a County Court having insolvency jurisdiction. District Judges have jurisdiction to deal with "Local Business" under paragraph 3.6 of the IPD, which expression is defined by paragraph 3.7.

25.12 If the application or petition is not "Local Business" then the entirety of those insolvency proceedings must be transferred. When considering a transfer, paragraphs 3.8 and 3.9 of the IPD are intended to give guidance and assist the reviewing judge with the case management decision. They are to be read in conjunction with the limitations set out in paragraphs 3.2 and 3.3.

25.13 If a debtor wishes to apply for a bankruptcy order this is now dealt with by the Adjudicator employed by the Insolvency Service. For further information see
https://www.gov.uk/apply-for-bankruptcy.

(4) DISTRIBUTION OF BUSINESS—CORPORATE (NON-INSOLVENCY)

1A-222 **25.14** The High Court, its District Registries and the County Courts have power to hear all non-insolvency corporate matters unless otherwise provided for in the CPR. In the High Court in the Rolls Building all shareholder disputes, schemes, capital reductions, Part IV transfer of business, cross-border mergers and other company law work begins with an ICC Judge.

If a derivative claim brought under 261-264 of the CA 2006 by a shareholder/member of a company in respect of a cause of action vested in the company is made in the High Court and its District Registries, then the derivative claim must be decided by a High Court Judge.

COURT RULES AND PRACTICE DIRECTIONS

1A-223 **25.15** Insolvency proceedings, whether personal or corporate, are governed by the Insolvency (England and Wales) Rules 2016 (SI 2016/1024) ("IR 2016"). The IPD provides further general guidance and explains the requirements for particular applications. The Civil Procedure Rules ("the CPR") apply as provided for by Rule 12.1, IR 2016. All insolvency proceedings must be allocated to the multi-track and accordingly the provisions of the CPR providing for directions questionnaires and track allocation do not apply. Attention is also drawn to –

> 25.15.1 Practice Direction 49B of the CPR, which requires the petitioner in a contributory's petition to indicate whether the petitioner consents or objects to a validation order under s.127 of the Insolvency Act 1986 in the standard form and makes consequential provision; and
>
> 25.15.2 Practice Direction 51P of the CPR, which provides for an express trials pilot for simple applications before ICC Judges, which will take no longer than 2 days to hear and where the costs of each party will not exceed £75,000.

25.16 Claims under the Company Directors Disqualification Act have their own prescribed rules, namely the Insolvent Companies (Disqualification of Unfit Directors) Proceedings Rules 1987 (SI 1987/2023), as amended. The CPR will apply to such claims, except when inconsistent with the 1987 Rules. Regard should also be had to the Practice Direction on Directors Disqualification.

25.17 "Unfair prejudice" petitions under section 994 of the Companies Act 2006 are governed the Companies (Unfair Prejudice Applications) Proceedings Rules 2009 (SI 2009/2469) as amended. The CPR again applies, except when inconsistent with the 2009 Rules or the Companies Act 2006. Attention is again drawn to Practice Direction 49B of the CPR, which provides that such petitions should not seek the winding up of the company unless that is the petitioner's preferred remedy or the only remedy to which the petitioner is entitled.

25.18 The CPR applies to all other companies cases. Attention is drawn to Practice Direction 49A, which sets out certain requirements for applications under companies legislation generally and also specific requirements in particular cases.

25.19 The Chief ICC Judge has published a Practice Note explaining the Court's approach in dealing with applications under the Companies (Cross-Border Mergers Regulations) 2007 for a certificate showing compliance with pre-merger steps in relation to a UK merging company: *https://www.judiciary.uk/publications/practice-note-on-cross-border-mergers-october-18/*.

(7) ISSUING PROCEEDINGS

1A-224 **25.20** In order to start proceedings it is necessary to file a petition, issue a claim or file an application commencing proceedings. This cannot be done without payment of the required fee, unless the relevant party has obtained remission of fees. A fee is also payable on filing an application within proceedings.

25.21 A file will be created when proceedings are started. In the Rolls Building all files for cases will be opened electronically using the CE-File system. Electronic filing of documents is compulsory for parties with legal representation and may be used by unrepresented parties. Attention is drawn to Practice Direction 51O of the CPR with regard to the operation of the electronic filing system. The CE-File system can be accessed at *https://efile.cefile-app.com*.

25.22 Requests to inspect the court file are made in insolvency proceedings by application under Rule 12.39, IR 2016 and, in company matters, under CPR Part 5.

LISTING FOR HEARINGS

1A-225 **25.23** Hearings before a High Court Judge will be listed as part of the general listing jurisdiction of the Chancery Judges' Listing Office ("Chancery Listing"). Chapter 21 will therefore apply. Listing queries should be directed to Chancery Listing.

25.24 ICC Judges will ordinarily hear matters of up to 10 days' duration but longer hearings may sometimes be accommodated. Trials proceeding under the Insolvency Express Trial Practice Direction (see above) will be listed for up to 2 days. Details can be found on the Daily List published at https://www.justice.gov.uk/courts/court-lists/list-cause-rolls2#Insolvency. Queries in relation to any hearings taking place before an ICC Judge should be directed to rolls.icl.hearings1@justice.gov.uk.

25.25 Listing before an ICC Judge will take place as directed by the court. Petitions made for relief under section 996 of the CA 2006 have automatic directions which will be sent to the parties by an ICC Judge listing officer. For all other matters before an ICC Judge the listing officer will list according to a time estimate and, if no time estimate is provided, it is likely that the listing officer will list an initial hearing for 15 minutes for directions.

25.26 The court may direct the filing of listing certificates before a final hearing and will list the case for hearing at a non-attendance pre-trial review. The ICC listing certificate may be obtained from the court office. The listing officer may make use of a trial window if appropriate.

25.27 Both the High Court Judges and the ICC Judges maintain interim applications lists in which applications may be made. To obtain an urgent hearing of an application before an ICC Judge, a certificate of urgency must be completed and signed by the solicitor/counsel with conduct of the application or by the litigant in person. The certificate must (i) state the nature of the application; (ii) explain why it is urgent; (iii) attach a draft order; and (iv) provide a time estimate for pre-reading and the hearing. A certificate of urgency with an explanation why the hearing is urgent and when the hearing is required, must be lodged prior to the hearing.

ICC INTERIM APPLICATIONS COURT AT THE ROLLS BUILDING

25.28 The ICC Interim Applications Court takes place on Thursdays, Fridays and every other **1A-226** Monday. The ICC Judges' listing officer (Claire Prosser) should be contacted in the event that an urgent application needs to be heard on any other day. She will seek to accommodate a hearing. The ICC Interim Applications Court will run in the same way as the High Court Judges' Interim Applications Court, which is not affected by the introduction of this list. It is intended that the list will be used to hear applications for:

1. an injunction to restrain presentation of a petition to wind up a company or to restrain advertisement of such a petition
2. an administration order
3. an appointment of a provisional liquidator
4. search and seizure orders pursuant to section 365 of the Insolvency Act 1986
5. an appointment of an interim receiver pursuant to section 286 of the Insolvency Act 1986
6. validation orders
7. other applications that are urgent, such as those made pursuant to section 125 of the Companies Act 2006.

25.29 Parties appearing in the ICC Interim Applications Court should report to the ICC Judges' clerks on the first floor before 10:30. The ICC Judges will work from hard copy documents and not from CE-file. Accordingly, in addition to the usual lodged bundles, any additional documents such as skeleton arguments or late-provided documents (whether or not they are also filed via CE-file) should be made available in hard copy, either via ICC Listing or to the ICC Judges' clerks on the first floor in the normal way. Bundles and skeleton arguments should be delivered by 10am on the day prior to the hearing.

25.30 Applications with a time estimate of more than two hours (including pre-reading time, judgment and consequentials) are generally not suitable for the ICC Interim Applications Court.

VALIDATION ORDERS

25.31 A validation order is a court order which allows a company to continue trading or a **1A-227** debtor to deal with their property notwithstanding a winding up order/bankruptcy petition being made against the applicant. Section 127 of the IA 1986 is applicable for a company and Section 284 of the IA 1986 is applicable for an individual debtor.

25.32 It is imperative that the urgent provisions for validation orders as set down in paragraphs 9.11 and 12.8 of the IPD are strictly complied with in order to allow the Court to deal with the application in a timely manner.

THE CO.IN SCHEME: HELP WITH WINDING-UP PETITIONS

25.33 The City Law School's Company Insolvency Pro Bono Scheme ('Co.IN') was set up in **1A-227.1** 2015 to provide free legal advice and representation to assist litigants in person (including a company or corporation that is not represented by a lawyer) using the Winding Up Court. The scheme is free and runs every Wednesday during term time from 10 am in consultation room 17 on the 2nd Floor of the Rolls Building where a Litigant in person will be able to speak to the Law School's barristers and students.

HEARINGS

25.34 Applications, trials and appeals before a High Court Judge are governed by Chapters 16, **1A-227.2** 21 and 25 respectively.

25.35 Chapter 21, paragraphs 21.19 to 21.112 , apply to all hearings and trials before an ICC Judge except hearings listed for 15 minutes or less, save that the place for delivery of documents for the purposes of paragraph 21.78 is the ICC counter on the first floor of the Rolls Building and the email address for filing skeleton arguments of under 25 pages for the purposes of paragraph 21.79 is rolls.icl.hearings1@justice.gov.uk. Hard copies of skeleton arguments should always be delivered, whether or not they have been emailed or uploaded to the CE File.

25.36 A hearing bundle must be lodged for all hearings before an ICC Judge or High Court Judge and in all claims where documents are 30 pages or more. In respect of bankruptcy petitions all the necessary procedural documents demonstrating compliance with the Insolvency Act 1986 and the IR 2016 must be produced and contained in a bundle lodged ready for the hearing.

25.37 There is a strict policy of "no bundle, no hearing". The person seeking a remedy at the hearing is responsible for the bundle being lodged but the parties should liaise and reach agreement as to content whenever practical.

ORDERS

1A-227.3 **25.38** Attention is drawn to Chapter 22. Responsibility for drawing up a minute of order lies with the applicant's legal representatives or, if the applicant is not legally represented, with the respondent's legal representatives. Minutes of orders, in both Word and PDF format, should be emailed to rolls.icl.hearings1@justice.gov.uk. If no party is legally represented then the court will draw the order. The court will also produce winding up orders and bankruptcy orders.

25.39 The judge's judicial title and the date of the order should appear below the court details. "Chief ICC Judge", "ICC Judge" or "Deputy ICC Judge", as appropriate, are acceptable abbreviations of the tiles of the ICC Judges and their deputies in orders and other documents.

COURT-TO-COURT COMMUNICATIONS IN CROSS-BORDER INSOLVENCY CASES

1A-227.4 **25.40** There is increasing international recognition that communication between courts in different jurisdictions may be of assistance in the efficient conduct of cross-border insolvency cases. Improved communication may lead to a co-ordinated approach between the courts and maximisation of benefit for all stakeholders of financially troubled enterprises.

25.41 There are, at present, three principal sets of guidelines for court-to-court communications which might be adopted, with appropriate modifications, in such cases. These are the American Law Institute/International Insolvency Institute Guidelines Applicable to Court-to-Court Communications in Cross-Border Cases, the EU Cross-Border Insolvency Court-to-Court Communications Guidelines the Judicial Insolvency Network Guidelines for Communication and Cooperation between Courts in Cross-Border Insolvency Matters:

> The ALI/III Guidelines are available at: *https://www.iiiglobal.org/sites/default/files/7-_ali.pdf*
> The EU Guidelines are available at: *http://www.ejtn.eu/PageFiles/16467/EU_Cross-Border_Insolvency_Court-to-Court_Cooperation_Principles.pdf*
> The JIN Guidelines (with minor amendments for use in England and Wales) are available at: *https://assets.publishing.service.gov.uk/government/uploads/system/uploads/attachment_data/file/612376/JIN_Guidelines.pdf*

25.42 In a cross-border insolvency case, the insolvency practitioner involved, together with any other interested parties, should consider, at an early stage in the proceedings, whether the Court should be invited to adopt one of these sets of guidelines for use in the proceedings, with such modifications as the circumstances of the case may require.

CHAPTER 28 SHORTER TRIALS AND FLEXIBLE TRIALS

GENERAL

Replace paragraph 28.1 with:

1A-235 **28.1** A Practice Direction made under rule 51.2 provided for a pilot of two schemes, the Shorter Trials Scheme and the Flexible Trials Scheme. Both schemes became permanent in October 2018 and they operate from all the B&PCs including those in the Rolls Building and those outside of London. The schemes can be found at PD 57AB. Although included within one Practice Direction, the two schemes are distinct.

CHAPTER 29 SPECIALIST WORK

(1) TRUSTS

VARIATION OF TRUSTS ACT 1958

Replace paragraph 29.24 with:

1A-247 **29.24** If the application is to be heard by a judge, it will be listed in the General list. The previous practice of listing these applications before a judge without reference to the Master no longer applies. Following the decision by Morgan J in *V v T* [2014] EWHC 3432 (Ch) it will be unusual for Variation of Trust cases to be heard in private. However, the Master or judge will consider at the hearing whether parts of the evidence should not be available for inspection on the file and whether additional safeguards are needed to protect children, born and unborn. Where the parties consider that a question of confidentiality or anonymity arises they should, when they are ready to issue proceedings, attend the Master at an AWN, having lodged the papers beforehand. A Variation of Trusts Confidentiality is at Form CH 43. Provided that there are prima facie grounds for protecting confidentiality the Master will be likely to order that access to the court file should be restricted, and that the parties should be anonymous, until the hearing. In such a case the Claim Form should be issued on an anonymised basis. The Master will also consider at the AWN whether there is a reason why the application should be heard by a judge. Where there are no issues of confidentiality or anonymity, and there are no other issues that the parties wish to raise, it is not necessary for the parties to attend the Master prior to issue; they should however include with a formal application notice a letter to the Master with case management suggestions, including whether the matter may be suitable for hearing by a judge.

Replace paragraph 29.25 with:

29.25 Applications under the Act will require the court to consider the current trusts that are to be varied. It will assist the court and save time if the parties' representatives can agree between themselves a single summary of the trusts (and their tax effects) and where appropriate, a summary of the documents and events that have led to the current trusts. Such summaries might appear in or be appended to the claimant's (or some other) witness statement, or be contained in a separate document filed with the skeleton arguments. If other summaries appear in the documents (e.g. in opinions prepared for litigation friends) which the court need not consider in light of the agreed summaries, their location should be identified in a pre-reading list with an indication that they need not be considered.

Replace paragraph 29.26 with:

29.26 Where any children or unborn beneficiaries will be affected by an arrangement under the Act, evidence must normally be before the court which shows that their litigation friends (in the case of children) or the trustees (in the case of unborn beneficiaries) support the arrangement as being for their benefit, and exhibits a written opinion to this effect. In complicated cases a written opinion is usually essential to the understanding of the litigation friends and the trustees, and to the consideration by the court of the merits and fiscal consequences of the arrangement. If the written opinion was given on formal instructions, those instructions must be exhibited. Otherwise the opinion must state fully the basis on which it was given. The opinion must be given by the advocate who will appear on the hearing of the application. A skeleton argument may not be needed where a written opinion has been put in evidence and no matters not appearing from the instructions or the opinion are to be relied on.

(2) PROBATE AND INHERITANCE

Add new title and paragraph 29.66.2:

GUARDIANSHIP (MISSING PERSONS) ACT 2017

29.66.2 Guardianship (Missing Persons) Act 2017
This Act came into force on 31 July 2019 and enables the Business and Property Courts to ap- **1A-258.1**
point a guardian to manage the property and financial affairs of a missing person (as that term is defined in section 1 of the Act). The definition includes a person who is held hostage or is in prison if they are unable to make or communicate decisions about their property or financial affairs.

An application to appoint a guardian may also be made in the Family Division.

The Act contains detailed provisions that need to be considered carefully before the claim is issued:

    (1)   The person was missing throughout a period of 90 days ending on the date the application was made (see section 3).

    (2)   The proposed guardian must be a suitable person (see section 4).

The court may appoint a guardian over all the missing person's property and financial affairs, or specified elements. The guardian may be given full or limited powers, and specific duties may be imposed.

The court may impose conditions and restrictions including a requirement for the guardian to give security before discharging any functions under the guardianship order and/or provide reports to the Public Guardian. It is likely that security will be required in most cases.

New rules have been grafted onto CPR Part 57 commencing with 57.24 and by adding Practice Direction 57C. The procedure is a hybrid version of the normal Part 8 procedure. Prescribed information must be included in the Part 8 claim form and in a witness statement that is filed on issue of the claim. The witness statement must provide evidence to satisfy the court that the statutory criteria in section 1 and 3 are met and that the court has jurisdiction based on the domicile or habitual residence of the missing person or the applicant where the applicant is the missing person's spouse or civil partner - section 2. In addition, the witness statement must explain why the proposed guardian is suitable by reference to the requirements of section 4 including the particular issues that are set out in section 4(2). The guardian does not, however, need to be a relative of the missing person and a professional person may be appointed.

The claimant must be a person who has a 'sufficient interest' in the missing person's affairs. The claimant may propose that he or she is appointed as guardian in which event both the sufficient interest and suitability criteria will have to be met by the applicant.

The missing person is named in the Part 8 claim form as the defendant. For obvious reasons the defendant does not normally need to be served with the claim. No other parties need be added to the claim even if it is known they wish to make representations. Instead, the rules require that notice of the claim is given to the missing person's spouse, civil partner, parent, child or sibling and any of them may intervene in the claim and participate as of right by giving formal notice of their wish to intervene. The claim must be advertised. Other persons who wish to intervene must apply to the court for permission.

The court will fix a directions appointment when the claim is issued. At the directions hearing, the court will wish to establish that (1) the claim and the evidence provide the information that is required by the Act and the CPR, and (2) will need to be satisfied that the claim has been notified and advertised. Any applications to intervene will be dealt with at the hearing. If there is a dispute about the appointment, or further steps are required, directions will be given and a disposal hearing date will be fixed. It is very unlikely the court will permit a trial of disputed issues of fact other than in exceptional circumstances. In a straightforward case, the court may be able to make an order appointing a guardian at the first hearing.

The court may hear an urgent application to appoint a guardian if the "urgency condition", as it is defined in section 3(3), is met. Applications may be made after the appointment of a guardian to vary or revoke the order and for other orders. These applications are made by issuing an application notice.

All claims and applications made under the Act in London, including urgent claims, will be dealt with by Chancery Masters unless, exceptionally, they are released to be heard by a High Court Judge. Attention is drawn to the Code of Practice issued by the Ministry of Justice in June 2019 pursuant to section 22 of the Act. It provides a useful summary of the provisions of the Act and examples of how the Act may operate in particular circumstances: *https://assets.publishing.service.gov. uk/government/uploads/system/uploads/attachment_data/file/822418/missing-people-code-of-practice.pdf*. Some useful guidance on managing a missing person's finances and property can be found here: *https://www.gov.uk/manage-missing-persons-finances*.

(6) PENSIONS

STARTING PROCEEDINGS

Add new paragraph 29.92:

1A-263   **29.92** Sometimes the outcome of litigation is relevant to a separate professional negligence claim against advisers. There are several options to consider to avoid the risk of points being re-argued in separate proceedings. The advisers can agree to be bound by the outcome of the litigation, or joined as defendants for the purpose of being bound (as in *Shannan v Viavi Solutions UK Ltd* [2016] EWHC 1530 (CH)). An alternative route is an application under CPR 19.8A for the court to direct notice of the claim to be served on the adviser.

Replace paragraph with:

REPRESENTATIVE BENEFICIARIES

1A-264   **29.93** The use of one or more representative beneficiaries to represent the interests of members under CPR rule 19.7(2) is a standard feature of most pensions claims. The number of representatives and classes represented should be kept to the minimum necessary to enable the court to be satisfied that it has heard full argument on behalf of all those interested. It is often convenient to make an "issue-based" representation order, that is for the representative to be appointed to represent all those interested in an issue being resolved in a particular way: see *Capita ATL v Zurkinskas* [2010] EWHC 3365 (Ch). If the trustees are in doubt as to who to join, see PD 64B paragraph 4.3.

29.94 Representative beneficiaries will almost always have to be funded at the expense of the scheme and for that purpose it will be necessary to obtain a prospective costs order. Details of a proposed order are usually agreed by the trustees' solicitors and solicitors for the proposed representative and put before the Master for approval at the first hearing. For the procedure generally see under Trusts (1 above) and note the reference to a model order annexed to PD 64A.

29.95 CPR rule 19.7(2) does not specifically require that the representative be a member of the class represented, although this is usually the case. The court's overriding concern is to see that the interests of all those represented are protected, and for this purpose the court will be willing to appoint a non-member of the class if the circumstances warrant it: see eg *Sovereign Trustees v Glover* [2007] EWHC 1750 (Ch) and *Walker Morris Trustees Ltd v Masterson* [2009] EWHC 1955 (Ch), in each of which solicitors were appointed representatives. In some circumstances a person may even act as a representative for a class although his personal interests are opposed to the position he is advancing: see *Thompson v Fresenius Kabi Ltd* [2013] Pens LR 157.

29.96 Moreover, in some cases the interests of some classes of members are aligned with those of the employer(s), and an employer can properly be appointed to represent their interests; in other cases, the trustees (who would normally be neutral) may agree to be appointed to represent the members or some class of them to save costs: see eg *Premier Foods v RHM Pension Trust* [2012] EWHC 447 (Ch), *Arcadia Group Ltd v Arcadia Group Pension Trust Ltd* [2014] EWHC 2683 (Ch). This procedure is a useful one, particularly on pure questions of construction or law where there are only two possible outcomes; it is not suitable for all cases and is unlikely for example to be suitable where there are questions as to what the trustees did, particularly if there is any criticism of the trustees' conduct.

29.97 If a compromise is proposed in proceedings in which a representative is to be or has been appointed under CPR rule 19.7, the court's approval is required, and the court may only approve the compromise where it is for the benefit of the represented persons; CPR rule 19.7(5) and (6). For this purpose it will almost invariably require an opinion on the merits of the proposed compromise from counsel instructed on behalf of the represented class. Such an opinion is normally confidential and not served on or shown to the other parties. The application for the court's approval should be in public, but discussion of the merits of the proposed compromise from the point of view of the represented class will usually take place in private and in the absence of the other parties.

29.98 A similar practice applies where a defendant acting as a representative does not consider it appropriate to oppose the relief sought. Examples of this have arisen in claims for rectification of pension scheme rules. In such unopposed applications for summary judgment, a practice has built up for the hearing to be held in open court, but submissions on behalf of the representative party as to the merits of the summary judgment application to be held in private and in the absence of the claimant: see eg *Misys Ltd & Anor v Misys Retirement Benefits Transfers Limited & Anor* [2012] EWHC 4250 (Ch) at [20] and *Konica Minolta Business Solutions (UK) Limited v Applegate & Ors* [2013] EWHC 2536 (Ch) at [7]. The position is however currently unsettled: in *Saga Group Limited v Paul* [2016] EWHC 2344 (Ch) at [22] the Court concluded that the applications should not be heard using the confidential approach, and in *Sovereign Trustees Limited v Lewis* [2016] EWHC 2593 (Ch) at [37] (heard before *Saga* but judgment given later) Chief Master Marsh observed that the confidential approach worked well before him.

Replace paragraph with:

CONSULTATION OR NOTIFICATION
29.99 Although there is no requirement to consult with or notify members of a pension scheme **1A-265** when it is proposed that a person be appointed under CPR 19.7(2) to represent their interests, in the context of unopposed summary judgment applications it has been said that notification is desirable or good practice: *Industrial Acoustics Company Ltd v Crowhurst* [2012] EWHC 1614 (Ch) at [60] and *CitiFinancial Europe Plc v Davidson* [2014] EWHC 1802 (Ch) at [7]. The scheme's trustees would ordinarily be the appropriate persons to notify members of what is proposed.

29.100 The same considerations would also apply where the court's approval is sought under CPR 19.7(6) to the settlement of a claim.

29.101 Where members have not been notified and are unaware of the proposed compromise, the court might decide to postpone the effective date of any order for a short period to allow any person affected by it to apply to the court if he or she considers that, due to circumstances which are particular to them, they should not be bound: *Smithson v Hamilton* [2008] EWCA Civ 996 at [13]-[15] (period 28 days), and *Archer v Travis Perkins PLC* [2014] EWHC 1362 (Ch) at [26]-[28] (period 42 days).

Replace paragraph with:

S 48 ADMINISTRATION OF JUSTICE ACT 1985
29.102 The jurisdiction conferred on the High Court by s.48 of the Administration of Justice **1A-266** Act 1985 may be invoked by trustees where any question of construction has arisen out of the terms of a trust. See generally under Trusts (1 above).

29.103 Whilst the jurisdiction is particularly well suited to construction issues arising in relation to a trust of modest value where a conventional inter partes application would be prohibitively expensive, it may be (and has been) successfully invoked in cases involving occupational pension schemes of substantial size where the question concerned has been sufficiently clear so as to be an appropriate one to deal with under s.48.

29.104 In the case of a pension scheme, the employer is not a necessary party to the application, nor will any order made either be directed to it (as opposed to, and affording protection to, the applicant trustees) or prevent a member from subsequently asserting a claim, either by legal proceedings or before the Pensions Ombudsman, which is inconsistent with an order made under s.48. The effect of an order under s.48 is to protect the trustees against any complaint that they have wrongly administered the scheme but it does not bind any of the members or potential beneficiaries of the scheme: see *re BCA Pension Plan* [2015] EWHC 3492 (Ch) at [36].

29.105 S.48 is intended for use in clear cases only; it will not provide, and an applicant therefore should not seek, a binding decision on the question of construction which has arisen. In a particular case the court may consider that, as a matter of discretion, it would be preferable to have the issue finally and bindingly resolved at a substantive hearing, as opposed to its merely being made the subject of directions to the trustees, especially where conflicting opinions have been expressed by different counsel advising the trustees: see *Greenwold v Pike* [2007] EWHC 2202 (Ch).

29.106 Where the court makes an order, it may require the trustees to notify the members in some suitable fashion: see generally *re BCA Pension Plan* [2015] EWHC 3492 (Ch) at [37]-[43].

Replace paragraph with:

APPEALS FROM THE PENSIONS OMBUDSMAN

1A-267 **29.107** Appeals from determinations or directions of the Pensions Ombudsman lie on a point of law to the High Court under s.151(4) of the Pension Schemes Act 1993, and are assigned to the Chancery Division by PD 52D paragraph 5.1(8). The permission of the High Court is required for such appeals under CPR rule 52.29.

29.108 Although the default time limit for filing an appellant's notice is 21 days from the date of the decision appealed against (CPR rule 52.4(2)(b)), the Ombudsman may direct a longer period (CPR rule 52.4(2)(a) and see CPR rule 52.1(3)(c) under which "lower court" includes the person from whose decision an appeal is brought) and has given a general direction for England and Wales that the person wishing to appeal must lodge the appeal within 28 days after the date of an Ombudsman determination.

29.109 The attention of appellants is drawn to PD 52D paragraph 3.4(1) that states the appellant must serve the appellant's notice on the person from whose decision the appeal is brought. Although there is no obligation under PD 52D paragraph 3.4(1) to do so, the Ombudsman's Office often finds it helpful to be kept informed of the progress of the appeal and copied into relevant correspondence.

29.110 Where scheme members appeal, they are frequently unrepresented. In such a case the respondent (trustees or employer or other as the case may be) should take it upon themselves to confirm both that the Ombudsman has been served with the appellant's notice and that the material put before the court includes all material that was before the Ombudsman and is potentially relevant to the appeal.

29.111 Attention is drawn to the power of the court to make an order to limit the recoverable costs in such an appeal under CPR 52.19 and that the application should be made as soon as practicable in relation to the progress of the appeal: see Coats UK Pension Scheme Trustees Ltd v A Styles & Others [2019] EWHC 35 (Ch).

29.112 It is desirable that the order made as a result of an appeal from a determination of the Pensions Ombudsman is clear about which aspects of the determination are upheld, set aside or remitted back to the Pensions Ombudsman for further determination. Therefore, where parties propose to compromise such an appeal, they should, where possible, liaise with the office of the Pensions Ombudsman about the wording of the Consent Order.

Replace section (7) Competition List (Ch. D) with:

(7) COMPETITION LIST (CH.D)

INTRODUCTION

1A-268 **29.113** Proceedings (other than those in the Commercial Court) relating to the application of competition law, namely the application of Articles 101 and 102 of the Treaty on the Functioning of the European Union ("TFEU") (formerly Articles 81 and 82 of the EC Treaty) and the equivalent provisions of the Competition Act 1998, must be brought in the Competition List in the Chancery Division. They are governed by CPR Part 30 and its Practice Direction.

29.114 Many Judges of the Chancery Division also sit in the Competition Appeal Tribunal ("CAT"), in their capacity as Chairmen of the CAT. This Guide discusses the jurisdiction of the CAT only insofar as it is relevant to the transfer of competition law claims from the High Court to the CAT and from the CAT to the High Court. Further information about the CAT is available on its website at *www.catribunal.org.uk.*

NATURE OF COMPETITION LAW CLAIMS

1A-269 **29.115** Claims relating to the application of competition law brought in the Chancery Division typically take the form of injunction applications seeking to restrain alleged breaches of competition law, or private actions for damages for alleged breaches of competition law.

29.116 Private actions for damages may be characterised as "follow-on" claims, "stand-alone" claims or a hybrid of both types of claims. So-called "follow-on" claims follow on from a pre-existing finding, by one of the UK competition authorities or by the European Commission (or by a court or tribunal on appeal from one of those bodies), that there has been an infringement of

UK or EU competition law. In contrast, "stand-alone" claims are claims in which the court is asked to make a finding of infringement.

29.117 Competition law claims are by their nature complex and frequently involve consideration of economic or technical issues.

PRACTICE DIRECTION – COMPETITION LAW

29.118 The Practice Direction on Competition Law (Claims relating to the application of Articles 81 and 82 of the EC Treaty (now Articles 101 and 102 of the TFEU) and Chapters I and II of Part I of the Competition Act 1998) sets out certain requirements in relation to competition law claims. Many of these requirements are derived from those provisions of Council Regulation (EC) No.1/2003 (on the implementation of the rules on competition laid down in the Treaty) which provide for co-operation between the European Commission and the national courts of EU Member States. **1A-270**

29.119 In addition to transfers of competition law claims (discussed in further detail below), the Practice Direction covers the following matters relevant to claims raising Article 101/102 issues:
- The requirement to serve a copy of the statement of case on the Competition and Markets Authority (formerly the Office of Fair Trading) at the same time as it is served on the other parties to the claim;
- The procedure by which national competition authorities and the European Commission may submit observations to the court on issues relating to the application of Articles 101 or 102;
- The obligation on the parties and the national competition authorities (where those authorities have been served with a copy of the statement of case) to notify the court of any decision, or contemplated decision, of the European Commission which has or would have legal effects in relation to the particular agreement, decision or practice in issue before the national court, in order to avoid a conflict with any such decision; and
- The requirement to notify relevant judgments to the European Commission.

TRANSFER OF COMPETITION LAW CLAIMS TO THE COMPETITION LIST FROM OTHER DIVISIONS OF THE HIGH COURT OR THE COUNTY COURT

29.120 Where a party's statement of case raises an issue relating to the application of competition law and the claim has not been commenced in the Chancery Division (or, if applicable, the Commercial Court), the claim must be transferred to the Competition List (Ch.D), in accordance with and subject to the provisions of CPR rule 30.8 and paragraph 2 of the Practice Direction on Competition Law. The claim, or part of the claim, may subsequently be transferred to another court if the issue relating to the application of competition law has been resolved, or the judge considers that the claim or part of the claim to be transferred does not involve any issue relating to the application of competition law. **1A-271**

TRANSFER OF COMPETITION LAW CLAIMS TO OR FROM THE CAT

29.121 In an appropriate case, competition law claims may, in whole or in part, be transferred from the Competition List to the CAT pursuant to section 16(1) of the Enterprise Act 2002 and the Section 16 Enterprise Act 2002 Regulations 2015 (S.I. 2015 No. 1643), and/or section 16(4) of the Enterprise Act 2002. Paragraphs 8.1-8.6 and 8.10-8.13 of PD 30 (as in force from 1 October 2015) make provision for such transfers. The High Court may order a transfer on its own initiative or on application by the claimant or defendant. When deciding whether to make an order, the court must consider all the circumstances of the case including the wishes of the parties. The first such transfer order was made in *Sainsbury's Supermarkets Ltd v MasterCard Incorporated and Others* [2015] EWHC 3472 (Ch), in which Barling J considered the reasons why such a transfer might be appropriate. **1A-272**

29.122 Similarly, the CAT may, in an appropriate case, direct that all or part of a claim before it be transferred to the Competition List, pursuant to section 16(5) of the Enterprise Act 2002. PD 30 paragraphs 8.7-8.9 make provision for such transfers. Following any such transfer, the High Court must allocate a case number and list the case for a case management hearing before a judge.

DAMAGES DIRECTIVE

29.123 Directive 2014/104/EU of the European Parliament and of the Council of 26 November 2014 on certain rules governing actions for damages under national law for infringements of the competition law provisions of the Member States and of the European Union, known as the Damages Directive, is due to be implemented in the UK by 27 December 2016. The implementation of the Damages Directive may necessitate amendments to the CPR prior to the end of 2016. **1A-273**

Replace section (8) Court Funds (Payments into and out of court) with:

(8) COURT FUNDS (PAYMENTS INTO AND OUT OF COURT)

29.124 Reference should be made to CPR Part 37 and PD 37, and the Court Funds Rules 2011. **1A-274**

PAYMENTS INTO COURT

—MORTGAGEES

1A-275   **29.125**   Mortgagees wishing to lodge surplus proceeds of sale in court under s.63 of the Trustee Act 1925 must in their witness statement, in addition to the matters set out in 37PD 6.1:

(1)   set out the steps they have taken to fulfil their obligation under s.105 of the Law of Property Act 1925 to pay other prior chargees (if any) and the mortgagor, and why those steps have not been successful;

(2)   exhibit office copy entries of the mortgaged property.

Failure to do so will usually result in their application being rejected by the court.

PAYMENTS OUT

—APPLICATION

1A-276   **29.126**   Applications under PD 37 for payment out of money held in court must be made by Part 23 application notice (Form N244). The application notice and the court fee should be sent to the Miscellaneous Payments Clerk – Masters' Appointments/Case Management Section. The following details must be included in Part C of the application notice:

•   The reasons why the payment should be made

•   A statement confirming that no-one else has any claim to the money (or if there is another claimant providing details of that person and their interest)

•   Bank details of the person to whom the payment out of court should be made including the name and address of the bank/building society branch, its sort code, and the account title and number

29.127   The Statement of Truth must be completed and signed.

29.128   Copies of documents which show an entitlement to the money in court and as to identity (as to which see below) must be exhibited to the application notice. The court may in some cases require certified copies or the original documents. Documents may be certified by a solicitor or any other person on the list of persons who may approve a passport application as long as the certifier provides his/her name and status legibly and signs each copy; or copies may be certified at a Post Office. Where an original document is sent, this should be stated in the covering letter and its return requested.

29.129   Approval is shown not by a formally drawn order, but by signing the payment schedule in Form CFO 200. Failure to set out what steps have been taken and why they were unsuccessful will usually result in the application being rejected by the court.

—DETERMINATION OF THE APPLICATION BY THE COURT

1A-277   **29.130**   If there is a dispute as to entitlement to money in court, the Master will generally transfer the matter to the County Court. If, exceptionally, it is appropriate for the case to be retained in the High Court in London (for example if significant sums are involved or there are other linked proceedings) the Master may order it to proceed by Part 8 claim form (see Chapter 8 above) and may list it for disposal or directions. If there is no agreement it may be necessary for there to be an inquiry into competing claims; for example, where moneys have been paid into court under the Trustee Act following sale by a mortgagee, there may need to be an inquiry into the beneficial interests of joint owners and/or priorities between other secured lenders. In all other cases (except as stated below) the application will be considered without a hearing and if the application makes out an entitlement to the funds in court, or part of them, the payment out of court will be approved.

29.131   Where the applicant is a joint owner of property the Master will normally allow payment out of one-half of the money in court, but not of the other half unless the joint owner consents.

29.132   If the application is made by a person with a benefit of a charging order, the Master will require to be satisfied

(1)   in the case of joint ownership, as to whether that charging order extends to the whole of the proceeds of sale or only to the share of the proceeds of sale of one of the co-owners;

(2)   that there are no persons with a prior interest e.g. legal or equitable chargees.

—EVIDENCE OF ENTITLEMENT

1A-278   **29.133**   The person claiming to be entitled to funds held in court must produce evidence of their entitlement to the fund. This may be one of the following documents:

•   CFO account statement

•   Sealed copy of court order

•   Where the person entitled to the funds has died, a sealed copy of the grant of representation (grant of probate or letters of administration)

•   Where there is more than one personal representative the written consent (or death certificate, if deceased) of every other representative (together with evidence of their identity – see below)

- Where the value of the estate is less than £5,000, a copy of the will (or written declaration of kinship if the person died intestate) and death certificate of the deceased, rather than a copy of the grant of representation
- In the case of money paid in by a bank or building society (as mortgagee), or by a trustee, the paying-in witness statement or affidavit
- Where the application is made by a dissenting shareholder, the relevant share certificates
- Where the applicant is the former land owner in an application for payment of monies paid into court following a compulsory purchase, documents evidencing title to the land at the relevant time and notice of the compulsory purchase order

—EVIDENCE OF IDENTITY

1A-279

29.134 The person claiming entitlement must normally produce evidence of their identity (unless the application is made on their behalf by a solicitor or other legal representative who should also be satisfied as to their client's identity). This may be one of the following documents:
- Passport or UK travel document
- Driving licence
- UK identity card for foreign nationals, residence permit or travel documents issued by the Home Office
- European Community or European Economic Area identity card
- Alternatively, a birth or adoption certificate may be provided, but is not absolute proof of identity and must be accompanied by one other supporting document:
- National insurance card or a letter from the Department of Work and Pensions showing NI number
- The front page of a benefits book or a letter concerning state pension and showing NI number
- P45, P60 or payslip
- Student union card
- Marriage certificate
- Decree nisi or decree absolute
- Bank or building statement issued in the last 3 months

—EVIDENCE OF NAME OR ADDRESS CHANGE

1A-280

29.135 Where the person claiming entitlement has changed their name, they must also produce
- Marriage or civil partnership certificate
- Decree nisi or decree absolute
- Deed poll declaration
- Adoption certificate

29.136 The evidence must show a clear link between the name shown on the evidence of entitlement and the person's current name.

29.137 Where the person claiming entitlement has changed their address, they must produce
- 2 of the following documents evidencing their previous address – utilities or council tax bill, or bank/building society statement from the relevant time
- Utilities bill or bank/building society statement issued within the last 3 months

29.138 Reference should be made to CPR Part 37 and the accompanying PD, 37 PD, and the Court Funds Rules 2011.

Chapter 30 Chancery business outside London

Replace paragraph 30.5 with:

1A-281

30.5 The Chancery Senior Circuit Judge in Wales is HHJ Milwyn Jarman QC. He is based at the Cardiff Civil Justice Centre, the address of which is 2 Park Street, Cardiff CF10 1ET and the telephone number of which is 029 2037 6400. HHJ Jarman also sits elsewhere in Wales on a regular basis. Emails can be sent to enquiries.cardiff.countycourt@justice.gov.uk.

Replace table with:

Birmingham	The Priory Courts, 33 Bull Street, Birmingham B4 6DS Chancery Listings: Christine Baker 0121 681 3160 Email:*chris.baker@justice.gov.uk* Shared inbox: *birmingham.chancery@justice.gov.uk*
Bristol	Bristol Civil Justice Centre, 2 Redcliff Street, Bristol BS1 6GR DX95903 BRISTOL 3 General switchboard: 0117 366 4800 Chancery listings: Amy Smallcombe 0117 366 4833 Email: amy.smallcombe@hmtcs.gsi.gov.uk *bristolchancerylisting@justice.gov.uk*

Cardiff	The Civil Justice Centre, 2 Park Street, Cardiff CF10 1ET Diary Manager for Wales: Annette Parsons 02920 376424 Email: *annette.parsons@justice.gov.uk* hearings.cardiff.countycourt@justice.gov.uk
Leeds	The Court House, 1 Oxford Row, Leeds LS1 3BG Chancery Listings: Richard Marsland 0113 3062461 Email: *Richard.marsland6@justice.gov.uk* Applications/orders: *orders@leeds.districtregistry.gsi.gov.uk* Skeletons: hearings.leeds.countycourt@justice.gov.uk
Liverpool	35 Vernon Street, Liverpool, Merseyside L2 2BX DX 702600 Liverpool Chancery Listings: Liz Taylor 0151 2962445 Email: *elizabethtaylor6@justice.gov.uk* No shared Inbox
Manchester	Manchester Civil Justice Centre, 1 Bridge Street West, Manchester, Greater Manchester M60 9DJ DX 72483 Manchester 44 Chancery Listings Manager: Julie Bagnall 0161 240 5223 Email: *julie.bagnall@justice.gov.uk* Shared Inbox *manchester.chancery@justice.gov.uk*
Newcastle	The Law Courts, Quayside, Newcastle-upon-Tyne NE1 3LA Chancery Listings: Brian Redhead 0191 2302056 Email: *brian.redhead@justice.gov.uk* Main Chancery contact: Helen Tait 0191 2012061 Email: *helen.tait@justice.gov.uk* Shared Inbox: civil.newcastle.countycourt@justice.gov.uk
Preston	The Law Courts, Openshaw Place, Ringway, Preston PR1 2LL Diary Manager: Bernadette Gregson 01772 844713 Email: *bernadettegregson@justice.gov.uk* Angela Moizer *centralisedcivillisting@justice.gov.uk*
Mold	Listings Managers (Based in Wrexham): Beth Sear 01978 317406 Tracey Patterson Email: *northwalescivillisting@justice.gov.uk*
Caernarfon	Caernarfon County Court & Family Court Hearing Centre Llanberis Road, Caernarfon, Gwynedd, LL55 2DF Listing staff: Jared Hughes 01286 684600 Email: enquiries@caernarfon.countycourt.gsi.gov.uk

CHAPTER 31 THE BUSINESS AND PROPERTY COURTS OF ENGLAND AND WALES

(11)   TECHNOLOGY & CONSTRUCTION COURT (QBD)

(A)   THE GENERAL TCC LIST.

Replace list with:

1A-284   This includes:
- Building and engineering disputes.
- Claims by and against architects, engineers, surveyors, accountants and other specialised advisers relating to the services they provide.
- Claims involving issues that are technically complex.
- Claims relating to the design, supply and installation of computers, software and related network systems.
- Claims relating to the supply and provision of materials, goods, plant and other services.
- Claims by and against local authorities relating to their statutory duties concerning the development of land or the construction of buildings.
- Dilapidation claims as between landlord and tenant.
- Environmental claims, including pollution and reclamation.
- Nuisance claims relating to land use.
- Claims arising out of fires, explosions and other catastrophic events.
- Insurance disputes relating to construction, engineering and technology.
- Contractual disputes involving oil and gas installations, onshore and offshore, and ship building.
- Any arbitration claim under the Arbitration Act 1996, including challenges to decisions of arbitrators in construction and engineering disputes and/or application for permission to appeal and appeals in such cases.

SECTION 1BA ADMINISTRATIVE COURT JUDICIAL REVIEW GUIDE

Replace the Administrative Court Judicial Review Guide with:
July 2019

Contents

Foreword to the 2019 Edition

This is the fifth edition of the Judicial Review Guide, which has become an invaluable resource **1BA-1** for all who are involved in proceedings before the Administrative Court. It covers all the stages of a claim for judicial review. Good practice is identified and pitfalls foreshadowed. I encourage all those who conduct judicial review cases (whether or not they are lawyers) to study it.

The production of the Guide is dependent on judges, lawyers and the staff of the Court. I am particularly indebted to Mr Justice Supperstone (as lead Judge of the Court), Mr Justice Lewis and Mrs Justice Farbey for their contributions; to Jessica Pressman, the Administrative Court Office lawyer who marshalled the amendments and to Jessica McDonald who assisted with the production of the Guide. David Gardner, formerly a lawyer in the Administrative Court office in Cardiff, was responsible for much of the original research and drafting of this Guide. A number of other judges and Court staff have also worked very hard to produce the Guide and I am grateful to all those, named and un-named, who have done so. The result of their labours is this important guide to a very significant part of the daily work of the High Court.

The Rt Hon Dame Victoria Sharp DBE
President of the Queen's Bench Division

Preface to the 2019 Edition

This Guide provides a general explanation of the work and practice of the Administrative **1BA-2** Court. It is designed to make it easier for parties to conduct judicial reviews in the Administrative Court, by drawing together into one place the relevant statutory provisions, rules of procedure, practice directions, and case law on procedural aspects of judicial review. It provides general guidance as to how litigation in the Administrative Court should be conducted in order to achieve the overriding objective of dealing with cases justly and at proportionate cost.

The Guide has been prepared with all Court users in mind, whether they are persons who lack legal representation (known as "litigants in person") or persons who have legal representation. We invite all Court users to follow this Guide when they prepare and present their cases.

In recent years, the Administrative Court has become one of the busiest specialist Courts within the High Court. It is imperative that Court resources (including the time of the judges who sit in the Administrative Court) are used efficiently. That has not uniformly been the case in the past where the Court has experienced problems in relation to applications claiming unnecessary urgency, over-long written arguments, and bundles of documents, authorities and skeleton arguments being filed very late (to name just a few problems). These and other bad practices will not be tolerated. This Guide therefore sets out in clear terms what is expected. Sanctions may be applied if parties fail to comply.

It is anticipated that in 2020 the Electronic Working Pilot Scheme will commence in the Administrative Court, using the CE-File electronic court file system. Court users will be able to file documents electronically direct to the court file. Many Court users will be familiar with the system, which is already in operation in the Rolls Building Courts and the Queen's Bench Division Central Office. This new edition of the Guide provides a summary of the system pending a detailed Practice Note.

This new edition also includes at Annex 6 the guidance for handing down judgments in Wales. The Upper Tribunal continues to undertake a significant number of judicial review cases. Annex 7 contains important information about its jurisdiction.

We are grateful to all those who provided constructive feedback on the 2018 Guide which we have reflected in the present edition. We continue to welcome feedback which should be sent to the Senior Legal Managers in the Administrative Court Office, by email to administrativecourtoffice. guide-feedback@hmcts.x.gsi.gov.uk. We plan to update this Guide from time to time, as appropriate.

The Honourable Mr Justice Supperstone, Judge in Charge of the Administrative Court
The Honourable Mr Justice Lewis
The Honourable Mrs Justice Farbey DBE
Royal Courts of Justice, July 2019

PART A:—PRELIMINARY MATTERS

1. INTRODUCTION

1.1. THE JUDICIAL REVIEW GUIDE

1BA-3   **1.1.1.** This Guide has been prepared under the direction of the lead Judge of the Administrative Court and provides a general explanation of the work and practice of the Administrative Court with particular regard to judicial review. The Guide is designed to make it easier for parties to conduct judicial reviews in the Administrative Court. The definition of public law and administrative law is beyond the scope of this Guide and reference should be made to the many academic and practitioner texts on the subject for further reading.

1.1.2. The Guide must be read with the Civil Procedure Rules ("CPR") and the supporting Practice Directions. Litigants and their advisers are responsible for acquainting themselves with the CPR; it is not the task of this Guide to summarise the CPR, nor should anyone regard this Guide as a substitute for the CPR.

1.1.3. The Guide does not have the force of law, but parties using the Administrative Court will be expected to act in accordance with it. Where relevant, parties should draw the Court's attention to a particular rule or case and not merely rely on referring to this Guide. The Guide is intended to be applicable in the Administrative Court and the Administrative Court Offices across England and Wales.

1.1.4. The contents of the Guide, including any websites, email addresses, telephone numbers and addresses, are correct at the time of publication. The Guide will be updated from time to time.

1.2. THE CIVIL PROCEDURE RULES

1BA-4   **1.2.1.** The overriding objective set out in CPR 1.1(1) is central to civil proceedings, including judicial reviews. It requires the parties and the Court to deal with cases justly and proportionately, including at proportionate cost.

1.2.2. The CPR are divided into Parts. A particular Part is referred to in the Guide as CPR Part 54, etc., as the case may be. Any particular rule within a Part is referred to, for example, as CPR 54.12(2). The current CPR can be viewed on the Government's website via *www.gov.uk/courts-tribunals/administrative-court*.

1.2.3. The judicial review procedure is mainly (but not exclusively) governed by CPR Part 54 and the associated practice directions. CPR Part 54 and the associated practice directions are required reading for any litigant considering judicial proceedings. More details on these provisions will be given throughout this Guide.

1.3. PRACTICE DIRECTIONS

1BA-5   **1.3.1.** Most Parts of the CPR have an accompanying practice direction or directions, and other practice directions deal with matters such as the pre-action Protocols.

1.3.2. The practice directions are made pursuant to statute and have the same authority as the CPR themselves. However, in case of any conflict between a rule and a practice direction, the rule will prevail. Each practice direction is referred to in the Guide with the number of any part that it supplements preceding it; for example, one of the practice directions supplementing CPR Part 54 is referred to as CPR PD 54A. A reference to a particular sub-paragraph of a practice direction will be referred to as, for example, CPR PD 54A paragraph 5.1.

1.3.3. The key associated practice directions to CPR Part 54 are CPR PD 54A (Judicial Review Practice), CPR PD 54D (Venue for Claims), and CPR PD 54E (Planning Court). These practice directions are required reading for any litigant considering judicial proceedings. More details on these provisions will be given throughout this Guide.

1.4. FORMS

1BA-6   **1.4.1.** CPR PD 4 lists the forms generally required to be used under the CPR.

1.4.2. The Practice Direction contains 3 tables. Table 1 lists the "N forms" that are referred to and required by the CPR and the Practice Directions. Tables 2 and 3 list forms that are not relevant to this Guide. Other forms may be provided by the Administrative Court Office and are not available online (for example, Form 86b – see paragraph 8.4 of this Guide).

1.4.3. The relevant N forms that are directly relevant to judicial review proceedings are:

N461	Judicial Review claim form
N461(PC)	Judicial Review claim form (Planning Court)
N462	Judicial Review acknowledgment of service
N462(PC)	Judicial Review acknowledgement of service (Planning Court)

| N463 | Judicial Review – application for urgent consideration |
| N463(PC) | Judicial Review – application for urgent consideration (Planning Court) |

1.4.4. The following general N forms are also required in a judicial review application:

N215	Certificate of service
N244	Application notice
N260	Statement of costs (Summary Assessment)
N279	Notice of discontinuance
N434	Notice of change of legal representative

1.4.5. The forms contained in CPR PD 4 are available in the various practitioners' textbooks and at the Administrative Court website: *www.gov.uk/courts-tribunals/administrative-court*.

1.4.6. There are a few forms which are not set out in the rules that practitioners must use. One form of importance in judicial review is that for an out of hours application (see paragraph 16.3 of this Guide).

1.5. FEES

1.5.1. By virtue of the Civil Proceedings (Fees) Order 2008 No. 1053 (L. 5) (as amended) the **1BA-7** Administrative Court Office is required to charge fees at certain stages in proceedings or when a party requests an order from the Court. The relevant fees (at the time of publication) are outlined in Annex 2.[1] Current fees can also be checked at the Administrative Court website at *www.gov.uk/courts-tribunals/administrative-court.*

1.5.2. Some litigants may be entitled to the remission of fees.[2] Guidance on whether you may be entitled to fee remission can be found on form EX160A and litigants can apply online at *www.gov.uk/help-with-court-fees.*This Guide will only refer to fees, but a litigant should be aware that fee remission is potentially available for all fees save for copying charges (except for vexatious litigants and persons subject to Civil Restraint Orders where different rules apply, see paragraph 4.6 of this Guide).

1.5.3. Court fees should not be confused with costs between parties, which can be considerably more than the Court fees. Costs are discussed in this Guide in chapter 23.

1.5.4. A litigant in person will be expected to comply with the requirements to use the right form and to pay fees, just like a represented litigant. Litigants in person should therefore make themselves familiar with those parts of this Guide which are relevant to their claim and with the applicable requirements.

1.6. CALCULATING TIME LIMITS

1.6.1. Any reference to days in the CPR or in this Guide will be a reference to clear, calendar **1BA-8** days, unless stated otherwise. Therefore, when calculating time limits, every day, including weekends and bank holidays, will count, except for the day of the act or order itself (see CPR 2.8 for more detail and examples).

1.6.2. Any reference in the CPR or in this Guide to service of a document does not mean the date that the document is actually received. The date of service is set as the second working day after the day that the document was sent.[3]

1.7. THE ADMINISTRATIVE COURT

1.7.1. The Administrative Court is part of the Queen's Bench Division of the High Court (one **1BA-9** of the three divisions of the High Court, together with the Chancery Division and Family Division). The Administrative Court hears the majority of applications for judicial review[4] and also some statutory appeals and applications which fall outside the remit of this Guide.

1.7.2. Judicial review is the procedure by which an individual, company, or organisation may challenge the act or omission of a public body and ensure that the public body meets its legal obligations.

1.7.3. The Rt Hon Dame Victoria Sharp is the President of the Queen's Bench Division. Mr Justice Supperstone is the judge in charge of the Administrative Court.

1.7.4. Some cases in the Administrative Court come before a Divisional Court, usually consisting of one Lord Justice of Appeal (or the President) and one High Court Judge. Further information about the Divisional Court can be found at paragraphs 6.3.1, 9.1.3.2, 13.3 and 23.11 of this Guide.

---

[1] The fees are set out in schedule 1 of the Civil Proceedings (Fees) Order 2008 (as amended).

[2] The fee remission provisions are set out in schedule 2 of the Civil Proceedings (Fees) Order 2008 (as amended).

[3] CPR 6.14 and CPR 6.26

[4] See paragraphs 5.5 and 5.6 of this Guide where the exceptions are discussed

1.7.5. Judicial reviews which challenge planning decisions are heard in the specialist Planning Court, a part of the Administrative Court.

1.8. THE ADMINISTRATIVE COURT OFFICE

1BA-10   1.8.1. The administration of judicial review cases in the Administrative Court is dealt with by the Administrative Court Office ("ACO"). All documentation must be filed with the ACO and all enquiries on cases must be directed to the ACO (not directly to the judiciary).

1.8.2. The ACO and its staff are a part of Her Majesty's Courts and Tribunals Service ("HMCTS"), which in turn is an executive agency of the Ministry of Justice ("MOJ"). There are ACOs in Birmingham Civil Justice Centre, Cardiff Civil Justice Centre, Leeds Combined Court Centre, Manchester Civil Justice Centre, and in the Royal Courts of Justice in London. Contact details for the ACOs can be found in Annex 1 to this Guide.

1.8.3. As outlined in CPR PD 2A paragraph 2 the ACO in London is open for business from 10 a.m. to 4.30 p.m. (10 a.m. to 4.00 p.m. for the other ACOs) on every day of the year except;

(a)   Saturdays and Sundays;

(b)   Good Friday;

(c)   Christmas Day;

(d)   A further day over the Christmas period determined in accordance with the table specifically annexed to the Practice Direction. This will depend on which day of the week Christmas Day falls;

(e)   Bank holidays in England and Wales;

(f)   Such other days as the Lord Chancellor, with the concurrence of senior judiciary, may direct.

1.9. THE JUDICIARY AND THE MASTER

1BA-11   1.9.1. The judiciary in the Administrative Court consists of the High Court Judges (The Honourable Mr/Mrs Justice ....) and other judges or practitioners who have been authorised to sit in the Administrative Court. This Guide will simply refer to judges rather than differentiating between these judges. The judges are addressed in Court as my Lord/my Lady.

1.9.2. In the Royal Courts of Justice there is also a Master of the Administrative Court, currently Master Gidden (addressed in Court as Master). Masters generally deal with interim and pre-action applications, and manage the claims so that they proceed without delay.

2.   THE PARTIES

1BA-12   2.1. This part of the Guide is intended to give guidance on who should be the parties in a claim for judicial review. Identifying the parties correctly ensures that pre-action discussions are occurring between the proper persons (see reference to the pre-action Protocol at paragraph 5.2 of this Guide). It also ensures that the proper parties are referred to on any Court documents.

2.2. THE PARTIES

1BA-13   2.2.1. Claimant(s)

2.2.1.1. Claimants tend to be persons aggrieved by the public law decisions of public bodies who wish to challenge those decisions in the Administrative Court (see reference to "standing" at paragraph 5.3.2 of this Guide).

2.2.1.2. The claimant in judicial review proceedings can be any individual or incorporated company (also known as a corporation). Partnerships are able to bring proceedings in the name of the partnership.

2.2.1.3. The Court may allow unincorporated associations (which do not have legal personality) to bring judicial review proceedings in their own name. But it is sensible, and the Court may require, that proceedings are brought in the name of one or more individuals, such as an office-holder or member of the association, or by a private limited company formed by individuals. A costs order may be, and often is, made against the party or parties named as claimant(s).

2.2.1.4. Public bodies can be claimants in judicial review proceedings. The Attorney General has a common law power to bring proceedings. Local authorities may bring proceedings by virtue of s.222 of the Local Government Act 1972.

2.2.2. Defendant(s)

2.2.2.1. The Defendant in judicial review proceedings is the public body / public office which made the decision under challenge (or failed to make a decision where that failure is challenged), not the individual within that public body or public office.

2.2.2.2. Where the decision is made by a Government Department it is the relevant Secretary of State who is the defendant. Therefore, even if the decision challenged is that of a civil servant working in, for example, the Home Office, the defendant would be the Secretary of State for the

Home Department.[1]

2.2.2.3. Where the decision maker is a Court or Tribunal it is the Court or Tribunal which must be the defendant. The opposing party in the underlying case is named as an 'Interested Party' (see below at 2.2.3).

2.2.3. Interested Parties

2.2.3.1. An interested party is defined as any person (including a corporation or partnership), other than the claimant or defendant, who is directly affected by the claim.[2] For example, where a claimant challenges the decision of a defendant local authority to grant planning permission to a third party, the third party has a direct interest in the claim and must be named as an interested party.

2.2.3.2. Where the defendant is a Court or Tribunal, any opposing party in the lower Court or Tribunal would be an interested party in the judicial review.[3]

2.2.3.3. Interested parties must be included in pre-action correspondence and named in the claim form. Interested parties must also be served with the claim form, as required by CPR 54.7(b).

2.2.4. Interveners

2.2.4.1. In judicial review proceedings the Court retains a power to receive evidence and submissions from any other persons. Any person can apply, under CPR 54.17(1), to make representations or file evidence in judicial review proceedings. Potential interveners should be aware that any application must be made promptly[4] and that there are costs considerations (see paragraph 23.7 of this Guide).

2.3. MULTIPLE CLAIMANTS / DEFENDANTS / INTERESTED PARTIES

2.3.1. A claim for judicial review may be brought by one claimant or, in appropriate **1BA-14** circumstances, by more than one claimant. It may, for example, be appropriate for the claim to be brought by more than one claimant where a number of different individuals are affected by the decision challenged.

2.3.2. A claim may be brought against one defendant or, in appropriate circumstances, against two or more defendants. This may, for example, be appropriate where two or more bodies are responsible for the decision under challenge.

2.3.3. There are, exceptionally, be appropriate circumstances in which a number of different challenges by different claimants against different defendants can be combined within one single claim for judicial review. This will, generally, only be appropriate if the different challenges can be conveniently dealt with together.

2.3.4. If a claimant considers that any person is directly affected by the claim, they must identify that person as an interested party and serve the claim form on that person.[5] A defendant must also identify in its acknowledgement of service a person who the defendant considers is an interested party because the person is directly affected[6] and the Court will consider making that person an interested party when considering permission.

2.3.5. Where a person who is a potential defendant or interested party has not been named or served with the claim form, the Court may direct that they be added as a party, that the claim be served on that person, and the person may make representations or lodge an acknowledgement of service if the person so wishes.[7]

2.4. CASE TITLES

2.4.1. In judicial review proceedings the case title differs from other civil proceedings to reflect **1BA-15** the fact that judicial review is the modern version of a historical procedure whereby Her Majesty's Judiciary, on her behalf, acted in a supervisory capacity. Technically a judicial review is brought by the Crown, on the application of the claimant, to ensure that powers are being properly exercised. The case title reflects this:[8]

---

[1] The whole system of departmental organisation and administration is based on the constitutional notion that the decision of a government official is constitutionally that of the Minister, who alone is answerable to Parliament. This principle is called the "Carltona principle" based on the case of *Carltona Ltd v Commissioners of Works* [1943] 2 All ER 560

[2] CPR 54.1(2)(f)

[3] CPR PD 54A

[4] CPR 54.17(2)

[5] CPR 54.6 and 54.7

[6] CPR 54.8(4)(1)

[7] CPR 19.2(2) & CPR 19.2(4). In an appropriate case, ACO lawyers would have power to make such an order under CPR 54.1A. For the requirement to serve the papers on a new party, see CPR PD 5A paragraph 3.1. For removal of parties, see CPR 19.2(3). In an appropriate case, ACO lawyers would have powers to make such an order under CPR 54.1A.

[8] This form of the case title is stipulated in *Practice Direction (Administrative Court: Establishment)* [2000] 1 W.L.R. 1654.

The Queen (on the application of Claimant X) -v- Defendant Y

2.4.2. The case title is sometimes written as follows:

R (on the application of Claimant X) -v- Defendant Y

Or

R (Claimant X) -v- Defendant Y

2.4.3. The Crown will not involve itself in any way in the claim on behalf of the Claimant. The inclusion of the Queen's name in the title is purely formal.

3.   Litigants in person

3.1. GENERAL

1BA-16   **3.1.1.** Many cases in the Administrative Court are now conducted by parties who do not have professional legal representation and who represent themselves ("litigants in person"). It is important for litigants in person to be aware that the rules of procedure and of practice apply to them in the same way as to parties who are represented by lawyers. The Court will have regard to the fact that a party is unrepresented and will ensure that that party is treated fairly, as explained below. Many forms of help are available for individuals who wish to seek legal advice before bringing claims for judicial review.

3.1.2. Represented parties must treat litigants in person with consideration at all times during the conduct of the litigation. Represented parties are reminded of the guidance published by the Bar Council, CILEx and the Law Society (see: *https://www.lawsociety.org.uk/support-services/advice/articles/litigants-in-person-new-guidelines-for-lawyers-june-2015/*).

3.1.3. Litigants in person must show consideration and respect to their opponents, whether legally represented or not, to their opponents' representatives, and to the Court.

3.2. OBLIGATION TO COMPLY WITH PROCEDURAL RULES

1BA-17   **3.2.1.** A litigant in person will be expected to comply with the Civil Procedure Rules ("CPR"), and the provisions of this Guide apply to them. Litigants in person should therefore make themselves familiar with those parts of this Guide which are relevant to their claim and also with the applicable provisions of the CPR.

3.2.2. For example, the requirement to provide all relevant information and facts (described at paragraph 14.1 of this Guide under the heading "Duty of Candour") applies to all litigants and includes documents and facts which are unfavourable to the litigant. This requirement applies to litigants in person in the same way as it applies to litigants with representation. Similarly, the requirement to set out grounds of challenge in a coherent and well-ordered Grounds of Claim (see paragraph 6.3.4.1 of this Guide) applies to litigants in person in the same way as it applies to litigants with representation. Litigants in person may be penalised if they do not comply with the rules.

3.2.3. Generally, it is the duty of all parties to litigation, whether represented or not, to bring relevant matters to the attention of the Court and not to mislead the Court. This means for example that parties must not misrepresent the law and must therefore inform the Court of any relevant legislation or previous Court decisions which are applicable to their case and of which they are aware (whether favourable or not to their case). In addition there is a particular duty when an application is made to the Court without the other party being present or notified in advance (usually in cases of urgency). Here the litigant is under a duty to disclose any facts or other matters which might be relevant to the Court's decision, even if adverse to their case, and specifically draw the Court's attention to such matters (described at paragraph 14.1 of this Guide under the heading "Duty of Candour").

3.2.4. A litigant in person must give an address for service in England or Wales in the claim form. It is essential that any change of address is notified in writing to the Administrative Court Office ("ACO") and to all other parties to the case, otherwise important communications such as notices of hearing dates may not arrive.

3.3. THE HEARING

1BA-18   **3.3.1.** It is very important that litigants in person give copies of any written document which sets out their arguments (known as a "skeleton argument") which they intend to rely on, and any other material (for example, reports of cases) in support of their arguments, to the Court and to their opponents in good time before the hearing. Litigants in person should familiarise themselves with the rules about skeleton arguments at chapter 17 of this Guide. If they do not follow these rules, the Court may refuse to hear the case, or may adjourn the case to allow the other party or parties proper time to consider and respond to the late skeleton or material, in which case the litigant in person may be ordered to pay the costs incurred by the adjournment.

3.3.2. Litigants in person should identify in advance of the hearing the points which they consider to be their strongest points, and they should put those points first in their skeleton argument and in any oral submissions to the Court.

3.3.3. At the hearing, the litigant in person will be asked to give their name(s) to the usher or in-court support staff if they have not already done so.

3.3.4. The case name will be called out by the court staff. The hearing will then begin.

3.3.5. At the hearing, the claimant usually speaks first, then the defendant speaks, and then the claimant has an opportunity to comment on what the defendant has said. Sometimes the judge may think it is sensible, depending on the circumstances, to vary that order and, for example, let the defendant speak first.

3.3.6. At the hearing, the judge may make allowances for any litigant in person, recognising the difficulties that person faces in presenting his or her own claim. The judge will allow the litigant in person to explain his or her case in a way that is fair to that person. The judge may ask questions. Any other party in court, represented or not, will also have an opportunity to make submissions to the judge. At the end of the hearing, the judge will usually give a ruling, which may be short. The judge will explain the order he or she makes. Representatives for other parties should also explain the court's order after the hearing if the litigant in person wants further explanation.

3.4. PRACTICAL ASSISTANCE FOR LITIGANTS IN PERSON

3.4.1. Neither the court staff nor the judges are in a position to give advice about the conduct of **1BA-19** a claim. There is however a great deal of practical help available for litigants in person.

3.4.2. The Personal Support Unit ("PSU") is a free and independent service based in a number of court buildings which supports litigants going through the court process without legal representation. The PSU does not give legal advice and will not represent a litigant, but will assist by taking notes, discussing the workings of the court process, and providing assistance with forms. There are PSUs in each of the court centres in which the majority of judicial reviews are heard (Birmingham Civil Justice Centre, Bristol Civil Justice Centre, Cardiff Civil Justice Centre, Leeds Combined Court Centre, Manchester Civil Justice Centre, and the Royal Courts of Justice in London) as well as some other court buildings. For more information see *https://www.thepsu.org/*.

3.4.3. The Citizens Advice Bureau ("CAB") provides advice on a wide range of issues at drop in centres, by telephone, and online (see *https://www.citizensadvice.org.uk/*).

3.4.4. There is a Citizens Advice Bureau at the Royal Courts of Justice which may be able to of-fer some advice. It is situated on the ground floor, on the left hand side of the main hall (see *http://www.rcjadvice.org.uk/*).

3.4.5. There are a number of guides available designed to help litigants in person. Amongst these are: the Bar Council Guide to representing yourself in Court (see: *http://www.barcouncil.org.uk/media/203109/srl_guide_final_for_online_use.pdf*) and the QB Interim Applications Guide (see: *https://www.judiciary.gov.uk/publications/guide-self-represented-qbd/*).

3.5. LEGAL REPRESENTATION AND FUNDING

3.5.1. There are a number of solicitors' firms in England and Wales that conduct judicial review **1BA-20** litigation. Further, there are a number of barristers in both England and Wales that will give advice without referral by a solicitor, acting on a direct access basis. Details of these legal professionals can be found on the Law Society (*http://www.lawsociety.org.uk/*) and Bar Council (*http://www.barcouncil.org.uk/*) websites respectively.

3.5.2. There are three ways that legal representation can be provided: fee paid representation, legal aid, and pro bono representation (free legal representation).

3.5.3. Fee Paid Representation

3.5.3.1. Legal representatives will act for a party that will pay their fees directly. Fee paid representation is generally conducted at an agreed hourly rate or by agreeing a fixed fee in advance.

3.5.3.2. Alternatively, some legal representatives will act for a party under a conditional fee agreement ("CFA"). CFAs are commonly known as "no win, no fee" agreements. The individual firm or barrister will be able to confirm the basis on which they will act.

3.5.3.3. Some lawyers will be prepared to undertake a specific piece of work for payment, short of representing the client for the whole of the case. For example, a lawyer may be prepared to draft a skeleton argument for the case which the litigant in person can then use for the hearing, or ap-pear at a particular hearing. This is sometimes called "unbundled" work.

3.5.4. Legal Aid (Civil Cases)

3.5.4.1. The individual firm or barrister will be able to confirm whether they can work on a legal aid basis and whether a particular claimant will be entitled to apply for legal aid.

3.5.4.2. There are three types of legal aid: legal help, which can be used to give limited, initial advice and assistance; investigative representation, which can be used to investigate a potential claim in greater depth than that under legal help; and full representation, which can be used to issue and conduct judicial review proceedings.

3.5.4.3. Litigants in person who may be eligible for legal aid can contact Civil Legal Advice ("CLA"). Litigants can telephone the CLA helpline to find their nearest CLA Information Point on 0345 345 4 345. This service is funded by the Legal Aid Agency ("LAA"). The LAA is open from Monday to Friday, 9am to 8pm, and on Saturday, 9am to 12:30pm. Members of the public can also text "legalaid" and their name to 80010 to get a call back. This costs the same as a normal text message. An online "eForm" process for applying for legal aid is available. Telephone 0300 200 2020 or email contactcivil@legalaid.gsi.gov.uk.

3.5.4.4. To obtain full representations, and thus engage the legal representative to conduct the judicial review proceedings, the claimant will be required to pass two eligibility tests:

3.5.4.5. Financial Eligibility: The Legal Aid Agency will assess the claimant's disposable income and capital. If the claimant's income and/or capital amount to more than the set sum then legal aid will not be available.

3.5.4.6. Merits Criteria: The Legal Aid Agency will consider the merits of the proposed claim. If the Legal Aid Agency considers that the proposed claim lacks the requisite merit then legal aid will not be available.

3.5.5. Legal Aid (Criminal Cases)

Judicial review proceedings are not incidental to lower court proceedings and thus any representation order granted in the lower court will not cover judicial review proceedings.[1] A representation order may not be granted by the Administrative Court itself, although legal aid may be available from the Legal Aid Agency.

3.5.6. Pro-Bono Advice and Representation

3.5.6.1. Some solicitors firms and barristers will offer limited free advice on the prospects of a claim. The individual solicitor or barrister will be able to confirm if they are prepared to give advice on such terms.

3.5.6.2. There are some specialist organizations that arrange for free advice and representation. The largest are:

3.5.6.2.1. The National Pro-Bono Centre (*http://www.nationalprobonocentre.org.uk/*);

3.5.6.2.2. The Bar Pro-Bono Unit (*http://www.barprobono.org.uk/*);

3.5.6.2.3. Law Works (*https://www.lawworks.org.uk/*).

3.5.6.3. A potential litigant should note that pro-bono organizations are overwhelmed with applications and cannot offer assistance to everyone. Further, the application process can be lengthy. The Administrative Court is unlikely to stay a claim or grant an extension of time to file a claim to await the outcome of an application for pro-bono advice or representation.

3.6. MCKENZIE FRIENDS

1BA-21 **3.6.1.** A litigant in person may have the assistance of a non-legally qualified person, known as a "McKenzie Friend". Where a McKenzie Friend assists, the litigant in person must be present at the hearing and will be responsible for the conduct of his or her case at that hearing. But the McKenzie Friend may provide some assistance.

3.6.2. Guidance on McKenzie Friends was given in *Practice Guidance (McKenzie Friends: Civil and Family Courts)*[2] which established that a McKenzie Friend may:

3.6.2.1. Provide moral support for litigant(s) in person;

3.6.2.2. Take notes;

3.6.2.3. Help with case papers; and

3.6.2.4. Quietly give advice on any aspect of the conduct of the case.

3.6.3. The Practice Note also established that a McKenzie Friend may not:

3.6.3.1. Act as the litigant's agent in relation to the proceedings;

3.6.3.2. Manage litigants' cases outside Court, for example by signing Court documents; or

3.6.3.3. Address the Court, make oral submissions or examine witnesses.

3.6.4. The Court can, however, give permission to a person who is not a party and who has no rights of audience to address the Court. But this is only done in exceptional cases, on an application being made, and where it is shown to be in the interests of justice that such permission should be given.

3.6.5. A litigant who wishes to attend a hearing with the assistance of a McKenzie Friend should inform the Court as soon as possible indicating who the McKenzie Friend will be. The proposed McKenzie Friend should produce a short curriculum vitae or other statement setting out relevant experience, confirming that he or she has no interest in the case and understands the McKenzie Friend's role and the duty of confidentiality.

3.6.6. The litigant in person and the McKenzie Friend must tell the Court if the McKenzie Friend is being paid for his or her assistance and be ready to give details of that remuneration. The Court may stop a McKenzie Friend from assisting if the Court believes there is good reason to do so in any individual case. It is unlawful for a person who is not authorised to do so to give paid or unpaid legal advice or representation in respect of immigration matters.[3]

3.6.7. If the Court considers that a person is abusing the right to be a McKenzie Friend (for example, by attending in numerous claims to the detriment of the litigant(s) and/or the Court) and

---

[1] Regulation 20(2)(a) of the Criminal Legal Aid (General) Regulations 2013

[2] [2010] 1 W.L.R. 1881, [2010] 4 All ER 272, and see *https://www.judiciary.gov.uk/publications/mckenzie-friends/*

[3] s.84 Immigration and Asylum Act 1999

this abuse amounts to an interference with the proper processes of the administration of justice, the Court may make an order restricting or preventing a person from acting as a McKenzie Friend.[1]

4. Vexatious Litigant Orders and Civil Restraint Orders

4.1. The Court has power to make a civil restraint order ("CRO") under CPR PD 3C in relation **1BA-22** to any person, alternatively to make an order under s.42 of the Senior Courts Act 1981 (a "vexatious litigant").

4.2. The effect of either of those orders is to require the person subject to that order to obtain the permission of the Court to start proceedings before they may commence a judicial review.

4.3. This application is distinct from the application for permission to apply for judicial review.

4.4. If a person who is subject to such an order fails to make an application for permission to start proceedings, the application for permission to apply for judicial review (or the application for an interim or pre-action order) will be dismissed without further order. The Court may also consider the filing of the application to be a contempt of Court.

4.5. The application for permission to start proceedings must be made by filing an application notice (N244 or PF244)[2] with the Administrative Court Office with the relevant fee.

4.6. The fee is not subject to fee remission and must be paid. If permission to start proceedings is later granted and the applicant is able to claim fee remission then the fee can be refunded.[3]

4.7. The application notice should state:[4]

4.7.1. The title and reference number of the proceedings in which the order was made;

4.7.2. The full name of the litigant and his/her address;

4.7.3. The fact that the litigant is seeking permission pursuant to the order to apply for permission to apply for judicial review (or whatever interim or pre-action order is sought);

4.7.4. Explain briefly why the applicant is seeking the order; and

4.7.5. The previous occasions on which the litigant has made an application for permission must be listed.[5]

4.8. The application notice must be filed together with any written evidence on which the litigant relies in support of his/her application.[6] Generally, this should be a copy of the claim papers which the litigant requests permission to file.

4.9. If the litigant is a vexatious litigant, there is no need to serve an application on any other intended litigants unless directed by the Court to do so.[7] It may be considered to be good practice to do so nonetheless.

4.10. If the litigant is subject to a CRO then notice of the application must be given to the other intended litigants, which must set out the nature and the grounds of the application, and they must be given 7 days to respond to the notice before the application for permission is filed. Any response must be included with the application.[8]

4.11. The application will be placed before a judge who may, without the attendance of the litigant:[9]

4.11.1. Make an order giving the permission sought;

4.11.2. Give directions for further written evidence to be supplied by the litigant before an order is made on the application;

4.11.3. Make an order dismissing the application without a hearing; or

4.11.4. Give directions for the hearing of the application.

4.12. The Court will dismiss the application unless satisfied that the application is not an abuse of process and there are reasonable grounds for bringing the application.[10]

4.13. For vexatious litigants, an order dismissing the application, with or without a hearing, is final and may not be subject to reconsideration or appeal.[11]

4.14. For those subject to a CRO, there is a right of appeal (see chapter 25 of this Guide for appeals), unless the Court has ordered that the litigant has repeatedly made applications for permission pursuant to the CRO which were totally without merit, and the Court directs that if the

---

[1] *Noueiri* [2001] 1 W.L.R. 2357

[2] CPR PD 3A paragraph 7.2, CPR PD 3C paragraph 2.6, CPR PD 3C paragraph 3.6, CPR PD 3C paragraph 4.6

[3] Paragraph 19(3), schedule 2, Civil Proceedings (Fees) Order 2008

[4] CPR PD 3A paragraph 7.3

[5] CPR PD 3A paragraph 7.5

[6] CPR PD 3A paragraph 7.4

[7] CPR PD 3A paragraph 7.7

[8] CPR PD 3C paragraph 2.4-2.6, CPR PD 3C paragraph 3.4-3.6, CPR PD 3C paragraph 4.4-4.6

[9] CPR PD 3A paragraph 7.6, CPR PD 3C paragraph 2.6, CPR PD 3C paragraph 3.6, CPR PD 3C paragraph 4.6

[10] s.42(3) of the Senior Courts Act 1981

[11] CPR PD 3A paragraph 7.6 and s.42(4) of the Senior Courts Act 1981

litigant makes any further applications for permission which are totally without merit, the decision to dismiss the application will be final and there will be no right of appeal, unless the judge who refused permission grants permission to appeal.[1]

5.   BEFORE STARTING THE CLAIM

5.1.   GENERAL CONSIDERATIONS

1BA-23   **5.1.1.** Before bringing any proceedings, the intending claimant should think carefully about the implications of so doing. The rest of chapter 5 of this Guide considers the practical steps to be taken before issuing a claim form, but there are a number of general considerations, including personal considerations.

5.1.2. A litigant who is acting in person faces a heavier burden in terms of time and effort than does a litigant who is legally represented, but all litigation calls for a high level of commitment from the parties. This should not be underestimated by any intending claimant.

5.1.3. The overriding objective of the CPR is to deal with cases justly and at proportionate cost. In all proceedings there are winners and losers; the loser is generally ordered to pay the costs of the winner and the costs of litigation can be large (see chapter 23 of this Guide for costs).

5.1.4. Part B of this Guide outlines the procedure when bringing a claim. This section will outline the considerations before bringing a claim, including the pre-action procedure, factors which may make bringing a claim inappropriate, costs protection, the timescales in which proceedings should be started, and the duties of the parties concerning the disclosure of documents.

5.2.   THE JUDICIAL REVIEW PRE-ACTION PROTOCOL

1BA-24   **5.2.1.** So far as reasonably possible, an intending claimant should try to resolve the claim without litigation. Litigation should be a last resort.

5.2.2. There are codes of practice for pre-trial negotiations. These are called "Protocols". The appropriate pre-action Protocol in judicial review proceedings is the Judicial Review Pre-action Protocol, which can be viewed on the Government's website via *https://www.justice.gov.uk/courts/procedure-rules/civil/protocol/prot_jrv*. This is a very important document which anyone who is considering bringing a claim should consider carefully.

5.2.3. It is very important to follow the Judicial Review Pre-action Protocol, if that is possible, before commencing a claim. There are two reasons for this. First of all, it may serve to resolve the issue without need of litigation or at least to narrow the issues in the litigation. Secondly, failure to follow the Protocol may result in costs sanctions being applied to the litigant who has not followed the Protocol.

5.2.4. A claim for judicial review must be brought within the relevant time limits fixed by the CPR. The Protocol process does not affect the time limits for starting the claim (see paragraph 5.4 of this Guide). The fact that a party is using the Protocol would not, of itself, be likely to justify a failure to bring a claim within the time limits set by the CPR or be a reason to extend time. Therefore, a party considering applying for judicial review should act quickly to comply with the Protocol but note the time limits for issue if the claim remains unresolved.

5.2.5. The Protocol may not be appropriate in urgent cases (e.g., where there is an urgent need for an interim order) but even in urgent cases, the parties should attempt to comply with the Protocol. The Court will not apply cost sanctions for non-compliance where it is satisfied that it was not possible to comply because of the urgency of the matter.

5.2.6. Stage one of the Protocol requires the parties to consider whether a method of alternative dispute resolution ("ADR") would be more appropriate. The Protocol mentions discussion and negotiation, referral to the Ombudsman and mediation (a form of facilitated negotiation assisted by an independent neutral party).

5.2.7. Stage two is to send the defendant a pre-action letter. The letter should be in the format outlined in Annex A to the Protocol. The letter should contain the date and details of the act or omission being challenged and a clear summary of the facts on which the claim is based. It should also contain the details of any relevant information that the claimant is seeking and an explanation of why it is considered relevant.

5.2.8. The defendant should normally be given 14 days to respond to the pre-action letter and must do so in the format outlined in Annex B to the Protocol. Where necessary the defendant may request the claimant to allow them additional time to respond. The claimant should allow the defendant reasonable time to respond, where that is possible without putting the time limits to start the case in jeopardy.

---

[1] CPR PD 3C paragraph 2.3(2) and 2.6(3), CPR PD 3C paragraph 3.3(2) and 3.6(3), CPR PD 3C paragraph 4.3(2) and 4.6(3). For the conditions under which an extended civil restraint order may be discharged, see *Middlesbrough Football & Athletic Co v Earth Energy Investments LLP and Millinder* [2019] EWHC 226 (Ch).

5.3. SITUATIONS WHERE A CLAIM FOR JUDICIAL REVIEW MAY BE INAPPROPRIATE

5.3.1. There are situations in which judicial review will not be appropriate or possible. These **1BA-25** should be considered at the outset. Litigants should refer to the CPR and to the commentary in academic works on administrative law. The following are some of those situations in outline:

5.3.2. Lack of Standing (or *Locus Standi*)

5.3.2.1. A person may not bring an application for judicial review in the Administrative Court unless that person has a "sufficient interest" in the matter to which the claim relates.[1]

5.3.2.2. The issue of standing will generally be determined when considering permission but it may be raised and determined at any stage.

5.3.2.3. The parties and/or the Court cannot agree that a case should continue where the claimant does not have standing.[2] Nor does the Court have a discretion. A party must have standing in order to bring a claim.

5.3.2.4. The sufficient interest requirement is case specific and there is no general definition.[3] Those whom a decision directly and adversely affects will seldom (if ever) be refused relief for lack of standing. Some claimants may be considered to have sufficient standing where the claim is brought in the public interest.

5.3.3. Adequate Alternative Remedy

5.3.3.1. Judicial review is often said to be a remedy of last resort (see *R (Archer) v Commissioners for Her Majesty's Revenue and Customs* [2019] EWCA Civ 1021 at [87] – [95]).[4] If there is another method of challenge available to the claimant, which provides an adequate remedy, the alternative remedy should generally be exhausted before applying for judicial review.

5.3.3.2. The alternative remedy may come in various guises. Examples include an internal complaints procedure or a statutory appeal.

5.3.3.3. If the Court finds that the claimant has an adequate alternative remedy, it will generally refuse permission to apply for judicial review.

5.3.4. The Claim is Academic

5.3.4.1. Where a claim is purely academic, that is to say that there is no longer a case to be decided which will directly affect the rights and obligations of the parties,[5] it will generally not be appropriate to bring judicial review proceedings. An example of such a scenario would be where the defendant has agreed to reconsider the decision challenged.

5.3.4.2. Only in exceptional circumstances where two conditions are satisfied will the Court proceed to determine an academic issue. These conditions are: (1) a large number of similar cases exist or are anticipated, or at least other similar cases exist or are anticipated; and (2) the decision in a judicial review will not be fact-sensitive.[6]

5.3.5. The Outcome is Unlikely to have been Substantially Different.

The Courts have in the past refused permission to apply for judicial review where the decision would be the same even if the public body had not made the error in question. Section 31(3C)-(3F) of the Senior Courts Act 1981 now provides that the Courts must refuse permission to apply for judicial review if it appears to the Court highly likely that the outcome for the claimant would not have been substantially different even if the conduct complained about had not occurred. The Court has discretion to allow the claim to proceed if there is an exceptional public interest in doing so.

5.3.6. The Claim Challenges a Decision of one of the Superior Courts.

5.3.6.1. The Superior Courts[7] are the High Court, the Court of Appeal, and the Supreme Court. They cannot be subject to judicial review.

5.3.6.2. Where the Crown Court is dealing with a trial on indictment it is a Superior Court and its actions are not subject to judicial review.[8] Otherwise, its functions are subject to judicial review.

---

[1] s.31(3) of the Senior Courts Act 1981

[2] This principle has been confirmed in a number of other cases, for example in *R. v Secretary of State for Social Services ex parte Child Poverty Action Group* [1990] 2 Q.B. 540 at 556 and more recently in *R (Wylde) v Waverley Borough Council* [2017] EWHC 466 (Admin) from paragraph 19 onwards.

[3] *Inland Revenue Commissioners v National Federation of Self-Employed and Small Businesses Ltd* [1982] A.C. 617

[4] See also *R. v Epping and Harlow General Commissioners ex parte Goldstraw* [1983] 3 All E.R. 257 at 262, *Kay v Lambeth London Borough Council* [2006] 2 A.C. 465 at 492 (paragraph 30), and *R. (Gifford) v Governor of Bure Prison* [2014] EWHC 911 (Admin) at paragraph 37.

[5] *R. v Secretary of State for the Home Department ex parte Salem* [1999] 1 AC 450

[6] *R. (Zoolife International Ltd) v The Secretary of State for Environment, Food and Rural Affairs* [2008] A.C.D. 44 at paragraph 36

[7] See the discussion of the differences between inferior and superior Courts in *R v Chancellor of St. Edmundsbury and Ipswich Diocese ex parte White* [1948] 1 K.B. 195

[8] ss.1, 29(3), and 46(1) of the Senior Courts Act 1981

5.4. TIME LIMITS

1BA-26   **5.4.1.** The general time limit for starting a claim for judicial review requires that the claim form be filed promptly and in any event not later than 3 months after the grounds for making the claim first arose.[1] It must not be presumed that just because the claim has been lodged within the three month time that the claim has been made promptly, or within time.[2]

5.4.2.   When considering whether a claim is within time a claimant should also be aware of two important points:

5.4.2.1.   The time limit may not be extended by agreement between the parties (although it can be extended by the Court, see paragraphs 5.4.4 and 6.3.4.4 of this Guide);[3]

5.4.2.2.   The time limit begins to run from the date the decision to be challenged was made (not the date when the claimant was informed about the decision).[4]

5.4.3.   There are exceptions to the general time limit rule discussed above. These include the following:

5.4.3.1.   Planning Law Judicial Reviews:[5] Where the claim relates to a decision made under planning legislation the claim must be started not later than six weeks after the grounds to make the claim first arose. Planning legislation is defined as the Town and Country Planning Act 1990, the Planning (Listed Buildings and Conservation Areas) Act 1990, the Planning (Hazardous Substances) Act 1990 and the Planning (Consequential Provisions) Act 1990.

5.4.3.2.   Public Contract Judicial Reviews:[6] Where the claim relates to a decision under the Public Contracts Regulations 2015 S.I. 2015/102, which governs the procedure by which public bodies may outsource public services (sometimes referred to as "procurement"), the claim must be started within the time specified by r. 92 of those Regulations, which is currently 30 days from the date when the claimant first knew or ought to have known that grounds for starting the proceedings had arisen. Note that this time limit begins to run from the date of knowledge, in contrast to the general rule where the relevant date is the decision date itself. For further guidance on Public Contract Judicial Reviews, see paragraph 5.7 of this Guide.

5.4.3.3.   Judicial Review of the Upper Tribunal:[7] Where the defendant is the Upper Tribunal the claim must be started no later than 16 days after the date on which notice of the Upper Tribunal's decision was sent to the applicant. Again, note the difference from the general rule: here the time limit is calculated from the date the decision was sent, not the date it was made.

5.4.3.4.   Judicial Review of a decision of a Minister in relation to a public inquiry, or a member of an inquiry panel.[8] The time limit for these challenges is 14 days unless extended by the Court. That shorter time limit does not apply to any challenge to the contents of the inquiry report, or to a decision of which the claimant could not have become aware until publication of the report.[9]

5.4.4.   Extensions of Time

5.4.4.1.   CPR 3.1(2)(a) allows the Court to extend or shorten the time limit even if the time for compliance has already expired.

5.4.4.2.   Where the time limit has already passed, the claimant must apply for an extension in section 8 of the claim form (form N461). The application for an extension of time will be considered by the judge at the same time as deciding whether to grant permission.

5.4.4.3.   The Court will require evidence explaining the delay. The Court will only extend time if an adequate explanation is given for the delay, and if the Court is satisfied that an extension of time will not cause substantial hardship or prejudice to the defendant or any other party, and that an extension of time will not be detrimental to good administration.

5.5. JUDICIAL REVIEW OF IMMIGRATION AND ASYLUM DECISIONS

1BA-27   **5.5.1.** Since 1st November 2013 the Upper Tribunal (Immigration and Asylum Chamber) ("UT(IAC)") has been the appropriate jurisdiction for starting a judicial review in the majority of decisions relating to immigration and asylum, not the Administrative Court (see Annex 1 for UT(IAC) contact details).

5.5.2.   The Lord Chief Justice's Direction[10] requires filing in, or mandatory transfer to, the

---

[1] CPR 54.5 (1)

[2] See for example *R. v Cotswold District Council ex parte Barrington Parish Council* [1998] 75 P. & C.R. 515

[3] CPR 54.5(2)

[4] *R. v Department of Transport ex parte Presvac Engineering* [1992] 4 Admin. L.R. 121

[5] CPR 54.5(5).

[6] CPR 54.5(6),

[7] CPR 54.7A(3)

[8] s.38 (1) of the Inquiries Act 2005

[9] s. 38(3) of the Inquiries Act 2005

[10] Lord Chief Justice's Direction; Jurisdiction of the Upper Tribunal under s.18 of the Tribunals, Courts and Enforcement Act 2007 and Mandatory Transfer of Judicial Review applications to the

UT(IAC) of any application for permission to apply for judicial review and any substantive application for judicial review that calls into question the following:

5.5.2.1. A decision made under the Immigration Acts or any instrument having effect, whether wholly or partly, under an enactment within the Immigration Acts, or otherwise relating to leave to enter or remain in the UK. The Immigration Acts are defined as: Immigration Act 1971, Immigration Act 1988, Asylum and Immigration Appeals Act 1993, Asylum and Immigration Act 1996, Immigration and Asylum Act 1999, Nationality, Immigration and Asylum Act 2002, Asylum and Immigration (Treatment of Claimants, etc.) Act 2004, Immigration, Asylum and Nationality Act 2006, UK Borders Act 2007, Immigration Act 2014, Immigration Act 2016; or

5.5.2.2. A decision of the Immigration and Asylum Chamber of the First-tier Tribunal, from which no appeal lies to the Upper Tribunal.

5.5.3. All other immigration and asylum matters remain within the jurisdiction of the Administrative Court.[1] Further, even where an application comes within the classes of claim outlined at paragraph 5.5.2 above, an application which comprises or includes any of the following classes must be brought in the Administrative Court:

5.5.3.1. A challenge to the validity of primary or subordinate legislation (or of immigration rules);

5.5.3.2. A challenge to the lawfulness of detention;

5.5.3.3. A challenge to a decision concerning inclusion on the register of licensed Sponsors maintained by the UKBA;

5.5.3.4. A challenge to a decision which determines British citizenship;

5.5.3.5. A challenge to a decision relating to asylum support or accommodation;

5.5.3.6. A challenge to the decision of the Upper Tribunal;

5.5.3.7. A challenge to a decision of the Special Immigration Appeals Commission;

5.5.3.8. An application for a declaration of incompatibility under the s.4 of the Human Rights Act 1998; and

5.5.3.9. A challenge to a decision which is certified (or otherwise stated in writing) to have been taken by the Secretary of State wholly or partly in reliance on information which it is considered should not be made public in the interests of national security.

5.5.4. Challenges to decisions made under the National Referral Mechanism for identifying victims of human trafficking or modern slavery[2] are not immigration decisions. They fall within the jurisdiction of the Administrative Court.

5.5.5. Annex 7 contains further information about judicial review in the Upper Tribunal and the UT(IAC) in particular.

5.6. JUDICIAL REVIEW OF FIRST-TIER TRIBUNAL DECISIONS

5.6.1. Since 3rd November 2008 the Upper Tribunal (Administrative Appeals Chamber) **1BA-28** ("UT(AAC)") has been the appropriate jurisdiction for starting a judicial review that challenges certain decisions of the First-tier Tribunal, not the Administrative Court (see Annex 1 for UT(AAC) contact details).

5.6.2. The Lord Chief Justice's Direction[3] requires filing in, or mandatory transfer to, the UT(AAC) of any application for permission to apply for judicial review and any substantive application for judicial review that calls into question the following:

5.6.2.1. Any decision of the First-tier Tribunal on an appeal made in the exercise of a right conferred by the Criminal Injuries Compensation Scheme in compliance with s.5(1) of the Criminal Injuries Compensation Act 1995 (appeals against decisions on reviews); and

5.6.2.2. Decisions of the First-tier Tribunal where there is no right of appeal to the Upper Tribunal and that decision is not an excluded decision within paragraph (b), (c), or (f) of s.11(5) of the 2007 Act (appeals against national security certificates).

5.6.3. The direction does not have effect where an application seeks a declaration of incompatibility. In that case the Administrative Court retains the jurisdiction to hear the claim.

Upper Tribunal under s.31A(2) of the Senior Courts Act 1981, dated 21st August 2013 and amended on 17th October 2014, available at *https://www.judiciary.uk/publications/lord-chief-justices-direction-regarding-the-transfer-of-immigration-and-asylum-judicial-review-cases-to-the-upper-tribunal-immigration-and-asylum-chamber/*

[1] See paragraph 5.5.4. of this Guide for an example

[2] See National Referral Mechanism Guidance: Adult (England and Wales) at *https://www.gov.uk/government/publications/human-trafficking-victims-referral-and-assessment-forms/guidance-on-the-national-referral-mechanism-for-potential-adult-victims-of-modern-slavery-england-and-wales*

[3] Lord Chief Justice's Direction Upper Tribunal: Judicial Review Jurisdiction, pursuant to s.18(6) of the Tribunals, Courts and Enforcement Act 2007

5.7. PUBLIC CONTRACT JUDICIAL REVIEWS

1BA-29 **5.7.1.** Where a decision made under the Public Contract Regulations 2015 is challenged, claimants may consider it necessary to bring proceedings for judicial review in the Administrative Court as well as issuing a claim in the Technology and Construction Court ("TCC"). Where this happens, the claim will, unless otherwise directed by the lead judge of the Administrative Court or of the TCC, proceed in the TCC before a TCC judge who is also designated to sit in the Administrative Court.

5.7.2. If this occurs, the claimant must:

5.7.2.1. At the time of issuing the claim form in the ACO, by letter to the ACO, copied to the lead judge of the Administrative Court and the lead judge of the TCC, request transfer of the judicial review claim to the TCC;

5.7.2.2. Mark that letter clearly as follows: "URGENT REQUEST FOR TRANSFER OF A PUBLIC PROCUREMENT CLAIM TO THE TCC";

5.7.2.3. If not notified within 3 days of the issue of the claim form that the case will be transferred to the TCC, contact the ACO and thereafter keep the TCC informed of its position.

5.7.3. This procedure is to apply only when claim forms are issued by the same claimant against the same defendant in both the Administrative Court and the TCC simultaneously (i.e. within 48 hours of each other).

5.7.4. When the papers are transferred to the TCC by the ACO in accordance with the procedure outlined above, the lead judge of the TCC will review the papers as soon as reasonably practicable. The lead judge of the TCC will then notify the claimant and the ACO whether he/she considers that the two claims should be case managed and/or heard together in the TCC.

5.7.5. If he or she decides that is so, the claim for judicial review will be case managed and determined in the TCC.

5.7.6. If he or she decides that the judicial review claim should not proceed in the TCC, he or she will transfer the judicial review claim back to the Administrative Court and give his/her reasons for doing so, and the claim for judicial review will be case managed and determined in the Administrative Court.

5.8. ABUSE OF PROCESS

1BA-30 **5.8.1.** It may be an abuse of process to file a judicial review in the Administrative Court, on the basis that under the Lord Chief Justice's practice direction it falls within its jurisdiction and not the jurisdiction of UT(IAC). An example would be a judicial review which purports to fall within the detention exception where there is no obvious distinct merit to that aspect of the claim.[1]

PART B:—THE CLAIM

6. STARTING THE CLAIM

6.1. OVERVIEW OF JUDICIAL REVIEW PROCEDURE

1BA-31 **6.1.1.** Judicial review is a two stage process which is explained further in this Guide. First the claimant must obtain permission (sometimes referred to as "leave") to apply for judicial review from the Court. If permission is granted by the Court, then the second stage is the substantive claim.

6.1.2. Unlike a number of other civil and criminal proceedings the judicial review process does not incorporate a case management conference, although one may be ordered by a judge. The Court expects the parties to liaise with each other and the ACO to ensure that the claim is ready for the Court. An open dialogue between the parties and the staff of the Administrative Court Office is essential to the smooth running of the case.

6.1.3. The following flow diagram may be used as a quick guide to the judicial review process. Full details of each stage are outlined later in this Guide.

---

[1] See *R (Ashraf) v Secretary of State for the Home Department* [2013] EWHC 4028 (Admin)

Judicial Review Process[1]

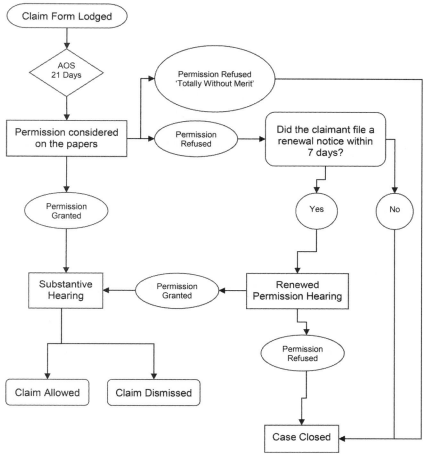

6.2. ISSUING THE CLAIM

6.2.1. All judicial review claims must be started by issuing a claim form in the ACO. Where a **1BA-32** claim form is received in the ACO on an earlier date than the date of issue, then, for the purposes of the judicial review time limits (see paragraph 5.4 of this Guide), the claim is begun on the earlier date.[2] This earlier date will also be noted on the claim form by the ACO. All other relevant time limits will run from the date of issue shown by the Court seal.

6.2.2. If the claimant has lodged the claim in the ACO in Cardiff, the claim may be lodged in Welsh or English.

6.2.3. When issuing the claim form, it must be accompanied by the relevant fee. If the relevant fee is not paid, the claim form and any accompanying documentation will be returned.

6.2.4. If the claim form is returned in accordance with 6.2.3 above, it is not considered to have been issued for the purposes of the judicial review time limits (see paragraph 5.4 of this Guide).

6.3. REQUIRED DOCUMENTATION

6.3.1. The claimant must file one copy of the completed judicial review claim form to be **1BA-33** retained by the ACO. If the claim is later listed before the Divisional Court a second/third copy will be required.

6.3.2. The claimant must also file an additional copy of the claim form for every defendant and interested party in the claim. The additional copies will be sealed and returned to the claimant

---

[1] © David Gardner, reproduced with kind permission of The University of Wales Press from *Administrative Law and the Administrative Court in Wales*

[2] CRP PD 7A paragraphs 5.1 and 5.2

to serve on the defendant(s) and interested parties (see paragraph 6.8 of this Guide for service, and see Annex 3 for a list of addresses for service on government departments).

6.3.3. The claimant is required to apply for permission to apply for judicial review in the claim form. The judicial review claim form automatically includes this application in section 4 of the claim form. The claimant must also specify the judicial review remedies sought (see chapter 11 of this Guide for remedies). There is space for this in the claim form at section 7.

6.3.4. The claim form must be accompanied by certain documents, which must be with the claim form when it is filed. The required documents are:

6.3.4.1. A detailed statement of the claimant's grounds for bringing the claim for judicial review (which can be outlined in section 5 of the claim form or in an attached document). This document should be as short as possible, while setting out the claimant's arguments. The grounds must be stated shortly and numbered in sequence. Each ground should raise a distinct issue in relation to the decision under challenge.[1] Arguments and submissions in support of the grounds should be set out separately in relation to each ground.

6.3.4.2. Where the claim includes a claim for damages under the Human Rights Act 1998, the claim for damages must be properly pleaded and particularised.[2]

6.3.4.3. A statement of the facts relied on (which can be outlined in section 9 of the claim form, or in an attached document, or in an attached document incorporated with the grounds in a detailed statement of facts and grounds);

6.3.4.4. Any application to extend the time limit for filing the claim form (which can be made in section 8 of the claim form or in an attached document);

6.3.4.5. Any application for directions (which can be made in section 8 of the claim form or in an attached document);

6.3.4.6. Any written evidence in support of the claim or application to extend time;

6.3.4.7. A copy of any decision letter or order that the claimant seeks to have quashed;

6.3.4.8. Where the claim for judicial review relates to a decision of a Court or Tribunal, an approved copy of the reasons for reaching that decision;

6.3.4.9. Copies of any documents on which the claimant proposes to rely;

6.3.4.10. Copies of any relevant statutory material; and

6.3.4.11. A list of essential documents for advance reading by the Court (with page references to the passages relied on).

6.3.5. The documentation must be provided in an indexed and paginated bundle.

6.3.6. One copy of the documentation bundle is to be provided to be retained by the Court.

6.3.7. As the ACO, since 28th February 2017, has only required one copy of the claim form, documentation bundle, and any other documentation filed, it must retain this documentation for the Court file. As such, claim documentation cannot be returned after the claim has finished. The parties should ensure they have made their own copies of the claim documentation for their reference. The exception to this is where a party has been required to file an original document (such as a deed or identification document). When returning this document, the ACO may copy the document before returning and retain the copy on the court file.

6.3.8. If the claim form is not accompanied by the documentation outlined at paragraph 6.3.4 above without explanation as to why and detail of when it will be provided, the ACO may, at its discretion, return the claim form without issuing it.

6.3.9. If the claim form is returned in accordance with paragraph 6.3.8 above, it is not considered to have been issued for the purposes of the judicial review time limits (see paragraph 5.4 of this Guide).

6.3.10. If the documentation required as outlined at paragraph 6.3.4 above is not filed with a claim form which is issued by the ACO, but at a later date, it has been filed out of time. As such, it must be accompanied by an application to extend time to file the documentation. Such an application must be made on an application notice with the relevant fee (see paragraph 12.7 of this Guide).

6.4. DUTY OF CANDOUR

1BA-34

6.4.1. There is a special duty which applies to parties to judicial review known as the "duty of candour" which requires the parties to ensure that all relevant information and all material facts are put before the Court.[3] This means that parties must disclose any information or material facts which either support or undermine their case.

6.4.2. It is very important that you comply with the duty of candour. The duty is explained in more detail below at paragraph 14.1 of this Guide.

---

[1] *R (Talpada) v SSHD* [2018] EWCA Civ 841 emphasised the need for a clear and succinct statement of the grounds, in the context of appeals, see [68]. See also *Hickey v Secretary of State for Work and Pensions* [2018] EWCA Civ 851 at [74].

[2] *R (Nazem Fayad) v SSHD* [2018] EWCA Civ 54 at [54] – [56]. Claims for damages that are not adequately particularised may give rise to consequences in costs for the claimant.

[3] See the discussion of this principle in *R. (Al-Sweady) v Secretary of State for Defence* [2010] H.R.L.R. 2 at 18

6.5. DISCLOSURE

6.5.1. The duty of candour ensures that all relevant information is before the Court. The general rules in civil procedure requiring the disclosure of documents do not apply to judicial review claims. However, the Court can order disclosure, exceptionally, in a particular claim. **1BA-35**

6.5.2. An application may be made in the course of a judicial review claim for disclosure of specific documents or documents of a particular class or type. A Court may order disclosure (under CPR 31.12(1)) of documents where this is necessary to deal fairly and justly with a particular issue.[1] An application under CPR 31.12(1) is made in accordance with the principles discussed in paragraph 12.7 of this Guide.

6.5.3. In practice, orders for disclosure of documents are rarely necessary in judicial review claims. The disclosure of documents may not, in fact, be necessary to allow the Court to consider a particular issue. Furthermore, a defendant may have disclosed the relevant documents (either before proceedings begin or as part of its evidence provided during proceedings (see paragraph 14.1 of this Guide on the duty of candour)).

6.6. WHERE TO ISSUE THE CLAIM (APPROPRIATE VENUE)

6.6.1. There are five ACOs in England and Wales in which a claim may be issued. They are situated in Birmingham Civil Justice Centre, Cardiff Civil Justice Centre, Leeds Combined Court Centre, Manchester Civil Justice Centre, and in the Royal Courts of Justice in London. Contact details for the ACOs can be found in Annex 1 to this Guide. **1BA-36**

6.6.2. The general expectation is that proceedings will be administered and determined in the region with which the claimant has the closest connection.[2] As such the claim should be filed in the ACO with which the claimant has the closest connection.

6.6.3. Any claim started in Birmingham will normally be determined at an appropriate Court in the Midlands, in Cardiff in Wales, in Leeds in the North-East of England, in London at the Royal Courts of Justice; and in Manchester, in the North-West of England.

6.6.4. Claims where the claimant has the closest connection to the South West of England should be issued in the ACO in Cardiff Civil Justice Centre. The administration of the claim will take place in Cardiff, but all hearings will (unless there are exceptional circumstances) take place in the South West of England (principally in Bristol).

6.6.5. Whilst it is not encouraged, the claimant may issue a claim in a different region to the one with which he/she has the closest connection. The claimant should outline why the claim has been lodged in a different region in section 4 of the claim form. The decision should be justified in accordance with the following considerations:

6.6.5.1. Any reason expressed by any party for preferring a particular venue;

6.6.5.2. The region in which the defendant, or any relevant office or department of the defendant, is based;

6.6.5.3. The region in which the claimant's legal representatives are based;

6.6.5.4. The ease and cost of travel to a hearing;

6.6.5.5. The availability and suitability of alternative means of attending a hearing (for example, by videolink);

6.6.5.6. The extent and nature of media interest in the proceedings in any particular locality;

6.6.5.7. The time within which it is appropriate for the proceedings to be determined;

6.6.5.8. Whether it is desirable to administer or determine the claim in another region in the light of the volume of claims issued at, and the capacity, resources and workload of, the Court at which it is issued;

6.6.5.9. Whether the claim raises issues sufficiently similar to those in another outstanding claim to make it desirable that it should be determined together with, or immediately following, that other claim; and

6.6.5.10. Whether the claim raises devolution issues and for that reason whether it should more appropriately be determined in London or Cardiff.

6.6.6. There are a number of exceptions to the general rule on venue outlined in paragraph 6.6.2 above. The exceptions can be found in CPR PD 54D paragraph 3.1. They are not repeated here as they do not relate to judicial review proceedings.

6.6.7. If the claim is issued in an ACO thought not to be the most appropriate, it may be transferred by judicial order, often made by an ACO lawyer. The Court will usually invite the views of the parties if it is minded to transfer the claim to a different venue. The defendant and any interested party can address the issue of venue in their summary grounds.

---

[1] As discussed in *R. v Secretary of State for Foreign and Commonwealth Affairs ex parte World Development Movement Ltd* [1995] 1 W.L.R. 386 at 396-397
[2] CPR PD 54D paragraph 5.2

6.7. FILING DOCUMENTS WITH THE COURT

1BA-37   **6.7.1.** The Administrative Court Office will accept the service of documents by email provided:

6.7.1.1. The document being filed does not require a fee;

6.7.1.2. The document, including attachments, does not exceed the maximum which the appropriate court office has indicated it can accept by email;[1]

6.7.1.3. The email, including any attachments, is under 10MB in size.

6.7.2. Where a document may be emailed it must be emailed to the appropriate ACO general inbox (see the contacts list at Annex 1).[2] Any party filing a document by email should not also file a hard copy unless instructed.

6.7.3. A document may be filed by fax where it needs to be filed urgently. Hearing bundles and/or documents which require a fee should only be faxed in an emergency and must be accompanied by an undertaking to pay the fee. Any party filing a document by fax should not also file a hard copy unless instructed.[3]

6.7.4. Paragraph 6.7.1 above also applies to skeleton arguments, which must be sent to the dedicated skeleton arguments email address for the relevant ACO (see the contacts list at Annex 1). Also see chapter 17 of this Guide on skeleton arguments.

6.7.5. Any document filed by fax or email after 4pm will be treated as filed on the next day on which the ACO is open.[4] If any party intends to file documents by fax, that party should first telephone the relevant ACO to ensure that the fax machine is available, and that there is someone there to receive the document.

6.7.6. An email sent to the Court must include the name, telephone number and address / email address for contacting the sender and it (including attachments) must be in plain or rich text format rather than HTML. Where proceedings have been started, it must also clearly state the Court's reference number for the case, the names of the parties and the date and time of any hearing to which the email relates.

6.7.7. The ACO or a judge may give instructions or order that a document is to be filed by email or fax in circumstances other than those outlined above.

6.7.8. It is anticipated that in 2020 the Electronic Working Pilot Scheme will commence in the Administrative Court, using the CE-File electronic Court file system and that Court users will be able to file documents electronically direct to the Court file.

6.7.9. Court users can sign up to use electronic filing by logging on to *https://efile.cefile-app.com*. Further practical guidance for users of CE-File can be found at *https://www.gov.uk/guidance/ce-file-system-information-and-support-advice*. Users are advised to familiarise themselves with the system before the start date.

6.7.10. All claims issued under the Pilot Scheme will be managed through CE-File and all documents filed will be held on CE-File. Some claims issued before the commencement of the Scheme are being migrated to CE-File, and parties can file documents in such cases electronically. Parties can also request that a claim be migrated to CE-File.

6.7.11. All historic claims held on CE-File will be allocated a new style claim number. The old claim number will not be recognised by CE-File.

6.7.12. Claims (including paper applications) will be managed as far as possible from CE-File. All documents filed with the Court will be scanned to the electronic file, and case management will be carried out using that file unless the volume of documents makes that impractical. If paper versions of documents are required, a direction will be given to lodge further paper copies, usually in the form of a bundle.

6.7.13. The Court will not maintain a paper file for claims filed and managed on CE-File. The only exception will be original documents that are required to be filed with the Court pursuant to an order or a provision of the CPR.

6.7.14. A hard copy hearing bundle will still be required for every hearing. Responsibility for lodging the hard copy hearing bundle will normally fall on the claimant or applicant. This general rule will apply whether or not the claimant or applicant is a litigant in person, unless a represented party has been directed by a judge or agreed in writing to assume responsibility for the production of the hard copy hearing bundle.

6.7.15. It is anticipated that a more detailed Practice Note may be issued during the course of Michaelmas Term 2019.

---

[1] In many instances, 50 pages, but parties should check with the appropriate court office. In London, the maximum number is 20.

[2] CPR PD 5B paragraph 2.1 and 2.2

[3] CPR PD5A paragraph 5.3

[4] CPR PD5A paragraph 5.3(6) and CPR PD 5B paragraph 4.2

6.8. SERVING THE CLAIM FORM

6.8.1. The claimant must serve a sealed copy of the claim form with a copy of the bundle of **1BA-38** documentation filed alongside the claim form on the defendant(s) and any interested parties within 7 days of the claim being issued.

6.8.2. The claim form is deemed to have been served on the second business day after it is sent by post, sent by document exchange, faxed, emailed, or delivered personally. The claimant may only serve by fax or email if the party being served has agreed to service in such a form.

6.8.3. All Government Departments should be served at the office as stipulated under the Crown Proceedings Act 1947 (reproduced at Annex 3 of this Guide). Local authorities should be served at their main offices with a note that papers should be directed to the authority's legal department (see CPR PD 54A, paragraph 6.2(b)).

6.8.4. If the party to be served is outside of the UK or the claimant wishes to apply to dispense with service of the claim form, there are separate provisions to those outlined at paragraph 6.8.2 above. In such scenarios the claimant should consider CPR 6.16 (for dispensing with service) and CPR 6.30 - 6.34, CPR 6.36 - 6.37, and CPR PD 6B (for serving outside of the UK).

6.8.5. Once the claimant has served the papers on the defendant(s) and any interested party or parties the claimant must confirm this with the ACO by filing a certificate of service (form N215) within 21 days of service of the claim form. If, after 28 days of lodging the claim form, the Administrative Court Office has not received a certificate of service or an acknowledgment of service from the defendant, then the case will be closed.

6.8.6. If a claim is closed because the claimant fails to file a certificate of service within time, the claim will only be reopened by judicial order. Such an order must be applied for on an application notice with the relevant fee (see paragraph 12.7 of this Guide). In the application the claimant must explain why the certificate of service was not filed on time, whether the failure caused any prejudice to any party or any delay to the judicial review process, and outline the reasons why the claim should be reopened.

6.8.7. CPR 39.8 provides that any communication between a party to proceedings and the Court must be disclosed to, and if in writing (whether in paper or electronic format), copied to, the other party or parties or their representatives (with some exceptions). If a party fails to comply with the rule, the Court may impose sanctions or return the communication to the sender without consideration of its content.

6.9. ADDITIONAL PROVISIONS FOR VEXATIOUS LITIGANTS OR PERSONS SUBJECT TO A CIVIL RESTRAINT ORDER

6.9.1. If a claimant is subject to a civil proceedings order made under s.42 of the Senior Courts **1BA-39** Act 1981 or is subject to a civil restraint order made under CPR 3.11 then the claimant must apply for permission to start proceedings before he/she may file an application for permission to apply for judicial review.

6.9.2. Such an application must be made on form N244 or PF244 and be accompanied by the relevant fee. This fee is not subject to fee remission, but it can be refunded if permission to start proceedings is granted.

6.9.3. The requirements for vexatious litigants or persons subject to a civil restraint order are discussed in greater detail in chapter 4 of this Guide.

6.10. AMENDING THE CLAIM AFTER IT HAS BEEN ISSUED BUT BEFORE PERMISSION TO APPLY FOR JUDICIAL REVIEW

6.10.1. If the claimant wishes to file further evidence, amend or substitute their claim form or **1BA-40** claim bundle, or rely on further grounds after they have been filed with the ACO then the claimant must apply for an order allowing them to do so. To apply, the claimant must make an application in line with the interim applications procedure discussed at paragraph 12.7 of this Guide.

6.10.2. The Court retains a discretion as to whether to permit amendments and will often be guided by the prejudice that would be caused to the other parties or to good administration.

6.10.3. In *R (Bhatti) v Bury Metropolitan Borough Council* [2013] EWHC 3093 (Admin) the Court warned that, where the defendant has agreed to reconsider the original decision challenged (thus effectively agreeing to quash the decision challenged without the intervention of the Court) it may not be appropriate to stay the claim or seek to amend the claim. Instead, it may be more appropriate to end the claim (see chapter 22 of this Guide) and, if the claimant seeks to challenge the new decision, to commence a new claim. The exceptions to this principle, where the Court may be prepared to consider the challenge to the initial decision, are narrow, and apply only where:

6.10.3.1. The case raises a point of general public importance; and

6.10.3.2. The point which was at issue in relation to the initial decision challenged remains an important issue in relation to the subsequent decision.[1]

---

[1] *R (Bhatti) v Bury Metropolitan Borough Council* [2013] EWHC 3093 and *R (Yousuf) v Secretary of*

6.10.4. If the defendant has agreed to and already made a new decision which the claimant seeks to challenge, it may be more convenient for the parties and the Court to amend the claim to allow for the new decision to be challenged.[1] The claimant should note the following guidance (as observed at paragraph 22 of *R (Hussain) v Secretary of State for Justice* [2016] EWCA Civ 1111):

6.10.4.1. The Court can impose a condition requiring the re-formulation of the claim and the re-preparation of any bundles of material, so as to eliminate any irrelevant surplus material and to work from a single set of papers. Any draft order or draft consent order seeking amendment of the claim in these circumstances should typically include a provision allowing for a new, amended claim bundle to be filed or, ideally, be accompanied by a copy of the proposed amended claim bundle.

6.10.4.2. The Court retains discretion to permit amendments and may make an assessment that overall the proper conduct of proceedings will best be promoted by refusing permission to amend and requiring a fresh claim to be brought.

6.10.4.3. The Court will be astute to check that a claimant is not seeking to avoid complying with the any time limits by seeking to amend rather than commence a fresh claim.

6.10.4.4. A claimant seeking permission to amend would also be expected to have given proper notice to all relevant persons, including interested parties.

7.   THE ACKNOWLEDGEMENT OF SERVICE

7.1.   THE ACKNOWLEDGEMENT OF SERVICE

1BA-41

7.1.1. Any defendant or interested party served with the claim form who wishes to take part in the application for permission to apply for judicial review must file and serve an acknowledgement of service.[2]

7.1.2. When filing an acknowledgement of service form N462 must be used.

7.1.3. Filing an acknowledgment of service is wise for any defendant and any interested party in order for the Court to know if that person intends to contest the claim, but it is not mandatory.

7.1.4. If a party fails to file an acknowledgment of service within the relevant time limit (see paragraph 7.2 below) this will have three effects on the claim:

7.1.4.1. The papers will be sent to a judge to consider whether to grant permission to the claimant to apply for judicial review without having heard from the party who has failed to file the acknowledgement of service;

7.1.4.2. In the event that the judge does not grant or refuse permission outright, but directs that permission falls to be considered at an oral hearing (see paragraph 8.2.5 of this Guide), or if the judge refuses permission and the claimant applies for reconsideration at an oral hearing (see paragraph 8.4 of this Guide), the party may not take part in that hearing without the permission of the Court;[3] and

7.1.4.3. The judge considering any substantive application for judicial review may consider that party's failure to submit an acknowledgement of service when considering costs (see chapter 23 of this Guide for costs).[4]

7.1.5. If the party does not file an acknowledgment of service and permission is subsequently granted (see paragraph 8.2.2 and chapter 10 of this Guide), the party may still take part in the substantive application for judicial review.[5]

7.1.6. If the claim was started in or has been transferred to the ACO in Cardiff, the acknowledgement of service and any evidence may be lodged in Welsh or English.

7.2.   TIME LIMITS

1BA-42

7.2.1. The acknowledgment of service must be filed at the ACO within 21 days of the claim papers being served.[6] The 21 day time limit may be extended or shortened by judicial order. If appropriate, a judge may also consider permission to apply for judicial review without waiting for an acknowledgment of service.

7.2.2. The parties cannot agree between themselves to extend the deadline,[7] it can only be extended by an order of the Court. An application for an extension of time must be made in accordance with the interim applications procedure and on payment of the relevant fee (see paragraph

---

State for the Home Department [2016] EWHC 663 (Admin)
  [1] R (Hussain) v Secretary of State for Justice [2016] EWCA Civ 1111
  [2] CPR 54.8(2)
  [3] CPR 54.9(1)(a)
  [4] CPR 54.9(2)
  [5] CPR 54.9(1)(b)
  [6] CPR 54.8(2)(a)
  [7] CPR 54.8(3)

12.7 of this Guide). Alternatively, the application can be made retrospectively in the acknowledgment of service in section D, provided permission has not already been considered.

7.2.3. The acknowledgment of service must be served on all other parties no later than 7 days after it was filed with the ACO.

7.2.4. As soon as an acknowledgement of service has been filed by each party to the claim, or upon the expiry of the relevant time limit, the papers will be sent to a judge who will consider whether to grant permission to apply for judicial review by considering the papers alone (see chapter 8 of this Guide).

7.2.5. The judicial review procedure does not allow for the claimant to respond to the acknowledgment of service during the paper application process. The ACO will not delay consideration of permission on the basis that the claimant may wish to reply. Any replies that are received before a case is sent to a judge to consider permission will be put before the judge but it is a matter for the judge as to whether he/she is willing to consider the reply.

7.3. CONTENTS

7.3.1. The acknowledgment of service must: **1BA-43**

7.3.1.1. Set out the summary grounds for contesting the claim, if the party does contest it.[1] These must be as concise as possible. The summary grounds of defence may be part of the acknowledgment of service in section C, or they may be included in an attached separate document.

7.3.1.2. State if the party is intending to contest the application for permission on the basis that it is highly likely that the outcome for the claimant would not have been substantially different if the conduct complained of had not occurred, by ticking the box in section A, and set out the summary of the grounds for doing so.[2]

7.3.1.3. State, in section B, the name and address of any person the party believes to be an interested party.[3]

7.3.1.4. State, in section E, if the party contests the claimant's application for an automatic costs limit under the Aarhus Convention (see paragraph 24.4 of this Guide), if one was made.

7.3.2. Evidence may be filed with the acknowledgment of service but it is not required.

7.3.3. If the party does not intend to contest the claim, they should make it clear in section C of the acknowledgment of service whether they intend to remain neutral or would in principle agree to the decision being quashed. This information will allow the Court to manage the claim properly. If the party does agree in principle to the decision being quashed, then the parties should attempt to agree settlement of the claim at the earliest opportunity.

7.4. DEFENDANT'S APPLICATIONS

When lodging the acknowledgment of service the party may request further directions or an   **1BA-44** interim order from the Court in section D.[4] Examples of applications that may be made at this stage are for the party's costs of preparing the acknowledgment of service and for the discharge of any previously made injunctions.

8.   PERMISSION TO APPLY FOR JUDICIAL REVIEW

8.1. THE APPLICATION

8.1.1. The claimant must obtain permission from the Court to apply for judicial review. If   **1BA-45** permission is granted, the claim will usually proceed to a full hearing on those grounds on which permission has been granted (this is often referred to as the substantive hearing – see chapter 10 of this Guide).

8.1.2. In the first instance the claim papers (comprising the papers filed by the claimant and any acknowledgment(s) of service) are sent to a judge. The judge will then consider the papers and determine whether to grant permission to apply for judicial review.

8.1.3. The Court will refuse permission to apply for judicial review unless satisfied that there is an arguable ground for judicial review having a realistic prospect of success,[5] although there are a number of orders the Court can make before ultimately determining this question (see paragraph 8.2 of this Guide).

8.1.4. Even if a case is thought to be arguable, the judge must refuse permission if the judge

---

[1] CPR 54.8(4)(a)(i)
[2] CPR 54.8(4)(a)(ia)
[3] CPR 54.8(4)(a)(ii)
[4] CPR 54.8(4)(b)
[5] Description of the test taken from *Sharma v Brown-Antoine* [2007] 1 W.L.R. 780

considers that the outcome for the applicant would not have been substantially different if the conduct complained of had not occurred.[1]

8.1.5. If the Court considers that there has been undue delay in bringing the claim, the Court may refuse permission.[2] Delay is discussed further at paragraph 5.4 of this Guide.

8.2.   COURT ORDERS ON PERMISSION

1BA-46

8.2.1. There are a number of different orders that may be made by the judge following consideration of the papers. The following are the most common orders made by judges considering permission to apply for judicial review, but they are not exhaustive.

8.2.2. Permission Granted

The judge has determined that there is an arguable case on one of more grounds. The case will proceed to a substantive hearing of the application for judicial review on those grounds on which permission is granted. In this event, the judge will usually give directions for the substantive hearing.

8.2.3. Permission Refused

The judge has determined that none of the grounds advanced by the claimant are arguable and as such the claim should not proceed to a substantive hearing. When permission is refused on the papers, the judge will record brief reasons for that decision in the order.[3] The judge may order the claimant to pay the defendant's costs of preparing an acknowledgement of service at this stage (see paragraph 23.4 of this Guide).

8.2.4. Permission Granted in Part

8.2.5. In some cases, the judge may decide that some of the grounds advanced by the claimant are arguable but others are not. The judge will direct the matter to proceed to a substantive hearing on the arguable grounds only.

8.2.6. The claimant can request that the refused grounds are reconsidered for permission at an oral hearing (see paragraph 8.4 of this Guide).

8.2.7. The claimant may not raise or renew grounds at the substantive hearing where permission has not already been granted unless the court (unusually) permits that to occur.[4]

8.2.8. Permission adjourned to an oral hearing on notice

The judge has made no determination on the application for permission. Instead the application for permission will be considered at an oral hearing in Court with the claimant and any other parties who wish to make representations to the Court attending. The hearing will take a similar form to that of a renewed permission hearing (see paragraph 8.4 of this Guide).

8.2.9. Permission adjourned to a "rolled up hearing".

8.2.9.1. The judge has made no determination on the application for permission. Instead the application for permission will be considered in Court with the substantive hearing to follow immediately if permission is granted.

8.2.9.2. In practice, at the rolled up hearing the judge will not necessarily consider permission then the substantive hearing one after another formulaically. The judge is more likely to hear argument on both points together and give a single judgment, but the manner in which the hearing is dealt with is within the discretion of the judge.

8.2.9.3. When preparing documentation for a rolled up hearing the parties should apply the same rules as apply when preparing for a substantive hearing (see chapter 9 of this Guide). This is because, despite the fact that permission has not yet been granted or refused, substantive consideration of the application for judicial review will, if appropriate, take place on the same day. Thus, the documentation before the Court should be the same as if the hearing was the substantive hearing.

8.2.9.4. Where a rolled up hearing is ordered the claimant will be asked by the ACO to sign an undertaking to pay the fee for the substantive application for judicial review which would then become payable in the event that the judge later grants permission.

8.2.10. The application for permission is to be resubmitted.

The judge has made no determination on the application for permission. Instead the judge will request the parties perform some act (such as file additional documents or representations) or await some other event (such as the outcome of a similar case). Once the act or event has been performed, or when the time limit for doing so has expired, the papers will be resubmitted to the judge to consider permission on the papers.

8.3.   TOTALLY WITHOUT MERIT ORDERS

1BA-47

8.3.1. If the judge considers that the application for permission is "totally without merit" then he/she may refuse permission and certify the claim as being totally without merit in the order.

---

[1] s.31(3C)-(3F) of the Senior Courts Act 1981
[2] s.31(6)(a) Senior Courts Act 1981
[3] CPR 54.12(2)
[4] *R (Talpada) v SSHD* [2018] EWCA Civ 841 at [23] and [68]

8.3.2. The term "totally without merit" has been defined broadly and applies to a case that is bound to fail, not one that is necessarily abusive or vexatious.[1]

8.3.3. Where a case is certified as totally without merit there is no right to a renewed oral hearing[2] (see paragraph 8.4 of this Guide) and the claim is concluded in the Administrative Court, albeit appeal rights do apply (see paragraph 25.3 of this Guide).

8.4. RECONSIDERATION AT AN ORAL HEARING

8.4.1. If permission is refused the claimant should consider the judge's reasons for refusing permission on the papers before taking any further action. **1BA-48**

8.4.2. If the claimant takes no further action then, seven days after service of the order refusing permission, the ACO will simply close the case. If the Court has directed the parties to file written submissions on costs or has given directions in relation to any other aspect of the case, the claim will remain open until the costs or that other aspect are resolved. If there is an interim or costs order in place at that time, and unless the Court has directed otherwise, it will continue in effect (even though the case is closed administratively) and the parties will have to apply to set aside that order (see paragraph 12.7 of this guide).

8.4.3. If, having considered the reasons, the claimant wishes to continue to contest the matter they may not appeal, but they may request that the application for permission to apply for judicial review be reconsidered at an oral hearing (often referred to as a renewed hearing).[3]

8.4.4. When the ACO serves an order refusing permission to apply for judicial review on the papers it will also include a renewal notice (Form 86b). If the claimant wishes to have their application for permission to apply for judicial review reconsidered at an oral hearing they should complete and send this form back to the ACO within seven days[4] of the date upon which it is served. A fee is payable. The claimant should send a copy of the Form 86b to any party that filed an acknowledgement of service.

8.4.5. The Claimant must provide grounds for renewing the application for permission and must in those grounds address the judge's reasons for refusing permission by explaining in brief terms why the claimant maintains those reasons are wrong. It is not sufficient simply to state that renewal is sought on the original grounds, without seeking to explain the asserted error in the refusing judge's reasons. If the refusing judge's reasons are not addressed, the judge may make an adverse costs order against the claimant at the renewal hearing and/or impose any other sanction which he/she considers to be appropriate.[5]

8.4.6. Upon receipt of the renewal notice the ACO will list an oral hearing (see paragraph 13.2.1 of this Guide on listing). The hearing cannot, without judicial order, take place without all parties being given at least two days' notice of the hearing.[6] The ACO will send notice to all parties of the date of the hearing.

8.4.7. The renewed hearing is normally a public hearing that anyone may attend and observe and will take place in Court before a judge. The only issue at the hearing is the arguability of the claim or particular grounds, so hearings are expected to be short, with the parties making succinct submissions.

8.5. TIME ESTIMATE FOR RENEWED APPLICATION:

8.5.1. The standard time estimate for a renewed permission application is 30 minutes to include the Court giving judgment, if that is appropriate, at the end of the hearing. **1BA-49**

8.5.2. If either party reasonably believes that the renewed application (including judgment) is likely to last more than 30 minutes, that party should inform the ACO as soon as possible of that fact, and of that party's revised time estimate (including judgment). Failure to inform the ACO may result in the hearing having to be adjourned on the hearing day for lack of Court time, in which event the Court will consider making a costs order against the party or parties which should have notified the Court of the longer time estimate.

8.5.3. Even where a party informs the Court that the renewed application is likely to take more than 30 minutes, the Court will only allocate such Court time as it considers appropriate, bearing in mind the pressure on Court time from other cases. In any event, it is rare that permission hearings will be allocated a time estimate over two hours.

---

[1] *R. (Grace) v Secretary of State for the Home Department* [2014] 1 W.L.R. 3432, and *Samia W v Secretary of State for the Home Department* [2016] EWCA Civ 82

[2] CPR 54.12(7)

[3] CPR 54.12(3)

[4] CPR 54.12(4)

[5] See, in an extradition context, *Roby Opalfvens v Belgium* [2015] EWHC 2808 (Admin), at [14]

[6] CPR 54.12(5)

8.6. PROCEDURE AT RENEWAL HEARINGS

1BA-50   **8.6.1.** The defendant and/or any interested party may attend the oral hearing. Unless the Court directs otherwise, they need not attend. If they have not filed an acknowledgement of service, they will have no right to be heard,[1] although the Court may nonetheless permit them to make representations (see paragraph 7.1.4 of this Guide).[2]

8.6.2. Where there are a number of cases listed before a judge in any day, an attempt will be made to give a time marking for each case. This may be shown on the daily cause list or the judge's clerk may contact the parties and/or their representatives. Alternatively, at the start of the day's list, the judge may release the parties and/or their representatives until a specific time later in the day.

8.6.3. At the hearing, the judge retains discretion as to how the hearing will proceed. Subject to that discretion, generally, the hearing will follow a set pattern:

8.6.3.1. The claimant will speak first setting out his/her grounds and why he/she contends they are arguable;

8.6.3.2. The defendant(s) will speak second setting out why the grounds are not arguable or other reasons why permission should not be granted;

8.6.3.3. Any interested parties will speak third to support or contest the application for permission;

8.6.3.4. The claimant is usually given a right to a short reply;

8.6.3.5. The decision refusing or granting permission, and, if appropriate, any further directions or orders will usually be announced at the conclusion of the hearing.

8.6.4. Any party before a hearing in the Administrative Court in Wales has the right to speak Welsh or English. The guidance outlined at paragraph 10.3 of this Guide also applies to permission hearings.

8.6.5. The test for granting permission at an oral hearing is the same as the one applied by the judge considering permission on the papers (see paragraph 8.1.3 of this Guide).

8.6.6. In the event that permission is refused at the renewal hearing then the claim has ended in the Administrative Court (subject to any appeal – see paragraph 25.3 of this Guide). In the event that the judge does give permission then the case will proceed to the substantive hearing, which will take place on a later date (unless the hearing was "rolled up" (see paragraph 8.2.6 of this Guide), in which case the substantive hearing will follow immediately). The date for the hearing may be ordered by the judge or listed by the ACO (see paragraph 13.2.2 of this Guide for listing).

8.7. ALTERNATIVE PROCEDURE WHERE THE UPPER TRIBUNAL IS THE DEFENDANT

1BA-51   **8.7.1.** In some claims the Upper Tribunal will be the appropriate defendant. This will generally only arise where the Upper Tribunal has refused permission to appeal against the decision of the First-tier Tribunal, because other decisions of the Upper Tribunal are subject to a right of appeal, which should be exercised instead of applying for judicial review. Where the claimant wishes to challenge the decision of the Upper Tribunal when it has refused permission to appeal from a decision of the First-tier Tribunal the judicial review procedure is amended by CPR 54.7A. The claimant should read all of CPR 54.7A. The most important points are outlined below.

8.7.2. The Court will only grant permission to apply for judicial review if it considers:

8.7.2.1. That there is an arguable case which has a reasonable prospect of success that both the decision of the Upper Tribunal refusing permission to appeal and the decision of the First Tier Tribunal against which permission to appeal was sought are wrong in law; and

8.7.2.2. That either the claim raises an important point of principle or practice or there is some other compelling reason to hear the claim.[3]

8.7.3. The general procedure in CPR Part 54 will apply, save for the following amendments:

8.7.3.1. The application for permission may not include any other claim, whether against the Upper Tribunal or not, and any such other claim must be the subject of a separate application;[4]

8.7.3.2. The claim form and the supporting documents must be filed no later than 16 days after the date on which notice of the Upper Tribunal's decision was sent to the applicant, not the normal three months;[5]

8.7.3.3. If the application for permission is refused on paper there is no right to a renewed oral hearing (see paragraph 8.4 of this Guide), albeit appeal rights do then apply (see paragraph 25.3 of this Guide).[6]

8.7.3.4. If permission to apply for judicial review is granted and if the Upper Tribunal or any interested party wishes there to be a hearing of the substantive application, it must make a request for such a hearing no later than 14 days after service of the order granting permission, in which

---

[1] CPR PD 54A paragraph 8.5
[2] CPR 54.9(1)(a)
[3] CPR 54.7A(7)
[4] CPR 54.7A(2)
[5] CPR 54.7A(3)
[6] CPR 54.7A(8)

case the ACO will list a substantive hearing. If no request for a hearing is made within that period, the Court will make a final order quashing the Upper Tribunal's decision without a further hearing.[1] The case will then return to the Upper Tribunal to consider permission to appeal again.

8.7.4. In claims against the Upper Tribunal there are discrete documents required by CPR 54.7A(4) that must be filed with the claim. If the documents required by CPR 54.7A(4) are not provided with the claim form the Court is unlikely to allow additional time for them to be submitted and may refuse permission to apply for judicial review on the grounds that it does not have sufficient information to properly consider the claim. The Court is very unlikely to order additional time to submit the documents in the absence of an application for extension of time to file the required documents (such applications, whilst not encouraged, should be made on the claim form, see paragraph 15.2 of this Guide for details, or by way of separate application, see paragraph 12.7 of this Guide for details).

8.7.5. The list of documents required by CPR 54.7A is as follows:

8.7.5.1. The decision of the Upper Tribunal to which the judicial review claim relates and any documents giving reasons for the decision;

8.7.5.2. The grounds of appeal to the Upper Tribunal and any documents sent with them;

8.7.5.3. The decision of the First-tier Tribunal, the application to that Tribunal for permission to appeal, and its reasons for refusing permission to appeal; and

8.7.5.4. Any other documents essential to the claim.

9. AFTER PERMISSION

9.1. DIRECTIONS FOR SUBSTANTIVE HEARING

9.1.1. When permission to apply for judicial review is granted, the claim will proceed to the substantive hearing on a later date. **1BA-52**

9.1.2. Unless the judge orders a particular date for the hearing, the ACO will list the substantive hearing as soon as practicable (see paragraph 13.2.2 of this Guide for listing; see also Annex 4 for the Administrative Court Listing Policy).

9.1.3. When granting permission a judge will often give directions as to how the case will progress to the substantive hearing, including:

9.1.3.1. The time within which the defendant or interested party or parties should file detailed grounds of resistance and any evidence on which they intend to rely at the hearing;

9.1.3.2. Who should hear the case, and specifically whether it should be heard by a Divisional Court (a Court with two or more judges),

9.1.3.3. Other case management directions including a timetable for skeleton arguments, trial bundles and authorities bundles to be lodged.

9.1.4. Judicial directions will supersede any standard directions. If the judge does not make any directions, the following standard directions apply:

9.1.4.1. The claimant must pay the relevant fee to continue the application for judicial review. Failure to do so within 7 days of permission being granted will result in the ACO sending the claimant a notice requiring payment within a set time frame (normally 7 more days). Further failure will result in the claim being struck out without further order.[2]

9.1.4.2. Any party who wishes to contest or support the claim must file and serve any detailed grounds and any written evidence within 35 days of permission being granted.[3] The defendant may rely on their summary grounds as the detailed grounds. If doing so they should inform the Administrative Court Office and the other parties in writing within the time set for filing the detailed grounds.

9.1.4.3. The claimant must file and serve a skeleton argument no less than 21 working days[4] before the substantive hearing (see paragraph 17.2 of this Guide for the contents of the skeleton argument).[5]

9.1.4.4. The defendant and any other party wishing to make representations at the substantive hearing must file and serve a skeleton argument no less than 14 working days before the substantive hearing.[6]

---

[1] CPR 54.7A(9)

[2] CPR 3.7(1)(d), (2), (3), & (4)

[3] CPR 54.14(1)

[4] CPR PD 54A paragraph 15 refers to "working" days. This is different from the normal presumption in the CPR that days means "calendar" days, save for periods of time of less than 5 days, see CPR 2.8(3). It is a feature of the CPR that if the judge, when granting permission, expressly orders the skeleton argument to be filed "21 days" before the substantive hearing, then it must be provided 21 *calendar* days, not working days, before the substantive hearing. This is because CPR 2.8(3) applies to all judicial orders.

[5] CPR PD 54A paragraph 15.1

[6] CPR PD 54A paragraph 15.2

9.1.4.5. The claimant must file a paginated and indexed bundle of all relevant documents required for the hearing of the judicial review when filing the skeleton argument[1] (21 working days before the hearing unless judicial order allows for a different time period). The bundle must include those documents required by the defendant and any other party who is to make representations at the hearing.[2] The parties should be liaising as far before the substantive hearing as possible to agree what is required in the agreed bundle.

9.2. AMENDING THE CLAIM

1BA-53
9.2.1. If the claimant wishes to file further evidence or rely on further grounds then the claimant must ask for the Court's permission to do so.[3] To seek permission the claimant must make an application in line with the interim applications procedure discussed at paragraph 12.7 of this Guide[4]

9.2.2. This rule also applies to other parties who are filing documents outside the 35 day time limit (discussed at paragraph 9.1.4.2 of this Guide).

9.2.3. The application may be dealt with in advance of the substantive hearing or at the hearing itself. The decision on when the application should be dealt with is ultimately a judicial one, but the parties should indicate a preference when lodging the application.

9.2.4. The Court retains a discretion as to whether to permit amendments. In *R (Bhatti) v Bury Metropolitan Borough Council* [2013] EWHC 3093 (Admin) the Court warned that, where the defendant intended to reconsider the original decision challenged, it may not be appropriate to seek a stay or to amend the claim. Instead, it may be more appropriate to end the claim (see chapter 22 of this Guide) and, if the claimant seeks to challenge the new decision, to commence a new claim. The exceptions to this principle, where the Court may be prepared to consider the challenge to the initial decision, are narrow, and apply only where:

9.2.4.1. The case raises a point of general public importance; and

9.2.4.2. The point which was at issue in relation to the initial decision challenged remains an important issue in relation to the subsequent decision.[5]

9.2.5. If the defendant has made a new decision which the claimant seeks to challenge, it may in some circumstances be more convenient for the Court to permit parties to amend the claim to allow a challenge to the new decision.[6] Where permission is granted to amend the claim after permission to apply for judicial review has been granted, the parties should ensure that the substantive hearing bundle only includes relevant documentation. Any documentation that is only relevant to the initial decision should not form part of the bundle. The claimant should note the following guidance (as observed at paragraph 22 of *R (Hussain) v Secretary of State for Justice* [2016] EWCA Civ 1111):

9.2.5.1. The Court retains discretion to permit amendments and may make an assessment that overall the proper conduct of proceedings will best be promoted by refusing permission to amend and requiring a fresh claim to be brought.

9.2.5.2. The Court will be astute to check that a claimant is not seeking to avoid complying with any time limits by seeking to amend rather than commence a fresh claim.

9.2.5.3. A claimant seeking permission to amend would also be expected to have given proper notice to all relevant persons, including interested parties.

9.3. ACTION IF AN INTERPRETER IS REQUIRED

1BA-54
9.3.1. If a party or witness requires an interpreter it is generally the responsibility of that party or the party calling the witness to arrange for the attendance of and to pay for the interpreter.

9.3.2. The ACO can arrange an interpreter to attend free of charge to the party seeking an interpreter's assistance where:

9.3.2.1. The party is a litigant in person who cannot address the Court in English (or Welsh if the case is proceeding in Wales) and the party cannot afford to pay for an interpreter, does not qualify for legal aid and does not have a friend or family member who the judge agrees can act as an interpreter; and

9.3.2.2. The judge agrees that an interpreter should be arranged free of charge to that party; or

9.3.2.3. In such other circumstances as ordered by the Court.

9.3.3. It is the responsibility of the party which requests an interpreter free of charge to that

---

[1] CPR PD 54A paragraph 16.1
[2] CPR PD 54A paragraph 16.2
[3] CPR 54.15 and CPR 54.16(2) respectively. See also *R (Talpada) v SSHD* [2018] EWCA Civ 841 at [23] and [68] and paragraph 8.4.2.3 above.
[4] See *Hickey v Secretary of State for Work and Pensions* [2018] EWCA CIV 851 at [73]-[74]
[5] *R (Bhatti) v Bury Metropolitan Borough Council* [2013] EWHC 3093, and see *R (Yousuf) v Secretary of State for the Home Department* [2016] EWHC 663 (Admin)
[6] *R (Hussain) v Secretary of State for Justice* [2016] EWCA Civ 1111

party to make the request in writing as soon as it becomes clear that a hearing will have to be listed and an interpreter is required.

9.3.4. The party which requests an interpreter free of charge must inform the ACO in writing that an interpreter is required and the party must state which language the interpreter will be required to translate into English and vice versa (or into Welsh and vice versa if the case is proceeding in Wales: see paragraph 10.3 of this Guide for use of the Welsh language).

9.3.5. Where the party does not notify the Court that an interpreter is required and a hearing has to be adjourned to arrange for an interpreter to attend on another occasion, the Court may make an adverse costs order against the party requiring an interpreter (see paragraph 23.1 of this Guide).

9.4. RESPONSIBILITY FOR PRODUCTION OF SERVING PRISONERS AND DETAINED PERSONS

9.4.1. Where a serving prisoner or a detained person is represented by counsel it is generally not expected that the serving prisoner or detained person will be produced at Court, unless the Court orders otherwise. **1BA-55**

9.4.2. Where the serving prisoner or detained person is acting without legal representation, it is the responsibility of the serving prisoner or detained person to arrange for their attendance at Court or for a video-link to be arranged between the Court and prison or detention centre. The serving prisoner or detained person must make the request that they be produced at Court for the hearing or that a video-link should be arranged, to the prison or detention centre authorities, as soon as they receive notice of the hearing. The prison or detention centre authorities are responsible for considering requests for production, for arranging production of a person at Court, and for arranging video-links.

9.5. SPECIFIC PRACTICE POINTS

Reference should be made to the guidance contained under Part C of this Guide, Specific Practice Points, which gives detailed guidance on skeleton arguments (at chapter 17), documents (at chapter 18) and authorities (at chapter 19). **1BA-56**

10. SUBSTANTIVE HEARING

10.1. FORMAT OF THE HEARING

10.1.1. The hearing is generally a public hearing which anyone may attend and observe. The hearing normally takes place before a single judge, unless the Court orders the case to be heard by a Divisional Court. **1BA-57**

10.1.2. The Court will decide how the hearing should proceed. Most hearings follow the following sequence:

10.1.2.1. The claimant will speak first setting out the arguments in support of the grounds of claim.

10.1.2.2. The defendant will speak second setting out the arguments in support of the grounds of defence;

10.1.2.3. Any interested parties and/or interveners will speak third to support, contest, or clarify anything that has been said; and

10.1.2.4. The claimant will have a right to reply to the other parties' submissions.

10.2. EVIDENCE

10.2.1. Evidence before the Court will nearly always consist of witness statements and written evidence without allowing oral evidence to be given and without cross examination of witnesses. **1BA-58**

10.2.2. The Court retains an inherent power to hear from witnesses.[1] If a party seeks to call or cross-examine a witness, an application should be made in accordance with the interim applications procedure outlined in section 12.7 of this Guide. As a matter of practice, it is only in very exceptional cases that oral evidence is permitted in a judicial review. Permission will be given only where oral evidence is necessary to dispose of the claim fairly and justly.[2]

---

[1] See the comments of Munby J (as he then was) in *R. (PG) v London Borough of Ealing* [2002] A.C.D. 48 at paragraphs 20 and 21.

[2] *R (Bancoult) v Secretary of State for Foreign and Commonwealth Affairs* [2012] EWHC 2115 at 14. An example of permission for cross examination being given is *R (Jedwell) v Denbighshire CC* [2015] EWCA Civ 1232. But the Court of Appeal has since reaffirmed that this should be viewed as an exceptional course, see Hallett LJ in *R (Talpada) v SSHD* [2018] EWCA Civ 841 at [2]; Underhill LJ at [54].

10.3. USE OF THE WELSH LANGUAGE

1BA-59   **10.3.1.** A hearing before the Administrative Court in Wales is subject to the provisions of s.22 of the Welsh Language Act 1993 and as such any person addressing the Court may exercise their right to speak in Welsh. This right applies only to hearings in Wales and so, if the party seeks to exercise this right they should start the claim in the ACO in Cardiff or seek transfer of the claim to the ACO in Cardiff.

10.3.2. Under the Practice Direction Relating to the Use of the Welsh Language in Cases in the Civil Courts in Wales, the Court may hear any person in Welsh without notice of the wish to speak in Welsh, providing all parties and the Court consent.[1]

10.3.3. In practice, the parties should inform the Court as soon as possible,[2] preferably when lodging the claim papers, if any person intends to speak in Welsh. This will allow the Court to make proper directions and allow the ACO in Cardiff to make practical arrangements.

10.3.4. There are bi-lingual judges who can consider such claims, but nonetheless, it is likely that an order will be made for simultaneous translation, where a translator appears in Court translating into English and Welsh.[3]

10.4. JUDICIAL REVIEW WITHOUT A HEARING

1BA-60   If all parties agree, the substantive consideration may take place without a hearing, and the judge will decide the claim by considering the papers alone. The parties should inform the ACO in writing if all parties have agreed to this course of action. The judge, on consideration of the papers, may refuse to make a decision on the papers and order an oral hearing.

10.5. THRESHOLD FOR RELIEF

1BA-61   **10.5.1.** To succeed in the claim the claimant must show that the defendant has acted unlawfully.

10.5.2. Even if a claimant establishes that the defendant has acted unlawfully, the Court has a discretion whether to grant a remedy or not.

10.5.3. The Court will not grant relief where it appears to the Court to be highly likely that the outcome for the claimant would not have been substantially different if the conduct complained of had not occurred.[4]

10.6. JUDGMENT AND ORDERS

1BA-62   **10.6.1.** When the hearing is concluded the Court will usually give judgment in one of two ways:

10.6.1.1. Orally, then and there, or sometimes after a short adjournment (this is referred to as an "ex tempore" judgment).

10.6.1.2. The Court may give judgment in writing sometime after the hearing (this is referred to as a "reserved" judgment).

10.6.2. A reserved judgment will be "handed down" at a later date. The hand down procedure is governed by CPR PD 40E. Unless the Court otherwise directs, at least two working days before the hand down date the judge will provide a copy of the judgment to legal representatives in the case.[5] That draft is confidential and any breach of that confidentiality is a contempt of court. The legal representatives may then propose any typographical corrections.[6]

10.6.3. After the draft judgment has been circulated the parties are obliged to attempt to agree the form of the final order and any consequential orders[7] (usually costs and permission to appeal – see chapters 23 and 25 of this Guide). The parties should submit an agreed order, which should include the terms of any orders made by the judge in Court and the terms of any agreed consequential orders, by 12 noon the day before the hand down date.[8] If the parties can agree a final order then they need not attend the hand down hearing.[9]

10.6.4. If consequential orders cannot be agreed then the Court will decide consequential orders by considering representations. This may be done in one of two ways:

---

[1] Paragraph 1.2 of the Practice Direction Relating to the Use of the Welsh Language in Cases in the Civil Courts in Wales

[2] Paragraph 1.3 of the Practice Direction Relating to the Use of the Welsh Language in Cases in the Civil Courts in Wales

[3] This was the format ordered in *R. (Welsh Language Commissioner) v National Savings and Investments* [2014] P.T.S.R. D8 and is in line with HMCTS's Welsh language scheme 2013-2016, paragraph 5.26.

[4] s.31(2A) of the Senior Courts Act 1981

[5] CPR PD 40E paragraph 2.3

[6] Ibid, paragraph 3.1

[7] Ibid, paragraph 4.1

[8] CPR PD 40E paragraph 4.2

[9] Ibid, paragraph 5.1

10.6.4.1. The parties may attend Court on the date of handing down and make representations orally. The Court will then decide on consequential orders. The parties should inform the ACO in good time if they intend to do this as time will need to be allocated for the judge to hear representations. Such a hearing would usually last for 30 minutes, rather than the 5 minutes set aside for a simple hand down; or

10.6.4.2. The parties may agree a final order that allows them to make written representations within a set time period on consequential orders, which the Court will then consider and, at a later date, make an order based on those written representations alone.

10.6.5. The final judgment will then be handed down in Court. In practice this is a short hearing at which the judge makes the final copy of the judgment available and endorses it. The judge will not read the judgment verbatim. The judge will adjourn any consequential matters which remain to be dealt with at a later date.

10.6.6. The Judge in Charge of the Administrative Court has approved the arrangements for handing down judgments in Wales at Annex 6 of this Guide, which should be followed.

10.6.7. The ACO will send sealed copies of any orders approved by the judge to the parties. Until an order has been approved and sealed the parties should not assume that any agreed orders will be approved. It is the sealed order itself that holds legal force as opposed to the judgment and it is the order that must be enforced if a party fails to comply with the terms.

10.6.8. All substantive judgments are made publicly available at the website www.bailii.org which does not charge a fee for access.

11. Remedies

11.1. When the claimant starts a claim he/she must state in section 7 of the claim form what **1BA-63** remedy he/she seeks from the Court in the event that he/she is successful. There are six remedies available to a successful claimant in judicial review proceedings, all of which are listed in sections 31(1) and 31(4) of the Senior Courts Act 1981 as well as CPR Part 54. This section of the Guide will discuss those remedies.

11.2. MANDATORY ORDER

11.2.1. A mandatory order is the order the Court can make to compel a public body to act in a **1BA-64** particular way.

11.3. QUASHING ORDER

11.3.1. A quashing order quashes, or sets aside, the decision, thereby confirming that the chal- **1BA-65** lenged decision has no lawful force and no legal effect.

11.3.2. After making a quashing order the Court will generally remit the matter to the public body decision maker and direct it to reconsider the matter and reach a fresh decision in accordance with the judgment of the Court.[1]

11.3.3. The Court has power to substitute its own decision for the decision which has been quashed.[2] This power is only exercisable against the decisions of the inferior Courts or Tribunals, only on the grounds of error of law, and only where there is only one possible decision now open to the decision maker.

11.4. PROHIBITING ORDER

11.4.1. A prohibiting order prohibits a public body from taking an action that the public body **1BA-66** has indicated an intention to take but has not yet taken.

11.5. ORDINARY DECLARATIONS

11.5.1. A declaration is a statement by the Court as to what the law on a particular point is or is **1BA-67** not. Using the declaratory remedy the Administrative Court can examine an act (including an act announced but not yet taken) of a public body and formally declare that it is lawful, or unlawful.

11.5.2. A declaration does not have any coercive effect although a public body is expected to comply with the declaration. A declaration can be a remedy on its own,[3] or can be granted in combination with other remedies.

11.5.3. A declaration will not be granted where the question under consideration is a hypothetical question, nor where the person seeking the declaration has no real interest in it, nor where the

---

[1] As outlined in s.31(5)(a) of the Senior Courts Act 1981 and CPR 54.19(2)(a)

[2] Under s.31(5)(b) of the Senior Courts Act 1981 and CPR 54.19(2)(b)

[3] CPR 40.20

declaration is sought without proper argument (e.g. in default of defence or on admissions or by consent).[1]

11.6.   DECLARATION OF INCOMPATIBILITY

1BA-68   **11.6.1.** If the Court determines that any Act of Parliament is incompatible with a Convention right - that is a right derived from the European Convention on Human Rights 1950 ("ECHR") which is incorporated into the law of the United Kingdom by the Human Rights Act 1998 - it may make a declaration of incompatibility.[2]

11.6.2. A declaration of incompatibility may be made in relation to subordinate legislation if the Court is satisfied that (disregarding any possibility of revocation) the Act of Parliament concerned prevents removal of the incompatibility.[3]

11.6.3. The principles behind ordinary declarations (see paragraph 11.5 of this Guide above), such as the requirement that a declaration will not be made in hypothetical circumstances, apply.[4]

11.6.4. A declaration of incompatibility does not affect the validity, continuing operation or enforcement of the provision in respect of which it is given and it is not binding on the parties to the proceedings in which it is made.[5] The declaration acts to inform Parliament of the incompatibility of that provision with a Convention right.

11.6.5. The claimant must state in the remedies section of the claim form (section 7) if they are applying for a declaration of incompatibility, giving precise details of the Convention right which has allegedly been infringed, and the domestic law provision which is said to be incompatible.[6]

11.6.6. The claimant should consider making the Crown, via the relevant Secretary of State, an interested party if a declaration of incompatibility is sought. In any event, where an application for a declaration of incompatibility has been made the Court may order that notice should be given to the Crown.[7] If the Court is considering making a declaration of incompatibility and the Crown is not already a party, the Court must inform the relevant Secretary of State and allow him/her at least 21 days[8] to consider whether to intervene and make representations.[9]

11.7.   INJUNCTIONS

1BA-69   **11.7.1.** An injunction is an order to act in a particular way (a positive injunction) or to refrain from acting in a particular way (a negative injunction). It is a remedy that is not confined to judicial review, although it is available in judicial review.

11.8.   DAMAGES

1BA-70   **11.8.1.** Whilst primarily a private law remedy, the Administrative Court has power to award damages.

11.8.2. The right to seek damages in judicial review proceedings is subject to two provisos:

11.8.2.1. The claimant may only seek damages if they are also seeking another remedy, not just damages alone;[10] and

11.8.2.2. The claimant may only seek damages if a private law claim for damages on the same basis would have succeeded (had it been brought in the County Court or appropriate division of the High Court).[11]

11.8.2.3. Where the claim includes a claim for damages under the Human Rights Act 1998, the claim for damages must be properly pleaded and particularized.[12]

11.8.3. Where the assessment and award of damages is likely to be a lengthy procedure the general practice of the Administrative Court is to determine the judicial review claim, award the other remedy sought (if appropriate), and then transfer the claim to either the County Court or appropriate division of the High Court to determine the question of damages.

---

[1] *Re F* [1990] 2 A.C. 1
[2] ss.4(1) and 4(2) of the Human Rights Act 1998
[3] ss.4(3) and 4(4) of the Human Rights Act 1998.
[4] See, for example, *Taylor v Lancashire County Council* [2005] 1 W.L.R. 2668
[5] s.4(6) of the Human Rights Act 1998
[6] CPR PD 16 paragraphs 15.1(2)(a), (c)(i), & (d)
[7] CPR 54A PD paragraph 8.2 & CPR PD 19A paragraph 6.1
[8] CPR 19.4A(1)
[9] s.5(1) of the Human Rights Act 1998
[10] CPR 54.3(2)
[11] s.31(4) of the Senior Courts Act 1981
[12] *R (Nazem Fayad) v SSHD* [2018] EWCA Civ 54 at [54] – [56]. Claims for damages that are not adequately particularised may give rise to consequences in costs for the claimant.

11.9. MULTIPLE REMEDIES

11.9.1. The Court may grant more than one remedy where it is deemed appropriate.　**1BA-71**

11.10. REMEDIES WHERE THE OUTCOME WOULD NOT HAVE BEEN SUBSTANTIALLY DIFFERENT

11.10.1. If the claimant is successful in judicial review proceedings, but the Court considers that **1BA-72** it is highly likely that the outcome for the claimant would not have been substantially different if the conduct complained of had not occurred, the Court must refuse to grant any form of relief, and may not award damages, in the claim for judicial review unless the Court considers it appropriate to do so for reasons of exceptional public interest.[1]

11.11. DISCRETIONARY REMEDIES

11.11.1. Remedies in judicial review proceedings are within the discretion of the Court.　**1BA-73**

11.11.2. Even where a claimant shows that a defendant has acted unlawfully, the Court may refuse to grant a remedy, in particular where:[2]

11.11.2.1. The claimant has delayed in filing the application for judicial review and the Court considers that the granting of the remedy sought would be likely to cause substantial hardship to, or would substantially prejudice the rights of any person, or would be detrimental to good administration.[3]

11.11.2.2. The error of law made by the public body was not material to the public body's decision.

11.11.2.3. The remedy would serve no useful practical purpose.

11.11.2.4. The claimant has suffered no harm or prejudice.

11.11.3. The principles on discretionary remedies discussed above do not apply to the award of damages.

12. Case Management

12.1. CASE MANAGEMENT IN THE ADMINISTRATIVE COURT

12.1.1. All proceedings in the Administrative Court, from the start of the claim to the end, are **1BA-74** subject to the overriding objective outlined in CPR 1.1. The overriding objective requires all cases to be dealt with justly and at proportionate cost.

12.1.2. Dealing with a case justly and at proportionate cost includes:[4]

12.1.2.1. Ensuring that the parties are on an equal footing;

12.1.2.2. Saving expense;

12.1.2.3. Dealing with it in ways which are proportionate to the amount of money involved, to the importance of the case, to the complexity of the issues, and to the financial position of each party;

12.1.2.4. Ensuring that it is dealt with expeditiously and fairly;

12.1.2.5. Allotting to it an appropriate share of the Court's resources, while taking into account the need to allot resources to other cases; and

12.1.2.6. Ensuring compliance with rules, practice directions and orders.

12.1.3. In ensuring that the overriding objective is complied with, the Court must actively manage cases,[5] which includes (but is not limited to) the following:

12.1.3.1. Encouraging the parties to co-operate with each other in the conduct of the proceedings;

12.1.3.2. Identifying the issues at an early stage;

12.1.3.3. Deciding promptly which issues need full investigation and trial and accordingly disposing summarily of the others;

12.1.3.4. Deciding the order in which issues are to be resolved;

12.1.3.5. Encouraging the parties to use an alternative dispute resolution procedure if the Court considers that appropriate and facilitating the use of such procedure;

12.1.3.6. Helping the parties to settle the whole or part of the case;

12.1.3.7. Fixing timetables or otherwise controlling the progress of the case;

12.1.3.8. Considering whether the likely benefits of taking a particular step justify the cost of taking it;

12.1.3.9. Dealing with as many aspects of the case as it can on the same occasion;

---

[1] s31(2A) Senior Courts Act 1981 and s31(2B) Senior Courts Act 1981
[2] See *R. (Baker) v Police Appeals Tribunal* [2013] EWHC 718 (Admin)
[3] s.31(6)(b) Senior Courts Act 1981
[4] CPR 1.1(2)
[5] CPR 1.4

12.1.3.10. Dealing with the case without the parties needing to attend at Court;

12.1.3.11. Making use of technology; and

12.1.3.12. Giving directions to ensure that the trial of a case proceeds quickly and efficiently.

12.1.4. The parties are required to help the Court to further the overriding objective.[1]

12.1.5. This chapter of the Guide is intended to provide more detail on what is expected from the Court, the ACO, and the parties in order to further the overriding objective.

12.2. DUTIES OF THE PARTIES

1BA-75

12.2.1. The parties must make efforts to settle the claim without requiring the intervention of the Court. This is a continuing duty and whilst it is preferable to settle the claim before it is started, the parties must continue to evaluate the strength of their case throughout proceedings, especially after any indication as to the strength of the case from the Court (such as after the refusal or grant of permission to apply for judicial review). The parties should consider using alternative dispute resolution (for example, mediation) to explore settlement of the case, or at least to narrow the issues in the case.

12.2.2. CPR Part 54 does not provide for a formal case management hearing in judicial review proceedings, although the parties may apply for an interim order or the Court may make case management orders with or without a hearing. It is not uncommon for the first time the parties appear in Court before the judge to be the final hearing of the claim. As such, the parties have a duty to ensure that they maintain effective, constructive, and regular communication with each other and the ACO (see also paragraph 14.1 of this Guide on the Duty of Candour).

12.2.3. The parties must comply with the procedural provisions in the CPR, the relevant Practice Directions and orders of the Court (including orders by an ACO lawyer). If a party knows they will not be able to do so they should inform the ACO and the other parties as soon as possible and make the application to extend the time limit as soon as possible (in accordance with the interim applications procedure in paragraph 12.7 of this Guide).

12.2.4. If a party is aware that they may need to apply for an interim order (extending time as per paragraph 12.2.3 above or for interim relief in accordance with chapter 15 of this Guide) they should inform the other parties and the ACO as soon as they know they may need to make the application. The application should then be made as quickly as possible. Delay in making an application and/or a failure to put the ACO and the other parties on notice, especially where it requires urgent consideration, is a factor which may weigh against the granting of the order.

12.2.5. The parties should, if possible, agree the form of any case management order and/or interim relief and file an agreed draft order (i.e. a draft consent order), which will be subject to the Court's approval. A fee is payable when submitting a draft consent order and the reasons for requesting the order should be included in an accompanying application notice (N244 or PF244). A draft order (even if is agreed by the parties) does not have the status of an order until it has been approved by the Court.

12.2.6. The parties should also comply with any requests from ACO staff members (such as requests for documents or information). Whilst these requests do not have the force of an order of the Court, failure to comply with such a request may be a factor considered by a judge or ACO lawyer that weighs against granting an interim order, permission to apply for judicial review, substantive relief, or costs.

12.2.7. If the parties are aware that a case is likely to settle without the further involvement of the Court they should inform the ACO as soon as possible.

12.2.8. The parties and their legal representatives should ensure compliance with the CPR, Practice Directions and rules. Of particular importance are: the duty of candour, the requirement to make full disclosure of all material facts (see paragraph 14.1 of this Guide), and the procedures for bringing urgent cases before the Court, see chapter 16 of this Guide.

12.3. ROLE OF THE ADMINISTRATIVE COURT OFFICE STAFF

1BA-76

12.3.1. The staff members in the ACO handle the day to day running of the ACO from the start of the process to the finish. One of their duties is to ensure that the cases are properly managed by requesting missing or late documents from the parties and by referring problematic issues to an ACO lawyer, the Master, or a judge.

12.3.2. The ACO staff members are not legally qualified and cannot give legal advice on the merits of the claim. Staff members may be able to assist with the basic judicial review procedure. However, any advice from a member of staff as to procedure must not be considered to circumvent any legal provision (be that provision in statute, case law, the CPR, or a Court order) or the provisions of this Guide. Parties and the Court are responsible for the conduct of proceedings and the parties will not be able to rely on the advice of the ACO as a reason for not complying with legal provisions.

12.3.3. The ACO staff may contact the parties to request information or specific documents if

---

[1] CPR 1.3

that information or document is required under the CPR or is thought to be necessary to allow the Court to properly consider or case manage the claim. The parties should comply with any requests unless they are unable to do so, when written reasons should be given for the failure.

12.3.4. The ACO staff have a duty to ensure that cases are being managed in accordance with the overriding objective. As such, where it appears that a case is not being managed in accordance with the overriding objective they have a duty to either make enquiries of the parties to establish the proper further course of action and/or to refer the case to an ACO lawyer or judge to consider further case management. Examples (but not an exhaustive list) of scenarios in which ACO staff may act as such are:

12.3.4.1. The claim appears to have been filed and/or issued in the Administrative Court under the judicial review provisions when it appears the claim should properly have been filed and/or issued in another Court or under a different provision;

12.3.4.2. The parties have failed to comply with procedural provisions in the CPR or a Court order;

12.3.4.3. The claim has been stayed for some time without a satisfactory update from the parties;

12.3.4.4. The staff member has concerns over the conduct of the parties.

12.4. ROLE OF THE ADMINISTRATIVE COURT OFFICE LAWYERS

12.4.1. An ACO lawyer must be a qualified solicitor or barrister. The role of the ACO lawyer is **1BA-77** as a non-partisan lawyer, subject to the duties of an officer of the Court (as all lawyers are). Therefore, whilst employed by HMCTS, their primary duty is to the Court. The role in itself is three-fold:

12.4.1.1. To provide advice on practice and procedure in the Administrative Court to whoever requires it; be that judges, ACO staff, practitioners, or litigants;

12.4.1.2. To provide legal research and updates for the judges of the Administrative Court; and

12.4.1.3. To communicate with the parties and exercise delegated judicial powers to ensure that cases in the Administrative Court are managed properly.

12.4.2. As an ACO lawyer is independent of the parties he/she cannot give advice on the merits of the claim. An ACO lawyer may draw the parties' attention to provisions or precedents that may have an impact on the claim. If this is done the parties should consider what is said, but this should not be considered to be formal legal advice or a determination on the law. The parties have responsibility for the conduct of their own claim and the decision on the law is the preserve of the judge who considers the claim.

12.4.3. An ACO lawyer has a duty to ensure that the case is managed in accordance with the overriding objective and may enter into discussions with the parties or make case management orders (when applied for, when a case is referred to them by an ACO staff member, or of his/her own volition) to further the overriding objective and properly manage the case. Any order of an ACO lawyer will always be made after consideration of the papers without a hearing.

12.4.4. The specific powers that the ACO lawyer may use are delegated by the President of the Queen's Bench Division[1] and include:

12.4.4.1. Determining when an urgent application should be referred to a judge.

12.4.4.2. Adding, removing, or correcting parties other than interveners.

12.4.4.3. Extending or abridging the time for the filing of any document required by the CPR, Practice Direction or court order.

12.4.4.4. Extending the time of any procedural step required of a party.

12.4.4.5. Directing the filing of any document required for the proper disposal of the case.

12.4.4.6. Dismissing a claim or application when a party has failed to comply with any order, rule or Practice Direction.

12.4.4.7. Determining applications for relief from sanctions.

12.4.4.8. Determining applications to stay proceedings by consent or otherwise.

12.4.4.9. Mandatory transfer of claims to the Upper Tribunal.

12.4.4.10. Order that the Court is minded to transfer the claim to a different region, which order will result in transfer in the event that no objection is received.[2]

12.4.4.11. Determining applications by solicitors to come off record.

12.4.4.12. Determining applications to vacate or adjourn hearings.

12.4.4.13. Determining any application for an agreed judgment or order for the disposal of the proceedings.[3]

12.4.5. If a party is not content with an order of the ACO lawyer then CPR 54.1A(5) provides that the party may request that the order is reviewed by a judge. Such a review may take place on

---

[1] CPR 54.1A(1)

[2] Where an objection is received the final decision on transfer will be taken by a judge.

[3] ACO lawyers will only be able to approve if permission has already been granted as they are subject to the restriction under CPR 54.1A(3)(a)

the papers or by way of an oral hearing in Court.[1] The choice of how the review takes place is the choice of the party requesting the review. The request for a review must be made by filing the request in writing (a letter or application notice may be used) within 7 days of the date on which the party was served with the ACO lawyer's order.[2] As long as the request is filed within 7 days (or such time as allowed by the order) there is no fee. If it is filed out of time then an application must be made to file the request out of time and it must be made on an application notice (N244 or PF244) with the relevant fee.

12.5. ROLE OF THE MASTER OF THE ADMINISTRATIVE COURT

1BA-78   **12.5.1.** The Master has the power to make any order allowed under the CPR unless the CPR expressly states that the Master may not make such an order. In judicial review proceedings this means that the Master generally deals with interim applications that do not come within the powers delegated to the ACO lawyers. This includes, but is not limited to:[3]

12.5.1.1. Making interim orders relating to case management or interim remedies (including applications to vary bail conditions, provided the prosecutor does not oppose the variation);

12.5.1.2. Determining liability for costs and making summary assessments of costs (see chapter 23 of this Guide for costs); and

12.5.1.3. Making orders relating to applications from vexatious litigants for permission to start or continue claims for judicial review (see paragraphs 4.10 and 4.11 of this Guide).

12.5.2. The Master may make orders with or without a hearing.[4]

12.5.3. The Master is under a duty to case manage the claim in accordance with the overriding objective. To this end the Master may request enquires are made of the parties by an ACO lawyer or ACO staff member or he/she may make case management orders (when applied for, when a case is referred to him/her by an ACO staff member or ACO lawyer, or of his/her own volition).

12.5.4. Any challenge to the terms of an order made by the Master without a hearing must be made by applying for reconsideration of the order at an oral hearing.[5] The application must be made on form N244 or PF244 and the relevant fee is payable. The hearing will be listed before a judge in Court. See paragraph 15.5 of this Guide for further details.

12.5.5. A challenge to an order made by the Master at an oral hearing must be made by appealing to a High Court judge (see paragraph 25.6 of this Guide on appeals).[6]

12.6. ROLE OF THE JUDICIARY

1BA-79   **12.6.1.** Judges of the Administrative Court have all the powers of the High Court under statute, the CPR, and under the inherent jurisdiction of the Court.

12.6.2. In ensuring that the overriding objective is complied with, the Court must actively manage cases (see paragraph 12.1 of this Guide).

12.6.3. Any challenge to the terms of a case management order made without a hearing must be made by applying for reconsideration at a hearing (see paragraph 15.5 of this Guide). Any challenge to an order made at an oral hearing must be appealed (see paragraph 25.6 of this Guide).

12.7. APPLICATIONS ONCE A CLAIM HAS COMMENCED

1BA-80   **12.7.1.** An application for directions or an interim order can be made at any time after commencement of the claim.[7] For pre-commencement applications, see paragraph 16.4 of this Guide; for applications for interim relief, chapter 15 of this Guide.

12.7.2. To make such an application:

12.7.2.1. The application must be filed with the ACO on an application notice (N244 or PF244 are the most commonly used).

12.7.2.2. The application must be accompanied by payment of the relevant fee.

12.7.2.3. The application must be accompanied by evidence stating why the direction or order is required.

12.7.2.4. A draft order should be enclosed with the application.

12.7.3. Where possible, a copy of the application, evidence and accompanying draft order should be sent to the proposed defendants and interested parties to give them notice that the application is being made. Where the application has been made without giving notice to the other parties then the evidence supporting the application should explain why the application has been made without giving notice.

---

[1] CPR 54.1A(5) & (6)
[2] CPR 54.1A(7)
[3] CPR 2.4(a) and CPR PD 2B paragraphs 3.1(c) and 3.1A
[4] CPR 23.8
[5] *R. (MD (Afghanistan)) v Secretary of State for the Home Department* [2012] 1 W.L.R. 2422
[6] CPR PD 52A paragraph 4.3
[7] CPR Part 23

12.7.4. In the application notice the applicant may request the application be considered at a hearing or by a judge considering the papers. In either event, the ACO will send the papers to a judge, master, or ACO lawyer to consider in the first instance. A judicial order may be made on the papers alone if it is thought that a hearing would not be appropriate. Otherwise, a hearing may be listed to hear the application. Such a hearing is usually listed at short notice (see paragraph 13.2.3 of this Guide).

12.7.5. It is the responsibility of each party to indicate the likely length of the hearing to determine the application (if the application is determined at a hearing). The length of hearing should include time for giving judgment.

12.7.6. If the parties are able to agree the form of any case management order then the application may be made by consent. If the parties can agree then this is preferable to making a contested application, although the Court retains discretion as to whether to grant or refuse the order or to make the order in a varied form. Applications made by consent in this way are made in accordance with the procedure outlined at paragraph 22.4 of the Guide (which deals with consent orders to end the claim, but the procedure is identical).

12.7.7. Where a rule or court order expressly states that the parties may make an "application" (for example, "*the claimant may make an application for permission to admit further evidence within 21 days*") then the procedure outlined in this paragraph will be applicable. If the application is made within any applicable time limit then the relief from sanction principles (see paragraph 12.9 of this Guide) will not apply. Where a rule or court order allows for "representations" (for example, "*the claimant may make representations on costs within 7 days*") then it is permissible to file the written representations without the need for the formal application process. Such representations, if emailed, should come in the form of an attached word document. If the representations are not received within any applicable time limit then an application must be made, in accordance with this paragraph and paragraph 12.9, to extend the time limit.

12.8. APPLICATIONS FOR THE CLAIM TO BE STAYED

12.8.1. If either party wishes to stay a claim, an application must be made to the Court for that **1BA-81** to occur (see paragraph 12.7 of this Guide for the procedure for making applications). Save in exceptional circumstances, an application for stay should be made on notice to the other parties, and their agreement to it should be sought before the application is made.

12.8.2. The duration of the proposed stay must be made clear in the application notice. Usually, a stay is sought pending the outcome of a particular event (for example, the conclusion of a related Tribunal appeal or a lead case in the Court of Appeal) or for a specific period of time (not usually exceeding a few weeks or months).

12.8.3. A stay will not normally be permitted to enable the defendant to reconsider the decision under challenge in the claim. Where the defendant agrees to reconsider, the judicial review should generally be withdrawn. A fresh claim can then be brought if the claimant wishes to challenge the reconsideration.[1] In any event, the Court's permission will be required to amend the claim form in light of any subsequent decision (see paragraphs 6.10 (pre-permission) and 9.2 (post-permission) of this Guide for further guidance on this principle).

12.9. RELIEF FROM SANCTIONS

12.9.1. Where a party has failed to comply with a provision under the CPR, a Practice Direction **1BA-82** or an order of the Court, which specifies a sanction for non-compliance or a sanction can otherwise be implied, and the party wishes to set aside the sanction, that party must apply for relief from sanction.[2] If they do not then the Court may refuse to consider that party's case[3] and/or make an adverse costs order against the party.[4] An implied sanction is a sanction that is not expressly imposed by a rule or direction but the consequence of a failure to comply would be the same as if the rule expressly imposed a sanction for non-compliance (for example, if a party fails to file an appeal notice or renewal notice within the relevant time period, and does not obtain an extension of

---

[1] See *R (Bhatti) v Bury Metropolitan Borough Council* [2013] EWHC 3093, and *R (Yousuf) v Secretary of State for the Home Department* [2016] EWHC 663 (Admin)

[2] CPR 3.8(1) and *R (Hysaj) v Secretary of State for the Home Department* [2014] EWCA Civ 1633. In Hysaj a failure to file an appellant's notice in time required an application to extend time to file the notice retrospectively or the appeal could not progress. The Court of Appeal held that the relief from sanctions provisions applied as the lack of ability to appeal unless an extension of time was granted was an implied sanction. In *R (Fayad) v SSHD* [2018] EWCA Civ 54 where the Court of Appeal confirmed at [22] that the approach to be adopted to applications for extension of time in judicial review cases was that set out in *Denton v TH White Ltd* [2014] EWCA Civ 906, citing Hysaj. See also *R (The National Council on Civil Liberties, Liberty) v SSHD and SSFCO (Procedural Matters)* [2018] EWHC 976 (Admin) at [3].

[3] CPR 3.4(2)(c)

[4] CPR 44.2(4)(a), CPR 44.2(5)(c) and CPR 44.4(3)(a)(i)

time from the Court, the claim cannot proceed; the implied sanction is therefore one of striking out).[1]

12.9.2. An application for relief from sanction must be made in line with the interim applications procedure (see paragraph 12.7 of this Guide). The application for relief from sanction may be considered by an ACO lawyer, the Master, or a judge.

12.9.3. When considering whether to grant an application for relief from sanction, the ACO lawyer, the Master, or a judge, must consider the principles outlined in *Mitchell v News Group Newspapers Ltd* [2013] EWCA Civ 1537 and *Denton v T.H. White Ltd* [2014] EWCA Civ 906[2]. These cases should be considered if making such an application, but, in summary, the Court will consider the application in three stages:

12.9.3.1. Identify and assess the seriousness and significance of the failure to comply with any rule or Court order. If the breach is neither serious nor significant, the Court is likely to grant relief.

12.9.3.2. Consider why the default occurred. If there is a good reason for it, the Court will be likely to decide that relief should be granted, but merely overlooking the deadline is unlikely to constitute a good reason.

12.9.3.3. Evaluate all the circumstances of the case, so as to enable the Court to deal justly with the application including consideration of the first two factors. Particular weight is to be given to the need for litigation to be conducted efficiently and at proportionate cost and to enforce compliance with rules, practice directions and orders.

12.10. ABUSE OF THE COURT'S PROCESS

1BA-83   **12.10.1.** The Court has a duty to ensure that the Court's process is not abused. If a party, a legal representative, or any other person acts in a way thought to be inappropriate the Court may, in an appropriate case:

12.10.1.1. Strike out statements of case;[3]

12.10.1.2. Make an adverse costs order requiring the person to pay a party's costs (see paragraph 23.1 of this Guide);[4]

12.10.1.3. Make a wasted costs requiring a legal representative to pay a party's costs (see paragraph 23.13 of this Guide);[5]

12.10.1.4. Refer a legal representative to their regulatory body to consider further sanctions;[6]

12.10.1.5. Make a Civil Restraint Order (see chapter 4 of this Guide).[7]

12.10.2. Before making any of the above orders, the Court will usually give the relevant party, legal representative, or third party the opportunity to make representations on the appropriateness of such an order.

12.10.3. Scenarios which may be considered to be an abuse of process include, but are not limited to:[8]

12.10.3.1. Acting in bad faith or with an improper purpose.

12.10.3.2. Attempting to re-litigate a decided issue.

12.10.3.3. Raising in subsequent proceedings matters which could and should have been litigated in earlier proceedings.

12.10.3.4. Starting proceedings or applying for an order after improper delay.

12.10.3.5. Persistent failure to comply with rules or orders of the Court.

12.10.3.6. Knowingly starting proceedings in the Administrative Court which ought to be issued in another Court or Tribunal.

12.10.3.7. Proceedings which are frivolous, vexatious, harassing or manifestly groundless.

12.11. COMMUNICATIONS WHICH ARE ABUSIVE OR WITHOUT PROPER PURPOSE

1BA-84   **12.11.1.** The ACO is generally in a position to communicate with the parties in person at the public counter, by telephone, email, or post (see Annex 1 for details) and will respond to communications if the communication so requires. The exception to this principle will apply if a person has been made subject to a notification of restricted communication.

12.11.2. Such a notification will be sent by the manager of the ACO if it is considered that the person has been communicating with the ACO in a manner which is:

---

[1] See *Sayers v Clarke Walker* [2002] EWCA Civ 645 and *Altomart Ltd v Salford Estates (No.2) Ltd* [2014] EWCA Civ 1408

[2] See, in addition, footnote 151

[3] CPR 3.4(1)(c)

[4] CPR 44.2(4)(a), CPR 44.2(5)(c) and CPR 44.4(3)(a)(i)

[5] Section 51(6) Senior Courts Act 1981 and CPR 46.8

[6] *R (Hamid) v SSHD* [2012] EWHC 3070 (Admin)

[7] CPR 3.11, CPR PD 3c, and CPR 23.12

[8] Examples taken from *Halsbury's Laws of England*, Vol.11 Civil Procedure (2015), Part 19, paragraph 1044, and from *R (Ashraf) v SSHD* [2013] EWHC 4028 (Admin)

12.11.2.1. Aggressive, intimidating, or harassing; or

12.11.2.2. Persistent, time consuming, and without proper purpose.

12.11.3. Such a notification will inform the persons that the form in which they may communicate with the ACO is restricted to the manner outlined in the notice, all other forms of communication will be ignored, and that a response to the permitted form of communication will only be made if the communication raises a new issue that requires the response of the ACO.

12.11.4. Notifications of restricted communication will be sent in writing to the last known address for the person subject to the notification.

12.11.5. The person subject to the notification may request in writing at any time that the ACO manager rescinds the notification at his/her discretion. Such a request should include reasons for the request and will be responded to in writing.

12.11.6. A notification of restricted communication is made by the manager of the ACO as an employee of HMCTS. Any complaint against such a notification must be made in accordance with the HMCTS complaints policy.

12.11.7. The Court, under its inherent jurisdiction to control its own proceedings, may also make, rescind, or vary a notification of restricted communication.

13. LISTING

13.1. LISTING POLICY

13.1.1. The Administrative Court has a listing policy that will be followed by the ACO when it **1BA-85** lists any hearing. The listing policy can be found at Annex 4 to this guide.

13.1.2. This section of the Guide will summarise the procedure in the policy, but the policy itself should be referred to for full details.

13.1.3. The policy is intended to be applied flexibly. The ACO may, where it considers it appropriate to do so, list cases otherwise than in accordance with the policy.

13.1.4. A particular case may be listed in a particular way by reason of a judicial order.

13.2. LISTING PROCEDURE

13.2.1. For permission hearings, hearings will usually be fixed for a date without seeking the **1BA-86** views of representatives. Several weeks' notice of the hearing will normally be given.

13.2.2. For substantive hearings, the ACO will usually consult with counsel's clerks to attempt to agree a suitable date for the hearing. This will generally occur in one of two ways:

13.2.2.1. In the ACO in London, the ACO will telephone or email either counsel's clerks and/or solicitors to arrange an appointment to fix the hearing. Five working days' notice will be given of the appointment. At the appointment if parties are unable to agree a date that is also acceptable to the Court, the ACO will list the matter for first available date convenient to the Court.

13.2.2.2. In the other ACOs, the ACO will either email or telephone counsel's clerks or solicitors for all sides to request the dates of availability for counsel on the Court record (that is to say the Court has been informed counsel is/are acting). Unless availability is provided over the telephone at the time of the initial contact the clerk will be informed that they must provide availability within 48 hours otherwise the ACO will list the matter for first available date convenient to the Court. If the availability of all counsel corresponds, the ACO will check for judicial availability and list accordingly; alternatively, if parties are unable to agree a date that is also acceptable to the Court, the ACO will list the matter for first available date convenient to the Court.

13.2.3. Interim relief hearings are usually listed in the same way as renewal hearings, but where interim relief is required urgently the hearing may be listed at short notice with little or no consultation as to the availability of the parties. The application will usually be fixed on the basis that it will take no longer than 30 minutes to hear, unless a different time estimate is required by a judge, master, or ACO lawyer. If a party considers that the application will require a longer hearing, the suggested time estimate must be confirmed as soon as possible, in writing with reasons, and is subject to the Court's approval.

13.2.4. Due to limited judicial time the ACO is unable to routinely take into account the availability of litigants representing themselves (litigants in person) or instructing solicitors.[1] However, if there are dates when a litigant in person is unable to attend and there are good reasons for not being able to attend then the litigant in person may inform the ACO in writing in advance and the ACO may be able to take this into account when listing.

13.2.5. A substantive hearing will be allocated a hearing time estimate by either the judge granting permission or the ACO. If a party considers that the application will require a longer hearing, the suggested time estimate must be confirmed as soon as possible, in writing with reasons, and is subject to the Court's approval.

---

[1] In extradition appeals, the Court will apply Criminal Practice Direction 50B.13. Therefore, save in exceptional circumstances, regard will not be given to an advocate's existing commitments.

13.2.6. Once the hearing has been listed, all parties will be sent a listing notice by the ACO which confirms the date, location, and time estimate for the hearing. The start time of the hearing will not be in the listing notice. Generally, Administrative Court hearings start at 10.30am, but this may be changed up until 2.00pm the day before the hearing. The parties should check the hearing time on the day before the hearing by telephoning the ACO or checking the hearing time online at *www.gov.uk/courts-tribunals/administrative-court.*

13.3. DIVISIONAL COURTS

1BA-87

13.3.1. Divisional Courts may be convened for any case in the High Court.[1]

13.3.2. A Divisional Court means that two or more judges sit together. Divisional Courts are generally only convened for cases that raise issues of general public importance or for criminal cases[2] where the case has some public interest, is not straightforward, or is likely to set a precedent. Generally, if permission to apply for judicial review is granted in such cases, a direction that the substantive claim will be heard by a Divisional Court will be made by the single judge at the permission stage.[3] However, a direction can be made at any time in such cases and it may be appropriate for an oral permission application and will generally be appropriate for rolled up hearings (see paragraphs 8.2.5, 8.2.6 and 8.4 of this Guide; and see *Thakrar v Crown Prosecution Service* [2019] EWCA Civ 874).

13.3.3. Criminal cases come before the Administrative Court in a variety of contexts whether in relation to actual or prospective criminal proceedings (such as a decision of the Director of Public Prosecutions not to prosecute a person for an alleged crime). Just because the decision under challenge has some connection to a criminal trial or sentence does not automatically mean that the judicial review proceedings are criminal in nature: a careful appraisal is necessary by reference to the circumstances of each case. The focus should be on the nature and character of the underlying litigation.[4]

13.3.4. If a judicial review is allocated to the Divisional Court, the listing arrangements will be different, particularly if the case is considered to be urgent. The ACO will not be able to offer as many suitable available dates for a hearing and will not generally take account of the availability of each party's counsel when listing the hearing.

13.4. APPLYING TO ADJOURN A LISTED HEARING

1BA-88

13.4.1. If a party wishes to apply to adjourn a listed hearing then the application must be made in one of the following ways:

13.4.1.1. By agreeing with all other parties that the hearing should be adjourned and filing a draft consent order for the approval of the Court,[5] one of the terms of which is that the hearing is adjourned. Such an order must be signed by all parties and must be accompanied by the relevant fee (although see paragraph 13.4.1.2 below). The parties may also include further directions sought in such a draft order. The parties should not assume that a hearing has been adjourned unless they have been informed by the ACO that the consent order has been approved. Reasons for the hearing being adjourned should be provided.

13.4.1.2. If the parties agree a consent order to adjourn the hearing, which does not seek other directions, and they file the draft consent order with the ACO more than 14 days before the hearing, then no fee is payable. The request should be made on form AC001. The other provisions noted at paragraphs 13.4.1.1 and 22.4 of this Guide will still apply.

13.4.1.3. If the parties cannot agree a consent order, then a party may make an application to adjourn the hearing in line with the interim applications procedure (see paragraph 12.7 of this Guide). Such an application must be made on form N244 or PF244 and be accompanied by the relevant fee. The application notice should include the reasons for the request, any attempts made to agree the request with the other parties, and any responses from the other parties to that request. A draft of the order sought should also be attached to the application.

13.4.2. The decision to adjourn a listed hearing is a judicial decision and cannot be taken by the ACO. The hearing will generally not be adjourned unless there are good reasons to do so, even where all parties agree that the hearing should be adjourned. Where the sole reason for seeking the adjournment is that counsel is/are not available for the hearing the application to adjourn will rarely be granted. Where the matter has been listed to be heard by a Divisional Court the Court will be very reluctant to grant an adjournment.

---

[1] s.66 of the Senior Courts Act 1981

[2] As there is no right of appeal to the Court of Appeal, see paragraph 25.5 of this Guide.

[3] CPR 54.10(2)(b)

[4] For the scope of what constitutes a criminal case, reference should be made to *Belhaj v Director of Public Prosecutions* [2018] UKSC 33, *R. (McAtee) v The Secretary of State for Justice* [2018] EWCA Civ 2851 and *Thakrar v Crown Prosecution Service* [2019] EWCA Civ 874.

[5] See paragraph 22.4 of this Guide for the procedure for filing a consent order in the context of ending a claim – the procedure is identical

PART C:—SPECIFIC PRACTICE POINTS

14. Duty of Candour

14.1. THERE IS A SPECIAL DUTY WHICH APPLIES TO PARTIES TO JUDICIAL REVIEW KNOWN AS THE "DUTY OF CANDOUR" WHICH REQUIRES THE PARTIES TO ENSURE THAT ALL RELEVANT INFORMATION AND FACTS ARE PUT BEFORE THE COURT.[1] THIS MEANS THAT PARTIES MUST DISCLOSE ANY INFORMATION OR MATERIAL FACTS WHICH EITHER SUPPORT OR UNDERMINE THEIR CASE.

14.1.1. This rule is needed in judicial review claims, where the Court's role is to review the **1BA-89** lawfulness of decisions made by public bodies, often on an urgent request being made, where the ordinary rules of disclosure of documents do not apply (see paragraph 6.5 and chapter 20 of this Guide on evidence) and where the witness statements are usually read (rather than being subject to cross examination by witnesses who are called to give their evidence orally).

14.1.2. The rule is particularly important where the other party has not had the opportunity to submit its own evidence or make representations (usually an urgent application – see chapter 16 of this Guide).

14.1.3. The Court will take seriously any failure or suspected failure to comply with the duty of candour. The parties or their representatives may be required to explain why information or evidence was not disclosed to the Court, and any failure may result in sanctions.

14.1.4. Claimants in judicial review proceedings must ensure that the Court has the full picture. In some circumstances, to ensure this, it is not sufficient simply to provide the relevant documents. Instead, a specific explanation of a document or an inconsistency must be given, usually by witness statement attested by the claimant.[2] (See also paragraph 16.5.3 of this Guide.)

14.1.5. Public authorities have a duty of candour and co-operation with the Court and must draw the Court's attention to relevant matters. A particular obligation falls upon both solicitors and barristers acting for public authorities to assist the Court in ensuring that these high duties are fulfilled. The Court will expect public authorities to comply with the duty of candour without being reminded of it. See *R. (Citizens UK) v The Secretary of State for the Home Department* [2018] EWCA Civ 1812.

14.1.6. The duty of candour is a continuing duty on all parties.

14.1.7. The duty means that a claimant must reassess the viability and propriety of a challenge in light of the defendant's acknowledgement of service and summary grounds.[3]

15. Interim Relief

15.1. WHEN IS INTERIM RELIEF APPROPRIATE?

15.1.1. A party (usually the Claimant) may request an interim remedy whilst the case is pending. **1BA-90** Common examples are:

15.1.1.1. An interim order stopping the action the defendant plans to take (e.g. to prevent removal from the UK, assuming that UTIAC has no jurisdiction in the matter, see paragraph 5.5 of this Guide);

15.1.1.2. An interim order requiring the defendant to act in a certain way (e.g. – to provide the claimant with accommodation).

15.1.2. Interim relief is usually requested in the claim form. But it can be applied for at any stage of proceedings and in exceptional cases can be applied for before proceedings are commenced. The procedure is outlined in CPR Part 23, supplemented in places by CPR Part 25 and CPR Part 54.

15.1.3. The Court may require the claimant to give undertakings as a condition of any interim relief:

15.1.3.1. The claimant may be required to give an undertaking in damages, so that if the defendant succeeds at the end of the day, and has suffered financial loss as a result of the relief ordered in the claimant's favour in the meanwhile, the claimant will have to compensate that loss; and

15.1.3.2. An undertaking operates as if it was a Court order, and breach of an undertaking is equivalent to breaching a Court order, which the Court can sanction by imposing an adverse costs order on the party in default, refusing to hear the application, striking out the claim and proceeding to consider committal for contempt of Court.

---

[1] See the discussion of this principle in *R. (Al-Sweady) v Secretary of State for Defence* [2009] EWHC 2387 (Admin) at paragraph 18.

[2] *R (Mohammed Shahzad Khan) v Secretary of State for the Home Department* [2016] EWCA Civ 416 at 45

[3] Ibid, 48

15.2. INTERIM RELIEF WHEN LODGING THE CLAIM

1BA-91   **15.2.1.** Interim relief is usually applied for at the same time as lodging the claim papers (see chapter 6 of this Guide on starting proceedings).

15.2.2. Such an application can be made by making the application in section 8 of the claim form (form N461). As with the statement of facts and grounds, the substance of the application can be contained in a separate document to which section 8 of the claim form refers.

15.2.3. The application for interim relief will be considered by the judge on the papers, usually at the same time as the application for permission to apply for judicial review. The advantage for all parties is that this process reduces paperwork, reduces Court time, and does not require an additional fee.

15.2.4. The judge considering the application for interim relief alongside permission may either make an order based on the papers alone or order that the application for interim relief be dealt with at a hearing in Court (see paragraph 13.2.3 of this Guide for listing of such hearings).

15.2.5. Where the circumstances of the case require urgent consideration of the application for permission to apply for judicial review and/or any interim relief, a different procedure applies. This is dealt with separately in this Guide (see chapter 16).

15.3. INTERIM RELIEF BEFORE COMMENCEMENT OF PROCEEDINGS

1BA-92   **15.3.1.** In exceptionally urgent circumstances a person may apply for interim relief before starting proceedings. See paragraph 16.4 of this Guide for the procedure where an urgent application is made before proceedings have been commenced.

15.4. INTERIM RELIEF IN ONGOING PROCEEDINGS

1BA-93   **15.4.1.** Where a claim has already been lodged but it subsequently becomes clear that an interim order is required, the party seeking interim relief should issue an application on form N244 or PF244. If the application is urgent, the party should make that clear in the application form, and indicate the timescale within which the judge is requested to consider the application in that application and, preferably, in a covering letter as well. Such an application, whether it is made urgently or not, should always, unless it is impracticable, be served on all the other parties. The Court is unlikely to consider the application unless the opposing party has been given an opportunity to respond to the application in writing.

15.5. RECONSIDERATION IF INTERIM RELIEF IS REFUSED

1BA-94   **15.5.1.** Where an application for an interim order has been refused without a hearing (that is to say that the judge made the order considering the papers alone), a party may request the decision be reconsidered.[1]

15.5.2. Reconsideration is requested by lodging an application notice (N244 or PF244) with the relevant fee within 7 days of service of the order made on the papers, unless the order allows for a different time limit.[2] The application must be served on all other parties.

15.5.3. If an application is made for reconsideration after refusal on the papers then reconsideration must take place at an oral hearing in Court (see paragraph 13.2.3 of this Guide on listing).

15.5.4. If reconsideration is required within a set time frame the application must make the relevant timescale clear in the application and, preferably, in a covering letter as well.

15.5.5. Where reconsideration of an order made on the papers is extremely urgent and cannot wait until the Court's sitting hours, then the application for reconsideration can be made by a party's legal representative to the out of hours judge in accordance with paragraph 16.3 of this Guide. In such circumstances the practitioner will be asked to undertake to pay the relevant fee on the next working day.

15.5.6. A party who wishes to challenge a decision made on the papers must apply for reconsideration in the Administrative Court before they can appeal (see chapter 25 of this Guide for appeals).[3]

---

[1] *R. (MD (Afghanistan)) v Secretary of State for the Home Department* [2012] EWCA Civ 194

[2] CPR 3.3(6)

[3] *R. (MD (Afghanistan)) v Secretary of State for the Home Department* [2012] EWCA Civ 194 at paragraph 21

15.6. CRITERIA FOR THE GRANT OF INTERIM RELIEF

15.6.1. When considering whether to grant interim relief while a judicial review claim is pending, the judge will consider:[1]   **1BA-95**

15.6.1.1. Whether there is a real issue to be tried. In practice, in judicial review claims, that involves considering whether there is a real prospect of succeeding at the substantive hearing, that is to say a more than a fanciful prospect of success;

15.6.2. Whether the balance of convenience lies in granting the interim order;

15.6.3. Any other factors the Court considers to be relevant.

15.6.4. Generally, there is a strong public interest in permitting a public authority's decision to continue, so the applicant for interim relief must make out a strong case for relief in advance of the substantive hearing.[2]

15.6.5. The Court will be reluctant to grant any form of interim relief without establishing the defendant's response to the application. The Court is likely, if time permits, to permit the defendant an opportunity to respond to the application. In an urgent case, this may be by abridging time for service of the acknowledgement of service or calling the matter in for a hearing on short notice.

15.6.6. If time does not permit the defendant to be heard, then the Court will consider granting relief for a very short period until the defendant has been able to make its submissions (in writing or at a hearing).

15.6.7. Sometimes, if the merits of the underlying claim are unclear and there is no particular urgency in granting relief, the Court will give directions for an "expedited" (speedy) determination of permission, or trial of the claim (possibly on the basis that permission should be "rolled up" with the substantive hearing – see paragraph 8.2.6 of this Guide). In this way, the Court can be sure that both parties have had a chance to put their arguments before the Court before any form of order granting (or refusing) relief is made.

15.7. REMOVALS CASES

15.7.1. There are particular rules relating to cases where a claimant challenges a decision to   **1BA-96**
remove him or her from the jurisdiction, see CPR PD 54A, paragraph 18. Such challenges would now generally fall within the jurisdiction of UTIAC. A person who makes an application for permission to apply for judicial review of a removal decision must file a claim form which must:

15.7.1.1. Indicate on the face of the claim form that the practice direction applies (which can be done by ticking the relevant box in section 4 of the claim form);

15.7.1.2. Attach to the claim form a copy of the removal directions and the decision to which the application relates;

15.7.1.3. Attach any document served with the removal directions including any document which contains the UK Border Agency's factual summary of the case; and

15.7.1.4. Contain or be accompanied by the detailed statement of the claimant's grounds for bringing the judicial review (or give the reasons why compliance with the last two conditions is not possible).

15.7.2. That person must send copies of the claim form to the UK Border Agency.

15.7.3. The Court has set out certain principles to be applied when such applications are made in *R (Madan) v Secretary of State for the Home Department* [2007] EWCA Civ 770, which were endorsed by the Court in *R (SB (Afghanistan)) v Secretary of State for the Home Department* [2018] EWCA Civ 215:[3]

15.7.3.1. Such applications must be made promptly on the intimation of a deportation decision and not await the actual fixing of removal arrangements;

15.7.3.2. The detailed statement of grounds must include a statement of all previous applications made in respect of that applicant's immigration status and indicate how the present state of the case differs from previous applications.

15.7.4. Counsel and solicitors appearing on the application, in the absence of the defendant, are under professional obligations to draw the judge's attention to any matter adverse to their client's case, including in particular any previous adverse decisions, and to take a full note of the judge's judgment or reasons, which should then be submitted to the judge for approval.

---

[1] *R. (Medical Justice) v Secretary of State for the Home Department* [2010] EWHC 1425 (Admin) and *American Cyanamid Company v Ethicon Limited* [1975] AC 396

[2] The position is different for cases involving removals from the UK involving claims of a breach of Articles 2 and 3 of the ECHR – see below at 15.7, and see *R (SB (Afghanistan)) v SSHD* [2018] EWCA Civ 215 at [78].

[3] See [55]-[56]. At [75], the Court suggested that a valid claim was one which was made at a time which afforded the Secretary of State a viable opportunity to appreciate that such a claim had been made and to take steps to address it.

16. URGENT CASES

16.1. GENERAL

1BA-97   **16.1.1.** The Administrative Court often deals with urgent cases. This is a very important part of the Court's work, and the availability of the Court to deal with urgent cases is in the public interest. However, the Court's experience in recent years is that some litigants and practitioners are misusing, and even abusing, the procedures for seeking urgent adjudication. The consequence of this is or may be that those claimants with genuinely urgent cases have had to wait longer than they needed to, because wholly unmeritorious and/or non-urgent cases are ahead of them in the queue.

16.1.2.   All litigants and their advisers are reminded of the rules relating to urgent applications which are summarised below. In particular,

16.1.2.1.   It is very important that litigants and their advisors state clearly on the Court forms what are the reasons for urgency (see paragraph 16.2 below).

16.1.2.2.   It is very important that litigants and their advisors comply with their duty of candour which requires them to disclose all relevant material to the Court (see paragraph 14.1 of this Guide).

16.1.3.   The CPR, Practice Directions and other obligations owed to the Court must be complied with. If they are not complied with, the party in default is likely to be made subject to an adverse costs order (for example, being made to pay some or all of the other party's legal costs, or being unable to recover their own legal costs, even if successful), and risks having their claim dismissed for non-compliance. Professional representatives may face applications for wasted costs, or be referred to their Regulator for consideration of disciplinary action, for failure to comply with their professional obligations.

16.1.4.   Professional representatives are reminded of the following passage from *R (Hamid) v Secretary of State for the Home Department* [2012] EWHC 3070 (Admin):

"[7] ... If any firm fails to provide the information required on the form and in particular explain the reasons for urgency, the time at which the need for immediate consideration was first appreciated, and the efforts made to notify the defendant, the Court will require the attendance in open court of the solicitor from the firm who was responsible, together with his senior partner. It will list not only the name of the case but the firm concerned. ..."

16.2. URGENT CONSIDERATION – FORM N463

1BA-98   **16.2.1.** Where the circumstances of the case require urgent consideration of the application for permission to apply for judicial review and/or any interim relief (which is not so urgent that it has been sought pre-action, but still sufficiently urgent that the Court is being asked to deal with it within a shortened timeframe), the Claimant may apply for urgent consideration at the same time as issuing the claim form.[1] These situations will generally be those where some irreversible action will take place if the Court does not act to prevent it, or where an expedited judicial review is required.

16.2.2.   The claimant must complete form N463 (a new version is available as of 26 March 2018), providing the following information (which is required to be inserted in the relevant boxes on that form):

16.2.2.1.   The circumstances giving rise to the urgency. If the representative was instructed late, an explanation must be provided as to why their client instructed them at the last moment. If the form is filed only shortly before the end of the working day, an explanation should also be provided as to why the application was not made earlier in the day;

16.2.2.2.   The timescale sought for the consideration of the application;

16.2.2.3.   The date by which any substantive hearing should take place;

16.2.2.4.   Efforts taken to put the defendant on notice of the application for urgent consideration;

16.2.2.5.   The grounds on which any interim order is sought.

16.2.3.   A draft of the order sought should be attached which sets out the relief sought and any directions for an expedited hearing.

16.2.4.   The full claim papers (see chapter 6 of this Guide on starting proceedings, i.e. claim form and required supporting documents) must be filed alongside the urgent application. Where the application for urgent consideration is filed at the same time as the claim papers there is no additional fee for the urgent application, it is covered by the fee to start proceedings.

16.2.5.   The claimant should serve the claim papers and the Form N463 with supporting documentation on the defendant and interested parties, advising them of the application and that they may make representations.

16.2.6.   The Administrative Court Office will have a judge available to consider any urgent application received between 10am and 4pm (4.30pm in London), Monday to Friday, excluding

---

[1] *Practice Statement (Administrative Court: Listing and Urgent Cases)* [2002] 1 W.L.R. 810

public holidays (see CPR PD 2A, paragraph 2.1). The judge may either make an order based on the papers alone or order that the application (or part of it) be dealt with at a hearing in Court (see paragraph 13.2.3 for listing of such hearings). In appropriate situations the Master or an ACO lawyer may consider the application and request further information or make an order.

16.2.7. It is not appropriate for any urgent application arising during court hours (see paragraph 16.2.6 above) in relation to a judicial review to be put before the judge in charge of the interim applications court in London ("Court 37"). The Administrative Court has a judge available to deal with immediate applications in the context of a judicial review. Court 37 deals with other Queen's Bench Division matters. If a matter is brought before Court 37 (or any inappropriate court) which should have been brought before the Administrative Court as a matter arising in judicial review proceedings (pre-claim or otherwise) then the judge is likely to refuse to deal with the application and direct the applicant to file proceedings in the Administrative Court Office unless doing so would cause any irreversible prejudice or harm.

16.2.8. Wherever possible the Court will want representations from the defendant before determining the application. In cases where interim relief is sought, the Court will generally make an order allowing the defendant a short time to file written submissions before deciding the application, unless irreversible prejudice would be caused to the claimant in the meanwhile; alternatively, the judge may list the matter for a hearing on notice to the defendant (see paragraph 13.2.3 of this Guide for listing). In cases where an expedited substantive hearing is sought, the Court may abridge time for service of the defendant's acknowledgement of service and request the defendant's views on the order sought, to enable the Court to take an early view on permission and any consequential case management directions.

16.2.9. If the matter is put before a judge who concludes that the application was not urgent, and is suitable for disposal according to the ordinary procedures of the Court, the judge may refuse to deal with the matter on an urgent basis, and may make an adverse costs order against the applicant or his legal representatives (see paragraph 23.1 of this Guide on costs).

16.2.10. If an urgent application is refused on the papers the applying party may request the decision be reconsidered at an oral hearing (see paragraph 15.5 of this Guide for the procedure). The application must be made by filing the application notice with the Administrative Court Office, not by applying in the interim applications court (or any other court).

16.3. OUT OF HOURS APPLICATIONS

16.3.1. In the event that an urgent application needs to be made outside the sitting hours of the **1BA-99** Administrative Court (see paragraph 16.2.6 of this Guide) and the application cannot wait until the sitting hours recommence, then the claimant may make the application to the out of hours High Court Judge. A High Court Judge is on call at all times to deal with very urgent applications which cannot wait until the next working day.

16.3.2. If a party needs to make an out of hours application to the Court, the acting barrister or solicitors should telephone 0207 947 6000[1] and speak to the Queen's Bench Division out of hours duty clerk.

16.3.3. The out of hours duty clerk will require the practitioner to complete the out of hours form, which can be downloaded from the Government website *https://www.gov.uk/government/publications/form-qbd-oha-out-of-hours-application-queens-bench-division* and emailed to qbdutyclerk@ejudiciary.net (Emails must not be sent to this address unless the out of hours duty clerk has invited you to do so.)

16.3.4. The out of hours judge may deal with the application on paper. Alternatively, the out of hours judge may telephone the representatives acting for the claimant to enable them to make their submissions orally before deciding the application. The representatives will be required to provide a telephone number on which they can be reached. The out of hours judge may also telephone any other party to the application if he or she considers that to be appropriate (this is often done in immigration cases where the application seeks a stay on removal).

16.3.5. The fact that a judge is being asked to make an order out of hours, usually without a hearing, and often without any representations from the defendant's representatives and in a short time frame, means that the duty of candour (to disclose all material facts to the judge, even if they are not of assistance to the claimant's case) is particularly important, see paragraph 14.1 of this Guide.

16.3.6. Legal representatives must consider very carefully whether an out of hours application really is required and should only make such an application if the matter really cannot wait until the next working day.

16.3.7. The out of hours service is not available to litigants in person.

---

[1] As required by CPR PD 54D paragraph 4.2 and CPR PD 25A paragraph 4.5

16.4. PRE-ACTION APPLICATIONS

1BA-100   **16.4.1.** In exceptionally urgent circumstances, a person may apply, typically for interim relief, before starting judicial review proceedings. The Court may only grant a pre-action order where:

16.4.1.1. The matter is urgent; or

16.4.1.2. It is otherwise necessary to do so in the interests of justice.[1]

16.4.2. The claimant should carefully consider whether the matter is really so urgent that an application should be made before the claim is started. It is much better to apply at the same time as lodging the claim papers if that is possible: this will make it easier for the Court to understand the issues and is likely to conserve legal costs.

16.4.3. The claimant should always try to reach an agreement with the public authority, even for a short period, before applying for pre-action interim relief. The Court will expect to be told about such efforts and why they have not succeeded, if the matter is brought before the Court instead.

16.4.4. If the matter really is urgent and no short-term compromise can be reached, then the claimant can make an application for a pre-action relief by filing an application notice (N244 or PF244) with the ACO.[2] The application must be accompanied by the relevant fee, must be supported by evidence establishing why the order is required,[3] and should enclose a copy of the draft order. Where possible a copy of the application, evidence, and draft order should be sent to the proposed defendants and interested parties to give them notice that the application is being made.[4] Where the application has been made without giving notice to the other parties then the evidence supporting the application should explain why the application has been made without giving notice.[5]

16.4.5. In the application notice the applicant may request the application be considered at a hearing or by a judge considering the papers. In either event, the ACO will send the papers to a judge, master, or ACO lawyer to consider in the first instance. A judicial order may be made on the papers alone if it is thought that a hearing would not be appropriate.[6] Otherwise, a hearing will be listed to consider the application. Such a hearing is usually listed at short notice.

16.4.6. Wherever possible the Court will want representations from the defendant before determining any application made in advance of issuing the claim form. Unless, by not granting that order, irreversible prejudice would be caused to the claimant, the Court will generally make an order allowing the defendant a short time period to file written representations or the Court will direct that the application should be dealt with at a hearing listed with notice being provided to the defendant.

16.4.7. The claimant will usually be required to undertake to file a claim form and grounds of claim, usually within a short period, or, if no satisfactory undertaking is offered, will be directed by the Court to do so.[7]

16.5. ABUSE OF THE PROCEDURES FOR URGENT CONSIDERATION

1BA-101   **16.5.1.** Where an application for urgent consideration or an out of hours application is made which does not comply with this Guide and/or it is manifestly inappropriate, the Court may make a wasted costs order or some other adverse costs order (see paragraphs 23.1 and 23.13 of this Guide respectively).

16.5.2. In *R. (Hamid) v Secretary of State for the Home Department* [2012] EWHC 3070 (Admin) (see paragraph 16.1.4 above) the Court held that where urgent applications are made improperly the Court may summon the legal representative to Court to explain his or her actions and would consider referring that person, or their supervising partner (if different) to the relevant regulator. Although concerns about the behaviour of legal representatives most often arise in the context of last-minute attempts to prevent a client's removal from the UK, the Hamid jurisdiction is not confined to that situation, nor is it confined to the situation in which the underlying claim is utterly without merit.[8] It extends to all cases, not just immigration cases. Examples (but not an exhaustive list) of applications which have been held to be inappropriate under the Hamid rule are:

16.5.2.1. The claimant's solicitor had delayed making the urgent application until the last minute and had not disclosed the full facts of the case in an attempt to use the urgent process to prevent his client's removal from the UK.[9]

16.5.2.2. The claimant's solicitor requested urgent interim relief against a decision that had

---

[1] CPR 25.2(2)(b).
[2] CPR 23.3(1)
[3] CPR 25.3(2)
[4] CPR 23.4(1)
[5] CPR 25.3(3)
[6] CPR 23.8(c)
[7] CPR 25.2(3)
[8] *Jetly v Secretary of State for the Home Department* [2019] EWHC 204 (Admin)
[9] *R. (Hamid) v Secretary of State for the Home Department* [2012] EWHC 3070 (Admin)

been made three years earlier.[1]

16.5.2.3. A practitioner advanced arguments that his client was suicidal and psychotic when they knew or ought to have known were false and/or inconsistent with their own medical evidence.[2]

16.5.2.4. A practitioner lodged an application with grounds that were opaque and brief and failed to set out any of the claimant's history of criminality.[3]

16.5.3. In *R. (Sathivel) v Secretary of State for the Home Department* [2018] EWHC 913 (Admin), the Divisional Court reminded legal practitioners of the relevant standard of professional and ethical behaviour required of those conducting proceedings on behalf of clients in the field of immigration and asylum law:

(a)   The duty owed by legal practitioners to the court is paramount.

(b)   This duty includes an obligation on legal representatives to ensure that they are fully equipped with all relevant documentation before commencing proceedings or making applications.

(c)   They must make real efforts to obtain documents from previously instructed solicitors.

(d)   They must act candidly and bring to the attention of the court or tribunal gaps in the evidence.

(e)   They must avoid delay in bringing urgent applications. They must not advance a case to the Court simply as part of an effort to cause delay.

(f)   The Court went on to give guidance about the procedure to be followed in Hamid cases and stated that, in future, the Court will not necessarily refer the matter to a Divisional Court under the Hamid jurisdiction before deciding to pass the file to the representative's regulatory body as a complaint.

(g)   The Court will in future consider referring a case to the regulatory body on the first occasion that the legal representative falls below the relevant standards.

16.5.4. Practitioners should be aware that the Court can identify those who are responsible for abusing the Court's processes by making adverse costs orders (see paragraph 23.1 of this Guide) or by activating the Hamid procedure outlined above which may lead to those practitioners being disciplined by their Regulator. If the Hamid procedure is activated any orders made in relation to the referral may be published and placed in the public domain and any such publication will include the explanation provided by the legal representative. Also see paragraph 12.10 of this Guide on abuse of the Court's process.[4]

17.   SKELETON ARGUMENTS

17.1.   GENERAL

17.1.1. A skeleton argument is a written document setting out a summary of the party's arguments in the case.   **1BA-102**

17.1.2. CPR PD 54A paragraph 15 requires each party to prepare a skeleton argument before any substantive hearing.

17.1.3. Parties should also prepare skeleton arguments before any interim hearing in the course of a judicial review (including any renewed permission or hearing for interim relief or directions), even where the issue is straightforward. A skeleton argument in such circumstances is not mandatory by virtue of any rule, but may be very helpful to the Court.

17.2.   CONTENT OF SKELETON ARGUMENT

17.2.1. The skeleton argument must include the following:[5]   **1BA-103**

17.2.1.1.   On the first page, a time estimate for the complete hearing, including delivery of judgment, and the judge's pre-reading.

17.2.1.2.   A list of issues.

17.2.1.3.   A list of the legal points to be taken (together with any relevant authorities with page references to the passages relied on)

17.2.1.4.   A chronology of events with page references to the bundle of documents.

17.2.1.5.   A list of essential documents for the advance reading of the Court (with page references to the passages relied on);

---

[1] *R. (Butt) v Secretary of State for the Home Department* [2014] EWHC 264 (Admin)

[2] *R (Okondu) v Secretary of State for the Home Department (wasted costs; SRA referrals; Hamid) IJR* [2014] UKUT 377 (IAC)

[3] *R (Okondu) v Secretary of State for the Home Department (wasted costs; SRA referrals; Hamid) IJR* [2014] UKUT 377 (IAC)

[4] See also *R (SB (Afghanistan)) v SSHD* [2018] EWCA Civ 215 at [54]-[56]; and *Vai Sui Ip v Solicitors Regulation Authority* [2018] EWHC 957 (Admin) where a Divisional Court upheld the sanction of striking off a solicitor for making abusive applications for judicial review of immigration decisions.

[5] CPR PD 54A paragraph 15.3

17.2.1.6. A time estimate for the advance reading suggested; and

17.2.1.7. A list of persons referred to in the claim.

17.2.2. It is helpful if the skeleton argument sets out the points to be made as clearly and as concisely as possible. Ideally, the skeleton argument should be in the following form:

17.2.2.1. The decision under challenge should be clearly identified, or the relevant failure to make a decision, if that is what is under challenge.

17.2.2.2. The relevant facts should be summarised including any relevant change of facts or circumstances since the claim form and supporting documentation were lodged.

17.2.2.3. The grounds for seeking judicial review (or interim relief, or any other order) should be set out under numbered headings. The grounds must be stated shortly and numbered in sequence. Each ground should raise a distinct issue in relation to the decision under challenge.[1]

17.2.2.4. Arguments and submissions in support of the grounds should be set out separately in relation to each ground.

17.2.2.5. Relevant legal principles should be set out. Lengthy extracts from EU Directives, international Conventions, statutes, case law and other sources should be avoided if possible. It is much more helpful to the Court if the skeleton states the proposition of law which the party contends for, and then refers to the source of or authority for that proposition, with short extracts quoted if that is appropriate. It is not usually necessary or helpful to cite more than one case in support of each proposition of law.

17.2.2.6. The remedy sought should be identified.

17.2.2.7. Any urgency, other matter relevant to the timing of the case, and any other relevant point, such as alternative remedy, should be identified.

17.3. FORMAT OF SKELETON ARGUMENT

1BA-104

17.3.2.1. A skeleton argument should be clearly typed and properly spaced. A font style of not less than 11-point should be used, and lines should be reasonably spaced (1.5 or double spacing is ideal).

17.3.2.2. Paragraphs should be numbered sequentially.

17.3.2.3. Pages should be numbered. It is rarely necessary for skeleton arguments to be any longer than 20 pages in length.

17.4. METHOD OF SERVICE

1BA-105

17.4.1. Skeleton arguments may be filed with the Court by email at the relevant email address set out in Annex 1 as long as they do not exceed the maximum which the appropriate court office has indicated it can accept by email (see paragraph 6.7 of this Guide).[2] Otherwise, they should be lodged at the Court in hard copy. Service by email is encouraged, wherever possible, and is likely to be of greatest assistance to the Court. Skeletons served by email should be served in the form of an attached word document (as opposed to pdf, any other format, or in the body of the email). There is no need to file a hard copy of the skeleton if filing by email.

17.4.2. Skeleton arguments should always be served on the other party or parties to the case, whether or not that party is in a position to provide a skeleton by way of exchange.

17.5. TIMING OF SERVICE OF SKELETON ARGUMENTS

1BA-106

17.5.1. Skeleton arguments must be served in good time before any hearing.

17.5.2. That means that the skeleton argument must be served on or before the date set by the Court, if directions are in place. The standard direction usually ordered by the Court for substantive hearings is that the claimant's skeleton argument is to be filed with the Court and served on the other parties not less than 21 days before the date of the hearing of the claim, and the defendant's skeleton argument is to be filed with the Court and served on the other parties not less than 14 days before the hearing date. (But see paragraph 9.1.4 of this Guide for computation of time for service of skeleton arguments.)

17.5.3. These standard directions may be varied by the Court, in which case the parties must comply with those specific directions.

17.5.4. For all other hearings where there are no standard directions (for example, hearings for renewal of permission), and in the absence of specific directions, skeleton arguments should be served at least 2 working days before the hearing is listed. If there is or may be a problem with compliance with that deadline, the ACO should be alerted as soon as possible.

17.5.5. Skeleton arguments should not be handed to the Court on the day of the hearing.

---

[1] *R (Talpada) v SSHD* [2018] EWCA Civ 841 emphasised the need for a clear and succinct statement of the grounds, in the context of appeals, see [68]. See also *Hickey v Secretary of State for Work and Pensions* [2018] EWCA Civ 851 at [74].

[2] CPR PD 5B, paragraph 2.2(b)

17.6. SANCTION FOR NON-COMPLIANCE

If the skeleton argument does not comply with this guidance, or is served late, the Court may **1BA-107** refuse to permit the party in default to rely on the skeleton; alternatively, the Court make an adverse costs order against the party in default (see paragraph 23.1 of this Guide on costs).[1]

18. DOCUMENTS

18.1. BUNDLES FOR SUBSTANTIVE HEARINGS

18.1.1. CPR 54A PD paragraph 16 requires the claimant to file a bundle of documents at the **1BA-108** same time as the claimant files his or her skeleton argument for the substantive hearing. The bundle of documents should contain all relevant documents, including any documents required to be included by the defendant and any other party who is to make representations at the hearing.

18.1.2. The Court expects, therefore, to have a joint bundle of documents for the judicial review which includes all the documents to which any party present at the hearing will refer. The Court does not expect to have documents handed up to it during the course of the hearing, save in exceptional circumstances (and always subject to the Court's permission to adduce documents or evidence in that way).

18.2. OTHER HEARINGS

18.2.1. In some instances, there will be no directions about the production of bundles (for **1BA-109** example, where an urgent application is made by one party) but that party should still make sure that all relevant documents are before the Court. Any bundle containing documents which are to be put before the Court should be served on the Court and the other party or parties in good time before the hearing.

18.2.2. Good time means at least three clear days before most ordinary hearings.

18.2.3. If the matter is urgent, the bundle should be served on the Court and the other party or parties no later than 1pm on the day before the hearing.

18.3. FORMAT OF COURT BUNDLES

18.3.1. Any collection of documents to go before the Court is a "bundle". Bundles should ide- **1BA-110** ally be secured in files which are sufficiently large to accommodate the documents contained in them. The pages should be numbered sequentially and indexed.

18.3.2. The bundle spines should be clearly marked with the reference number of the case and name of the parties.

18.3.3. Photocopying should be 2-sided in portrait format (not landscape).

18.3.4. Photocopies must be legible.

18.3.5. Documents should be presented in chronological order.

18.3.6. In cases where the documents are extensive (as a guideline, more than 500 pages), the parties should endeavour to agree a "core bundle" of key documents. In those cases, consideration should be given to including only the important and relevant parts of a long document in the Court bundle and not copying the whole of that document.

18.3.7. The judge may refuse to read a bundle which does not comply with these requirements, or direct that a revised bundle is submitted which does comply, in which event the judge may disallow the costs or make a different adverse costs order.

18.4. TIMING OF LODGING OF TRIAL BUNDLES

18.4.1. Trial bundles must be lodged in good time before any hearing. **1BA-111**

18.4.2. That means that the trial bundle must be lodged on or before the date set by the Court if directions are in place. The direction usually ordered by the Court for substantive hearings is that the trial bundle must be filed and served not less than 4 weeks before the date of the hearing.

18.4.3. For substantive hearings, where there are no directions, trial bundles must be lodged when the claimant is due to lodge a skeleton argument (see paragraph 9.1.4.5 of this Guide for more detail) For all other hearings, or where there are no specific directions in place, any documents must be filed at Court as soon as possible and in good time before the hearing.

18.4.4. Any unavoidable submission of late bundles should clearly state the date of the hearing on the bundles. The bundles should be accompanied by a letter to the ACO setting out the reasons for late submission. Failure to make it clear that the bundles relate to an imminent hearing may result in the bundles not being placed before the judge in advance of the hearing.

---

[1] See as an example *R (National Council of Civil Liberties, Liberty) v SSHD and SSFCA (Procedural Matters)* [2018] EWHC 976 (Admin) at [17]

18.5. SANCTION FOR NON-COMPLIANCE

1BA-112   **18.5.1.** If the trial bundle or bundle of documents does not comply with this guidance, or is served late, the Court may refuse to allow the party in default to rely on the bundle of documents; alternatively, it may make an adverse costs order against the party in default (see paragraph 23.1 of this Guide on costs).

19.   AUTHORITIES

19.1. GENERAL

1BA-113   **19.1.1.** Parties are encouraged to limit the number of authorities (i.e. cases) cited, to those which are really necessary for the fair disposal of the claim, and which establish the particular principle of law contended. In most cases, it is unnecessary to adduce more than 10 authorities, and some cases will require fewer, if any, authorities.
19.1.2. Where extensive authorities are cited, it is preferable to agree a core bundle of authorities, itself not exceeding 10 authorities.

19.2. FORMAT OF AUTHORITIES BUNDLES

1BA-114   **19.2.1.** Bundles of authorities should be paginated or tabbed and indexed.
19.2.2. Photocopying should be 2-sided in portrait format (not landscape).
19.2.3. Copies should be legible.
19.2.4. Authorities which have been reported should be produced in their reported form. Transcripts are only acceptable where the case has not been reported.

19.3. AGREEMENT OF CONTENTS AND SERVICE OF AUTHORITIES BUNDLES

1BA-115   **19.3.1.** A party should always notify the other party or parties of any authorities on which he or she intends to rely at the hearing, in good time before the hearing, and ensure that copies of those authorities are available for that party at the hearing.
19.3.2. The Court will usually give directions for a joint bundle of authorities to be filed in advance of any substantive hearing. If there are no such directions in place, the parties are required to work together to arrive at a joint list of authorities, and to ensure that a bundle of those authorities is filed at Court in good time before any hearing. If agreement cannot be reached, separate bundles will have to be filed by each party in which event there should be no duplication in the two sets of bundles.
19.3.3. All authorities on which the parties intend to rely at the substantive hearing should be included in the bundles of authorities, even if those authorities were filed at Court with the claim form, acknowledgement of service or detailed grounds. The Court will not necessarily have the permission or earlier bundles available at the substantive hearing.

19.4. SANCTION FOR NON-COMPLIANCE

1BA-116   **19.4.1.** If the bundle of authorities does not comply with this guidance, or is served late, the Court may refuse to allow the party in default to rely on those authorities, may require the bundle to be adjusted to meet the Court's requirements, and/or may make an adverse costs order against the party in default (see paragraph 23.1 of this Guide on costs).

20.   EVIDENCE

20.1. WITNESS EVIDENCE

1BA-117   **20.1.1.** Witness statements must comply with the CPR.[1] Specifically, they must
20.1.1.1. Be in the witness' own words;
20.1.1.2. State that person's full name and address;
20.1.1.3. State which of the statements in it are made from the witness' own knowledge, and which are matters of information or belief (also stating what is the source of matters of information or belief);
20.1.1.4. Be produced on A4 paper, and legible, with numbered pages and paragraphs.
20.1.2. Witness statements must include a statement of truth in the following terms: "*I believe that the facts stated in this witness statement are true*". The witness must not sign that statement of truth unless he or she holds an honest belief in the truth of the statements made in the witness statement.
20.1.3. Proceedings for contempt of Court may be brought against a person if he or she makes

---

[1] CPR PD 32.17-25

or causes to be made a false statement in a document verified by a statement of truth, without an honest belief in its truth.[1]

20.1.4. In judicial review proceedings, it is rare for a witness to be called to give oral evidence: see paragraph 10.2 of this Guide.

20.2. EXPERT EVIDENCE

20.2.1. Sometimes a party will wish to rely on expert evidence to advance its case although this is **1BA-118** unusual in judicial review.

20.2.2. Expert evidence must be restricted to that which is reasonably required to resolve the proceedings.[2]

20.2.3. Experts owe an overriding duty to the Court. It is the duty of an expert to help the Court on matters which are within their expertise. That duty overrides any obligation owed to the person from whom the expert received instructions or by whom the expert was paid.[3]

21. SANCTIONS

21.1. The Court has at its disposal various means to enforce compliance with the CPR, Practice **1BA-119** Directions and Court orders. The following is a summary. Details of the various means, and when they may be used, are set out elsewhere in this Guide.

21.2. COSTS SANCTIONS

21.2.1. So far as costs sanctions are concerned, the Court has a discretion on whether to award **1BA-120** costs to or against a party. The Court can sanction non-compliance by ordering the party in default to pay the other side's costs, or by disallowing the costs by the party in default even if that party is successful in the claim (see paragraph 23.1 of this Guide).

21.2.2. The Court can make a wasted costs order in appropriate circumstances, if the non-compliance has been the fault of the party's legal representatives. A wasted costs order falls to be paid by those legal representatives (see paragraph 23.13 of this Guide).

21.2.3. If the Court does make a costs order in favour of one of the parties, the Court can order that costs should be paid on the "indemnity" basis, which means that in quantifying those costs, the party in whose favour the order has been made gets the benefit of the doubt on any question going to the reasonableness or proportionality of those costs (see paragraph 23.2.4 of this Guide).

21.3. PROCEDURAL SANCTIONS

21.3.1. If Court documents are filed out of time according to the CPR, Practice Directions, or **1BA-121** the Court's directions, that party must file an application for an extension of time. The Court will only grant that extension if it is satisfied that it is appropriate to do so, according to the rules (see paragraphs 12.7 and 12.9 of this Guide)

21.3.2. If no extension of time is granted, the party in default will not be able to rely on the late-filed documents, and that may be to that party's disadvantage. If the Court does grant an extension of time, it may be on the basis that the party in default should pay some or all of the other party's costs (see paragraph 23.1 of this Guide).

21.3.3. If there are no directions in place relating to the serving and filing of documents, but nonetheless documents are filed late (for example a skeleton argument on an application for directions), then the Court may refuse to consider those documents, which may disadvantage the party which seeks to rely on them (see, for example, paragraphs 17.5 and 18.4 of this Guide).

21.4. OTHER SANCTIONS

21.4.1. The Court can summon before it professional representatives who appear to have abused **1BA-122** the procedure for urgent consideration pursuant to *Hamid*, and if not satisfied of the explanation given, may refer those professional representatives to their disciplinary body with a view to further action being taken (see paragraph 16.5 of this Guide).

---

[1] CPR 32.14

[2] CPR 35.1. See also CPR 54.16.8 for guidance on the circumstances when expert evidence may be admissible in a claim for judicial review.

[3] CPR 35.3

PART D:—ENDING THE CLAIM

22. Ending a Claim

22.1. INTRODUCTION

1BA-123   Once a claim has been started then there are a set number of ways to end the claim. They broadly fit into three categories: where the case is determined by the Court, where the case is discontinued and where the case is settled by consent. A claim cannot be ended by simply writing to the Court asking to withdraw the claim.

22.2. DETERMINED BY THE COURT

1BA-124   Where the Court makes a final determination, and produces a Court order, the case will have concluded in the Administrative Court (subject only to an appeal to the Court of Appeal, see CPR Part 52 and chapter 25 of this Guide). Such a determination will generally be one of the following:

22.2.1. Permission to apply for judicial review is refused (either at an oral hearing or on the papers where the claim is held to be totally without merit or reconsideration is not requested).

22.2.2. The substantive claim is dismissed.

22.2.3. The substantive claim is allowed.

22.3. DISCONTINUANCE

1BA-125   **22.3.1.** A case may be ended by discontinuing the claim, which may be done at any point in the proceedings.[1]

22.3.2. Discontinuance requires the claimant to file a notice of discontinuance (form N279) and serve it on all parties.[2] There is no Court fee payable when discontinuing.

22.3.3. The claimant may discontinue the claim in relation to all or some of the parties.[3]

22.3.4. The Court's permission is required to discontinue where the claimant has obtained an interim injunction[4] or any party has given an undertaking to the Court.[5] This can be done by filing the notice of discontinuance, referring to the fact that permission is required, and the ACO will forward the notice to a judge to give permission without a hearing (unless the judge orders a hearing and representations). In other cases, permission is not required.

22.3.5. The discontinuance will take effect from the date on which the notice of discontinuance is served on the defendant(s).[6]

22.3.6. By filing a notice of discontinuance the claimant accepts that he/she is liable for the defendant's costs up until that date[7] (unless the parties have agreed a different costs order) and a costs order will be deemed to have been made on the standard basis[8] (see paragraph 23.2.3 of this Guide). The claimant may apply to reverse the general rule that they are liable for costs and/or may claim their costs. Any such application must demonstrate a good reason for departing from the general rule. A good reason will normally exist if the defendant has behaved unreasonably. Any such application must be made in accordance with the interim applications procedure (see paragraph 12.7 of this Guide).

22.4. CONSENT ORDERS AND UNCONTESTED PROCEEDINGS

1BA-126   **22.4.1.** Subject to the approval of the Court, the parties may agree to end the claim by filing two copies of a draft, agreed order with the ACO, together with a short statement of the matters relied on as justifying the proposed agreed order and copies of any authorities or statutory provisions relied on, and accompanied by the relevant fee.[9] The Court will only approve the order if it is satisfied that the order should be made; if not so satisfied, a hearing date may be set.

22.4.2. The terms of the order can include anything that the parties wish the Court to approve, but will generally include the following:

22.4.2.1. The draft order must note (often in the header to the order as well as in the recitals) that the order is made 'By Consent'.[10]

---

[1] CPR 38.2(1)
[2] CPR 38.3(1)
[3] CPR 38.2(3)
[4] CPR 38.2(2)(i)
[5] CPR 38.2(2)(ii)
[6] CPR 38.5(1)
[7] CPR 38.6(1)
[8] CPR 44.9(1)(c)
[9] CPR PD 54A paragraph 17. See Annex 2 of this Guide for the fee.
[10] CPR 40.6(7)(b)

22.4.2.2. The draft order must be signed by the legal representative for every party to the claim (including interested parties), or by the party themselves where they are acting in person.[1]

22.4.2.3. Where the claim has been finally determined the consent order must detail the manner of determination, which includes:

22.4.2.3.1. The claim is 'withdrawn'. The effect of this is to leave the challenged decision in place (unless the defendant has voluntarily withdrawn the decision, thus removing the claimant's need to obtain the relief of the Court).

22.4.3. The parties agree that the decision challenged should be quashed (see paragraph 11.3 of this Guide). The consent order should make provision for determining costs, otherwise a deemed costs order will apply (see paragraph 23.8 of this Guide for deemed costs orders). This is generally done in one of three ways:

22.4.3.1. By providing for an agreed, set sum to be paid between the parties.

22.4.3.2. By allowing the parties to agree the quantum of costs after the consent order has been finalised, with a fall-back option of applying for detailed assessment of costs, for example – the Claimant is to pay the Defendant's reasonable costs, to be subject to detailed assessment if not agreed (see paragraph 23.3.4 of this Guide for detailed assessment).

22.4.3.3. By making provision for summary assessment of costs on the papers. Such a provision should follow the ACO Costs Guidance, which is outlined at paragraph 23.5 of this Guide.

22.4.3.4. Where the agreement relates to an order for costs only, the parties need only file a document signed by all the parties setting out the terms of the proposed order (a fee is payable).

22.5. SETTLEMENTS ON BEHALF OF CHILDREN AND PROTECTED PARTIES

22.5.1. Where a claim is made by or on behalf of, or against, a child or a protected party[2] no settlement, compromise or payment and no acceptance of money paid into Court shall be valid without the approval of the Court.[3] **1BA-127**

22.5.2. To obtain the Court's approval, an application must be made in accordance with the procedure described at paragraph 12.7 of this Guide.

22.6. OTHER POINTS OF PRACTICE

22.6.1. The parties have an obligation to inform the Court if they believe that a case is likely to settle as soon as they become aware of the possibility of settlement.[4] Such information allows judges and staff to allocate preparation time and hearing time accordingly. Failure to do so may result in the Court making an adverse costs order against the parties (see paragraph 23.1 of this Guide for costs). **1BA-128**

22.6.2. When a case is closed by the ACO the file may be immediately reduced in size for storage (or "broken up"). Particulars of claim and witness statements are retained on the closed file but all exhibits, written evidence, and authorities are confidentially destroyed. The reduced file is retained for three years after the case is closed before it too is confidentially destroyed.

23. COSTS

23.1. LIABILITY FOR COSTS

23.1.1. The Court has a discretion as to whether costs are payable by one party to another.[5] There are provisions which guide this discretion. **1BA-129**

23.1.2. Where the Court decides to make an order for costs, the general rule is that the unsuccessful party will be ordered to pay the costs of the successful party, subject to the abovementioned discretion of the Court.[6]

23.1.3. In deciding whether to make an order contrary to the general rule, the Court must have regard to all the circumstances of the case, including the conduct of the parties and whether a party has succeeded on part of his or her case even if he/she has not been wholly successful.

23.1.4. The conduct of the parties includes (but is not limited to):[7]

23.1.4.1. Conduct before as well as during the proceedings, and in particular the extent to

---

[1] CPR PD 54A paragraph 17(1).

[2] CPR 21.1

[3] CPR 21.10

[4] *Yell Ltd v Garton* [2004] C.P. Rep. 29

[5] s.51(1) of the Senior Courts Act 1981 and CPR 44.2(1)

[6] CPR 44.2(2)(a) and *R. (M) v Croydon London Borough Council* [2012] EWCA Civ 595, at paragraphs 58 – 65. The fact that one party is publicly funded is "not necessarily irrelevant" to the exercise of discretion on costs, see *ZN (Afghanistan) v SSHD* [2018] EWCA Civ 1059 at [91]-[92] and [106].

[7] *R (KR) v Secretary of State for the Home Department* [2012] EWCA Civ 1555

which the parties followed the pre-action Protocol (see paragraph 5.2 of this Guide).

23.1.4.2. Whether it was reasonable for a party to raise, pursue or contest a particular allegation or issue.

23.1.4.3. The manner in which a party has pursued or defended his/her case and whether he/she has wholly or partly exaggerated his claim.

23.1.5. As a result of the provisions above, where a party has failed to comply with orders of the Court or other procedural rules (such as those outlined in this Guide) the Court may reduce the amount of costs to which a successful party would normally be entitled. Further, in such a scenario, a liable party may be required to pay more than would normally be considered to be reasonable had the breach of the provision not occurred.

23.1.6. Liability to pay costs is not necessarily an all or nothing decision and a judge may require one party to pay a percentage of the other party's costs, thus deciding that the losing party is, for example, liable to pay 80% of the other party's costs. A successful party's costs may be reduced if they lose on one or more of the issues in the case but there is no rule requiring a reduction in these circumstances.

23.2. REASONABLE COSTS AND THE BASIS OF THE ASSESSMENT

1BA-130 **23.2.1.** The Court will not allow costs which have been unreasonably incurred or are unreasonable in amount.[1] In determining if costs are reasonable the Court will have regard to all the circumstances of the case.[2]

23.2.2. The basis of the assessment is important when determining whether the costs claimed are reasonable. In determining the basis of the assessment the Court has two options; the standard basis or on an indemnity basis.

23.2.3. The Standard Basis

23.2.3.1. Most costs orders are made on the standard basis. Where a Court is silent as to the basis on which it is assessing costs, the presumption is that assessment is on the standard basis.[3]

23.2.3.2. Where the amount of costs is to be assessed on the standard basis, the Court will only allow costs which are proportionate to the matters in issue. Where there is doubt as to whether costs were reasonable and proportionate in amount the Court will determine the question in favour of the paying party.[4] Costs incurred are proportionate[5] if they bear a reasonable relationship to:

23.2.3.2.1. The sums in issue in the proceedings;

23.2.3.2.2. The value of any non-monetary relief in issue in the proceedings;

23.2.3.2.3. The complexity of the litigation;

23.2.3.2.4. Any additional work generated by the conduct of the paying party; and

23.2.3.2.5. Any wider factors involved in the proceedings, such as reputation or public importance.

23.2.4. The Indemnity Basis

23.2.4.1. This basis is reserved as a sanction. The Court will apply indemnity costs in those cases where the losing party has acted unreasonably in bringing or maintaining the claim or in any other way.

23.2.4.2. Where the amount of costs is to be assessed on an indemnity basis, the Court will resolve any doubt which it may have as to whether costs were reasonably incurred or were reasonable in amount in favour of the receiving party.[6] There is no requirement that the costs be proportionate, as appears in the standard basis assessment.

23.3. MANNER OF ASSESSMENT AND POTENTIAL COSTS ORDERS

1BA-131 **23.3.1.** Where the Court orders a party to pay costs to another party, it may either make a summary assessment of the costs or order detailed assessment of the costs.[7]

23.3.2. Where the Court does not proceed to summary assessment and does not mention the manner of assessment in a costs order then the costs order is presumed to order detailed assessment.[8]

23.3.3. Summary Assessment

23.3.3.1. Summary assessment involves a judge determining the amount of costs payable by the liable party. The judge will then make an order for the amount of costs to be paid, for example: The Claimant is to pay the Defendant's costs in the sum of £5,000.

23.3.3.2. The parties must lodge a statement of costs not less than 24 hours before the hearing at which costs will be assessed or with the papers where an application is to be determined without

---

[1] CPR 44.3(1)
[2] CPR 44.4(1)
[3] CPR 44.3(4)(a)
[4] CPR 44.3(2)
[5] According to CPR 44.3(5)
[6] CPR 44.3(3)
[7] CPR 44.6(1)
[8] CPR PD 44 paragraph 8.2

a hearing (unless a judge has ordered a different timescale).[1]

23.3.3.3. The Court is not entitled to summarily assess the costs of a receiving party who is a child or protected party unless the legal representative acting for the child or protected party has waived the right to further costs.[2]

23.3.3.4. Unless a judge orders otherwise, any costs order must be complied with within 14 days of the costs order,[3] although the parties may vary this time limit and agree their own payment terms without seeking the agreement of the Court.

23.3.4. Detailed Assessment

23.3.4.1. Detailed assessment involves a costs judge considering the claim for costs in accordance with the procedure in CPR Part 47. Guidance on the procedure can be found in the Senior Courts Costs Office Guide, which can be found online at the following website;
https://www.gov.uk/government/publications/senior-courts-costs-office-guide.

23.3.4.2. Where detailed assessment has been ordered by the Administrative Court in London, the application for detailed assessment of costs must be started at the Senior Courts Costs Office in London.

23.3.4.3. Where detailed assessment has been ordered by any of the Administrative Courts outside of London, the application for detailed assessment of costs must be started in the District Registry associated with the relevant ACO. For example, a judicial review determined by the Administrative Court in Cardiff would result in any detailed costs assessment being started in the District Registry in Cardiff Civil Justice Centre.[4] Western Circuit cases administered by the ACO in Cardiff but heard on the Western Circuit must also be lodged in the District Registry in Cardiff.

23.3.4.4. It should be noted that detailed assessment proceedings cease to be Administrative Court proceedings and a new case number will be assigned to the proceedings. The ACO will not have any further involvement with the case.

23.4. COSTS AT THE PERMISSION STAGE

23.4.1. There is a discrete procedure on applying for and considering costs when a judge is considering permission to apply for judicial review, although this procedure may be varied by judicial order:[5]   **1BA-132**

23.4.1.1. If permission has been granted, either on the papers or at an oral hearing, then the claimant's costs are deemed to be costs in the case, and the question of whether the claimant will be able to recover those costs will depend on the outcome of the case.

23.4.1.2. Where a proposed defendant or interested party wishes to seek costs at the permission stage, the acknowledgment of service should include an application for costs and should be accompanied by a schedule setting out the amount claimed;

23.4.1.3. The judge, if refusing permission on the papers, should include in the refusal a decision whether to award costs in principle or not, and an indication of the amount which he/she proposes to assess summarily. This will be a final order on costs unless representations in writing are filed as per the procedure below.[6]

23.4.1.4. The claimant or defendant should be given 14 days to respond in writing to the in principle costs order and should serve a copy on the other parties.

23.4.1.5. The other parties will normally have 14 days to reply in writing to any such response, and to the order proposed by the judge;

23.4.1.6. Any submissions on costs that are filed in accordance with the above will be put before a judge to consider and make an award on the papers. If the Claimant also seeks reconsideration of the refusal of permission at an oral hearing then any objections to costs that have been previously ordered may be considered at the renewal hearing. The Court may confirm or vary the earlier order as to costs.

23.4.1.7. If the parties file costs representations outside of the above time limits they must apply for an extension of time to file the costs submissions in accordance with the procedure at paragraph 12.7 of this Guide.

23.4.2. If permission to apply for judicial review is refused there are additional principles which the Court will generally apply:[7]

23.4.2.1. A successful defendant or other party at the permission stage who has filed an acknowledgment of service should generally recover the costs of doing so from the claimant, whether or not they attend any permission hearing.

23.4.2.2. A defendant or other party who attends and successfully resists the grant of permission at a renewal hearing should not generally recover from the claimant the costs of attending, but

---

[1] CPR PD 44 paragraph 9.5(4)(b)
[2] CPR PD 44 paragraph 9.9
[3] CPR 44.7(1)(a)
[4] *Public Services Ombudsman for Wales v Heesom* [2015] EWHC 3306 (QB)
[5] *R. (Ewing) v Office of the Deputy Prime Minister* [2006] 1 W.L.R. 1260
[6] See *R (Jones) v Nottingham City Council* [2009] EWHC 271 (Admin)
[7] *R. (Mount Cook Land Ltd) v Westminster City Council* [2004] C.P. Rep. 12

will still be entitled to the costs of preparing the acknowledgment of service.[1]

23.4.2.3. A Court, in considering an award of costs against an unsuccessful claimant at a permission hearing, should only depart from the general principles above if it is considered that there are exceptional circumstances for doing so.

23.4.2.4. Exceptional circumstances may consist in the presence of one or more of the features in the following non-exhaustive list:

23.4.2.4.1. The hopelessness of the claim.

23.4.2.4.2. The persistence in it by the claimant after having been alerted to facts and/or of the law demonstrating its hopelessness.

23.4.2.4.3. The extent to which the Court considers that the claimant, in the pursuit of his application, has sought to abuse the process of judicial review (see paragraph 12.10.3 of this Guide for examples of abuse of process).

23.4.2.4.4. Whether, as a result of the deployment of full argument and documentary evidence by both sides at the hearing, the unsuccessful claimant has had, in effect, the advantage of an early substantive hearing of the claim.

23.4.2.4.5. Whether the unsuccessful claimant has substantial resources which it has used to pursue the unfounded claim and which are available to meet an order for costs.

23.4.2.4.6. Whether the permission was refused at a rolled up hearing, in which event the defendant, who has prepared for a substantive hearing, may be awarded costs.

23.5. COSTS AFTER SETTLING

1BA-133

23.5.1. The onus lies on the parties to reach agreement on costs wherever possible and in advance of asking the Court to resolve costs (in order to support the overriding objective and ensure that efficient use is made of Court time). The parties should not, therefore, make submissions to the Court on costs following a compromise of proceedings without first seeking to agree costs through reasoned negotiation, mindful of the overriding objective to the CPR, the amount of costs actually at stake, and the principles set out in *M v Croydon* [2012] EWCA Civ 595, paragraphs 59-63.

23.5.2. In considering costs as part of a settlement, the parties should bear in mind that the Court may already have decided the issue of costs of the application for permission. Where this decision amounts to a final order (see procedure outlined above at paragraph 23.4.1) the Court should not be asked to revisit those costs in any submissions on costs following settlement.

23.5.3. Where a claim has settled (see paragraph 22.4 of this Guide) but the parties have been unable to agree costs, the parties should follow the ACO Costs Guidance dated April 2016 which is reproduced at annex 5 to this Guide.

23.5.4. In accordance with that Costs Guidance (see paragraph 23.5.3 and annex 5 to this Guide), the costs section of the consent order should state:

23.5.4.1. Within 28 days of the order, the defendant may file with the Court and serve on all other parties, submissions as to what the appropriate costs order should be. If the defendant does not file submissions, the order will be that the defendant will pay the claimant's costs of the claim on the standard basis, to be the subject of detailed assessment if not agreed.

23.5.4.2. Where the defendant does file submissions within 28 days, the claimant or any other party may file and serve submissions within 14 days of service of those submissions. If neither the claimant nor any other party files such submissions in response, the costs order will be in the terms sought by the defendant.

23.5.4.3. Where submissions are filed by the claimant or any other party, the defendant shall have 7 days in which to file and serve a reply. The matter shall then be put before the judge for a decision on costs or further order.

23.5.5. In accordance with that Costs Guidance (see paragraph 23.5.3 and annex 5 to this Guide), the submissions must:

23.5.5.1. Confirm that the parties have used reasonable endeavours to negotiate a costs settlement.

23.5.5.2. Identify what issues or reasons prevented the parties agreeing costs liability.

23.5.5.3. State the approximate amount of costs likely to be involved in the case.

23.5.5.4. Identify the extent to which the parties complied with the pre-action Protocol.

23.5.5.5. State the relief the claimant sought (i) in the claim form and (ii) obtained.

23.5.5.6. Address specifically how the claim and the basis of its settlement fit the principles in *M v Croydon London Borough Council* and *Tesfay* [2016] EWCA Civ 415 (see paragraph 23.5.6 below), including the relationship of any step taken by the defendant to the claim.

23.5.6. In accordance with that Costs Guidance, the submissions must be made in documentation as outlined below:

23.5.6.1. Submissions should be of a normal print size and should not normally exceed two A4 pages in length unless there is good reason to exceed this, which is properly explained in the submissions.

---

[1] See *R (Davey) v Aylesbury Vale DC (Practice Note)* [2008] 1 WLR 878

23.5.6.2. Submissions should be accompanied by the pre-action Protocol correspondence (where this has not previously been included as part of the documents supporting the claim), the correspondence in which the costs claim is made and defended, along with any other correspondence necessary to demonstrate why the claim was brought in the light of the pre-action Protocol correspondence or why the step which led to settlement was not taken until after the claim was issued.

23.5.6.3. Unless advised otherwise, the parties should assume that the Court has the claim papers originally lodged by the parties. Further copies of these should not be provided unless requested by the Court.

23.5.7. The following is a short summary of how the Court will consider what order on costs to make, based on *M v Croydon London Borough Council* and *Tesfay*.

23.5.7.1. Where a claimant has been wholly successful in terms of the relief sought the claimant will generally recover all his/her costs, unless there is some good reason to the contrary.

23.5.7.2. Where a claimant has only succeeded in part the judge will normally determine how reasonable the claimant was in pursuing the unsuccessful relief (the defendant has refused to adhere to the demands of the claimant but the claim has settled anyway), how important the unsuccessful relief was compared with the successful relief, and how much the costs were increased as a result of the claimant pursuing the unsuccessful relief.

23.5.7.3. Where there has been some compromise which does not actually reflect the claimant's claims the default position will generally be no order for costs. However, in some cases, the judge may look at the underlying claim and inquire whether it was tolerably clear who would have won if the matter had not settled. If it is, then that may well strongly support the contention that the party who would have won did better out of the settlement, and therefore did win.

23.6. INTERESTED PARTIES AND COSTS

23.6.1. The Court does not generally order an unsuccessful claimant to pay two sets of costs of the substantive claim (typically the costs incurred by the defendant and an interested party), although the Court may order two sets of costs to be paid, in particular where the defendant and the interested party have different interests which require separate representation.[1] If the claimant is acting in the public interest rather than out of personal gain then it is less likely that the court will order the second set of costs.[2] **1BA-134**

23.6.2. The Court may, however, and often does, order an unsuccessful claimant to pay two sets of costs of preparing acknowledgements of service at the permission stage.[3]

23.7. INTERVENERS AND COSTS

23.7.1. A person may apply to file evidence or make representations at a hearing[4] (see paragraph 2.2.4 of this Guide). Such a person is commonly referred to as an intervener and there are specific rules governing whether an intervener can recover its costs or be ordered to pay costs, summarised below.[5] **1BA-135**

23.7.2. A relevant party, that is to say a claimant or defendant in substantive or permission judicial review proceedings,[6] cannot be ordered to pay an intervener's costs[7] unless there are exceptional circumstances that make such a costs order appropriate.[8]

23.7.3. If the Court is satisfied that any one of four conditions is met, the Court must order the intervener to pay any costs specified in an application by a claimant or defendant that the Court considers have been incurred by them as a result of the intervener's involvement in that stage of the proceedings.[9] The four conditions are:

23.7.3.1. The intervener has acted, in substance, as the sole or principal applicant, defendant, appellant or respondent.

23.7.3.2. The intervener's evidence and representations, taken as a whole, have not been of significant assistance to the Court.

23.7.3.3. A significant part of the intervener's evidence and representations relates to matters that it is not necessary for the Court to consider in order to resolve the issues that are the subject of the stage in the proceedings.

23.7.3.4. The intervener has behaved unreasonably.

---

[1] *Bolton MDC v Secretary of State for the Environment* [1995] 1 WLR 1176

[2] *R (John Smeaton on behalf of Society for the Protection of Unborn Children) v The Secretary of State for Health* [2002] EWHC 886 (Admin), paragraphs 31 – 41.

[3] *R (Luton Borough Council) v Central Bedfordshire Council* [2014] EWHC 4325 (Admin)

[4] CPR 54.17

[5] s.87 of the Criminal Justice and Courts Act 2015

[6] See above, s.87(9) and (10)

[7] See above, s.87(3)

[8] See above, s.87(4)

[9] See above, s.87(5)

23.7.4. If the intervener becomes a party, the costs provisions above no longer apply and are deemed never to have applied.[1]

23.8. ORDERS WHICH DO NOT MENTION COSTS

1BA-136   **23.8.1.** Where an order does not mention costs then a deemed costs order is presumed to have been made. There are two scenarios in the Administrative Court where deemed costs orders apply. Those two scenarios are:

23.8.1.1. Subject to paragraph 23.8.1.2 below, where an order is silent as to costs and makes no provision for how costs are to be assessed, then the Court is deemed to have ordered that there be no order for costs.[2]

23.8.1.2. Where the Court makes an order granting permission to appeal, an order granting permission to apply for judicial review, or any other order or direction sought by a party on an application without notice, and the order does not mention costs, it will be deemed to include an order that the costs are in the case, and will be determined according to the outcome of the claim.[3]

23.8.2. Any party may apply to vary the deemed costs order made in accordance with paragraph 23.8.1.2 above (but not 23.8.1.1).[4] Such an application must be made in accordance with the interim orders procedure (see paragraph 12.7 of this Guide).

23.9. SETTING ASIDE COSTS ORDERS

1BA-137   Save for deemed costs orders (see paragraph 23.8.2 above) any costs order where the parties have had the opportunity to make representations before the order was made, be that a costs order on the papers or after an oral hearing, is a final costs order.[5] The Administrative Court may not set it aside or reconsider the order at a hearing. If challenged, the order must be appealed (see chapter 25 of this Guide for appeals).

23.10. COSTS WHEN THE CLAIMANT HAS THE BENEFIT OF LEGAL AID

1BA-138   **23.10.1.** Costs orders can be made against persons who have the benefit of legal aid (subject to the principles discussed earlier in this section of the Guide). Where the Court does make such an order it will order that the person with the benefit of legal aid must pay the costs of the requesting party and the Court may set the amount to be paid, but the Court will note that the person with the benefit of legal aid is subject to costs protection in accordance with s.26 of the Legal Aid, Sentencing, and Punishment of Offenders Act 2012.

23.10.2. As a result of the costs protection, the person with the benefit of legal aid is not automatically liable for the costs. If the person awarded costs wishes to require the person with the benefit of legal aid to pay those costs they must apply for an order from the Senior Courts Costs Office or, where the costs order was made by an Administrative Court not in London, he/she must apply to the relevant associated District Registry.

23.11. COSTS FROM CENTRAL FUNDS (CRIMINAL CASES)

1BA-139   **23.11.1.** In judicial reviews relating to a criminal cause or matter, where a claimant is successful, a Divisional Court may make a costs order, which shall be for payment out of central funds (that is to say, it will be paid by the Ministry of Justice).[6]

23.11.2. The costs order is made in such amount as the Court considers reasonably sufficient to compensate for any expenses properly incurred in the proceedings, unless the Court considers that there are circumstances that make it inappropriate to recover the full amount when the Court may order a lesser amount in a sum the Court considers just and reasonable.

23.11.3. The costs order may not require the payment out of central funds of an amount that includes legal costs unless those costs were incurred in proceedings in the Court below (Magistrates' Court or Crown Court on appeal against conviction or sentence).

23.11.4. There is no power for a single judge to order costs be paid out of central funds. Where a claimant seeks an order for costs from central funds when appearing before a single judge, the judge will adjourn the matter to be considered on the papers by a Divisional Court, constituted of the single judge who heard the case and another judge.

23.11.5. When making the costs order, the Court will fix the amount to be paid out of central

---

[1] See above, s.87(11)

[2] CPR 44.10(1)(a)(i)

[3] CPR 44.10(2)

[4] CPR 44.10(3)

[5] *R. (Jones) v Nottingham City Council* [2009] A.C.D. 42 and *R. (Bahta) v Secretary of State for the Home Department* [2011] C.P. Rep. 43

[6] s16(6) and 17 of the Prosecution of Offences Act 1985

funds in the order if it considers it appropriate to do so.[1] Where the Court does not fix the amount to be paid out of central funds in the order it must describe in the order any reduction required and the amount must be fixed by means of a determination made by or on behalf of the Court by the Senior Courts Costs Office.[2]

23.11.6. If the claimant has the benefit of a representation order or a legal aid certificate (see paragraph 3.5.4 of this Guide) then he/she cannot claim costs out of central funds.[3]

23.11.7. Where an order for costs from central funds has been made the claimant must forward the order to the Senior Courts Costs Office, which will arrange for payment of the amount specified.

23.12. COSTS AGAINST COURTS OR TRIBUNALS OR CORONERS

Where the defendant in judicial review proceedings is a Court, Tribunal or Coroner, the Administrative Court will generally not make costs orders against the defendant where the defendant has not acted obstructively or improperly and only makes representations neutrally on the procedure or law. In such cases, it will often be appropriate for the Court to make a costs order against the interested party (see paragraph 2.2.3 of this Guide) which took the underlying administrative decision that generated the proceedings before the Court or Tribunal whose decision is challenged. For example, in judicial review proceedings against the Upper Tribunal in immigration cases, the Court may make a costs order against the Secretary of State for the Home Department who will generally be named as an interested party. Where a Court, Tribunal or Coroner does contest the claim, it become liable for costs, subject to the principles discussed in this section of the Guide.[4] **1BA-140**

23.13. WASTED COSTS ORDERS

23.13.1. In appropriate cases the Court has power to order that a legal representative should pay the costs of an opposing party or that a specified sum for costs is disallowed.[5] These orders are referred to as wasted costs orders. **1BA-141**

23.13.2. A wasted costs order may be made against the receiving party's own legal representatives or against the representatives of the paying party.[6]

23.13.3. An application for a wasted costs order may be made by the party who suffered the wasted costs or may be ordered of the Court's own volition.

23.13.4. When considering whether to make a wasted costs order, the Court will consider three points:[7]

23.13.4.1. Did the legal representative (or any employee of the representative) act improperly, unreasonably or negligently?

23.13.4.2. If so, did the conduct cause the party who incurred the costs to incur unnecessary costs or has the conduct caused costs incurred by a party prior to the conduct to be wasted?

23.13.4.3. If so, is it just in all the circumstances to order the legal representative to compensate the subject of the wasted costs for the whole or part of the relevant costs?

23.13.5. The Court will give the legal representative a reasonable opportunity to make written submissions or, if the legal representative prefers, to attend a hearing before it makes such an order.[8]

23.13.6. Unless there is good reason otherwise, wasted costs applications should generally be considered by the Court at the end of proceedings.[9]

23.14. COSTS WHERE A PARTY IS REPRESENTED PRO BONO

Section 194 of the Legal Services Act 2007 makes provision for the recovery of costs where the representation has been provided pro bono (free of charge to the represented party), see paragraph 3.5.6 of this Guide.[10] Where such an order is made, the costs awarded in favour of that party will not be payable to the party's legal representatives but to a charity, the Access to Justice Foundation. **1BA-142**

---

[1] See above, s.16(6C)

[2] See above, s.16(6D)

[3] See above, s.21(4A)

[4] *R (Faqiri) v The Upper Tribunal (Immigration and Asylum Chamber) v The Secretary of State for the Home Department* [2019] EWCA Civ 151

[5] s.51(6) of the Senior Courts Act 1981 and CPR 46.8

[6] *Brown v Bennett* [2002] 2 All ER 273

[7] CPR PD 46 paragraph 5.5 and *Re a Barrister Wasted Costs Order) (No 1 of 1991)* [1993] QB 293

[8] CPR 46.8(2)

[9] *Filmlab Systems International Ltd v Pennington* [1994] 4 All ER 673

[10] CPR 46.7

24.   JUDICIAL REVIEW COSTS CAPPING ORDERS

24.1.   INTRODUCTION

1BA-143   A judicial review cost capping order ("JRCCO")[1] may take a number of forms. Usually, the order will specify a limit on the amount that a claimant can be ordered to pay in respect of the other side's costs if the claimant loses (e.g the claimant's liability for costs will be capped at £5,000). Where a JRCCO is granted the order must be coupled with an order placing a limit on the amount that a claimant who is successful can recover from a defendant even if the claimant ultimately wins the case (sometimes called a reciprocal costs capping order).[2]

24.2.   JRCCOS: GENERAL PRINCIPLES

1BA-144   **24.2.1.** A JRCCO may only be granted after permission to apply for judicial review has been granted (see paragraph 8.2.2 of this Guide);[3]

24.2.2. A JRCCO may only be applied for by a claimant, not a defendant, interested party, or intervener;[4]

24.2.3. The court may only make a JRCCO if it is satisfied that:[5]

24.2.3.1. The proceedings are public interest proceedings. Public interest proceedings are defined[6] to mean that the issue which is the subject of the proceedings is of general public importance. Further, the public interest requires the issue to be resolved and the proceedings are likely to provide an appropriate means of resolving it. When considering this issue, the court must have regard[7] to the number of people likely to be directly affected if relief is granted, how significant the effect on those people is likely to be, and whether the proceedings involve considera-tion of a point of law of general public importance.

24.2.3.2. In the absence of the order, the claimant would withdraw the application for judicial review or cease to participate in the proceedings and it would be reasonable to do so.

24.2.4. The court must have regard,[8] when considering whether to make a JRCCO, to the following:

24.2.4.1. Whether, in the absence of the order, the claimant would withdraw the application for judicial review or cease to participate in the proceedings and it would be reasonable to do so.

24.2.4.2. The financial resources of the parties to the proceedings, including the financial resources of any person who provides, or may provide, financial support to the parties;

24.2.4.3. The extent to which the claimant is likely to benefit if relief is granted (see chapter 11 of this guide for final remedies);

24.2.4.4. The extent to which any person who has provided, or may provide, the applicant with financial support is likely to benefit if relief is granted;

24.2.4.5. Whether legal representatives for the applicant for the order are acting free of charge; and

24.2.4.6. Whether the claimant is an appropriate person to represent the interests of other persons or the public interest generally.

24.3.   JRCCOS: PROCEDURE[9]

1BA-145   **24.3.1.** An application for a JRCCO must normally be contained in the claim form at section 8 or it must accompany the claim form in a separate document.[10]

24.3.2. The application must be supported by evidence setting out:[11]

24.3.2.1. Why a JRCCO should be made, having regard, in particular, to the matters at paragraph 24.2.3 and 24.2.4 above.

---

[1] Defined in s.88(2) of the Criminal Justice and Courts Act 2015 as" an order limiting or remov-ing the liability of a party to judicial review proceedings to pay another party's costs in connection with any stage of the proceedings".

[2] s.89(2) of the Criminal Justice and Courts Act 2015

[3] s.88(3) of the Criminal Justice and Courts Act 2015

[4] s.88(4) of the Criminal Justice and Courts Act 2015

[5] Further to s.88(6) of the Criminal Justice and Courts Act 2015

[6] s.88(7) of the Criminal Justice and Courts Act 2015

[7] Under s. 88(8) of the Criminal Justice and Courts Act 2015

[8] Further to s.89(1) of the Criminal Justice and Courts Act 2015

[9] The relevant procedure in this section of the Guide is found in the Criminal Justice and Courts Act 2015 and supplemented where appropriate by the guidance on protective costs order procedure in *R. (Corner House Research) v Trade and Industry Secretary* [2005] 1 W.L.R. 2600 and *R. (Buglife) v Thurrock Thames Gateway Development Corp* [2009] C.P. Rep. 8 at paragraphs 29 – 31.

[10] CPR PD 46 paragraph 10.2 and *R. (Corner House Research) v Trade and Industry Secretary* [2005] 1 W.L.R. 2600

[11] CPR 46.17(1)(b)

24.3.2.2. A summary of the claimant's financial resources, unless the court has dispensed with this requirement.[1] The summary must provide details of the following:[2]

24.3.2.2.1. The claimant's significant assets, liabilities, income and expenditure; and

24.3.2.2.2. Any financial support which any person has provided or is likely to provide to the claimant, the aggregate amount which has been provided and which is likely to be provided.

24.3.2.3. The costs (and disbursements) which the claimant considers the parties are likely to incur in the future conduct of the proceedings.

24.3.2.4. If the claimant is a body corporate, whether it is able to demonstrate that it is likely to have financial resources available to meet liabilities arising in connection with the proceedings. Where it cannot the court must consider giving directions for the provision of information about the body's members and their ability to provide financial support for the purpose of the proceedings.[3]

24.3.3. If the defendant wishes to resist the making of the JRCCO it should set out its reasons in the acknowledgment of service. Similarly, any representations on a reciprocal costs capping order (capping both parties' costs) should be made in the acknowledgment of service.

24.3.4. The claimant will usually be liable for defendant's costs incurred in a successful resistance to an application for a JRCCO.

24.3.5. If the judge grants permission to apply for judicial review on the papers the judge will then consider whether to make the JRCCO on the papers and if so, in what terms. If the judge does not grant permission to apply for judicial review the judge cannot make a JRCCO (see paragraph 24.2.1 above).

24.3.6. If the judge grants permission to apply for judicial review, but refuses to grant the JRCCO, and the claimant requests that the decision is reconsidered at a hearing (see paragraph 15.5 of this Guide for the procedure), that hearing should generally be limited to an hour and the claimant will face liability for costs if the JRCCO is again refused.

24.3.7. When the Court reconsiders at a hearing whether or not to make a JRCCO, the paper decision should only be revisited in exceptional circumstances.[4]

24.3.8. An application for a JRCCO can be made at any time, not just when lodging the claim, although it is discouraged. When the preferred procedure, outlined above, cannot be utilised, a party may still apply for a JRCCO. In such circumstances the application should be made in accordance with the application procedure outlined at paragraph 12.7 of this Guide.

24.4. ENVIRONMENTAL LAW CLAIMS[5]

24.4.1. There are limits on the amount of costs that a party may be ordered to pay in what are known as Aarhus Convention claims (that is, certain claims involving environmental issues). **1BA-146**

24.4.2. These provisions only apply where the claimant is a member of the public.[6] Members of the public includes natural persons, corporations and unincorporated associations[7] (see paragraphs 2.2.1.2 and 2.2.1.3 of this Guide), but does not include public bodies (see paragraph 2.2.1.4 of this Guide).

24.4.3. An Aarhus Convention claim, as far as judicial review proceedings are concerned, is a judicial review claim which deals with subject matter within the scope of articles 9(1), 9(2), or 9(3) of the Convention on Access to Information, Public Participation in Decision Making and Access to Justice in Environmental Matters ('the Aarhus Convention').[8] The convention can be found online: *http://ec.europa.eu/environment/aarhus/*

24.4.4. Where the claimant believes that his or her claim is an Aarhus Convention claim and they wish to apply for a costs cap under these provisions they must:

24.4.4.1. Note that fact in part 6 of the claim form;[9]

24.4.4.2. File and serve with the claim form a schedule of the claimant's financial resources which takes into account any financial support which any person has provided or is likely to provide to the claimant and which is verified by a statement of truth.[10]

24.4.5. If the claimant does not comply with 24.4.4 above then they are taken to have either indicated that the Aarhus Convention does not apply or that they have opted out of these costs cap-

---

[1] CPR 46.17(3)

[2] CPR PD 46 paragraph 10.1

[3] CPR 46.18

[4] *R. (Buglife) v Thurrock Thames Gateway Development Corp* [2009] C.P. Rep 8 at paragraph 31

[5] It should be noted that the provisions on costs caps in environmental law cases changed on the 28th February 2017. The provisions below reflect these changes, but for judicial claims lodged before that date the parties should refer to the old rules as outlined in the 2016 Guide.

[6] CPR 45.41(2)(a)

[7] CPR 45.41(2)(a)&(b) and article 2.4 of the Aarhus Convention

[8] CPR 45.41(2)(a)(i)&(ii)

[9] CPR 45.42(1)(a)

[10] CPR 45.42(1)(b)

ping provisions (they may also do the latter even if they indicate the convention does apply). In either case the costs cap will not apply.[1]

24.4.6. Where the claimant complies with 24.4.4 above, the costs limit is automatically in place, subject to the provisions below.[2]

24.4.7. The current costs limit is £5,000 where the claimant is claiming only as an individual and not as, or on behalf of, a business or other legal person. In all other cases the limit is £10,000. Where a defendant is ordered to pay costs, the limit is £35,000.[3]

24.4.8. The court may vary or remove the limits outlined at paragraph 24.4.7 above.[4] The court may vary such an amount or remove such a limit only if satisfied that to do so would not make the costs of the proceedings prohibitively expensive for the claimant and, in the case of a variation which would reduce a claimant's maximum costs liability or increase that of a defendant, without the variation the costs of the proceedings would be prohibitively expensive for the claimant.[5]

24.4.9. Proceedings are to be considered prohibitively expensive if the likely costs (including any court fees which are payable by the claimant) either[6] exceed the financial resources of the claimant or are objectively unreasonable having regard to:

24.4.9.1. The situation of the parties;

24.4.9.2. Whether the claimant has a reasonable prospect of success;

24.4.9.3. The importance of what is at stake for the claimant;

24.4.9.4. The importance of what is at stake for the environment;

24.4.9.5. The complexity of the relevant law and procedure; and

24.4.9.6. Whether the claim is frivolous.

24.4.10. When the court considers the financial resources of the claimant for these purposes, it must have regard to any financial support which any person has provided or is likely to provide to the claimant.[7]

24.4.11. Where the defendant intends to challenge the assertion that the Aarhus Convention applies and, therefore, that the costs limit does not apply, the procedure to challenge the assertion can be found at CPR 45.45:

24.4.11.1. The defendant must indicate if he refutes the assertion in the acknowledgment of service at section E.

24.4.11.2. The defendant must set out the defendant's grounds for such denial.

24.4.11.3. Where the defendant argues that the claim is not an Aarhus Convention claim, the Court will determine that issue at the earliest opportunity, usually at the same time as considering permission to apply for judicial review on the papers.

24.4.12. In any proceedings to determine whether the claim is an Aarhus Convention claim, as per paragraph 24.4.11 above:[8]

24.4.12.1. If the court holds that the claim is not an Aarhus Convention claim, it will normally make no order for costs in relation to those proceedings.

24.4.12.2. If the court holds that the claim is an Aarhus Convention claim, it will normally order the defendant to pay the claimant's costs of those proceedings to be assessed on the standard basis, and that order may be enforced even if this would increase the costs payable by the defendant beyond the amount stated at paragraph 24.4.7 above or any variation of that amount.

25.   APPEALS

25.1.   APPEALS IN CIVIL CASES

1BA-147   Parties may seek to appeal to the Court of Appeal. Permission to appeal is required. Appeals in civil cases are discussed below from paragraphs 25.2 – 25.4

25.2.   CHALLENGING THE GRANT OF PERMISSION

1BA-148   **25.2.1.** Where permission to bring a judicial review has been granted:

25.2.1.1. Neither the defendant nor any other person served with the claim form may apply to the Administrative Court to set aside an order giving permission to bring a judicial review.[9]

25.2.1.2. If the defendant or another interested party has not been served with the claim form, they may apply to the Administrative Court to set aside permission, but the power to set aside permission is exercised sparingly and only in a very plain case.[10]

---

[1] CPR 45.42(1)&(2)
[2] CPR 45.42(1)
[3] CPR 45.43(2)&(3)
[4] CPR 45.44(1)
[5] CPR 45.44(2)
[6] See CPR 45.44(3)
[7] CPR 45.44(4)
[8] See CPR 45.45(3)
[9] CPR 54.13
[10] See *R v Secretary of State ex p Chinoy* (1992) 4 Admin L Rep 457

25.3. APPEALS AGAINST THE REFUSAL OF PERMISSION

25.3.1. Where permission to apply for judicial review has been refused after a hearing in the **1BA-149** Administrative Court, the claimant may appeal to the Court of Appeal, but permission to appeal must be obtained from the Court of Appeal.[1]

25.3.2. Where permission has been refused by the Administrative Court on the papers, and there is no right to request reconsideration of that refusal at an oral hearing before the Administrative Court, the applicant can apply to the Court of Appeal for permission to appeal.[2]

25.3.3. An appeal (including the application for permission to appeal) against the refusal of permission to apply for judicial review must be lodged with the Court of Appeal within 7 days of the date of the decision, or within the time limit ordered by the Administrative Court.[3] This is also the case where permission has been refused and the right to renewal has been removed (cases where the Upper Tribunal is the defendant (see paragraph 8.7 of this Guide) and totally without merit cases (see paragraph 8.3 of this Guide)),[4] although in these cases the 7 days begins from the date of service of the order, not the date of the decision.[5]

25.3.4. The Court of Appeal may, instead of giving permission to appeal, give permission to apply for judicial review, in which event the case will proceed in the Administrative Court unless the Court of Appeal orders otherwise.[6]

25.4. APPEALS AGAINST SUBSTANTIVE DECISIONS

25.4.1. Permission to appeal against the Court's decision following the substantive hearing is **1BA-150** required and it can be granted by the Administrative Court. The application will need to be made at the hearing at which the decision to be appealed is made unless the court directs the application to be made later.[7] The Court may adjourn the question of permission to another date or to be considered on written representations, but it must make an order doing so at the time of the hearing.

25.4.2. In the event that permission to appeal is refused by the Administrative Court, a second application can be made to the Court of Appeal itself in the appellant's notice (form N161).[8] The application for permission can be made to the Court of Appeal even if permission to appeal was not sought from the Administrative Court. Any party seeking to appeal should submit grounds of appeal that are focused, clear and concise.[9] Parties should follow the relevant provisions of the CPR and Practice Directions on appeals

25.4.3. An appeal (including any application for permission to appeal) against a substantive decision of the Administrative Court must be lodged with the Court of Appeal within 21 days of the date of the decision or within the time limit ordered by the Administrative Court.[10]

25.4.4. Permission to appeal will only be granted if the Court finds that the appeal would have a real prospect of success or there is some other compelling reason why the appeal should be heard.[11]

25.4.5. Further information on appeals to the Court of Appeal can be provided by the Civil Appeals Office (see Annex 1 for contact details).

25.5. APPEALS IN CRIMINAL CASES

25.5.1. There is no right of appeal from the Administrative Court to the Court of Appeal in **1BA-151** cases relating to any criminal cause or matter.[12]

25.5.2. The only route of appeal from the Administrative Court is to the Supreme Court. An appeal to the Supreme Court is only possible where two conditions are satisfied. First, the Administrative Court must certify that the case raises a point of law of general public importance.[13] The second is that permission to appeal must be granted.

25.5.3. An application for permission to appeal to the Supreme Court and for a certificate of a

---

[1] CPR 52.8(1), and see *Glencore Energy UK Ltd v Commissioners of HM Revenue and Customs* [2017] EWHC 1587 (Admin)
[2] CPR 52.8(2)
[3] CPR 52.8(3)
[4] CPR 52.8(2)
[5] CPR 52.8(4)
[6] CPR 52.8(5)
[7] CPR 52.3(2)(a)
[8] CPR 52.3(3) and CPR 52.12(1)
[9] *Hickey v The Secretary of State for Work and Pensions* [2018] EWCA Civ 851
[10] CPR 52.12(2)
[11] CPR 52.6(1)
[12] s.18(1)(a) of the Senior Courts Act 1981
[13] s.1(2) of the Administration of Justice Act 1960

point of law must be made to the Administrative Court within 28 days of the decision challenged or the date when reasons for the decision are given.[1]

25.5.4. The application for a certificate of a point of law and for permission to appeal may be made in the same application. The procedure is the same as the interim applications procedure (see paragraph 12.7 of this Guide). The Court may decide to grant the certificate even if it decides to refuse permission to appeal. The certificate will be used in any application to the Supreme Court itself for permission to appeal.

25.5.5. The right of appeal to the Supreme Court applies only to substantive decisions. There is no appeal from the decision of the Court if permission to apply for judicial review is refused.[2]

25.5.6. Further information on appeals to the Supreme Court can be obtained from the Supreme Court (see Annex 1 for contact details).

25.6. APPEALING CASE MANAGEMENT ORDERS

1BA-152 **25.6.1.** The principles applied above at paragraphs 25.1 – 25.4 (for civil cases) and 25.5 (for criminal cases) apply for appeals against case management orders, although paragraph 15.5 of this Guide on reconsideration of interim orders made without a hearing should be considered before appealing.

25.6.2. The time limit for appealing remains 21 days in civil cases, but the proceedings in the Administrative Court will not necessarily await the decision of the Court of Appeal. If the parties wish the Administrative Court proceedings to be stayed pending the decision of the Court of Appeal they must apply for a stay (see paragraph 12.8 of this Guide).

25.6.3. Permission to appeal is generally granted more sparingly in appeals against case management orders as not only will the Court consider whether the appeal would have a real prospect of success or there is some other compelling reason why the appeal should be heard, but it will generally also consider the significance of the decision, the costs involved in appealing, the delay or disruption likely to be caused to the Administrative Court proceedings, and whether the point would be better dealt with at or after the substantive hearing.

25.7. APPEALS AGAINST AN INTERIM ORDER MADE BY THE MASTER

1BA-153 **25.7.1.** An appeal against the order of the Master made at an oral hearing may be appealed to a High Court Judge. If the Master's decision is made on the papers the provisions on reconsideration at paragraph 15.5 of this Guide should be considered.

25.7.2. The application for permission to appeal must be filed on form N161 and lodged with the Administrative Court Office. The parties should also consider the guidance in paragraphs 25.1 – 25.4 above, which, save for any references to the Court of Appeal, would equally apply to appeals against the Master's decisions.

ANNEX 1 –

CONTACT DETAILS

THE ADMINISTRATIVE COURT OFFICES

Website

1BA-154 *www.gov.uk/courts-tribunals/administrative-court*

Birmingham

> The Administrative Court Office
> Birmingham Civil and Family Justice Hearing Centre Priory Courts
> 33 Bull Street
> Birmingham
> West Midlands B4 6DS
> DX 701987 Birmingham 7

Telephone Number: 0121 681 4441
General Email: administrativecourtoffice.birmingham@hmcts.x.gsi.gov.uk
Skeleton Arguments Email: administrativecourtofficebirmingham.skeletonarguments@hmcts.x.gsi.gov.uk

---

[1] s.2(1) of the Administration of Justice Act 1960
[2] *Re Poh* [1983] 1 All ER 287

Leeds

> The Administrative Court Office
> Leeds Combined Court Centre
> The Courthouse
> Oxford Row Leeds
> West Yorkshire LS1 3BG
> DX: 703016 Leeds 6

Telephone Number: 0113 306 2578
General Email: administrativecourtoffice.leeds@hmcts.x.gsi.gov.uk
Skeleton Arguments Email: administrativecourtofficeleeds.skeletonarguments@hmcts.x.gsi.gov.uk

London

> The Administrative Court Office Royal Courts of Justice
> Strand
> London WC2A 2LL
> DX 44450 Strand

Telephone Number: 020 7947 6655
The Administrative Court public counter is open from 10:00-16:30. From 15:00 only urgent applications can be issued.
General Email: administrativecourtoffice.generaloffice@hmcts.x.gsi.gov.uk
Skeleton Arguments Email: administrativecourtofficelondon.skeletonarguments@hmcts.x.gsi.gov.uk
List Office Email: administrativecourtoffice.listoffice@hmcts.x.gsi.gov.uk
Case Progression Email administrativecourtoffice.caseprogression@hmcts.x.gsi.gov.uk
Case progression (Crime and Extradition only) Email: administrativecourtoffice.crimex@hmcts.x.gsi.gov.uk

Manchester

> The Administrative Court Office
> Manchester Civil and Family Justice Centre 1 Bridge Street
> West Manchester M60 9DJ
> DX 724783 Manchester 44

Telephone Number: 0161 240 5313
General Email: administrativecourtoffice.manchester@hmcts.x.gsi.gov.uk
Skeleton Arguments Email: administrativecourtofficemanchester.skeletonarguments@hmcts.x.gsi.gov.uk

Wales and the Western Circuit

> The Administrative Court Office Cardiff Civil Justice Centre,
> Park Street, Cardiff, CF10 1ET
> DX 99500 Cardiff 6

Telephone Number: 02920 376460
General Email: administrativecourtoffice.cardiff@hmcts.x.gsi.gov.uk
Skeleton Arguments Email: administrativecourtofficecardiff.skeletonarguments@hmcts.x.gsi.gov.uk

Upper Tribunal (Administrative Appeals Chamber)

> Upper Tribunal (Administrative Appeals Chamber) 5th Floor Rolls Building
> 7 Rolls Buildings, Fetter Lane London EC4A 1NL
> DX 160042 STRAND 4

Telephone Number: 020 7071 5662
Email adminappeals@Justice.gov.uk

Upper Tribunal (Immigration and Asylum Chamber)
For the UT(IAC) – Judicial Reviews Only:
For London:

> Upper Tribunal (Immigration and Asylum Chamber), IA Field House
> 15 Breams Buildings London EC4A 1DZ

For UT(IAC) judicial reviews in Birmingham, Cardiff, Leeds, or Manchester, see the contact details for the Administrative Court Office in that area above.
For UT(IAC) – All non-judicial review cases:
Lodging Appeals:

> Upper Tribunal (Immigration and Asylum Chamber), IA Field House
> 15 Breams Buildings London EC4A 1DZ

Unless advised otherwise, all other correspondence to:

> Upper Tribunal (Immigration and Asylum Chamber) Arnhem Support Centre
> PO Box 6987
> Leicester LE1 6ZX

Facsimile: 0116 249 4130
Customer Service Centre (Enquiry Unit) telephone: 0300 123 1711

Senior Courts Costs Office

> Senior Courts Costs Office Royal Courts of Justice Strand
> London WC2A 2LL
> DX 44454 Strand

Telephone Number: 020 7947 6469/ 6404 / 7818 Email: SCCO@justice.gov.uk
Website: *https://www.gov.uk/courts-tribunals/senior-courts-costs-office*

Court of Appeal (Civil Division)

> Civil Appeals Office Room E307
> Royal Courts of Justice Strand
> London WC2A 2LL
> DX: 44450 Strand

Telephone Number: 020 79477121/6533

Supreme Court

> The Supreme Court Parliament Square London SW1P 3BD
> DX 157230 Parliament Sq 4

Telephone Number: 020 7960 1500 or 1900
Facsimile: 020 7960 190

Annex 2 –

Forms and Fees

	Act / Application	Form*	Fee**	Ref**
1BA-155	Application for permission to apply for judicial review	N461 (Judicial Review Claim Form)	£154.00	1.9(a)
	Reconsideration of permission at an oral hearing	86b	£385.00	1.9(aa)
	Continuing judicial review after permission has been granted Any fee paid under 1.9(aa) is deducted	-	£770.00	1.9(b)
	Appeal	N161 (Appellant's Notice)	£240.00	2.4

Act / Application	Form*	Fee**	Ref**
Acknowledgment of Service	N462 (JR)	£0.00	-
Interim Application	N244 (Application Notice)	£255.00	2.6
Consent Order	N244 & Consent Order	£100.00	2.7
Discontinuance	N279 (Notice of Discontinuance)	£0.00	-
Urgent Consideration (within 48 hours of lodging claim)	N463 (Application for Urgent Consideration)	£255.00 (unless made when lodging when the fee is £0.00)	2.6

* = current forms can be found at www.gov.uk/courts-tribunals/administrative-court
** = schedule 1, Civil Proceedings Fee Order 2008 (as amended). The fees above were correct on 14th June 2019.

Annex 3 –

Addresses for Service of Central Government Departments[1]

Government Department	Solicitor for Service
Advisory, Conciliation and Arbitration Service, Cabinet Office, Commissioners for the Reduction of National Debt, Crown Prosecution Service (Civil), Department for Business, Energy and Industrial Strategy, Department for Communities and Local Government, Department for Digital, Culture, Media and Sport, Department for Education, Department for Environment, Food and Rural Affairs, Department for Exiting the European Union, Department for International Development, Department for International Trade, Department for Transport, Forestry Commission, The Treasury Solicitor, Department of Health, Foreign and Commonwealth Office, Health and Safety Executive, Home Office, Department of Communities and Local Government, Ministry of Defence, Ministry of Justice, National Savings and Investments (NS&I), Northern Ireland Office, Office for Budget Responsibility, Privy Council Office, Public Works Loan Board, Serious Fraud Office, Statistics Board (UK Statistics Authority) The National Archives, Wales Office (Office of the Secretary of State for Wales)	Government Legal Department One Kemble Street London WC2B 4TS [Editorial Note: Subject to change from September 2019. Check for updated information.]
Crown Prosecution Service (Acting as a public prosecutor)	Rose Court, 2 Southwark Bridge, London, SE1 9HS
Competition and Markets Authority	Director of Litigation Competition and Markets Authority Victoria House Southampton Row London WC1B 4AD

1BA-156

[1] Taken from published list by David Lidington, Chancellor of the Duchy of Lancaster and Minister for the Cabinet Office on the 4th April 2018. Also found at annex 2 to CPR PD 66.

Government Department	Solicitor for Service
Department for Work and Pensions	Legal Director's Office Department for Work and Pensions Caxton House Tothill Street London SW1H 9NA
Food Standards Agency	Director of Legal Services Food Standards Agency Aviation House 125 Kingsway London WC2B 6NH
Her Majesty's Revenue and Customs	General Counsel and Solicitor to Her Majesty's Revenue and Customs HM Revenue and Customs South West Wing Bush House, Strand London WC2B 4RD
National Crime Agency	The Legal Adviser National Crime Agency Units 1-6 Citadel Place Tinworth Street London SE11 5EF
Office for Standards in Education, Children's Services and Skills (Ofsted)	Deputy Director, Legal Services Ofsted Clive House 70 Petty France Westminster London SW1H 9EX

ANNEX 4 –

LISTING POLICY FOR THE ADMINISTRATIVE COURT

NOTE ON THE POLICY

1BA-157   This policy replaces the general listing policy for all Administrative Court Offices as outlined in Annex C of *Practice Statement* [2002] 1 All ER 633 and the listing policy for the Administrative Court Office for Wales and the Western Circuit version 3.1.

This is a consolidated listing policy for the Administrative Court Offices ("ACOs") in the Royal Courts of Justice in London, Birmingham Civil Justice Centre, Cardiff Civil Justice Centre, Leeds

Combined Court Centre and Manchester Civil Justice Centre. The terms "Regions", "regional courts" and "regional ACOs" as used in this listing policy mean the Administrative Court Centres and Offices in Cardiff, Birmingham, Leeds and Manchester.

The policy is designed to be used as guidance for officers when listing cases in the Administrative Court. It has the approval of The Honourable Mr. Justice Supperstone, Judge in Charge of the Administrative Court.

It should further be noted that this policy may be amended in any individual case by judicial order.

June 2018

1   URGENT AND/OR INTERIM APPLICATIONS AND HEARINGS

1 The interim/urgent application process will begin when a claim form and urgent consideration notice (N461 and N463[299]) or a general application notice (N244 or PF244 and in extradition cases, EX244) is received by the ACO and any relevant fee is paid. If consideration is sought within a set time period this should be made apparent by the applying party in the application and in any covering letter which accompanies it.

2 Urgent non-extradition applications are issued within working hours in the following way:

a. **London:** Under CPR PD 54A paragraph 5.9 and CPR PD 5A paragraph 2.2, the ACO requires the parties to file any urgent or interim application in a hard copy bundle. The only exception to this principle is under CPR PD 5A paragraph 5.3 which allows urgent applications to be filed by fax. However, it is appreciated that, for urgent claims with a large quantity of documents, it may be impractical to file the claim by fax. In such circumstances, the party making the application should contact the ACO to discuss whether sending the application by email may be acceptable. If the ACO agrees to receive the application by email then a hard copy must still be provided to remain compliant with CPR PD 54A paragraph 5.9 and CPR PD 5A paragraph 2.2, but the ACO will not wait for the hard copy before processing the urgent application. Court users who wish to lodge an urgent application without payment of the court fee are required to follow the procedure in the document entitled "Urgent Applications requiring an Undertaking" attached as Annex 1 to this policy.

b. **Regions:** The practice at a. above for London should be followed except that Court users who wish to lodge an urgent application without payment of the court fee are required to follow the procedure in the document entitled "Urgent Applications requiring an Undertaking in the Regions" attached as Annex 2 to this policy.

3 In urgent extradition cases, the *Criminal Practice Directions 2015*[1] apply. Crim PD 50B.16 provides that the Court will deal with requests for an expedited appeal without a hearing. Requests for expedition must be made in writing either within the appeal notice or by application notice EX244 and clearly marked with the Administrative Court reference number. The request for expedition must be lodged with the Administrative Court Office or emailed to the appropriate email address: administrativecourtoffice. crimex@hmcts.x.gsi.gov.uk. Notice must be given to the other parties. Once the ACO agrees to receive the application by email, the applicant will email a copy of the application and/or claim form to the appropriate court. On receipt, the officer will issue the application and process.

4 Out of Hours Urgent Applications: applications issued out of hours are *not* covered by this policy. CPR PD 54D, paragraph 4.2 makes provision for urgent applications out of hours.

5 Once issued, the officer will provide the case number, by email if the application has been issued by email (see above). That case number is to be quoted by the applicant on the hard copies of documents that will follow by post.

6 Any application for urgent consideration will be dealt with in the following way:

• If the application is to be considered on papers immediately, without an oral hearing, the application is likely to be sent directly to the "immediates judge"; alternatively, it may be sent to the ACO lawyer in the first instance.

• If the application is not immediate but urgent, the officer may send the application to an ACO lawyer to consider initial directions (CPR 54.1A) and the ACO lawyer may refer the application to a Judge without making an order; alternatively, the officer may refer the application to a Judge directly.

7 If the case requires urgent listing for oral hearing, the Judge will usually give directions including a timetable for listing. Alternatively, the officer will consult with the ACO lawyer who may consult with a Judge before approving a timetable for listing the application. The officer will list the case within that timetable and without checking the availability of the parties. The time estimate for hearing the application is assumed to be 30 minutes unless a different time estimate is requested by the parties and is approved by the court.

---

[1] [2015] EWCA Crim 1567 (as amended) and see
https://www.justice.gov.uk/courts/procedure-rules/criminal/rulesmenu-2015;
https://www.judiciary.gov.uk/wp-content/uploads/2015/09/crim-pd-2015.pdf

8 A listing notice will be sent by the officer by post, but it may also be sent by fax or email if the parties require early notice of the hearing due to its proximity.

9 If the case does not require urgent listing, then the officer will list the case, adopting the process in the permission hearing policy below. At least 3 days' notice of the hearing must be given unless a judicial order provides otherwise.

2   Permission Hearings Judicial Review and Statutory Appeals & Applications

10 Upon receipt of a renewal notice (Form 86B), appeal notice (with the relevant fee) or a Judge's order adjourning permission into Court, the officer will proceed to list. In London, the hearing will generally be listed within three weeks of the Form 86B being lodged. Outside London, the time scale may be longer. The time estimate for renewal hearings is assumed to be 30 minutes unless a different time estimate is requested by the parties and is approved by the court.

11 Hearings will usually be fixed at the Court's convenience without taking counsel's availability into consideration.

3   Substantive Hearings (including Rolled Up Hearings) Judicial Review and Statutory Appeals & Applications

12 Once permission is granted, the claimant must pay the relevant fee for continuation within the statutory time limit (if the fee is not paid within that time, the case will be closed and will not be listed). Once the case enters the warned list (on the warned list[1] date), the officer will proceed to list the case. Where a rolled-up hearing has been ordered, the claimant must give an undertaking to pay the continuation fee if permission is ultimately granted; once the undertaking is given, the officer will proceed to list the case (if the undertaking is not given, the case will be closed and will not be listed).

13 Substantive hearings should ideally be listed to be heard within the following time scales:
- Judicial Review Substantives – within 9 months of issue
- Extradition Substantives - within 2 months of issue
- Planning s.288 and other Statutory Reviews - within 6 months of issue (see section 6. below)
- Planning Judicial Review Substantives - within 10 weeks of the date of expiry of the period for the submission of detailed grounds by the Defendant or Interested Party (see section 6. below).

14 The listing period for planning cases will only be extended in exceptional circumstances and with the agreement of the ACO manager or ACO lawyer.

15 The court will list substantive hearings in the following way:
a. **London:** the officer will either email or telephone counsel's clerks or solicitors for all sides to arrange an appointment to fix. The officer will allow 5 working days' notice for the appointment. At the appointment, if the availability of all counsel corresponds, then every effort will be made to list on that/those date(s) but only if that date is also suitable for the Court and is within the listing period. The relevant time limit will not be extended due to the unavailability of counsel alone. If the available dates do not correspond, and/or the date(s) is/are unsuitable for the Court the case will be listed at the ACO's convenience.
b. **Regions:** the officer will either email or telephone counsel's clerks or solicitors for all sides to request the dates of availability for counsel for the three month period after the warned list date. Unless availability is provided at the time of the initial contact the clerk will be informed that they must provide availability within 48 hours or the case will be listed, with or without those dates at the Court's convenience. The officer is not required to follow up on the enquiry. The sooner the clerks/solicitors respond the better as judicial availability may change. If the availability of all counsel corresponds, the officer will check for judicial availability on that/those date(s). If a Judge is available on the said date(s) then the case will be listed accordingly.
  i.   If counsels' dates do correspond every effort will be made to list on that/those date(s).
  ii. The officer will attempt to list the case in the most geographically appropriate hearing centre, considering judicial availability for that Court centre.
  iii. Only in exceptional circumstances will cases that relate to a particular geographical region not be heard at that region.
  iv. If the available dates do not correspond, and/or the date(s) is/are unsuitable for the Court the case will be listed at the ACO's convenience.

16 The relevant time limit will not be extended due to the unavailability of counsel alone.

17 The court will endeavour to take a litigant in person's availability into account when listing

---

[1] The warned list begins on the first day on which the ACO could list the case taking into account the time allowed by the CPR or judicial order for the parties to file documents.

if dates are provided in writing and in advance and a satisfactory explanation is given as to why a date is unsuitable. Due to operational reasons, this may not be possible in all cases.

18 Only the availability of counsel or solicitor with higher rights of audience on the Court record will be checked. If a party did not provide the Court with the details of their advocate, then the case will be listed at the Court's convenience.

4 DIVISIONAL COURTS

19 Where a party considers that a claim or application should be dealt with by a Divisional Court, then that party should notify the ACO in writing as soon as possible, i.e. usually in or with the claim form or application, or the acknowledgment of service or response to an application.

20 Although parties may make representations as to the suitability of a case to be heard before the Divisional Court, the decision whether a case should be listed before the Divisional Court and if so, the constitution of that Court, are matters for the Court.

21 The ACO will not be able to offer as many suitable available dates for a hearing and will not generally take account of the availability of each party's counsel when listing the hearing.

5 VACATING FIXTURES

22 A case can only be adjourned or vacated by judicial order.

23 If the application to vacate is made more than 14 days before the fixed hearing and all the parties consent to the adjournment then a fee is not payable. If the application is made with the consent of all parties (except in extradition matters where *Criminal Practice Direction* 50D.4 applies) and received by the court less than 14 days before the date of hearing, a fee is payable. Form N244 or PF244 (EX244 in extradition) accompanied by a draft consent order should be filed. A consent order should also include reasons for the hearing being adjourned. A consent order to adjourn without reasons attached is unlikely to be approved.

24 Even when all the parties consent to the adjournment, parties must always assume that the hearing remains listed until they are advised otherwise by the court. The hearing will generally not be adjourned unless there are good reasons to do so, even where all parties agree that the hearing should be adjourned. Where the sole reason for seeking the adjournment is that counsel is/are not available for the hearing, the adjournment will rarely be granted. Where the matter has been listed to be heard by a Divisional Court the Court will be very reluctant to grant an adjournment

25 In all other cases, an application notice should be filed with the court at least 3 days prior to the hearing (unless good reasons are provided for the late filing of the application)

26 A decision whether to grant or refuse an application to adjourn can be taken by a lawyer under delegated powers. If a party is not content with an order of the ACO lawyer then CPR 54.1A(5) provides that the party may request that the order is reviewed by a judge. Such a review may take place on the papers or by way of an oral hearing in Court. The request for a review must be made by filing the request in writing (a letter or application notice may be used) within 7 days of the date on which the party was served with the ACO lawyer's order. As long as the request is filed within 7 days (or such time as allowed by the order) there is no fee. If it is filed out of time then an application must be made to file the request out of time and it must be made on an application notice (N244 or PF244) with the relevant fee.

6 PLANNING COURT

27 The Planning Court is a "specialist list" of which the Planning Liaison Judge is in charge (CPR 54.22). The work covered by the Planning Court is defined in CPR 54.21.

28 The policy set out in paragraphs 1 to 26 above generally applies to cases in the Planning Court subject to the points set out below and any other alterations which may from time to time be laid down by the Planning Liaison Judge.

29 Cases in the Planning Court generally fall into three broad categories:-

(i)   Statutory review claims (a) under PD8C[1] (where permission to apply is required and an Acknowledgment of Service must be accompanied by summary grounds of defence) and (b) under PD8A para 22[2] (where neither permission nor summary grounds are required);

(ii)   *Appeals under s.289 of TCPA 1990* against decisions on enforcement notice appeals and tree replacement orders (under section s.208)[3] where permission is required (see PD 52D para 26);

---

[1] 307 claims under section 287 or 288 of TCPA 1990, s63 of the Planning (Listed Buildings and Conservation Areas) Act 1990, s.22 of the Planning (Hazardous Substances) Act 1990 and s.113 of the Planning and Compulsory Purchases Act 2004.

[2] A statutory application to quash an "order, scheme, certificate or plan" eg. to quash a CPO or an order for a road scheme under the Highways Act 1980

[3] s.65 of the Planning (Listed Building and Conservation Areas) Act 1990.

(iii)   *Planning judicial reviews* (including challenges to neighbourhood plans under s.61N of TCPA 1990).

30   The Planning Liaison Judge designates those cases which are "significant" according to para 3.2 of PD 54E.

31   For "significant" claims, para 3.4 of PD 54E sets the following target timescales which the parties should prepare to meet, subject to the overriding objective of the interests of justice: -

(a)   applications for permission to apply for judicial review or planning statutory review are to be determined within three weeks of the expiry of the time limit for filing of the acknowledgement of service;

(b)   oral renewals of applications for permission to apply for judicial review or planning statutory review are to be heard within one month of receipt of request for renewal;

(c)   applications for permission under section 289 of the Town and Country Planning Act 1990 are to be determined within one month of issue;

(d)   planning statutory reviews are to be heard within six months of issue; and

(e)   judicial reviews are to be heard within ten weeks of the expiry period for the submission of detailed grounds by the defendant or any other party as provided in CPR 54.14.

32   The objective is to deal with other cases not designated as "significant", within the general timescales set out above for the Administrative Court.

33   Claims in the Planning Court are only dealt with by judges who have been nominated by the President of the Queen's Bench Division. Certain judges are nominated to hear "significant" cases whilst other judges may only hear "other cases" (CPR 52.22).

Listing of substantive hearings for the Planning Court in London

34   The list office does not wait until a case enters the Warned list. Instead, once the Court fee to continue the proceedings has been paid, the list office emails a window of suitable dates to the parties and encourages them to agree a mutually convenient date. The appointment to fix procedure is used only when necessary.

Listing of substantive hearings for "significant" cases in London

35   Having regard to the limited availability of judges authorised to hear "significant" cases, the listing policy is necessarily stricter. "Significant" cases are listed primarily by reference to the availability of a judge authorised to hear such cases. They are listed for hearings between Tuesdays to Thursdays only of any sitting week. The Court will offer the parties 3 dates within the timescales set by PD 54E. If parties are unable to agree one of those 3 dates, the case is listed without further consultation.

Regional Offices

36   The regional offices generally apply the same policy.

Hearings for oral renewal of applications for permission

37   Hearings are usually fixed at the Court's convenience without taking counsel's availability into consideration.

38   Unless the parties otherwise notify the Administrative court Office and the court agrees hearings of renewed applications for permission are listed for 30 minutes (including the time needed for any judgment). Sometimes hearings of renewal applications have had to be adjourned when a significantly increased time estimate is provided too late and cannot be accommodated because of other work already listed. The fixing letter therefore states:

"This application has been fixed in accordance with our listing policy and on the basis that it will take no longer than 30 minutes to hear. If you have already indicated that this application will require a hearing of longer than 30 minutes, I would be grateful if you could confirm this with the List Office, **in writing**. Otherwise on receipt of this letter you must confirm your current time estimate.

This is a mandatory requirement. If it becomes necessary to adjourn because of a late increased time estimate, quite apart from any costs sanction, the solicitors and counsel involved may be required to appear before the Court to explain the failure to comply with the instruction above. Furthermore, the case will be re-listed for the earliest possible opportunity in accordance with the availability of a Judge and *not* the availability of counsel."

Administrative Court in London Urgent Applications requiring an Undertaking

Court Users who wish to lodge an urgent application without payment of the court fee are required to follow the procedure set out in this notice. This facility is to be used in exceptional circumstances as a result of unavoidable emergency by solicitors/barristers with rights to participate in litigation only.

The cut off time for using this procedure is 4.30pm.

Court Users are encouraged to use the HMCTS fee account facility to avoid unnecessary process and delay in issuing court proceedings.

To create an account please contact:

MiddleOffice.DDServices@liberata.gse.gov.uk

Procedure to be followed for undertaking:

Step 1: Email the required documents (set out below) to:

administrativecourtoffice.generaloffice@hmcts.x.gsi.gov.uk

Step 2: Wait for the Court to process your application and email you a sealed claim form for service. Please note if you do not provide all of the documents set out below your application will not be processed.

Step 3: Post the required fee to the Court ensuring the Court will receive the fee within 5 days in line with the undertaking agreement and please clearly state the Court reference so we can allocate it once received.

Documents required:

- Undertaking form (EX160B). This form can be obtained from the gov.uk website at the following link: *http://formfinder.hmctsformfinder.justice.gov.uk/ex160b-eng.pdf*
- A covering letter explaining in full the emergency and why to use this service is unavoidable.
- Urgent Consideration form (N463). You must ensure **all** sections of the form are completed. Failure to do so will result in your application not being issued; you must also state the reasons for urgency on this form.
- Judicial Review claim form (N461). You must ensure all necessary sections of the form are completed and the statement of truth is signed.
- Grounds in support of your application.
- Decision document. If you are unable to provide this you must clearly state in Section 10 on the N461 the reasons why and what date you expect to be able to lodge it with the Court.
- A draft of the order sought that sets out the relief sought and any directions for an expedited hearing should be attached.

You are no longer be required to send hard copies of the required documents to the Court, see the recent change in CPR 54A9D 5.9.

The claimant must file *one* copy of a paginated and indexed bundle containing all the documents referred to in paragraphs 5.6 and 5.7 (claim forms and any additional documents).

Failure to prepare your documentation in accordance with the requirements could delay your urgent application from being considered.

Points to note:

1. Practitioners and parties are reminded to comply with the Civil Procedure Rules and Practice Directions. In particular see CPR PD 5A and 5B.

2. Practitioners should note the warning issued by the Divisional Court about late and unmeritorious claims in *R (Hamid) v Secretary of State for the Home Department* [2012] EWHC 3070. Failure to comply with the warning may require the attendance in open court of the solicitor from the firm who was responsible, together with his/her partner. The Court will list not only the name of the case but the firm concerned.

3. The Administrative Court deals with a high volume of urgent applications each day. Please do not contact the Court unless at least 30 minutes has elapsed from lodging your undertaking, and you have not received a response from the Court. If no response has been received from the Court after 30 minutes, you are at liberty to telephone or email the court in the first instance or to contact the Delivery Manager by email,Oludotun.Onasanya@hmcts.x.gsi.gov.uk. The delivery manager will aim to respond as soon as possible, although this may not always be possible. Any emails that are received seeking to escalate the matter outside of the above will not be actioned.

Failure to treat court staff with respect and to adhere to the above guidance will result in the Director/ Partner of the practices' firm being called before the Master of the Administrative Court to explain the firm's actions.

[Annex 2 to Administrative Court Listing Policy]

Regional Administrative Court Offices and Regional Upper Tribunal (Immigration and Asylum Chamber) Offices

Urgent Applications requiring an Undertaking in the Regions

Court Users who wish to lodge an urgent application without payment of the court fee are required to follow the procedure set out in this notice. This facility is to be used by Solicitors/ Barristers with rights to participate in litigation only in exceptional circumstances as a result of unavoidable emergency.

The cut off time for using this procedure is 4pm.

In Administrative Court claims court users are encouraged to use the HMCTS fee account facility to avoid unnecessary process and delay in issuing court proceedings.

To create an account please contact:

MiddleOffice.DDServices@liberata.gse.gov.uk

Regrettably, the fee account facility does not apply to cases brought in the Upper Tribunal. Applicants for UT cases should contact the Office to make payment by credit/debit card, fee undertaking or fee remission as appropriate.

Procedure to be followed for undertaking:

Step 1: Email the required documents (set out below) and contact the relevant office to confirm receipt of the email:

administrativecourtoffice.cardiff@hmcts.x.gsi.gov.uk

Tel: 02920 376 460

administrativecourtoffice.birmingham@hmcts.x.gsi.gov.uk

Tel: 0121 681 4441

administrativecourtoffice.leeds@hmcts.x.gsi.gov.uk

Tel: 0113 306 2578

administrativecourtoffice.manchester@hmcts.x.gsi.gov.uk

Tel: 0161 240 5313

Step 2: Wait for the Court to notify you that your application has been issued. Please note if you do not provide all of the documents set out below your application will not be processed. The Court will post *one* copy of the sealed claim form to the claimant to effect service.

Step 3: Post the required fee to the Court ensuring the Court will receive the fee within 5 days in line with the undertaking agreement and please clearly state the Court reference so we can allocate it once received.

The claimant must file *one* copy of a paginated and indexed bundle containing all the documents.

Failure to prepare your documentation in accordance with the requirements could delay your urgent application from being considered.

Documents required:

- Undertaking form (EX160B). This form can be obtained from the gov.uk website at the following link: *http://formfinder.hmctsformfinder.justice.gov.uk/ex160b-eng.pdf*
- A covering letter explaining in full the emergency and why the use of this service is unavoidable.
- Urgent Consideration form (N463 (Admin Court) or T483 (UTIAC)). You must ensure **all** sections of the form are completed. Failure to do so will result in your application not being issued; you must also state the reasons for urgency on this form.
- Judicial Review form (N461 (Admin Court) or T480 (UTIAC)). You must ensure all necessary sections of the form are completed and the statement of truth is signed.
- Grounds in support of your application.
- Decision document. If you are unable to provide this you must clearly state in Section 10 (on the N461 or T480) the reasons why and what date you expect to lodge it with the Court.
- A draft of the order sought that sets out the relief sought and any directions for an expedited hearing should be attached.

Points to note:

1. Practitioners and parties are reminded to comply with the Civil Procedure Rules and Practice Directions. In particular see CPR PD 5A and 5B.
2. Practitioners should note the warning issued by the Divisional Court about late and unmeritorious claims *in R (Hamid) v Secretary of State for the Home Department* [2012] EWHC 3070. Failure to comply with the warning may require the attendance in open court of the solicitor from the firm who was responsible, together with his/her partner. The Court will list not only the name of the case but the firm concerned.

Failure to treat court staff with respect and to adhere to the above guidance will result in the Director/ Partner of the practices' firm being called before the Master of the Administrative Court to explain the firm's actions.

Annex 5 –

ACO Costs Guidance April 2016

Guidance as to how the parties should assist the Court when applications for costs are made following settlement of claims for judicial review – April 2016

WHEN THIS GUIDANCE APPLIES

1. This guidance is applicable where the parties to judicial review have agreed to settle the **1BA-158** claim but are unable to agree liability for costs and have submitted that issue for determination by the Court.

2. It applies to all consent orders submitted for approval by the court after 18 April 2016.

3. Previous guidance is withdrawn.

THE PROBLEM

4. The Court faces a significant number of cases, poorly considered and prepared by the parties, which can consume judicial time far beyond what is proportionate to deciding a costs issue after the parties have settled the case. The judicial and other Court resources applied to these cases must be proportionate to what is at stake. That requires efficiency and co-operation from the parties. At the same time, parties want to have the costs orders resolved fairly and quickly.

HOW THE PARTIES SHOULD ASSIST THE COURT BEFORE SENDING IN SUBMISSIONS ON COSTS

5. The onus lies on the parties to reach agreement on costs wherever possible, and in advance of asking the Court to resolve the issues, in order to support the overriding objective and ensure that efficient use is made of judicial time. See *M v Croydon* [2012] EWCA Civ 595, paragraphs 75-77.

6. The parties should not make submissions to the Court on costs following a compromise of the proceedings without first seeking to agree the allocation of costs through reasoned negotiation, mindful of the overriding objective to the CPR, the amount of costs actually at stake and the principles set out in *M v Croydon*, paragraphs 59-63. This should give them a clear understanding of the basis upon which they have failed to reach agreement, so as to focus their submissions to the court on the points in dispute.

7. Liability for costs between the parties will depend on the specific facts in each case but the principles are set out in *M v Croydon*, paragraphs 59-63 (annexed at the end of this guidance) and *Tesfay* (2016) EWCA Civ 415.

The fair and efficient operation of this Guidance and the Timetable detailed below assume that in the 28 day period between the date of the Court's order and the Defendant's submissions, the parties will have ascertained by communication between themselves who is seeking what costs order and why as well as the basis of any disagreement between them, so that all submissions are then as focused and succinct as possible to assist the Court in speedier decision-making.

8. The procedure timetabled below starts with the Defendant because it is so often said that the Claimant does not know why a costs order in its favour is resisted. However it is to be hoped that only one set of submissions per side will be necessary. The cost correspondence between the parties can be annexed to the submissions. Submissions are expected not to exceed 2 sides of A4 at reasonable font size, in the absence of very good reason.

THE TERMS OF CONSENT ORDERS

9. Following a settlement the terms of consent orders require the approval of the court. Unless there are specific contrary reasons given with the proposed consent order, the court is very unlikely to approve the draft without varying its terms so as to expressly incorporate the provisions of this Guidance.

TIMETABLE

10. Within 28 days of the service of the order upon the parties, the Defendant may file with the Court, and serve on all other parties, submissions as to what the appropriate order for costs should be.

11. Where the Defendant does not file submissions in accordance with 11 above the Defendant will be ordered to pay the Claimant's costs of the claim on the standard basis and for these to be the subject of detailed assessment if not agreed. However, if the Court considers that such an order would be wrong or unfair in all the circumstances, it shall make such other costs order as it sees fit, or it may require submissions from any party in the case within a specified time, or extend time for the service of the Defendant's submissions.

12.   Where submissions are filed and served by the Defendant, the Claimant or any other party may file and serve submissions in reply within 14 days of the service of those submissions.

13.   Where no submissions are filed by the Claimant or by any other party in accordance with the above, the Court will make the Order sought by the Defendant. However, if the Court considers that such an order would be wrong or unfair in all the circumstances, it shall make such other costs orders as it sees fit, or it may require submissions from any party in the case within a specified time, or extend time for the service of the Claimant's or other party's submissions.

14.   Where submissions are filed by the Claimant or by any other party, the Defendant shall have 7 days in which to file and serve a reply. If the Court thinks it necessary in the interests of justice, it may seek any further submissions from any party. A party may also apply for permission within 14 days of the service of previous submissions to lodge further submissions provided it explains what new point has arisen in those previous submissions to which it needs to reply. A short timetable can be expected for any such submissions.

CONTENT OF SUBMISSIONS

15.   Submissions should:
- confirm that the parties have used reasonable endeavours to negotiate a costs settlement;
- identify what issues or reasons prevented the parties agreeing costs liability;
- state the approximate amount of costs likely to be involved in the case;
- clearly identify the extent to which the parties complied with the pre-action protocol;
- state the relief the claimant (i) sought in the claim form and (ii) obtained;
- address specifically how the claim and the basis of its settlement fit the principles in *M v Croydon*, and *Tesfay* including the relationship of any step taken by the defendant to the claim.

DOCUMENTS

16.   Submissions should be of a normal print size and should not normally exceed two A4 pages in length unless there is compelling reason to exceed this which is properly explained in the submissions.

17.   Submissions should be accompanied by the pre-action protocol correspondence (where this has not previously been included as part of the documents supporting the claim), the correspondence in which the costs claim is made and defended, along with any other correspondence necessary to demonstrate why the claim was brought in the light of the pre-action protocol correspondence or why the step which led to settlement was not taken until after the claim was issued.

18.   Unless advised otherwise, the parties should assume that the Court has the claim form and grounds, the acknowledgment of service and evidence lodged by the parties. Further copies of these should not be provided unless requested by the Court.

Case No: C1/2011/1716

Neutral Citation Number: [2012] EWCA Civ 595
IN THE COURT OF APPEAL (CIVIL DIVISION)
ON APPEAL FROM THE HIGH COURT OF JUSTICE
QUEEN'S BENCH DIVISION, ADMINISTRATIVE COURT
THE HON MR JUSTICE LINDBLOM
Case CO/1468/2009

Royal Courts of Justice
Strand, London, WC2A 2LL
Date: 8th May 2012

Before:
THE MASTER OF THE ROLLS
LADY JUSTICE HALLETT DBE
(VICE-PRESIDENT OF THE QUEEN'S BENCH DIVISION)
and
LORD JUSTICE STANLEY BURNTON
Between:
M

Appellant

- and -
MAYOR AND BURGESSES OF THE
LONDON BOROUGH OF CROYDON

Respondents

(Transcript of the Handed Down Judgment of
WordWave International Limited
A Merrill Communications Company
165 Fleet Street, London EC4A 2DY
Tel No: 020 7404 1400, Fax No: 020 7404 1424
Official Shorthand Writers to the Court)

Robert Latham (instructed by *Hansen Palomares*) for the *Appellant, M*
Catherine Rowlands (instructed by *Policy & Corporate Services Department of Croydon LBC*) for
the *Respondent, Croydon LBC*
Hearing date: 14 March 2012
Judgment

THE MASTER OF THE ROLLS:

59. In my view, however, on closer analysis, there is no inconsistency in either case, essentially for reasons already discussed. Where, as happened in *Bahta*, a claimant obtains all the relief which he seeks, whether by consent or after a contested hearing, he is undoubtedly the successful party, who is entitled to all his costs, unless there is a good reason to the contrary. However, where the claimant obtains only some of the relief which he is seeking (either by consent or after a contested trial), as in *Boxall* and *Scott*, the position on costs is obviously more nuanced. Thus, as in those two cases, there may be an argument as to which party was more 'successful' (in the light of the relief which was sought and not obtained), or, even if the claimant is accepted to be the successful party, there may be an argument as to whether the importance of the issue, or costs relating to the issue, on which he failed.

60. Thus, in Administrative Court cases, just as in other civil litigation, particularly where a claim has been settled, there is, in my view, a sharp difference between (i) a case where a claimant has been wholly successful whether following a contested hearing or pursuant to a settlement, and (ii) a case where he has only succeeded in part following a contested hearing, or pursuant to a settlement, and (iii) a case where there has been some compromise which does not actually reflect the claimant's claims. While in every case, the allocation of costs will depend on the specific facts, there are some points which can be made about these different types of case.

61. In case (i), it is hard to see why the claimant should not recover all his costs, unless there is some good reason to the contrary. Whether pursuant to judgment following a contested hearing, or by virtue of a settlement, the claimant can, at least absent special circumstances, say that he has been vindicated, and, as the successful party, that he should recover his costs. In the latter case, the defendants can no doubt say that they were realistic in settling, and should not be penalised in costs, but the answer to that point is that the defendants should, on that basis, have settled before the proceedings were issued: that is one of the main points of the pre-action protocols. Ultimately, it seems to me that *Bahta* was decided on this basis.

62. In case (ii), when deciding how to allocate liability for costs after a trial, the court will normally determine questions such as how reasonable the claimant was in pursuing the unsuccessful claim, how important it was compared with the successful claim, and how much the costs were increased as a result of the claimant pursuing the unsuccessful claim. Given that there will have been a hearing, the court will be in a reasonably good position to make findings on such questions. However, where there has been a settlement, the court will, at least normally, be in a significantly worse position to make findings on such issues than where the case has been fought out. In many such cases, the court will be able to form a view as to the appropriate costs order based on such issues; in other cases, it will be much more difficult. I would accept the argument that, where the parties have settled the claimant's substantive claims on the basis that he succeeds in part, but only in part, there is often much to be said for concluding that there is no order for costs. That I think was the approach adopted in *Scott*. However, where there is not a clear winner, so much would depend on the particular facts. In some such cases, it may help to consider who would have won if the matter had proceeded to trial, as, if it is tolerably clear, it may, for instance support or undermine the contention that one of the two claims was stronger than the other. *Boxall* appears to have been such case.

63. In case (iii), the court is often unable to gauge whether there is a successful party in any respect, and, if so, who it is. In such cases, therefore, there is an even more powerful argument that the default position should be no order for costs. However, in some such cases, it may well be sensible to look at the underlying claims and inquire whether it was tolerably clear who would have won if the matter had not settled. If it is, then that may well strongly support the contention that the party who would have won did better out of the settlement, and therefore did win.

ANNEX 6 –

HANDING DOWN ADMINISTRATIVE COURT JUDGMENTS IN WALES

INTRODUCTION

1BA-159   **1.** There is a strong principle, reflected in CPR PD 54D, that Welsh Administrative Court cases are heard in Wales. That extends to the hand-down of judgments. Usually, the judge will still be sitting in Wales, and he/she will hand-down the judgment in open court in the usual way. Where the judge has heard a case in Wales but is sitting outside Wales at the time of the judgment hand-down, then, if the judge cannot conveniently return to Wales to perform the hand-down, the default position is that he/she will hand-down the judgment by video-link. There are such facilities in all of the court buildings in which the Administrative Court is likely to sit in Wales.

2. The following protocol should be followed.

ARRANGEMENTS FOR HANDING DOWN

3. Once a judge has finalised the draft judgment, the judge or the judge's clerk should contact the Administrative Court Office in Wales[1] to confirm:
- The date on which they wish to hand down;
- The court centre outside Wales from which they intend to hand down (e.g. RCJ, Birmingham Civil Justice Centre).
- The court room within that court centre from which they intend to hand down the judgment, confirming that that court room has video link facilities.
- The court centre in Wales in which they wish to hand-down via video link: this should be the court centre where the case was heard.

4. The ACO in Wales will confirm whether they have video link facilities available for handing down.[2]

5. If facilities are not available, then the ACO in Wales and the judge/judge's clerk will liaise to find a date on which facilities are available for video link hand down in both court centres.

6. Once a date has been agreed, the ACO in Wales will inform the parties that hand-down will take place by video link and the relevant court centres, either of which they may attend.

THE HAND DOWN

7. The ACO in Wales will arrange for a video link test between the two court centres to take place the day before the hand down.

8. Copies of the final judgment must be sent by the judge or judge's clerk to the ACO in Wales in advance of the hand-down to ensure that copies can be made available to any attendees at the hand-down. The ACO in Wales must ensure that so far as possible the embargo is respected, and the judgment is not made available until judgment has been formally handed down.

9. For the hand-down itself, the court centre at which the judge is sitting will dial in to the other court centre to hand-down judgment.

ANNEX 7–

JUDICIAL REVIEW IN THE UPPER TRIBUNAL

A7.1   THE UPPER TRIBUNAL'S JUDICIAL REVIEW JURISDICTION

1BA-160   **A7.1.1** The Upper Tribunal's judicial review jurisdiction is conferred by section 15 of the Tribunals, Courts and Enforcement Act 2007 ("TCEA"). The existence of the jurisdiction depends upon certain conditions being met, as explained in section 18 of the TCEA.

A7.1.2 The UT has power to grant a mandatory, prohibiting or quashing order, a declaration and an injunction. Relief granted by the UT has the same effect as corresponding relief granted by the High Court and is enforceable as if it were relief granted by that Court. In deciding whether to grant relief the UT must apply the same principles that the High Court would apply in deciding whether to grant relief on an application for judicial review.

A7.1.3 Like the position in the High Court, section 16 of the TCEA provides that an application for judicial review may be made only if the applicant has obtained permission. Section 16 also contains provisions in the same terms as section 31(2A of the Senior Courts Act 1981, restricting

---

[1] Telephone: 02920 376460. Email: administrativecourtoffice.cardiff@hmcts.x.gsi.gov.uk

[2] This will be done immediately if the enquiry is made by telephone and relates to a hand down in Cardiff Civil Justice Centre or within 24 hours if the enquiry is made by email or relates to another Court centre in Wales.

the grant of relief where the UT considers it highly likely the outcome would not have been substantially different even if the conduct complained of had not occurred.[1]

A7.2 TRANSFERS OF JUDICIAL REVIEW APPLICATIONS

A7.2.1 As explained at paragraph 5.5 of the Guide, the effect of the Lord Chief Justice's Direction is that most applications for judicial review of immigration (and asylum) decisions are filed in the Upper Tribunal (Immigration and Asylum Chamber) ("UT(IAC)") and, if filed in the High Court, must be transferred to the UT(IAC). If an application is made to the UT(IAC) for judicial review of a decision that is not covered by the Direction, or which is specifically exempted by it (see 5.5.3), then, subject to what is said in the following paragraph, the UT(IAC) must transfer the application to the High Court.[2]

A7.2.2 If certain conditions specified in section 31A(4) and (5) of the Senior Courts Act 1981 are met, the High Court may by order transfer [a judicial review application] to the Upper Tribunal if it appears to the High Court to be just and convenient to do so".[3] This power is routinely exercised in order to transfer to the UT(IAC) a judicial review made by a person who claims to be a minor from outside the United Kingdom, challenging a local authority's assessment of that person's age.

A7.2.3 The UT has power to permit or require an amendment which, if made, would give rise to an obligation to transfer the proceedings to the High Court. Except with the permission of the UT, additional grounds may not be advanced if they would give rise to an obligation to transfer.

The UT therefore has power to decide whether to retain jurisdiction over the judicial review application. If the judicial review application has been transferred to the UT by the High Court under that Court's power of transfer, and the amendment or additional grounds would not have prevented the High Court from exercising that power, if the amendment or grounds had been in place prior to transfer, then the UT will transfer the application back to the High Court only if the UT considers it just and convenient to do so.[4]

A7.3 OUT OF HOURS APPLICATIONS

A7.3.1 The out of hours procedure described in paragraph 16.3 of the Guide applies to urgent applications in immigration judicial review proceedings that cannot wait until the next working day. For this purpose, the out of hours High Court judge sits as a judge of the UT.

SECTION 2   SPECIALIST PROCEEDINGS

SECTION 2A   COMMERCIAL COURT

PART 58—COMMERCIAL COURT

Related sources

Delete the tenth bullet point (beginning "For two years").

2A-3

---

[1] See paragraph 11.10 of this Guide.
[2] TCEA s. 18(3).
[3] Section 31A(3) of the Senior Courts Act 1981.
[4] UT r 33A.

Editorial note

2A-9.1

Replace "Bridgehouse (Bradford No.2) Ltd v BAE Systems Plc [2018] 10 WLUK 444" with:
   Bridgehouse (Bradford No.2) Ltd v BAE Systems Plc [2018] EWHC 3719 (Comm)

COMMERCIAL COURT GUIDE

O.   ARBITRATION

O.8   CHALLENGING THE AWARD

CHALLENGE BY WAY OF APPEAL

2A-154

Replace paragraph O8.2 with:
   O8.2   If permission to appeal is granted, skeleton arguments should be served in accordance with the timetable for applications in section F.[1]

CHALLENGING AN AWARD FOR SERIOUS IRREGULARITY

Replace the first paragraph in O8.5 with:
   O8.5   If the nature of the challenge itself or the evidence filed in support of it leads the Court to consider that the claim has no real prospect of success, the Court may exercise its powers under rule 3.3(4) and/or rule 23.8(c) to dismiss the application without a hearing. If a respondent considers that the case is one in which the Court could appropriately deal with the application without a hearing it should within 21 days file a respondent's notice to that effect together with a skeleton argument (not exceeding 15 pages) and any evidence relied upon. The applicant may file a skeleton/evidence in reply within 7 days of service of the respondent's notice and skeleton argument. Where the Court makes an order dismissing the application without a hearing the applicant will have the right to apply to the Court to set aside the order and to seek directions for the hearing of the application[2]. If such application is made and dismissed after a hearing the Court may consider whether it is appropriate to award costs on an indemnity basis.

SECTION 2B   CIRCUIT COMMERCIAL COURTS

CIRCUIT COMMERCIAL (MERCANTILE) COURT GUIDE

5.   PARTICULARS OF CLAIM, DEFENCE AND REPLY

2B-22   *Add new title before paragraph 5.12 and update the following cross reference "PD59 para.6.2" to "PD59 para.6.1":*

EXTENDING PERIOD FOR A DEFENCE

SERVING AND FILING A REPLY

Replace paragraph 5.13 with:
   5.13   Any reply must be served and filed within 21 days after service of the defence: rule 59.9.

---

   [1] As for the procedure on any application for permission to appeal from a refusal of permission on paper, in *Midnight Marine v Thomas Miller* [2018] EWHC 3431 (Comm); [2019] 1 Lloyd's Rep. 399 Males J held that there was no reason why the application should not be dealt with on paper by the judge who had refused permission to appeal. It should not be listed for an oral hearing before a different judge.
   [2] In *Midnight Marine v Thomas Miller* [2018] EWHC 3431 (Comm); [2019] 1 Lloyd's Rep. 399 Males J held that at any renewal hearing the question would simply be whether there was a real prospect of success such that the case should be allowed to go to a full hearing. Such hearings should therefore be short, typically no more than 30 minutes; they should, where possible, be listed before the judge who had dismissed the application without a hearing; there should be no need for further written submissions, save for a succinct explanation of what was wrong with the judge's reasons for dismissal; and respondents should not generally attend, or should not recover their costs if they did. In those respects, such hearings would be similar to the oral renewal of applications for permission to apply for judicial review. after a refusal on paper

A claimant who does not file a reply does not admit what is pleaded in the defence and a claimant who files a reply that does not deal with something pleaded in the defence is not taken to admit it. A reply is necessary when the Claimant wishes to allege facts (or rely upon a legal provision or argument) which have not been pleaded in the claim. Accordingly, it should not be served simply to repeat what is pleaded in the particulars of claim. Proper consideration should be given to the question of a reply as soon as the defence has been served. The reply should be served before case management information sheets are provided to the Court. This will enable the judge to see all the pleaded issues before the Case Management Conference ("CMC") and will assist the parties in preparing for it. In some cases, more than 21 days may be needed for the service and filing of a reply (whether or not accompanied by a defence to counterclaim). In such a case, the defendant and the claimant may agree that the period for serving and filing a reply shall be extended by up to 21 days. However, any such agreement and brief reasons must be in writing and notified to the court. An application to the court is required for any further extension. If the parties are able to agree a further extension, a draft consent order should be provided together with a brief explanation of the reasons for the extension. However, if the effect of any agreed extension for the service of the reply would result in the reply being served after the date fixed for the CMC, the parties must on not less than 3 clear days' notice apply to the Court for the CMC to be adjourned.

Appendix A

Court Addresses and other Information for Circuit Commercial (Mercantile) Courts

1. London and South East

Judge

Replace Judge details with:
    His Honour Judge Pelling QC **2B-35**
    Clerk: Jas Kahlon
    Email: Jas Kahlon@jusice.gov.uk
    Tel: 0207 947 6339

3. North East (Leeds)

Listing, Enquiries and Video-conferencing

Replace the first line with:
    Head of section: Sandie Umarji **2B-37**

Users' Committee for the Business & Property Courts in Leeds

Replace with:
    Chair: Mr Justice Snowden. Contact via: sandie.umarji@justice.gov.uk

4. North East (Newcastle upon Tyne)

Judges

Replace Clerk contact details with:
    Email: Helen.Tait@justice.gov.uk **2B-38**
    Tel: 0191 201 2061

Listing, Enquiries and Video-conferencing

Replace Email with:
    Email: Helen.Tait@justice.gov.uk

Users' Committee

Replace with:
    Chair: Mr Justice Snowden. Contact via: Helen.Tait@justice.gov.uk Tel: 0191 201 2061
    User observations and suggestions: Email to newcastlechancery@justice.gov.uk marked FAO His Honour Judge Kramer

5.   NORTH WEST (LIVERPOOL)

Judges

Replace with:

2B-39   His Honour Judge Pearce. HHJs Hodge, Davies, Eyre QC, and Halliwell are also authorised to hear Circuit Commercial cases.

Listing and Enquiries

Replace contact with:
   Circuit Commercial Manager: Alison Blunsden (alison.blunsden@justice.gov.uk) Email (for filing and enquiries): Enquiries.liverpool.countycourt@justice.gov.uk

Replace fax with:
   Fax (Goldfax): 01264 785 132 (not a dedicated fax so clearly mark "Circuit Commercial Court")

Video-conferencing

Replace contact with:
   Contact: Stephen Christiansen

Replace email with:
   Email: stephen.christiansen@justice.gov.uk

Users Committee

Replace with:
   Please contact Alison Blunsden.

6.   NORTH WEST (MANCHESTER)

Judges and Listing

Replace first line with:

2B-40   His Honour Judge Pearce. HHJs Hodge, Davies, Eyre QC, and Halliwell are also authorised to hear Circuit Commercial cases.

8.   WALES (CARDIFF)

Address

Replace with:

2B-42   Cardiff Circuit Commercial Court
         Cardiff Civil Justice Centre
         2 Park Street
         Cardiff
         CF10 1ET
         DX 99500 Cardiff 6

Judge

Replace Clerk contact details with:
   Email: barry.sharples@justice.gov.uk
   Tel: 029 2037 6411
   Fax: 029 2037 6475

Replace Listing Clerk email with:
   Email: amanda.barrago@justice.gov.uk

9. Wales (Mold)

Address

Replace with:

Law Courts
Civic Centre
Mold
Flintshire
CH7 1AE
DX 702521 Mold 2

2B-43

Judge and Listing

After the first line, add new line:
His Honour Judge Jarman QC is also authorised to hear Circuit Commercial cases

Replace Email with:
Email: northwalescivillisting@justice.gov.uk

SECTION 2C   PROCEEDINGS IN THE TECHNOLOGY AND CONSTRUCTION COURT

TECHNOLOGY AND CONSTRUCTION COURT GUIDE

Editorial note

To the end of the paragraph, add:
From 25 February 2019, electronic filing via CE file has been extended to the Business and **2C-39.1** Property Courts outside London (Birmingham, Bristol, Cardiff, Leeds, Liverpool, Manchester, Newcastle).

Editorial note

Replace the last sentence (beginning "Michael J Lonsdale") with:
Bresco Electrical Services Ltd (In Liquidation) v Michael J Lonsdale (Electrical) Ltd [2019] EWCA Civ **2C-44.1** 27 (company in insolvent liquidation seeking to refer dispute to adjudication but adjudication would be futile because the decision would not be enforced).

Add new paragraph 2C-46.1:

Editorial note

From January 2019, the Disclosure Pilot for the Business and Property Courts, Practice Direc- **2C-46.1** tion 51U, applies to proceedings in the Technology and Construction Court.

SECTION 2D   ADMIRALTY JURISDICTION AND PROCEEDINGS

Part 61—Admiralty Claims

Replace r.61.1(2) with:

Scope and interpretation[1]
(2) In this Part—   **2D-6**
    (a) "admiralty claim" means a claim within the Admiralty jurisdiction of the High Court as set out in section 20 of the Senior Courts Act 1981;

---

[1] Amended by the Civil Procedure (Amendment No.5) Rules 2001 (SI 2001/4015) and the Civil Procedure (Amendment No.2) Rules 2009 (SI 2009/3390), the Civil Procedure (Amendment) Rules 2017 (SI 2017/95) and the Civil Procedure (Amendment) Rules 2019 (SI 2019/342).

(b)   "the Admiralty Court" means the Admiralty Court of the Queen's Bench Division of the High Court of Justice;

(ba) "the Admiralty Judge" means the judge in charge of the Admiralty Court and any other judge authorised to sit in the Admiralty Court;

(bb) "the Admiralty Registrar" means the holder of the office of this name listed in column 1 of Part II of Schedule 2 to the Senior Courts Act 1981 or any person who is authorised to exercise the powers of this office in accordance with s.91(1) of the Act;

(bc) "claim in personam" means an admiralty claim, other than a claim in rem, brought in accordance with section 21(1) of the Senior Courts Act 1981

(c)   "claim in rem" means a claim in an admiralty action in rem brought in accordance with section 21(2) to (5) of the Senior Courts Act 1981;

(d)   "collision claim" means a claim within section 20(3)(b) of the Senior Courts Act 1981;

(e)   "limitation claim" means a claim under the Merchant Shipping Act 1995 for the limitation of liability in connection with a ship or other property;

(f)   "salvage claim" means a claim—

   (i)   for or in the nature of salvage;

   (ii) for special compensation under; Article 14 of Schedule 11 to the Merchant Shipping Act 1995

   (iii) for the apportionment of salvage; and

   (iv) arising out of or connected with any contract for salvage services;

(g)   "caution against arrest" means a caution entered in the Register under rule 61.7;

(h)   "caution against release" means a caution entered in the Register under rule 61.8;

(i)   "the Register" means the Register of cautions against arrest and release which is open to inspection as provided by Practice Direction 61;

(j)   "the Marshal" means the Admiralty Marshal;

(k)   "ship" includes any vessel used in navigation;

(l)   "the Registrar" means the Admiralty Registrar; and

(m)   "electronic track data" means a digital or electronic recording of the track of a vessel (including any associated visual or aural recordings) as recorded by, for example, ship or shore-based AIS (Automatic Identification System), ECDIS (Electronic Chart and Display Information System), or a voyage data recorder.

Add new paragraph 2D-6.1:

Note

2D-6.1   Paragraph (2)(ba)–(bc) inserted and para.(2)(c), (k), (l) amended by the Civil Procedure (Amendment) Rules 2019 (SI 2019/342) r.10, with effect from 6 April 2019.

Replace r.61.2(3) with:

Admiralty claims[1]

(3) Rule 30.5 applies to claims in the Admiralty Court except that the **2D-16** Admiralty Court may order the transfer of a claim to—

(a) the Commercial Court;

(b) a Circuit Commercial Court; or

(c) [Omitted]

(d) any other appropriate court.

Add new paragraph 2D-16.1:

Note

Paragraph (3)(a), (b) amended and para.(3)(c) revoked by the Civil Procedure (Amendment) **2D-16.1** Rules 2019 (SI 2019/342) r.11, with effect from 6 April 2019.

Replace r.61.4 with:

Special provisions relating to collision claims[2]

61.4—(1) This rule applies to collision claims. **2D-29**

(2) A claim form need not contain or be followed by particulars of claim and rule 7.4 does not apply.

(3) An acknowledgment of service must be filed.

(4) A party who wishes to dispute the court's jurisdiction must make an application under Part 11 within 2 months after filing his acknowledgment of service.

(4A) Every party must—

(a) within 21 days after the defendant files their acknowledgment of service; or

(b) where the defendant applies under Part 11, within 21 days after the defendant files their further acknowledgment of service,

disclose any electronic track data which is or has been in its control, in accordance with Part 31, and, where every party has electronic track data in its control, each must provide copies, or permit inspection, of that electronic track data within 7 days of a request by another party to do so.

(5) Every party must—

(a) within 2 months after the defendant files the acknowledgment of service; or

(b) where the defendant applies under Part 11 within 2 months after the defendant files the further acknowledgment of service,

file at the court a completed collision statement of case in the form specified in Practice Direction 61.

(6) A collision statement of case must be—

(a) in the form set out in Practice Direction 61; and

(b) verified by a statement of truth.

(7) A claim form in a collision claim in personam may not be served out of the jurisdiction unless—

(a) the case falls within section 22(2)(a), (b) or (c) of the Senior Courts Act 1981; or

---

[1] Amended by the Civil Procedure (Amendment No.5) Rules 2001 (SI 2001/4015), the Civil Procedure (Amendment No.4) Rules 2005 (SI 2005/3515), the Civil Procedure (Amendment) Rules 2014 (SI 2014/407), the Civil Procedure (Amendment No.2) Rules 2017 (SI 2017/889) and the Civil Procedure (Amendment) Rules 2019 (SI 2019/342).

[2] Amended by the Civil Procedure (Amendment No.5) Rules 2001 (SI 2001/4015), the Civil Procedure (Amendment) Rules 2008 (SI 2008/2178) and the Civil Procedure (Amendment No.2) Rules 2009 (SI 2009/3390), and Civil Procedure (Amendment) Rules 2017 (SI 2017/95) and the Civil Procedure (Amendment) Rules 2019 (SI 2019/342).

   (b)   the defendant has submitted to or agreed to submit to the jurisdiction; and

the court gives permission in accordance with Section IV of Part 6; or

   (c)   rule 6.33 applies.

   (8)   Where permission to serve a claim form out of the jurisdiction is given, the court will specify the period within which the defendant may file an acknowledgment of service and, where appropriate, a collision statement of case.

   (9)   Where, in a collision claim in rem ("the original claim")—

   (a)   (i)   a counterclaim; or

         (ii)   a cross-claim in rem

         arising out of the same collision or occurrence is made; and

   (b)   (i)   the party bringing the original claim has caused the arrest of a ship or has obtained security in order to prevent such arrest; and

         (ii)   the party bringing the counterclaim or cross claim is unable to arrest a ship or otherwise obtain security,

the party bringing the counterclaim or cross claim may apply to the court to stay the original claim until sufficient security is given to satisfy any judgment that may be given in favour of that party.

   (10)   The consequences set out in paragraph (11) apply where a party to a claim to establish liability for a collision claim (other than a claim for loss of life or personal injury)—

   (a)   makes an offer to settle in the form set out in paragraph (12) not less than 21 days before the start of the trial;

   (b)   that offer is not accepted; and

   (c)   the maker of the offer obtains at trial an apportionment equal to or more favourable than his offer.

   (11)   Where paragraph (10) applies the parties will, unless the court considers it unjust, be entitled to the following costs—

   (a)   the maker of the offer will be entitled to—

         (i)   all his costs from 21 days after the offer was made; and

         (ii)   his costs before then in accordance with the apportionment found at trial; and

   (b)   all other parties to whom the offer was made—

         (i)   will be entitled to their costs up to 21 days after the offer was made in accordance with the apportionment found at trial; but

         (ii)   will not be entitled to their costs thereafter.

   (12)   An offer under paragraph (10) must be in writing and must contain—

   (a)   an offer to settle liability at stated percentages;

   (b)   an offer to pay costs in accordance with the same percentages;

   (c)   a term that the offer remain open for 21 days after the date it is made; and

   (d)   a term that, unless the court orders otherwise, on expiry of that period the offer remains open on the same terms except that the offeree should pay all the costs from that date until acceptance.

Add new paragraph 2D-29.1:

Note

2D-29.1   Paragraphs (7), (9), (11)(a)(ii), (b)(i) amended by the Civil Procedure (Amendment) Rules 2019 (SI 2019/342) r.12, with effect from 6 April 2019.

Replace r.61.6(2) with:

Security in claim in rem[1]

(2) Unless the terms on which security has been given provide otherwise, **2D-42** the court may order that—

- (a) the amount of security be reduced, and may stay the claim until the order is complied with; or
- (b) the amount of security be increased, and may give the claimant permission to arrest or re-arrest the property proceeded against to obtain further security.

Add new paragraph 2D-42.1:

Note

Paragraph (2) substituted by the Civil Procedure (Amendment) Rules 2019 (SI 2019/342) r.13, **2D-42.1** with effect from 6 April 2019.

Add new r.61.8(3A):

Release and cautions against release[2]

(3A) A caution against release— **2D-48**

- (a) is valid for 12 months after the date it is entered in the Register; and
- (b) may be renewed for a further 12 months by filing a further request.

Add new paragraph 2D-48.1:

Note

Paragraph (3A) inserted by the Civil Procedure (Amendment) Rules 2019 (SI 2019/342) r.14, **2D-48.1** with effect from 6 April 2019.

Replace r.61.11 with:

Limitation claims[3]

61.11—(1) This rule applies to limitation claims. **2D-73**

(2) A claim is started by the issue of a limitation claim form as set out in Practice Direction 61.

(3) The—

- (a) claimant; and
- (b) at least one defendant

must be named in the claim form, but all other defendants may be described.

(4) The claim form—

- (a) must be served on all named defendants and any other defendant who requests service upon him; and
- (b) may be served on any other defendant.

(5) The claim form may not be served out of the jurisdiction unless—

- (a) the claim falls within section 22(2)(a), (b) or (c) of the Senior Courts Act 1981;
- (b) the defendant has submitted to or agreed to submit to the jurisdiction of the court; or
- (c) the Admiralty Court has jurisdiction over the claim under any applicable Convention; and

the court grants permission in accordance with Section IV of Part 6; or

---

[1] Amended by the Civil Procedure (Amendment No.5) Rules 2001 (SI 2001/4015) and the Civil Procedure (Amendment) Rules 2019 (SI 2019/342).

[2] Amended by the Civil Procedure (Amendment No.5) Rules 2001 (SI 2001/4015) and the Civil Procedure (Amendment No.2) Rules 2009 (SI 2009/3390) and the Civil Procedure (Amendment) Rules 2019 (SI 2019/342).

[3] Amended by the Civil Procedure (Amendment No.5) Rules 2001 (SI 2001/4015), the Civil Procedure (Amendment) Rules 2008 (SI 2008/2178) and the Civil Procedure (Amendment No.2) Rules 2009 (SI 2009/3390) and the Civil Procedure (Amendment) Rules 2019 (SI 2019/342).

    (d)   rule 6.33 applies.

(6) An acknowledgment of service is not required.

(7) Every defendant upon whom a claim form is served must—

    (a)   within 28 days of service file—

        (i)   a defence; or

        (ii) a notice that the defendant admits the right of the claimant to limit liability; or

    (b)   if the defendant wishes to—

        (i)   dispute the jurisdiction of the court; or

        (ii) argue that the court should not exercise its jurisdiction,

file within 14 days of service (or where the claim form is served out of the jurisdiction, within the time specified in rule 6.35) an acknowledgment of service as set out in Practice Direction 61.

(8) If a defendant files an acknowledgment of service under paragraph (7)(b) he will be treated as having accepted that the court has jurisdiction to hear the claim unless he applies under Part 11 within 14 days after filing the acknowledgment of service.

(9) Where one or more named defendants admits the right to limit—

    (a)   the claimant may apply for a restricted limitation decree in the form set out in Practice Direction 61; and

    (b)   the court will issue a decree in the form set out in Practice Direction 61 limiting liability only against those named defendants who have admitted the claimant's right to limit liability.

(10) A restricted limitation decree—

    (a)   may be obtained against any named defendant who fails to file a defence within the time specified for doing so; and

    (b)   need not be advertised, but a copy must be served on the defendants to whom it applies.

(11) Where all the defendants upon whom the claim form has been served admit the claimant's right to limit liability—

    (a)   the claimant may apply to the Admiralty Registrar for a general limitation decree in the form set out in Practice Direction 61; and

    (b)   the court will issue a limitation decree.

(12) Where one or more of the defendants upon whom the claim form has been served do not admit the claimant's right to limit, the claimant may apply for a general limitation decree in the form set out in Practice Direction 61.

(13) When a limitation decree is granted the court—

    (a)   may—

        (i)   order that any proceedings relating to any claim arising out of the occurrence be stayed;

        (ii) order the claimant to establish a limitation fund if one has not been established or make such other arrangements for payment of claims against which liability is limited; or

       (iii) if the decree is a restricted limitation decree, distribute the limitation fund; and

    (b)   will, if the decree is a general limitation decree, give directions as to advertisement of the decree and set a time within which notice of claims against the fund must be filed or an application made to set aside the decree.

(14) When the court grants a general limitation decree the claimant must—

    (a)   advertise it in such manner and within such time as the court directs; and

    (b)   file—

        (i)   a declaration that the decree has been advertised in accordance with paragraph (a); and

    (ii)   copies of the advertisements.

(15) No later than the time set in the decree for filing claims, each of the defendants who wishes to assert a claim must file and serve his statement of case on—

    (a)   the limiting party; and

    (b)   all other defendants except where the court orders otherwise.

(16) Any person other than a defendant upon whom the claim form has been served may apply to the court within the time fixed in the decree to have a general limitation decree set aside.

(17) An application under paragraph (16) must be supported by a declaration—

    (a)   stating that the applicant has a claim against the claimant arising out of the occurrence; and

    (b)   setting out grounds for contending that the claimant is not entitled to the decree, either in the amount of limitation or at all.

(18) The claimant may constitute a limitation fund by

    (a)   making a payment into court;

    (b)   providing security in such form and on such terms as considered adequate by the court; or

    (c)   a combination of (a) and (b),

the procedure for which, in each case, is set out in Practice Direction 61.

(19) A limitation fund may be established before or after a limitation claim has been started.

(20) If a limitation claim is not commenced within 75 days after the date the fund was established—

    (a)   the fund will lapse;

    (b)   all money in court (including interest) will be repaid to the person who made the payment into court; and

    (c)   any security provided will be discharged.

(21) Money paid into court under paragraph (18) will not be paid out, nor will any security provided be discharged, except under an order of the court.

(22) A limitation claim for—

    (a)   a restricted decree may be brought by counterclaim; and

    (b)   a general decree may only be brought by counterclaim with the permission of the court.

Add new paragraph 2D-73.1:

Note

    Paragraphs (5), (20)(a), (20)(b), (21) amended, para.(18) substituted and para.(20(c) inserted by **2D-73.1** the Civil Procedure (Amendment) Rules 2019 (SI 2019/342) r.15, with effect from 6 April 2019.

Constituting a limitation fund

Replace paragraph with:

    CPR r.61.11(18) states that a claimant may constitute a fund by making a payment into court. In **2D-76.1** an unreported case, *Daina Shipping Co v MSC Mediterranean Shipping Co* [2012] Fo. 255 the Admiralty Judge, Teare J held that a limitation fund could be constituted by a guarantee contained in a letter of undertaking to the court provided by a well-known, foreign-based protection and indemnity insurer. The Court of Appeal has decided that on its proper construction art.11.2 of the Limitation of Liability for Maritime Claims Convention 1976 as enacted by s.185(1) of the Merchant Shipping Act 1995 provides that a limitation fund may be constituted by producing a guarantee which is considered by the court to be adequate security for the fund, see *Kairos Shipping v Enka & Co. (The "Atlantic Confidence")* [2014] EWCA Civ 217; [2014] 1 Lloyds Rep. 586. Rule 61.11(18) was amended by Civil Procedure (Amendment) Rules 2019 (SI 2019/342), with effect from 6 April 2019 to rectify the lacuna in this rule identified by these cases. It did so by substituting a new rule that makes provision for both making a payment into court and for providing such other security, such as a guarantee, or a combination of the two.

Replace r.61.13 with:

Assessors[1]

2D-83   **61.13   The court may sit with assessors when hearing—**
   (a)   **collision claims;**
   (b)   **other claims involving issues of navigation or seamanship; or**
   (c)   **a reference as defined in paragraph 13.1 of Practice Direction 61,**
and, whenever it does so, the parties will not be permitted to call expert witnesses unless the court orders otherwise.

Add new paragraph 2D-83.1:

Note

2D-83.1   Amended by the Civil Procedure (Amendment) Rules 2019 (SI 2019/342) r.16, with effect from 6 April 2019.

PRACTICE DIRECTION 61—ADMIRALTY CLAIMS

Case management

Replace paragraph 2.1 (where "Admiralty judge" has been changed to "Admiralty Judge") with:

2D-89   **2.1**   After a claim form is issued the Registrar will issue a direction in writing stating—
   (1)   whether the claim will remain in the Admiralty Court or be transferred to another court; and
   (2)   if the claim remains in the Admiralty Court—
      (a)   whether it will be dealt with by—
         (i)   the Admiralty Judge; or
         (ii)   the Registrar; and
      (b)   whether the trial will be in London or elsewhere.

Replace paragraph 2.3 (where "Admiralty judge" has been changed to "Admiralty Judge") and add new paragraphs 2.4 and 2.5:

   2.3   Where the Registrar directs that the claim will be dealt with by the Admiralty Judge, case management directions will be given and any case management conference or pre-trial review will be heard by the Admiralty Judge.
   2.4   Where it is directed that a claim is to be dealt with by the Registrar, it is the Registrar who will give directions, conduct any case management conference and any pre-trial review, and try the claim.
   2.5   Appeals from all decisions and judgments of the Registrar are to the Admiralty Judge, unless otherwise ordered (and subject to article 4(1)(a) of the Access to Justice 1999 (Destination of Appeals) Order 2016, S.I. 2016 No. 917).

Add new paragraph 2D-94.1:

Claims in personam

2D-94.1   **3A.1**   This section applies to Admiralty claims in personam (defined in rule 61.1(2)(bc) as an admiralty claim other than a claim in rem). Subject to the provisions of Part 61 and this practice direction relating to limitation claims and to collision claims, the following provisions apply to such claims.
   3A.2   All such claims will proceed in accordance with Part 58 (Commercial Court).
   3A.3   The claim form must be in Form ADM1A and must be served by the claimant.
   3A.4   The claimant may be named or may be described, but if not named in the claim form must identify themselves by name if requested to do so by any other party.

---

   [1] Amended by the Civil Procedure (Amendment No.5) Rules 2001 (SI 2001/4015) and the Civil Procedure (Amendment) Rules 2019 (SI 2019/342).

3A.5 The defendant must be named in the claim form.

3A.6 Any person who files a defence must identify themselves by name in the defence.

Before paragraph 4.7, insert paragraph title "Fast track collision claims". **2D-95.1**

Add new paragraph 2D-95.1.1:

Shorter and flexible trials of collision cases

4.8 In a collision action to which rule 61.4(4A) and paragraph 4.7 of this **2D-95.1.1** practice direction do not apply, the parties will be expected to consider whether the claim is suitable to tried in accordance with Practice Direction 57AB (Shorter and Flexible Trial Schemes).

4.9 Practice Direction 57AB applies to collision claims with the following modifications—

   (1)   paragraphs 2.09 to 2.34 do not apply and paragraphs 4.1 to 4.6 of this practice direction will apply instead; and

   (2)   at the case management conference, in exercising its powers under PD57AB, the court will consider the options in paragraph 4.7(1)(a) to (i) above.

Sale by the court and priorities

Replace paragraph 9.3 (where "Admiralty judge" has been changed to "Admiralty Judge") with:

9.3 An order for sale before judgment may only be made by the Admiralty **2D-112** Judge.

Replace paragraph 9.4 (where "Admiralty judge" has been changed to "Admiralty Judge") with:

9.4 Unless the Admiralty Judge orders otherwise, a determination of priorities may only be made by the Admiralty Judge.

Limitation claims

Replace paragraph 10.1 with:

10.1 The claim form in a limitation claim must be— **2D-114**

   (1)   in form **ADM15**; and

   (2)   accompanied by a declaration—

      (a)   setting out the facts upon which the claimant relies; and

      (b)   stating the names and addresses (if known) of all persons who, to the knowledge of the claimant, have claims against him in respect of the occurrence to which the limitation claim relates (other than named defendants and interested parties),

   verified by a statement of truth.

Replace paragraph 10.8 with:

10.8 On an application under rule 61.11(12) the Registrar may—

   (1)   grant a general limitation decree; or

   (2)   if he does not grant a decree—

      (a)   order service of a defence; and

      (b)   [Omitted]

      (c)   make such other case management directions as may be appropriate.

Add new paragraph 10.9A:

10.9A A limitation fund may be constituted by—

   (1)   making a payment into court;

   (2)   providing court-approved security; or

   (3)   a combination of (1) and (2).

Replace paragraph 10.10 with:

10.10 Where a limitation fund is established by making a payment into

court, the sum paid in must be—
(1)   the sterling equivalent of the number of special drawing rights to which [the claimant] claims to be entitled to limit his liability under the Merchant Shipping Act 1995; together with
(2)   interest from the date of the occurrence giving rise to his liability to the date of payment into court.

Replace paragraph 10.12 with:
10.12   An application under paragraph 10.11(2)(b)—
(1)   may be made without notice; and
(2)   must be supported by evidence proving, to the satisfaction of the court, the sterling equivalent of the appropriate number of special drawing rights on the date of payment into court.

Replace paragraph 10.13 with:
10.13   The claimant must give notice in writing to every defendant and interested party whose address the claimant knows, of—
(1)   any payment into court specifying—
　　(a)   the date of the payment in;
　　(b)   the amount paid in and how it has been calculated;
　　(c)   the amount and rate of interest included; and
　　(d)   the period to which it relates; and
(2)   any excess amount (and interest) paid out to him under paragraph 10.11(2)(b).

Add new paragraphs 10.13A to 10.13J:
10.13A   Where a claimant wishes to establish a limitation fund (in whole or in part) by providing security, the claimant must apply to the court for an order approving the security. The application may be made on paper and without notice, but the applicant should first seek to agree the provider, form, nature, and terms of the proposed security with any named defendant and any interested party before making the application (unless the circumstances of the case make that impracticable).
10.13B   An application under paragraph 10.13A must be—
(1)   accompanied by the proposed security or a draft thereof; and
(2)   supported by evidence of—
　　(a)   the adequacy of the proposed security; and
　　(b)   if the proposed security is expressed in sterling, the sterling equivalent of the appropriate number of special drawing rights on the date the application is made.
10.13C   The court shall approve the proposed security if it is satisfied that it is adequate in all the circumstances (including its form, nature, terms, and the financial standing of the person offering it).
10.13D   Where a limitation fund is established (in whole or in part) by providing court-approved security, the security may be expressed in special drawing rights or sterling. If the security is expressed in sterling, the amount of the security shall be the same as if the fund were being constituted by payment in to court and paragraphs 10.10 and 10.11(1) above shall apply in an equivalent sense.
10.13E   The claimant must give notice in writing to every named defendant and any interested party whose address is known of any court-approved security lodged at court, specifying—
(1)   the terms of the security;
(2)   the date on which the security was lodged at court;
(3)   how the amount of security was calculated;
(4)   the amount and rate of interest included, and the period to which it relates,

and shall provide on request any person so notified with a copy of the security so lodged and the application made under paragraph 10.13A.

10.13F An application to set aside the court's approval of a security may be made by—

(1) any person (whether a defendant, an interested party or another), who was not given notice of the claimant's application under paragraph 10.13A; or

(2) any person (whether a defendant, an interested party or another) if circumstances relevant to the adequacy of the security have changed since it was approved by the court.

10.13G An application under paragraph 10.13F(1) must be—

(1) made on notice to the provider of the security, all claimants, all named defendants, and all interested parties (whose addresses are known);

(2) supported by evidence setting out the reasons why the court's approval of the security should be set aside; and

(3) made within 21 days of receipt by the applicant of notice given under paragraph 10.13E (if such notice was given to the applicant) or as soon as reasonably practicable (if no such notice was given to the applicant).

10.13H An application under paragraph 10.13F(2) must be—

(1) made on notice to the provider of the security, all claimants, all named defendants, and all Interested Parties (whose addresses are known);

(2) supported by evidence setting out the change in circumstances justifying the setting aside of the court's approval of the security; and

(3) made as soon as reasonably practicable after discovery of the change of circumstances.

10.13I On an application under paragraph 10.13F, the court may—

(1) confirm its approval of the adequacy of the security;

(2) set aside its approval of the adequacy of the security; and/or

(3) require the fund to be reconstituted in such manner and on such terms as it thinks fit.

10.13J If a claimant has constituted a fund by payment in of money, it may apply at any time for an order permitting the reconstitution of the fund (in whole or in part) by means of a court-approved security. Any such application shall be made in accordance with paragraphs 10.13A to 10.13E, and paragraphs 10.13F to 10.13I shall apply to any order made.

Add new paragraph 2D-114.1:

Editorial note

Paragraphs 10.13A to 10.13J were inserted by CPR Update 104, with effect from 6 April 2019. **2D-114.1**
This addressed a deficiency in CPR Pt 63 and its PD noted in *The Atlantik Confidence* [2014] EWCA Civ 217; [2014] 1 W.L.R. 3883, CA.

Delete paragraphs 2D-121 to 2D-123.

References to the Registrar

Replace paragraph 13.2 with:

13.2 Unless the court orders otherwise, where a reference has been **2D-124** ordered—

(1) if particulars of claim have not already been served, the claimant must file and serve particulars of claim on all other parties within 14 days after the date of the order;

(2) any party opposing the claim must file a defence to the claim within 14 days after service of the particulars of claim on him;

(3) the rules concerning statements of case shall apply to the particulars of claim, the defence and any other statements of case served in the reference; and

(4)   all documents which the claimant (or counterclaimant) in a reference intends to rely on in order to show that the sums claimed were properly incurred and paid ('vouchers') shall be appended to their first statement of case in the reference and cross referenced to the sums being claimed, unless there is a compelling reason not to do so.

OTHER ADMIRALTY PRACTICE DIRECTIONS AND STATEMENTS

Replace Practice Note with:

Practice Note (Admiralty: Assessors' Remuneration) of 1 September 2019

2D-142   1.   This guidance is issued by Mr Justice Teare with the agreement of Sir Terence Etherton, Master of the Rolls, and Dame Victoria Sharpe, President of the Queen's Bench Division. It is issued as a Practice Note and not as a Practice Direction. It replaces Practice Note (Admiralty: Assessors' Remuneration) of 1 April 2018.

2.   In the absence of special directions given in a particular case the level of remuneration which should normally be paid to Trinity Masters and nautical and other assessors summoned to assist the Court of Appeal, the Admiralty Court on the trial of an action, or a Divisional Court of the Queen's Bench Division is as follows:

(1)   Full day's attendance at hearing: £790;

(2)   Half day's attendance at hearing: £395;

(3)   Attendance at court when case is not heard: £158 per hour;

(4)   Consultation with the court on a day when there is no hearing: £395;

(5)   Attendance to hear reserved judgment (including any consultation with the court on the same day): £199;

(6)   If notice of attendance is countermanded less than two days before the hearing: £395; and

(1)   Assessors should receive reasonable sums for their travelling expenses and subsistence;

(2)   Where there is a cross appeal, or where appeals are heard together, or where actions are consolidated or tried together, the proceedings should be treated as one appeal or action as the case may be;

(3)   In the absence of special directions given in a particular case, the remuneration and expenses should be paid by the appellant or the party setting down the action as the case may be without prejudice to any right to recover from any other party the amount so paid on assessment.

3.   The figures specified in paragraph 2 above are subject to annual adjustment.

4.   The guidance in this Practice Note takes effect on 1 September 2019 and is to apply to all actions and appeals the hearing of which begin on or after that date. For guidance concerning actions and appeals the hearing of which began before 1 September 2019 see the Practice Note (Admiralty: Assessors' Remuneration) of 1 April 2018.

SECTION 2E   ARBITRATION PROCEEDINGS

PART 62—ARBITRATION CLAIMS

Family Court claims

Replace paragraph with:

2E-6.1   Pending rule/practice direction amendments special provision has been made for arbitration claims arising out of family court cases. On 23 November 2015 the President of the Family Court, Sir James Munby, issued *Practice Direction (Family Court: Interface with Arbitration)* [2016] 1 W.L.R. 59. This concerns the interface between the Family Court and arbitrations conducted in accordance with the provisions of the Arbitration Act 1996 where the parties to a post-relationship breakdown financial dispute have agreed to submit issues for decision by an arbitrator whose award is to be binding upon them. The text of the guidance is at: *https://www.judiciary.gov.uk/publications/practice-guidance-arbitration-in-the-family-court* [Accessed 6 February 2016]. It should be noted that notwithstanding its description in the W.L.R. as a Practice Direction, the guidance issued by the President is not a Practice Direction: it was not issued, as would have been necessary for it to be a Practice Direction, with the concurrence of the Lord Chancellor. In *BC v BG* [2019] EWFC 7; [2019] 2 F.C.R. 187 (Ms Clare Ambrose) the court held that the primary means for challenging an arbitration award obtained under the Family Law Arbitration Financial Scheme should be through the powers of the Arbitration Act 1996 and that the decision in *J v B (Challenge to Arbitral Award)* [2016] EWHC 324 (Fam); [2016] 1 W.L.R. 3319; [2016] 2 WLUK 643 was limited to the grounds of a vitiating mistake or supervening event and did not create an open-ended discretion to re-open an award without regard to the restrictions and safeguards imposed by the 1996 Act.

III.   Enforcement

Service of enforcement proceedings

Replace paragraph with:
   Where service of enforcement proceedings is required by s.12 of State Immunity Act 1978, it is **2E-40.1**
not mandatory for an arbitration claim or an order permitting the enforcement of an arbitration
award to be served in accordance with the provisions of s.12. Orders permitting the enforcement of
an arbitration award had to be served, pursuant to CPR r.62.18(8)(b) and r.6.44, but the court had
jurisdiction in an appropriate case to dispense with service in accordance with r.6.16 and/or r.6.28:
General Dynamics United Kingdon v State of Libya [2019] EWCA Civ 1110 (also see Vol.1 para.6.28.1).

Arbitration Act 1996

A party to an arbitration agreement

To the end of the fourth paragraph, after "Andrew Smith J", add:
   followed in *Minister of Finance (Inc) v International Petroleum Investment Co* [2019] EWHC 1151 **2E-107**
(Comm)

"… the Court may by order extend the time for taking that step"

Replace "Haven Insurance v EUI [2018] EWCA Civ 2494" with:
   Haven Insurance v EUI [2018] EWCA Civ 2494; [2019] Lloyd's Rep. I.R. 128   **2E-122**

Scope of section 47

Replace the second paragraph with:
   In *Sucafina SA v Nicola Rotenberg* [2012] EWCA Civ 637; [2012] 2 Lloyd's Rep. 54; [2012] 2 All **2E-207**
E.R. (Comm) 952; [2013] Bus. L.R. 158; [2012] 2 C.L.C. 203 the Court of Appeal upheld the deci-
sion of Eder J. that a failure to pay arbitral fees did not affect the nature of two interim awards as
awards which were final and binding on those issues with which they dealt. In *ZCCM Investments
Holdings Plc v Kansanshi Holdings Plc* [2019] EWHC 1285 (Comm); [2019] 2 Lloyd's Rep. 29
Cockerill J considered the authorities dealing with the question of whether a document is a
procedural ruling or an award.

Application

In the fourth line, after "of the district", replace "registry." with:
   registry (in the Commercial Court and the London Circuit Commercial Court, the application is **2E-250**
to a judge).

Editorial note

Replace the second paragraph with:
   Hearings in s.67 challenges may be in public, and the judgments in respect of such challenges **2E-256**
will be in public and will usually not be anonymised: *Chung v Silver Dry Bulk Co Ltd* [2019] EWHC
1479 (Comm) per Moulder J.

To the end of the paragraph, add:
   In *Soletanche Bachy France SAS v Aqaba Container Terminal (Pvt) Co* [2019] EWHC 362 (Comm);
[2019] 1 Lloyd's Rep. 423 Sir Michael Burton held that even if it was a nullity for the arbitrators to
accept corrections out of time, that did not amount to a substantive absence of jurisdiction although
it would amount to a plain irregularity by the arbitrators which, if there had been a substantial
injustice, the court could correct.

"On the ground of serious irregularity"

In the third paragraph, replace "RJ v HB [2018] EWHC 2833 (Comm)" with:
   RJ v HB [2018] EWHC 2833 (Comm); [2018] 6 Costs L.R. 1347   **2E-262**

After the third paragraph, add new paragraph:
   Similarly in *P v D* [2019] EWHC 1277 (Comm) Sir Michael Burton held that arbitrators had
breached their duty under the Arbitration Act 1996 s.33 to act fairly and impartially as between the
parties by reaching a decision on a core issue without the losing party's main witness being cross-
examined on that issue and by basing their decision on a case which had not been argued.

*In the ninth paragraph (beginning "Where an award is challenged"), after "3383 (Comm) (Flaux", replace
"J))." with:*
   J); *ZCCM Investments Holdings Plc v Kansanshi Holdings Plc* [2019] EWHC 1285 (Comm); [2019] 2
Lloyd's Rep. 29).

After the ninth paragraph, add new paragraph:
   In *Pakistan v Broadsheet LLC* [2019] EWHC 1832 (Comm) the court (Moulder J) held that the giving of "inadequate reasons" by an arbitration tribunal in relation to an arbitration award did not amount to a serious irregularity leading to a substantial injustice for the purposes of a challenge under the Arbitration Act 1996 s.68(2)(c) or (h).

Remission and setting aside

Replace "RJ v HB [2018] EWHC 2833 (Comm)" with:
2E-263   *RJ v HB* [2018] EWHC 2833 (Comm); [2018] 6 Costs L.R. 1347

Appeals to the Court of Appeal

Replace the fifth paragraph with:
2E-268   Save in exceptional circumstances only a High Court judge can grant permission to appeal to the Court of Appeal: *Henry Boot Construction (UK) Ltd v Malmaison Hotel (Manchester) Ltd* [2000] 2 Lloyd's Rep. 625; [2001] Q.B. 388; [2001] 1 All E.R. 257, CA. In *Midnight Marine v Thomas Miller* [2018] EWHC 3431 (Comm); [2019] 1 Lloyd's Rep. 399 Males J held that there was no reason why the application should not be dealt with on paper by the judge who had refused permission to appeal. For the application to be listed for an oral hearing before a different judge was unnecessarily wasteful.

Section 80(5)

Replace paragraph with:
2E-292   Paragraph (2)(a) of CPR r.3.1 (The court's general powers of court management) states that the court may "extend or shorten the time for compliance with any rule, practice direction or court order (even of the application is made after the time for compliance has expired)" (for commentary, see Vol.1, para.3.1.2). The manner in which this discretion should be exercised for the purpose of extending time limits for proceedings under the 1996 Act to which s.80(5) relates (in particular in ss.67 to 69) was considered by Colman J in *Kalmneft JSC v Glencore Iternational AG* [2002] 1 All E.R. 76; [2002] 1 Lloyd's Rep.128. In *Nagusina Naviera v Allied Maritime Inc* [2002] EWCA Civ 1147; [2003] 2 C.L.C. 1, CA, the Court of Appeal was referred to the guidance given by Colman J and did not dissent from it. Since then that guidance given by Colman J has been followed consistently by the Commercial Court; the leading modern iteration is *Terna Bahrain Holding Company WLL v Al Shamsi* [2012] EWHC 3283 (Comm); [2013] 1 Lloyd's Rep. 86, where the principles derived from this line of authority were summarised. The doubts expressed by Eder J in *S v A* [2016] EWHC 846 (Comm); [2016] 1 Lloyd's Rep. 604 (as to whether this approach was consistent with the principles given in the recent decisions of the Court of Appeal in *Mitchell v News Group Newspapers Ltd* [2013] EWCA Civ 1537 and *Denton v TH White Ltd* [2019] 1 Lloyd's Rep. 569; [2014] EWCA Civ 906.) have not gained traction. In *State A v Party B* [2019] EWHC 799 (Comm), the factors were considered and Sir Michael Burton indicated that where fresh evidence was being relied upon, those factors had to allow for some leeway: the longer the delay, the more transformational that evidence would have to be.

"… be enforced … as a judgment" s.101(2)

After the first paragraph, add new paragraph:
2E-353   In *General Dynamics v Libya* [2019] EWCA Civ 1110, the Court of Appeal held that it was not mandatory for an arbitration claim or an order permitting the enforcement of an arbitration award to be served in accordance with the provisions of s.12. Orders permitting the enforcement of an arbitration award had to be served, pursuant to CPR r.62.18(8)(b) and r.6.44, but the court had jurisdiction in an appropriate case to dispense with service in accordance with r.6.16 and/or r.6.28.

SECTION 2F   INTELLECTUAL PROPERTY PROCEEDINGS

PART 63—INTELLECTUAL PROPERTY CLAIMS

Brexit

Replace paragraph with:
2F-1.1.1   At the time of writing, the Plant Breeders' Rights (Amendment etc.) Regulations (EU Exit) 2019 (SI 2019/204) will revoke Council Regulation (EC) 2100/94 (see the Schedule to the 2018 Regula-

tions) on Brexit. This is anticipated to render reference to the Council Regulation in r.63.1(2)(j)(vii) redundant. Further revisions to Pt 63 should also be anticipated in respect of reference to the Office for Harmonisation in the Internal Market in respect of both Council Regulation (EC) 207/2009 and 6/2002. Both would be expected to become redundant. It is anticipated that r.63.1(2)(e) will be retained as the patent regime, including that in respect of supplementary licence protection, will form part of retained EU law (see further *Guidance - Patents if there's no Brexit Deal* (Dept. of Business, Energy & Industrial Strategy (24 September 2018) *https://www.gov.uk/government/publications/patents-if-theres-no-brexit-deal/patents-if-theres-no-brexit-deal* [Accessed 13 February 2019]). The Department's Guidance note also states that supplementary licence protection applications pending and pending patent applications on Exit Day will be unaffected, suggesting that transitional and saving provisions to Pt 63 may also be anticipated. Further reference should also be made to one further statutory instrument, the Patents (Amendment) (EU Exit) Regulations 2019 (SI 2019/801) and a further draft statutory instrument, the Trade Marks (Amendment etc.) (EU Exit) Regulations 2018.

See Vol.1 para.5.0.1.1 for detail on the amendments to the CPR and its PDs in the event of a no-deal exit.

V. Intellectual Property Enterprise Court[1]

Small claims in the Intellectual Property Enterprise Court

After the third paragraph, add new paragraph:

2F-17.21.1 In *Twentieth Century Fox Film Corps v Cyclone Events Ltd* (IPEC), 13 June 2019, unrep., in refusing an application to re-allocate a claim from the multi-track to the small claims track, the court, amongst other matters, concluded that:

- the matters to be considered under r.26.8 are not necessarily to be accorded equal weight. Instead it is a matter for the court to determine the weight to give each in the circumstances of a case; and
- "the circumstances of the parties" under r.26.8(1)(i), include the issue of access to justice (the defendants submitting, unsuccessfully, that their access to justice would be compromised by the exposure to, and need to fund, costs in the multi-track).

Replace Patents Court Guide:

PATENTS COURT GUIDE
Issued April 2019

By authority of the Chancellor of the High Court

1. INTRODUCTION

2F-127 This guide applies to the Patents Court only. The Intellectual Property Enterprise Court has its own guide to which users of that court are referred.

The general guidance applicable to matters in the Chancery Division, as set out in the Chancery Guide, also applies to patent actions unless specifically mentioned below. Thus practitioners should consult this guide together with the Chancery Guide.

"PD63" refers to the Practice Direction - Patents and Other Intellectual Property Claims which supplements CPR Part 63.

2. ALLOCATION

2F-128 Actions proceeding in the Patents Court are allocated to the multi-track (Part 63.1(3)). Attention is drawn to Part 63.8 and PD63.5 (case management). Since October 2014, claims issued in the Patents Court have received claim numbers with the prefix HP-.

3. THE JUDGES OF THE PATENTS COURT

2F-129 The judges of the Patents Court and their clerks are set out in Annex A to this guide, together with their contact details.

Trials of cases with a technical difficulty rating of 4 or 5 will normally be heard by Arnold J, Birss J or Henry Carr J or by suitably qualified deputy High Court judges.

4. JUDGES ABLE AND WILLING TO SIT OUT OF LONDON

2F-130 If the parties so desire, for the purpose of saving time or costs, the Patents Court will sit out of London. Before any approach is made to the Chancery Listing Officer, the parties should discuss

---

[1] Heading amended by the Civil Procedure (Amendment No.7) Rules 2013 (SI 2013/1974) r.26(h) with effect from 1 October 2013.

between themselves the desirability of such a course. If there is a dispute as to venue, the court will resolve the matter on an application. Where there is no dispute, the Chancery Listing Officer should be contacted as soon as possible so that arrangements can be put in place well before the date of the proposed hearing.

5. INTELLECTUAL PROPERTY COURT USERS' COMMITTEE

2F-131   This committee (the "IPCUC") considers the problems and concerns of intellectual property litigators and litigants. Membership of the committee includes the judges of the Patents Court, representatives of the Intellectual Property Bar Association, the Intellectual Property Lawyers Association, the Chartered Institute of Patent Attorneys, the Chartered Institute of Trade Mark Attorneys and the IP Federation. Anyone having views concerning the improvement of intellectual property litigation is invited to make his or her views known to the committee, preferably through the relevant professional representative on the committee. They may also be communicated to the secretary, whose details are in Annex A to this guide.

PROCEDURE IN THE PATENTS COURT

6. STATEMENTS OF CASE

TIME LIMITS

2F-132   **6.1** In general, the time limits set out in Part 15 apply to litigation of patents and registered designs. However, Part 63.7 modifies Part 15 in respect of the time limits for filing defences and replies.

CONTENT OF STATEMENTS OF CASE

6.2 In general, statements of case (i.e. the pleadings of all parties) must comply with the requirements of Part 16. Furthermore, they should comply with Part 63.6 and PD63.4. Copies of important documents referred to in a statement of case (e.g. an advertisement referred to in a Particulars of Infringement or documents cited in Grounds of Invalidity) should be served with the statement of case. Where any such document requires translation, a translation should be served at the same time.

SERVICE ON THE COMPTROLLER-GENERAL OF PATENTS, DESIGNS AND TRADE MARKS ("THE COMPTROLLER")

6.3 Parties are reminded of the requirement in Part 63.14(3) that, where a remedy is sought that would if granted affect an entry in any United Kingdom Patent Register (for example the revocation of a patent or registered design), they are required to serve on the Comptroller: the claim form, counterclaim or application notice; any other relevant statement of case such as grounds of invalidity (including any amended statement of case); and any accompanying documents. In addition, PD63.14.1 requires that, when such an order is made, the party in whose favour the order is made must serve it on the Comptroller within 14 days.

NOTIFICATION OF THE EUROPEAN UNION INTELLECTUAL PROPERTY OFFICE

6.4 Parties are reminded of the requirement in PD63 para.15.4 to inform the Court when judgment becomes final on a counterclaim for a declaration of invalidity of a registered Community design that paragraph 15.4 applies and that a copy of the judgment needs to be sent to the European Union Intellectual Property Office.

INDEPENDENT VALIDITY OF CLAIMS

6.5 Where one party raises the issue of validity of a patent, the patentee (or other relevant party) should identify which of the claims of the patent are alleged to have independent validity as early as possible.

7. ACTIVE CASE MANAGEMENT AND STREAMLINED PROCEDURE

2F-133   **7.1** The claimant should apply for a case management conference ("CMC") within 14 days of the date when all defendants who intend to file and serve a defence have done so (PD63.5.3). If the claimant fails to do so, then any other party may apply for a CMC (PD63.5.6). Any party may apply in writing for a CMC prior to the above periods. Where a case has been transferred from another division or from another court, the claimant must file for a CMC within 14 days of the transfer (PD63.5.4).

7.2 Almost invariably CMCs in the Patents Court will be conducted by a judge. However, in the limited circumstances set out in PD63.5.2(2) (see also para.15 below), a Master may conduct a CMC. Bundles in accordance with PD63.5.9 should be filed with the court.

7.3 In general, parties should endeavour to agree directions prior to the date fixed for the CMC. Although the court has the right to amend directions which have been agreed, this will only happen where there is good reason for doing so. A specimen order for directions is Annex B to this Guide.

7.4 In accordance with the overriding objective, the court will actively manage the case. In making any order for directions, the court will consider all relevant matters and have regard to the overriding objective with particular emphasis on proportionality, the financial position of the parties, the degree of complexity of the case, the importance of the case and the amount of money at stake.

7.5 The parties are reminded of their continuing obligation to assist the court to further the overriding objective. Moreover, it is the duty of the parties' advisors to remind litigants of the existence of mediation or other forms of alternative dispute resolution as a possible means to resolve disputes. In particular, the parties should consider:

(a) The need for and/or scope of any oral testimony from factual or expert witnesses. The court may confine cross-examination to particular issues and to time limits. The parties should consider whether oral testimony of witnesses should be given by video facility.

(b) The need for, and scope of, any disclosure of documents. The requirements of Part 31.5(3)-(5) relating to disclosure reports apply to actions in the Patent Court.

(c) The need for any experiments, process or product descriptions.

(d) The need for an oral hearing or whether a decision can be made on the papers. If an oral hearing is considered to be appropriate, the court may order that the hearing be of a fixed duration.

(e) Whether all issues should be tried together or whether it would be advantageous for one or more issues to be tried in advance of the remaining issues.

(f) Whether there is a need for a document setting out the basic undisputed technology (a "technical primer", as to which see para. 13.6 below), and if so, its scope and the steps to be taken to achieve agreement of it.

(g) Whether a scientific adviser should be appointed.

(h) The technical complexity of the action. Technical complexity is measured on a scale of 1 to 5, with 1 being the least complex and 5 the most.

(i) Whether a costs-capping order should be made.

(j) Whether there should be a stay of proceedings for mediation or other form of alternative dispute resolution.

(k) Whether the case is of sufficient value that it ought to be exempt from the costs management provisions in Part 3.12-3.18.

STREAMLINED PROCEDURE

7.6 Any party may at any time apply to the court for a streamlined procedure in which:

(a) all factual and expert evidence is in writing;

(b) there is no requirement to give disclosure of documents;

(c) there are no experiments;

(d) cross-examination is only permitted on any topic or topics where it is necessary and is confined to those topics;

or for any variant on the above.

7.7 Prior to applying for a streamlined procedure, the party seeking it should put its proposal to other parties in the proceedings and should endeavour to agree a form of order.

7.8 If the parties agree to a streamlined procedure, the proposed form of order should be put to the judge for approval as a paper application.

8. ADMISSIONS

8.1 With a view to early elimination of non-issues, practitioners are reminded of the necessity of making admissions as soon as possible. This should be done as early as possible, for instance, in a defence or reply. Thus, in a defence, a party may admit the acts complained of or that his article/process has certain of the features of a claim. In a reply a patentee may be able to admit prior publication of cited documents. For the effect of admissions, see Part 14. **2F-134**

8.2 Parties should also consider serving a notice to admit facts in accordance with Rule 32.18 for the purpose of identification of points not in dispute: for example, by asking whether or not the defendant disputes that his article/process has certain features of the claim the real dispute can be narrowed. Thus the ambit of disclosure and of witness and expert statements will be narrowed.

8.3 Parties are reminded that when deciding the issue of costs, a court can take into account the conduct of the parties, including whether it was reasonable for a party to contest a particular issue, see Rule 44.2(5)(b).

8.4 The position should be kept under constant review. If there is any alteration in the admissions that can be made, the identity of the claims said to have independent validity, or the claims alleged to be infringed, that information should be communicated forthwith to the other parties.

9. ALTERNATIVE DISPUTE RESOLUTION ("ADR")

9.1 While emphasising its primary role as a forum for deciding patent and registered design cases, the Patents Court encourages parties to consider the use of ADR (such as, but not confined to, mediation and conciliation) as an alternative means of resolving disputes or particular issues **2F-135**

within disputes. A fuller list of the different types of ADR can be found in section 2.12 of the Guide to the Intellectual Property Enterprise Court.

9.2 Settlement of disputes by ADR has many advantages including significant saving of costs and providing parties with a wider range of solutions than can be offered by litigation. Legal representatives should consider and advise their clients as to the possibility of attempting to resolve the dispute via ADR. In an appropriate case, the Patents Court may stay a case for a specified period of time to encourage and enable the parties to use ADR.

10. APPLICATIONS FOR INTERIM INJUNCTIONS AFFECTING THE NATIONAL HEALTH SERVICE

2F-135.1   **10.1** Attention is drawn to PD25A para. 5.2, which requires the Court, when making an order for an interim injunction, to consider whether to require the applicant to give an undertaking to pay any damages sustained by a person other than the respondent who suffers loss as a result of the order. Where a party seeks an interim injunction which would affect dealings in a pharmaceutical product or medical device purchased by the National Health Service ("NHS"), the Court will consider whether the applicant should give such an undertaking in favour of the NHS. The applicant must notify the Department of Health by email to patents@dhsc.gov.uk of (i) the application when it is made and (ii) any order made following the application as soon as practicable. Notification to this email address will amount to notice to all four NHS agencies in England, Scotland, Wales and Northern Ireland.

DISCLOSURE

2F-136   **11.1** Parties are obliged to provide disclosure in accordance with Part 31 as modified by Rule 63.9 and PD63.6.1-6.3 and as modified by Practice Direction 51U – Disclosure Pilot for the Business and Property Courts.

PROCESS AND/OR PRODUCT DESCRIPTION

11.2 Where appropriate, parties are encouraged to provide a process and/or product description ("PPD") instead of standard disclosure relating to processes or products which are alleged to infringe or are otherwise relevant to proceedings.

11.3 Subject to 10.5 below, PPDs must be adequate to deal with the nature of the allegation that has been advanced by the other party or parties. The parties have joint responsibility at an early stage to determine the nature of the case advanced so that the PPD is adequate to deal with that case.

11.4 Parties should bear in mind when preparing a PPD that they may be called on to prove it at trial. Any material omission or inaccuracy could result in a costly adjournment with consequential adverse orders, including as to costs. A PPD ought to be accompanied by a signed written statement which:

(i)   states that the person making the statement is personally acquainted with the facts to which the description relates;

(ii)   verifies that the description is a true and complete description of the product or process; and

(iii) contains an acknowledgement by the person making the statement that he or she may be required to attend court in order to be cross-examined on the contents of the description.

11.5 Insofar as a party is not able to verify that the PPD is a true and complete description of all relevant aspects of its product or process (for example because it does not make certain components in its product and does not know how they work), then the correct course is for the party to verify such parts as it is able, and to serve a disclosure list (which may or may not contain any documents) in relation to the remainder.

DESCRIPTIONS AND DRAWINGS OF PROCESSES OR PRODUCTS

11.6 Parties are encouraged to agree descriptions and drawings of processes and/or products which are the subject of infringement proceedings or are alleged to constitute relevant prior art.

MODELS OR APPARATUS OF PROCESSES OR PRODUCTS

11.7 If a party wishes to adduce a model or apparatus at trial, it should, if practicable, ensure that directions for such are given at the first CMC (PD63 para. 8.1). Parties should endeavour to view and agree the accuracy of such models or apparatus where possible well in advance of the date of trial.

INSPECTION ON TERMS AS TO CONFIDENTIALITY

11.8 It is often the case in patent cases that one or both parties disclose documents which they are only willing permit inspection of on terms as to confidentiality. Parties should endeavour to agree confidentiality clubs and agreements. Specimen confidentiality agreements form Annex C to this Guide; these specimen agreements may need adaptation to suit the circumstances of a particular case.

General Matters Relating to Hearings of Applications and Trials

12. ARRANGEMENTS FOR LISTING

12.1 Attention is drawn to the Practice Statement: Listing of Cases for Trial in the Patents Court **2F-137** issued by the Judge in Charge of the Patents Court on 7 December 2015 reproduced in Annex D to this Guide.

12.2 The Chancery Listing Officer is responsible for the listing of all work of the Patents Court. The Chancery Listing Officer and his staff are located in the Rolls Building. The office is open to the public from 10.00 am to 4.30 pm each day. The telephone number is 020 7947 7717 and the fax number is 0870 739 5868.

12.3 Appointments to fix trials and interim applications are dealt with between 11.00 am and 12.00 noon each working day. The applicant should first obtain an appointment from the Chancery Listing Officer and give 3 clear days' notice to all interested parties of the date and time fixed.

12.4 A party should not seek to list an application or cause the opposing advocate or counsel's clerk to "pencil in" a date for hearing prior to raising with the proposed respondent the subject-matter of the application so that, where possible, agreement may be reached on the subject-matter of the application. Applicants who fail properly to consult with the respondents prior to listing an application may be met with an adverse costs order.

SHORT APPLICATIONS

12.5 Short applications (i.e. those estimated to last no more than 1 hour) will usually be heard before the normal court day starts at 10.30 am e.g. at 9.30 or 10 am. These can be issued and the hearing date arranged at any time by attendance at the Chancery Listing Office. Attention is drawn to PD63.5 about the filing of documents and skeleton arguments.

URGENT APPLICATIONS AND WITHOUT NOTICE APPLICATIONS

12.6 A party wishing to apply without notice to the respondent(s) should contact the Chancery Listing Office. In cases of emergency in vacation or out of normal court hours, the application should be made to the duty Chancery judge.

INTERIM INJUNCTION HEARINGS AND EXPEDITED TRIALS

12.7 Applicants for interim remedies (in particular, interim injunctions) and respondents are encouraged to consider whether an expedited (speedy) trial would better meet the interests of justice. Applications for expedited trials may be made at any time but should be made as soon as possible and notice given to all parties. Parties are reminded that varying degrees of expedition are possible. Some cases may warrant extreme expedition, others a lesser degree.

12.8 When an application for an interim injunction is made the applicant should, where practicable, make prior investigations with the Chancery Listing Officer about trial dates on an unexpedited and expedited basis having regard to the estimated length of trial.

PRE-TRIAL REVIEWS (PTRS)

12.9 As with other cases in the Chancery Division, a pre-trial review should be held between 4-6 weeks before trial in all cases estimated to last five days or more. An important issue to be discussed at the per-trial review will be the trial timetable.

SEPTEMBER TRIALS

12.10 The Patents Court will endeavour, if the parties so desire and the case is urgent, to hear trials in September.

13. TIME ESTIMATES AND TECHNICAL COMPLEXITY RATINGS

13.1 In providing appropriate time estimates, parties must appreciate the need to give realistic **2F-138** and accurate time estimates and ensure that the time estimate includes a discrete reading time for the court to read the papers prior to the hearing of the application or trial. In general, the court will wish to read the skeleton arguments, the patent (where relevant), the prior art (where relevant), expert reports and other key documents (e.g. substantive witness statements). Advisors should bear in mind the technical difficulty of the case when considering the reading time estimate. The court will consider the imposition of guillotines where time estimates are in danger of being exceeded.

13.2 Similarly, in proving technical complexity ratings, the parties must appreciate the need to give realistic and accurate estimates of the technical complexity of the case. The technical complexity rating should take account of the complexity of both the patent and the prior art as well as the complexity of the infringement issues and likely evidence.

REVISED TIME ESTIMATES AND TECHNICAL COMPLEXITY RATINGS

13.3 Where parties and their legal advisors consider that a time estimate that has been provided (e.g. at the CMC) has become unrealistic, they have a duty to notify the new time estimate to the

Chancery Listing Office or, where appropriate, the judge's clerk as soon as possible. The same applies to estimates of technical complexity.

14. DOCUMENTS AND TIMETABLE

2F-139   **14.1** Bundling for the hearing of applications and trials is of considerable importance and should be approached intelligently. The Direction in Annex E on Standard Trial Bundles in the Patents Court shall be followed. Subject to that, the general guidance given in Appendix 6 Chapter 21 of the Chancery Guide, paragraphs 21.34 to 21.72, should be followed. Solicitors or patent attorneys who fail to follow this Direction and the general guidance do so may be required to explain why and may be penalised personally in costs.

14.2 If it is known which judge will be taking the hearing, papers for the hearing should be lodged directly with that judge's clerk. If there is insufficient time to lodge hard copies before the deadline, documents of significance (and particularly skeleton arguments) should be supplied by e-mail to the clerk of the judge concerned, followed up by clean hard copies.

14.3 It is the responsibility of both parties to ensure that all relevant documents are lodged with the clerk of the judge who will be taking the hearing by noon two days before the date fixed for hearing unless some longer or shorter period has been ordered by the judge or is prescribed by this guide.

14.4 The judges request that all important documents also be supplied to them on a USB stick in a format convenient for the judge's use (normally the current or a recent version of Microsoft Word for Windows or as a text searchable pdf). These will usually include skeleton arguments, important patents, prior art, the witness statements and expert reports.

14.5 Prior to trial, parties should ensure that they comply with the requirements of PD63.9 concerning the provision of a trial timetable, trial bundle and reading guide for the judge. The trial timetable should be detailed and set out the times and dates that witnesses will be required to give evidence, as well as any days that any witness is unavailable to give evidence.

14.6 The parties are encouraged to produce a technical primer setting out the agreed basic undisputed technology relevant to the case. This should be produced in advance of the expert reports to avoid substantially the same material being described by each expert. Ideally primers should be agreed documents. Generally, where the parties are not able to agree whether to include a particular issue ought to be included in the primer, rather than having a "marked-up" primer showing the areas of dispute, the issue should be omitted and dealt with by the experts in their reports. Where a technical primer has been produced, the parties should identify those parts which are agreed to form part of the common general knowledge. Usually, this should be done either in, or shortly after exchange of, the expert reports, but in any event a reasonable time prior to trial.

14.7 Skeleton arguments should be lodged in time for the judge to read them before an application or trial.

(a)   In the case of applications, this should normally be 10:30am the previous working day (or, in the case of short applications, 3pm)

(b)   In the case of trials, this should normally be at least two working days before commencement of the trial. In substantial cases, a longer period (to be discussed with the clerk to the judge concerned) may be needed.

14.8 Skeleton arguments which refer to confidential information should where possible do so in a separate confidential appendix. If that is not practicable, a redacted non-confidential version of the skeleton argument should be filed at the same time as the confidential version. Similarly, redacted non-confidential versions of witness statements and experts reports which contain confidential information should be filed wherever practicable.

14.9 Where any party wishes to put documents to a witness in cross-examination, these should generally be supplied to the witness sufficient time in advance so that the witness has time to consider them before giving evidence. Generally, documents for cross-examination should be supplied at least 48 hours before the witness gives evidence. However, more time may be required depending on the nature and number of the documents intended to be relied upon. The number of documents should be kept within manageable bounds. In the case of documents over 4 pages long, there should be an indication of which parts will be put to the witness.

14.10 Following the evidence in a substantial trial, a short adjournment may be granted to enable the parties to summarise their arguments in writing before oral argument.

TRANSCRIPTS

14.11 In trials where a transcript of evidence is being made and supplied to the judge, the transcript should be supplied by e-mail and in hard copy. Where real time transcription is being used, the Court should be provided with a terminal.

15. TELEPHONE APPLICATIONS

2F-140   **15.1** For short (20 minutes or less) matters, the judges of the Patents Court are willing to hear applications by telephone conference in accordance with the Practice Direction under Part 23. The party making the application is responsible for setting up the telephone application and informing the parties, Counsels' clerks and Chancery Listing of the time of the conference call.

15.2 It is possible for the application to be recorded, and if recording by the court rather than by BT (or other service provider) is requested, arrangements should be made with the Chancery Listing Officer. The recording will not be transcribed. The tape will be kept by the clerk to the judge hearing the application for a period of six months. Arrangements for transcription, if needed, must be made by the parties.

15.3 This procedure should be used where it will save costs.

MISCELLANEOUS

16. JURISDICTION OF MASTERS

16.1 Masters have only a limited jurisdiction in patent matters (see PD63.5.2(2)). Generally it is **2F-141** more convenient for consent orders (on paper or in court) to be made by a judge even where a Master has jurisdiction to do so.

16.2 Where a Master makes a consent order disposing of an action which has been fixed, it is the duty of all the parties' representatives to inform the Chancery Listing Officer that the case has settled. Where the validity of the patent was in issue, the Comptroller should also be informed.

17. CONSENT ORDERS

17.1 The court is normally willing to make consent orders without the need for the attendance **2F-142** of any parties. A draft of the agreed order and the written consent of all the parties' respective solicitors or counsel should be supplied to the Chancery Listing Office. Unless the judge considers a hearing is needed, he will make the order in the agreed terms by initialling it. It will be drawn up accordingly and sent to the parties.

18. DRAFT JUDGMENTS

18.1 Many judgments, particularly after a full trial, will be reserved and handed down at a later **2F-143** date, as advised by the Chancery Listing Office. Prior to that, the practice has arisen to provide the parties' legal representatives (or litigants in person) with a copy of the draft judgment for advocates to notify the court of typographical and obvious errors (if any). The text may be shown, in confidence, to the parties, but only for the purpose of obtaining instructions and on the strict understanding that the judgment, or its effect, is not to be disclosed to any other person, or used in the public domain, and that no action is taken (other than internally) in response to the judgment. Reference is invited to PD40E paras 2.1 to 2.9.

19. ORDERS FOLLOWING JUDGMENT

19.1 Where a judgment is made available in draft before being given in open court the parties **2F-144** should, in advance of that occasion, exchange drafts of the desired consequential order. It is highly undesirable that one party should spring a proposal on the other for the first time when judgment is handed down. Where the parties are agreed as to the consequential order and have supplied to the judge a copy of the same signed by all parties or their representatives, attendance at the handing down of the judgment is not necessary. If it is not possible for there to be an effective hearing to determine the consequential relief when a judgment is handed down, the hearing will be adjourned for a short period which should not exceed 28 days. A standard order for such situations is Annex F to this guide.

19.2 Advocates are reminded of their responsibility to draft, agree and lodge orders for sealing promptly following any hearing. In the event of dispute as to the wording of an order, consideration should be given as to whether the matter may be resolved by the court on paper. In the event that a hearing is required, the hearing should be listed as soon as practicable.

20. APPEALS FROM THE COMPTROLLER

PATENTS

20.1 By virtue of statute, these lie only to the High Court (and not the Intellectual Property **2F-145** Enterprise Court). They are now governed by Part 52 (see Rule 63.16(1)). Permission to appeal is not required. Note that the Comptroller must be served with a Notice of Appeal (Rule 63.16(3)). The appellant has the conduct of the appeal and he or his representative should, within 2 weeks of lodging the appeal, contact the Chancery Listing Officer with a view to arranging a hearing date. The appellant must ensure that the appeal is set down as soon as is reasonably practicable after service of the notice of appeal. Parties are reminded that the provisions about the service of skeleton arguments apply to appeals from the Comptroller.

REGISTERED DESIGNS

20.2 Appeals in registered designs cases may be brought before the High Court or the Appointed Person. Appeals to the High Court are assigned to the Patents Court (Rule 63.16(2)). Permission to appeal is not required. Note that the Comptroller must be served with a Notice of Appeal (Rule 63.16(3)).

APPEALS ON PAPER ONLY

20.3 The court will hear appeals on paper only if that is what the parties desire. If the appellant is willing for the appeal to be heard on paper only, he should contact the respondent and United Kingdom Intellectual Property Office at the earliest opportunity to discover whether such a way of proceeding is agreed. If it is, the Chancery Listing Office should be informed as soon as possible. The parties (and the Chancery Listing Officer if he/she desires) should liaise amongst themselves for early preparation of written submissions and bundles and provide the court with all necessary materials.

21. APPEALS TO THE COURT OF APPEAL

2F-146   **21.1** The Court of Appeal has issued guidance as to the procedure for all intellectual property appeals, including appeals from the Patents Court. This is reproduced in Annex G to this guide.

ANNEX A:

CONTACT DETAILS

1.   The judges of the Patents Court, their clerks and their contact details

2F-147   Mann J (Clerk: Susan Woolley - tel 020 7947 7964; *Susan.Woolley@justice.gov.uk*)
Morgan J (Clerk: Supriya Saleem - tel 020 7947 6419; *Supriya.Saleem@justice.gov.uk*)
Norris J (Clerk: Pauline Drewett - tel 020 7073 1789; *Pauline.Drewett@justice.gov.uk*)
Arnold J [Judge in charge of the Patents Court] (Clerk: Pauline Drewett - tel 020 7073 1789; *Pauline.Drewett@justice.gov.uk*)
Roth J (Clerk: Caroline Reid - tel 020 7071 5694; *Caroline.Reid@justice.gov.uk*)
Birss J (Clerk: Gwilyn Morris – tel 020 7947 7379; *Gwilyn.Morris2@justice.gov.uk*)
Nugee J (Clerk: Gary Clark – tel 020 7947 7200; *Gary.Clark@justice.gov.uk*)
Henry Carr J (Clerk: Jas Kahlon – tel 020 7947 6339; *Jas.Kahlon@justice.go.uk*)

2.   Secretary of the Intellectual Property Court Users Committee and current contact details

Michael Burdon, Simmons & Simmons LLP, CityPoint, One Ropemaker Street, London, EC2Y 9SS Tel: 020 7628 2020 Fax: 020 7628 2070.

ANNEX B:

SPECIMEN ORDER FOR DIRECTIONS

(A) COMMENTARY

2F-148   A draft order is annexed below covering most normal eventualities. The directions are intended only as a guide and are not "standard directions". Not all paragraphs will be applicable in every case.

(B) ORDER FOR DIRECTIONS

UPON the parties' legal advisors having advised the litigants of the existence of mediation as a possible means of resolving this claim and counterclaim
IT IS ORDERED THAT

(1) TRANSFER

1. [This claim and counterclaim be transferred to the Intellectual Property Enterprise Court.] (If this order is made, no other order will generally be necessary, though it will generally be desirable for procedural orders to be made at this time to save the costs of a further conference in the Intellectual Property Enterprise Court.)

(2) SERVICE ON THE COMPTROLLER

2. The [claimants/defendants] shall serve on the Comptroller: (a) the claim form, counterclaim or application notice; (b) any other relevant statement of case (including any amended statement of case); and (c) any accompanying documents of any claim for a remedy which would, if granted, affect an entry in any United Kingdom Patent Office register.

(3) COSTS MANAGEMENT

3. These proceedings are exempt from the costs management provisions contained in section II of CPR 3 and Practice Direction 3E.

(4) AMENDMENTS TO STATEMENTS OF CASE

4. The claimants have permission to amend their claim form shown in red on the copy [annexed to the application notice/as signed by the solicitors for the parties/annexed hereto] and [to re-serve the same on or before [date]/and that re-service be dispensed with] and that the defendants have permission to serve a consequentially amended defence within [number] days [thereafter/hereafter] and that the claimants have permission to serve a consequentially amended reply (if so advised) within [number] days thereafter.

(5) FURTHER INFORMATION AND CLARIFICATION

5.(a)   The [claimants/defendants] do on or before [date] serve on the [defendants/claimants] the further information or clarification of the [specify statement of case] as requested by the [claimants/defendants] by their request served on the [defendants/claimants] on [date] [and/or]

(b)   The [claimants/defendants] do on or before [date] serve on the [defendants/claimants] [a response to their request for further information] [do answer the requests in their request for further information] or clarification of the [identify statement of case] served on the [defendants/claimants] on [date].

(6) ADMISSIONS

6. The [claimants/defendants] do on or before [date] state in writing whether or not they admit the facts specified in the [defendants'/claimants'] notice to admit facts dated [date].

(7) SECURITY

7. The claimants/defendants do provide security for the defendants'/claimants' costs for its claim/counterclaim in the sum of £[state sum] by [paying such sums into court] [specify manner in which security to be given] and that:

(i)   in the meantime the claim [counterclaim] be stayed [and/or];

(ii)   unless security is given as ordered by the above date, the claim [counterclaim] be struck out without further order with the defendants'/claimants' costs of the claim [counterclaim] to be the subject of detailed assessment if not agreed.

(8) LISTS OF DOCUMENTS

8.(a)   The claimants and the defendants respectively do on or before [state date] make and serve on the other of them a list in accordance with form N265 of the documents in their possession custody or control which they are required to disclose in accordance with the obligation of standard disclosure in accordance with Part 31 as modified by paragraph 5 of the Practice Direction—Patents etc. supplementing Part 63.

(b)   In respect of those issues identified in Schedule [number] hereto disclosure shall be limited to those [documents/categories of documents] listed in Schedule [number].

(9) INSPECTION

9. If any party wishes to inspect or have copies of such documents as are in another party's control, it shall give notice in writing that it wishes to do so and such inspection shall be allowed at all reasonable times upon reasonable notice and any copies shall be provided within [number] working days of the request upon the undertaking of the party requesting the copies to pay the reasonable copying charges.

(10) EXPERIMENTS

10.(a)   Where a party desires to establish any fact by experimental proof, including an experiment conducted for the purposes of litigation or otherwise not being an experiment conducted in the normal course of research, that party shall on or before [date] serve on all the other parties a notice stating the facts which it desires to establish and giving full particulars of the experiments proposed to establish them.

(b)   A party upon whom a notice is served under the preceding sub-paragraph shall within [number] days, serve on the party serving the notice a notice stating in respect of each fact whether or not that party admits it.

(c)   Where any fact which a party wishes to establish by experimental proof is not admitted that party shall apply to the court for further directions in respect of such experiments.

[*Or where paragraph 9 of the Practice Direction - Patents etc. supplementing CPR Part 63 has been complied with.*]

10.(a)   The claimants/defendants are to afford to the other parties an opportunity, if so requested, of inspecting a repetition of the experiments identified in paragraphs [specify them] of the notice[s] of experiments served on [date]. Any such inspection must be requested within [number] days of the date of this order and shall take place within [number] days of the date of the request.

(b)   If any party shall wish to establish any fact in reply to experimental proof that party shall on or before [date] serve on all the other parties a notice stating the facts which it desires to establish and giving full particulars of the experiments proposed to establish them.

(c)   A party upon whom a notice is served under the preceding sub-paragraph shall within [number] days serve on the party serving the notice a notice stating in respect of each fact whether or not that party admits it.

(d)   Where any fact which a party wishes to establish by experimental proof in reply is not admitted the party may apply to the court for further directions in respect of such experiments.

(11) NOTICE OF MODELS, ETC.

11.(a)   If any party wishes to rely at the trial of this claim and counterclaim upon any model or apparatus, that party shall on or before [date] give notice thereof to all the other parties; shall afford the other parties an opportunity within [number] days of the service of such notice of inspecting the same and shall, if so requested, furnish the other party with copies or illustrations of such model or apparatus.

(b)   No further or other model or apparatus shall be relied upon in evidence by either party save with consent or by permission of the court.

(12) PRODUCT OR PROCESS DESCRIPTION

12.(a)   The defendants/claimants do provide a written description together with relevant drawings of the following [product(s)] [process(es)] to the claimants/defendants by [date].

    i.   [description of product or process];

    ii.   [description of product or process]; etc.

(b)   The description served under paragraph (a) shall be accompanied by a signed written statement which shall:

    (i)   state that the person making the statement is personally acquainted with the facts to which the description relates;

    (ii)   verify that the description is a true and complete description of the product or process; and

    (iii)   contain an acknowledgement by the person making the statement that he may be required to attend court in order to be cross-examined on the contents of the description.

(13) TECHNICAL PRIMER

13. The parties shall use their best endeavours to agree on or before [date] a single technical primer setting out the basic undisputed technology.

(14) SCIENTIFIC ADVISER

14. A.B is appointed a scientific adviser to assist the court in this claim and counterclaim, his/her costs to be met in the first instance in equal shares by the parties and to be costs in the claim and counterclaim, subject to any other order of the trial judge.

(15) WRITTEN EVIDENCE AND CIVIL EVIDENCE ACT NOTICES

15.(a)   Each party shall on or before [date] serve on the other parties [signed] written statements of the oral evidence which the party intends to lead on any issues of fact to be decided at the trial, such statements to stand as the evidence in chief of the witness unless the court otherwise directs;

(b)   Each party shall on or before [date] serve on the other parties [signed] written statements of the oral evidence which it intends to lead at trial in answer to facts and matters raised in the witness statements served on it under paragraph (a) above;

(c)   Each party may call up to [number] expert witnesses in this claim and counterclaim provided that the said party:

    (i)   supplies the name of such expert to the other parties and to the court on or before

[date]; and

(ii)   no later than [date]/[[number days] before the date set for the hearing of this claim and counterclaim] serve upon the other parties a report of each such expert comprising the evidence which that expert intends to give at trial.

(iii)   no later than [date]/[[number of days] before the date set for the hearing of this claim and counterclaim] serve upon the other parties any report of such expert in reply to a report served under paragraph 15(c)(ii) above.

[(d)   The claimant shall, with the cooperation of the other parties, arrange for the experts to meet on or before [date] to determine on what issues they agree and on what they disagree and the experts shall before [date] file a report stating where they agree and where they disagree and in the latter case, their reasons for disagreeing].

16. Each party shall, no later than [date], serve upon the other parties any Civil Evidence Act Notices upon which it intends to rely at trial.

(16) ADMISSIBILITY OF EVIDENCE

17. A party who objects to any statements of any witness being read by the judge prior to the hearing of the trial, shall serve upon each other party a notice in writing to that effect setting out the grounds of the objection.

(17) NON-COMPLIANCE

18. Where either party fails to comply with the directions relating to experiments and written evidence it shall not be entitled to adduce evidence to which such directions relate without the permission of the court.

(18) PRE-TRIAL REVIEW

19. There shall be a pre-trial review shall take place not more than [] weeks prior to the date of the trial of this action.

(19) TRIAL BUNDLES

20. Each party shall no later than [28] days before the date fixed for the trial of this claim and counterclaim serve upon the other parties a list of all the documents to be included in the trial bundles. The claimants shall no later than [21] days before the date fixed for trial serve upon the defendants ... sets of the bundles for use at trial.

21. The claimants must file with the court no later than [4] days before the date fixed for the trial:

(i)   the trial bundle; and

(ii)   a reading guide for the judge.

(20) TRIAL

22. The trial of these proceedings shall be before an assigned judge alone in [London], estimated length [number] days which shall include a pre-trial reading estimate for the judge of [number] days. The technical difficulty rating is [].

(21) LIBERTY TO APPLY

23. The parties are to be at liberty on three days' notice to apply for further directions and generally.

(22) COSTS

24. The costs of this application are to be costs in the claim and counterclaim.

25. This Order shall be served by the [] on the [].

SERVICE OF THE ORDER

The court has provided a sealed copy of this order to the serving party: [NAME] at [ADDRESS] [REFERENCE]

ANNEX C:

SPECIMEN CONFIDENTIALITY AGREEMENTS

THIS AGREEMENT is dated .... and made
BETWEEN:

2F-148.1

(1)   *[.]*, (the "*Party 1*"), registered in England and Wales as company number • and having its registered office at •; and

(2)   *[.]*, (the "*Party 2*"), registered in England and Wales as company number • and having its registered office at •.

BACKGROUND:

(A)   Party 2 intends to receive Confidential Information from Party 1 relating to the Purpose.

(B)   The parties have agreed to comply with this agreement in connection with the disclosure and use of Confidential Information.

1. INTERPRETATION

1.1 Definitions:

"Confidential Information" means has the meaning given in clause 2.

"Discloser" means Party 1, being the party that discloses its Confidential Information, directly or indirectly, to the Recipient.

"Dispute" means UK High Court Action No. [•] and any appeals.

"Purpose" means for the purpose of the Dispute.

"Recipient" means Party 2, being the party that receives Confidential Information, directly or indirectly, from the Discloser.

"Representative(s)" means in relation to each party:

(A)   its officers and employees that need to know the Confidential Information for the Purpose;

(B)   its professional advisers who are engaged to advise that party in connection with the Purpose; and

(C)   any other person to whom the Discloser agrees in writing that Confidential Information may be disclosed in connection with the Purpose.

1.2 Interpretation

(A)   A reference to writing or written includes documents created or stored in electronic form.

(B)   Any obligation on a party not to do something includes an obligation not to allow that thing to be done.

2. CONFIDENTIAL INFORMATION

2.1 Confidential Information means all information which the Discloser or its Representatives identify as confidential and discloses, or makes available, to the Recipient or its Representatives after the date of this agreement. The Confidential Information includes any information, findings, data or analysis derived from Confidential Information but excludes any information referred to in clause 2.2

2.2 Information is not Confidential Information if:

(A)   it is, or becomes, generally available to the public other than as a direct or indirect result of the information being disclosed by the Recipient or its Representatives in breach of this agreement;

(B)   it was available to the Recipient on a non-confidential basis prior to disclosure by the Discloser;

(C)   it was, is, or becomes available to the Recipient on a non-confidential basis from a person who, to the Recipient's actual knowledge, is not under any confidentiality obligation in respect of that information;

(D)   it was lawfully in the possession of the Recipient before the information was disclosed by the Discloser;

(E)   it is developed by or for the Recipient independently of the information disclosed by the Discloser;

(F)   the parties agree in writing that the information is not confidential; or

(G)   the Court orders that the information is not confidential.

3. CONFIDENTIALITY OBLIGATIONS

3.1 In return for the Discloser making Confidential Information available to the Recipient, the Recipient undertakes to the Discloser that it shall:

(A)   keep the Confidential Information secret and confidential;

(B)   not use or exploit the Confidential Information in any way except for the Purpose;

(C)   not disclose or make available any Confidential Information in whole or in part to any person to whom the Discloser has not disclosed the Confidential Information for the Purpose, except as expressly permitted by, and in accordance with this agreement;

(D)   apply the same security measures and degree of care to the Confidential Information as the Recipient applies to its own confidential information, which the Recipient warrants as providing adequate protection from unauthorised disclosure, copying or use; and

(E)   ensure that its Representatives who receive the Confidential Information comply with these obligations

4. MANDATORY DISCLOSURE

4.1 Subject to the provisions of this clause 4, the Recipient may disclose Confidential Information to the minimum extent required by:

(A)   an order of any court of competent jurisdiction or any regulatory, judicial, governmental or similar body or any taxation authority of competent jurisdiction;

(B)   the rules of any listing authority or stock exchange on which its shares are listed or traded; or

(C)   the laws or regulations of any country to which its affairs are subject.

4.2   Before the Recipient discloses any Confidential Information pursuant to clause 4.1 it shall, to the extent practicable and permitted by law, use all reasonable endeavours to give the Discloser as much notice of this disclosure as possible.

5. DESTRUCTION OF CONFIDENTIAL INFORMATION

5.1 At the conclusion of the Dispute, including any appeals, the Recipient shall, if requested by the Discloser, promptly:

(A)   destroy all documents and materials containing, reflecting, incorporating or based on the Confidential Information;

(B)   to the extent technically practicable, erase all the Confidential Information from its computer and communications systems and devices used by it, or which is stored in electronic form;

(C)   ensure that its Representatives who receive the Confidential Information comply with these obligations; and

(D)   certify in writing to the Discloser that it has complied with the requirements of this clause 5.1.

5.2   Nothing in clause 5.1 shall require the Recipient to return or destroy any documents and materials containing or based on the Confidential Information that the Recipient is required to retain by applicable law, or to satisfy the requirements of a regulatory authority or body of competent jurisdiction or the rules of any listing authority or stock exchange, to which it is subject. The Recipient's legal representatives can retain one complete set of all documents which would otherwise be required to be destroyed. The provisions of this agreement shall continue to apply to any documents and materials retained by the Recipient pursuant to this clause 5.2

6. GENERAL

6.1   Assignment and other dealings.

Neither party shall assign, transfer, mortgage, charge, subcontract, declare a trust over or deal in any other manner with any of its rights and obligations under this agreement.

6.2   Entire agreement.

(A)   This agreement constitutes the entire agreement between the parties and supersedes and extinguishes all previous agreements, promises, assurances, warranties, representations and understandings between them, whether written or oral, relating to its subject matter.

(B)   Each party agrees that it shall have no remedies in respect of any statement, representation, assurance or warranty (whether made innocently or negligently) that is not set out in this agreement. Each party agrees that it shall have no claim for innocent or negligent misrepresentation or negligent misstatement based on any statement in this agreement.

6.3   Variation.

No variation of this agreement shall be effective unless it is in writing and signed by the parties (or their authorised representatives).

6.4   Waiver.

No failure or delay by a party to exercise any right or remedy provided under this agreement or by law shall constitute a waiver of that or any other right or remedy, nor shall it prevent or restrict the further exercise of that or any other right or remedy. No single or partial exercise of such right or remedy shall prevent or restrict the further exercise of that or any other right or remedy.

6.5   Governing law.

This agreement and any dispute or claim (including non-contractual disputes or claims) arising out of or in connection with it or its subject matter or formation shall be governed by and construed in accordance with the law of England and Wales.

6.6 Jurisdiction.

Each party irrevocably agrees that the courts of England and Wales shall have exclusive jurisdiction to settle any dispute or claim (including non-contractual disputes or claims) arising out of or in connection with this agreement or its subject matter or formation and hereby submits to the jurisdiction of the courts of England and Wales for this purpose.

This agreement has been entered into on the date stated at the beginning of it.

Signed by [NAME OF AUTHORISED
SIGNATORY] for and on behalf of [NAME   ....
OF PARTY 1]   Authorised Signatory

Signed by [NAME OF AUTHORISED
SIGNATORY] for and on behalf of [NAME   ....
OF PARTY 2]   Authorised Signatory

2F-148.2

THIS AGREEMENT is dated .... and made
BETWEEN:
(1) *[.]*, (the "*Discloser*"), registered in England and Wales as company number • and having its registered office at •; and
(2) *[.]*, (the "*Recipient*"), of •.
BACKGROUND:
(A) The Recipient intends to receive Confidential Information from the Discloser relating to the Purpose.
(B) The parties have agreed to comply with this agreement in connection with the disclosure and use of Confidential Information.

1. INTERPRETATION

1.1 Definitions:

"Confidential Information" means has the meaning given in clause 2.
"Discloser" is the party that discloses its Confidential Information, directly or indirectly, to the Recipient.
"Dispute" means UK High Court Action No. [•] and any appeals.
"Purpose" means for the purpose of the Dispute.
"Recipient" is the party that receives Confidential Information, directly or indirectly, from the Discloser.

1.2 Interpretation

(A) A reference to writing or written includes documents created or stored in electronic form.
(B) Any obligation on a party not to do something includes an obligation not to allow that thing to be done.

2. CONFIDENTIAL INFORMATION

2.1 Confidential Information means all information which the Discloser or its professional advisers identify as confidential and discloses, or makes available, to the Recipient after the date of this agreement. The Confidential Information includes any information, findings, data or analysis derived from Confidential Information but excludes any information referred to in clause 2.2

2.2 Information is not Confidential Information if:
(A) it is, or becomes, generally available to the public other than as a direct or indirect result of the information being disclosed by the Recipient in breach of this agreement;
(B) it was available to the Recipient on a non-confidential basis prior to disclosure by the Discloser;
(C) it was, is, or becomes available to the Recipient on a non-confidential basis from a person who, to the Recipient's actual knowledge, is not under any confidentiality obligation in respect of that information;
(D) it was lawfully in the possession of the Recipient before the information was disclosed by the Discloser;
(E) it is developed by or for the Recipient independently of the information disclosed by the Discloser;
(F) the parties agree in writing that the information is not confidential; or
(G) the Court orders that the information is not confidential.

3. CONFIDENTIALITY OBLIGATIONS

3.1 In return for the Discloser making Confidential Information available to the Recipient, the Recipient undertakes to the Discloser that it shall:
(A) keep the Confidential Information secret and confidential;
(B) not use or exploit the Confidential Information in any way except for the Purpose;

(C)   not disclose or make available any Confidential Information in whole or in part to any person to whom the Discloser has not disclosed the Confidential Information for the Purpose, except as expressly permitted by, and in accordance with this agreement;

(D)   apply the same security measures and degree of care to the Confidential Information as the Recipient applies to its own confidential information, which the Recipient warrants as providing adequate protection from unauthorised disclosure, copying or use; and

4. MANDATORY DISCLOSURE

4.1 Subject to the provisions of this clause 4, the Recipient may disclose Confidential Information to the minimum extent required by:

(A)   an order of any court of competent jurisdiction or any regulatory, judicial, governmental or similar body or any taxation authority of competent jurisdiction;

(B)   the rules of any listing authority or stock exchange on which its shares are listed or traded; or

(C)   the laws or regulations of any country to which its affairs are subject.

4.2 Before the Recipient discloses any Confidential Information pursuant to clause 4.1 it shall, to the extent practicable and permitted by law, use all reasonable endeavours to give the Discloser as much notice of this disclosure as possible.

5. DESTRUCTION OF CONFIDENTIAL INFORMATION

5.1 At the conclusion of the Dispute, including any appeals, the Recipient shall, if requested by the Discloser, promptly:

(A)   destroy all documents and materials containing, reflecting, incorporating or based on the Confidential Information;

(B)   to the extent technically practicable, erase all the Confidential Information from its computer and communications systems and devices used by it, or which is stored in electronic form; and

(C)   certify in writing to the Discloser that it has complied with the requirements of this clause 5.1.

5.2 Nothing in clause 5.1 shall require the Recipient to return or destroy any documents and materials containing or based on the Confidential Information that the Recipient is required to retain by applicable law, or to satisfy the requirements of a regulatory authority or body of competent jurisdiction or the rules of any listing authority or stock exchange, to which it is subject. The provisions of this agreement shall continue to apply to any documents and materials retained by the Recipient pursuant to this clause 5.2

6. GENERAL

6.1   Assignment and other dealings.

Neither party shall assign, transfer, mortgage, charge, subcontract, declare a trust over or deal in any other manner with any of its rights and obligations under this agreement.

6.2   Entire agreement.

(A)   This agreement constitutes the entire agreement between the parties and supersedes and extinguishes all previous agreements, promises, assurances, warranties, representations and understandings between them, whether written or oral, relating to its subject matter.

(B)   Each party agrees that it shall have no remedies in respect of any statement, representation, assurance or warranty (whether made innocently or negligently) that is not set out in this agreement. Each party agrees that it shall have no claim for innocent or negligent misrepresentation or negligent misstatement based on any statement in this agreement.

6.3   Variation.

No variation of this agreement shall be effective unless it is in writing and signed by the parties (or their authorised representatives).

6.4   Waiver.

No failure or delay by a party to exercise any right or remedy provided under this agreement or by law shall constitute a waiver of that or any other right or remedy, nor shall it prevent or restrict the further exercise of that or any other right or remedy. No single or partial exercise of such right or remedy shall prevent or restrict the further exercise of that or any other right or remedy.

6.5   Governing law.

This agreement and any dispute or claim (including non-contractual disputes or claims) arising out of or in connection with it or its subject matter or formation shall be governed by and construed in accordance with the law of England and Wales.

6.6   Jurisdiction.

Each party irrevocably agrees that the courts of England and Wales shall have exclusive jurisdiction to settle any dispute or claim (including non-contractual disputes or claims) arising out of or in connection with this agreement or its subject matter or formation and hereby submits to the jurisdiction of the courts of England and Wales for this purpose.

This agreement has been entered into on the date stated at the beginning of it.

Signed by [NAME OF AUTHORISED
SIGNATORY] for and on behalf of [NAME   ....
OF DISCLOSER]   Authorised Signatory
Signed by [NAME OF RECIPIENT]   ....

ANNEX D:

PRACTICE STATEMENT: LISTING OF CASES FOR TRIAL IN THE PATENTS COURT
Issued 7 December 2015

2F-148.3   The Patents Court endeavours bring patent cases on for trial where possible within 12 months of the claim being issued. To this end, the following procedure will be adopted.

1.   The parties will be expected (a) to start to consider potential trial dates as soon as is reasonable practicable after the service of the proceedings and (b) to discuss and attempt to agree trial dates with each other when seeking to agree directions for trial.

2.   The starting point for listing trials is the current applicable Trial Window advertised by the Chancery List Office. Patent cases will be listed on the basis that the Trial Windows are divided as follows: estimated hearing time (excluding pre-reading and preparation of closing submissions) up to 5 days; estimated hearing time (excluding pre-reading and preparation of closing submissions) 6 to 10 days; and estimated hearing (excluding pre-reading and preparation of closing submissions) over 10 days.

3.   Where it will enable a case to be tried within 12 months, or shortly thereafter, the Court may list a trial up to one month earlier than the applicable Trial Window without the need for any application for expedition.

4.   The Court will use its case management powers in a more active manner than hitherto, with a view to dealing with cases justly and at proportionate cost in accordance with CPR rule 1.1. This may have the effect of setting limits on hearing times that enable cases to be listed promptly. For example, the Court may direct that a case estimated at 6 days will be heard in 5 days, and may allocate time between the parties in a manner which enables that to be achieved.

5.   Where it makes a significant difference to the time which cases must wait to be listed for trial and it will not cause significant prejudice to any party, cases may be listed without reference to the availability of counsel instructed by the parties.

These steps do not exclude the possibility of cases being expedited where expedition is warranted. Nor do they exclude the possibility of the parties opting to use the streamlined procedure or the Shorter Trial pilot scheme or the Flexible Trial pilot scheme.

This Practice Statement is issued with the concurrence of the Chancellor of the High Court. It supersedes the Practice Statement issued on 28 January 2015.

Arnold J
Judge in Charge of the Patents Court

ANNEX E:

STANDARD TRIAL BUNDLES IN THE PATENTS COURT

Introduction

2F-148.4   The objective of this direction is to have a standard arrangement of bundles so that, as every document is produced in the course of the litigation, it is put in its place in the standard arrangement and the bundles do not subsequently have to be re-arranged or re-ordered, and the lawyers can continue using the same bundles, from the CMC up to and during the trial (recognising that for some interim applications it may be appropriate to have an application bundle specific for the hearing in addition to the standard bundles). Therefore, all that will be needed for trial would be preparation of additional copies for the judge, witnesses and stenographer.

There is a conflict between the need to avoid re-doing bundles as a case progresses, which requires documents to be added to the end of existing bundles, and the desire for documents to be in a sensible order, which in pleadings or technical literature bundles may not follow the order in which the documents are produced in the litigation. It has to be accepted that this direction requires a degree of prescriptiveness, but there also needs to be some sensible flexibility and co-operation between the parties' solicitors, particularly in multi-patent cases.

A new document should generally be added to the end of an existing bundle, and bundles should generally not require re-ordering; the new document either adds to an existing bundle or starts a new bundle. Therefore, whenever any party serves a document they should also serve a new index page for the bundle(s) in which the document being served is to be placed. Amended documents should replace the unamended version in the bundle, and Responses to Part 18 Requests and Responses to Notices to Admit should replace the Request or Notice in the bundle.

Confidentiality

Confidential material can appear in a number of places — within a skeleton, pleading, PPD, witness statement or exhibit to a witness statement. The objective is that all confidential material is contained in a separate confidential bundle, with a redacted version or cross-referenced page in the relevant main bundle.

The preferred practice is that sections of a document which contain confidential information are contained in a separate confidential annex or exhibit, which is placed in the separate confidential bundle. In some cases, where this is not feasible, the party serving a document should provide a redacted version to go in the main bundle, and include a full version containing the confidential material (highlighted or underlined), or at least particular sections containing the confidential information, for inclusion in the confidential bundle. This has the additional advantage that the parties will then have redacted versions of witness statements or expert reports, which can be made available in Court under CPR 32.13.

In cases where the confidential material is voluminous or confidentiality regimes are complex the parties should agree as early as possible on the way in which it can be dealt with.

Cross-referencing

It should be possible to include bundle references (in bold) for all documents referred to in witness statements and expert reports, since the location in the bundles of all exhibits will be determined when the evidence is finalised. Separate side annotation can thus be avoided.

All references to exhibits and other documents, including those in reply evidence, should refer to the actual bundle and tab number.

Duplication of exhibits

Where more than one of a party's witnesses or experts refers to the same document, it should be exhibited to only one statement or report, and the others should refer to that exhibit.

If the defendant's witnesses refer to documents which are also exhibited to the claimant's evidence, the duplicated exhibit should be removed from the defendant's exhibits bundle and replaced by a placeholder which cross-refers to the claimant's exhibits bundle.

Technical literature

Copies of all technical literature and other documents referred to in an expert report or witness statement should be provided in the bundles, usually as exhibits or in the technical literature bundle, but possibly elsewhere (eg prior art bundle).

Since in most cases there is little technical literature, the default position is to exhibit technical literature to an expert report or witness statement.

If it appears to either party's solicitors that there is likely to be a suitable amount of technical literature for a separate bundle, they should raise it with the other side. If they all agree, then there will be a separate Technical Literature bundle, Bundle L.

Since cross-references to the bundles are included in expert reports and witness statements when served, the bundle(s) L need to be divided between:

i.   publications referred to in Claimant's evidence in chief,
ii.   publications referred to in Defendant's evidence in chief
iii.   publications referred to in Claimant's evidence in reply
iv.   publications referred to in Defendant's evidence in reply

Rearranging the literature into chronological order following service of the reply evidence should be avoided; it would involve re-jigging the bundle(s), and re-doing the cross-references in the expert reports and witness statements, at a busy period in a case, and is an expenditure of time which this direction is designed to avoid.

Amendment of the patent

If the patentee applies to amend the patent in suit, the parties will need to agree where the relevant documents will be included in the bundles (eg proposed amended specification and claims in the "A.n" series of bundles, statements of case in the "B.n" etc series: or in some cases, all in one separate bundle may be more sensible).

Pagination

Separate pagination should be used within in each tab. Where a document already has clear page numbers, like a technical publication, then it does not need separate pagination. Documents (eg bundles of correspondence) should be paginated before service.

Standard bundles

A.1	**Patent(s)** (usually comb-bound)
A.2	**Priority documents and application(s) as filed** (when priority and added matter are in issue).
B.1	**Pleadings, Orders and Notices**. This will include pleadings, documents referred to in the pleadings (except the pleaded prior art), orders, lists of documents, PPDs, any technical primer and any Civil Evidence Act Notices (without annexed documents).

The bundle should be filled chronologically for the pleadings. Thereafter, tabs can be held open for documents which the parties know will be served (eg Order for Directions, Lists of Documents, Product/Process Description, Primer) and other documents can be added chronologically after these tabs.

To avoid re-arranging the bundle, Part 18 Requests should be added to the end of the bundle at the time of service, and replaced by the Response when served. The same applies *mutatis mutandis* to Admissions.

[NB: for the judge, a comb-bound copy of the technical primer should be provided.]

B.2	**Pleaded Prior Art.**
C.1	**Claimant's Evidence**. This bundle will include both fact and expert evidence (including witness statements served with a Civil Evidence Act Notice). Reply evidence should be added to bundle **C.1** when it is served.
C.2, C.3, etc.	**Exhibits to the Claimant's evidence**

The principle with exhibits is that the exhibits to each witness statement or report are contained in one bundle (or section of a bundle), and the tab numbers follow the exhibit numbers, even when split over two bundles.

All documents referred to in a statement or report should be referred to as exhibits; to refer to some as annexes or appendices can cause confusion.

The preference is that each bundle contains the exhibits of one witness/expert, so that reply exhibits can be added to the end. This avoids the inconvenience of subdividing bundles, which would result in two runs of tab numbers.

Where this is not practicable, it may be better to abandon the principle of tab numbers matching exhibit numbers, in the interest of avoiding two runs of the same tab numbers in a single bundle. In such a case, reply exhibits would have to follow the exhibits to all the evidence in chief, as trying to insert each witness's reply exhibits immediately after their exhibits in chief will require too much rearrangement of bundles.

If one expert's exhibits go over more than one (sensibly filled) bundle then it should continue to the next bundle (C.2/C.3, and so on).

CONF-C	This bundle will include the claimant's documents which contain confidential information of either Party.
D.1	**Defendant's Evidence** (as above).
D.2, D.3, etc.	**Exhibits to the Defendant's Evidence** (as above).
CONF-D	This bundle will include the defendant's confidential documents (as above).
E.	**Documents referred to in Civil Evidence Act Notices** (or E.1, E.2 etc. if more than one bundle)(other than witness statements).
F, G.	**Selected documents from Claimant's / Defendant's Disclosure** (to the extent not exhibited to witness statements)
H.	**Documents from Interim Hearings** (only if required). These could include, for example, evidence from interim injunctions or other interim applications, transcripts of hearings, or interim judgments to the extent that these are going to be referred to at trial. Where evidence in the form of witness statements is included, the exhibits should be in a separate bundle **H.2**.
I.	**Selected Inter-Solicitor correspondence** (only if and to the extent required)
L.	**Technical Literature** (if agreed by parties).
S.	**Skeletons**

T.   **Transcripts**

X.   **Documents handed up at trial**

CXX[witness initials] — those documents provided by the Claimant for cross examination

DXX[witness initials] — those documents provided by the Defendant for cross-examination

Any other documents which are case specific can be included with the parties' agreement in bundles using any of the remaining letters.

Notes on bundles

Bundle indices

There is no need to repeat the whole title of the action on the index: it is better to aim to get the entire index to a bundle on one sheet.

An index should be intelligent: thus "Exhibit AGS3 to the first affidavit of Anthony Graham Snooks" is not as helpful as "AGS3 - 1989 Accounts".

It should be made clear in the index if documents are amended, redacted/non-confidential or contain confidential information.

Front- and back-sheets

Front- and back-sheets should be discarded from copy documents in the bundles. For exhibits, the exhibit number should instead be written in the top right-hand corner of the first page. This makes it easier to identify the document when looking for it in the bundle.

Bundle labels

Bundles should be clearly labelled with a brief description of their contents. There is no need to repeat the entire title of the action. Ideally a large sticker, legible at a distance (e.g. "B.1 PLDGS") should be used. Remember people have to find bundles in a rack or stand.

A similar sticker should appear in the top left inside of the bundle - so that the reader can see which bundle he is looking at without having to look at the front.

Binders

All bundles should be strong enough for practical use. Both ring binders (preferably with locking devices) and lever-arch are suitable. Do not use large lever-arch files for a small quantity of documents. In the case of both, do not overload. Binding techniques which mean that the bundle will not lie open should be avoided.

Different colours for different volumes aids ready identification, although clear labels can do the same job. A different colour for the confidential bundles is much encouraged.

Annex F:

Specimen order on handing down of judgment

UPON THIS ACTION [AND COUNTERCLAIM] having been tried before the Honourable **2F-148.5** [Mr/Mrs] Justice [] on the [] of []

AND UPON the Court handing down Judgment on [DATE]

IT IS ORDERED THAT:

1. The hearing to determine the appropriate form of Order following the handing-down of Judgment in these proceedings ('the Form of Order Hearing') be adjourned to the first available date convenient to the parties but no later than [DATE].
2. Such adjournment is an adjournment within paragraph 4.1(a) of the Practice Direction 52A to Part 52; and accordingly the time for making any application for permission to appeal be extended until the Form of Order Hearing and pending that hearing the time for service of any Appellant's Notice shall not run.
3. Until the Form of Order Hearing the documents [referred to in / scheduled to] the Order dated [] shall remain confidential and shall only be used for the purpose of these proceedings notwithstanding that they have been, or may have been, read to or by the Court or referred to at a hearing which has been held in public.
4. Costs are in the case.
5. This Order shall be served by the [] on the [].

Service of the Order

The court has provided a sealed copy of this order to the serving party: [] at [ADDRESS] [REFERENCE]

ANNEX G:

PROCEDURE IN INTELLECTUAL PROPERTY APPEALS IN THE COURT OF APPEAL

Applications for Permission to Appeal

2F-148.6   The appellant's notice, skeleton argument and bundle should be lodged as required by CPR PD52C, sections 2, 4 and 7.

Appeals

Where permission to appeal has been given by the lower court or granted by the Court of Appeal:

- The Civil Appeals Office will ask the parties to provide an agreed time estimate where possible or, where agreement cannot be reached, separate time estimates for the hearing of the appeal together with an agreed time estimate for any necessary pre-reading.
- The case will then be referred to the Supervising Lord Justice for listing directions.
- Once the appeal is listed, the parties will be asked to lodge an agreed timetable for the filing of skeleton arguments, appeal bundles and bundles of authorities for approval by the Supervising Lord or Lady Justice.
- Any subsequent request by the parties to amend the approved timetable will be referred to the Supervising Lord or Lady Justice for determination.

Replace The Intellectual Property Enterprise Court Guide:

THE INTELLECTUAL PROPERTY ENTERPRISE COURT GUIDE
Issued July 2019

By authority of the Chancellor of the High Court

1.   GENERAL

1.1   Introduction

2F-149   This is the Guide to the Intellectual Property Enterprise Court (the IPEC). The Guide is written for all users of the IPEC, whether a litigant in person (i.e. a litigant who acts on their own behalf without professional representation) or a specialist intellectual property litigator. It aims to help users and potential users of the IPEC by explaining how the court's procedures work and providing guidelines where appropriate.

The IPEC is part of the High Court. It is one of the Business and Property Courts of England and Wales. It hears only cases concerning intellectual property.

The IPEC aims to provide a procedure for intellectual property litigation which is speedier and less costly than is the case in the rest of the High Court. It is also designed to safeguard parties from the risk of paying large sums in costs to the opposing party at the conclusion of the proceedings. The intention is to ensure that parties without the benefit of large financial resources are not deterred from seeking access to justice because of the high cost of litigation.

1.2   Multi-track and small claims track

The IPEC has two sets of procedures or 'tracks'. They are known as 'the IPEC a multi-track' track and 'the IPEC small claims track. They differ in that the small claims track deals with cases of a simpler nature with a claim for a lower level of damages.

The IPEC multi-track, litigants may claim up to £500,000 in compensation for infringement of their rights. This cap on compensation may be waived by agreement of the parties. At the end of the trial the losing party may be required to pay the winning party's legal costs, but with very limited exceptions such costs will not exceed £50,000. The procedure not only caps the overall costs which a losing party will have to pay, it also limits costs payable for each stage of the proceedings. These 'costs caps' – limiting the extent of any adverse order on costs – form a significant feature of the IPEC.

The small claims track is for suitable claims in which the compensation sought is no more than £10,000. Generally, at the end of the case the losing party will be required to pay little or none of the winning party's legal costs. There is thus even greater protection from an adverse order on costs in the event that a party is not successful. The procedure in the small claims track is shorter and less formal than in the multi-track, and the court fees are lower.

As of October 2019, there will be district judges based in each of the six Business and Property Court centres out of London, namely Birmingham, Bristol, Cardiff, Leeds, Manchester and Newcastle, who will be able to hear matters in the IPEC small claims track. Such matters can be issued using the Business and Property Courts' electronic filing system (see Annex A). Appeals from decisions in the IPEC small claims track will be filed at the relevant appeal centre indicated in

Practice Direction 52B (see section 2.2 of this Guide) and a judge of the multi-track will be made available to hear the appeal, whether locally or in London depending on the circumstances of the case and on judge availability.

Guidance is given below as to whether the multi-track or small claims track is likely to be the more appropriate forum for a dispute.

The focus of this Guide is the IPEC multi-track. In the remainder of the Guide, unless expressly stated otherwise 'the IPEC' will mean the IPEC multi-track.

Guide to the IPEC small claims track

There is a separate Guide for the IPEC's small claims track, available at
www.gov.uk/government/publications/intellectual-property-enterprise-court-a-guide-to-small-claims.

1.3 Intellectual property cases

The IPEC hears intellectual property cases of any kind. For the most part this means cases concerning patents, registered designs, unregistered designs, trade marks, passing off, copyright, database rights, performance protection rights, trade libel and breach of confidence. There are other intellectual property rights less often relied on, such as moral rights, semiconductor topography rights and the protection of plant varieties, and all of these may also be litigated in the IPEC. The IPEC deals with disputes which involve matters other than intellectual property, such as contractual claims, but only if associated with an intellectual property claim.

1.4 Remedies

All the remedies available elsewhere in the High Court can be claimed in the IPEC. These include preliminary and final injunctions, orders for the payment of damages or an account of profits, the latter being an order that a defendant found to infringe should disclose and pay over the profits made from the infringement. Search and seizure orders, asset freezing orders and orders requiring the dissemination of a judgment (such as publication on a website) may also be granted in the IPEC.

1.5 The judges

The Presiding Judge of the IPEC is a specialist circuit judge. Nominated barristers and solicitors, all experienced in intellectual property law, sit as deputy IPEC judges. Judges who sit in the Patents Court also sit in the IPEC when the need arises.

1.6 Trials outside London

Particularly where it would save costs, IPEC trials will be heard outside London. If the parties wish the trial to be heard at a place other than London, they should contact the clerk of the Presiding IPEC Judge as soon as possible so that arrangements can be put in place well before the date of the proposed hearing. (Contact details are given at the end of this Guide.) Before making such an approach, the parties should discuss this between themselves.

If there is disagreement between the parties as to where the trial should be heard, an application should be made to the court to resolve the matter. Parties should be aware that generally a trial will not be heard outside London unless the parties are able to agree on an alternative location.

Subject to very limited exceptions, IPEC judges will not sit outside London for applications, including case management conferences. This is because it is impractical for a short hearing. However, applications may be heard by phone or may be resolved in writing by the court without any hearing, subject to the approval of the judge.

1.7 Representation

A person may represent themselves in litigation in the IPEC as 'a litigant in person'. However, intellectual property disputes can be complex and litigants will often benefit from the assistance of a professional representative.

Solicitors and Patent and trade mark attorneys[1] are all entitled to represent clients in the IPEC. These professionals may additionally instruct barristers to help prepare the case and/or to argue the case in court. In some instances, a barrister may accept instructions directly from the public.

Each of these professions has its own qualifications and a particular set of skills. It may be appropriate to instruct more than one legal representative to act as a team.

A company or other corporation may be represented at trial by an employee, whether or not the employee is director, provided the employee has been authorized by the company and the court gives permission, see CPR Part 39 rule 6.

---

[1] The rights of patent attorneys and trade mark attorneys to conduct litigation and appear in the IPEC are determined by the Intellectual Property Regulation Board (IPREG) (*www.ipreg.org.uk*). Attorneys with an Intellectual Property Litigation Certificate may conduct litigation and appear in the IPEC.

IP Pro Bono

Where a person bringing or defending a case in the IPEC cannot afford to pay for their own legal representative, they may be eligible to seek free or 'pro bono' advice. A scheme has been set up which provides free professional assistance for those involved in intellectual property litigation who do not have the resources to pay for advice. The IP Pro Bono scheme was organized with the IPEC particularly in mind. It has a website at which explains how the scheme works and how a party may obtain free assistance from a professional adviser experienced in the relevant area of intellectual property law. Those who wish to use the scheme should apply as soon as is reasonably possible.

2.   CIVIL PROCEDURE RULES

2.1   The CPR

2F-150   Like all proceedings in the High Court, procedure in the IPEC is governed by the Civil Procedure Rules ('the CPR') which can be found at: *www.justice.gov.uk/courts/procedure-rules/civil/rules.*

Those unfamiliar with civil litigation will find the CPR lengthy and complex. This is an unfortunate and usually unavoidable consequence of the wide scope of rules needed to regulate civil litigation. It would be unwise for a litigant to navigate the rules in detail without informed advice. Users of the IPEC should be aware that this Guide cannot and does not attempt to cover every issue which may arise in the course of litigation.

However, it is the goal of this Guide to provide users with the basic information needed to use the court. To that end, the rules which are most relevant to litigants in the IPEC will be referred to below in the course of explaining how the IPEC works so that users may consult the rules themselves if they wish to.

2.2   Abbreviations

The CPR are divided into numbered Parts. Each Part has numbered rules. Most Parts have at the end of them guidelines relevant to that Part, called 'practice directions'.

By way of example, rule 23 of Part 63 will be referred to as 'Part 63 rule 23'. The practice direction at the end of Part 63 will be referred to as 'PD 63' and its paragraphs as 'PD 63 para.1', and so on.

2.3   Rules of particular relevance to the IPEC

- Part 63 applies to all intellectual property claims. It includes rules specific to intellectual property cases and also modifies some Parts of the CPR which would otherwise apply generally to all claims.
- Practice Direction 63 (PD 63) supplements Part 63.
- Part 63 and PD 63 are arranged in sections as follows:
    - Section I relates to proceedings which concern patents and registered designs. It is applicable to proceedings in the IPEC which relate to those rights.
    - Section II allocates all other IP cases to particular courts including the Chancery Division, the IPEC and certain County Courts where there is a Chancery District Registry.
    - Section III deals with service of documents and participation by the Comptroller.
    - Section IV does not relate to proceedings in the IPEC.
    - Section V relates to all proceedings started in or transferred to the IPEC. This section contains the procedural rules which are particular to the IPEC.
- Attention is drawn to two other parts of the CPR which contain provisions specific to the IPEC:
    - Part 30 and in particular PD 30 paras. 9.1 and 9.2. These apply to the transfer of proceedings to and from the IPEC. Part 30 rule 5, when applied to IPEC transfers, is modified by Part 63 rule 18.
    - Part 45 Section IV and Section IV of PD 45 relate to costs in the IPEC.

3.   THE COURT IN WHICH TO BRING PROCEEDINGS

3.1   The options

2F-151   A litigant wishing to start an intellectual property claim must decide on the court in which to bring the proceedings. First, should the claim be brought in the IPEC or elsewhere in the High Court?

If the case is to be brought in the IPEC there is a second decision to be made: should it be started in the IPEC multi-track or the IPEC small claims track?

3.2   The IPEC or elsewhere in the High Court

The following guidelines are provided to assist users in determining whether a case is suitable for the IPEC:

- The financial resources of the parties. A party may have limited financial resources and may therefore require the lower cost of litigating in the IPEC and the protection of costs caps in order to gain access to justice. If this can be shown, it is likely to be treated as a strong (though not overriding) reason to have the case heard in the IPEC. This will be particularly the case if the court reaches the view that there is a risk of a better funded opponent being able to bring unfair financial pressure to bear should the case be heard outside the IPEC. That said, a party wishing for the proceedings to be in the IPEC remains under an obligation to tailor their case to ensure that all the issues in the proceedings will not give rise to a trial lasting more than 2 days, or at the most 3 days.
- The overall complexity of the claim. Where the claim is such that it will require a trial of more than 2 days, it is unlikely to be suitable for the IPEC. Exceptionally, a trial of 3 days may be permitted. A litigant with a complex claim or complex defence and/or counterclaim, as the case may be, who wishes the case to be heard in the IPEC, should give strong consideration to pruning their case down to the essentials. A failure to do so may result in the action being heard elsewhere in the High Court purely because there are too many issues for a 2 or 3 day trial.
- The nature of the evidence. If it is anticipated that a large number of witnesses will be required on either or both sides, all to be cross-examined, there may be a significant risk that the limit of a 2 or 3 day trial will be exceeded.
- The value of the claim. Aside from the £500,000 limit on damages or account of profits, the value of the claim, though relevant, is generally not a major factor in the evaluation of whether a case is suitable for the IPEC. This is in part because it is often difficult to give an accurate estimate of the overall value.

A defendant sued in the general Chancery Division is entitled to apply to have the case transferred to the IPEC, and vice versa. This should be raised in correspondence first. If the parties agree that the case should be transferred, it still requires the approval of a judge in the court in which the case is currently listed but it is likely to happen. If there is no agreement, an application to transfer must be made. This should be done, at the latest, at the case management conference. The case management conference (CMC) is a preliminary hearing which is discussed further below.

Parties may take the joint view that a case which would not normally be suitable for the IPEC should nonetheless be heard there. They are also free to agree that the £500,000 limit on compensation for infringement will be waived. In such a case the court will usually accommodate the parties' wish provided that the trial will not take excessively longer than is usual for an IPEC trial.

3.3 The IPEC multi-track or small claims track

Where a claimant has decided to bring their case in the IPEC, consideration should be given to whether it should be in the IPEC multi-track or small claims track.

The small claims track never hears cases involving patents, registered designs, semiconductor topography rights or plant varieties. A claim in relation to those rights can only be brought in the IPEC multi-track (or the Patents Court).

Broadly speaking, if the case does not concern any of those rights and the compensation sought does not exceed £10,000, the claim will be heard in the small claims track. However, £10,000 does not constitute a hard and fast ceiling; the small claims track is entitled to order compensation above that amount. So although the level of damages (or defendant's profits) at stake is important, other matters also have to be taken into account.

If a case involves a point of law of some complexity or importance, or if it requires extensive cross-examination or for other reasons the trial is liable to last more than one day, the case will be unsuitable for the small claims track even if less than £10,000 is claimed in compensation. On the other hand, a straightforward case with no significant issue of law that can easily be heard in less than a day may be suitable for the small claims track even if the claimant seeks somewhat more than £10,000.

A defendant sued in either track may apply to have the case transferred. Before doing so, the defendant should seek the agreement of the claimant as to which track is appropriate.

Where the court is called upon to decide whether the case should be heard in the multi-track or the small claims track, in addition to the matters already discussed the size of the party seeking to have the case heard in the small claims track is often a significant factor. The court is more likely to allocate a case to the small claims track where an individual or a small company with limited financial means would benefit from the less formal procedure in the small claims track and/or the greater protection from exposure to an adverse costs order, provided the opposing side would still have sufficient opportunity to present their case. Another factor could be that judges who hear IPEC small claims are based more locally to the parties, thus affording a saving in costs.

CPR Part 63 rule 27 deals with allocation to the small claims track.

4. PROCEDURE IN THE IPEC

4.1 Before starting proceedings

2F-152   Attention is drawn to the Practice Direction – Pre-Action Conduct, which can be found at *http://www.justice.gov.uk/courts/procedure-rules/civil/rules/pd_pre-action_conduct*. This sets out steps to be taken before starting a claim.

Paragraph 6 of the practice direction is of particular relevance and is set out here:

"**Steps before issuing a claim at court**

6. Where there is a relevant pre-action protocol, the parties should comply with that protocol before commencing proceedings. Where there is no relevant pre-action protocol, the parties should exchange correspondence and information to comply with the objectives in paragraph 3, bearing in mind that compliance should be proportionate. The steps will usually include –

(a)   the claimant writing to the defendant with concise details of the claim. The letter should include the basis on which the claim is made, a summary of the facts, what the claimant wants from the defendant, and if money, how the amount is calculated;

(b)   the defendant responding within a reasonable time - 14 days in a straight forward case and no more than 3 months in a very complex one. The reply should include confirmation as to whether the claim is accepted and, if it is not accepted, the reasons why, together with an explanation as to which facts and parts of the claim are disputed and whether the defendant is making a counterclaim as well as providing details of any counterclaim; and

(c)   the parties disclosing key documents relevant to the issues in dispute."

It should be noted that this practice direction, including paragraph 6, was drafted to apply generally in civil litigation, not just in the IPEC. In the context of IPEC proceedings there is no 'relevant pre-action protocol' as mentioned in the first sentence, so the remainder of the paragraph applies. With regard to 6(b), defendants in an IPEC case are expected to respond within 14 days save in exceptional circumstances.

Threats

Potential claimants should be aware that while they should notify the intended defendant of their proposed claim, this should not take the form of an unjustified threat of infringement proceedings. In relation to some intellectual property rights a party making such a threat can be sued. It is beyond the scope of this Guide to explain the (sometimes fine) distinction between informing another party of your intellectual property right and threatening to bring proceedings for its infringement. It is wise to seek professional advice.

4.2 Starting proceedings

Proceedings are started when the court issues a claim form. To have this done, the intended claimant must complete Form N1 and send it to the court. Form N1 and notes for completing it can be found at *www.gov.uk/government/publications/form-n1-claim-form-cpr-part-7*.

Form N1 and any other document can be filed with the court online, see Section 5 of this Guide 'General Arrangements' below. Alternatively, the form may be posted to the IPEC or presented at the public counter on the ground floor of the Rolls Building. The Rolls Building is a court building in London which contains the IPEC. Its address, which is also the address of the IPEC, is given in Annex A at the end of this Guide.

4.3 Service of the claim form

'Service' of a document means delivering it to another party in the proceedings. This is to be distinguished from 'filing' a document with the court.

A copy of the claim form should be served by the claimant on each defendant together with a response pack. A response pack consists of the documents that a defendant will need to read and complete in order to make its initial response to the claim. It contains (a) a form for defending the claim, (b) a form for admitting the claim and (c) a form for acknowledging service. The response pack is supplied to the claimant by the court along with the claim form.

CPR Part 6 and the associated practice direction deal with how to make sure that documents are correctly served. A typical means of service on a company is by first class post to the company's principal or last known place of business, although CPR Part 6 rule 3 sets out a number of alternative methods. These include email provided that the party being served, or their solicitor, has previously indicted in writing that they are willing to be served by email.

If the relief sought involves a change to any UK registered right (such as its revocation or amendment), attention is also drawn to Part 63 rule14(3), which requires that copies of certain documents should also be sent to the UK Intellectual Property Office.

It is good practice for a claimant to serve their Particulars of Claim with the claim form.

4.4 Response by the defendant

A defendant served with Particulars of Claim has a choice as to how to respond. They may serve their Defence within 14 days of service of the Particulars of Claim. More usually a defendant will file an Acknowledgment of Service with the court. This is a form contained within the response pack which will have been served on the defendant along with the claim form. Filing an Acknowledgment of Service extends the time allowed for serving the Defence (see below). If the defendant wishes to challenge the jurisdiction of the court, they should only file an Acknowledgment of Service.

CPR Part 10 rule 3 sets out the period for filing an Acknowledgment of Service. Generally it must be done within 14 days of service of the claim form or, if the claim form states that the Particulars of Claim are to follow, within 14 days of service of the Particulars of Claim. The CPR only requires the Acknowledgement of Service to be filed with the Court, although subsequent documents, such as the Defence, must both be filed with the Court and served on the other parties (see Part 15 rule 6). It is always helpful to send a copy of any document filed with the court to the other party to ensure that those documents are received by the other party in a timely manner.

4.5 Statements of Case

(a) Introduction

The statements of case are the documents in which each party sets out their case, often called pleadings. For the claimant this will be the Particulars of Claim. The defendant responds with the Defence. Alternatively, the defendant can serve a Defence and Counterclaim where the defendant wishes not only to defend the claim but also to respond with a claim of their own. The claimant may then serve a Reply or a Reply and Defence to Counterclaim, as appropriate.

Part 63 rule 20(1) requires that a statement of case in the IPEC must set out concisely all the facts and arguments upon which the party serving the statement relies. This is sometimes misunderstood. All relevant facts and arguments must be stated. But they should not be set out in a manner which includes every detail. There will be an opportunity by the time of the trial to explain to the court everything that matters. A good approach is to make the statement of case as concise as is possible, while considering whether any argument proposed to be run at trial and the basis for it will come as a surprise to an opponent who has read the statement of case. If not, the statement of case has probably been drafted in sufficient detail.

Copies of important documents referred to in a statement of case (e.g. a patent, a design registration or an image of a design, or a contract relied on) should be served with the statement of case. Where any such document requires translation, a translation should be served at the same time.

(b) Time limits for filing and serving statements of case

The relevant time limits are unfortunately dispersed across different Parts of the CPR. The following is a summary guide.

The better practice is for a claimant to file and serve the Particulars of Claim with the court together with the claim form. However, the Particulars of Claim can be served up to 14 days later (Part 7 rule 4(1)). If served later, the Particulars of Claim must be filed with the court no later than 7 days after service on the defendant (Part 7 rule 4(3)).

If no Acknowledgement of Service has been filed by the defendant, the period for filing the Defence with the court is 14 days after service of the Particulars of Claim (Part 15 rule 4(1)(a)). If an Acknowledgement of Service has been filed, then the time limit for filing the Defence depends on whether the Particulars of Claim confirms that paragraph 6 of the Pre-Action Conduct Practice Direction (set out above) has been complied with. The time limit is 42 days if it does and 70 days if it does not (Part 63 rule 22(2) and (3)). In the event that the defendant also wishes to make a counterclaim against the claimant, this should follow on from the Defence in the same document and should be headed 'Counterclaim' (PD 20 para. 6.1).

The Defence (or Defence and Counterclaim) must be served on every other party (Part 15 rule 6). This should be done at the same time as filing the Defence. The CPR does not specify a time limit for serving the Defence but undue delay may cause adverse consequences in costs later.

The time limit for the claimant filing a Reply with court is 28 days from the service of the Defence. The same time limit applies to service of the Reply on other parties (Part 63 rule 22(4)).

If the claimant has been served with a Defence and Counterclaim it must respond with a Reply and Defence to Counterclaim. This should follow on from the Reply in the same document and should be headed 'Defence to Counterclaim' (PD 20 para. 6.2). The time limits for a Reply and Defence to Counterclaim are the same as for a Reply.

An optional final statement of case from the defendant is a Reply to the Defence to Counterclaim. This must be both filed and served 14 days from the service of the Defence to Counterclaim (Part 63 rule 22(5)).

Some time limits are stricter than others in the IPEC. The parties are not at liberty to extend the time limits set out in Part 63 rule 22 without the prior consent of the judge. An application for an extension of time must be made before the expiry of the relevant period and set out good reasons why the extension is required. Such applications are almost always dealt with without a hearing.

(c)   Content of statements of case for different types of claim
The following is guidance on the preparation of a statement of case for particular types of claim.

Patent proceedings
- A statement of case alleging infringement of a patent must (a) state which of the claims are alleged to be infringed and (b) give at least one example of the defendant's infringing product or process.
- A statement of case alleging that a patent is invalid must specify the grounds on which the validity of the patent is challenged, including any challenge to a priority date. All prior art relied on must be specified and a copy of each item of prior art must be attached to the pleading. Only very rarely will more than 3 items of prior art be permitted. If it is alleged that a patent does not disclose the invention clearly and completely enough for it to be performed, the pleading must state which aspects of the invention cannot be made to work and in which respects the invention cannot be made to work.
- A statement of case served in response to an allegation that the patent is invalid must state which claims are said to be independently valid.
- By the time the pleadings are closed and before the case management conference (CMC, see below), it should be clear which claims are in issue. They will be the claims which are alleged to be infringed and the claims which are alleged to have independent validity. The parties should bear in mind that at the CMC the court may require the number of claims in issue to be reduced, so consideration should be given to which of them is or are the most important to the party's case.
- Before the CMC the claim or claims in issue should be broken down into suitable integers (i.e. separate parts). The party alleging infringement should create a document stating which integers of the claim are embodied in the allegedly infringing product or are incorporated in the allegedly infringing process. This is often best done by a chart. In the case of a product claim the argument on infringement can be made even more clearly by using a diagram to identify where each integer of the claim is to be found in the allegedly infringing product. (It is not necessary to wait until pleadings are closed to do this. Particularly where it is apparent which claim or claims will be in issue, it is helpful to create the claim chart in the Particulars of Claim).
- Likewise the party alleging that a patent is invalid because it lacks novelty or inventive step over prior art should create a chart identifying which integers of the claim are present in the pleaded prior art. Again, sometimes a diagram of a prior art product may make the point even more clearly. It is helpful to create the chart as part of the Defence, but this must be done before the CMC at the latest.
- All parties should state what they understand to be the inventive concept – the core of the invention – in relation to the patent claim(s) in issue. The inventive concept may well form an essential part of arguments at trial and each side's definition should be clear by the time of the CMC.
- There should be a statement from both sides as to the facts which are said to be relevant common general knowledge. The nature and characteristics of the skilled person should be identified.

Registered design proceedings
- Where the defendant alleges the registered design is not new or lacks individual character, the Defence must specify the details of any prior design relied on, including full details of the date on which and the manner in which the prior design was made available to the public.
- The parties should be aware that at the CMC the number of items of prior art relied on may be limited by the court. If a party wishes to allege that an item of prior art is typical of other items available to the public and that all such items are relevant to the design corpus, consideration should be given as to how such typicality is to be proved at trial.
- Both the Particulars of Claim and the Defence should set out the relevant party's case as to the nature and characteristics of the informed user.

UK unregistered design right proceedings
- The Particulars of Claim should unambiguously identify the design or designs relied on. There is usually no difficulty if the design is of a specified entire article. If the claimant relies on the design of part of an article, or a combination of parts, the design in question must be clearly identified. A marked diagram may be essential.
- The claimant should bear in mind that at the CMC the court is likely to impose a limit on the number of designs relied on. Five is a usual maximum.
- The clamant should set out in their Particulars of Claim the significant features of each

design relied on. The claimant should identify which of the significant features are to be found in the allegedly infringing article and where. For clarity it may be appropriate to do this by means of an annotated diagram.

- In the Defence, the defendant should indicate whether they agree the list of significant features of the claimant's design and, if appropriate, add to the list. By reference to the list, the defendant should identify which of the significant features are admitted to be present in the design of the accused article. It may convenient to use a chart to do this (though it is not obligatory).
- If the defendant alleges that the design in issue lacks originality (in the copyright sense), one item of prior art should be identified in support of the allegation. The defendant should identify where each of the significant features is to be found in that item of prior art. It may be appropriate to use an annotated diagram.
- If the defendant alleges that the design in issue or any part of it is commonplace, all prior art relied on should be identified. By any clear and convenient means, the defendant should indicate which of the significant features of the design in issue are to be found in each item of prior art. Parties should be aware that the number of items of prior art which may be relied on may be limited by the court at the CMC.
- If alleged, the defendant should clearly identify which of the significant features of the design constitute a method or principle of construction, or are features which either (i) enable the article to be connected to, or place in, around or against, another article so that either article may perform its function, or (ii) are dependent upon the appearance of another article of which the article is intended by the designer to form an integral part. Any clear and convenient means of identification may be used.
- It may be helpful for the claimant to respond in the Reply.

Trade Mark proceedings
- Similarities relied on between a mark and a sign will not generally require elaboration. But in an appropriate case some detail may be necessary in relation to allegations that goods or services are similar. Parties to trade mark cases should identify the nature and characteristics of the average consumer (if relevant).

Copyright proceedings
- A defence of independent design in a copyright case should to be addressed in appropriate detail.

(d) Statements of truth
Attention is drawn to Part 63 rule 21, which modifies Part 22 in its application to the IPEC. The statement of truth must be made by a person with knowledge of the facts alleged (or by persons who between them have such knowledge). If more than one person signs the statement of truth, the individuals should indicate in some suitable manner which parts of the statement of case they are verifying. The knowledge of the person signing the statement of truth should be direct knowledge, so it will seldom be appropriate for that person to be a legal advisor.

Part 32 rule 14 sets out the consequences of verifying a statement of case containing a false statement without an honest belief in its truth, and to the procedures set out in PD 32 para. 28.

4.6 Case management
The case management conference (CMC) is a preliminary hearing in court which gives the judge, with the assistance of the parties, the opportunity to manage the conduct of the case. This is so that the proceedings will move forward to the trial in an efficient way proportionate to the nature of the dispute.

At the CMC the court will identify the issues of fact and law to be resolved at the trial and will decide whether to make orders under paragraph 29.1 of PD 63. These include orders permitting the filing of further material in the case such as disclosure, witness statements, experts' reports and skeleton arguments. The trial date will be fixed at the CMC as will the date on which judgment is to be handed down (unless this falls within a court vacation, in which case the date of judgment will be given at the end of the trial).

(a) Directions questionnaire
No directions questionnaire is required.

(b) The application for the case management conference
The claimant should apply for a CMC within 14 days after all defendants who intend to file and serve a Defence have done so. Where a case has been transferred from another court, the claimant should apply for a CMC within 14 days of the transfer. However, any party may apply for a CMC at any point if there is good reason. In particular, if the claimant has failed to apply for a CMC within 14 days of service of the Defence, the defendant should do so.

An application for a CMC is made in the same was as any other application to the court (see below). Once the application has been made, the judge's clerk will contact the parties to fix a date which is available in the court diary and which is convenient to the parties.

(c)   Preparation for the CMC

In advance of the hearing a bundle of documents (see Annex C) should be filed with the court at the Rolls Building (address in Annex A). Two days before the CMC is usually sufficient. See section 5.5 of the Guide below on the preparation of bundles.

The CMC is a particularly important part of the IPEC procedure. No material may be filed in the case by way of evidence, disclosure or written submissions unless permission is given by the judge. The first and last opportunity to obtain such permission is likely to be at the CMC. Save in exceptional circumstances the court will not permit a party to submit material in addition to that ordered at the CMC (Part 63 rule 23(2)). A cost-benefit test is applied to the filing of material in support of a case, see PD 63 para 29.2(2).

It is important that before the CMC the parties have given full consideration to the following:

The issues

The issues in dispute. These should clearly emerge from the statements of case. The parties must draw up a list of issues which the court will have to resolve at trial. It is not necessary to list every sub-issue that may arise and this should not be done. The parties will be permitted to argue at trial any point which is both covered by the pleadings and which the opposing side should reasonably contemplate as falling within one or more of the listed issues. The trial judge may refuse to hear argument at trial on a point which does not satisfy those criteria.

Disclosure

Whether disclosure of documents by the opposing side will be required and if so, which documents and why. Only specific disclosure is available in the IPEC, i.e. disclosure of either particular documents or particular classes of documents, often identified by reference to one or more of the list of issues. Usually, whether or not other disclosure is ordered, the parties will be expected to disclose any 'known adverse documents' within the meaning of paragraph 2 of PD 51U (which can be found at *www.justice.gov.uk/courts/procedure-rules/civil/rules/practice-direction-51u-disclosure-pilot-for-the-business-and-property-courts#2*).

The disclosure pilot scheme in operation in other Business and Property Courts does not apply to the IPEC.

Evidence of fact

Whether there is a need for evidence from one or more witnesses of fact and if so, the number of witnesses that will be required and, in broad terms, the factual matters which each witness will address. Generally, each issue of fact should be covered by only one witness. Where possible a single witness should deal with as many matters as possible so that the number of witnesses is kept to a minimum.

Expert evidence

Whether there is a need for evidence from one or more experts and if so, the number of experts that will be required and, in broad terms, the topics on which each expert will express an opinion. If expert evidence is permitted at all, only where it is clearly shown that different and distinct areas of expertise are relevant to the issues at trial will more than one expert be allowed.

Experiments, process descriptions, samples

Whether there is a need for any party to perform any experiments, provide a process description or supply a sample of any product or design.

Timetable

The timetable for the stages up to trial, in particular the dates for disclosure of documents, factual evidence and where appropriate, expert evidence, the supply of samples and any other relevant event. The court will not usually approve a timetable containing an automatic right to serve evidence in reply, but it may include a date by which the parties may apply to the court serve evidence in reply. Such an application, when later made, must state the topics in the evidence of the opposing side to be addressed in reply.

Draft order

The parties should attempt to agree a proposed order for directions, including the list of issues, to be made at the CMC in advance of the hearing. If agreed, a draft should be supplied to the court with the bundle of documents. If not agreed, each of the parties' proposed orders should be supplied with the bundle. In such a case it is helpful to have a single document marked up to show the alternative proposals of the parties.

(d) The hearing of the CMC

The CMC will almost always be conducted as a hearing in court. Where all parties consent, the judge may determine the CMC on paper. But even where the proposed order has been agreed by the parties the judge may require submissions in court to be sure that the issues have been correctly identified and that the directions are appropriate.

An example CMC order is attached to this Guide at Annex B.

(e) Amendments to a statement of case

On occasion a party may wish to amend its statement of case. If the other parties agree then generally no difficulties arise. If not, permission to amend may be sought at or before the CMC. Amending a statement of case after the CMC is difficult under the IPEC procedure, so parties must be sure by the time of the CMC that their pleadings are in final form.

(f) Alternative dispute resolution

The parties are required to give consideration to alternative dispute resolution (ADR) before the CMC. Either party may apply for time in which to pursue ADR before the proceedings progress further. Unless the court is satisfied that ADR is likely to be futile, time will usually be given. ADR is considered in more detail below.

(g) Costs in a multi-party case

If the case includes more than one defendant or group of defendants who are separately represented, the parties should consider the question of the likely effect of the costs capping provisions. If in doubt the parties should raise the matter at the CMC.

(h) Security for costs

In certain circumstances it is open to a defendant to seek security for costs. This means requiring the claimant to safeguard a sum of money to ensure that, in the event that the defendant were to win the action, the defendant's entitlement to its costs is secured. The rules relating to security for costs are set out at Part 25 rules 12-14.

(i) Expression of a preliminary, non-binding opinion on the merits

If it is likely to assist the parties in reaching a settlement, the IPEC is willing to express a preliminary and non-binding opinion on the merits of the case. This is often call an 'early neutral evaluation'. The court will almost certainly not take this course unless agreed by both sides. If there is agreement, the request to give the non-binding opinion should be made in advance of the CMC so that the court may consider whether it is appropriate. It is unlikely to be appropriate, for example, if the outcome of the proceedings will largely depend on unpredictable evidence that may emerge at trial.

4.7 Applications

An application to the court, including an application for a CMC, is made according to the procedure set out in Part 63 rule 25. This rule applies Part 23 with modifications, so Part 23 must also be considered. In brief, Part 23 requires the applicant to serve an application notice, a standard Form N244 in which the applicant states their intention to apply to the court and which sets out the nature of the application. Form N244 can be downloaded at:

www.gov.uk/government/publications/form-n244-application-notice

With the exception of applications made at the CMC, once the application notice is received by the party on whom it is served – the respondent – the respondent to the application must file and serve a response on all relevant parties within 5 working days of service of the application notice, see Part 63 rule 25(2). This rule is specific to the IPEC and is significant. If 5 working days elapse and the respondent has done nothing, the applicant is entitled to ask the court to make the order sought without further delay. It is therefore imperative that there is a response as soon as possible. Usually it is sufficient to contact the applicant and state the respondent's position with regard to the application. If a resolution cannot be agreed, the applicant will contact the court and arrange a hearing.

An applicant should take care to serve the application notice on the respondent. If the applicant notifies the court that 5 working days have elapsed without a response, it is important also to inform the court of the date on which the application notice was served and how this was done. Unless the court is shown that 5 working days have undoubtedly elapsed since service of the application notice, no action will be taken by the court.

Applications for judgment in default

If a defendant fails to file either an Acknowledgment of Service or a Defence within two weeks of service on it of the Particulars of Claim the claimant may make an application for judgment in default. This is an application to have judgment in the entire claim entered against the defendant because the defendant has not engaged with the court process.

A claimant may also make an application for a default judgment if the defendant files an

Acknowledgment of Service but fails to file a Defence within the relevant time limit (see above).

An application for judgment in default which seeks an order for an injunction must be made by an application notice. This will allow the defendant the usual 5 working days in which to respond. Such applications can generally be dealt with on paper. It is important to satisfy the court (a) that the claim form and Particulars of Claim were properly served and the date on which this was done and (b) the date and means of service of the application notice for judgment in default.

If judgment in default is granted, the order will be served on the defendant. The defendant has the right to apply to set aside such an order. This is done by filing an application notice. Setting aside an order for judgment in default will not follow automatically. Broadly speaking, the court will have to be satisfied that the defendant has an arguable defence and that the defendant ought to be given the opportunity to advance their defence. The longer the defendant takes in seeking to set aside a judgment in default, the less likely it is that the judgment will be set aside.

4.8   Urgent applications

An application for an interim injunction or other urgent relief, should be made by filing an application notice in the usual way (save in cases of extreme urgency, discussed below). Once the application notice has been served, the applicant should contact the judge's clerk (see Annex A). The clerk will find a date for the hearing which is appropriate to the urgency of the matter and, if possible, is convenient to all parties. In the meantime, the parties should make every effort to agree a timetable for evidence to be filed and served in relation to the application and any question of relief pending the hearing. Failing agreement, the judge's clerk should be informed. The court will then finalise the timetable and deal with any application for relief pending the hearing. This may be done on paper, by a phone application, or in a short hearing, as appropriate.

In cases of extreme urgency, an application may be made without an application notice. This is done by contacting the clerk to the IPEC. No such application will be entertained unless the judge is given very good reason why the matter is extremely urgent.

The court will always fix a date and time for hearings appropriate to the urgency of the application.

This may mean that the application will be heard by a judge other than the Presiding Judge of the IPEC. The convenience of the parties and their advisors will be taken into account but will not be of paramount importance.

4.9   The trial

At the trial the court will take an active part in controlling the proceedings and setting limits on the time allocated during a trial. To facilitate this process the parties are required to file a timetable for the conduct of the trial shortly in advance. If agreed by the judge, this timetable is likely to be enforced strictly. Unless there is good reason not to, the court will allocate equal time to the parties.

Trial on paper

In an appropriate case and if the parties consent, the trial may be conducted on paper, i.e. there is no hearing. The judgment is delivered in the usual way once the judge has read the papers.

4.10   Costs

There is no requirement for costs budgets in the IPEC.

Costs are subject to the cap provided by Part 45 rules 45.30-45.32. With certain limited exceptions the court will not order a party to pay total costs of more than £50,000 on the final determination of a claim in relation to liability and no more than £25,000 on an inquiry as to damages or account of profits.

Tables A and B of PD 45 Section IV set out the maximum amount of scale costs which the court will award for each stage of a claim.

There are exceptions: court fees, costs relating to enforcement of an order and wasted costs are excluded from the costs cap (Part 45 rule 31(4A)). Any recoverable VAT is not included in the capped costs (Part 45 rule 31(5)).

In the IPEC all costs are assessed summarily (Part 45 rule 41(3)). To enable the court to assess costs, the parties should prepare a statement of costs in advance of any hearing in which costs will be claimed. It is essential that the statement of costs breaks down the costs by reference to the stage of the claim in which they were incurred, see Table A and B of PD 45 Section IV.

Costs of an interim application

Costs of the case management conference or any other interim hearing will almost always be reserved to the conclusion of the trial (Part 63 rule 26(1)). The most usual exception arises when a party is found to have has behaved unreasonably. In such a case the court may make an order for costs at the conclusion of the hearing, to be paid shortly thereafter. These costs will be awarded in addition to the totality of the capped costs which the receiving party is entitled to at the end of the trial, see Part 45 rule 32.

4.11 Alternative dispute resolution

Settlement of a dispute by alternative dispute resolution (ADR) has many advantages. It can result in significant saving of costs. It also has the potential to provide the parties with a wider range of solutions than can be offered by litigation. For example, while the solution to litigation is usually limited to 'win/lose' on the issues put in front of the court, ADR may provide a creative 'win/win' solution, as some forms of ADR can explore other ways for the parties to co-operate. ADR can also explore settlement in several countries at the same time.

Legal representatives should consider and advise their clients as to the possibility of seeking to resolve the dispute via ADR. This should be recorded in a recital to the order made at the case management conference (see Annex B). In an appropriate case, the IPEC judge will adjourn a case for a specified period of time to encourage and enable the parties to use ADR.

There are many forms of ADR. Most of these are not free. They include:

(a) Mediation – This involves the appointment of a trained mediator to see whether a legally binding agreement can be negotiated. The parties will usually sign a framework agreement for the procedure of the mediation. Mediation can involve the mediator meeting with both parties together and/ or meeting the parties in separate rooms and shuttling between them. The UKIPO offers a specialist IP mediation service (details on the Intellectual Property Office website). Other mediation services are also available.

(b) Intellectual Property Office Opinions – The UK Intellectual Property Office runs a scheme to give non-binding opinions on patent infringement and patent validity. The opinion is given on the basis of written papers provided by the party applying for the opinion. The other party has the right to file observations but does not become a party to proceedings before the IPO. The parties can optionally agree to be bound by the outcome of any such opinion.

(c) Arbitration – This involves the appointment of an arbitrator under a set of procedural rules. The arbitrator will then make a binding decision on the case. Arbitration replaces the court action, but the decision of the arbitrator is private to the parties. Note that since arbitration is a private matter between the parties, arbitrators cannot revoke intellectual property rights.

(d) Conciliation – This involves the use of a third party to see whether agreement may be reached or to offer a non-binding opinion on the dispute. Some trade bodies offer conciliation services.

(e) Early Neutral Evaluation – This means appointing an expert to give a non-binding opinion about one or more issues in a dispute (unless the parties have asked the court to give an early neutral evaluation, see above). Although not binding, such opinions may assist the parties in reaching a settlement of the case.

(f) Binding expert determination – The parties may agree to appoint an expert to make a legally binding decision about one or more issues in a dispute.

5. General arrangements

5.1 Filing documents with the court

(a) Filing documents online

Documents may be filed at the court online. A guide as to how this may be done is at **2F-152.1** www.gov.uk/guidance/ce-file-system-information-and-support-advice.

This does not apply to bundles of documents to be used at the hearing of an application or at the trial. These must be taken or sent in hard copy to the court (see (b) and (c) below).

(b) Posting documents to the court

Documents may be posted to the court at the address given at Annex A below.

(c) Filing in person

Documents may also be filed by presenting them at the public counter of the Rolls Building, the court building in which the IPEC is located. The address is given at Annex A below.

5.2 Court fees

Fees are charged by the court for starting proceedings, for the trial and for making an application. The current fees are set out at www.gov.uk/government/publications/fees-in-the-civil-and-family-courts-main-fees-ex50.

5.3 Arrangements for listing

(a) Applications including the case management conference

Once the application notice has been filed and served on the opposing side, the applicant should contact the judge's clerk (contact details given below) in order to fix a date for the hearing.

If the matter is urgent, the clerk should be notified, giving reasons for the urgency. Where possible a date be fixed which is convenient to the parties. However, if one or both parties offer only a limited range of suitable dates, the court may fix a date without reference to both parties' convenience, particularly where otherwise there would be an unreasonable delay before the hearing.

(b) Trials
Trial dates are fixed at the case management conference (CMC). Parties attending the CMC should have their diaries and other necessary information available so that an appropriate date for the trial is fixed, such information to include the availability of witnesses. After the CMC the court will contact the parties confirming the trial date and requesting payment of the trial fee. The trial fee must be paid within 14 days of the trial date being set.

5.4 Time estimates for applications
The parties must provide time estimates for all applications in respect of which a hearing is sought. Parties must appreciate the need to give a realistic time estimate.

Where parties and their legal advisors consider that a time estimate provided by the opposing side is not realistic, they have a duty to notify the judge's clerk as soon as possible, giving their own time estimate.

5.5 Documents bundles and skeletons for the trial and applications
The preparation of papers for the hearing of applications and trials is important and should be approached intelligently. Annex C provides guidance to the preparation of the bundle of documents for use at trial or an application. This should be followed. Legal representatives and litigants in person who fail to do so may be required to explain why and may be penalised personally in costs.

It is the responsibility of both parties to ensure that all relevant documents are lodged by noon two working days before the date fixed for hearing unless some longer or shorter period has been ordered by the judge.

At the trial it is the responsibility of the claimant to prepare the bundles. A timetable for doing this will be set out in the order following the CMC. For an application it falls to the applicant to prepare the bundle in good time so that a copy may be provided to the court by noon two working days before the hearing and to the opposing side.

Where the party responsible for preparing the bundles is a litigant in person and the opposing side is professionally represented, it is helpful for the professional representatives to offer to undertake the task of preparing the bundles.

Bundles should be taken or sent to the court at the Rolls Building. Skeleton arguments should be supplied by email to the judge's clerk. Where the matter is urgent, the judge's clerk may be asked whether documents may be sent by email.

It is helpful if all important documents in trial bundles are also supplied on a USB stick or via e-mail in a format convenient for the judge's use (normally the current or a recent version of Microsoft Word or as a text searchable pdf). These will usually include skeleton arguments, important patents and drawings, the witness statements and expert reports.

Skeleton arguments should be lodged in time for the judge to read them before an application or trial. Any skeleton argument must also be served on the other parties in the case. In the case of applications, if a skeleton argument is used, it should normally be filed by 10:30am the previous working day (or, in the case of short applications, 3pm).

In the case of trials, the deadline for filing skeleton arguments will be stated in the order following the CMC. The court will frequently be assisted by a chronology of relevant facts in the trial skeleton It should be included in the skeleton unless the chronology is short enough to be self-evident or would contribute nothing of value.

5.6 Telephone applications
The IPEC will hear applications by telephone conference in accordance with the PD 23 and PD 63 para. 30.1. The party making the application must first contact the judge's clerk to seek the consent of the judge. If consent is given, that party is responsible for setting up the telephone application and informing the parties, counsels' clerks (where barristers are instructed) and the judge's clerk of the time of the conference call.

It is possible for the application to be recorded, and if recording by the court rather than by British Telecom (or other service provider) is requested, arrangements should be made with the judge's clerk. The recording will not be transcribed. The tape will be kept by the judge's clerk for a period of six months. Arrangements for transcription, if needed, must be made by the parties.

This procedure may be used where it will save costs but it is not suitable for all applications.

5.7 Consent Orders
The court will usually make orders proposed with the consent of all parties without the need for the parties to attend. A draft of the agreed order and the written consent of all the parties or their respective legal representatives should be supplied to the judge's clerk. Unless the judge assigned to

hear the application considers a hearing is needed, he or she will make the order in the agreed terms by signing it. It will be drawn up accordingly and sent to the parties.

5.8 Evidence at the trial

Evidence will usually be given by witnesses present at the trial. However, the judge may give permission for a party to provide evidence by video link. Permission must be sought well in advance of the trial, generally at the CMC, so that the court may make suitable arrangements.

Where a transcript of the evidence is made, it should be supplied to the judge by e-mail and in hard copy.

5.9 Draft judgment

Many judgments, particularly after a trial, will be reserved and handed down at a later date. Usually the parties' legal representatives (or litigants in person) will be provided with a copy of the draft judgment in advance of the date of handing down so that they may notify the court of typographical and obvious errors (if any). The text may be shown, in confidence, to the parties, but only for the purpose of obtaining instructions and on the strict understanding that the judgment, and its effect, are not to be disclosed to any other person or used in the public domain, and that no action is taken (other than internally) in response to the judgment. If the parties would prefer not to be shown the draft judgment on this basis they should inform the court at the time the judgment is reserved.

5.10 Order following judgment

There will often be a hearing after the judgment has been handed down in order to finalise the order to be made in consequence of the judgment. This may be immediately after the judgment is handed down or may be at a later date. The timing may depend on other commitments of the court. The parties should contact the court to be notified of or to arrange the date. The parties must exchange drafts of the desired consequential order in advance of the hearing. Where the parties are agreed as to the consequential order and have supplied to the judge a copy signed by all parties or their representatives, no hearing will be necessary.

5.11 Enforcement

A party seeking to enforce an injunction or procedural order should make an application to the court.

Enforcement of Financial Element of an Order

Enforcement of a financial element of an order (an order entitling a party to receive payment from another party) will be done by a district judge. Special provisions apply. A party seeking to enforce a financial element must take or send the documents set out below **in hard copy** at The Rolls Building, 7 Rolls Buildings, Fetter Lane, London EC4A 7NL. The documents should be contained in a bundle which is clearly marked for the attention of the IPEC Small Claims Track sitting in the Thomas More Building. The relevant documents are:
- the enforcement application;
- any evidence in support of the application;
- the sealed judgment or order of which enforcement is sought;
- any appeal notice or appeal order; and
- any order staying the proceedings.

5.12 Appeals

An order of an IPEC judge may be appealed. This applies equally to orders made following a trial and those made in response to an application to the court. All appeals go the Court of Appeal, see PD52A, Section3, Table 1. No party has an absolute right to appeal, permission must be obtained. Permission to appeal may and generally should be sought from the judge who made the order. If the judge refuses to give permission, the party may instead seek permission from the Court of Appeal.

NOTE THAT this does not apply to appeals from decisions in the IPEC Small Claims Track. All appeals from the IPEC Small Claims Track go to an enterprise judge, i.e. a judge of the IPEC multi-track, see CPR 63.19(3).

Costs in the Court of Appeal

There is no automatic capping of costs in the Court of Appeal. However, the Court of Appeal has a discretion to make an order limiting the costs which a successful party may recover from the unsuccessful party on appeal. See CPR Part 59 rule 19. The discretion will be exercised with regard to (a) the means of both parties, (b) all the circumstances of the case and (c) the need to facilitate access to justice. Exceptionally, an order limiting costs may not be made if the appeal raises an issue of principle or practice upon which substantial sums may turn.

An appellant who wishes to have the appeal costs capped should apply to the Court of Appeal as soon as is practicable.

5.13   Information available on the Internet

A link to 'Intellectual Property Enterprise Court' (and links to other courts) can be found at: *www.gov.uk/courts-tribunals*. If you follow that link you can also find links to copies of this Guide and the Guide to the Intellectual Property Enterprise Court Small Claims Track.

The Civil Procedure Rules (CPR) and Practice Directions are at: *www.justice.gov.uk/courts/procedure-rules/civil/rules*

Statutes and other legislation are at: *www.legislation.gov.uk*

www.justice.gov.uk/courts/court-lists provides links to two useful sites. The first is 'Intellectual Property Enterprise Court Diary'. If you click on that you will find the diary for trials (but not applications) to be heard in the IPEC and a record of past trials. The second is 'Business and Property Courts Rolls Building Cause List'. If you follow that link to 'Intellectual Property List (ChD)' a list of all IP court hearings, including those heard in the IPEC. After about 2pm the website shows the hearings for the following day.

Judgments of the IPEC are usually available at the bailii website at: *http://www.bailii.org/ew/cases/EWHC/IPEC*

Annex A

Contact details

The Intellectual Property Enterprise Court

2F-152.2   The home of the IPEC is in the Rolls Building at this address:

> The Rolls Building
> 7 Rolls Building Fetter Lane
> London
> EC4A 1NL
> DX160040 Strand 4

The IPEC is presided over by a specialist circuit judge, at present His Honour Judge Hacon.

The judge's clerk and clerk to the Intellectual Property Enterprise Court is at present Irram Khan. Her contact details are:

> irram.khan@justice.gov.uk
> Tel: 020 7947 6265

Filing documents online

Documents may be filed at the court online. A guide as to how this may be done is at *www.gov.uk/guidance/ce-file-system-information-and-support-advice*.

This does not apply to bundles of documents to be used at the hearing of an application or at the trial. These must be taken or sent in hard copy to the court (see above).

Postal application to issue process

Applications should be addressed to the Issue Section at the Rolls Building (address above) and clearly marked Intellectual Property Enterprise Court.

The public counter

The public counters are on the ground floor of the Rolls Building (address above). The counters are open Monday to Friday (except public holidays) from 10am-4.30pm.

General Enquiries

Apart from the issuing of proceedings, all communications with the Court should be addressed to the Clerk to the Intellectual Property Enterprise Court.

Please note that the court cannot give legal advice.

IP Pro Bono

A person with limited financial resources (including firms and companies if they qualify) may be entitled to free professional advice regarding any IP matter, whether concerning the IPEC or not. The IP Pro Bono scheme is designed to help such persons. It may be contacted at: *www.ipprobono.org.uk.*

Intellectual Property Enterprise Court Users Committee

The IPEC has a Users' Committee which considers the problems and concerns of intellectual property litigators in the IPEC. Membership of the committee includes the judges of the Intellectual Property Enterprise Court and of the Patents Court, representatives of each of the Intellectual Property Office, European Patent Office, Intellectual Property Bar Association, IP Chambers Clerks, the Intellectual Property Lawyers Association, the Chartered Institute of Patent Attorneys, the Institute of Trade Mark Attorneys, the IP Federation, the British Copyright Council, the Pro Bono Committees and IP Academics.

Anyone having views concerning the improvement of intellectual property litigation in the Intellectual Property Enterprise Court is invited to make his or her views known to the committee, preferably through the relevant professional representative on the committee or its secretary.

The current secretary is:

Luke Maunder,
Bristows,
100 Victoria Embankment,
London
EC4Y 0DH
Tel: 020 7400 8000
Fax: 020 7400 8050
Email: luke.maunder@bristows.com

Annex B

Example CMC Order

UPON HEARING the Case Management Conference on [date]   **2F-152.3**
UPON the issues to be determined at trial being identified in the Schedule to this order ("the Issues")

AND UPON the parties' legal advisors having informed their clients of alternative dispute resolution as a possible means of resolving these proceedings

IT IS ORDERED THAT:

Split trial

1. The trial shall determine only issues of liability, namely those set out in the schedule to this order. All issues of quantum, should they arise, will be resolved at a second trial.

Disclosure

2. Disclosure in accordance with the following paragraphs shall be given by 4pm on [date].

3. The claimant shall make and serve on the defendant a list in accordance with form N265 of documents in their control which relate to [Issues identified by number].

4. The defendant shall make and serve on the claimant a list in accordance with form N265 of the documents in their control which relate to [Issues identified by number].

5. Each party's list of documents shall also include all known adverse documents within the meaning of paragraph 2 of Practice Direction 51U.

6. If any party wishes to inspect or have copies of such documents as are in another party's control it shall give notice in writing that it wishes to do so and such inspection shall be allowed at all reasonable times upon reasonable notice and any copies shall be provided within 7 days of the request, upon the undertaking of the party requesting the copies to pay the reasonable copying charges.

Evidence

7. The statements of case shall stand as evidence in chief.

8. The claimant may file [number] witness statements dealing with issues [Issues identified by number].

9. The defendant may file [number] witness statements dealing with issues [Issues identified by number].

10. The witness statements shall be filed and exchanged on or before 4pm on [date].

11. The parties may apply to serve witness statements in reply on or before 4pm on [date]. An application must identify the matters in the opposing party's evidence of fact to be addressed.

12. The parties may each serve an expert's report dealing with [Issues identified by number] on or before 4pm on [date].

13. The parties may apply to serve an expert's report in reply on or before 4pm on [date]. An application must identify the matters in the opposing party's expert evidence to be addressed.

14. The witnesses may be cross-examined at trial.

TRIAL

15. The claimant shall no less than 4 weeks before the date of the trial serve on the other parties a list of all documents that it proposes to include in the trial bundle.

16. The other parties shall each no less than 3 weeks before the date of the trial serve on the claimant a list of any additional documents that it proposes should be included in the trial bundle.

17. The claimant shall no less than 2 weeks before the date of the trial serve on the other parties an agreed bundle of documents for use at the trial and no less than 1 week before the date of the trial file the agreed bundle with the court. The bundle shall be prepared in accordance with to the IPEC Guide.

18. Time estimates for the cross-examination and speeches of the parties, a reading guide for the judge shall be filed by 4pm on [date].

19. The parties shall file and exchange skeleton arguments, on or before 4pm on [date].

20. The time allocated for the trial is [ ] day(s).

21. The trial of the Claim shall take place on [date].

22. Judgment in the action shall be handed down on [date].

COSTS

23. Costs are reserved to the trial.

SCHEDULE—LIST OF ISSUES

The following list adopts the abbreviations used in the Statements of Case.

Trade Mark

1. Whether, because the Trade Mark is similar to the Earlier Trade Mark and is registered for goods identical with or similar to those for which the Earlier Trade Mark is registered, there exists a likelihood of confusion on the part of the public.
2. Whether the Sign has been used in the course of trade.
3. Whether the Sign is similar to the Trade Mark.
4. Whether the Trade Mark has a reputation in the United Kingdom.
5. Whether use of the Sign has taken unfair advantage of the distinctive character or the repute of the Trade Mark.
6. Whether such use was without due cause.

Passing Off

7. Whether the claimant owns goodwill in its business associated in the mind of the public with the Trade Mark.
8. Whether the defendant has misrepresented that its goods are connected in the course of trade with the claimant's business.
9. If so, whether such misrepresentation has caused the claimant damage.

ANNEX C

GUIDELINES ON BUNDLES

GENERAL

2F-152.4 **1.** The 'bundle' is the name given to the one or more files containing the documents to be used at a trial or other hearing. Preparation of the bundle is primarily the responsibility of the claimant in the case of a trial bundle and the applicant in the case of other hearings unless the court has directed otherwise. This must be done in consultation with the other parties. It is the duty of all parties to co-operate in order to agree the content of the bundle in good time before the trial or other hearing.

2. In no circumstances should rival bundles be presented to the court.

TYPICAL CONTENTS OF A BUNDLE

3. Below is set out a typical list of the documents that should go into the bundle for the trial, for the case management conference (CMC) or for any other hearing. Some hearings will not require all the indicated documents. For example, at the CMC there will not normally yet exist any experts' reports, disclosure documents or earlier orders of the court and there may be no witness statements. The parties are also free to agree that types of document other than those listed below should go into the bundle if it is important for the judge to see them.

Statements of Case
Claim Form and Particulars of Claim
Defence and Counterclaim
Reply and Defence to Counterclaim
Part 18 Requests for further information and Responses
Orders
All earlier orders of the court made in the proceedings
Evidence
Witness statements
Experts' reports
Exhibits
Documents exhibited to the statements of case, witness statements and experts' reports
Disclosure
Documents produced in disclosure on which any party seeks to rely
Correspondence
Correspondence between parties or their legal advisors may be included, but **strictly only to the extent that will be relevant at the trial or other hearing**.

AVOIDANCE OF DUPLICATION

4. No more than one copy of any one document should be included, unless there is good reason for doing otherwise.

CHRONOLOGICAL ORDER

5. In general the documents in each of the categories (statements of case, witness statements, orders, etc) should be arranged in date order starting with the earliest document.

6. The sequence of exhibits in an exhibits file (see paragraph 18 below) should reflect the order in which they are referred to in the relevant statement of case, witness statement or expert's report.

PAGINATION OF A BUNDLE FOR A TRIAL

7. The bundle prepared for a trial may be paginated continuously from start to finish, i.e. beginning with 1 for the first page of the first file and continuing the numbering up to the last page of the last file. Alternatively, each file may be paginated continuously from the first to the last page. One or other of these modes of pagination must be used for the trial bundle. It is not necessary for other hearings.

8. These page numbers should be inserted in bold figures, at the bottom of the page and in a form that can clearly be distinguished from any other pagination on the document.

FORMAT AND PRESENTATION

9. Where possible the documents should be in A4 format.

10. Where the colour of any image or writing in a document is important, the document must be copied in colour.

11. Documents in a foreign language should be translated; the translation should immediately follow the document translated. The translation should be agreed or, if it cannot be agreed, each party's proposed translation should be included.

12. Subject to paragraph 18 below, the bundle should contain the minimum convenient number of files with appropriate use of dividers for each file. The size of each file should be tailored to its contents. It is not useful to have a large lever-arch file with just a few pages inside; on the other hand bundles should not be overloaded as they tend to break. **No bundle should contain more than 300 pages.**

13. Large documents, such as plans, should be placed in a file in a way such that the document is easily accessible.

14.   Each file in the bundle should have a list of contents at the front. It is not necessary to put the full heading of the action on the contents list. Documents should be identified briefly but enough to know what each document is, e.g. "AGS3 – Defendant's Accounts".

15.   The contents list of a correspondence file need not identify each letter, email etc. if these are presented in chronological order.

16.   Labels on the outside of files should use **large and clearly visible** lettering, e.g. "File A. Statements of Case." A label should be used on the front as well as on the spine.

17.   A label should also be stuck on to the front inside cover of a file, in such a way that it can be clearly seen even when the file is open.

EXHIBITS IN A SEPARATE BUNDLE

18.   Exhibits to statements of case, witness statements or experts' reports should generally be put in a separate bundle so that the reader can see both the text of the statement and the document referred to at the same time. This need not be done if there are very few exhibits; in such cases exhibits should immediately follow the document to which they are exhibited.

SECTION 2FA   FINANCIAL LIST

PART 63A—FINANCIAL LIST

Editorial introduction

2FA-1.1   *In the penultimate line of the first paragraph, after "two-year period, commencing", replace "in" with:*
from 1

Financial List claims

2FA-2.1   *In the fourth paragraph, after "There were two", replace "key" with:*
central

Effect of rule

The Financial List judges

2FA-5.1   *Replace the first list with:*
The Chancellor, currently Sir Geoffrey Vos;
Mr Justice Hildyard;
Mr Justice Mann;
Mr Justice Marcus Smith;
Mr Justice Nugeel;
Mr Justice Snowden and
Mr Justice Zacaroli.

Replace the second list with:
The Judge in charge of the Commercial Court, currently Mr Justice Teare;
Mr Justice Andrew Baker;
Mr Justice Butcher;
Mr Justice Knowles;
Mr Justice Males; and
Mr Justice Phillips.

SECTION 2G   COMPANIES ACT PROCEEDINGS

PRACTICE DIRECTION 49A—APPLICATIONS UNDER THE COMPANIES ACTS AND RELATED LEGISLATION

This Practice Direction supplements CPR Part 49

Section II. Particular applications under the 2006 Act

Proceedings under section 955 (Takeovers—enforcement by the court)

Replace paragraph with:

16. Proceedings for an order under section 955 may be started by a Part 7 **2G-22** or a Part 8 claim form, as appropriate.

Companies Court

Note on listing and criteria for the transfer of work from the ICC Judges to The County Court sitting in Central London

Replace "(7)(c)" with: **2G-39**

(c)   applications to rectify the register by reason of omission or mis-statement in any statement or notice delivered to the registrar of companies (s.859M Companies Act 2006) or to replace an instrument or debenture delivered to the registrar of companies (s.859N Companies Act 2006).

Applications to extend time for registering a charge or to rectify an omission or mis-statement

At the end of the fourth paragraph (beginning "The claim form"), replace "ICC Judge" with:

registrar   **2G-45**

Unfair Prejudice Applications (2006 Act Pt 30)

In the tenth paragraph (beginning "Following consultation with the"), after "directions in the", add:

prescribed form (see para.2G-46.2)   **2G-46.1**

In the eleventh paragraph, after "The rationale for", replace "doing so" with:

automatic directions

In the eleventh paragraph, after list item (c), insert new paragraphs:

Practitioners should note that the Disclosure Pilot set out in PD 51U applies to Unfair Prejudice petitions: see *Message from the Chief Insolvency and Companies Court Judge* dated 6 February 2019 (see para.51UPN.2). The automatic directions have recently been updated to reflect this.

On the approach to be adopted to the Disclosure Pilot, see generally In the *UTB LLC v Sheffield United Ltd (Re Blades Leisure Ltd)* [2019] EWHC 914 (Ch), paras 11-25, 65, and 75-80.

SECTION 3   OTHER PROCEEDINGS
SECTION 3A   HOUSING

Law of Property Act 1925

No forfeiture notice before determination of breach.

Add new paragraph at end:

Note also that a s.146 notice can only be served after the right of re-entry has become enforce- **3A-16** able under the provisions of the lease. In *Toms v Rubery* [2019] EWCA Civ 128, a lease required a landlord to give a tenant 14 days to remedy a breach of covenant before a right of re-entry became enforceable. As the s.146 notice had been sent before the tenant had been given that time to remedy the breach, it had not been validly served.

Defective Premises Act 1972

"Landlord's duty of care ..."

Replace paragraph with:

3A-55 Section 4 imposes on landlords a duty of care to all persons who might reasonably be affected by defects in the premises. The duty is to take such care as is reasonable in all the circumstances to see that they are reasonably safe from personal injury or from damage to their property (see, e.g. *Clarke v Taff Ely BC* (1983) 10 H.L.R. 44, QBD and *Rogerson v Bolsover DC* [2019] EWCA Civ 226; [2019] H.L.R. 24). The duty is owed if the landlord has the express or implied right under the agreement to enter the premises to carry out any description of maintenance or repair of the premises (e.g. *McAuley v Bristol City Council* [1992] 1 All E.R. 749; (1991) 23 H.L.R. 586; [1991] 46 E.G. 155, CA). See too the Rent Act 1977 ss.3(2) and 148 (below); and the Housing Act 1988 s.16 (below).

County Courts Act 1984

Possession to be given at expiration of specified period

Replace paragraph with:

3A-305 An order for possession under subs.(3) must be suspended as provided by that subsection. In *Golding v Martin* [2019] EWCA Civ 446; [2019] L. & T.R. 16, an order which, contrary to the provisions of s.138, was unconditional and did not provide for the possibility of payment of the arrears and costs or state that it would take effect in not less than four weeks from the date of the order was set aside.

Subsection (4) provides that the period may be extended at any time before possession of the land is recovered "in pursuance of the order" under subs.(3). There is some authority for the proposition that recovery of possession "in pursuance of the order" means recovery under a warrant for possession and not by other means (*Gadsby and Mitchell v Price and Harrison* [1985] C.L.Y. 1877).

Housing Act 1985

Equality Act 2010

Add new paragraph at end:

3A-378 For the effect of the public sector equality duty contained in Equality Act 2010 s.149, upon possession claims where alleged drugs problems at premises are in issue, see *Powell v Dacorum BC* [2019] EWCA Civ 23; [2019] H.L.R. 21 and *Forward v Aldwyck Housing Group Ltd* [2019] EWHC 24 (QB); [2019] H.L.R. 20. See too *London and Quadrant Housing Trust v Patrick* [2019] EWHC 1263 (QB); 23 May 2019 (Turner J).

"member of the tenant's family"

Replace "Haringey LBC v Simawi [2018] EWHC 2733 (QB)" with:

3A-412 *Haringey LBC v Simawi* [2018] EWHC 2733 (QB); [2019] H.L.R. 13

3A-460 *Replace (1)(c) with:*

Meaning of "long tenancy"

(c) any tenancy granted in pursuance of Part V (the right to buy), including any tenancy granted in pursuance of that Part by virtue of section 17 of the Housing Act 1996 (the right to acquire).

Note

Replace paragraph with:

3A-461 Amended by the Housing Act 1988 s.140, Sch.17, para.40; and the Housing Act 1996 (Consequential Provisions) Order 1996 (SI 1996/2325) art.5, Sch.2, para.14; and the Housing Act 1996 (Consequential Amendments No.2) Order 1997 (SI 1997/627) Sch.2, para.3; and (subject to transitional and saving provisions in Sch.3 thereof) by the Housing and Regeneration Act 2008 (Consequential Provisions) Order 2010 (SI 2010/866) Sch.2, para.26 with effect from 1 April 2010; and the Abolition of the Right to Buy and Associated Rights (Wales) Act 2018 (Consequential Amendments and Savings Provisions) Regulations 2019 (SI 2019/110) reg.3(a), with effect from 26 January 2019 subject to savings specified in SI 2019/110 reg.5.

Sch.1, para.6—private sector leasing

Replace the second paragraph with:

3A-503 See *Tower Hamlets LBC v Abdi* (1992) 91 L.G.R. 300; (1993) 25 H.L.R. 80, CA; *Hackney LBC v*

Lambourne (1993) 25 H.L.R. 172, CA; *Haringey LBC v Hickey* [2006] EWCA Civ 373; [2006] H.L.R. 36; and *Mohamed v Barnet LBC* (2019) EWHC 1012 (QB). For the interrelationship between Sch.1, paras 4 and 6, see *City of Westminster v Boraliu* [2007] EWCA Civ 1339; [2008] 1 W.L.R. 2408.

Landlord and Tenant Act 1985

Change title of paragraph: **3A-535**

Commencement and application

Add new paragraphs at end:
It applies to all new tenancies and replacement tenancies with terms of less than seven years (including new periodic tenancies) granted on or after 20 March 2019. It also applies to all tenancies which began as fixed term tenancies before 20 March 2019, but which become periodic tenancies after that date. As from 20 March 2020, it applies to all periodic tenancies (including statutory periodic tenancies, secure tenancies, assured tenancies and protected tenancies). It does not apply to licences.

It implies a covenant by the landlord that the dwelling:
(a)   is fit for human habitation at the time the lease is granted or otherwise created or, if later, at the beginning of the term of the lease, and
(b)   will remain fit for human habitation during the term of the lease.

It is not possible for a landlord to contract out of this implied covenant. The implied covenant applies to the demised premises and, if the dwelling forms part of a building (a flat in a block, or a room in an HMO), to all parts of the building in which the landlord has an estate or interest (s.9A(6)), e.g. the common parts, or the retained parts such as outside walls, windows, roof etc.

Sections 9A(2) and 9A(3) provide exceptions to liability on the landlord's part where unfitness is caused by the tenant's failure to behave in a tenant-like manner or the tenant's breach of covenant; where the dwelling is destroyed or damaged by fire, storm, flood or other inevitable accident; where the tenant is entitled to remove the item in question from the dwelling; where carrying out works or repairs would put the landlord in breach of any obligation imposed by any enactment; or where the works require the consent of a third party and the landlord has made reasonable endeavours to get that consent, but it has not been given.

In determining fitness, regard shall be had to the matters listed in s.10, viz. repair, stability, freedom from damp, internal arrangement, natural lighting, ventilation, water supply, drainage and sanitary conveniences, facilities for preparation and cooking of food and for the disposal of waste water; and any of the 29 hazards set out in the Housing Health and Safety Rating System (England) Regulations 2005. The property shall be regarded as unfit for human habitation if, and only if, it is so far defective in one or more of those matters that it is "not reasonably suitable for occupation in that condition". Although there is no express provision in ss.9A to 10 requiring a tenant to give notice of unfitness, the same principles considered by the House of Lords in *O'Brien v Robinson* [1973] A.C. 912, noted at para.3A-553, are likely to be applied within the demised premises, although landlords are likely to be deemed to have notice of unfitness within the common parts or other areas retained by them.

Note

To the end of the paragraph, add:
See commentary at para.3A-535. **3A-541**

Note

To the end of the paragraph, add:
See commentary at para.3A-535. **3A-543**

Note

To the end of the paragraph, add:
See commentary at para.3A-535. **3A-545**

Housing Act 1988

"private registered provider of social housing"

Replace paragraph with:
Subsections (1A) and (1B), which were inserted by Localism Act 2011 s.164, provide that a court **3A-893.1** cannot make an order for possession of a property let by a private registered provider of social housing with a fixed term of at least two years, unless the landlord has given the tenant at least six months' notice in writing stating that they do not intend to grant another tenancy and informing the tenant how they can obtain help and advice. Those subsections do not apply in relation to an assured shorthold tenancy that: (a) was granted before the day on which the amendment came into

force; or (b) came into being by virtue of s.5 of the Housing Act 1988 (periodic tenancy arising on termination of fixed term) on the coming to an end of an assured shorthold tenancy within para.(a). (See Localism Act 2011 s.164(2).) Section 21(1B) is only a bar to a court making an order for possession where the term of an assured shorthold tenancy has expired by effluxion of time. There is no requirement that the landlord give six months' notice during a fixed term (*Livewest Homes Ltd v Bamber* [2019] EWCA Civ 1174; 10 July 2019).

Add new paragraph 3A-893.6:

Tenants' Fees

3A-893.6 Tenant Fees Act 2019 s.1 provides that landlords must not require tenants or persons acting on their behalf to make prohibited payments in connection with tenancies of housing. Those payments which are permitted (and so not prohibited payments) are listed in Sch.1, viz. rent, deposits, holding deposits, payments in the event of a default, payments on variation, assignment or novation of a tenancy, payments on termination of tenancies, payments in respect of council tax, utilities, television licences or communication services. Under s.17, if a landlord breaches that provision and a prohibited payment is made, no section 21 notice may be given in relation to the tenancy so long as all or part of the prohibited payment has not been repaid. Guidance issued by the government is available at *https://www.gov.uk/government/publications/tenant-fees-act-2019-guidance*. The Act was brought into force on 1 June 2019.

Recovery of possession—the notice requirements

Replace "Barrow v Kazim [2018] EWCA Civ 2414" with:
3A-894 Barrow v Kazim [2018] EWCA Civ 2414; [2019] H.L.R. 14

Replace the last paragraph with:
  Section 21 notices may be given before the fixed term expires. The section 21 notice requirements, as amended by the Deregulation Act 2015, now apply to all assured shorthold tenancies, whenever granted. Landlords of assured shorthold tenants must use a prescribed form of s.21 notice. The notice is prescribed by the Assured Tenancies and Agricultural Occupancies (Forms) (England) (Amendment) Regulations 2019 (SI 2019/915). A new prescribed Form 6A, took effect from 1 June 2019. This must be used for all section 21 notices from 1 June 2019 (or at least for all tenancies and renewal tenancies that post-date 1 October 2015). It is strongly arguable that using the previous form 6A after 31 May 2019 would result in the section 21 notice being invalid, because the information about the Tenant Fees Act is relevant information. The Assured Tenancies and Agricultural Occupancies (Forms) (England) Regulations 2015 (SI 2015/620) provide that a notice in "a form substantially to the same effect" as the prescribed form is valid—see para.2. However, neither the Assured Shorthold Tenancy Notices and Prescribed Requirements (England) Regulations 2015 (SI 2015/1646) nor the Assured Shorthold Tenancy Notices and Prescribed Requirements (England) (Amendment) Regulations 2015 (SI 2015/1725) contains a similar provision. There is now no requirement that the date specified in the notice is the last day of a period of the tenancy. However, a notice under s.21(1) or s.21(4) cannot be served during the first four months of a tenancy (with the exception of replacement tenancies as defined in s.21(7) or statutory periodic tenancies arising under s.5(2)). Possession claims may not be begun later than six months from the date of service of the s.21 notice. If landlords comply with these requirements (and subject to the restrictions referred to in paras 3A-893.1 to 3A-893.4), they are automatically entitled to possession. See too *Elias v Spencer* [2010] EWCA Civ 246, 29 January 2010, unrep. The court has no power to suspend possession orders, apart from the Housing Act 1980 s.89(1).

Section 21 and ECHR art.8

Replace "FJM v United Kingdom Application No.76202/16," with:
3A-895 FJM v United Kingdom (Admissibility) (76202/16) [2019] H.L.R. 8,

Tenancies granted on or after 1 October 2015

Replace the second paragraph with:
3A-896.1 Landlords of assured shorthold tenancies granted on or after 1 October 2015 must use a prescribed form of s.21 notice. The notice is prescribed by the Assured Tenancies and Agricultural Occupancies (Forms) (England) (Amendment) Regulations 2019 (SI 2019/915). A new prescribed Form 6A, took effect from 1 June 2019. This must be used for all section 21 notices from 1 June 2019 (or at least for all tenancies and renewal tenancies that post-date 1 October 2015). It is strongly arguable that using the previous form 6A after 31 May 2019 would result in the s.21 notice being invalid, because the information about the Tenant Fees Act is relevant information. The Regulations do not apply to a statutory periodic assured shorthold tenancy which came into being under s.5(2) on the expiry of a fixed term tenancy on or after 1 October 2015 if the original assured shorthold tenancy was granted before that date. Note though that from 1 October 2018, the prescribed form must be used whenever the tenancy was granted.

In the third paragraph, replace "Assured Shorthold Tenancy Notices and Prescribed Requirements (England) (Amendment) Regulations 2015 (SI 2015/1725)" with:
Assured Tenancies and Agricultural Occupancies (Forms) (England) (Amendment) Regulations 2019 (SI 2019/915)

Housing Act 1996

Restriction on termination of tenancy for failure to pay service charge

Add new paragraph at end:
A landlord may, during the period when prevented from exercising a right of re-entry by s.81, **3A-1054** waive the right to forfeit a lease for non-payment of service charges (*Stemp v 6 Ladbroke Gardens Management Ltd* [2018] UKUT 375 (LC)).

"reasonable to continue to occupy"

Replace the last paragraph with:
For the interaction between the public sector equality duty and Housing Act 1996 s.177, see **3A-1251** *Lomax v Gosport BC* [2018] EWCA Civ 1846; [2018] H.L.R. 40 and *Kannan v Newham LBC* [2019] EWCA Civ 57; [2019] H.L.R. 22. See too *London and Quadrant Housing Trust v Patrick* [2019] EWHC 1263 (QB); 23 May 2019 (Turner J).

Vulnerable

Replace the last paragraph with:
In *Hotak v Southwark LBC* [2015] UKSC 30; [2015] 2 W.L.R. 1341 the Supreme Court held that **3A-1324** the public sector equality duty (Equality Act 2010 s.149) is complimentary to the duty under Pt 7. It requires, however, the decision maker to focus very sharply on whether the applicant is under a disability or has any other relevant protected characteristic, the extent of such disability, the likely effect of the disability when taken together with any other features on the applicant if and when homeless and whether the applicant is as a result vulnerable. In many cases the decision maker would comply with the duty under s.149 by properly considering whether an applicant was vulnerable within the meaning of s.189. There would, however, undoubtedly be cases where a decision, which was otherwise lawful, would be unlawful because the decision maker had failed to comply with the public sector equality duty. For cases involving the interaction between the public sector equality duty and Housing Act 1996 (in other contexts), see *Lomax v Gosport BC* [2018] EWCA Civ 1846; [2018] H.L.R. 40 and *Kannan v Newham LBC* [2019] EWCA Civ 57; [2019] H.L.R. 22.

Affordability

Replace paragraph with:
The question of whether accommodation is affordable and accordingly whether it is reasonable **3A-1345** to continue to occupy it is not to be "judged on a Micawber test as to whether one's income exceeds, or fails to measure up to, the rent one is required to pay" (per Sir Thomas Bingham M.R. in *R. v Croydon LBC Ex p. Graham* (1994) 26 H.L.R. 286, CA, where the applicant had not acted unreasonably in moving (without prospect of homelessness) to cheaper suitable accommodation. See too *R. v Tower Hamlets LBC Ex p. Ullah* (1992) 24 H.L.R. 680, QBD, *R. v Leeds City Council Ex p. Adamiec* (1992) 24 H.L.R. 138, QBD, and *R. v Westminster City Council Ex p. Ali* (1997) 29 H.L.R. 580, QBD. In *Samuels V Birmingham City Council* [2019] UKSC 28; 12 June 2019, the Supreme Court stated that in any assessment affordability must be based upon full income and expenses, including any housing benefit income and rent liability. Assessment of 'reasonable living expenses' "requires an objective assessment; it cannot depend simply on the subjective view of the case officer", and must be on the basis of an indefinite period of future occupation. The Code of Guidance makes clear that amounts will vary "according to the circumstances and composition of the applicant's household". Where an applicant cares for children, the question is what are her reasonable living expenses (other than rent), that being determined having regard to both her needs and those of the children, including the promotion of their welfare. A council officer's subjective view as to what an applicant should be doing with their household budget is not valid as an approach. The question is rather whether the household expenses are objectively at a reasonable level.

Duty to persons with priority need who are not homeless intentionally

Replace "Sambotin v Brent LBC [2018] EWCA Civ 1826" with:
Sambotin v Brent LBC [2018] EWCA Civ 1826; [2019] H.L.R. 5   **3A-1374**

"secure that accommodation is available for occupation"

In the fourth paragraph (beginning "In addition,"), replace "Alibkhiet v Brent LBC; Adam v City of Westminster [2018] EWCA Civ 2742" with:
Alibkhiet v Brent LBC; Adam v City of Westminster [2018] EWCA Civ 2742; [2019] H.L.R. 15   **3A-1375**

"cease to be subject to the duty"

3A-1376
In the last paragraph, replace "Sambotin v Brent LBC [2018] EWCA Civ 1826" with:
Sambotin v Brent LBC [2018] EWCA Civ 1826; [2019] H.L.R. 5

Referral of case to another local housing authority

3A-1402
In the last paragraph, replace "Sambotin v Brent LBC [2018] EWCA Civ 1826" with:
Sambotin v Brent LBC [2018] EWCA Civ 1826; [2019] H.L.R. 5

Reconsideration of review

3A-1428
In the first paragraph, replace the first two sentences with:
Local authorities have no statutory obligation to conduct second reviews (*R. (B) v Redbridge LBC* [2019] EWHC 250 (Admin). Applicants, may ask for extra-statutory reviews or updated decisions as to issues such as suitability, but there is no requirement that local authorities must conduct them. If local authorities fail, on request, to reconsider reviews, the remedy for applicants is to appeal the original review decision in the county court in accordance with s.204.

Appeals

3A-1430
After the first paragraph, add new paragraph:
It is "wrong in principle" to attempt to challenge earlier un-appealed review decisions in subsequent homelessness applications "in the absence of exceptional circumstances" (*Godson v Enfield LBC* [2019] EWCA Civ 486, following *Tower Hamlets LBC v Rahanara Begum* [2005] EWCA Civ 116.

"extension of time for bringing appeal"

3A-1441
To the end of the first paragraph, before the last sentence, add:
Being unrepresented may not, by itself, be a "good reason" (*Tower Hamlets LBC v Al Ahmed* [2019] EWHC 749 (QB).

Add Renting Homes (Fees etc.)(Wales) Act 2019:

Renting Homes (Fees etc.) (Wales) Act 2019

(2019 ANAW 2)

ARRANGEMENT OF SECTIONS

Paragraph numbers marked with a "+" denote content that is available on White Book on Westlaw UK or the Civil Procedure CD.

SECTION 3B   BUSINESS TENANCIES

Landlord and Tenant Act 1954

s.30(1)(f) intention of landlord to demolish or reconstruct

Replace the fourth paragraph with:
   Intention needs to be distinguished from motive. Motive and purpose as such are irrelevant. **3B-182**
However, they may be "investigated at trial as evidence for the genuineness of [the landlord's]
professed intention to carry out the works". So, where a landlord's only purpose in carrying out the
works was to obtain possession from the tenant, the landlord did not satisfy the test in s.30(1)(f).
See *S Franses Ltd v Cavendish Hotel (London) Ltd* [2018] UKSC 62 and Lord Sumption at [19]:
      "the landlord's intention to demolish or reconstruct the premises must exist independently of
      the tenant's statutory claim to a new tenancy, so that the tenant's right of occupation under a
      new lease would serve to obstruct it. The landlord's intention to carry out the works cannot
      therefore be conditional on whether the tenant chooses to assert his claim to a new tenancy
      and to persist in that claim. The acid test is whether the landlord would intend to do the
      same works if the tenant left voluntarily" .

Delete the penultimate paragraph (beginning "In Dogan v Semali").

SECTION 3C   CONTEMPT OF COURT

A. AN OUTLINE OF THE LAW OF CONTEMPT OF COURT

2.   *Principal forms of contempt liability*

(a)   Contempt "in the face of the court"

Replace "Hughes Jarvis Ltd v Searle [2019] EWCA Civ 1" with:
   Hughes Jarvis Ltd v Searle [2019] EWCA Civ 1; [2019] 1 W.L.R. 2934   **3C-6**

(c)   Interference with the due administration of justice

(i)   Interference generally

Replace "R. v Yaxley-Lennon [2018] EWCA Crim 1856; [2018] 2 Cr. App. R. 30" with:
   R. v Yaxley-Lennon [2018] EWCA Crim 1856; [2019] 1 W.L.R. 5400; [2018] 2 Cr. App. R. 30   **3C-9**

(d)   Contempt by witnesses

Replace "Hughes Jarvis Ltd v Searle [2019] EWCA Civ 1," with:
   Hughes Jarvis Ltd v Searle [2019] EWCA Civ 1; [2019] 1 W.L.R. 2934,   **3C-14**

(ii)   Witness refusing to give evidence

To the end of the first paragraph, add:
   A criminal defendant and a respondent to an application for contempt enjoy not only the **3C-16**
privilege against self-incrimination enjoyed by all witnesses, but also the right to silence which carries with it the absolute right not to go into the witness box: see *Douherty v Chief Constable of Essex
Police* [2019] EWCA Civ 55 at [19]-[23].

(e)   Contempt of court and enforcement of judgments etc by order of committal

(iv)   Enforcement by committal order of order for court attendance of debtor

To the end of the paragraph, add:
   See most-recently the discussion in *Attorney-General v Yaxley-Lennon* [2019] EWHC 1791 (QB).   **3C-21**

(f) Corporations and contempt liability

3C-24.1

Replace "Integral Petroleum SA v Petrogat FZE [2018] EWHC 2686 (Comm)" with:
Integral Petroleum SA v Petrogat FZE [2018] EWHC 2686 (Comm); [2019] 1 W.L.R. 574

3. Jurisdiction

(a) High Court

(iii) Concurrent jurisdiction

3C-30

To the end of the paragraph, add:
and the decision of the Divisional Court in *Solicitor-General v Holmes* [2019] EWHC 1483 (Admin).

(b) Crown Court

3C-32

Replace "National Crime Agency v A [2018] EWHC 2534 (Admin) (Supperstone J)." with:
National Crime Agency v A [2018] EWHC 2534 (Admin); [2018] 1 W.L.R. 5887 (Supperstone J).
In *R. (Gopee) v Southwark Crown Court* [2019] EWHC 568 (Admin), the Divisional Court preferred to reconstitute itself as the Court of Appeal (Criminal Division)in order to allow an appeal out-of-time to a Victim Surcharge Order that had been wrongly imposed administratively as part of the sentence for contempt of court.

(c) County Court

3C-33

Replace "Hughes Jarvis Ltd v Searle [2019] EWCA Civ 1" with:
Hughes Jarvis Ltd v Searle [2019] EWCA Civ 1; [2019] 1 W.L.R. 2934

4. Procedure

3C-35

Replace the second paragraph with:
As to the role of the Law Officers in bringing contempt proceedings, see Vol.1 para.81.18.6, and the recent decisions of the Divisional Court in *Attorney General v Yaxley-Lennon* [2019] EWHC 1791 (QB) and *Solicitor General v Holmes* [2019] EWHC 1483 (Admin).

5. Penalties for contempt and kindred offences

3C-36

After the third paragraph, add new paragraph:
The principles of sentencing for contempt of court, and the proper approach to appellate review of sentencing, were reviewed by the Court of Appeal in *Liverpool Insurance Company Ltd v Zafar* [2019] EWCA Civ 392; [2019] 1 W.L.R. 3833.

Replace "Phonographic Performance Ltd v Ellis (T/A BLA BLA BAR) [2018] EWCA 2812" with:
Phonographic Performance Ltd v Ellis (T/A BLA BLA BAR) [2018] EWCA 2812; [2019] Bus. L.R. 542; [2019] E.M.L.R. 13

6. Appeal in cases of contempt of court

3C-37

Replace "R. v Yaxley-Lennon [2018] EWCA Crim 1856; [2018] 2 Cr. App. R. 30" with:
R. v Yaxley-Lennon [2018] EWCA Crim 1856; [2019] 1 W.L.R. 5400; [2018] 2 Cr. App. R. 30

(c) The appeal court's powers

3C-40

Replace the first paragraph with:
Section 13(3) of the 1960 Act states that a court to which an appeal is brought under s.13 may reverse or vary the order or decision of the court below, and may make such other order "as may be just" (s.13(3)). Section 13(3) encompasses the appellate court's power to order a re-hearing, and to impose bail conditions pending re-hearing (*R. v Yaxley-Lennon* [2018] EWCA Crim 1856; [2019] 1 W.L.R. 5400; [2018] 2 Cr. App. R. 30, at paras 78 and 86). The appeal court has a complete discretion, fettered only by the need to do justice. The court must take into account the interests of (a) the contemnor, (b) the "victim" of the contempt, and (c) other users of the court (for whom maintenance of the authority of the court is of supreme importance) (*M v P*, [1993] Fam 167, CA, at p 178 per Lord Donaldson M.R; *In re Scriven* [2004] EWCA Civ 683, at para.30). The interests of the contemnor include ensuring that they have been informed in sufficiently clear terms of what has been found against them. When the civil division of the Court of Appeal is hearing appeals in contempt cases, it will adopt the same principles and approach in relation to sentencing as the criminal division of the Court of Appeal (*Robinson v Murray* [2005] EWCA Civ 935, [2006] 1 F.L.R. 365, CA). The Court of Appeal will not interfere if the sentence fell within the permissible bracket (*Patel v Devjee* [2006] EWCA Civ 1211 and *Liverpool Insurance Company Ltd v Zafar* [2019] EWCA Civ 392; [2019] 1 W.L.R. 3833.).

(e) Direct appeals to the Supreme Court—exclusion of contempt decisions

Replace paragraph with:

In the Administration of Justice Act 1969 it is provided that, where the High Court grants the **3C-40.2**
appropriate certificate under s.12, a party may apply to the Supreme Court under s.13 for permission to appeal from the High Court directly to that Court (see paras 9B-30 and 9B-33 below). Such appeals are colloquially known as "leapfrog appeals" because an appeal to the Court of Appeal is "leapfrogged". It is expressly provided that no certificate may be granted under s.12 in respect of a decision or order by the High Court in the exercise of its jurisdiction to punish for contempt (s.15(4)). Under similar statutory arrangements in ss.14A and 14B of the Tribunal, Courts and Enforcement Act 2007, in ss.37ZA and 37ZB of the Employment Tribunal Act 1996, and in ss.7B and 7C of the Special Immigration Appeals Commission Act 1997, inserted in those statutes by the Criminal Justice and Courts Act 2015, provision is made for appeals directly to the Supreme Court from, respectively, the Upper Tribunal, the Employment Appeal Tribunal, and the Special Immigration Appeals Commission, and in each situation decisions made by those bodies in the exercise of their jurisdictions to punish for contempt are excluded. However, the non-availability of "leapfrog appeals" (under s.12 Administration of Justice Act 1969) from the High Court to the Supreme Court in matters of contempt of court should not be confused with the normal "non-leapfrog" route of appeal directly to the Supreme Court under s.13(2)(c) of the Administration of Justice Act 1960, from decisions of the Divisional Court, or a single judge of the High Court made on appeal, or the Court Martial Appeal Court.

C. Contempt of Court Act 1981

Meaning of "substantial risk" and "seriously impeded or prejudiced"

To the end of the fifth paragraph (beginning "On an application"), add:

However, a submission that such prejudice is necessary—as opposed to being merely sufficient— **3C-51**
was described as "fundamentally misconceived" by the Divisional Court in *Attorney General v Yaxley-Lennon* [2019] EWHC 1791 (QB) at [72].

Postponement of reports of proceedings

Replace "R. v Sarker [2018] EWCA Crim 1341; [2018] Crim. L.R. 843" with:

R. v Sarker[2018] EWCA Crim 1341; [2018] 1 W.L.R. 6083; [2018] Crim. L.R. 843   **3C-58**

To the end of the ninth paragraph, add:

In *Attorney General v Yaxley-Lennon* [2019] EWHC 1791 (QB) at [45]-[66], the Divisional Court considered that "subjective recklessness", without any actual knowledge of the order postponing reporting, was sufficient to ground contempt.

Consent of the Attorney General

Replace "R. v Yaxley-Lennon [2018] EWCA Crim 1856; [2018] 2 Cr. App. R. 30" with:

R. v Yaxley-Lennon[2018] EWCA Crim 1856; [2019] 1 W.L.R. 5400; [2018] 2 Cr. App. R. 30   **3C-64**

Confidentiality of jury's deliberations

Replace the first paragraph with:

As it extends to England and Wales, this section was repealed by the Criminal Justice and Courts **3C-66**
Act 2015 s.74(2) with effect from 13 April 2015 (SI 2015/778). By s.74(1) of that Act additions were made to the Juries Act 1974 (ss.20D to 20G) for the purpose of making it a criminal offence for a person intentionally to disclose a jury's deliberations, or to solicit or to obtain such information. The equivalent offences in respect of an inquest jury are now to be found in s.33 and Sch.6 of the Coroners and Justice Act 2009, as amended.

Interests of justice

To the end of the penultimate paragraph, add:

, upheld on appeal [2019] EWCA Civ 350   **3C-72**

Term of imprisonment or fine for contempt

Replace "R. v Yaxley-Lennon [2018] EWCA Crim 1856; [2018] 2 Cr. App. R. 30" with:

R. v Yaxley-Lennon[2018] EWCA Crim 1856; [2019] 1 W.L.R. 5400; [2018] 2 Cr. App. R. 30   **3C-87**

To the end of the third paragraph, add:
   The principles of sentencing for contempt of court, and the proper approach to appellate review of sentencing, have been recently reviewed by the Court of Appeal in *Liverpool Victoria Insurance Company Ltd v Zafar* [2019] EWCA Civ 392; [2019] 1 W.L.R. 3833.

In the fifth and final paragraphs, replace "Phonographic Performance Ltd v Ellis (t/a Bla Bla Bar) [2018] EWCA Civ 2812" with:
   Phonographic Performance Ltd v Ellis (t/a Bla Bla Bar) [2018] EWCA Civ 2812; [2019] Bus. L.R. 542; [2019] E.M.L.R. 13

SECTION 3D   PROCEEDINGS UNDER THE HUMAN RIGHTS ACT 1998

Human Rights Act 1998

Section 1(1)

In the second paragraph, after "since the Convention", replace "is" with:
3D-3   in the context of this Act means the Convention

Section 2(1)

In the penultimate paragraph, after "[69]-[81] (not disapproved", add:
3D-9   of

Section 2(1)(b)

In the first paragraph, after "Human Rights to", add:
3D-10   issue a

Section 6(1)

Add new paragraph at end:
3D-24   In *Re Finucane's Application for Judicial Review (Northern Ireland)* [2019] UKSC 7 the Court dealt with whether the s.6 requirement that it is unlawful for a public authority to act in a manner incompatible with Convention rights could support an action when the Act was not in force at the time of the incident complained of. Reference was made by the Court to the jurisprudence of the ECtHR relating to the procedural aspect of art.2 of the ECHR. The principle that even though the period should not normally exceed 10 years this was not an immutable rule, had been applied by the UKSC in *Re McCaughey's Application for Judicial Review* [2011] UKSC 20 and thus was the relevant test to determine this issue. Furthermore, following *Brecknell v United Kingdom* (2008) 46 E.H.R.R. 42, in the context of art.2 investigations, any information with the potential to undermine the conclusions of an earlier investigation would prompt revival, and trigger s.6 even where the incident occurred before the introduction of the Act.

Add new paragraph 3D-31.1:

Section 7(1)
3D-31.1   In *Re Jordan's Application for Judicial Review* [2019] UKSC 9 it was held that no court could remove the right under s.7(1)(a) to bring proceedings against a public authority—that right is only subject to the limitation in s.7(5). However, courts are entitled to exercise court management powers, including ordering a stay in proceedings, provided three aspects of ECHR rights are considered:
   (i)   ECHR rights must be applied in a way which makes them practical and effective, not theoretical and illusory.
   (ii)   The s.7(1) right is a civil right within the meaning of art.6 and therefore must be considered within a reasonable time.
   (iii)   A legitimate aim must be pursued, and there must be a reasonable relationship of proportionality between the means and the aim, as the stay engages the right of effective access to court protected by art.6.

Sections 7(2) and (9)–(14) "the appropriate court or tribunal"

To the end of the paragraph, add:

In *Big Brother Watch v United Kingdom (58170/13)* [2018] 9 WLUK 157 the ECtHR held that the **3D-32** Investigatory Powers Tribunal (IPT) is, as a general rule, capable of offering redress to applicants complaining of both specific incidences of surveillance and the general Convention compliance of surveillance regimes (para.265). Accordingly, the IPT is considered a domestic remedy that must be exhausted before a matter can be determined by the ECtHR, unless special circumstances can be shown absolving applicants from the requirement to exhaust this remedy.

Sections 8(3) and 8(4)

In the final paragraph, fourth line, replace "reading" with:

read in **3D-40**

Replace s.10(1)(a) with:

REMEDIAL ACTION

Power to take remedial action

10.—(1) This section applies if— **3D-45**
    (a) a provision of legislation has been declared under section 4 to be incompatible with a Convention right and, if an appeal lies—
        (i) all persons who may appeal have stated in writing that they do not intend to do so;
        (ii) the time for bringing an appeal has expired and no appeal has been brought within that time; or
        (iii) an appeal brought within that time has been determined or abandoned; or

Section 12(3)

Replace paragraph with:

In *Cream Holdings Ltd v Bannerjee* [2004] UKHL 44; [2005] 1 A.C. 253 it was held that, at this **3D-49** interlocutory stage, the test of likelihood was higher than the normal threshold for the grant of an interlocutory injunction in *American Cyanamid v Ethicon Ltd* [1975] A.C. 396 (whether the claim had a "real prospect" of success) but not so high as being that the claim was "more likely than not" to succeed, which standard was unworkable in practice. The standard is a flexible one: the degree of likelihood of success at trial needed to satisfy s.12(3) must depend on the circumstances. There is no automatic priority, or presumption that art.10 ECHR has greater weight than art.8, and the court should evaluate whether it is necessary in any given case to qualify the one right in order to protect the other: *Campbell v MGN Ltd* [2004] UKHL 22; [2004] 2 A.C. 457; [2004] 2 W.L.R. 1232, para.55 (Lord Hoffmann) and para.141 (Baroness Hale). See also *Douglas v Hello! Ltd* [2001] Q.B. 967, para.150 per Keene L.J. and *Mahmud v Galloway & McKay* [2006] EWHC 1286; [2006] E.M.L.R. 26.See also *Boehringer Ingelheim Ltd v Vetplus Ltd* [2007] EWCA Civ 583; [2007] Bus. L.R. 1456; [2007] H.R.L.R. 33; *ETK v News Group Newspapers* [2011] EWCA Civ 439 at [10]. In *Birmingham City Council v Afsar* [2019] EWHC 1560 (QB) it was held that s.12(3) could apply where a case concerned an injunction against public protests as opposed to "publication". Section 12(3) formed part of a code expressly designed to address cases where relief was sought that might interfere with freedom of expression, and the narrow construction of the section was wrong.

After the first paragraph, add new paragraph:

In *Boyd v Ineos Upstream Ltd* [2019] EWCA Civ 515 at [34] the Court set out principles for applying s.12(3) to grant of an injunction in the context of unknown persons:
1. There must be a sufficiently real and imminent risk of a tort being committed to justify quia timet relief;
2. It must be impossible to name the persons who are likely to commit the tort unless restrained;
3. It must be possible to give effective notice of the injunction and for the method of such notice to be set out in the order;
4. The terms of the injunction must correspond to the threatened tort and not be so wide that they prohibit lawful conduct;
5. The terms of the injunction must be sufficiently clear and precise as to enable persons potentially affected to know what they must not do;
    and
6. The injunction should have clear geographical and temporal limits.

SECTION 3E INSOLVENCY PROCEEDINGS

PRACTICE DIRECTION—INSOLVENCY PROCEEDINGS

Editorial note

Paragraph 17 Appeals

3E-21.1 *To the end of the first paragraph, add:*
If a party is not ready to make an application for permission to appeal at the decision hearing, it is necessary to ask for the hearing to be formally adjourned; in the absence of adjournment the lower court will no longer be seised of the matter. In addition to applying for a formal adjournment of the hearing, the party should at the same time seek an extension of time for filing the appellant's notice: see *McDonald v Rose* [2019] EWCA Civ 4 paras 21-22.

INSOLVENCY PROCEEDINGS: GENERAL

Jurisdiction and distribution of business

Bankruptcy

3E-22 *Replace (7)(c) with:*
(c)   applications to rectify the register by reason of omission or mis-statement in any statement or notice delivered to the Registrar of Companies (s.859M Companies Act 2006) or to replace an instrument or debenture delivered to the Registrar of Companies (s.859N Companies Act 2006).

The EC Regulation on Insolvency Proceedings

3E-23 *Add new paragraph at end:*
Preparations for Brexit are now underway: see Insolvency (Amendment) EU Exit) Regulations 2019 (SI 2019/146), in exercise of the powers conferred by s.8(1) of the European Union (Withdrawal) Act 2018 and s.2(2) of the European Communities Act 1972. These regulations will only apply in the event that no deal is reached.

Procedure

3E-24 *Replace paragraph with:*
Insolvency proceedings are governed primarily by the Insolvency Act 1986 and the Insolvency (England and Wales) Rules 2016 (SI 2016/1024) (formerly the Insolvency Rules 1986) and not by the CPR. However, where the Act and the Rules do not make provision for procedure, the CPR may be invoked (r.12.1 Insolvency (England and Wales) Rules 2016 (formerly rr.7.51–7.51A Insolvency Rules 1986)). All insolvency proceedings are multi-track (r.12.1(2) Insolvency (England and Wales) Rules 2016 (formerly r.7.51A(3) of the Insolvency Rules 1986)). On the impact of the new Disclosure Pilot (Practice Direction 51U) see: *In the Matter of Blades Leisure Ltd* [2019] EWHC 914 (Ch), paras 11-25, 65 and 75-80. See too, Message from the Chief Insolvency and Companies Court Judge at para.51UPN.2.

Urgent applications

3E-26 *To the end of the paragraph, add:*
With effect from January 2019, an Insolvency and Companies Court Interim Applications Court has been introduced. This takes place on Thursdays, Fridays and every other Monday in term time. The ICC Judges' listing officer (Claire Prosser) should be contacted in the event that an urgent application needs to be heard on any other day. She will seek to accommodate a hearing. The ICC Interim Applications Court is run in the same way as the High Court Judges' Interim Applications Court, which is not affected by the introduction of this list. It is intended that the list will be used to hear applications for:
1.   an injunction to restrain presentation of a petition to wind up a company or to restrain advertisement of such a petition
2.   an administration order
3.   an appointment of a provisional liquidator
4.   search and seizure orders pursuant to section 365 of the Insolvency Act 1986
5.   an appointment of an interim receiver pursuant to section 286 of the Insolvency Act 1986
6.   validation orders
7.   other applications that are urgent, such as those made pursuant to section 125 of the Companies Act 2006.

Parties appearing in the ICC Interim Applications Court should report to the ICC Judges' clerks on the first floor before 10:30. Please note that the ICC Judges work from hard copy documents and not from CE-file. Accordingly, in addition to the usual lodged bundles, any additional documents such as skeleton arguments or late-provided documents (whether or not they are also filed via CE-file) should be made available in hard copy, either via ICC Listing or to the ICC Judges' clerks on the first floor in the normal way. Applications with a time estimate of more than two hours (including pre-reading time, judgment and consequentials) are generally not suitable for the ICC Interim Applications Court.

Winding-up petitions (Parts IV and V Insolvency Act 1986)

Jurisdiction

In the third line, after "the county court", replace "of the" with:
  in the insolvency **3E-55**

Hearing of the petition

Dismissal of the petition

Replace the first paragraph with:
  If the petitioner fails to appear, if the petitioner accepts that the petition debt is capable of **3E-68** dispute, or if the petition debt has been paid and no creditor or contributory seeks substitution, the court will generally dismiss the petition. It may also dismiss the petition for failure to gazette or for some other failure to comply with the Insolvency Rules 1986 (e.g. rr.7.10 and 7.12 IR 2016, formerly rr.4.11(6) and 4.14(3) IR 1986).

Double barrelled order

In the first line, replace "ICC Judge of companies" with:
  Registrar of Companies **3E-70**

Applications for relief from the effects of s.127

To the end of the paragraph, add:
  . On the defences of change of position and estoppel, see *Officeserve Technologies Ltd (In liquida-* **3E-82** *tion) v Annabel's (Berkeley Square) Ltd* [2018] EWHC 2168 (Ch).

Bankruptcy (Part IX Insolvency Act 1986)

Petition

In the second paragraph, second line, after "the Practice Direction).", add:
  An order for substituted service of a petition can only be made prospectively and not **3E-105** retrospectively: see *Ardawa v Uppal (As Trustee in Bankruptcy of the Appellant)* [2019] EWHC 456 (Ch) per Roth J.

SECTION 3F PERSONAL INJURY

Damages Act 1996

Delete paragraph 3F-35.2, "Commencement".

Note

Replace paragraph with:
  Section A1 was inserted by the Civil Liability Act 2018 s.10(1), with effect from 20 December **3F-36** 2018, subject to 2018 c.29 s.10(3). Section 1 repealed by the Civil Liability Act 2018 s.10(4)(a), with effect from 20 December 2018.

MIB Unidentified Drivers

Editorial Note
  In circumstances where a person is insured to drive a vehicle, but injury is caused in **3F-107** circumstances where the vehicle but not the driver can be identified so as to be served, then it may not be appropriate to plead a direct claim against the insurer. See *Cameron v Liverpool Victoria Insur-*

ance [2019] UKSC 6 where it was observed that Directive 2009/103 art.18 required the provision of a direct right of action against the insurer in respect of the underlying wrong of the person responsible and not just a liability to satisfy judgments entered against that person. However, the motorist was not trying to assert a direct right against the insurer for the underlying wrong. Her claim against the insurer was for a declaration that it was liable to meet any judgment against the other driver. Her claim against the driver was for damages, but the right that she asserted against him on the instant appeal was a right to sue him without identifying him or observing rules of court designed to ensure that he was aware of the proceedings. Nothing in the Directive required the UK to recognise such a right. Nor did art.10 require recourse to the MIB to be unnecessary in a case where the car, although not the driver, had been identified. While the MIB's indemnity was slightly smaller than the insurer's, it was consistent with the Directive (paras 27–30).

SECTION 3G   GENERAL DATA PROTECTION REGULATION

INTRODUCTION

Introduction

To the end of the list, add new bullet point:
3G-1 •   *Buivids v Datu valsts inspekcija* (C-345/17)

The General Data Protection Regulation 2016

Editorial note

Replace "Jehovah's Witnesses versus the Finnish Data Protection Authority (C-25/17)" with:
3G-3   *Tietosuojavaltuutettu v Jehovan todistajat* (C-25/17)

Add new paragraph at end:
In *Ittihadieh v 5-11 Cheyne Gardens RTM Co Ltd* [2017] EWCA Civ 121 it was held that activities relating to the management of a private block of flats in which the data controller resides fall within the scope of the exemption because they directly concern his private life and also directly concern his household.

Editorial note

At the end of the fourth paragraph, replace "definition." with:
3G-7   definition: see recital (27).

In the seventh paragraph, replace "The Common Services Agency and the Scottish Information Commissioner [2008] UKHL 47" with:
Common Services Agency v Scottish Information Commissioner [2008] UKHL 47

Replace the penultimate paragraph with:
"Data processors" carried no liability for compliance under the DPA 1998. This has changed and the question of whether a party is a data controller or a data processor has become correspondingly important. There is limited previous case law on the point.

Editorial note

At the end of the paragraph, replace "law. See South Lanarkshire Council v Scottish Information Commissioner [2009] UKSC 55." with:
3G-8.1   law; i.e. that the processing be "reasonably" necessary. See *South Lanarkshire Council v Scottish Information Commissioner* [2013] UKSC 55; [2013] 1 W.L.R. 2421 and *Cooper v National Crime Agency* [2019] EWCA Civ 16.

Editorial note

Replace the third paragraph with:
3G-11   Under s.8(2) DPA 1998 data controllers could take into account whether the supply of the data would involve "disproportionate effort" and be relieved of the obligation to provide information in such cases. The case law established that, while 8(2) did not apply directly to searches, the concept

of proportionality applied to the extent of the searches to be conducted by the data controller. This was most recently confirmed in *Dawson-Damer v Taylor Wessing* [2017] EWCA Civ 74; [2017] 1 W.L.R. 3255 and *Ittihadieh v 5-11 Cheyne Gardens RTM Co Ltd* [2017] EWCA Civ 121; [2018] Q.B. 256, although the courts also made clear that searches must be thorough and properly carried out. There is no provision expressly addressing disproportionate effort in art.12. Article 12(5) allows for requests to be refused or a charge made where the requests are manifestly unfounded or excessive, but this must be read in light of the general principle of proportionality under EU law. It seems likely – although not certain – that requests which would have been treated as engaging disproportionate effort under the DPA 1998 will be treated as excessive under the new provision. To that extent previous case law may remain relevant. Article 12(5) applies to all the individual rights, not only to subject access.

Exemptions

Replace the second paragraph with:
The exemption for legal professional privilege was considered in *Dawson-Damer v Taylor Wessing* [2017] EWCA Civ 74, *Gurieva v Community Safety Development UK Ltd* [2016] EWHC 643 (QB), *Holyoake v Candy* [2017] EWHC 52 (QB) and *Rudd v Bridle* [2019] EWHC 893 (QB). The exemption for public appointments was considered in *Ranger v House of Lords Appointment Commission* [2015] EWHC 45 (QB). The exemption for national security was considered in *Norman Baker MP v Secretary of State for the Home Department* [2001] U.K.H.R.R. 1275 and *R. (on the application of SSHD) v Information Tribunal* [2006] EWHC 2958 (Admin). The exemption relevant to the prevention or detection of crime was considered in *R. (Alan Lord) v Secretary of State for the Home Department* [2003] EWHC 2073 (Admin) and *Zaw Lin v Commissioner of Police of the Metropolis* [2015] EWHC 2484 (QB). The regulatory proceedings exemption was considered in *Rudd v Bridle* [2019] EWHC 893 (QB).

To the end of the paragraph, add:
Guidance on the application of the journalism exemption to non-traditional journalistic contexts has adopted a narrow approach, emphasising that the mere communication of material to others, even the public at large, does not render the controller a journalist: see *NT1 and NT2 v Google LLC* [2018] EWHC 799 (QB) and *Rudd v Bridle* [2019] EWHC 893 (QB).

Searches and disclosure

After the first paragraph, add new paragraphs:
The right to understand the purposes of the processing need not be provided by reference to **3G-15.1** each individual item of personal data. The principle of proportionality, having regard to the range of contexts of processing, entitles the controller to provide this at a higher level by reference to the essence of what the controller is doing with the data. The right to know the "recipients or categories of recipient" has been interpreted such that the right is focussed upon the category or class of recipient rather than individual identities (which may be third party personal data). Where the subject seeks "available information as to their source", that requires the disclosure of the actual source and not a description or category of source. For the only judicial discussion of these issues, see: *Ittihadieh v 5-11 Cheyne Gardens RTM Co Ltd* [2017] EWCA Civ 121; [2018] Q.B. 256.

Although commonly misused and misunderstood, it is a basic proposition that the right of subject access is a right of access to the data subject's personal data alone and is not a de facto right to disclosure of copy documents. The controller may extract the data from documents, rather than providing redacted documents, if it wishes to do so. See the authorities collated in *Ittihadieh v 5-11 Cheyne Gardens RTM Co Ltd* [2017] EWCA Civ 121; [2018] Q.B. 256. The limited nature of the right in this respect also means that there is no duty to provide material which is not personal data in order to render the data itself intelligible: *Rudd v Bridle* [2019] EWHC 893 (QB) (although see the references in art.12(1) to transparency and intelligibility for the basis for a possible wider argument under the GDPR).

Purpose

In the first paragraph, replace the last sentence with:
It has now been authoritatively established that a controller may not rely upon the motive or purpose of the data subject in order to limit or refuse their right of subject access: *Dawson-Damer v Taylor Wessing* [2017] EWCA Civ 74; [2017] 1 W.L.R. 3255, save for circumstances in which the exercise of the right would fall within the EU law doctrine of abuse of rights: *Ittihadieh v 5-11 Cheyne Gardens RTM Co Ltd* [2017] EWCA Civ 121; [2018] Q.B. 256.

Editorial note

At the end of the paragraph, replace "Shell Petroleum NV, the Shell Transport and Trading Company and Shell Nederland Verkoopmaatschappij BV v European Commission (T-33/06)." with:
Shell Petroleum NV, the Shell Transport and Trading Company and Shell Nederland Verkoopmaatschappij **3G-40** *BV v European Commission (T-343/06).*

Data Protection Act 2018

Add new paragraph 3G-46.1

Editorial note

3G-46.1   In *UKIP v Information Commissioner* [2019] UKUT 662 (AAC) the Upper Tribunal considered the equivalent information notice powers under the DPA 1998 and emphasised that an information notice is not to be approached as though it were a criminal indictment, even if breach might subsequently lead to criminal sanctions (see now s.144). The notice must be read fairly and objectively, as a whole. The Upper Tribunal explained that although the notice must state why the Commissioner requires the information, that did not require a detailed explanation and such a statement was entitled to be at a fairly high level of generality.

In *Doorstep Dispensaree Ltd v Information Commissioner* (EA/2018/0265) the First-tier Tribunal considered the restriction in s.143(6) preventing a notice overruling the privilege against self-incrimination. It is for the controller served with the notice to raise the issue; it does not invalidate the notice—and the Commissioner would often not be able to know in advance whether the privilege was engaged or not – but when raised must be taken into account by the Commissioner when considering whether there has been a breach of the notice's terms. The notice could be cancelled and reissued in amended terms: s.142(8).

Editorial note

Replace paragraph with:

3G-64.1   A data subject who wishes to vindicate his rights under the GDPR or DPA 2018, or challenge the legality of the processing of his personal data by a controller, may bring civil proceedings to do so by virtue of s.167. These may be in the form of Part 7 or Part 8 claims, depending on the degree of factual dispute. Where the controller is a public authority, it is generally likely to be the case that a civil claim under Pts 7 or 8 will be more appropriate than a claim for judicial review under Pt 54. The availability of the right to bring civil proceedings under s.167 will usually amount to an adequate alternative remedy (indeed, a clearly better remedy where there are factual issues) such as to lead to the refusal of permission: see *R. (Hussain) v Secretary of State for the Home Department* [2016] EWCA Civ 1111 and *R. (Segalov) v Chief Constable of Sussex Police & Chief Constable of Greater Manchester Police* [2018] EWHC 3187 (Admin).

In several cases under the DPA 1998 the courts considered whether the right to apply for an order—invariably in the context of subject access rights—could be displaced. In *Kololo v Commissioner of Police for the Metropolis* [2015] EWHC 600 (QB) the court rejected a submission that the access regime under the Crime (International Co-operation) Act 2003 was an alternative legal remedy. In *Johnson v Medical Defence Union* [2004] EWHC 2509 (Ch) the court held that the fact that documents were unavailable to the claimant under the right of subject access did not preclude access under the disclosure rules of CPR Pt 31.

In cases where the claim challenges the non-disclosure of personal data in response to a subject access request—whether because the controller says that the data is not personal data or because an exemption has been applied—it may be necessary for the court to examine the disputed data to resolve the issue. That has been so even where it necessarily places the data subject claimant at a procedural disadvantage: *Lin v Commissioner of Police for the Metropolis* [2015] EWHC 2484 (QB). In cases of claimed legal professional privilege, there are specific threshold tests before the court will review the information to go behind a solicitor's assertion of privilege: see *Holyoake v Candy* [2017] EWHC 52 (QB), and contrast with the refusal to accept the assertion in *Rudd v Bridle* [2019] EWHC 893 (QB) where the reasoning was clearly insufficient. There was a clear statutory power for this necessary function of the court to be able to test the controller's case under the DPA 1998 in s.15(2). For no explained reason, the DPA 2018 does not replicate an equivalent provision. Yet it would prohibit the court from resolving the issues in dispute if it were necessary to examine the withheld data, but it could not do so without also disclosing the data to the claimant and thereby undermining the whole purpose of the proceedings: see, e.g. *Roberts v Nottinghamshire Healthcare NHS Trust* [2008] EWHC 1934 (QB). In sufficiently serious cases, consideration may be given to the appointment of a special advocate, as occurred in *Roberts*: see *Lin*.

Section 167(2) gives the court a remedial discretion. That discretion must be exercised to further the purpose of the legislation, and the starting point is that where a breach has been established, compliance should be ordered. On this, and setting out a range of possibly relevant factors, see: *Ittihadieh v 5-11 Cheyne Gardens RTM Co Ltd* [2017] EWCA Civ 121; [2018] Q.B. 256.

SECTION 3H   CONSUMER CREDIT AND CONSUMER LAW

Impact of Brexit

At the end of the first paragraph, replace "day", 29 March 2019." with:
day".

3H-3.1

After the first paragraph, add new paragraph:
See Vol.1 para.5.0.1.1 for detail on the amendments to the CPR and its PDs in the event of a no-deal exit.

Consumer Rights Act 2015

Replace paragraph and add new paragraph 3H-1090.1:

3H-1090

CHAPTER 3

DUTY OF LETTING AGENTS TO PUBLICISE FEES ETC.

Duty of letting agents to publicise fees etc

83.—(1) A letting agent must, in accordance with this section, publicise details of the agent 's relevant fees.

(2) The agent must display a list of the fees—
- (a) at each of the agent 's premises at which the agent deals face-to-face with persons using or proposing to use services to which the fees relate, and
- (b) at a place in each of those premises at which the list is likely to be seen by such persons.

(3) The agent must publish a list of the fees on the agent 's website (if it has a website).

(3A) Subsection (3C) applies to an agent who—
- (a) is carrying on letting agency work in relation to a dwelling-house in England, and
- (b) advertises the dwelling-house on a third party website as a dwelling-house which a landlord is seeking to let on a tenancy.

(3B) Subsection (3C) also applies to an agent who, on a third party website, advertises letting agency work carried on by the agent in relation to dwelling houses in England.

(3C) The agent must ensure that—
- (a) a list of the agent's relevant fees is published on the third party website, or
- (b) there is a link on that website to a part of the agent's website where a list of those fees is published.

(4) A list of fees displayed or published in accordance with subsection (2), (3) or (3C) must include—
- (a) a description of each fee that is sufficient to enable a person who is liable to pay it to understand the service or cost that is covered by the fee or the purpose for which it is imposed (as the case may be),
- (b) in the case of a fee which tenants are liable to pay, an indication of whether the fee relates to each dwelling-house or each tenant under a tenancy of the dwelling-house, and
- (c) the amount of each fee inclusive of any applicable tax or, where the amount of a fee cannot reasonably be determined in advance, a description of how that fee is calculated.

(5) Subsections (6) and (7) apply to a letting agent engaging in letting agency or property management work in relation to dwelling-houses in England.

(6) If the agent is required to be a member of a client money protection scheme for the purposes of that work, the duty imposed on the agent by subsection (2), (3) or (3C) includes a duty to display or publish, with the list of fees, a statement that—

   (a)   indicates that the agent is a member of a client money protection scheme, and

   (b)   gives the name of the scheme.

(7) If the agent is required to be a member of a redress scheme for dealing with complaints in connection with that work, the duty imposed on the agent by subsection (2), (3) or (3C) includes a duty to display or publish, with the list of fees, a statement—

   (a)   that indicates that the agent is a member of a redress scheme, and

   (b)   that gives the name of the scheme.

(8) The appropriate national authority may by regulations specify—

   (a)   other ways in which a letting agent must publicise details of the relevant fees charged by the agent or (where applicable) a statement within subsection (6) or (7);

   (b)   the details that must be given of fees publicised in that way.

(9) In this section—

"client money protection scheme" means a scheme which enables a person on whose behalf a letting agent holds money to be compensated if all or part of that money is not repaid to that person in circumstances where the scheme applies;

"redress scheme" means a redress scheme for which provision is made by order under section 83 or 84 of the Enterprise and Regulatory Reform Act 2013.

"third party website", in relation to a letting agent, means a website other than the agent's website.

3H-1090.1   *Note* —Subsections (3A)–(3C) inserted and subss.(4), (6), (7), (9) amended by the Tenant Fees Act 2019 (c.4) ss.18(2)–(6), 19, with effect from 1 June 2019.

Replace paragraph and add new paragraph 3H-094.1:

Enforcement of the duty

3H-1094   **87.**—(1) It is the duty of every local weights and measures authority in England and Wales to enforce the provisions of this Chapter in its area.

(1A) The duty in subsection (1) is subject to section 26 (enforcement by the lead enforcement authority) of the Tenant Fees Act 2019.

(2) If a letting agent breaches the duty in section 83(3) (duty to publish list of fees etc on agent 's website), that breach is taken to have occurred in each area of a local weights and measures authority in England and Wales in which a dwelling-house to which the fees relate is located.

(2A) If a letting agent breaches the duty in section 83(3C) (duty to publish list of fees etc on third party website), that breach is taken to have occurred in each area of a local weights and measures authority in England in which a dwelling-house to which the fees relate is located.

(3) Where a local weights and measures authority in England and Wales is satisfied on the balance of probabilities that a letting agent has breached a duty imposed by or under section 83, the authority may impose a financial penalty on the agent in respect of that breach.

(4) A local weights and measures authority in England and Wales may impose a penalty under this section in respect of a breach which occurs in England and Wales but outside that authority 's area (as well as in respect of a breach which occurs within that area).

(5) But a local weights and measures authority in England and Wales may impose a penalty in respect of a breach which occurs outside its area and in the

area of a local weights and measures authority in Wales only if it has obtained the consent of that authority.

(6) Only one penalty under this section may be imposed on the same letting agent in respect of the same breach, subject to subsection (6A).

(6A) More than one penalty may be imposed on the same letting agent by a local weights and measures authority in England in respect of a breach which occurs in England where—

    (a) the breach continues after the end of 28 days beginning with the day after that on which the final notice in respect of the previous penalty for the breach was served, unless the letting agent appeals against that notice within that period, or

    (b) if the letting agent appeals against that notice within that period, the breach continues after the end of 28 days beginning with the day after that on which the appeal is finally determined, withdrawn or abandoned.

(6B) Subsection (6A) does not enable a penalty to be imposed after the final notice in respect of the previous penalty has been withdrawn or quashed on appeal.

(6C) In subsections (6A) and (6B) "final notice" has the meaning given by paragraph 3(2) of Schedule 9.

(7) The amount of a financial penalty imposed under this section—

    (a) may be such as the authority imposing it determines, but

    (b) must not exceed £5,000.

(8) Schedule 9 (procedure for and appeals against financial penalties) has effect.

(9) A local weights and measures authority in England must have regard to any guidance issued by the Secretary of State or the lead enforcement authority (if not the Secretary of State) about—

    (a) compliance by letting agents with duties imposed by or under section 83;

    (b) the exercise of its functions under this section or Schedule 9.

(10) A local weights and measures authority in Wales must have regard to any guidance issued by the Welsh Ministers about—

    (a) compliance by letting agents with duties imposed by or under section 83;

    (b) the exercise of its functions under this section or Schedule 9.

(11) The Secretary of State may by regulations made by statutory instrument—

    (a) amend any of the provisions of this section or Schedule 9 in their application in relation to local weights and measures authorities in England;

    (b) make consequential amendments to Schedule 5 in its application in relation to such authorities.

(12) The Welsh Ministers may by regulations made by statutory instrument—

    (a) amend any of the provisions of this section or Schedule 9 in their application in relation to local weights and measures authorities in Wales;

    (b) make consequential amendments to Schedule 5 in its application in relation to such authorities.

(13) For provisions about enforcement of this Chapter by the lead enforcement authority, see sections 24 to 26 of the Tenant Fees Act 2019.

(14) In this section "lead enforcement authority" has the meaning given by section 24(1) of the Tenant Fees Act 2019.

Note —Subsection (1A), (13), (14) inserted and subs.(9) amended by the Tenant Fees Act 2019 **3H-1094.1** (c.4) s.29(1), with effect from 15 April 2019. Subsection (6) amended and subss.(1A), (2A), (6A)-

(6C) inserted by the Tenant Fees Act 2019 (c.4) ss.18(7), 19, 20, with effect from 1 June 2019.

Replace paragraph 10 with:

SECTION 77

SCHEDULE 5

INVESTIGATORY POWERS ETC.

PART 2

THE ENFORCER'S LEGISLATION

Enforcer's legislation: duties and powers mentioned in paragraph 9(1)(a)

3H-1105   10.   The duties and powers mentioned in paragraph 9(1)(a) are those arising under any of the following provisions—

section 26(1) or 40(1)(b) of the Trade Descriptions Act 1968 (including as applied by regulation 8(3) of the Crystal Glass (Descriptions) Regulations 1973 (SI 1973/1952) and regulation 10(2) of the Footwear (Indication of Composition) Labelling Regulations 1995 (SI 1995/2489));

section 9(1) or (6) of the Hallmarking Act 1973;

paragraph 6 of the Schedule to the Prices Act 1974 (including as read with paragraph 14(1) of that Schedule);

section 161(1) of the Consumer Credit Act 1974;

section 26(1) of the Estate Agents Act 1979;

Article 39 of the Weights and Measures (Northern Ireland) Order 1981 (SI 1981/231 (NI 10));

section 16A(1) or (4) of the Video Recordings Act 1984;

section 27(1) of the Consumer Protection Act 1987 (including as applied by section 12(1) of the Fireworks Act 2003 to fireworks regulations under that Act and by regulation 18 of the Standardised Packaging of Tobacco Products Regulations 2015 (SI 2015/829) to those Regulations);

section 215(1) of the Education Reform Act 1988;

section 107A(1) or (3) or 198A(1) or (3) of the Copyright, Designs and Patents Act 1988;

regulation 31 of the Package Travel and Linked Travel Arrangements Regulations 2018 (SI 2018/634) ;

section 30(4) or (7) or 31(4)(a) of the Clean Air Act 1993;

paragraph 1 of Schedule 2 to the Sunday Trading Act 1994;

section 93(1) or (3) of the Trade Marks Act 1994;

section 8A(1) or (3) of the Olympic Symbol etc (Protection) Act 1995;

regulation 5C(5) of the Motor Fuel (Composition and Content) Regulations 1999 (SI 1999/3107);

paragraph 1(1)(b) or (2)(b) or 2 of Schedule 9 to the Radio Equipment and Telecommunications Terminal Equipment Regulations 2000 (SI 2000/730);

paragraph 1(a) of Schedule 10 to the Personal Protective Equipment Regulations 2002 (SI 2002/1144);

section 3(1) of the Christmas Day Trading Act 2004;

regulation 10(1) of the General Product Safety Regulations 2005 (SI 2005/1803);

regulation 10(1) of the Weights and Measures (Packaged Goods) Regulations 2006 (SI 2006/659);

regulation 13(1) or (1A) of the Business Protection from Misleading Marketing Regulations 2008 (SI 2008/1276);

regulation 19(1) or (1A) of the Consumer Protection from Unfair Trading Regulations 2008 (SI 2008/1277);

paragraph 2 or 5 of Schedule 5 to the Supply of Machinery (Safety) Regulations 2008 (SI 2008/1597);

section A11(7)(a) of the Apprenticeships, Skills, Children and Learning Act 2009;

regulation 32(2) or (3) of the Timeshare, Holiday Products, Resale and Exchange Contracts Regulations 2010 (SI 2010/2960);

regulation 10(1) of the Weights and Measures (Packaged Goods) Regulations (Northern Ireland) 2011 (SR 2011/331);

regulation 11 of the Textile Products (Labelling and Fibre Composition) Regulations 2012 (SI 2012/1102);

regulation 6(1) of the Cosmetic Products Enforcement Regulations 2013 (SI 2013/1478);

regulation 23(1) of the Consumer Contracts (Information, Cancellation and Additional Charges) Regulations 2013 (SI 2013/3134);

section 87(1) of this Act;

section 93(1) or (2) of this Act;

regulation 7(1) of the Packaging (Essential Requirements) Regulations 2015;

regulation 53 of the Tobacco and Related Products Regulations 2016 (SI 2016/507);

regulation 52(1)(a)(ii) or (b)(ii) of the Electromagnetic Compatibility Regulations 2016 (SI 2016/1091);

regulation 55(1) or (2) of the Simple Pressure Vessels (Safety) Regulations 2016 (SI 2016/1092);

regulation 61(1) or (2) of the Lifts Regulations 2016 (SI 2016/1093);

regulation 41(1) or (2) of the Electrical Equipment (Safety) Regulations 2016 (SI 2016/1101);

regulation 67(1) or (2) of the Pressure Equipment (Safety) Regulations 2016 (SI 2016/1105);

regulation 62 of the Non-automatic Weighing Instruments Regulations 2016 (SI 2016/1152);

regulations 70 of the Measuring Instruments Regulations 2016 (SI 2016/1153);

regulation 66(1) or (2) of the Recreational Craft Regulations 2017 (SI 2017/737).

section 6 of the Tenant Fees Act 2019

section 7 of the Tenant Fees Act 2019

section 26 of the Tenant Fees Act 2019

Note

Replace the third paragraph with:

Schedule 5 para.10 amended by the Packaging (Essential Requirements) Regulations 2015 (SI **3H-1111** 2015/1640) reg.15 with effect from 1 October 2015; the Consumer Rights Act 2015 (Consequential Amendments) Order 2015 (SI 2015/1726) Sch.1(1) para.6 with effect from 1 October 2015; the Consumer Rights (Enforcement and Amendments) Order 2016 (SI 2016/1259) Sch.1 para.2(2), with effect from 11 January 2017 subject to transitional and saving provisions as specified in SI 2016/1259 art.4; the Electromagnetic Compatibility Regulations 2016 (SI 2016/1091) reg.76(4)(a), with effect from 8 December 2016 subject to savings specified in SI 2016/1091 reg.75(3); the Simple Pressure Vessels (Safety) Regulations 2016 (SI 2016/1092) reg.78(7), with effect from 8 December 2016 subject to transitional provisions as specified in SI 2016/1092 reg.77(3); the Lifts Regulations 2016 (SI 2016/1093) reg.83(12)(c), with effect from 8 December 2016 subject to savings specified in SI 2016/1093 reg.83(3); the Electrical Equipment (Safety) Regulations 2016 (SI 2016/1101) Sch.7 para.11, with effect from 8 December 2016; the Pressure Equipment (Safety) Regulations 2016 (SI 2016/1105) Sch.12 para.12(a), with effect from 8 December 2016 subject to savings specified in SI 2016/1105 reg.90(3); the Non-automatic Weighing Instruments Regulations 2016 (SI 2016/1152) reg.4(8), with effect from 28 December 2016 in relation to an instrument for use for any of the purposes specified in reg.3(2) subject to transitional and consequential provisions specified in SI 2016/1152 reg.4; the Measuring Instruments Regulations 2016/1153, with effect from 28 December 2016; the Enterprise Act 2016 s.25(2), with effect from 1 April 2017; and the Recreational Craft Regulations 2017 (SI 2017/737) reg.84, with effect from 3 August 2017. Schedule 5 para.10 amended by the Tenant Fees Act 2019 (c.4) ss.6(6), 7(4), with effect from 1 June 2019; and the Tenant Fees Act 2019 (c.4) s.26(10), with effect from 15 April 2019 (except for the purpose specified in SI 2019/857 reg.2(c)); 1 June 2019 (otherwise). Schedule 5 para.11 amended by the Non-automatic Weighing Instruments Regulations 2016 (SI 2016/1152) reg.4(9), with effect from 28 December 2016 in relation to an instrument for use for any of the purposes specified in reg.3(2) subject to transitional and consequential provisions specified in SI 2016/1152 reg.4; and the Consumer Rights (Enforcement and Amendments) Order 2016 (SI 2016/1259) Sch.1 para.2(3), with effect from 11 January 2017 subject to transitional and saving provisions as specified in SI 2016/1259 art.4; and the Package Travel and Linked Travel Arrangements Regulations 2018 (SI 2018/634) reg.38(5)(b), with effect from 1 July 2018.

Add new paragraph at end:

Paragraph 10 further amended by the Consumer Rights Act 2015 (Enforcement) (Amendment) Order 2019 (SI 2019/1074) art.2, with effect from 23 July 2019.

SECTION 3L   EUROPEAN PROCEDURES (CPR PART 78)

PART 78—EUROPEAN PROCEDURES

Brexit

Replace paragraph with:

In the absence of any change to the relevant provisions brought about as a result of agreement **3L-1.1** between the United Kingdom and the Member States of the European Union before the day on which the United Kingdom leaves the European Union, the Civil Procedure Rules 1998 (Amendment) (EU Exit) Regulations 2019 (SI 2019/521) will revoke CPR 78 with effect from the date on which those Regulations come into force. That date ("exit day") is defined at s.20 of the European Union (Withdrawal) Act 2018. Exit day was originally specified at as 29 March 2019 at 11pm. The specified date was then changed, first by the European Union (Withdrawal) Act 2018 (Exit Day) (Amendment) Regulations 2019 (SI 2019/718) reg.2(2) to 11pm on 12 April 2019 subject to an extension which might have been granted in accordance with art.1 of the European Council Decision (EU) 2019/476. In the event of an extension, "exit day" would move to 22 May 2019 at 11pm. By reg.2(2) of European Union (Withdrawal) Act 2018 (Exit Day) (Amendment) (No.2) Regulations 2019 (SI 2019/859) "exit day" was changed again to 31 October 2019 at 11pm. The Practice Direction updates consequent upon the 107th update to the CPR will revoke PD 78 when those updates come into force on "exit day". Transitional provisions set out at reg.27 of the Civil Procedure Rules 1998 (Amendment) (EU Exit) Regulations 2019 (SI 2019/521) may apply. Whether the transitional provisions apply or not is to be determined by reg.16 to 18 of The European Enforcement Order, European Order for Payment and European Small Claims Procedure (Amendment etc.) (EU Exit) Regulations 2018 (SI 2018/1311), which themselves come into force on "exit day". Those Regulations will, by reg.8 and 9, revoke Regulation 1896/2006 (the foundation of section I of CPR 78) and by reg.10 revoke regulation 861/2007 (the foundation of section II of CPR 78). The Cross-Border Mediation (EU Directive) Regulations 2011 (SI 2011/1133) implementing the EU Mediation Directive (Directive 2008/52) (the foundation of section III of CPR 78) will be revoked (subject to savings set out at reg.2) by the Cross-Border Mediation (EU Directive) (EU Exit) Regulations 2019 (SI 2019/469) which again come into force on "exit day".

The draft Agreement on the withdrawal of the United Kingdom of Great Britain and Northern Ireland from the European Union and the European Atomic Energy Community endorsed by the European Council on 25 November 2018 would (if accepted by Parliament or otherwise agreed upon) extend EC Regulation 1896/2006 and EC Regulation 861/2007 (see art.67.3(d) and (e)) broadly to 31 December 2020 (the end date of the "transition period" see art.126). Directive 2008/52/EC would be extended in the same way by art.69.1(b).

SECTION 3M PREVENTION OF TERRORISM PROCEEDINGS (CPR PTS 76, 79, 80 & 88)

PART 79—PROCEEDINGS UNDER THE COUNTER-TERRORISM ACT 2008, PART 1 OF THE TERRORIST ASSET-FREEZING ETC. ACT 2010 AND PART 1 OF THE SANCTIONS AND ANTI-MONEY LAUNDERING ACT 2018[1]

Editorial introduction

Add new paragraph at end:

3M-52 The Part was further extended to cover sanctions-related decisions made under the Sanctions and Anti-Money Laundering Act 2018 (2018 Act). This was done via the Civil Procedure (Amendment) (EU Exit) Rules 2019 (SI 2019/147), which came into force on 1 March 2019, which were rules made under powers conferred by s.40 of the 2018 Act. The 2018 Act, not all of which is yet in force, was passed in anticipation of the UK exiting the EU because the UK's implementation of UN and other multilateral sanctions regimes has hitherto largely relied on the European Communities Act 1972. Once the UK leaves the EU, it will be unable to continue to use the European Communities Act 1972 to implement sanctions and would find itself in breach of international law by being unable to implement UN sanctions and without power to implement sanctions which have not been put in place at UN level. The 2018 Act thus aims to create a domestic framework of relevant powers to remedy this problem. See generally the Explanatory Notes to the 2018 Act. Under the 2018 Act, sanctions regulations may be made where the Minister considers it appropriate to do so for either; (a) the purposes of compliance with a UN obligation; (b) the purposes of compliance with any other international obligation; or (c) for a purpose stated within s.1(2) of the Act, which include furthering the prevention of terrorism in the UK or elsewhere, the interest of national security, or of international peace and security and providing accountability for, or be a deterrent to, gross violations of human rights, or otherwise promote compliance with international human rights law or respect for human rights. All sanctions regulations made by the appropriate Minister must set out the purpose for which they are made (s.1(3)). There are additional requirements for regulations made for a purpose which is not compliance with a UN or other international obligation, and these additional requirements are detailed in s.2. Different types of sanction are set out in s.1(5), which are then explained further in ss.3–8 of the 2018 Act. Sections 23–25, 27–29 and 36–37 set out procedures for requests to the appropriate Minister to have a designation reviewed. Section 38 then provides that the appropriate person may apply to the High Court for a decision made under those sections to be set aside. Pursuant to s.38(4) and (5) the principles applicable on an application for judicial review apply to the determination of such an application and the judicial review remedies are available. Section 39 makes provision in relation to damages and s.40 provides that the closed material procedure provided for in the Counter-Terrorism Act 2008 may be used (with listed modifications) in respect of proceedings under s.38 and on a claim arising from any matter to which such an application relates.

---

[1] Amended by the Civil Procedure (Amendment) (EU Exit) Rules 2019 (SI 2019/147).

SECTION 3O   EMPLOYMENT

Employment Tribunals Extension of Jurisdiction (England and Wales) Order 1994

Scope of the contractual jurisdiction of employment tribunals

After the seventh paragraph (beginning "Thirdly, former employers"), add new paragraph:
   In *Read v Ryder Ltd* UKEAT/0144/18, the EAT held that an employer's claim can only be **3O-0.14** presented if the employee's claim has, in one form of words or another, been expressly brought under the 1994 Order, or could only have been brought under the 1994 Order. It is not sufficient that a claim which is expressly brought under the separate jurisdiction relating to unlawful deduction from wages, or which could be construed as having been brought under the wages jurisdiction, could also have been brought under the 1994 Order.

Other areas of overlapping jurisdiction between courts and employment tribunals

Wages

Replace "Agarwal and Anderson [2018] EWCA Civ 2084" with:
   Agarwal and Anderson [2018] EWCA Civ 2084; [2019] I.C.R. 433; [2019] I.R.L.R. 657   **3O-0.15**

SECTION 4   SUPREME COURT OF THE UNITED KINGDOM AND JUDICIAL COMMITTEE OF THE PRIVY COUNCIL

SECTION 4A   SUPREME COURT OF THE UNITED KINGDOM APPEALS

Doctrine of precedent

Replace "Willers v Joyce [2016] UKSC 44; [2016] 3 W.L.R. 534" with:
   Willers v Joyce [2016] UKSC 44; [2018] A.C. 779   **4A-0.5**

Supreme Court Rules 2009

Application to reopen judgment

Replace "R (Bancoult) v Secretary of State for Foreign and Commonwealth Affairs (No.4) [2016] UKSC 35; [2016] 3 W.L.R. 157" with:
   R. (Bancoult) v Secretary of State for Foreign and Commonwealth Affairs (No.4) [2016] UKSC 35; **4A-28.2** [2017] A.C. 300

Effect of rule

Replace "Gohil v Gohil [2015] UKSC 61; [2015] 3 W.L.R. 1085" with:
   Gohil v Gohil [2015] UKSC 61; [2016] A.C. 849   **4A-29.1**

PRACTICE DIRECTION 10—DEVOLUTION JURISDICTION

General note

Replace the second paragraph in 10.1.5 with:
   10.1.5   As to **(a)** above, sections 32A and 33 of the Scotland Act 1998 provide **4A-192** for the scrutiny of Bills of the Scottish Parliament by the Supreme Court. Section 11 of the Northern Ireland Act 1998 provides for the scrutiny of Bills of

the Northern Ireland Assembly. Section 112 of the Government of Wales Act 2006 provides for the scrutiny of Bills of the National Assembly for Wales.

SECTION 4B JUDICIAL COMMITTEE OF THE PRIVY COUNCIL APPEALS

Practice Directions

Replace "Willers v Joyce [2016] UKSC 44; [2016] 3 W.L.R. 534" with:

4B-0.4   *Willers v Joyce* [2016] UKSC 44; [2018] A.C. 779

SECTION 5 EUROPEAN JURISDICTION

GENERAL

Brexit

Revocation of European legislation relating to jurisdiction and the Brussels and Lugano Conventions

Replace the first and second paragraphs with:

5-0   The effect of Brexit will, subject to transitional provisions or an Exit Deal, see fundamental changes to legislation relating to European jurisdiction. Part 5 of the Civil Jurisdiction and Judgments (Amendment) (EU Exit) Regulations 2019 (SI 2019/479) will, assuming it comes into force, revoke:

- Council Decision of 28 May 2001 (2001/470/EC) establishing a European Judicial Network in civil and commercial matters;
- Council Regulation (EC) No.44/2001 on jurisdiction and the recognition and enforcement of judgments in civil and commercial matters;
- Council Decision of 20 September 2005 (2005/790/EC) on the signing, on behalf of the Community, of the Agreement between the European Community and the Kingdom of Denmark on jurisdiction and the recognition and enforcement of judgments in civil and commercial matters;
- Council Decision of 27 April 2006 (2006/325/EC) concerning the conclusion of the Agreement between the European Community and the Kingdom of Denmark on jurisdiction and the recognition and enforcement of judgments in civil and commercial matters;
- Council Decision of 15 October 2007 (2007/712/EC) on the signing, on behalf of the Community, of the Convention on jurisdiction and the recognition and enforcement of judgments in civil and commercial matters;
- Council Decision of 27 November 2008 (2009/430/EC) concerning the conclusion of the Convention on jurisdiction and the recognition and enforcement of judgments in civil and commercial matters;
- Regulation (EU) No.1215/2012 of the European Parliament and of the Council of 12 December 2012 on jurisdiction and the recognition and enforcement of judgments in civil and commercial matters (recast);
- Regulation (EU) No.542/2014 of the European Parliament and of the Council of 15 May 2014 amending Regulation (EU) No.1215/2012 as regards the rules to be applied with respect to the Unified Patent Court and the Benelux Court of Justice; and
- Commission Delegated Regulation (EU) No.2015/281 of 26 November 2014 replacing Annexes I and II of Regulation (EU) No.1215/2012 of the European Parliament and of the Council on jurisdiction and the recognition and enforcement of judgments in civil and commercial matters.

Parts 2 and 3 of the 2019 regulations make corresponding amendments to primary and subordinate legislation. Part 2 removes references in inter alia the Civil Jurisdiction and Judgments Act 1982 to the Judgments Regulation (recast) and the Brussels and Lugano Conventions. The 2019 regulations will effect amendments to the Civil Jurisdiction and Judgments Act 1982 (Interim Relief) Order 1997, the Civil Jurisdiction and Judgments Act 1982 (Gibraltar) Order 1997, The Civil Jurisdiction and Judgments (Authentic Instruments and Court Settlements) Order 2001, and The Civil Jurisdiction and Judgments Order 2001.

The Service and Evidence Regulations

Replace paragraph with:
   The Service of Documents and Taking of Evidence in Civil and Commercial Matters (Revocation and Saving Provisions) (EU Exit) Regulations 2018 (SI 2018/1257) revoke the EU Service Regulation (1393/2007) and the Taking of Evidence Regulation (1206/2001), subject to saving provisions relating to outstanding requests for documents to be served or evidence to be taken in the UK, where those requests were received in the UK before exit day. Thereafter, the Hague Conventions on Evidence and Service will apply (see para.34.0.2 and the explanatory memorandum to the draft regulations, para.2.11). As in relation to the other changes foreshadowed by the Brexit statutory instruments, the draft Withdrawal Agreement provides for a longer saving period than the draft regulations, and if agreed, would extend application of the Service and Evidence Regulations to any request received before the end of the transition period (draft art.68).

Applicable law under Rome I and II Regulations

Replace paragraph with:
   In contrast to the overhaul of jurisdictional provisions, European legislation relating to the conflict of laws will remain in force following Britain's departure from the EU. The Rome I and II Regulations and the 1980 Rome Convention, which govern the law applicable to contractual and non-contractual obligations, are preserved by s.3 of the European Union (Withdrawal) Act 2018 in combination with the Law Applicable to Contractual Obligations and Non-Contractual Obligations (Amendment etc.) (EU Exit) Regulations 2019 (SI 2019/834). Regulation 3 also amends the Contracts (Applicable Law) Act 1990, so that the general provision in s.6 of the Withdrawal Act relating to the interpretation of retained EU law, will apply to the Rome Convention.
   See Vol.1 para.5.0.1.1 for detail on the amendments to the CPR and its PDs in the event of a no-deal exit.

SECTION 6   ADMINISTRATION OF FUNDS, PROPERTY AND AFFAIRS
SECTION 6A   COURT FUNDS

Administration of Justice Act 1982

Note

To the end of the paragraph, add:
   Subs.(2)(b)(ii) amended the Insurance Companies Act 1958 which has now been repealed.　　**6A-16.1**

Court Funds Rules 2011

Editorial note

After the penultimate sentence, add:
   At present forms cannot be accepted electronically and, therefore, all forms submitted by post to **6A-25** CFO must be signed with a wet signature.

Editorial note

After the penultimate sentence, add:
   At present forms cannot be accepted electronically and, therefore, all forms submitted by post to **6A-44** CFO must be signed with a wet signature.

Editorial note

After the penultimate sentence, add:
   At present forms cannot be accepted electronically and, therefore, all forms submitted by post to **6A-47** CFO must be signed with a wet signature.

Editorial note

After the penultimate sentence, add:
   At present forms cannot be accepted electronically and, therefore, all forms submitted by post to **6A-50** CFO must be signed with a wet signature.

Editorial note

Replace paragraph with:

6A-52   The correct form of request under r.27 is a **Form 201** completed by the claimant except under r.27(2) where a **Form 202** completed by the defendant is also required. At present forms cannot be accepted electronically and, therefore, all forms submitted by post to CFO must be signed with a wet signature. Both forms are available under *Court Funds Forms* in the online *Civil Procedure Forms Volume.*

Editorial note

After the penultimate sentence, add:

6A-61   At present forms cannot be accepted electronically and, therefore, all forms submitted by post to CFO must be signed with a wet signature.

Editorial note

Replace paragraph with:

6A-74   The correct form of notification of transfer is a **Form 211**. At present forms cannot be accepted electronically and, therefore, all forms submitted by post to CFO must be signed with a wet signature. The form can be found under Court Funds Forms in the online *Civil Procedure Forms Volume.*

INVESTMENTS ON BEHALF OF CHILDREN AND PROTECTED BENEFICIARIES

Funds held in court in Scotland

Replace second paragraph with:

6A-217   After that, they are transferred to the Queen's and Lord Treasurer's Remembrancer, Scottish Government Building, 1B-Bridge, Victoria Quay, Edinburgh EH6 6QQ (tel: 0300 020 3512 or 0131 243 3210; email: COQLTR@copfs.gov.uk). Enquires concerning Scottish estates which have fallen to the Crown should also be made to the Queen's and Lord Treasurer's Remembrancer. Other enquires may be made to the National Records of Scotland, HM General Register House, 2 Princes Street, Edinburgh EH1 3YY (tel: 0131 334 0380).

SECTION 6C   NON-CONTENTIOUS PROBATE

Non-Contentious Probate Rules 1987

Replace amendment note with:

(SI 1987/2024)

[As amended by the Non-Contentious Probate (Amendment) Rules 1991 (SI 1991/1876); the Non-Contentious Probate (Amendment) Rules 1998 (SI 1998/1903); the Non-Contentious Probate (Amendment) Rules 1999 (SI 1999/1015); the Non-Contentious Probate (Amendment) Rules 2003 (SI 2003/185); the Non-Contentious Probate (Amendment) Rules 2009 (SI 2009/1893); the Child Arrangements Order (Consequential Amendments to Subordinate Legislation) Order 2014 (SI 2014/852); the Non-Contentious Probate (Amendment) Rules 2016 (SI 2016/972); the Non-Contentious Probate (Amendment) Rules 2017 (SI 2017/1034); the Non-Contentious Probate (Amendment) Rules (SI 2018/1137); and the Non-Contentious Probate (Amendment) Rules 2019 (SI 2019/1057).]

SECTION 7 LEGAL REPRESENTATIVES—COSTS AND LITIGATION FUNDING
SECTION 7A1 LITIGATION FUNDING BEFORE APRIL 1, 2013

Funding Arrangements

Insurance Premiums

Transferring from legal aid

To the end of the paragraph, add:

As examples of decisions as to the reasonableness of transferring, see *EPX (A Child) v Milton* **7A1-64.1**
Keynes University Hospital NHS Trust [2019] EWHC 1508 (QB) and *AB v Mid-Cheshire Hospitals NHS Foundation Trust* [2019] EWHC 1889 (QB).

SECTION 7A2 LITIGATION FUNDING AFTER APRIL 1, 2013

Introduction

Replace the second paragraph with:

The amendments made by the 2012 Act will not apply to claims for damages in respect of dif- **7A2-1**
fuse mesothelioma until the Lord Chancellor has carried out a review of the likely effect of the amendments in relation to such proceedings, and published a report of the conclusions of the review. The commencement of the amendments was deferred in relation to publication and privacy proceedings: see the Legal Aid, Sentencing and Punishment of Offenders Act 2012 (Commencement No.5 and Saving Provision) Order 2013 (SI 2013/77), which lists the proceedings excluded and provides a definition of "publication and privacy proceedings". However in respect of such proceedings s.44 (success fees) but not s.46 (after the event insurance premiums) came into force on 6 April 2019: Legal Aid, Sentencing and Punishment of Offenders Act 2012 (Commencement No.13) Order 2018 (SI 2018/1287). The commencement of the amendments was deferred until 6 April 2016 in relation to certain insolvency proceedings: the Legal Aid, Sentencing and Punishment of Offenders Act 2012 (Commencement No.12) Order 2016 (SI 2016/345) art.2 (see further Vol.1 para.48.0.2.4).

Courts and Legal Services Act 1990

Note

Replace the first paragraph with:

Substituted, together with s.58A, by the Access to Justice Act 1999 s.27. Amended by SI 2003/ **7A2-4**
1887, SI 2005/3429 and (with effect from 1 April 2013) by the Legal Aid, Sentencing and Punishment of Offenders Act 2012 s.44 which inserted ss.58(4A) and (4B). The amendments made by the 2012 Act will not apply to claims for damages in respect of diffuse mesothelioma until the Lord Chancellor has carried out a review of the likely effect of the amendments in relation to such proceedings, and published a report of the conclusions of the review. The amendments made by the 2012 Act were deferred until 6 April 2019 in relation to publication and privacy proceedings and, in respect of certain insolvency proceedings, were deferred until 6 April 2016. All proceedings which can be the subject of an enforceable conditional fee agreement under s.58, other than proceedings under s.82 of the Environmental Protection Act 1990, are specified for the purposes of s.58(4)(a) by r.2 of the Conditional Fee Agreements Order 2013. For the purposes of s.58(4)(c), r.3 of that Order prescribes a maximum success fee of 100 per cent. Regulations 4 and 5 of the Order provide that the additional conditions shall apply to claims for personal injuries and that the maximum limit of the success fee in such claims shall be 25 per cent in proceedings at first

instance and 100 per cent in all other proceedings of general damages for pain, suffering, and loss of amenity and damages for pecuniary loss, other than future pecuniary loss, net of any sums recoverable by the CRU. The amendments made by the Legal Aid, Sentencing and Punishment of Offenders Act 2012 s.44 were brought into force for certain purposes by the Legal Aid, Sentencing and Punishment of Offenders Act 2012 (Commencement No.12) Order 2016 (SI 2016/345) art.2, with effect from 6 April 2016.

Note

7A2-6

Replace the pre-penultimate sentence (beginning "The amendments made") with:
   The amendments to this section made by the 2012 Act were deferred until 6 April 2019 in relation to publication and privacy proceedings and, in respect of certain insolvency proceedings, were deferred until 6 April 2016.

Conditional Fee Agreements Order 2013

Risk assessment

7A2-19.1

To the end of the paragraph, add:
   Affirmed on appeal: [2019] EWCA Civ 527

Recovery of Costs Insurance Premiums in Clinical Negligence Proceedings (No.2) Regulations 2013

The assessment of premiums

7A2-25.2

To the end of the paragraph, add:
   However where the recoverable part of a block-rated premium has been assessed as reasonable, it should be left out of the assessment of the proportionality of the total costs, on the ground that it was an unavoidable cost: *West v Stockport NHS Foundation Trust* [2019] EWCA Civ 1220.

SECTION 7C   THE SOLICITORS ACT 1974

Solicitors Act 1974

"Costs payable in discharge of a liability properly incurred by the solicitor on behalf of the party to be charged with the bill"

7C-95 *In the sixth line of the first paragraph, omit "after the event insurance premiums (Herbert v HH Law Ltd [2018] EWHC 580 (QB))".*

After the case citation for Blair & Girling, in the sixth line of the second paragraph, add:
   after the event insurance premiums (*Herbert v HH Law Ltd* [2019] EWCA Civ 527)

SECTION 8   LIMITATION

Limitation Act 1980

Date from which limitation calculated

8-3.1

Replace paragraph with:
   Matthew v Sedman [2019] EWCA Civ 475 it was held that when a deadline expired at midnight on a given day, any cause of action arising from a failure to meet the deadline arose on the stroke of midnight, not on the following day. Therefore the following day was not excluded when calculating the expiry of the relevant limitation period. In contrast, when the cause of action accrued partway through a day, it was well established that the day on which the cause of action accrued was excluded.

Date when action "brought"

Replace "Grant v Dawn Meats (UK) [2018] EWCA Civ 2212" with:
  Grant v Dawn Meats (UK) [2018] EWCA Civ 2212; L.T.L. 16/20/2018 **8-3.2**

Accrual of cause of action

Add new paragraphs at end:
  In *Bostani v Pieper* [2019] EWHC 547 (Comm), it was held that a Tomlin order was a simple **8-12.1**
contract for the purposes of the Limitation Act 1980 and therefore was subject to the six-year time
limit.
  In *Doyle v PRA Group (UK) Ltd* [2019] EWCA Civ 12; L.T.L. 23/1/19 the Court of Appeal held
that where a debtor defaulted on a credit card agreement regulated by the Consumer Credit Act
1974, the creditor's cause of action accrued from the date specified in the notice of default
required by s.87(1) of the 1974 Act.

Add new paragraph 8-17.1:

Section 8(1)—"a speciality"
  A seal was no longer necessary to make a deed a "speciality" for the purposes of s.8, provided **8-17.1**
the deed complied with the formalities required of a deed by the Law of Property (Miscellaneous
Provisions) Act 1989 s.1: *Liberty Partnerships Ltd v Tancred* [2018] EWHC 2707 (Comm); [2019] 2
W.L.R. 923.

Add new paragraph 8-48.0 after paragraph 8-48:

Section 15(1) and (6)—"Possession"
  In an adverse possession claim, the act of paving an area of land constituted a sufficient degree **8-48.0**
of exclusive physical control as to amount to "possession" for the purposes of the 1980 Act s.15(1)
and s.15(6). When considering how an occupying owner might have dealt with the land, the nature
and character of the land itself were important and it was not an absolute requirement that the
land be enclosed: *Thorpe v Frank* [2019] EWCA Civ 150; L.T.L 14/2/2019.

Section 21—actions for breach of trust and actions for breach of fiduciary duty

After the third paragraph, add new paragraph:
  In *Lloyds Banking Group Pensions Trustees Ltd v Lloyds Bank Plc* [2018] EWHC 2839 (Ch); [2019] **8-60**
Pens. L.R. 5, a claim by a beneficiary to receive late payment of arrears to be paid by the trustee
out of trust property was a claim to recover trust property within s.21(1)(b) of the 1980 Act;
consequently there was no limitation period.

Discretionary power to override time limits in actions for personal injuries or death

Replace paragraph with:
  Section 33, which is derived verbatim from s.2D of the 1939 Act, provides a most important and **8-90**
substantial change in the law of limitation relating to actions for personal injuries or death. It does
so by conferring on the court a discretionary power to direct that the provisions of ss.11 or 12 shall
not apply to the action or shall not apply to any specified cause of action to which the action relates
(s.33(1)). In *Ellis v Heart of England NHS Foundation Trust* [2018] EWHC 3505 (Ch); [2019] P.I.Q.R.
P8 it was held that the court should not import into s.33 the case law post-dating *Mitchell v News
Group Newspapers Ltd* [2013] EWCA Civ 1537 and *Denton v TH White Ltd* [2014] EWCA Civ 906.
The court may not disapply s.12(1), i.e. that provision which prevents dependants from recovering,
where at the date of his death the deceased could not have maintained an action, except where the
only reason why the deceased could not have recovered was the time bar under s.11. Accordingly,
the court may still, in that particular case, exercise its jurisdiction in favour of the dependants to
disapply s.11 (see s.33(2) and (4)). Similar provisions have now been added in relation to s.11A (see
the Consumer Protection Act 1987 Sch.1). In *Kimathi v Foreign & Commonwealth Office* [2018]
EWHC 1305 (QB) the judge held that fear alone did not amount to personal injury and therefore
s.33 did not apply.

Section 33(3)(a)—delay

Add new paragraph at end:
  In *HMG3 Ltd v Dunn* [2019] EWHC 882 (QB); L.T.L. 10/4/2019 it was held that although the **8-94.2**
deceased's diagnosis in 2008 had given him and his wife knowledge of a potential claim for
asbestosis, their delay in acting was understandable and excusable in human terms, given what they
had to cope with, and would cause no additional prejudice to the employers.

Section 33(3)(b)—effect of delay on the evidence

Replace "Kiwathi v Foreign & Commonwealth Office [2018] EWHC 2066 (QB)" with:
  Kimathi v Foreign & Commonwealth Office [2018] EWHC 2066 (QB) **8-94.3**

Procedural issues

To the end of the first paragraph, add:

8-94.7   In *PRs of the Estate of Hutson deceased v Tata Steel UK Ltd* [2019] EWHC 1608 (QB), Turner J held that in a group action involving allegations that former employees had been exposed to dust and fumes during their employment resulting in occupational diseases, the overriding objective was not best served by determining limitation defences in some of the cases as a preliminary issue.

Scope and operation of this section

Add new paragraph at end:

8-104   In *Chandra v Brooke North (A Firm)* [2013] EWCA Civ 1559 the Court of Appeal held that if a party wished to amend pleadings to add a claim that was said to be statute-barred, the court must compare the proposed amendments with the original particulars of claim, not the claim form. In *Hyde and Murphy v Nygate* [2019] EWHC 1516 (Ch) it was held that insolvency proceedings did not permit a wider approach to the question of whether proposed amendments to a claim amounted to a new claim for limitation purposes. The court must confine its analysis to comparing the unamended pleading with the proposed amended pleading.

SECTION 9   JURISDICTIONAL AND PROCEDURAL LEGISLATION
SECTION 9A   MAIN STATUTES

Senior Courts Act 1981

Delete paragraph 9A-56.1, "Appeal on point not raised at trial".

"costs ... shall be in the discretion of the court"

To the end of the last paragraph, add:

9A-202   Costs may be awarded in a foreign currency. Such an order may be made where payment in a foreign currency most truly reflects the claimant's loss, such that it is the most appropriate means to compensate the receiving party for costs incurred (*Cathay Pacific Airlines Ltd v Lufthansa Technik AG* [2019] EWHC 715 (Ch), unrep.).

County Courts Act 1984

Interest on judgment debts, etc.

Replace the first paragraph with:

9A-565   The County Court (Interest on Judgment Debts) Order 1991 (SI 1991/1184) (as amended) was made by the Lord Chancellor in exercise of powers conferred by this section. For text of the Order, see Vol.2 para.9B-70 below. For explanation of the effect of this Order, in particular as to fixing of date of judgment of a costs order for calculation of interest purposes, see Vol.1 paras 16AI.16 to 16AI.18 and para.40.8.1.

Civil Procedure Act 1997

Replace paragraph with:

RULES AND DIRECTIONS

Civil Procedure Rules

9A-738   **1.**—(1)   There are to be rules of court (to be called " Civil Procedure Rules") governing the practice and procedure to be followed in—
   (a)   the civil division of the Court of Appeal,
   (b)   the High Court, except in relation to its jurisdiction under the Extradition Act 2003, and

(c)   the county court.

(2)   Schedule 1 (which makes further provision about the extent of the power to make Civil Procedure Rules) is to have effect.

(3)   The power to make Civil Procedure Rules is to be exercised with a view to securing that the civil justice system is accessible, fair and efficient.

Replace paragraph with:

Rule Committee

2.—(1)   Civil Procedure Rules are to be made by a committee known as the **9A-740** Civil Procedure Rule Committee, which is to consist of the following persons —
- (a)   the Head of Civil Justice;
- (b)   the Deputy Head of Civil Justice (if there is one);
- (c)   the persons currently appointed in accordance with subsections (1A) and (1B).

(1A)   The Lord Chief Justice must appoint the persons falling within paragraphs (a) to (d) of subsection (2).

(1B)   The Lord Chancellor must appoint the persons falling within paragraphs (e) to (g) of subsection (2).

(2)   The persons to be appointed in accordance with subsections (1A) and (1B) are
- (a)   either two or three judges of the Senior Courts,
- (b)   one Circuit judge,
- (c)   either one or two district judges,
- (ca)   one person who is a judge of the Senior Courts, a Circuit judge or a district judge and who has particular experience of the law applicable in Wales,
- (d)   one person who is a Master referred to in Part II of Schedule 2 to the Senior Courts Act 1981,
- (e)   three persons who have a Senior Courts qualification (within the meaning of section 71 of the Courts and Legal Services Act 1990), including at least one with particular experience of practice in the county court,
- (f)   three persons who have been authorised by a relevant approved regulator to conduct litigation in relation to all proceedings in the Senior Courts, including at least one with particular experience of practice in the county court, and
- (g)   two persons with experience in and knowledge of the lay advice sector and consumer affairs.

(2A)   In subsection (2)(f) "relevant approved regulator" is to be construed in accordance with section 20(3) of the Legal Services Act 2007.

(3)   Before appointing a person in accordance with subsection (1A), the Lord Chief Justice must consult the Lord Chancellor.

(4)   Before appointing a person in accordance with subsection (1B), the Lord Chancellor must consult the Lord Chief Justice and, if the person falls within paragraph (e) or (f) of subsection (2), must also consult any body which—
- (a)   has members who are eligible for appointment under that paragraph, and
- (b)   is an authorised body for the purposes of section 27 or 28 of the Courts and Legal Services Act 1990.

(5)   The Lord Chancellor may reimburse the members of the Civil Procedure Rule Committee their travelling and out-of-pocket expenses.

(6)   The Civil Procedure Rule Committee must, before making or amending Civil Procedure Rules—

(a)   consult such persons as they consider appropriate, and

(b)   meet (unless it is inexpedient to do so).

(7)   The Civil Procedure Rule Committee must, when making Civil Procedure Rules, try to make rules which are both simple and simply expressed.

(8)   Rules made by the Civil Procedure Rule Committee must be signed by at least eight members of the Committee and be submitted to the Lord Chancellor, who may allow or disallow them.

(9)   The Lord Chief Justice may nominate a judicial office holder (as defined in section 109(4) of the Constitutional Reform Act 2005) to exercise his functions under this section.

(9)   If the Lord Chancellor disallows rules under subsection (8), he must give the Civil Procedure Rule Committee written reasons for doing so.

9A-741   *Change title of paragraph:*

Rule-making process

Replace paragraph with:

This section establishes the Civil Procedure Rule Committee and deals with its membership. Provisions in the Senior Courts Act 1981 and the County Courts Act 1984 dealing with the constitution of the former two Rule Committees were repealed when the 1997 Act came into force.

For extended commentary on the process for making Civil Procedure Rules, see Section 12 (CPR: Application, Amendment and Interpretation) paras 12-3 and 12-38, below. Practice directions are not made by the Rule Committee, although as a matter of practice they are considered by it before they are made by the Master of the Rolls, as the Lord Chief Justice's nominee, with the concurrence of the Lord Chancellor or relevant Minister for Justice (see s.5 below and commentary following).

Subsection (2)(c) was amended by the Civil Procedure Act 1997 (Amendment) Order 2006 (SI 2006/1847), increasing to two the number of district judges that may be appointed to the Committee. Courts Act 2003 s.62 provides for the appointment of the Head and Deputy Head of Civil Justice, referred to in s.2(1). Subsection (2)(ca) was inserted by The Civil Procedure Act 1997 (Amendment) Order 2017 (SI 2017/1148) to make provision for a judge with experience of the law of Wales to be a member of the Rule Committee. This section and section 3 were to be amended by Courts Act 2003, s.85. Those amendments have not as yet been brought into force. If they are brought into force they will, themselves, be subject to amendment by Constitutional Reform Act 2005, Sch.4, para.265.

Note there are two subsections entitled 2(9), the first was introduced by Constitutional Reform Act 2005, Sch.4, para.263(6), the second by Sch. 4, para. 385(2). No doubt this was a slip in the 2005 Act.

9A-744   *Replace paragraph with:*

Section 2: supplementary

3.—(1)   Rules made and allowed under section 2 are to—

(a)   come into force on such day as the Lord Chancellor may direct, and

(b)   be contained in a statutory instrument to which the Statutory Instruments Act 1946 is to apply as if it contained rules made by a Minister of the Crown.

(2)   A statutory instrument containing Civil Procedure Rules shall be subject to annulment in pursuance of a resolution of either House of Parliament.

Delete paragraphs 9A-745 and 9A-746.

SECTION 9B   OTHER STATUTES AND REGULATIONS

County Courts (Interest on Judgment Debts) Order 1991

Replace paragraph with:

The general rule

2.—(1) Subject to the following provisions of this Order, every judgment **9B-71** debt under a relevant judgment shall, to the extent that it remains unsatisfied, carry interest under this Order from the date on which the relevant judgment was given, unless the court orders otherwise.

(2) In the case of a judgment or order for the payment of a judgment debt, other than costs, the amount of which has to be determined at a later date, the judgment debt shall carry interest from that later date, unless the court orders otherwise.

(2A) The court may order that interest shall begin to run from a date before the date on which the relevant judgment is given.

(3) Interest shall not be payable under this Order where the relevant judgment—

    (a) is given in proceedings to recover money due under an agreement regulated by the Consumer Credit Act 1974;

    (b) grants—

        (i) the landlord of a dwelling house, or

        (ii) the mortgagee under a mortgage of land which consists of or includes a dwelling house,

a suspended order for possession.

(4) Where the relevant judgment makes financial provision for a spouse or a child, interest shall only be payable on an order for the payment of not less than £5,000 as a lump sum (whether or not the sum is payable by instalments).

For the purposes of this paragraph, no regard shall be had to any interest payable under section 23(6) of the Matrimonial Causes Act 1973.

(5) A judgment debt under a relevant judgment of, or registered in, the family court does not carry interest under this Order if by virtue of any other enactment it does not carry interest.

Note

Replace paragraph with:

Paragraph 2(5) inserted by the Crime and Courts Act 2013 (County Court and Family Court: **9B-71.1** Consequential Provision) Order 2014 (SI 2014/1773), art.6, with effect from 4 July 2014. Paragraphs (1) and (2) amended, and para.(2A) inserted by the County Courts (Interest on Judgment Debts) (Amendment) Order 2019 (SI 2019/903), art.2, with effect from 27 May 2019. Also see Vol.1 para.16AI.16, para.40.8.1 and Vol.2 para.9A-565.

High Court and County Courts Jurisdiction Order 1991

Brexit

Replace paragraph with:

At the time of writing, the European Enforcement Order, European Order for Payment and **9B-928.1** European Small Claims Procedure (Amendment etc.) (EU Exit) Regulations 2018 (SI 2018/1311) on exit day, will amend the High Court and County Courts Jurisdiction Order 1991 to omit reference to the European Order for Payment and European Small Claims Procedure Regulations. They will also effect savings for proceedings under these Regulations which commenced before exit day to continue to be governed by them.

See Vol.1 para.5.0.1.1 for detail on the amendments to the CPR and its PDs in the event of a no-deal exit.

Note

To the end of the paragraph, add:

9B-940   Art.8(1)(b) amended by High Court and County Courts Jurisdiction (Amendment) Order 1999 (SI 1999/1014).

Transfer to the High Court for execution

Replace paragraph with:

9B-941   The original figure in art.8(1)(b) was £2000 and was reduced by High Court and County Courts Jurisdiction (Amendment) Order 1996 (SI 1996/3141) to £1000. This has been further reduced by High Court and County Courts Jurisdiction (Amendment) Order 1999 (SI 1999/1014) to £600.

"enforced ... in the High Court"

In the final line, replace "grounds" with:

9B-942   goods

Justice and Security Act 2013

Effect of this section

After the ninth paragraph (beginning "In Belhaj v Director of Public Prosections"), add new paragraph:

9B-1408   For an example of a case where the conditions set out above were not even remotely made out, see *Coghlan v Chief Constable of Greater Manchester* [2018] EWHC 1784 (QB).

To the end of the penultimate paragraph, add:

, and *HTF, ZMS v Ministry of Defence* [2018] EWHC 1623 (QB), at [12]–[19].

SECTION 10   COURT FEES

Civil Proceedings Fees Order 2008

Add new paragraphs 10-3.2 and 10-3.2.1:

10-3.2   **3A.—**(1) In proceedings under the Guardianship (Missing Persons) Act 2017—

      (a) fee 2.4(a) (application on notice where no other fee is specified); and

      (b) fee 2.5(a) (application by consent or without notice where no other fee is specified);

are not payable by the Public Guardian.

    (2) For the purpose of this regulation, "Public Guardian" has the meaning given in section 57 of the Mental Capacity Act 2005.

10-3.2.1   *Note* —Inserted by the Court Fees (Miscellaneous Amendments) Order 2019 (SI 2019/1063) art.4(2), with effect from 22 July 2019.

Replace the entries for 6 and 10 with:

ARTICLE 3   SCHEDULE 1

FEES TO BE TAKEN

10-7

Column 1 Number and description of fee	Column 2 Amount of fee (or manner of calculation)
6 Determination in the Senior Court of costs incurred in the Court of Protection	
6.1 On the filing of a request for detailed assessment.	£85
6.2 On an appeal against a decision made in detailed assessment proceedings.	£65

Column 1 Number and description of fee	Column 2 Amount of fee (or manner of calculation)
6.3 On a request or application to set aside a default costs certificate.	£65
FEES PAYABLE IN HIGH COURT ONLY	
10 Miscellaneous proceedings or matters	
Bills of Sale	
10.1 On filing any document under the Bills of Sale Acts 1878 and the Bills of Sale Act (1878) Amendment Act 1882 or on an application under section 15 of the Bills of Sale Act 1878 for an order that a memorandum of satisfaction be written on a registered copy of the bill.	£28
Searches	
10.2 For an official certificate of the result of a search for each name, in any register or index held by the court; or in the Court Funds Office, for an official certificate of the result of a search of unclaimed balances for a specified period of up to 50 years.	£50
10.3 On a search in person of the court's records, including inspection, for each 15 minutes or part of 15 minutes.	£11
Judge sitting as arbitrator	
10.4 On the appointment of an eligible High Court judge as an arbitrator or umpire under section 93 of the Arbitration Act 1996	£610
10.5 For every day or part of a day (after the first day) of the hearing before an eligible High Court judge, so appointed as arbitrator or umpire.	£610
Where fee 10.4 has been paid on the appointment of an eligible High Court judge as an arbitrator or umpire but the arbitration does not proceed to a hearing or an award, the fee will be refunded.	

SECTION 11   OVERRIDING OBJECTIVE OF CPR

C.   Giving Effect to the "Overriding Objective"—Generally (rr.1.1 and 1.2)

2.   *General Application of "Overriding Objective" as Demonstrated in Decided Cases*

Replace the sixth paragraph with:

11-6   The overriding objective is not applicable where legal rights are involved (*Dicker v Scammell* [2003] EWHC 1601 (QB); [2003] N.P.C. 90, *Bhusate v Patel* [2019] EWHC 470 (Ch) and *Cowan v Foreman* [2019] EWCA Civ 1336. Nor can it confer jurisdiction if manifestly there is none (*Russell-Cooke Trust Co v Prentis* [2003] EWHC 1435 (Ch). Further, the CPR being rules of court, cannot (neither by means of the overriding objective provisions in them nor by any other provision) extend the jurisdiction of the court from that which the law provides (*Jaffray v The Society of Lloyds* [2007] EWCA Civ 586; [2008] 1 W.L.R. 75).

E.   Duty of the Parties (r.1.3)

In the fourth paragraph, replace "Khudados v Hayden [2007] EWCA Civ 1316; [2008] C.P. Rep. 12, CA, and Phoenix Healthcare Distribution Ltd v Woodward [2018] EWHC 2152 (Ch), unrep." with:

11-15   *Khudados v Hayden* [2007] EWCA Civ 1316; [2008] C.P. Rep. 12, CA.

Replace the seventh paragraph with:

There is no general duty upon one party to actual or potential civil proceedings to point out the mistakes of another party or his legal advisers, but each case depends on its facts; see *Thames Trains Ltd v Adams* [2006] EWHC 3291 (QB), (Nelson J) (where the authorities are summarised); *The Stolt*

Loyalty [1993] 2 Lloyd's Rep. 281 (Clarke J); *Bethell Construction Ltd v Deloitte & Touche* [2011] EWCA Civ 1321, CA; *Barton v Wright Hassall LLP* [2018] UKSC 12; [2018] 1 W.L.R. 1119; and *Woodward v Phoenix Healthcare Distribution Ltd* [2019] EWCA Civ 985, CA. In *Beever v Ryder Plc* [2012] EWCA Civ 1737; [2013] 2 Costs L.O. 364, the defendant alerted the court, but not the claimant, to the latter's failure to file a costs estimate with the allocation questionnaire. Thereupon the court, on its own initiative, made an unless order with which the claimant failed to comply with the result that the claim was struck out. The Court of Appeal stated that the defendant's action was a "breach of good practice" and, as such, a factor to be taken into account when determining whether the claimant should be granted relief from sanction. Presumably, where one party (A) is aware that court staff have made an error in discharging the court's responsibilities in relation to the handling of a claim, by which his opponent (B) is or may be prejudiced, and A has reason to believe that B is unaware of the error and the procedural consequences of it for him or is unsure whether he is and does, A is not by virtue of r.1.3 or on any other ground under a duty clearly to alert B to his predicament. However, A's reluctance in that respect may be a matter which the court will find difficult to ignore when determining applications made by B for relief from the consequences of the court's mistakes; see e.g. *Power v Meloy Whittle Robinson Solicitors* [2014] EWCA Civ 898, (where claimant, prejudiced by court's mis-service of claim form, making application for service by an alternative method). And see *OOO Abbott v Econowall UK Ltd* [2016] EWHC 660 (IPEC); [2017] F.S.R. 1, (HHJ Hacon), where it was noted that while parties are not required to inform their opponents of mistakes they have made, this is subject to the overriding objective and the obligation to ensure that parties and the court have a clear, common understanding of the real issues in dispute and as to the proper procedural arrangements for the effective progress of the claim. A failure to ensure this is the case can lead to unnecessary and disproportionate cost and delay to the parties, to the court, and have an adverse effect on other litigants. Where parties become aware of a genuine misunderstanding on a significant issue they should take reasonable steps to dispel it. And see *Freeborn v Marcal (t/a Dan Marcal Architects)* [2017] EWHC 3046 (TCC); [2017] 6 Costs L.R. 1103, where it was stressed that in all but the most serious cases parties should work together to avoid unnecessary procedural, satellite, litigation arising from procedural error. In *Higgins v ERC Accountants & Business Advisers Ltd* [2017] EWHC 2190 (Ch), referring to the decision in *OOO Abbott*, it was held that the defendant was under no obligation to remind the claimant in long-running litigation that they had not served the claim form i.e., there was no duty to inform their opponent of procedural mistakes they had made to which they had not contributed. This point was confirmed by *Woodward v Phoenix Healthcare Distribution Ltd* [2019] EWCA Civ 985, CA, where it was held that there was no positive duty on a defendant to warn a claimant that service had been defective. It also confirmed that the duty not to engage in technical game-playing, as set out at para.41 of *Denton v T H White Ltd* [2014] EWCA Civ 906; [2014] W.L.R. 3926, was focused on the elimination of meretricious resistance to relief from sanction applications that were bound to succeed.

SECTION 12   CPR: APPLICATION, AMENDMENTS AND INTERPRETATION

C.   Statutory Instruments Amending CPR

4.   *Amendments and Transitional Arrangements in Amending Statutory Instruments*

(b)   2014 to date

Add new paragraphs at the beginning:

12-34   Civil Procedure (Amendment No.3) Rules 2019 (SI 2019/1118) came into force on 1 October 2019. It amended the definition of Aarhus Convention claim in r.45.42(2)(a) and substituted a new CPR Pt 53, which established the Media and Communications List as a specialist High Court list.

Civil Procedure (Amendment No.2) Rules 2019 (SI 2019/1034) came into force on 31 July 2019. It introduced a new Section VII to CPR Pt 57 and made a minor amendment to r.57.24.

Civil Procedure (Amendment) Rules 2019 came into force on 6 April 2019. It made a number of technical amendments. It reintroduced reference to r.5.4A in the contents to CPR Pt 5. It clarified the application of costs and expenses in CPR Pt 21. It corrected the wording of CPR Pt 61 and also introduced provision to rectify a lacunae in the rules that had been identified in *The Atlantik Confidence* [2014] 1 Lloyd's Rep 586, CA. It also substantively amended CPR Pt 39.

The Civil Procedure Rules 1998 (Amendment) (EU Exit) Regulations 2019 (SI 2019/521) come into force on exit day i.e., the day on which the United Kingdom withdraws from the European Union. On exit day, various amendments, including the making of transitional provisions, are made to CPR Pts 5, 6, 8, 12, 13, 25, 30, 31, 32, 34, 63, 68, 75, and 78. The amendments are necessitated by the fact that, assuming the UK leaves the EU without entering into a Withdrawal Agreement (a no-deal Brexit), a EU law will either cease to have effect in UK law or will be retained in modified form only.

The Civil Procedure (Amendment) Rules 2019 (SI 2019/342) came into force on 6 April 2019. It made various amendments, including ones to clarify costs and expenses recoverability under Pt 21, to revise Pt 39, and update Pt 61 to render its language consistent with the Senior Courts Act 1981 and to make provision for the giving of security in admiralty claims to rectify a lacunae in the rules identified in the *Cosmotrade SA v Kairos Shipping Ltd (The Atlantik Confidence)* [2014] 1 Lloyd's Rep. 586, CA.

The Civil Procedure (Amendment) (EU Exit) Rules 2019 (SI 2019/147) came into force on 1 March 2019. These rules were not made by the Civil Procedure Rule Committee under powers contained in the Civil Procedure Act 1997. They were made by the Lord Chancellor under a rule-making power contained in s.40 of the Sanctions and Anti-Money Laundering Act 2018. They amend CPR Pt 79 to enable closed material proceedings to be applied to challenges to decisions made under the 2018 Act concerning the imposition of sanctions.

SECTION 13   RIGHTS OF AUDIENCE

F.   Right of Audience for Parties Acting in Person

Replace "Ndole Assets Ltd v Designer M&E Services UK Ltd [2018] EWCA Civ 2865" with:
   Ndole Assets Ltd v Designer M&E Services UK Ltd [2018] EWCA Civ 2865; [2019] B.L.R. 147   **13-12**

G.   Right of Audience Granted by the Court in Relation to the Proceedings

4.   Exercise of the Discretion

(c)   McKenzie Friend

Replace "In re F (Children) [2012] EWCA Civ 726, CA," with:
   In re F (Children) [2013] EWCA Civ 726, CA,   **13-18**

SECTION 15   INTERIM REMEDIES

A.   Interim Injunctions

2.   Principles and Guidelines to be Applied (American Cyanamid Co. Case)

(a)   Principles—a serious question to be tried

After the penultimate paragraph, add new paragraph:
   When seeking an injunction against Persons Unknown, proper consideration must be given to   **15-8**
compliance with s.12(3) of the Human Rights Act 1998. In *Boyd v Ineos Upstream Ltd* [2019] EWCA Civ 515, Longmore LJ at [34] (admittedly tentatively) identified the requirements as follows: (1) there must be a sufficiently real and imminent risk of a tort being committed to justify quia timet relief; (2) it is impossible to name the persons who are likely to commit the tort unless restrained; (3) it is possible to give effective notice of the injunction and for the method of such notice to be set out in the order; (4) the terms of the injunction must correspond to the threatened tort and not be so wide that they prohibit lawful conduct; (5) the terms of the injunction must be sufficiently clear and precise as to enable persons potentially affected to know what they must not do; and (6) the injunction should have clear geographical and temporal limits.

Change title of the section and replace paragraph with:

9.   Cross-Undertaking as to Damages

The court is normally only prepared to grant an interim injunction if the applicant is prepared   **15-25**
to offer a cross-undertaking in damages (so-called to identify that the undertakings are given by,

and are binding on, the applicant). The court has no power to order a party to give a cross-undertaking: it is something that an applicant must be prepared to give in return for the grant of an injunction. As a matter of practice, however, a cross-undertaking is required for the protection not only of the respondent, but of any other person who may suffer loss in consequence of the order: see PD 25A paras 5.1 and 5.2 (see Vol.1 para.25APD.5).

(b)   Undertakings in interim injunctions generally

Replace the second paragraph with:

15-27   A cross-undertaking is not given by the applicant to the respondent; it is given by the applicant to the court (*F. Hoffmann-La Roche & Co A.G. v Secretary of State for Trade and Industry* [1975] A.C. 295, HL, at p.361 per Lord Diplock; *Fletcher Sutcliffe Wild Ltd v Burch* [1982] F.S.R. 64). The terms of the cross-undertaking are for the court. Three things follow from this. First, where it is a matter for doubt, the proper interpretation of the cross-undertaking is not a matter of divining the mutual understanding of the parties to the proceedings. Secondly, it may be enforced by one who is not a party to the proceedings in those circumstances where it is given, not merely for the benefit of the respondent, but for his benefit as well (as to which, see further below) (*SmithKline Beecham Plc v Apotex Europe Ltd* [2005] EWHC 1655 (Ch); [2006] 1 W.L.R. 872; [2006] 2 All E.R. 53, at para.43 per Lewison J. (in this case the development and extent of undertakings generally is explained)). Thirdly, when an undertaking given to the court (for example to issue a claim form) is not complied with, there must be an enquiry by the court as to why that happened and what, if any, sanction or consequential order should be imposed (*Gray v UVW* [2010] EWHC 2367 (QB); [2010] 10 WLUK 464 (Tugendhat J)). In the case of injunctions to prevent significant environmental damage under the Aarhus Convention (see CPR r.45.41(2)), the court will, in considering whether to require a cross-undertaking in damages, have regard to the need not to make continuing with the claim prohibitively expensive for the applicant: see PD 25A para.5.3 (see Vol.1 para.25APD.5).

Delete the twelfth paragraph (beginning "The use of the word "damages"") and delete the penultimate and last paragraphs.

(g)   Fortifying undertaking

In the first sentence, after "the court may", replace "impose a condition to the effect that the claimant's undertaking should be fortified by his" with:

15-32   impose, as a condition for granting or continuing the injunction, a requirement that the applicant's undertaking should be fortified by

Replace the second paragraph with:
   A defendant should normally apply for the security at the time when the injunction is granted (or, if granted without notice) on the return date. The court has no power subsequently to impose such an additional term on the grant of an injunction (*Commodity Ocean Transport Corp. v Basford Unicorn Industries Ltd (The Mito)* [1987] 2 Lloyd's Rep. 197).
   An application for fortification of a cross-undertaking needs to be made whilst the injunction in respect of which it is given is continuing. Requiring fortification is adjunct to the undertaking offered by a claimant, and is only "required" in the sense of being the price which the claimant will have to pay if they want their order to operate in the future. There is no jurisdiction to grant an application for fortification once the injunction has been discharged: *Napp v Dr Reddy's Laboratories (UK) Ltd* [2019] EWHC 1009 (Pat) (Henry Carr J).

10.   Interim Injunctions in Particular Proceedings

(d)   Injunctions in restraint of trade

After the second paragraph, add new paragraph:

15-48.1   The Supreme Court in *Egon Zehnder Ltd v Tillman* [2019] UKSC 32 has overturned a century of authority and permitted the severance of offending words from a post-termination restrictive covenant, the basis being that removal of the words would not generate any major change in the overall effect of all the post termination restraints in the contract. The burden of showing this falls on the employer.

After the sixth paragraph (beginning "Where a defendant"), add new paragraph:
   Guidance was given as to the exercise of the jurisdiction to grant springboard injunctions in *Forse v Secarma Ltd* [2019] EWCA Civ 215, including that such injunctions are not punitive, but are intended to prevent the wrongdoer from benefitting from any commercial advantage wrongly achieved. Such injunctions must be no greater in scope and for no greater period than is reasonable to remove the unfair advantage secured by the defendant, and the court must estimate what that period will be, and limit the relief accordingly. The judge must state the grounds for the conclusions reached, and should avoid being too prescriptive because the evidence will be incomplete and untested at the interim stage. See especially at [33] and [57]-[60] (per Sir Terence Etherton MR).

B. Freezing Injunctions

5. "Domestic" Freezing Injunctions

(a) Relevant factors

(ii) Court's jurisdiction over substantive claim

At the end of the paragraph, delete the brackets and replace the words with:

15-67 The court will, as a matter of discretion, grant a worldwide freezing order to assist in enforcing an overseas arbitration award only in special or exceptional circumstances where the justice of the case so requires, thus departing from the normal guideline that the Court should confine itself to its own territorial area: *Rosseel NV v Oriental Shipping Ltd* [1990] 1 W.L.R. 1387.

(b) Assets excepted

(i) Payments in the ordinary course of business—Angel Bell orders

To the end of the second paragraph, add:

15-71 In *Koza Ltd v Akcil* [2019] EWCA Civ 891, three further propositions were added: a) The test is objective, so the question is to be considered against accepted commercial standards and practices for the running of a business; b) The question is not whether the transaction is ordinary or proper, but whether it is carried out in the ordinary and proper course of the company's business; c) These questions are to be answered in the specific factual context in which they arise.

To the end of the last paragraph, add:

In *Michael Wilson & Partners v Emmott* [2019] EWCA Civ 219, the Court of Appeal at [57]-[59] confirmed Tomlinson LJ's approach in *Nomihold* at [33] as the correct starting point providing "helpful and appropriately nuanced general guidance" and said that a decision applying it is a discretionary matter reached on a fact specific basis, with which the Appeal Court would be slow to interfere.

(ii) Living expenses and ordinary debts

To the end of the first paragraph, add:

15-72 It is not enough for the Defendant merely to assert that any other funds are or might be injuncted without identifying such other funds and their nature, form and location. This is so the court can determine, if it decides funds should be released for this purpose, which funds should be used: *Fundo Soberano de Angola v Dos Santos* [2018] EWHC 3624 (Comm) (Popplewell J at [13]).

(f) Freezing orders in aid of arbitration award

After the first paragraph, add new paragraph:

15-80.1 The court can grant permission to serve out of the jurisdiction a claim to enforce the award in the same manner as a judgment, irrespective of the place where the award was made. Where permission to enforce the award is sought and obtained, the court can in principle grant a worldwide freezing order, and a claim for such relief does not need to be included within the arbitration claim form: *Eastern European Engineering Ltd v Vijay Construction (Pty) Ltd* [2018] EWHC 1539 (Comm) (Butcher J). For commentary on post-judgment WFOs, see para.15-85 below.

6. "Worldwide" Freezing Injunctions

(d) Post-judgment WFO

Add new paragraphs at end:

15-85 Enforcement of arbitration awards is governed by CPR r.62.17 et seq., see Vol.2 para.2E-37. The court can grant a worldwide or domestic freezing order, even if such a claim is not included in the arbitration claim form: *Eastern European Engineering Ltd v Vijay Construction (Pty) Ltd* [2018] EWHC 1539 (Comm) (Butcher J). Granting such a WFO is a matter for the court's discretion, to be exercised only in special or exceptional circumstances where the justice of the case so requires, to depart from the normal guideline that the Court should confine itself to its own territorial area: *Rosseel NV v Oriental Shipping Ltd* [1990] 1 W.L.R. 1387.

For discussion of whether the payments in the ordinary course of business exception should be in place in post judgment freezing order cases, see para.15-71.

C. Search Orders

3. Grounds for Making Order

Replace the second and third paragraphs with:

15-91 Although in the *Anton Piller* case Lord Denning spoke of "an extreme case", in practice orders are granted far too routinely for them to be regarded as exceptional. However, the court still insists on a clear showing of fraud, dishonesty, contumacy, or imminent removal or destruction of property or evidence. The overriding principle is that of necessity. No order ought to be made unless it is necessary in the interests of justice. The so-called "balance of convenience" test, which plays a leading role in most decisions to grant interlocutory injunctions, has little, if any role to play in an application to grant a search order. Consistent with the principle of necessity, the cases have established the following conditions for the making of an order (see 1992 Consultation Paper, paras 2.4, et seq., and the summary in *Indicii Salus Ltd v Chandrasekaran* [2006] EWHC 521 (Ch) at [85]).

(1) There must be a strong prima facie case of a civil cause of action. Suspicion that there may be a cause of action should not be enough. A scrutiny of the merits of the claimant's case is an essential preliminary to the grant of a search order. It is not sufficient for the applicant to show merely a "serious question to be tried" (as is sufficient in applications for orthodox interlocutory injunctions).

(2) The damage to the claimant to be avoided by the grant of an order must be serious. If an order is sought in order to forestall the destruction of evidence, the evidence in question must be of major, if not critical, importance.

(3) There must be clear evidence that the defendants had in their possession incriminating documents or things.

(4) The risk of destruction or removal of evidence must be a good deal more than merely possible. (In *Booker McConnell v Plascow Plc* [1985] R.P.C. 425 at 441, CA, Dillon LJ referred to "a real possibility", which he contrasted with "extravagant fears which seem to afflict all claimants who have complaints of breach of confidence, breach of copyright or passing-off".) The fact that a respondent can be shown to have behaved improperly will not always justify an order. There must be a real reason to believe that the respondent will disobey an injunction for the preservation of the evidence in question.

(5) The harm likely to be caused by the execution of the order to the respondent and his business affairs must not be excessive or out of proportion to the legitimate object of the order. This precondition is particularly relevant where the seizure of trading stock or the perusal by the claimant of confidential commercial documents will be the effect of execution of the order and is strongly analogous to the principle of proportionality as applied by the European Court of Human Rights.

This summary was expressly approved by Vos C in *MX1 v Farazhad* [2018] 3 WLUK 744, unrep., at [40]-[41], subject to assuming, which is correct, that what was then a reference to 'danger' in the second criterion ought to read as 'damage' On the accuracy of that point, see Ormerod LJ's judgment in *Anton Piller* at [62]; *Lock International Plc v Beswick* [1989] 1 W.L.R. 1268 at 1280; and, *Indicii Salus Ltd v Chandrasekaran* [2006] EWHC 521 (Ch) at [85].).

If any of these pre-conditions is absent, the weight of judicial authority suggests that an application for the grant of a search order should be refused. If each of these preconditions appears to be present, an order will not necessarily be justified. The court will still have to weigh in the balance the claimant's need for the order against the injustice to the respondent in making the order ex parte without any opportunity for the respondent to be heard. The judge who hears the application for the order should keep in mind that, in as much as audi alteram partem is a requirement of natural justice, the making of an ex parte mandatory order always risks injustice to the absent and unheard respondent. The order should not be made unless it appears that, without the order, the claimant will be likely to suffer a greater injustice than that which the court, by making the order, will be inflicting on the respondent (see *Columbia Picture Industries v Robinson* [1987] Ch. 38). The court requires proportionality between the perceived threat to the claimant's rights and the remedy granted. The fact that there is overwhelming evidence that the defendant has behaved wrongfully in his commercial relationships does not necessarily justify a search order. People whose commercial morality allows them to take a customer list will not necessarily disobey an order of the court requiring them to deliver it up. Not everyone who is misusing confidential information will destroy documents in the face of a court order requiring him to preserve them (*Lock International Plc v Beswick* [1989] 1 W.L.R. 1268) (Hoffmann J)).

The search order has been described by Donaldson LJ in *Bank Mellat v Nikpour* (1985) 2 F.S.R. 87 at [92] as one of the law's "nuclear weapons." The making of an intrusive order ex parte allowing searches of premises or vehicles is contrary to normal principles of justice and can only be done when there is a paramount need to prevent a denial of justice to the claimant: Hoffmann J described the jurisdiction to permit a search of the defendant's dwelling as being "the absolute extremity of the court's powers": *Lock International Plc v Beswick* [1989] 1 W.L.R. 1268 at 1281. The court has therefore developed a less intrusive version, known as a doorstep delivery-up order, for when the evidence does not satisfy the high threshold for a search order. In *Hyperama Plc v Poulis* [2018] EWHC 3483 (QB) Pepperall J required the doorstep delivery up of electronic devices, to be retained uninspected until after the inter partes hearing.

APPENDIX 1   COURTS DIRECTORY

List of District Registries

Replace table with:

Name of place	Districts defined by reference to areas served by hearing centres of the County Court
Aberystwyth	Aberystwyth
Barnsley	Barnsley
Barnstaple	Barnstaple
Barrow in Furness	Barrow in Furness
Basingstoke	Basingstoke
Bath	Bath
Bedford	Bedford
Birkenhead	Birkenhead
Birmingham (Chancery)	Birmingham
Blackburn	Blackburn
Blackpool	Blackpool
Blackwood	Blackwood
Boston	Boston
Bournemouth	Bournemouth and Poole
Bradford	Bradford
Brighton	Brighton
	Lewes
Bristol (Chancery)	Bristol
	Weston-super-Mare
Burnley	Burnley
Bury St Edmunds	Bury St Edmunds
Caernarfon (Chancery)	Caernarfon
	Porthmadog
Cambridge	Cambridge
Canterbury	Canterbury
Cardiff (Chancery)	Cardiff
Carlisle	Carlisle
Carmarthen	Carmarthen
	Llanelli
Chatham	Medway
	Dartford
Chelmsford	Chelmsford
	Hertford
Chester	Chester
Chesterfield	Chesterfield
Coventry	
	Coventry
	Nuneaton
	Warwick
Crewe	Crewe
Croydon	Bromley
	Croydon
Darlington	Darlington

Name of place	Districts defined by reference to areas served by hearing centres of the County Court
Derby	Derby
Doncaster	Doncaster
	Rotherham
Dudley	Dudley
Durham	Durham
Eastbourne	Eastbourne
Exeter	Exeter
Gloucester	Gloucester and Cheltenham
Great Grimsby	Great Grimsby
Guildford	Aldershot and Farnham
	Guildford
Harrogate	Harrogate
Hastings	Hastings
Haverfordwest	Haverfordwest
Hereford	Hereford
Huddersfield	Huddersfield
Ipswich	Ipswich
Kingston upon Hull	Kingston upon Hull
Lancaster	Lancaster
Leeds (Chancery)	Leeds
Leicester	Leicester
Lincoln	Lincoln
Liverpool (Chancery)	Liverpool
Luton	Luton
Maidstone	Maidstone
Manchester (Chancery)	Manchester
Mansfield	Mansfield
Margate	Thanet
Merthyr Tydfil	Merthyr Tydfil
Middlesbrough	Middlesbrough
Milton Keynes	Aylesbury
	Milton Keynes
Mold (Chancery)	Mold
Newcastle upon Tyne (Chancery)	Newcastle upon Tyne
Newport (Gwent)	Newport (Gwent)
Newport (Isle of Wight)	Newport (Isle of Wight)
Northampton	Northampton
Norwich	Norwich
Nottingham	Nottingham
Oxford	Oxford
Peterborough	Peterborough
Plymouth	Plymouth
Pontypridd	Pontypridd
Portsmouth	Portsmouth
Port Talbot	Port Talbot
Prestatyn	Prestatyn
Preston (Chancery)	Preston
Reading	Reading
	Slough
Romford	Basildon
	Romford
St. Helens	St. Helens

Name of place	Districts defined by reference to areas served by hearing centres of the County Court
Salisbury	Salisbury
Scarborough	Scarborough
Sheffield	Sheffield
Skipton	Skipton
Southampton	Southampton
Southend-on-Sea	Southend-on-Sea
South Shields	North Shields
Stafford	Stafford
Stockport	Stockport
Stoke on Trent	Stoke on Trent
Sunderland	Gateshead
	Sunderland
Swansea	Swansea
Swindon	Swindon
Taunton	Taunton
Telford	Telford
Torquay	Torquay and Newton Abbot
Truro	Bodmin
	Truro
Wakefield	Wakefield
Walsall	Walsall
Welshpool	Welshpool and Newtown
Weymouth	Weymouth
Wigan	Wigan
Winchester	Winchester
Wolverhampton	Wolverhampton
Worcester	Worcester
Workington	West Cumbria
Worthing	Horsham
	Worthing
Wrexham	Wrexham
Yeovil	Yeovil
York	York

Note

Replace paragraph with:
 Table substituted by the Civil Courts Order 2014 (SI 2014/819), with effect from 22 April 2014. **AP-6**
Amended by the Civil Courts (Amendment) Order 2016 (SI 2016/974) art.2(3), with effect from
31 October 2016. Entries relating to "Halifax" revoked by the Civil Courts (Amendment No.2)
Order 2016 (SI 2016/1068) art.2(2)(a)(i), (b), with effect from 28 November 2016; entries relating
to "Tunbridge Wells" revoked by the Civil Courts (Amendment No.2) Order 2016 (SI 2016/1068)
art.2(2)(a)(ii), (b), with effect from 9 December 2016; entries relating to "Scunthorpe" revoked by
the Civil Courts (Amendment No.2) Order 2016 (SI 2016/1068) art.2(2)(a)(iii), (b), with effect
from 13 January 2017; entries relating to "Hartlepool" revoked by the Civil Courts (Amendment
No.2) Order 2016 (SI 2016/1068) art.2(2)(a)(iv), (b), with effect from 30 January 2017; and entry
in the second column relating to "Reigate" revoked by the Civil Courts (Amendment No.2) Order
2016 (SI 2016/1068) art.2(2)(c), with effect from 31 March 2017; entry relating to Llangefni and
reference to corresponding County Court Centre revoked by the Civil Courts (Amendment) Order
2017 (SI 2017/574) art.2.(2)(a)(i), (b), with effect from 12 May 2017; entries relating to Bolton and
Bury and references to corresponding County Court Centre revoked by the Civil Courts (Amendment) Order 2017 (SI 2017/574) art.2.(2)(a)(ii), (iii), (b), with effect from 2 June 2017; entry relating to Kendal and reference to corresponding County Court Centre revoked by the Civil Courts
(Amendment) Order 2017 (SI 2017/574) art.2.(2)(a)(iv), (b), with effect from 30 June 2017; entry
relating to Oldham and reference to corresponding County Court Centre revoked by the Civil
Courts (Amendment) Order 2017 (SI 2017/574) art.2.(2)(a)(v), (b), with effect from 14 July 2017;
entry in the second column relating to Kettering County Court revoked by the Civil Courts (Amendment) Order 2017 (SI 2017/574) art.2.(2)(c), (b), with effect from 7 July 2017; entries relating to

Chichester and Colchester in the first column and entries relating to Chichester, Colchester and Clacton, Chippenham and Trowbridge and Banbury revoked by the Civil Courts (Amendment) Order 2019 (SI 2019/889) art.2, with effect from 30 April 2019.

County Court Directory

County Court Directory

Schedule: County Court Directory

AP-9 *In the table, omit the entries for Chichester County Court hearing centre, Chippenham and Trowbridge County Court hearing centre and Colchester County Court hearing centre. Replace the entries for Brighton, Merthyr Tydfil and Pontypridd County Court hearing centres with:*

Column 1 County Court Hearing Centre	Column 2 District Registry, Chancery District Registry, Circuit Commercial Court Or Civil Trial Centre	Column 3 Civil Trial Centre to Which Cases Allocated to the Multi-Track Will Be Transferred	Column 4 Additional Proceedings	Column 5 Civil Trial Centres — Feeder Courts
Brighton	DR CTC		I C/LLP CEA	Hastings, Horsham, Lewes, Worthing
Merthyr Tydfil	DR	Cardiff	I C/LLP	
Pontypridd	DR	Cardiff	I C/LLP	

INDEX

This index has been prepared using Sweet & Maxwell's Legal Taxonomy. Main index entries conform to keywords provided by the Legal Taxonomy except where references to specific documents or non-standard terms (denoted by quotation marks) have been included. These keywords provide a means of identifying similar concepts in other Sweet & Maxwell publications and online services to which keywords from the Legal Taxonomy have been applied. Readers may find some minor differences between terms used in the text and those which appear in the index. Suggestions to *sweetandmaxwell.taxonomy@tr.com*.

(All references are to paragraph numbers)

Paragraph numbers marked "+" denote online/CD content; those within [...] refer to Volume 2

Paragraph numbers marked "+" denote online/CD content; those within […] refer to Volume 2

Paragraph numbers marked "+" denote online/CD content; those within [...] refer to Volume 2

Paragraph numbers marked "+" denote online/CD content; those within [...] refer to Volume 2

Paragraph numbers marked "+" denote online/CD content; those within [...] refer to Volume 2

Paragraph numbers marked "+" denote online/CD content; those within [...] refer to Volume 2

Paragraph numbers marked "+" denote online/CD content; those within [...] refer to Volume 2

Paragraph numbers marked "+" denote online/CD content; those within [...] refer to Volume 2

Paragraph numbers marked "+" denote online/CD content; those within [...] refer to Volume 2

Paragraph numbers marked "+" denote online/CD content; those within [...] refer to Volume 2

Paragraph numbers marked "+" denote online/CD content; those within [...] refer to Volume 2

Paragraph numbers marked "+" denote online/CD content; those within [...] refer to Volume 2

Paragraph numbers marked "+" denote online/CD content; those within [...] refer to Volume 2

Paragraph numbers marked "+" denote online/CD content; those within [...] refer to Volume 2